FUNDAMENTALS OF THE
ESOTERIC PHILOSOPHY

FUNDAMENTALS
OF THE
ESOTERIC
PHILOSOPHY

G. DE PURUCKER

THEOSOPHICAL UNIVERSITY PRESS
PASADENA, CALIFORNIA

THEOSOPHICAL UNIVERSITY PRESS
PASADENA, CALIFORNIA 91109
1979

First edition published in 1932
Second and Revised Edition copyright © 1979
by Theosophical University Press

Library of Congress Catalog Card Number 78-74258

Hardcover ISBN 0-911500-63-4
Softcover ISBN 0-911500-64-2

Manufactured in the United States of America

FOREWORD

In 1924 Katherine Tingley inaugurated within the esoteric body of the Theosophical Society a series of studies in *The Secret Doctrine* by H. P. Blavatsky, with Gottfried de Purucker as lecturer. In spite of the fact that he had not studied under Mme. Blavatsky, as had several among those present, she knew of none better prepared than he to interpret this work "from the esoteric standpoint." Moreover, she felt assured that after she was gone he would be there to "carry on these lessons," which ultimately would be published "for later generations."

At the first meeting on January 4th, Katherine Tingley set the tone of the gatherings by appealing to all present to cast aside everything of a personal and limiting nature and "get more in harmony with our higher self — with that part that is eternal and that is trying to open the way for us." Those attending should enter, "as did the neophytes of ancient days, in the spirit of self-forgetfulness," remembering that these studies were not being held primarily to enlarge the intellectual understanding of the student, but rather as an "earnest spiritual effort" to open the heart to the higher consciousness and stimulate the intuition for service in the daily life. After the lectures Katherine Tingley spoke for a few minutes and usually called upon different ones for their comments, herself giving the closing remarks. The members then left as they had come, in silence, which to her had marvelous potency for inner growth.

It was in this atmosphere of reverence for truth and for the lightbringers of mankind that G. de Purucker elucidated the spiritual principles upon which the "secret doctrine" of the ages rests. *Fundamentals of the Esoteric Philosophy* represents the stenographic record of those lectures given from 1924 to 1927, with periodic interruptions during Katherine Tingley's absence on lecture tours in the United States or Europe. In 1931 the transcripts were turned over to A. Trevor Barker for editing prior to publication in London, the quotations heading the chapters having been selected by Joseph H. Fussell, friend and colleague of the author.

What makes this book significant among the many expositions of *The Secret Doctrine* that have appeared since 1888? Not least, perhaps, is the inspired treatment of the vast evolutionary process that encompasses the rhythmic rebirth of worlds, of humans, and of every living being, for the purpose of bringing into actuality the fullness of godhood infolded within every god-spark. Propelled by ancient habit we too, in our cyclic descent into earthly life, follow the same cosmic routes traveled by all monads until, the lessons of planetary experience mastered, we graduate as self-evolved divinities. How the One becomes the many, how spirit irradiates every particle of matter, is the old story — now retold with a wondrous clarity so that the reader discovers he has at hand those key-teachings that will enable him to test for himself whether or not any religious or philosophic concept, ancient or modern, is in harmony with "that primeval spiritual and natural revelation" accorded the first thinking humans on earth. Throughout, like a golden sheen on the far horizon of time, he perceives the oneness of humanity's spiritual inheritance and our commonality of divine origin and goal. Further, there is wide scholarship here: not only are the terms from the Sanskrit, Hebrew, and other ancient literatures explained etymologically, but they are given richer interpretation in the light of Dr. de Purucker's knowledge of our early racial history and of the traditional lore and sacred scriptures of Orient and Occident.

For many, however, the greatest gift of all is his restorative trust in the dignity and nobility of man. We are indeed knights errant of eternity, bent on the ancient quest for a wisdom we know exists but which seems ever to elude our grasp. In being reminded of that quest, there is generated a devotion to truth and to the compassionate line of teachers — a devotion that has power to move the soul, to lead us life after life toward those encounters that will purify and strengthen the character and fit us better to serve humanity's cause.

The revision of this second edition has been undertaken with exceeding care and, while the few passages that pertained strictly to the esoteric nature of the sessions have been deleted as have some of the repetitions that are inevitable when a series of addresses is published almost verbatim, the lecture material has been left practically intact.

To have condensed and systematized the presentation would have foiled the intent of the author. Intangibly, yet step by step, he builds atmosphere as he touches on this teaching or that, carries the thought for a distance and then turns to another teaching, seemingly different, yet relevant to the larger picture he is unfolding. In a later chapter or two he may return to the earlier themes, develop them for a time, then again move on to other doctrines. Dr. de Purucker remarks more than once that in this he is deliberately following the ancient esoteric method of imparting sacred truths: repetition of the salient thought, but always with sufficient variation and enlargement of vision to draw the student on so that the mind will not set itself in molds. The mind that remains fluid is more responsive to intuition and the flow of light that may spontaneously illumine the soul when the inner nature is attuned.

It is of interest that the original edition of *Fundamentals of the Esoteric Philosophy* published in 1932 did not include the first two lectures, but began with the third one. Their omission no doubt was inadvertent; but, providentially, a few years after the author's death Kirby Van Mater, archivist for the Society, turned up the two missing lectures among papers which presumably had been returned with other material to headquarters from the European centers to which Katherine Tingley had sent them in 1924, to be shared with "appreciative minds." The pertinent portions of these meetings are now incorporated as sections i and ii of chapter 1, preceding section iii which originally appeared as the first chapter of the 1932 edition. The present volume is enhanced by their inclusion, for they amplify and deepen Dr. de Purucker's interpretation of the three fundamental propositions with which H. P. Blavatsky opens her magnum opus and which "pervade the entire system of thought" she proceeds to outline.

We acknowledge with gratitude the efficient help of all in our printing and editorial departments, with a special word of commendation to Raymond Rugland for his meticulous care in resetting the entire book in a more readable typeface; to James T. Belderis for redrawing the many diagrams; and to William T. S. Thackara for maintaining excellence in every phase of the book's physical production; for the several proofreadings required, deep appreciation to Elsa-Brita Titchenell, Manuel Oderberg, Ingrid Van Mater, and A. Studley and Eloise Hart; likewise to John P. Van Mater, librarian, for assistance to Mrs. Titchenell and Mr. Oderberg in checking the numerous quotations and references from original sources. It goes without saying that the close cooperation of the editorial committee, A. Studley Hart, Ida P. Moffett, and Sarah Belle Dougherty (who also prepared the enlarged index), made the task of editing the text for publication incomparably lighter.

After a near half-century, *Fundamentals of the Esoteric Philosophy* remains an excellent introductory study of theosophy for today's readers in search of the very truths that disciples of olden times, holding the fuel of devotion in their hands, sought to learn of sages and rishis.

GRACE F. KNOCHE

April 27, 1979
Pasadena, California

CONTENTS

PART ONE

FUNDAMENTALS OF THE
ESOTERIC PHILOSOPHY

PART ONE

ONE

I

. . . neither the collective Host (Demiurgos), nor any of the working powers individually, are proper subjects for divine honours or worship. All are entitled to the grateful reverence of Humanity, however, and man ought to be ever striving to help the divine evolution of *Ideas*, by becoming to the best of his ability a *co-worker with nature* in the cyclic task. The ever unknowable and incognizable *Karana* alone, the *Causeless* Cause of all causes, should have its shrine and altar on the holy and ever untrodden ground of our heart — invisible, intangible, unmentioned, save through "the still small voice" of our spiritual consciousness. Those who worship before it, ought to do so in the silence and the sanctified solitude of their Souls; making their spirit the sole mediator between them and the *Universal Spirit*, their good actions the only priests, and their sinful intentions the only visible and objective sacrificial victims to the *Presence*.

— H. P. BLAVATSKY, *The Secret Doctrine*, I, 280

WE SHOULD all feel deeply and gratefully sensible of the occasion which is here given to us to approach along the paths of thought the doctrines which from immemorial time have enlightened the intellect of our fellow students, have given courage to strong hearts under persecution, and have directed the forces of the world along the lines which men hold dearest — the lines of religion and the ethical principles which govern human conduct.

Personally I am deeply sensible of the responsibility which Katherine Tingley has put upon me, to say words which shall be simple, condensed, clear, helpful. Her instructions are to take the literary masterpiece of Helena Petrovna Blavatsky's life, her *Secret Doctrine*, and from beginning to end of it touch, if possible, upon every main doctrine therein contained, and produce a record and interpretation of its teachings which all minds can understand and which will be helpful to all members of the School both here and throughout the world.

The subject is a great one: great in scope, great in possibilities. I approach the duty given me with a true awe, with my heart filled with reverence for these venerable doctrines which from times so far back that "the mind of man runneth not to the contrary" of them have provided the world with its religions, its philosophies, its sciences, its arts, its ethics, and therefore its governments.

The Secret Doctrine is accurately named. It is the teaching which in all times has been held secret and esoteric. The world religions of the past and present may be proved to have sprung from it; the great religious philosophies of the Indian Peninsula, most easily so. The teachings of pre-Spanish America, of Europe in pagan times so called; the legends, the myths, the fairy tales in all the countries of the world, which we may exemplify by the teachings in the Scandinavian Eddas and the Anglo-Saxon Epics — these great works which so many people think to be only sagas or stories — are sprung in their origin from the secret wisdom which H. P. Blavatsky has imbodied and outlined in her masterly work.

These things are important to remember. The human mind has never produced in any part of the world merely wild and unbased, unfounded or merely mythical statements of religion. Religion, like everything else, begins with ideas and ends with dogmas and myths. In all dogmas may be found the seed of the esoteric root from which they sprang. In the Christian religion — whose dogmas have been man-made and have been christened God-made — its dogmas too are founded to a large extent upon the ancient pagan teachings, and therefore ultimately upon the esoteric truths imbodied in this vast collection of teachings which H. P. Blavatsky has called *The Secret Doctrine*. In it she has attempted to bring back in outline only, rarely in detail, some fundamental principles of this archaic doctrine, the same all over the world, the same in all times; interpreted variously by various men in various nations.

H. P. Blavatsky opens her work by enouncing three fundamental propositions, three basic facts. It seems to me that a correct understanding of these postulates would eliminate the many misunderstandings that exist today among men regarding the basic truths in religious thought. They unify, they separate never.

First, is her enunciation of an inscrutable Principle; the second postulate in the proem of *The Secret Doctrine* is that the universe is the playground, as it were, the field, the arena, the scene, of incessant, eternal, never-ceasing periodicity: that is to say, cyclical movement, the manifesting of the eternal life in the cyclical appearance and disappearance of worlds — stars, planets, and the other celestial bodies in the cosmic container which men so vaguely and inaccurately call space. She tells us, voicing the teaching of the ancient wisdom, that these worlds come and go like sparks, mystically called the "sparks of eternity." The life cycle of each of the greater bodies is of necessity of immense duration; and when we speak of time, human understanding demands that we shall have some measure by which we can understand what we mean by time, and by common consent the period of the earth's revolution around the sun, which we call one year, has been taken as an arbitrary measure.

The third postulate — by no means the least in importance, that which is easiest to understand and which for us perhaps is most pregnant with truth — is that the universe and all in it are one immense, eternal organism. Let us be careful here lest we fall into the doctrine called monism which teaches, briefly, that everything in the universe is ultimately derived from one material cause. Equally must we avoid falling into the erroneous doctrine of monotheism, or the teaching that the universe and all in it are the creation by the fiat and caprice of an infinite and eternal personal God. The former doctrine is simply materialism; the latter almost equally materialistic.

This third fundamental proposition tells us not merely that the universe is one with all that is in it, but more particularly that the being of man — his body, his bodies; his soul, his souls; and his spirit — is but the offspring, the fruitage of forces. Here we come upon one of the teachings most necessary for us to understand in the magnificent sweep of theosophical philosophy, that of hierarchies; that is to say, that the kosmos, the universe, while one organism, is nevertheless formed of steps or gradations of beings, consciousnesses or intellects, of all various kinds, in which the universal life manifests, and that these are interrelated, correlated and coordinated, and work together in one unity towards one common object and end.

We see thus that we are not merely children of earth, beings like butterflies, born of a day; but verily sparks of the heart of being, of the central fire of the universal life. If we could feel this wonderful truth in our hearts, and if we could carry our feeling into our daily lives, no force would be greater to govern our conduct than it; nothing could better mold our destinies or put us upon a nobler path of achievement and service.

Realizing that we are one unity with all that is; that universal brotherhood is a fact of being, rooted in the very heart of things, unescapable, not to be avoided; and that our acts and thoughts act and react with inevitable consequence in all that we think and do — not only upon ourselves, the thinkers and actors, but on all other beings everywhere — how different might the lives of men be! Here, more than in the first two fundamental propositions, do we find the true religious, scientific, and philosophical basis of morals. No man can work unto himself; inevitably, inviolably he works unto others likewise. What he does affects others. These teachings are realities, real things.

Let us have the knowledge of it, let us realize that every thought is a thing which eventuates now or at some later day in an action; that the accumulation of thoughts along any one line shall produce its proper effect or effects; that in the chain of being one thing leads to another, and that our moral and physical responsibility is precisely something that we can never escape. When man realizes that he is responsible and inevitably will be called to an accounting, and that at any instant selfishness of motive or godlike love and compassion direct his acts, then we shall have every right to look for a regenerated mankind.

II

In resuming our talk of last week, in which we considered the three fundamental postulates of the esoteric philosophy which H. P. Blavatsky outlined in the first pages of *The Secret Doctrine*, we must remember that we are dealing with subjects so abstract, so abstruse, that to attain to a simplification of them is a task beset with many difficulties, surrounded as it is with the forces of prejudice, and demanding also the use of such words that all minds will understand at least the main thought imbodied in our talks.

With regard to this question of words, no science or philosophy, no religious thought, can attempt to interpret itself to the world without having its own complete technical vocabulary; otherwise it is faced with misconstruction, misunderstanding, frequent needless opposition. For this reason certain words have been used, largely drawn from the Oriental religions, because there and there only, as regards religions which still live, do we find thoughts and the proper treatment of them which also exist in the ancient wisdom, today called theosophy. Scarcely one of these terms, however, has been properly interpreted or understood, precisely because they are for the most part Sanskrit words — not merely words from that language, but words which have also received color and meaning and application in religions which still use them. Even English terms have meanings varying according to the places where we find them. Hence, as said before, it will be necessary in studying *The Secret Doctrine* carefully to set forth the meaning in which these words are used — a meaning philosophic, a meaning religious, and a meaning current in the popular walks of life. But first it would seem good to quote from H. P. Blavatsky the paragraph occurring at the bottom of page 13, preceding her treatment of these fundamental propositions:

Before the reader proceeds to the consideration of the Stanzas from the Book of Dzyan which form the basis of the present work, it is absolutely necessary that he should be made acquainted with the few fundamental conceptions which underlie and pervade the entire system of thought to which his attention is invited. These basic ideas are few in number, and on

their clear apprehension depends the understanding of all that follows;
therefore no apology is required for asking the reader to make himself
familiar with them first, before entering on the perusal of the work itself.

These three propositions may be called a synopsis of the entire
system of esoteric philosophy. They are an epitome of the religious
and philosophic reasoning of the human soul from times vanishing
into unknown antiquity. Necessarily, therefore, are they very
difficult to understand, and in some of their reaches they cannot
be understood fully by the human mind. For instance, while we
cannot say with reference to this first proposition what this Principle *is*, nevertheless we can talk about it, talk around it, say what
it is *not*, as H. P. Blavatsky herself does when, after saying that in
the words of the Upanishad it is "unthinkable and unspeakable,"
she proceeds to speak of it and to give the ancient teaching about
it as it was understood by the greatest minds of olden times.

This first proposition is expressed by her as follows:

An Omnipresent, Eternal, Boundless, and Immutable PRINCIPLE on
which all speculation is impossible, since it transcends the power of human
conception and could only be dwarfed by any human expression or similitude. It is beyond the range and reach of thought — in the words of
Mandukya [Upanishad], "unthinkable and unspeakable."

What do we mean by *principle*, as a word? It has many
meanings: it may mean a rule of conduct; it may be used in the
sense of cause; or in its etymological meaning as beginning. The
word *prince* is from the same Latin root, meaning the head of the
men of his state, the beginning of justice, the fountain of law
and order.

Now what does H. P. Blavatsky mean in choosing the word
principle? Are we to understand that it is used in the sense of
a pure abstraction, as when one says six or long? Six what? Or
what is it which is long? Words so used are pure abstractions;
they have no application and no meaning unless connected with
some object. In other words, they signify nothing in especial;
and therefore if we choose to understand H. P. Blavatsky's use of
this word *principle*, in the sense of a pure abstraction without
application to any subject of thought or thing, then we must
conclude that the Principle of which she speaks is pure nothing-

ness — not *no thing*, but *nothing* in the ordinary sense. When she speaks of a Principle, however, she uses it with a purpose and a meaning; hence Principle does not mean nothingness. Yet we cannot call this All, this Mystery, this Space — which are other words that she gives it — by the name of any *thing*. On the other hand, it is not a being, it is not an entity, it is nothing limited, no matter how great or how apparently boundless.

Properly to understand why and how ancient thinkers used words such as this, we introduce here a key to ancient wisdom, and it is this: the thought of ancient times the world over was *anthropocentric*, not as defined in dictionaries today, meaning that man is the highest goal of creation in the ordinary Christian sense, or that the universe revolves around man as the most important thing in creation. This sense is by usage a permissible one, but it is not the sense in which the word is used when we apply it to this ancient key. Here is the meaning, difficult to understand, but very important for the proper interpretation of the wisdom set forth in *The Secret Doctrine*. A man thinks. He thinks with his own thoughts from what is in himself. He cannot think in the mind of another man. Perforce, by the necessities of his own being, his thoughts follow the cast or bent of his own nature: spring from within him, as from a fountain, and this, as applied to the religious and philosophic thought of the ancients is the meaning of the word anthropocentric, as we shall use it.

The word itself is from the Greek, *anthropos*, "man" in the general sense, like the German word *Mensch*, not man in the individual sense. It means that the ancients looked upon their religious philosophy and their philosophic systems as springing *from within man himself*, hence they were anthropocentric. Similar to this was their treatment of the phenomena of nature, which was based on the phenomenal fact that the earth was the apparent center of the solar system. So is any other planet. We have remnants of this system in our own languages today, when we speak of the "rising" and the "setting" of the sun, and so forth.

Now, then, treating the ancient wisdom from the anthropocentric position, the ancient thinkers realized that to render forth the thoughts which sprang up within them they must use human language, human similes, human metaphors. Only in this fashion could they receive some degree of the attentive consideration which they, as teachers of this ancient wisdom, merited. Hence we find the application of the anthropocentric idea to this word *principle* — a word which can be used both as an abstraction or in a concrete material sense.

Obviously H. P. Blavatsky did not use *principle* in a material sense. What, then, did she mean to convey? That this Principle beyond the reach of human thought must be all that which passes human understanding and which for that reason we can only call the All — a word simply expressing our ignorance, it is true; but it does express the fact that this ineffable Principle is All. Ultimately from it we sprang, back to it we are journeying through the aeons of illimitable time. All thoughts ultimately came from it, but by no fiat of a thinking mind, however great. The ancient philosophy tells us that we may liken the first stirrings of being in this All to the life germ in an egg. How marvelous it is that a thing which, when chemically analyzed, consists of but a few elements of matter, yet if not disturbed or destroyed, under proper conditions, brings forth a living being!

Many are the religions which have treated of this Principle in varying ways. Let us first take the Hebrew in illustration of the thought, because from it, largely, sprang the Christian doctrines. Since most of us were born in Christian countries, the doctrines which that church has had are most familiar to us, and this, perhaps, is a sufficient excuse for choosing it as our first illustration. "In the beginning," that is to say, "In the Principle," and so translated in the Greek Septuagint, "God made the world and the world was without form and void, and the Spirit of God moved upon the waters." Now here is a wonderful thing. The thought in those lines is by no means well expressed philosophically, but it does contain the esoteric teaching as we have it here in *The Secret Doctrine:* "In the beginning" — "In the Principle" — "In the All." The next statement is that "God" (the original Hebrew is *Elohīm*) made the earth and the earth was formless and void. What does *void* mean? Let me remind you that the word here means more than "empty"; it means properly, in this application, *intangible, immaterial,* as we would say, an astral world, a spiritual world, even.

"And the spirit of Elohīm moved upon the waters." What waters? Where were the waters upon which "Elohīm" or the "Gods" moved? Why should they move upon the "waters"? *Water* is a term used in the ancient religions as signifying space, the waters of space. We have here a treatment of an immaterial world, brought forth from the All by powers, by gods if you like — the word matters nothing — and of the spirit, the force of these beings, moving over or within this intangible and immaterial globe or world.

Turning to the Farther Orient and taking up the Sanskrit teachings as expressed in the Veda — the most ancient and highly revered religious and philosophical works of Hindustan — we find in the translation of Colebrooke the following:

> Nor Aught nor Naught existed; . . .

Think of the thought in this. Neither some thing nor no thing existed.

> . . . yon bright sky
> Was not, nor heaven's broad roof outstretched above.
> What covered all? what sheltered? what concealed?
> Was it the water's fathomless abyss?

Again the reference to the waters of space.

> There was not death — yet there was naught immortal,
> There was no confine betwixt day and night;
> The only One breathed breathless by itself,
> Other than It there nothing since has been.
> Darkness there was, and all at first was veiled
> In gloom profound — an ocean without light —
> The germ that still lay covered in the husk
> Burst forth, one nature, from the fervent heat.

See the marvelous attempt to render into ordinary human language, into commonplace figures of speech, however beautiful, thoughts whose subtility and profundity the human mind can reach towards, grasp for, attempt to reach — and yet must largely fail. And nevertheless we sense, we feel, as it were by an inner consciousness, the existence, the reality, the actuality, of that which we know is, and fail to tell.

Here we have a statement that "no thing" was and "not no thing" was. To this, by reason of our anthropocentric understanding, we can give no human name; yet, as the mind works analogically, the Veda tells us that the germ of life arose in It as It then was. So is It now, nothing less, nothing gone, nothing added; always the same so far as we can see, and yet changing ever. Utter immobility is death. In It death exists not. Motion, as we understand it, is life, and yet in It such life in reality exists not. It is in reality neither in motion nor motionless. All we can liken It to, following the anthropocentric rule, is utter space, containing unending motion *as we understand it,* in infinity, in eternity — and all these are but words, an open confession of the inability of the human mind to reach it. Yet how noble, how proud, a statement it is of the mighty forces of the human spirit which can reach up, and even get some intimation of the unutterable.

On page two of the first volume of her work, H. P. Blavatsky says: "It is the ONE LIFE, eternal, invisible, yet Omnipresent, without beginning or end, yet periodical in its regular manifestations, . . ."

Is it possible inwardly to conceive the immensity of this spacial All and our kosmos, our universe, as hanging from It by a thread of spirit — our universe, not alone our dust speck of earth, but the universe comprised within the encircling zone of the Milky Way — and the numberless other universes hanging from It? So, when we read "periodical in its regular manifestations," we inevitably follow the anthropocentric law of our being and reason as men.

The All itself never manifests; It is the *Unmanifest;* but it is true nevertheless that from It manifestation proceeds. To what can we liken It then? What were the pictures, the metaphors, by which the ancients explained the manifest proceeding from the unmanifest — the material from the immaterial, life from not-life, personality from nonpersonality, being, entity, from nonbeing and nonentity? Here is one figure: the world-principle is the sun. The sun sends forth innumerable rays of light; we may assume that the sending forth is eternal and in all directions; and that the rays of light are part of that which sends them forth. Thus did the ancients liken the sun to this All. The sun itself in their philosophy was but the material manifestation on this plane of a hierarchic series which had its roots again inmeshed in something still higher than itself, and so forth. How did they describe this Principle, this Unspeakable, in the Vedas? Silence and darkness surrounded the thought and they simply called it *Tat;* the English translation is "that" — not even "God," not even "the Shining One"; it was limited by no adjective, simply *That.*

Another figure was the World Tree, even more universal than that of the sun, found in the Hindu scriptures, in the ancient American Maya, Inca, Toltec symbols, found also in ancient Europe and preserved to this day in the Scandinavian Eddas. The World Tree — how is it imagined? It was figured as growing from above downwards, its roots rooted in That, and its trunk, its manifold branches, and its twigs, and its leaves, and its flowers, stretching downwards in all directions and representing the manifesting and manifested life, the incalculable things into which this cosmic river, this spiritual flood of being, runs.

Suppose a tip at the end of the lowest, utmost branch, the tip of a leaf: it draws its life from the leaf, the leaf from the twig, the twig from the branch, the branch from a larger branch, the larger branch from a larger one still, it from the trunk, the trunk from the roots, the roots — why proceed further? We can continue indefinitely. But the ancients, with their deep religious faith, simply said *That* when referring to that which transcends human power of conception. Thus, when H.P.B. says here, "yet periodical in its regular manifestations," so must we understand it. It is her own teaching that It manifests never, but from It springs all life. "Between which periods runs the dark mystery of non-Being" — what is this state? Is it dark per se? Is it an unsolvable mystery? Is it nothingness? What right have we to think so, so to conceive it? These are words used of necessity anthropocentrically, following the ancient rule, knowing that man can use no terms understandable by himself and his fellows except those which follow the psychological laws of his own being. Therefore, and we quote further:

> . . . between which periods reigns the dark mystery of [to us] non-Being; unconscious [to us], yet absolute Consciousness; unrealisable [by us], yet the one self-existing reality; truly, "a chaos to the sense, a Kosmos to the

reason." Its one absolute attribute, which is ITSELF, eternal, ceaseless Motion [to us], is called in esoteric parlance the "Great Breath," which is the perpetual motion of the universe, in the sense of limitless, ever-present SPACE."

III

In our last two meetings we studied the three fundamental postulates in H. P. Blavatsky's *Secret Doctrine*. Therein we are taught that there exists in man a link with the Unutterable, a cord, a communication, that extends from It to the inner consciousness; and that link — such is the teaching as it has come down to us — is the very heart of being. It arises in that supersensory Principle, that unutterable Mystery which H. P. Blavatsky defines in the first fundamental proposition as above human mind. Becoming one with that link, we can transcend the powers of ordinary human intellect, and reach (even if it be by striving out, upward, towards) that Unutterable, which is, we know — though it is beyond human power to express it in words, or beyond human thought — the concealed of the concealed, the life of life, truth of truth, the ALL.

Here is the thought, it seems to me, which illustrates so well Katherine Tingley's words in this regard. They struck me as very beautiful, profoundly suggestive. She said:

Thinking towards the unthinkable is a wonderful, spiritualizing force; one cannot think toward it without a disposition either to think more or feel more — without opening up the inner consciousness of man. And when that inner consciousness is awakened, the soul finds itself closer to the infinite laws, closer to THAT, or that Great Center that no words can express.

By striving towards this inwards, towards the Inmost, we can attain to some conception, if not understanding, of the infinite Principle of all that is. From It, in the course of endless duration, there spring into manifestation at the end of the great universal or cosmic pralaya, the beginnings of things. These beginnings eventuate in the forms of life and being described in the second and third fundamental propositions.

This inmost link with the Unutterable was called in ancient India by the term self, which has been often mistranslated "soul."

The Sanskrit word is *ātman,* and applies, in psychology, to the human entity. The upper end of the link, so to speak, was called *paramātman* or the "supreme self," the permanent self — words which describe neatly and clearly to those who have studied this wonderful philosophy somewhat of the nature and essence of the thing which man is, and the source from which, in that beginning-less and endless duration, he sprang. Child of earth and child of heaven, he contains both in himself.

We pass now from considering the first proposition to the second and the third. And in order that we may understand what we mean when we use certain words, it will be useful to illustrate our usages of such words. Let us take up the remarkably well-translated book entitled *The Song Celestial,* the work of Sir Edwin Arnold. It is a translation into English verse of the *Bhagavad-Gītā.* That work is an episode or an interlude found in the sixth book of the *Mahābhārata,* the greater of the two great Hindu epics; and in the style of the Hindu writings it comprises a dissertation on religious, philosophical, and mystical subjects. Sir Edwin's *Song Celestial,* in book the second, has the following:

> . . . The soul which is not moved,
> The soul that with a strong and constant calm
> Takes sorrow and takes joy indifferently,
> Lives in the life undying! That which is
> Can never cease to be; that which is not
> Will not exist. To see this truth of both
> Is theirs who part essence from accident,
> Substance from shadow. Indestructible,
> Learn thou! the Life is, spreading life through all;
> It cannot anywhere, by any means,
> Be anywise diminished, stayed, or changed.
> But for these fleeting frames which it informs
> With spirit deathless, endless, infinite,
> They perish. . . .
> Never the spirit was born; the spirit shall cease
>   to be never;
>   Never was time it was not; End and Beginning
>   are dreams!
> Birthless and deathless and changeless remaineth
>   the spirit for ever;
>   Death hath not touched it at all, dead though
>   the house of it seems!

Now these words are exquisitely beautiful. They nevertheless contain a mistranslation, a misrendering of the text of this wonderful little work. In the first place, Sir Edwin translates the Sanskrit word *tat,* first by the word "soul" and next by the word "spirit." Of course, analogically, it has a reference to the soul and the spirit of man; but the Sanskrit of it does not point particularly to the soul of man. I will read a translation in prose of these same verses, made with no attempt at poetic thought, no attempt to use beautiful language, but simply to express the thought:

The man whom these do not lead astray, O Bull among men! who is the same in pain and pleasure, and of steady soul, he partakes of immortality.

There is no existence for the unreal; there is no nonexistence for the Real. Moreover, the ultimate characteristic of both these is seen by those who perceive true principles.

Know That to be indestructible by which this whole universe was woven.

The Sanskrit word for "That" is *tat,* as already explained. The figure is that of the weaving of a web.

The destruction of this Imperishable, none is able to bring about.

These mortal bodies are said to be of the imbodied Eternal, Indestructible, Immeasurable One. . . .

He who knows It as the slayer, and he who thinks It to be the slain: both of them understand not. It slays not, nor is it slain.

It is not born, nor does it ever die; It was not produced, nor shall it ever be produced.

It is unborn, constant, everlasting, primeval. It is unhurt when the body is slain.

The application that the writer in the *Bhagavad-Gītā* makes is to the link which we have spoken of, the deathless, undying principle within us, and he describes it by the word That, and contrasts it with the manifested universe which, following the ancient teachings of India, was invariably spoken of as This — the Sanskrit word is *idam.*

The sages of olden times left on record the inner teaching of the religions of the peoples among whom they lived. This inner teaching was the esoteric philosophy, the theosophy of the period. In Hindustan this theosophy is found in the Upanishads, a part of the Vedic literary cycle. The word itself implies "secret doctrine" or "secret teachings." From the Upanishads and from other parts of the Vedic literature, the ancient sages of India produced what is called today the *Vedanta* — a compound Sanskrit word meaning "the end (or completion) of the Veda" — that is to say, instruction in the final and most perfect exposition of the meaning of the Vedic tenets.

In ancient Greece there were various schools and various Mysteries, and the theosophy of ancient Greece was held very secret; it was taught in the Mysteries and it was taught by different teachers to select bodies of their disciples. One of such great teachers was Pythagoras; another was Plato; and this theosophy was more or less clearly outlined and imbodied, after the fall of the so-called pagan religions, in what is today called the Neoplatonic philosophy. It represents actually the inner teachings of Pythagoras, Plato, and the inner sense of those mystical doctrines which passed current in Greece under the name of the Orphic poems.

Of the theosophy of Egypt we have but scanty remainings, such as exist in what is called "The Book of the Dead." Of the theosophy of ancient America, of the Incan, the Mayan, empires we have next to nothing. The theosophy of ancient Europe has passed away. All that remains to us is a certain number of mystical writings such as the Scandinavian Eddas, and the Germanic books, which are represented, for instance, in the sagas found written in the old High German and in the Anglo-Saxon tongues.

A study of the doctrines contained in the Upanishads, in "The Book of the Dead," in the Neoplatonic philosophy, in the Scandinavian Eddas, and elsewhere, shows that they had one common basis, one foundation, one common truth. Various men in various ages taught the same truth, using different words and different figures, different metaphors; but underneath always was the ancient doctrine, the secret wisdom.

The theosophy of the Jews was imbodied in what was later called the Qabbālāh, from a Hebrew word meaning "to receive"; that is to say, it was the traditional doctrine handed down or received (according to the statements of the Qabbālāh itself) through the prophets and the sages of Jewry, and was said to have been first taught by "God Almighty to a select company of angels in Heaven."

We must remember, when we approach the teachings of the ancient wisdom, that the ancient teachers spoke and thought and taught *anthropocentrically;* that is, that they all insisted on following the psychological laws of the human mind and therefore taught in human figures of speech, often using quaint metaphors, very odd, and yet so instructive as figures of speech. How wise that was, because thus they were able to carry on the teachings, and did so in such fashion that least of all did this anthropocentric system encourage the dogmatic rulings that have most truly blasted all that was best in the teachings of the Christian Church. These tropes, these metaphors, were so quaint that the mind understood almost instantly that they were but the vehicle imbodying the truth. Let us remember this, and our work becomes immensely more easy.

Now let us take the Qabbālāh as a sample of the manner in which one theosophy — the Jewish — approaches the mystery of how the Unmanifest produces the manifest, how from that which is endless and beginningless duration sprang forth matter, space in the sense of material extension, and time.

But first let me quote from another Sanskrit work, the *Kena-Upanishad.* Speaking of this unutterable Mystery, it says:

> The eye reacheth it not, language reacheth it not, nor does thought reach to it at all; verily, we know not nor can we say how one should teach it; it is different from the known, it is beyond the unknown. Thus have we heard from the men of olden times, for they taught it to us.   — 1, 3–4

The great Śankarāchārya, perhaps the most famous of Indian commentators on the Upanishads and the marvelously beautiful system of philosophy drawn from them called the Vedanta, says, commenting on the *Aitareya-Upanishad:*

> There is the One, sole, alone, apart from all duality, in which there appear not the multitudinous illusory presentments of unreal bodies and conditions of this universe of merely apparent reality; passionless, unmoving, pure, in utter peace; knowable only by the lack of every adjective epithet; unreachable by word or by thought.

The Qabbālāh, the traditionary teaching of the sages among the Jews, is a wonderful teaching; it contains in outline or in epitome every fundamental tenet or teaching that the Secret Doctrine contains. The teachings of the Qabbālāh are often couched in very quaint and sometimes amusing language; sometimes its language rises to the height of sublimity. What does the *Zohar*, the second of the great books that remain of the Qabbālāh (the word *Zohar* itself meaning "splendor"), have to say of the manner in which the Jewish religious books should be studied? It says this (iii, 152a):

> Woe be to the son of man who says that the Torah [the Hebrew Bible, especially the Pentateuch, or rather the first four books of the Bible excluding *Deuteronomy*, the fifth] contains common sayings and ordinary narratives. If this were the case we might in the present day compose a code of doctrines from profane writings which would excite greater respect. If the Law contains ordinary matter, then there are nobler sentiments in profane codes. Let us go and make a selection from them and we shall be able to compile a far superior code. No! Every word of the Law has a sublime sense and a heavenly mystery. . . . As the spiritual angels had to put on earthly garments when they descended to this earth, and as they could neither have remained nor be understood on the earth without putting on such a garment, so it is with the Law. When it descended on earth, the Law had to put on an earthly garment, in order to be understood by us, and the narratives are its garment. . . . Those who have understanding do not look at the garment but at the body [the esoteric meaning] beneath; whilst the wisest, the servants of the heavenly King, those who dwell on Mount Sinai, look at nothing but the soul —

i.e., at the ultimate secret doctrine or sacred wisdom hid under the "body," under the exoteric narratives or stories of the Bible.

In these days, when modernists and fundamentalists quarrel — quarrel unnecessarily about exoteric superficialities, about things which arise out of the egoism of men, about the dogmatic teachings of the Christian Church, every one of them probably based on ancient pagan esoteric philosophy — it is an immense pity that they do not know and understand that this ·teaching of the Qabbālāh as expressed in the *Zohar* is a *true* one; for under every garment is the life. As Jesus taught in parables, so the Bible was written in figures of speech, in metaphors.

TWO

WHERE IS REALITY? TRUTH CAN BE KNOWN. MAN'S COMPOSITE
NATURE ACCORDING TO DIFFERENT SYSTEMS: THREEFOLD,
FOURFOLD, FIVEFOLD, OR SEVENFOLD.

The fundamental Law in that system, the central point from which all
emerged, around and toward which all gravitates, and upon which is hung
the philosophy of the rest, is the One homogeneous divine SUBSTANCE-
PRINCIPLE, the one radical cause.

    . . . "Some few, whose lamps shone brighter, have been led
       From cause to cause to nature's secret head,
       And found that one first Principle must be. . . ."

It is called "Substance-Principle," for it becomes "substance" on the plane
of the manifested Universe, an illusion, while it remains a "principle" in the
beginningless and endless abstract, visible and invisible SPACE. It is the
omnipresent Reality: impersonal, because it contains all and everything. *Its
impersonality is the fundamental conception* of the System. It is latent in
every atom in the Universe, and is the Universe itself.

                         — *The Secret Doctrine*, I, 273

It is the True. It is the Self, and thou art it.
                         — *Chhāndogya-Upanishad*, 6, 14, 3

The Tao which can be expressed in words is not the eternal Tao; the
name which can be uttered is not its eternal name. Without a name, it is the
Beginning of Heaven and Earth; with a name, it is the Mother of all things.
Only one who is eternally free from earthly passions can apprehend its spiritual essence; he who is ever clogged by passions can see no more than its
outer form. These two things, the spiritual and the material, though we call
them by different names, in their origin are one and the same. This same-
ness is a mystery — the mystery of mysteries. It is the gate of all spirituality.
                   — *The Sayings of Lao Tzŭ* (Lionel Giles, trans.)

WE OPEN volume I of H. P. Blavatsky's *Secret Doctrine*
at page 13, to the second paragraph, which is as
follows:

The reader has to bear in mind that the Stanzas given treat only of the
Cosmogony of our own planetary System and what is visible around it, after

a Solar Pralaya. The secret teachings with regard to the Evolution of the Universal Kosmos cannot be given, since they could not be understood by the highest minds in this age, and there seem to be very few Initiates, even among the greatest, who are allowed to speculate upon this subject. Moreover the Teachers say openly that not even the highest Dhyani-Chohans have ever penetrated the mysteries beyond those boundaries that separate the milliards of Solar systems from the "Central Sun," as it is called. Therefore, that which is given relates only to our visible Kosmos, after a "Night of Brahmâ."

We choose this as the general text of our study this evening, as it seems not only appropriate but necessary to open our study of the more secret matters of which *The Secret Doctrine* treats, by asking in what manner or by what method do we obtain an understanding and a realization of these doctrines? Do they come to us as dogmatic teachings, or are they derived, following the definition that Webster gives of theosophy in his dictionary, by inner spiritual communion with "God"? There is something in Webster's definition which is true. The theosophist does believe that man has within himself the faculty of approaching divine things, of raising the inner man so that he can thereby obtain a more accurate mental representation of *things as they are,* or of reality.

On the other hand, if everyone did this, without proper and capable guidance and leading and teaching, extreme vanity and human conceit as well as many other forces in the human economy would inevitably lead to an immense diversity of opinions and teachings and doctrines, each man believing that he had the truth and he only, and hence that those who followed him and preached his views should form with him a special "church" or "sect" of their own. The words themselves would probably be avoided, but it would amount to that.

Therefore, here we find the use, the benefit, the appositeness, of the theosophical doctrines, to the effect that these teachings have come down to us from immemorial antiquity — transmitted from one Teacher to another — and that originally they were communicated to the nascent human race, when once it became self-conscious, by beings from a higher sphere, beings who themselves were of divine origin; and further, that this communication or emanation of their spiritual and higher intellectual selves into us, gave us our own higher principles. For the Teachers have told us that these doctrines have been checked or proved age after age, generation after generation, by innumerable spiritual seers, to use H. P. Blavatsky's own words — checked in every respect, checked as to fact, as to origin, checked as to operation on the human mind.

Now then, the faculties by which man can attain a knowledge of truth, of the real, can be called upon or evoked at any moment in any place, provided the right conditions are made, so that the striving soul may thus reach successfully upward or *inward*, and *know*. Sometimes in the most simple teachings are found the most divine truths. And why? Because the simple teachings are the fundamental ones.

Consider for a moment, therefore, the seven principles of man in their connection with the seven principles of the universe. The seven principles of man are a likeness or copy of the seven cosmic principles. They are actually the offspring of the seven cosmic principles, limited in their action in us by the workings of the law of karma, but running in their origin back into That which is beyond, into that which is the essence of the universe or the universal; in, beyond, within, to the Unmanifest, to the Unmanifestable, to that first Principle which H. P. Blavatsky enunciates as the leading thought of the wisdom-philosophy of *The Secret Doctrine*.

These principles of man are reckoned as seven in the philosophy by which the human, spiritual, and psychical economy has been explained to us in the present age. In other ages these principles or parts of man were differently reckoned — the Christian reckons them as body, soul, and spirit, and does not know the difference between the soul and the spirit; and many say that the soul and spirit are the same.

Some of the Indian thinkers divided man into a basic fourfold entity, others into a fivefold. The Jewish philosophy as found in the Qabbālāh teaches that man is divided into four parts:

1. The highest and most spiritual of all, that principle or part which is to us a mere breath of being, they called *neshāmāh*.

2. The second principle was called *rūahh* or spiritual soul,

spelled sometimes *rūach* according to another method of trans-literation.

3. The astral soul (or vital soul) was called *nephesh*, the third next lower, which man has in common with the brutes.

4. Then comes the *gūph* or physical vehicle, the house in which all these others dwell.

Over all, and higher than all, higher than the *neshāmāh* — which is not an emanation of this Highest, not a creation, not an evolution, but of which it was the *production* in a sense which we shall later have to explain — there is the Ineffable, the Boundless, called *Eyn* (or *Ain*) *Sōph*.

The Sanskrit terms which have been given to the seven principles of man in the theosophical philosophy are as follows, and we can get much help from explaining the original Sanskrit meanings of them, and illustrating the sense in which those words were used, and why they were chosen.

1. The first principle is called the *sthūla-śarīra*. *Sthūla* means "coarse," "gross," not refined, heavy, bulky, fat in the sense of bigness. *Śarīra* comes from a root which can best be translated by saying that it is that which is "easily dissolved," "easily worn away"; the idea being something transitory, foamlike, full of holes, as it were. Note the meaning hid in this: it is very important.

2. The second principle let us call the *linga-śarīra*. *Linga* is a Sanskrit word which means "characteristic mark"; hence model, pattern. It forms the model or pattern on which the physical body is built — this physical body, composed mostly of porosity, if the expression be pardoned; the most *unreal* thing we know, full of holes, foamy, as it were. We will revert to this thought later.

3. The third principle, commonly called the life-principle, is *prāna*. Now this word is used here in a general sense. There are, as a matter of fact, a number of life-currents, vital fluids. They have several names. One system gives the number as three; another as five, which is the commonly accepted number; another as seven; another twelve, as is found in some Upanishads; and one old writer even gives them as thirteen.

4. Then there is the *kāma* principle; the word *kāma* means "desire." It is the driving or impelling force in the human econ-

omy; colorless, neither good nor bad, only such as the mind and soul direct its use.

5. Then comes *manas;* the Sanskrit root of this word means "to think," "to cogitate," "to reflect" — mental activity, in short.

6. Then comes *buddhi,* or the spiritual soul, the vehicle or carrier of the highest principle of all, the ātman. Now *buddhi* comes from a Sanskrit root *budh.* This root is commonly translated "to enlighten," but a better translation is "to awaken" and, hence, "to understand"; *buddha,* the past participle of this root is applied to one who is spiritually "awakened," no longer living a living death, but awakened to the spiritual influence from within or from "above." Buddhi is the principle in us which gives us spiritual consciousness, and is the vehicle of the most high part of man. This highest part is the ātman.

7. This principle *(ātman)* is a universal one; but during incarnations its lowest parts, if we can so express it, take on attributes, because it is linked with the buddhi as the buddhi is linked with the manas, as the manas is linked to the kāma, and so on down the scale.

Ātman is also sometimes used of the universal self or spirit which is called in the Sanskrit writings Brahman (neuter), and the Brahman or universal spirit is also called the *Paramātman,* a compound Sanskrit term meaning the "highest" or most universal ātman. The root of ātman is hardly known. Its origin is uncertain, but the general meaning is that of "self."

Beyond Brahman is the *Parabrahman: para* is a Sanskrit word meaning "beyond." Note the deep philosophical meaning of this: there is no attempt here to limit the Illimitable, the Ineffable, by adjectives; it simply means "beyond the Brahman." In the Sanskrit Vedas and in the works deriving therefrom and belonging to the Vedic literary cycle, this *beyond* is called That, as this world of manifestation is called This. Other expressive Sanskrit terms are *sat,* the "real"; and *asat,* the "unreal" or the manifested universe; in another sense *asat* means "not *sat,*" i.e., even beyond (higher than) *sat.*

This Parabrahman is intimately connected with *Mūlaprakriti,* "root-nature." Their interaction and intermingling cause the first nebulous thrilling, if the words will pass, of the universal life when spiritual desire first arose in It in the beginnings of things. Such is the old teaching, employing of necessity the old anthropocentric tropes, clearly understood to be only human similes; for the conceptions of the seers of ancient times, their teachings, their doctrines, had to be told in human language to the human mind.

Now then, a man can reach inward, going "upward" step by step, climbing higher as his spiritual force and power wax greater and more subtil, until he reaches beyond his normal faculties, and steps beyond the Ring-pass-not, as H. P. Blavatsky calls it in her *Secret Doctrine*. Where and what is this Ring-pass-not? It is, at any period of man's consciousness, the utmost reach that his spirit can attain. There he stops, and looks into the Beyond — into the Unmanifested from which we came. The Unmanifest is in us; it is the Inmost of the Inmost in our souls, in our spirits, in our essential beings. We can reach *towards* it. We can actually reach it never.

Now where is reality? Is the real, is the true, to be found in these lower vestures of materiality? Or is it to be found in the state of being from which everything came?

The ancient Stoics in their wonderful philosophy taught, and the same teaching originated in the esoteric philosophy of Hellas or Greece — as found later in the Neoplatonic teachings — these ancient Stoics taught that truth *can* be known; that the most real thing, the greatest thing, was to be found in ever-receding vistas, as the spirit of man strived inward and beyond, veil after veil falling away as the "wise man" (their technical term) advances in the evolution of his soul. They taught that the material universe was illusory precisely as the Hindu speaks of *māyā;* and the Stoic understood that this apparently dense, gross, heavy, material universe is phenomenally unreal, mostly built up of holes, so to say — a teaching which is reechoed today in the writings and thoughts of the more intuitional of our scientists.

The Stoics taught that the ether was denser than the most dense material thing, fuller than the most full material thing — using human words, of course. To us, with our human eyes, trained only to see objects of illusion, it appears to be the most diaphanous, the thinnest, the most ethereal. What was the reality, the real, behind this All? The *real* thing? They said it was God, life of life, truth of truth, root of matter, root of soul, root of spirit. When the Stoic was asked: What is God? he nobly answered: What is God *not?*

Turning now to the ancient wisdom of Hindustan, to the Upanishads — going back far beyond the time when the ancient Brahmanic teachings and the Brahmanas became what they are today, to the time when real men taught real things — let us take from the *Chhāndogya-Upanishad,* mainly in the sixth lecture, a conversation between a father and his son. The son asks:

"If a man who has slept in his own house, rises and goes to another village, he knows that he has come from his own house. Why then do people not know that they have come from the Sat?" [A Sanskrit word meaning the Real, the Ineffable, of which we have spoken.]

And the father teaches his son as follows:

"These rivers, my son, run, the eastern toward the east, the western toward the west. They go from sea to sea. They become indeed sea. And as those rivers, when they are in the sea, do not know, I am this or that river,

"In the same manner, my son, all these creatures, when they have come from the True [that is, the Real] know not that they have come from the True [on account of the māyā]. Whatever these creatures are here, whether a lion, or a wolf, or a boar, or a worm, or a midge, or a gnat, or a mosquito, that they become again and again."

Now listen:

"That which is that subtile essence, in it all that exists has its self. It is the True. It is the Self, and thou, O Śvetaketu, art it." "Please, Sir, inform me still more," said the son. "Be it so, my child," the father replied.

Now the son is supposed to ask, "How is it that living beings, when in sleep or death they are merged again in the Sat, are not destroyed? Waves, foam, and bubbles arise from the water, and when they merge again in the water, they are gone."

"If someone were to strike at the root of this large tree here," says the father, "it would bleed, but live. If he were to strike at its stem, it would bleed, but live. If he were to strike at its top, it would bleed, but live. Pervaded by the living Self that tree stands firm, drinking in its nourishment and rejoicing;

"But if the life (the living Self) leaves one of its branches, that branch withers; if it leaves a second, that branch withers; if it leaves a third, that branch withers. If it leaves the whole tree, the whole tree withers. In exactly the same manner, my son, know this." Thus he spoke:

"This (body) indeed withers and dies when the living Self has left it; the living Self dies not. That which is that subtle essence, in it all that exists has its self. It is the True. It is the Self, and thou, O Śvetaketu, art it."

"Please, Sir, inform me still more," said the son. "Be it so, my child," the father replied.

"Fetch me from thence a fruit of the Nyagrodha tree." "Here is one, Sir." "Break it." "It is broken, Sir." "What do you see there?" "These seeds, almost infinitesimal." "Break one of them." "It is broken, Sir." "What do you see there?" "Not anything, Sir."

The father said: "My son, that subtle essence which you do not perceive there, of that very essence this great Nyagrodha tree exists. Believe it, my son. That which is the subtle essence, in it all that exists has its self. It is the True. It is the Self, and thou, O Śvetaketu, art it." "Please, Sir, inform me still more," said the son. "Be it so, my child," the father replied.

"Place this salt in water, and then wait on me in the morning." The son did as he was commanded. The father said to him: "Bring me the salt, which you placed in the water last night." The son having looked for it, found it not, for, of course, it was melted. The father said: "Taste it from the surface of the water. How is it?" The son replied: "It is salt." "Taste it from the middle. How is it?" The son replied: "It is salt." "Taste it from the bottom. How is it?" The son replied: "It is salt." The father said: "Throw it away and then wait on me." He did so; but salt exists for ever. Then the father said: "Here also, in this body, forsooth, you do not perceive the True (Sat), my son; but there indeed it is.

"That which is the subtle essence [that is, the saltiness of the salt], in it all that exists has its self. It is the True. It is the Self, and thou, O Śvetaketu, art it." "Please, Sir, inform me still more," said the son. "Be it so, my child," the father replied.   — 6, 10–13 (Max Müller trans.)

Let us turn to another part of this Upanishad, to the eighth lecture. And we read as follows: "Harih, Om." Hari is the name of several deities — of Śiva and Vishnu — but here, apparently, it is used for Śiva, which is preeminently the divine protector of the mystic occultist. Om is a word considered very holy in the Brahmanical literature. It is a syllable of invocation, and its general usage — as elucidated in the literature treating of it, which is rather voluminous for this word Om has attained to almost divinity — is that it should never be uttered aloud, or in the presence of an outsider, a foreigner, or a non-initiate, but it should be uttered in the silence of one's heart. We also have reason to believe, however, that it was uttered, and uttered aloud in a monotone by the disciples in the presence of their teacher. This word is always placed at the beginning of any scripture that is considered of unusual sanctity.

The teaching is, that prolonging the uttering of this word, both of the *O* and the *M*, with the mouth closed, it reechoes in and arouses vibration in the skull, and affects, *if the aspirations be pure*, the different nervous centers of the body for great good.

The Brahmanas say that it is an unholy thing to utter this word in any place which is unholy. I now read:

> There is this city of Brahman [that is, the heart and the body], and in it the palace, the small lotus (of the heart), and in it that small ether.

The Sanskrit word which Müller, the translator, has not given here for "small ether," doubtless because he knew not how to translate it, is *antarākāśa*, a compound Sanskrit word meaning "within the *ākāśa*." I read again:

> Now what exists within that small ether, that is to be sought for, that is to be understood. And if they should say to him: "Now with regard to that city of Brahman, and the palace in it, i.e. the small lotus of the heart, and the small ether within the heart, what is there within it that deserves to be sought for, or that is to be understood?"
>
> Then he should say: "As large as this ether (all space) is, so large is that ether within the heart. Both heaven and earth are contained within it, both fire and air, both sun and moon, both lightning and stars; and whatever there is of him (the Self) here in the world, and whatever is not (i.e. whatever has been or will be), all that is contained within it."
>
> And if they should say to him: "If everything that exists is contained in that city of Brahman, all beings and all desires (whatever can be imagined or desired), then what is left of it, when old age reaches it and scatters it, or when it falls to pieces?"
>
> Then he should say: "By the old age of the body, that (the ether, or Brahman within it) does not age; by the death of the body, that (the ether, or Brahman within it) is not killed. That (the Brahman) is the true Brahma-city (not the body). In it all [true] desires are contained. It is the Self, free from sin, free from old age, from death and grief, from hunger and thirst, which desires nothing but what it ought to desire, and imagines nothing but what it ought to imagine. Now as here on earth people follow as they are commanded, and depend on the object which they are attached to, be it a country or a piece of land,

"And as here on earth, whatever has been acquired by exertion, perishes, so perishes whatever is acquired for the next world by sacrifices and other good actions performed on earth. Those who depart from hence without having discovered the Self and those true desires, for them there is no freedom in all the worlds. But those who depart from hence, after having discovered the Self and those true desires, for them there is freedom in all the worlds."   — Ibid., 8, 1

THREE

THE DOCTRINE OF MĀYĀ; OBJECTIVE IDEALISM THE BASIS OF MORALS:
ROOTED IN THE SPIRITUAL UNITY — THE DIVINITY — OF THE
ALL. THE SELF AND THE "SELVES."

Maya or illusion is an element which enters into all finite things, for everything that exists has only a relative, not an absolute, reality, since the appearance which the hidden noumenon assumes for any observer depends upon his power of cognition. To the untrained eye of the savage, a painting is at first an unmeaning confusion of streaks and daubs of colour, while an educated eye sees instantly a face or a landscape. Nothing is permanent except the one hidden absolute existence which contains in itself the noumena of all realities. The existences belonging to every plane of being, up to the highest Dhyan-Chohans, are, in degree, of the nature of shadows cast by a magic lantern on a colourless screen; but all things are relatively real, for the cogniser is also a reflection, and the things cognised are therefore as real to him as himself. Whatever reality things possess must be looked for in them before or after they have passed like a flash through the material world; but we cannot cognise any such existence directly, so long as we have sense-instruments which bring only material existence into the field of our consciousness. Whatever plane our consciousness may be acting in, both we and the things belonging to that plane are, for the time being, our only realities. As we rise in the scale of development we perceive that during the stages through which we have passed we mistook shadows for realities, and the upward progress of the Ego is a series of progressive awakenings, each advance bringing with it the idea that now, at last, we have reached "reality"; but only when we shall have reached the absolute Consciousness, and blended our own with it, shall we be free from the delusions produced by Maya.
— *The Secret Doctrine*, I, 39–40

The Universe is called, with everything in it, MAYA, because all is temporary therein, from the ephemeral life of a fire-fly to that of the Sun. Compared to the eternal immutability of the ONE, and the changelessness of that Principle, the Universe, with its evanescent ever-changing forms, must be necessarily, in the mind of a philosopher, no better than a will-o'-the-wisp. Yet, the Universe is real enough to the conscious beings in it, which are as unreal as it is itself.   — Ibid., I, 274

I N TAKING up again our study of *The Secret Doctrine* at the
point we reached a fortnight ago, I open the first volume
at page 17, and read the third fundamental postulate — at
least a portion of it:

The fundamental identity of all Souls with the Universal Over-Soul, the
latter being itself an aspect of the Unknown Root; and the obligatory pilgrimage for every Soul — a spark of the former — through the Cycle of
Incarnation (or "Necessity") in accordance with Cyclic and Karmic law,
during the whole term. In other words, no purely spiritual Buddhi (divine
Soul) can have an independent ;(conscious) existence before the spark
which issued from the pure Essence of the Universal Sixth principle, — or the
OVER-SOUL, — has (a) passed through every elemental form of the phenomenal
world of that Manvantara, and (b) acquired individuality, first by natural
impulse, and then by self-induced and self-devised efforts (checked by its
Karma), thus ascending through all the degrees of intelligence, from the
lowest to the highest Manas, from mineral and plant, up to the holiest archangel (Dhyani-Buddha).

Paul, the Apostle of the Christians "to the Gentiles," as they
call him, according to the Christian Gospels in Acts 17, verses
23–28, spoke to an assembly of the Athenians on Mars Hill, commonly called the Areopagus, and he said the following (the
translation being ours):

For as I passed by and beheld your devotions, I found an altar with this
inscription: "To the Unknowable God.". . . For in It we live and move and
have our being, as certain also of your own poets have said, "For we are
also of Its line."

The poets of whom Paul speaks were probably Cleanthes the
Stoic, and Aratus. It is perhaps well to mention that the sense of
"unknowable," as used in connection with this word *agnostos*, is
that employed by Homer, by Plato, and by Aristotle. This Greek
word *agnostos* also permits the translation "unknown," but merely
because the Unknown in this connection is the Unknowable.

The Athenians had raised an altar to the Ineffable, and with
the true spirit of religious devotion they left it without further
qualification; and Paul, passing by and seeing it, thought he saw
an excellent chance to "make hay while the sun shone," and
claimed the Unknowable, to which this altar had been raised, as
the Jewish God, Jehovah.

A fortnight ago we stated how it was that man could form some conception of that ineffable Principle of which H. P. Blavatsky speaks as being the first of the three fundamental postulates necessary in order to understand the true teachings of the esoteric wisdom; and we saw that man has in himself a faculty transcending the ordinary human intellectual power — something in him by which he can raise himself upwards or, perhaps better, *inwards*, towards the inmost center of his own being, which in very truth *is* that Ineffable: from It we came, back to It we are journeying through the aeons of time.

All the ancient philosophers taught the truth concerning this same fundamental principle, each in his own way, each with different terms, each in the language of the country where it was promulgated, but always there was taught the central truth: that in the inmost being of man there lives a divinity, and this divinity is the offspring of the Highest, and that man can become a god in the flesh, or he can sink lower even than the common average of humanity so that he becomes at first obsessed or beset, and finally possessed by the daemons of his own lower nature and by those of the lower sphere; and by these particular daemons we mean the elemental forces of life, of chaotic life, or of the material sphere of being.

Again, how is it that man cannot see these truths intimately and immediately? We all know the answer is, on account of the illusion under which his mind labors, the illusion which is a part of himself, not cast upon him from the outside: he *sees*, for instance, and his mind reacts to the vision, and the reaction is conducted along the lines of the illusion which, taking the ancient Sanskrit word, is called māyā.

This is a technical term in the ancient Brahmanical philosophy. Let us examine its root. What does the word *māyā* come from? It comes from a Sanskrit root *mā*, meaning "to measure," and by a figure of speech it comes to mean to effect, or to form, and hence to limit. There is an English word *mete*, meaning "to measure out," from the same Indo-European root. It is found in the Anglo-Saxon as the root *met*, in the Greek as *med*, and in the Latin also in the same form.

Now māyā, as a technical term, has come to mean — ages ago

in the Brahmanical philosophy it was understood very differently from what it is now usually understood to be — the fabrication by man's mind of ideas derived from interior and exterior impressions, and hence the *illusory* aspect of man's thoughts as he considers and tries to interpret and understand life and his surroundings — and thence was derived the sense which it technically bears, illusion. It does *not* mean that the exterior world is nonexistent; if it were, it obviously could not be illusory; it *exists,* but *is* not. It is "measured out" or it stands out to the human spirit as a mirage. In other words, we do not see clearly and plainly and in their reality the vision and the visions which our mind and senses present to the inner life and eye.

The familiar illustrations of māyā in the Vedanta, which is the highest form that the Brahmanical teachings have taken and which is so near to our own teaching in many respects, were such as follows: a man at eventide sees a coiled rope on the ground and springs aside, thinking it a serpent. The rope is there, but no serpent.

Another illustration is what is called the "horns of the hare." When a hare is seen at eventide its long ears seem to project from its head in such fashion that it appears even to the seeing eye as being a creature with horns. The hare has no horns, but there is then in the mind an illusory belief that an animal with horns exists there.

That is what māyā means: not that a thing seen does not exist, but that we are blinded and our mind perverted by our own thoughts and our own imperfections, and do not as yet arrive at the real interpretation and meaning of the world, of the universe around us. By ascending inwardly, by rising up, by inner aspiration, by an elevation of soul, we can reach upwards or rather inwards toward that plane where truth abides in fullness.

Bernard of Clairvaux, the French mystic of the Middle Ages, said that one way of doing this, and he spoke truly, was by "emptying the mind," pouring out the trashy stuff it contains, the illusory beliefs, the false views, the hatreds, suspicions, carelessness, etc., and that by emptying out all this trash, the temple within is cleansed, and the light from the god within streams forth into the soul — a wonderful figure of thought.

It may be asked: what relationship has our philosophy to the many so-called idealistic systems of Europe, particularly in Germany, and represented by Bishop Berkeley in Britain? The answer is that there are points of contact, naturally, because the men who evolved these systems of philosophy were earnest men, and no man can earnestly think and strive upwards without arriving at some visions of truth, some faint perceptions of the inner life — but none of these systems of idealism is exactly the idealism of theosophy. Theosophy is not an absolute idealism; it does not teach that the external universe is *absolutely* nonexistent and that all external phenomena merely exist in the mind.

Theosophy is not exactly either the idealism of Kant nor the wonderful pessimistic idealism of Schopenhauer — wonderful as this great thinker was, and wonderful precisely because he derived his knowledge (and confessed it openly) from the Orient. The idealism of theosophy is nearest to the philosophy of the German philosopher von Schelling, who taught (principally) that truth was to be perceived by receding inwards and taking it from the spirit, and that the outward world is "dead mind" or perhaps rather *inert* mind — not the mind of the thinker obviously, but the mind of the Deity. Now this is called objective idealism because it recognizes the external object as having existence: it is not nonexistent, as absolute idealism would put it.

H. P. Blavatsky says on page 631 of the first volume of *The Secret Doctrine:*

Esoteric philosophy, teaching an *objective* Idealism — though it regards the objective Universe and all in it as *Maya,* temporary illusion — draws a practical distinction between collective illusion, *Mahamaya,* from the purely metaphysical stand-point, and the objective relations in it between various conscious *Egos* so long as this illusion lasts.

The teaching is that māyā is thus called from the action of Mūlaprakriti, or "root-nature," the coordinate principle of that other line of coactive consciousness which we call Parabrahman. We remember that from the moment when manifestation begins, it acts dualistically, that is to say, that everything in nature from that point onwards is crossed by pairs of opposites, such as long and short, high and low, night and day, good and evil, consciousness and nonconsciousness, etc., and that all these things are essentially māyic or illusory — real while they last, but the lasting is not eternal. It is through and by these pairs of opposites that the self-conscious soul learns truth.

What is the basis of morals? This is the most important question that can be asked of any system of thought. Is morality based on the dicta of man? Is morality based on the conviction in most men's hearts that for human safety it is necessary to have certain abstract rules which it is merely *convenient* to follow? Are we mere opportunists? or is morality, ethics, based on truth, which it is not merely expedient for man to follow, but needful? Surely upon the latter.

And in the third fundamental postulate which we read at the opening of our study this evening, we find the very elements, the very fundamentals, of a system of morality greater than which, profounder than which, more persuasive than which, perhaps, it would be impossible to imagine anything.

On what, then, is morality based? And by morality I mean not merely the opinion which some pseudophilosophers have, that morality is more or less that which is good for the community, based on the mere meaning of the Latin word *mores,* good customs as opposed to bad. No; morality is that instinctive hunger of the human heart to do righteousness, to do good to every man because it is good and satisfying and ennobling to do so.

When man realizes that he is one with all that is, inwards and outwards, high and low; that he is one with them, not merely as members of a community are one, not merely as individuals of an army are one, but like the molecules of our own flesh, like the atoms of the molecule, like the electrons of the atom, composing one unity — not a mere union but a spiritual *unity* — then he sees truth.

Every one of us belongs to, and is an inhering part of, that sublime and ineffable Mystery — the ALL — which contains and is individual and spiritual unity.

We have all of us one inward universal self, and each one has also his individual ego. The ego springs from the self and the self is the Ineffable, the Inmost of the Inmost, one in all of us — giving each one of us that sense of selfhood; although by extension of meaning we also speak, and properly speak, of the lower self, because this is a tiny ray from the Highest. Even the evil man has in himself not merely the spark of the divine, but the very ray of divinity itself: he is both the selfish ego and the universal self.

Why then are we taught that when we attain selflessness, we attain the divine? Precisely because selflessness is the attribute of the Paramātman, the universal self, where all personality vanishes. *Paramātman* is a Sanskrit compound meaning "highest" or "supreme self."

If we examine our own spirits, if we reach inwards, if we stretch ourselves inwards, as it were, towards the Inmost, every one of us may know that as he goes farther, farther, farther in, the self becomes selfless, the light becomes pure glory.

What a thought, that in the heart of each one of us there dwells, there lives, the ever-unfolding, the constant, the eternal, the changeless, knowing no death, knowing no sorrow, the very divinity of *all!* How it dignifies human life! What courage does it give to us! How does it clear away all of the old moldy superstitions! What unspeakable visions of reality, of the truth, do we obtain when we go inwards, after having emptied the mind, as Bernard says, of all the mental trash that encumbers it!

When man has reached the state where he realizes this and has so emptied his mind that it is filled only with the self itself, with the selfless selfhood of the Eternal — what did the ancients call this state? What did they call such a man himself? They called the state, *bodhi;* and they called the human, *buddha;* and the organ in and by which it was manifested, *buddhi.* All these words came from a Sanskrit root meaning "to awaken." When man has awakened from the living death in which we live, when he has cast off the toils of mind and flesh and, to use the old Christian term, has put on the "garments of eternity," then he has awakened, he is a buddha. And the ancient Brahmanical teachings, found today even in the Vedanta, state that he has become one with — not "absorbed," as is constantly translated — but has *become* one with the self of selves, with the Paramātman, the supreme self.

Turning again to the *Chhāndogya Upanishad,* one of the most important of the 108 or more Upanishads — the very word *upani-*

shad signifies esoteric treatise — we read from the eighth lecture, seventh, eighth, and ninth sections:

Prajāpati said —

We interrupt by saying that *prajāpati* is a Sanskrit word meaning "governor" or "lord" or "master of progeny." The word is applied to many of the Vedic gods, but in particular to Brahmā — that is to say, the third step from Parabrahman — the evolver-creator, the first and most recondite figure of the triad consisting of Brahmā, Vishnu, and Śiva. Brahmā is the emanator or evolver, Vishnu the sustainer or preserver, and Śiva, which may be translated euphemistically perhaps as "beneficent," the regenerator. This name is very obscure. However:

Prajāpati said: "The Self which is free from sin, free from old age, from death and grief, from hunger and thirst, which desires nothing but what it ought to desire, and imagines nothing but what it ought to imagine, that it is which we must search out, that it is which we must try to understand. He who has searched out that Self and understands it, obtains all worlds and all desires."

We interrupt to ask why? Because this self of selves, this Inmost, is all worlds: it is all, it is everything. Now to quote:

The Devas (gods) and Asuras (demons) both heard these words, and said: "Well, let us search for that Self by which, if one has searched it out, all worlds and all desires are obtained."

Thus saying Indra went from the Devas, Virochana from the Asuras, and both, without having communicated with each other, approached Prajāpati, holding fuel in their hands, as is the custom for pupils approaching their master.

They dwelt there as pupils for thirty-two years. Then Prajāpati asked them: "For what purpose have you dwelt here?"

They replied: "A saying of yours is being repeated, viz. 'the Self which is free from sin, free from old age, from death and grief, from hunger and thirst, which desires nothing but what it ought to desire, and imagines nothing but what it ought to imagine, that it is which we must search out, that it is which we must try to understand. He who has searched out that Self and understands it, obtains all worlds and all desires.' Now we both have dwelt here because we wish for that Self."

Prajāpati said to them: "The person that is seen in the eye, that is the Self. This is what I have said. This is the immortal, the fearless, this is Brahman."

Interrupting: the self that is seen in the eye is a figure of speech not infrequently found in the ancient Sanskrit writings; it signifies that sense of an indwelling presence that one sees when he looks into the eyes of another.

They asked: "Sir, he who is perceived in the water, and he who is perceived in a mirror, who is he?"
He replied: "He himself indeed is seen in all these."

[Eighth Section] "Look at your Self in a pan of water, and whatever you do not understand of your Self, come and tell me."
They looked in the water-pan. Then Prajāpati said to them: "What do you see?"
They said: "We both see the self thus altogether, a picture even to the very hairs and nails."
Prajāpati said to them: "After you have adorned yourselves, . . . look again into the water-pan."
They, after having adorned themselves, having put on their best clothes and cleaned themselves, looked into the water-pan.
Prajāpati said: "What do you see?"
They said: "Just as we are, well adorned, with our best clothes and clean, thus we are both there, Sir, well adorned, with our best clothes and clean."
Prajāpati said: "That is the Self, this is the immortal, the fearless, this is Brahman."
Then both went away satisfied in their hearts.
And Prajāpati, looking after them, said: "They both go away without having perceived and without having known the Self, and whoever of these two, whether Devas or Asuras, will follow this doctrine will perish."

Interrupting: they saw māyā and not the self.

Now Virochana, satisfied in his heart, went to the Asuras and preached that doctrine to them, that the self (the body) alone is to be worshipped, that the self (the body) alone is to be served, and that he who worships the self and serves the self, gains both worlds, this and the next.
Therefore they call even now a man who does not give alms here, who has no faith, and offers no sacrifices, an Asura, for this is the doctrine of Asuras. They deck out the body of the dead with perfumes, flowers, and fine raiment by way of ornament, and think they will thus conquer that world.

[Ninth Section] But Indra, before he had returned to the Devas, saw this difficulty.

Interrupting: the difficulty now comes which Indra saw.

As this self (the shadow in the water) is well adorned, when the body is well adorned, well dressed, when the body is well dressed, well cleaned, if the body is well cleaned, that self will also be blind, if the body is blind, lame, if the body is lame, crippled, if the body is crippled, and will perish in fact as soon as the body perishes. Therefore I see no good in this (doctrine).

Taking fuel in his hand he came again as a pupil to Prajāpati. Prajāpati said to him: "Maghavat (Indra), as you went away with Virochana, satisfied in your heart, for what purpose did you come back?"

He said: "Sir, as this self (the shadow) is well adorned, when the body is well adorned, well dressed, when the body is well dressed, well cleaned, if the body is well cleaned, that self will also be blind, if the body is blind, lame, if the body is lame, crippled, if the body is crippled, and will perish in fact as soon as the body perishes. Therefore I see no good in this (doctrine)."

"So it is indeed, Maghavat," replied Prajāpati; "but I shall explain him (the true Self) further to you. Live with me another thirty-two years."

Indra was able to see beyond the māyā of the personal self, and therefore was searching for the real, for the true, the self itself.

The translation is Max Müller's. It may be well to add in conclusion that all translations which have been made and may hereafter be made are made by ourself, from any one of the ancient languages, and if any quotation is taken from another translator, his name will be given.

FOUR

FROM PRIMORDIAL POINT TO UNIVERSE AND MAN. HOW DOES
MANIFESTATION ARISE? MANVANTARA AND PRALAYA.

The *Scintillas* are the "Souls," and these Souls appear in the three-fold
form of Monads (units), atoms and gods — according to our teaching. "Every
atom becomes a visible complex unit (a molecule), and once attracted into
the sphere of terrestrial activity, the Monadic Essence, passing through the
mineral, vegetable, and animal kingdoms, becomes man." (Esot. Catechism.) Again, "God, Monad, and Atom are the correspondences of Spirit,
Mind, and Body *(Atma, Manas, and Sthula Sarira)* in man." In their septenary aggregation they are the "Heavenly Man" (see *Kabala* for the latter
term); thus, terrestrial man is the provisional reflection of the Heavenly. . . .
"The Monads *(Jivas)* are the Souls of the Atoms, both are the fabric in which
the Chohans (Dhyanis, *gods*) cloth themselves when a form is needed."
(Esot. Cat.)   — *The Secret Doctrine*, I, 619

Parabrahm (the One Reality, the Absolute) is the field of Absolute Consciousness, *i.e.*, that Essence which is out of all relation to conditioned
existence, and of which conscious existence is a conditioned symbol. But
once that we pass in thought from this (to us) Absolute Negation, duality
supervenes in the contrast of Spirit (or consciousness) and Matter, Subject
and Object.

Spirit (or consciousness) and Matter are, however, to be regarded, not
as independent realities, but as the two facets or aspects of the Absolute
(Parabrahm), which constitute the basis of conditioned Being whether
subjective or objective. . . .

Hence it will be apparent that the contrast of these two aspects of the
Absolute is essential to the existence of the "Manifested Universe." Apart
from Cosmic Substance, Cosmic Ideation could not manifest as individual
consciousness, since it is only through a vehicle of matter that consciousness
wells up as "I am I," a physical basis being necessary to focus a ray of the
Universal Mind at a certain stage of complexity. Again, apart from Cosmic
Ideation, Cosmic Substance would remain an empty abstraction, and no
emergence of consciousness could ensue.

The "Manifested Universe," therefore, is pervaded by duality, which is,
as it were, the very essence of its EX-istence as "manifestation." But just as
the opposite poles of subject and object, spirit and matter, are but aspects

of the One Unity in which they are synthesized, so, in the manifested Universe, there is "that" which links spirit to matter, subject to object.

This something, at present unknown to Western speculation, is called by the occultists Fohat. It is the "bridge" by which the "Ideas" existing in the "Divine Thought" are impressed on Cosmic substance as the "laws of Nature."

— Ibid., I, 15–16

BEFORE we open our study this evening, it should be said with reference to the nature of these studies, that they are a simplification of *The Secret Doctrine* in the sense of an explanation and unfolding of the meaning of the teachings that the book contains. In order to achieve these ends, it will be of course necessary to bring to bear upon these doctrines, for comparison and in order to show analogy or identity, lines of thought from the great religions of the world and from the great minds of ancient times; because these, in their essence, have sprung from the central source of men's thought and religion which we today call theosophy.

Yet before we can really embark upon the study of *The Secret Doctrine* itself, as a book, it will be necessary during the course of our studies to clear from our path certain stumbling blocks which are in the way of each of us; certain ideas and so-called principles of thought which have been instilled into our minds from childhood, and which, on account of the psychological effect they have on our minds, really prevent us from grasping the truths of being that H. P. Blavatsky has so masterly given us.

In addition, it will be necessary to investigate certain very ancient principles of thought, and to penetrate more deeply into the real meaning of the ancient religions and philosophies than has ever been done in any modern books, because those books have been written by men who know nothing about the esoteric philosophy, men who were mostly rebels against the barren ecclesiasticism of the Christian Church; who, in order to gain freedom from those chains of ecclesiasticism, actually went too far the other way, and saw nothing but priestcraft and evildoing in these old religions and in the acts and teachings of the men who taught them, priests, philosophers, or scientists.

Another point always to keep in mind is, that we are actually undertaking the study of the very doctrines which formed the core of the heart of the teachings of the Mysteries of ancient days.

These Mysteries were divided into two general parts, the Lesser Mysteries and the Greater.

The Lesser Mysteries were very largely composed of dramatic rites or ceremonies, with some teaching; the Greater Mysteries were composed of, or conducted almost entirely on the ground of, study, and later were proved by personal experience in initiation. In the latter was explained, among other things, the secret meaning of the mythologies of the old religions, as for instance the Greek.

The active and nimble mind of the Greeks produced a mythology which for grace and beauty is perhaps without equal, but it nevertheless is very difficult to explain; the Mysteries of Samothrace and of Eleusis — the greater ones — explained among other things what these myths meant. These myths formed the basis of the *exoteric* religions; but note well that exotericism does not mean that the thing which is taught exoterically is in itself false, but merely that it is a teaching given without the key to it. Such teaching is symbolic, illusory, touching on the truth: the truth is there, but without the key to it — which is the esoteric meaning — it yields no proper sense.

We now read from *The Secret Doctrine*, volume I, page 43:

> The Secret Doctrine teaches the progressive development of everything, worlds as well as atoms; and this stupendous development has neither conceivable beginning nor imaginable end. Our "Universe" is only one of an infinite number of Universes, all of them "Sons of Necessity," because links in the great Cosmic chain of Universes, each one standing in the relation of an effect as regards its predecessor, and being a cause as regards its successor.
>
> The appearance and disappearance of the Universe are pictured as an outbreathing and inbreathing of "the Great Breath," which is eternal, and which, being Motion, is one of the three aspects of the Absolute — Abstract Space and Duration being the other two. When "the Great Breath" is projected, it is called the Divine Breath, and is regarded as the breathing of the Unknowable Deity — the One Existence — which breathes out a thought, as it were, which becomes the Kosmos. (See "Isis Unveiled.") So also it is when the Divine Breath is inspired again the Universe disappears into the bosom of "the Great Mother," who then sleeps, "wrapped in her invisible robes."

A fortnight ago we were studying the question of māyā and the relationship of the inner being of man to the ineffable Essence;

it remains for us briefly to study how man, who has a *personal* element in him, sprang forth from the very essence of *impersonality*, if one may so call it. We can say at once that the Infinite and Impersonal *never becomes finite and personal*. How, then, does the spirit of man (already the first film over the face of the Absolute, as it were) come into being? Let us remember that the manifestation of worlds and, deductively, of the beings who inhabit those worlds, took place in the extension of matter popularly called space. A center, first, is localized — a very poor word to use! — and is, de facto, not infinite, not eternal; if it were, it could neither manifest nor come into outward existence, for this is limitation. The Eternal, the Ineffable, the Infinite, does not ever manifest at all, either partially or in toto. Words themselves are misleading in treating of these subjects; but what can we say? We must use human expressions in order to convey our meaning.

How then arose manifestation? The ancient wisdom tells us the following: in the seeds of life remaining in space from a planet which had previously run its manvantara and had passed into latency or prakriti-pralaya, there came (when the hour struck for manifestation to begin again) into being in these seeds of life the activity called in Sanskrit *trishnā* ("thirst," if you like, desire for manifestation), thus forming the center around which was to gather a new universe. It had by karmic necessity its particular place in space and was to produce its particular kind of progeny — gods, monads, atoms, men, and the three elementary, or elemental, kingdoms of the world as we see it around us — from the karmic seeds which were brought over and which were lying latent from the preceding manvantara.

The universe reimbodies itself (it does not "reincarnate," which means coming into *flesh*), following precisely the analogical lines that the soul of man does in reincarnating, making the necessary allowances for varying conditions. As man is the product of his former life, or rather of his lives, so is a universe, a solar system, a planet, an animal, an atom — the very great as well as the so-called infinitesimal — the fruitage, the flower, of what went before. Each of these bears its load of karma precisely as the soul of man does.

The teachings relating to the evolving of the inner planes of being, which precede and produce the outer planes, are very esoteric and belong to a study higher than we venture to approach at the present time, but we can form some general idea of how it is done, by analogy and by comparison with the life of man.

When manifestation begins, what is called duality supervenes. It would seem to be a procession something like this, were we to symbolize it by a diagram.

Consider this uppermost straight line a hypothetical plane: it may be, humanly speaking, immeasurable miles in depth or in extension, but mere extension has nothing to do with the general concept. Above it stretches the infinitude of the Boundless, and below the diagram is the Boundless, and inwards through it is the Boundless, interpenetrating everywhere; but for purposes of our present illustration we will say that it is above.

Let us place anywhere we may please a point A, another one A', and a third A''. We have now reached, after a long period of latency or pralaya has passed, a period of manifestation or man-vantara. Such a point as A, or A' or A'', we will call the Primordial Point, the first breaking-through into the cosmic plane below; the spirit-force above arising into activity in the seeds of being and forcing its way down into the lower life of manifestation — *not pushed or moved by anything outside of itself* — is driven into manifestation by the karmic life of its own essential being, by the thirst of desire or blossoming forth, like a fresh upspringing in early summer of a flower, in which the tendency in manifestation is outward. This first appearance is conceived of in philosophy as the first or Primordial Point; this is the name given to it in the Jewish theosophy called the Qabbālāh.

From the moment that the point, the seed of life, the germ of being — all these are but names for the one thing, the spiritual atom, the spiritual monad, call it what you will — bursts through into the lower life as it were, differentiation or duality sets in and continues thenceforward to the end of the Great Cycle, forming the two side lines of the diagrammatic triangle. We may call one AB, the Brahmā (masculine), and the other AC, the Prakriti or nature (feminine). Brahmā is frequently also called *Purusha*, a Sanskrit word meaning "man," the Ideal Man, like the Qabbalistic Adām Qadmōn, the primordial entity of

THE BOUNDLESS

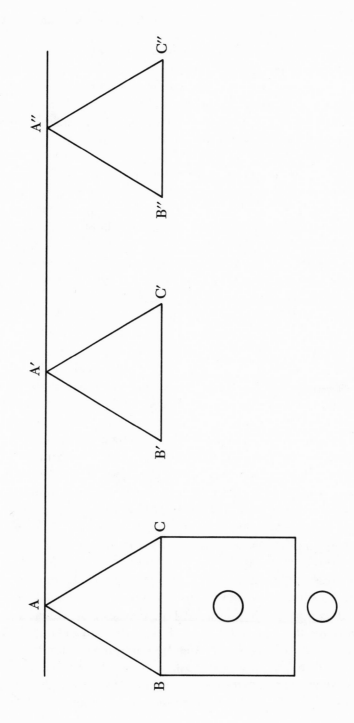

space, containing in Prakriti or nature all the septenary scales of manifested being.

At all times, from the very first instant when duality sets in, there is an unceasing attraction between these two lines or poles, and they join. Remember that this symbol is merely a paradigm or representation. Absolutely, it would be absurd to say that life and beings proceed into manifestation as geometric triangles only; but we can represent it *symbolically* to our minds in this fashion. When these two join, the Father and the Mother, spirit (or reality) and illusion (or māyā), Brahmā (or Purusha) and Prakriti (or nature), their union produces the Son. In the Christian scheme they give the spiritual or primordial Son the name of Christos; in the Egyptian scheme Osiris and Isis (or her twin sister Nephthys, which is merely the more recondite side of Isis) produce their son Horus, the spiritual sun, physically the sun or the light-bringer; and so similarly in the different schemes that the ancient world has handed down to us.

From the interaction of these three, by interpolar action, by the spiritual forces working in and out, two other lines fall down-wards — according to the mystical way in which this scheme of emanation is taught — and they also join and form the square, or the manifested kosmos.

Now from the central or Primordial Point is born or proceeds the sun of life. By it and through it is our union with the Ineffable. Man may be down here a physical being on earth, or anywhere else a luminous, ethereal entity, but it matters not where he is or what his body: for once the *seven* principles of his being are in action, man the thinking entity is produced, linked by his seventh principle, and his sixth, with that sun of life.

To every "man" of the unnameable multitudes of self-conscious beings belonging to this kosmos or universe, there extend respec-tively upwards or downwards two natures: one of which is a ray of spirit connecting him with the divine of the divinest, and from that extending upwards in all directions and linking him in every sense of the word with the Ineffable, the Boundless, which is, therefore, the core of his being, the center of his essence.

The appearance and evolution of man as a human being on this planet Terra follow the same line of nature's wonderful analogical working that a planet does in space, or a sun does with its brothers of a solar system, the planets. Man, thus being in very truth a child of Infinity, the offspring of the Ineffable, has latent within himself the capacity of the universe.

And on this fact depends what we have so often been told of the getting of powers. The very method by which we do *not* get them, the very way of missing and losing them, is to run after them, strange as it may sound, because this is the impulse of vanity and selfishness. If we, then, selfishly seek them, what do we get? We get the action of the lower powers upon us; it is a growing thirst for sensation which we do get, and this leads us towards and into the nether abyss of Matter, the opposite pole of the Boundless, if it is followed.

But in the great soul who has passed by and thrown off this thirst for personal acquisition, in whom the grasping spirit for self is no longer dominant, who feels his oneness with everything that is, who feels that every human being, yea the very pismire that laboriously crawls up a sand-knob only to tumble down again, is *himself* — no metaphor but an actuality: a different body, but the same life, the same essence, the same things latent in it as in him — in him indeed lies the power of ascending the ladder of being, drawn by the link with the Highest in his innermost nature. He and they are both filled full of latent powers and forces, and he and they may become in time very gods, blazing, as it were, with power like the sun; and the only way is utter selflessness, because selflessness, paradoxical as it may sound, is the only way to the self, the self universal. The personal self shuts the door before us.

Of course we cannot crush out of our being the sense of self-hood, nor is that desirable; but in the lowest aspect it takes upon itself the forms of all selfishness, until the being of the man who follows the left-hand path, or the path downwards, ends in what the early Christians — stealing from the Greeks — called Tartarus, the place of disintegration.

When man ascends beyond the reach of matter, he has cast off the bondage of māyā, or illusion. Let us remember that when manifestation opens, Prakriti becomes or rather is māyā; and

Brahmā, the Father, is the spirit of the consciousness, or the individuality. These two are really one, yet they are also the two aspects of the one life-ray acting and reacting upon itself, much as a man himself can say, "I am *I*." He has the faculty of self-analysis, or self-division; all of us know it, we can feel it in ourselves. One side of us, in our thoughts, can be called the Prakriti or the material element, or the māyāvi element, or the element of illusion; and the other, the spirit, the individuality, the god within.

Yet as man sees life, as he runs his eye down the scale of beings, he sees it through māyā; in fact, he is the child of māyā on one side, as he is of the spirit on the other. Both are in him. His lesson is to learn that the two are one and that they are not separate; then he no longer is deceived. His lesson is to understand that māyā, the great deluder, is the famous snake or serpent of antiquity, which leads us out from the Garden of Eden (employing a Biblical metaphor), through experience and suffering to learn what illusion *is* — and is *not*.

Also matter, which is the māyāvi manifestation of Prakriti on this plane (and I mean here physical matter), itself is not substantial. The most dense and rigid things we can think of, perhaps, are the metals, and actually they are, perhaps, the most porous, the most foamlike, the most evanescent, as seen from the other or higher side of being, from the other side of the plane. So well is this now understood that our more intuitive scientists are telling us that space, which seems to us so thin and tenuous, is in reality more rigid than the hardest steel. Why is it that electricity prefers metals as a path to common wood, or cotton wool, or some other such thing?

Before we go further, it would seem necessary to study a little what we mean by the words manvantara and pralaya. Let us take *manvantara* first. This word is a Sanskrit compound, and as such means nothing more than between two Manus; literally, "manu-between." Manu, or dhyāni-chohan, in the esoteric system, is the entities collectively which appear first at the beginning of manifestation and from which, like a cosmic tree, everything is derived or born. Manu actually is the (spiritual) tree of life of any planetary chain, of manifested being. Manu is thus, in one sense, the Third Logos; as the Second is the Father-Mother, the Brahmā and

Prakriti; and the First is what we call the Unmanifest Logos, or Brahman (neuter) and its cosmic veil Pradhāna.

Pradhāna is also a Sanskrit compound, meaning that which is "placed before"; and from this, it has become a technical term in philosophy, and means what we would call the first filmy appearance of root-matter, "placed before" or rather around Brahman as a veil. Root-matter is Mūlaprakriti, root-nature, and corresponding to it as the other or active pole is Brahman (neuter). That from which the First or Unmanifest Logos proceeds is called Parabrahman, and Mūlaprakriti is *its* kosmic veil. *Parabrahman* is another Sanskrit compound, meaning "beyond Brahman." *Mūlaprakriti,* again, as said above, is a Sanskrit compound meaning *mūla,* "root," *prakriti,* "nature."

First, then, the Boundless, symbolized by the ◯; then Parabrahman, and Mūlaprakriti its other pole; then lower, Brahman and its veil Pradhāna; then Brahmā-Prakriti or Purusha-Prakriti (Prakriti being also māyā); the manifested universe appearing through and by this last: Brahmā-Prakriti, Father-Mother. In other words, the Second Logos, Father-Mother, is the producing cause of manifestation through their Son, which in a planetary chain is Manu. A manvantara, therefore, is the period of activity between any two Manus, on any plane, since in any such period there is a root-Manu at the beginning of evolution, and a seed-Manu at its close, preceding a pralaya.

Pralaya: this is also a Sanskrit compound, formed of *laya,* from a Sanskrit root *lī,* and the prefix *pra.* What does *lī* mean? It means "to dissolve," "to melt away," "to liquefy," as when one pours water upon a cube of salt or of sugar. The cube of salt or of sugar vanishes in the water; it dissolves, changes its form; and this may be taken as a symbol of what pralaya is: a crumbling away, a vanishing away of matter into something else which is yet in it, and surrounds it, and interpenetrates it. That is pralaya, usually translated as the state of latency, state of rest or repose, between two manvantaras or life cycles. If we remember distinctly the meaning of the Sanskrit word, our minds take a new bent in direction, follow a new thought; we get new ideas; we penetrate into the arcanum of the thing that takes place.

Now there are many kinds of manvantaras; also many kinds of

pralayas. There are, for instance, the universal manvantara and the universal pralaya, and these are called *prākritika,* because it is the pralaya or vanishing away, melting away, of Prakriti or nature. Then there is the solar pralaya. Sun in Sanskrit is *sūrya,* and the adjective from this is *saurya;* hence, the saurya-pralaya, or the pralaya of the solar system. Then, thirdly, there is the terrestrial or planetary pralaya. The Sanskrit word for earth is *bhūmi,* and the adjective corresponding to this is *bhaumika:* hence, the bhau-mika-pralaya. Then we can say that there is the pralaya or death of the individual man. Man is *purusha;* the corresponding adjective is *paurusha:* hence, the paurusha-pralaya, or death of man. So, then, we have given examples of various pralayas: first of the prākritika, or dissolution of nature; next the solar pralaya, the saurya; next the bhaumika, or the passing away of the earth; and then the paurusha, or the death of man. And these adjectives apply equally well to the several kinds of manvantaras or life cycles.

There is another kind of pralaya which is called *nitya.* In its general sense, it means "constant" or "continuous," and can be exemplified by the constant or continuous change — life and death — of the cells of our bodies. It is a state in which the indwelling and dominating entity remains, but its different principles and *rūpas,* or "bodies," undergo continuous change. Hence it is called nitya. It applies to the body of man, to the outer sphere of earth, to the earth itself, to the solar system, and to all nature.

It is likewise represented by a symbol that H. P. Blavatsky has given us from the Oriental wisdom, the outbreathing and inbreathing of Brahman. This symbol, by the way, is not solely Indian. It is found in the ancient Egyptian texts, where one or another of the gods, Khnumu, for instance, breathes forth from his mouth the cosmic egg. It is also found alluded to in the Orphic Hymns, where the cosmic serpent breathes forth as an egg the things which are to be, or the future universe. Everywhere, especially where ancient religion or philosophy has longest retained its hold, there do we find the symbol of the cosmic egg. Religions of less age and of less influence do not so often employ it. The cosmic egg was found as a symbol in Egypt; it was found in Hindustan; it was found in Peru, where the "Mighty Man," the Sanskrit

Purusha, the Ideal Man, was called Manco Capac, and his wife and sister was called Mama Ocllo, which means "Mother Egg": these brought the universe into being, becoming later the sun and the moon respectively.

Why did the ancients symbolize the beginning of manifestation under the form of an egg? Let us ask: is it not a fine symbol? As the egg producing the chick contains the germ of life (laid by its mother, the hen, and fructified by the other pole of being), so the cosmic egg, which is the Primordial Point, also contains the germ of life. The egg itself also can be called the germ of life, and the germ of life within the egg can be called the inner germ — that more subtil point which receives those impulses of which we have spoken before, coming down from the highest center of communication between the outward world and the inner, the lines of inner magnetic action and reaction. And when the chick within the egg is formed, it bursts its shell and comes forth into the light of day, precisely as we saw was the case with the Primordial Point. When the karmic hour had struck, it burst forth, as it were, into other spheres of manifestation and activity. The ancients, carrying the figure still farther, even spoke of heaven as a domelike affair, as the upper part of an eggshell.

Let us think more deeply of these ancient symbols. The ancients were not fools. There is a deep meaning in these olden figures of speech. Why did Homer speak of his Olympus, the abode of Zeus and the gods, as being brazen, like brass, one of the hardest and most intractable things that the Greeks knew? Why did Hesiod speak of the same as made of iron? Because they realized that the life here in matter and of matter, was based upon an evanescent substratum, and that the lower world of matter is, as has been so often said, evanescent, foamy, full of holes, as it were, and unreal.

FIVE

To make of Science an integral *whole* necessitates, indeed, the study of spiritual and psychic, as well as physical Nature. Otherwise it will ever be like the anatomy of man, discussed of old by the profane from the point of view of his shell-side and in ignorance of the interior work. . . .

The duty of the Occultist lies with the *Soul and Spirit* of Cosmic Space, not merely with its illusive appearance and behaviour. That of official physical science is to analyze and study its *shell* — the *Ultima Thule* of the Universe and man, in the opinion of Materialism.

With the latter, Occultism has nought to do. It is only with the theories of such men of learning as Kepler, Kant, Oersted, and Sir W. Herschel, who believed in a Spiritual world, that Occult Cosmogony might treat, and attempt a satisfactory compromise. But the views of those physicists differed vastly from the latest modern speculations. Kant and Herschel had in their mind's eye speculations upon the origin and *the final destiny,* as well as the present aspect, of the Universe, from a far more philosophical and psychic standpoint; whereas modern Cosmology and Astronomy now repudiate anything like research into the mysteries of being. The result is what might be expected: complete failure and inextricable contradictions in the thousand and one varieties of so-called scientific theories, and in this theory as in all others.

The nebular hypothesis, involving the theory of the existence of a primeval matter, diffused in a nebulous condition, is of no modern date in astronomy as everyone knows. Anaximenes, of the Ionian school, had already taught that the sidereal bodies were formed through the progressive condensation of a primordial *pregenetic* matter, which had almost a negative weight, and was spread out through Space in an extremely sublimated condition. — *The Secret Doctrine,* I, 588, 589–90

THERE are three points which it would seem necessary to touch upon slightly before we begin our evening's study. The first is with regard to the question of morals, that is to say, right conduct based upon right views, right thinking. We have touched upon this matter at nearly every meeting because the line, the path, of duty — of right conduct based upon right views — is the path of all who would tread onward to the ancient wisdom and to the ancient Mysteries. The great thinkers, philosophers, and religious men, of all ages, have told us the same thing.

These meetings are not for purposes of intellectual study only, or to amuse ourselves with abstruse and mystic knowledge; but mainly, firstly, principally, for the purpose of gaining a right foundation for right views which shall govern human conduct. When we have this foundation we have the beginnings of all laws. We can affect the world by our own views and by our own acts; and, further, we shall be able in time to affect for good even the governments of the world, not directly and immediately perhaps, but at least indirectly and in the course of time. All the horrible things that perplex and confuse and distress mankind today arise wholly, almost, out of a lack of right views, and hence, a lack of right conduct. We have the testimony of the Greek and Roman initiates and thinkers that the ancient Mysteries of Greece taught men, above everything else, to live rightly and to have a noble hope for the life after death.

Next, the second point: in our last meeting we touched upon the ancient Mysteries, and we took as examples those of Greece from which the Romans derived their own Mysteries, but we touched upon one point only, the mythological aspect; and this mythological aspect comprises only a portion — a relatively small portion — of what was taught in the Mystery Schools, principally at Samothrace and at Eleusis. At Samothrace was taught the same Mystery-teaching that was current elsewhere in Greece, but here it was more developed and recondite; and the foundation of these Mystery-teachings was morals. The noblest and greatest men of ancient times in Greece were initiates in the Mysteries of these two seats of esoteric knowledge.

In other countries farther to the east they had other Mystery Schools or "colleges," and this word college by no means necessarily meant a mere temple or building; it meant "association," as in our modern word colleague, associate. The Teutonic tribes of northern Europe, the Germanic tribes — which included Scandinavia — had their Mystery-colleges also; and teacher and neophytes stood on the bosom of Mother Earth, under Father

Ether, the boundless sky, or in subterranean receptacles, and taught and learned. We state here at once that the core, the heart, the center, of the ancient Mysteries was the abstruse problems dealing with death. These teachings we still have, and they will be forthcoming.

The third point is with regard to the paradigms or diagrams which we may find necessary to use from time to time in order to illustrate certain teachings. Remember that these paradigms are relative and changeable; they are not hard and fast or absolute things. This fact must be kept always clear in the mind, and around them the mind should *never* be allowed to crystallize. Why? Because any paradigm, any particular combination of geometrical lines, can illustrate different thoughts or things: for instance, the paradigm of the triangle from which hangs the square (as used at our last meeting) can apply equally as well to the highest combined principle in man, the spiritual-mental monad, as to the lower principles into which the monad falls at the beginning of incarnation or manifestation, and from which it will resurrect when the first chimes of the pralayic bells are heard in the ākāśic spaces.

We will now resume our study. We take up, as our general theme, the same two paragraphs on page 43 of volume I of *The Secret Doctrine*, which we read at our last meeting:

The Secret Doctrine teaches the progressive development of everything, worlds as well as atoms; and this stupendous development has neither conceivable beginning nor imaginable end. Our "Universe" is only one of an infinite number of Universes, all of them "Sons of Necessity," because links in the great Cosmic chain of Universes, each one standing in the relation of an effect as regards its predecessor, and being a cause as regards its successor.

The appearance and disappearance of the Universe are pictured as an outbreathing and inbreathing of "the Great Breath," which is eternal, and which, being Motion, is one of the three aspects of the Absolute — Abstract Space and Duration being the other two. When the "Great Breath" is projected, it is called the Divine Breath, and is regarded as the breathing of the Unknowable Deity — the One Existence — which breathes out a thought, as it were, which becomes the Kosmos. (See "Isis Unveiled.") So also is it when the Divine Breath is inspired again the Universe disappears into the bosom of "the Great Mother," who then sleeps "wrapped in her invisible robes."

It was the intention to take up this evening the dawn of manifestation as it is found in the Hebrew Book of Beginnings called Genesis, and to study this and to show its similarity and likeness, and the fundamental identity of truth on which it is based, as compared with the other religions of the world. But in view of the fact that we were obliged at our last study to touch upon the first coming-into-being of the veil cast over the face of the Ineffable, it would seem best this evening to undertake, if we have time, a short sketch of what in science is called the nebular theory, how far the esoteric teachings run with it, and where and when they part from it.

The nebular theory, as originally taught in science by the Frenchman Laplace — but derived by him from the great German thinker and philosopher, Immanuel Kant — stated that the space which is now occupied by the planets of the solar system was originally filled with a very tenuous form of matter, in a highly incandescent or burning state. Let us say just here that this particular theory of Laplace as regards incandescence has never been proved, that it is not subject in all respects to mathematical demonstration, and cannot be, and that it itself, if taken as a whole, forms one of the greatest proofs against the truth of the nebular theory *as it was then stated*, and as it has since been modified in some degree by modern thinkers.

Laplace further stated that this nebula was in a condition of slow rotation, or circular moving, in the same direction in which the planets now move around in their orbits, and in the same direction in which the planets and the sun now move around their axes. In other words, the present orbital revolution and rotation of the planets are derived from this mechanical, original, circular motion of the primal nebula.

Laplace likewise stated that this hot, immense object cooled, and as it cooled it shrank, according to a certain law of heat, and this shrinking, according to a law of dynamics, increased the velocity of rotation and the momentum of any point on its surface. Now, as everyone knows, the parts of a wheel which are nearest the periphery, the circumference, move with the greatest momentum and the greatest speed, though no faster, in another sense, than do the particles at the hub. This increase of rapidity in whirling around grew so great that a time came when the centrifugal force overcame the centripetal or cohesive force, and then this whirling nebula threw off a ring, and this ring also continued going around, and condensing, and finally formed a sphere or ball which became the outermost planet, Neptune. And so progressively the other planets came into being, the core of the nebula remaining as our sun. In brief, as the nebular body contracted and condensed its matter, the same phenomenon occurred again in the same way, and thus the second outermost planet, Uranus, was thrown off, and so on until all the planets had come into being as spheres. Now some of these tenuous, still nebulous planets, by contracting and thus increasing their rotational velocity, themselves evolved rings around themselves, which in their turn were thrown off from their parent-planets, and following the same course as their parent-planets became spheres, which thus became the satellites, the moons of the respective planets; while the center of the *original* nebula condensed into the (supposedly) incandescent or fiery ball which is the sun.

When H. P. Blavatsky first brought the theosophical teachings to the Western world, questions of cosmogony, or the beginning and primal development of the universe, came much to the fore and she was asked, and her Teachers were also asked through her, in what respect the nebular theory ran side by side with and "corroborated" the exposition of the theory of the occultists, the esoteric theory; and the answer then given was called "an evasive answer." It aroused criticism and some angry language.

Why, it was asked, if the Teachers know these wonderful truths, had not they illuminated the world with the splendor of their teachings? Why did they keep them and other things hid? No teaching can be bad for man if it is *true*, it was argued — which was a very foolish argument, indeed, so far as it goes, because many teachings are true, and are yet utterly unfit for the average man to have. However, we are going to investigate that question tonight.

The nebular theory, the Teachers said, was in its *main outlines*, and in certain respects only, fairly representative of what the esoteric teaching was, but it yet, for all that, had vital defects; and these defects they did not entirely specify nor did they fully outline them. But they gave clear hints where the defects lay and what they were; and they also gave a clear, logical, and concise reason for their reticence, which was obligatory and unavoidable.

Now the main defect in the theory of Laplace was that it was a purely mechanical, purely mechanistic, purely materialistic hypothesis, in some respects uncorroborable even by mathematics, and based upon nothing but the fact that in the vast abysses of space, astronomers, investigating wastes of stellar light, found nebulae and nebulosities and, adopting Kant's idea, argued dogmatically upon it. But, nevertheless, there was truth in the nebular theory — there was *some* truth. Now what is that truth? And what was the most vital defect? The most vital defect, first, was the fact — as hinted above — that the theory omitted all action of spiritual beings in the universe as the drivers, the agents, the mechanics or mechanicians of the mechanism which undoubtedly exists. We are taught that the esoteric philosophy does not deny mechanical action in the universe, but declares that where there is mechanical action there is government or, specifically, mechanicians at work, producing the movements of the mechanism, in accordance with karma. There must be "law"-givers or "law"-makers or "law"-impulsors, if the expression may be used; and behind these there must be the universal life. In other words, the vital defect was that this nebular theory omitted the first truth of all being — that the gods were behind the kosmos, spiritual beings, spiritual entities — the name matters nothing. Not God, but gods.

"Nature" is imperfect, hence of necessity makes "mistakes," because its action derives from hosts of entities at work — what we see around us all the time is proof of it. "Nature" is not perfect. If it had sprung from the "hands of the immutable Deity," hence perfect and immutable like its parent, knowing no change, it would be a perfect work. It is much to the contrary, as we know, and its imperfections or "mistakes" arise from the fact that the beings existing in and working in and controlling and *making* nature extend in endless hierarchies from the Inmost of the Inmost, from the Highest of the Highest, downwards for ever, upwards for ever, in all degrees of imperfection and of perfection, which is precisely what we see in the scenes of manifestation surrounding us. Our intuition tells us the truth concerning this, and we should trust it.

This was well known to the ancients. The Stoics expressed it and taught it in their magnificent philosophy. The Stoics of Rome and of Greece originally expressed it by what they called theocrasy. Theocrasy has a compound meaning — *theos*, "a god," "divine being," and *krasis*, meaning "an intermingling" — an intermingling of everything in the universe, intermingling with everything else, nothing possibly separable from the rest, the Whole. It is the cardinal heresy of the Oriental religions today, notably in that of the Buddhists, if a man thinks that he is separate or separable from the universe. This is the most fundamental error that man can make. The early Christians called it the "sin against the Holy Ghost." If we look around us and if we look within, we realize that we are one entity, as it were, one great human host, one living tree of human life, woven inseparably *into* and *from* nature, the All.

The next defect of the nebular theory was that the nebula was declared to be in its earliest stages incandescent, burning. The esoteric teaching is that it is indeed glowing, but glowing with a cold light, the same as, or similar to, that of the firefly, if you like. There is no more heat in a nebula than there is in the light of the firefly. This light in the nebula, this luminosity, is not from combustion of any kind; but, then, what *is* it from? It is from the indwelling *daivī-prakriti*, "divine nature or light," in its manifestation *on that plane*, the same light which in sentient beings manifests in a higher form as *consciousness* in all its degrees, running from dull physical consciousness up through the soul and the ego; through the self up into the selfless self of the Paramātman, the "supreme self" — a mere expression of convenience as meaning the acme or summit of a hierarchy, because really there is no *supreme* self, which would mean a limit, hence finiteness. If there were, there would be a lowest self. Self is boundless, endless, the very heart of being, the foundation and dimensionless core of all that is.

Next, the third vital defect: the planets and the sun were not evolved or born in the manner stated by the nebular theory. How are the sun and the planets born? (Let me say here by way of parenthesis that this subject should come much later in our study, but there is a reason for referring to it now.) Every solar or planetary body, the sun and planets in our solar system and analogically everywhere else, is the *child or rather the result or reimbodiment of a former cosmic entity* which, upon entering into its pralaya, its prākritika-pralaya — the dissolution of its lower principles — at the end of its long life cycle, exists in space in the higher activity of its spiritual principles and in the dispersion of its lowest principles, which latter latently exist in space as skandhas, in what is called in Sanskrit a *laya*-condition, from the root *lī*, meaning "to dissolve" or "to vanish away." Hence, a laya-center is a point of disappearance — the mystical *point* where a thing disappears from one plane, if you like, and passes onwards to reappear on another plane.

To repeat an illustration which we used in our last meeting: pour water on a cube of sugar or salt, and watch it dissolve — vanish as a *cube* or discrete entity. It has entered its laya-state as a *cube* or entity of sugar or salt. The form of it has gone, and itself — the sugar or salt — has entered into something else. When the *higher principles* of a cosmic body enter into something else, what is that something else into which they enter? They enter into the highest cosmic aether first, and in due course go still higher into the intense activity of the spiritual planes; there long aeons are passed in states and conditions to us almost unimaginable. In due course of time they begin their downward course into matter again, or reimbodiment, and finally, by attraction, re-collect their old skandhas hitherto lying latent, and thus form for themselves a new body, by passing into manifestation through and by the laya-center where those skandhas were waiting.

Those lower principles were meanwhile in nirvana, what we would call devachan after the death of man, for devachan as a state applies not to the highest or heavenly or divine monad, but only to the middle principles of man, to the personal ego, or the personal soul, in man. Applied to us this condition is the state of devachan — the "land of the gods," if you like; but applied to a cosmic body it is the state of nirvana. *Nirvāna* is a Sanskrit compound, *nir*, "out," and *vāna* the past participle passive of the root *vā*, "to blow," i.e., literally "blown out."

So badly has the meaning of the ancient Indian thought (and even its language, the Sanskrit) been understood, that for many years very erudite European scholars were discussing whether being "blown out" meant actual entitative annihilation or not. I remember once talking with a Chinese savant (he happened to be a Buddhist) and he told me that the state of man after death was "like this" — and he took up a lighted candle which was on the table and blew upon it, and the light went out. And he said, "*That* way." He was right, because he was referring to the lower principles in man. *They* (not we, our monadic or entitative essence) are merely the vehicle in which we live; and when we die, our physical body is "blown out," breaks up, enters into its pralaya or dissolution, and its molecules, its particles, go into the laya-state, and pass a certain time there until nature calls them forth again; or, to put it more accurately in another way, until the indwelling impulse in each physical monadic particle through the *thirst for active being* rises forth into manifestation again, and it reenters some body of appropriate kind and of similar evolutional degree.

This is one — and only one — facet of the secret of the much misunderstood doctrine of transmigration into animals. The lower elements, the astral body and the astral dregs of the animal or physical man, become the principles — *not the latent higher,* but the intermediate principles — of the beast world. They are human dregs cast off by man.

The cosmic dust resulting from the dissolution of a former world rests in a laya-center; while the highest principles of that world or planetary chain are in their paranirvana, and remain there until the *divine* thirst for active life on the highest plane of descent, which rearises in the cosmic monad of a planet or sun, pulls, pushes, or urges, or impels, that monad to the spiritual frontiers of manifestation; and when it arrives at those frontiers, it bursts through them as it were, or breaks through, or goes through, or cycles downward through, into the plane below it, and thus again and again through many planes, till finally the cycling monad reaches and touches or lightens all those lower elements which are remaining in the laya-center: *awakens* them, *reawakens* them, *revivifies* them, *recalls* them into being, *reilluminates* them from within; and this produces the luminosity or nebulosity seen in so many parts of interstellar space. Therefore, it is, actually, *daivī-prakriti,* "divine nature," divine light, in one of its lowest forms — the seventh, counting downwards — and this same light, or force, on this *our* plane in one of its very lowest forms is electricity and magnetism. Our Teachers have told us that the physical universe here in which we live — the stones, metals, trees, etc. — is *corporealized light.* They are all formed of atoms, and these atoms, so to speak, are the mystic atoms of this light, the corpuscular part of light, because light *is* corpuscular: it is not a mere mode of motion or a wave or something else. Light (our light) is a body, as much a body as electricity — one of its forms — is a body, i.e., material, or subtil matter.

Now, then, when this nebula of which we have been speaking — let us give it the scientific name — has attained the point of development or evolution downwards into manifestation where the reimbodying principles of the former world or cosmos or sun or planet, as the case may be, have sufficiently entered into it, it begins to rotate by a characteristic energy, similar to electromagnetism, inherent in itself. Plato tells us that circular motion is one of the first signs of entitative, free, existence — a saying which is often laughed at by our young savants of science and quondam bigwigs of a transitory era of dogmatic thinking. Plato defines *being* as a "body which is capable of acting and being acted upon." It is a good definition to remember, for it implies both passive and active existence — or manifestation. He said that with reference to the highest essence of the cosmos — the primal Principle of which H. P. Blavatsky speaks as the ineffable *That* — it is not "a" being, hence limited, possessing bounds, because neither does it act nor is it acted upon. It is *All*, eternally, endlessly *All*.

So this cosmic nebula drifts from the place where it first was evolved, the guiding impulse of karma directing here and directing there, this luminous nebulosity moving circularly, and contracting, passing through other phases of nebular evolution, such as the spiral stage and the annular, until it becomes spherical, or rather a nebular series of concentric spheres. The nebula in space, as just said, takes often a spiral form, and from the core, the center, there stream forth branches, spiral branches, and they look like whirling wheels *within* wheels, and they whirl during many ages. When the time has come — when the whirling has developed *pari passu* with the indwelling lives and intelligences within the cosmic nebula — then the annular form appears, a form like a ring or concentric rings, with a heart in the center, and after long aeons, the central heart becomes the sun or central body of the new solar system, and the rings the planets. These rings condense into other bodies, and these other bodies are the planets circulating around their elder *brother,* the sun; elder, because he was the first to condense into a sphere.

The idea of modern scientists that the nebular sun threw off the planets, and that the earth after partial solidification threw off the moon, and that the other planets having moons did likewise, is not the teaching of the esoteric philosophy. It has never been proved, and it is criticized daily by men as eminent as those who propounded these theories. The nebular theory as propounded and modified from time to time, science has never proved; scientists have never been able to prove why so much heat could develop and be retained in so tenuous, so diaphanous an object. Why, if the luminosity arises from combustion of gaseous matter, does it not burn itself out? It had billions of years, countless ages, in which to burn out, and the sky is dotted with nebulae which have not burned out yet; and similarly with regard to the sun. The sun is formed of the same matter as the nebulae, later becoming cometary matter. The sun does not burn; it has no more heat in it than has a pane of glass which transmits the solar ray.

The sun is not in combustion: it is the generator and storehouse of the mighty ocean of force and forces which feed our entire solar system. Matter is corporealized or crystallized force; force, inversely, may be called subtil matter — or matter in its fourth, fifth, sixth, and seventh states, for *force and matter are one.* The sun is a storehouse and generator of forces, and is itself force in its first and second states — i.e., matter in its sixth and seventh states, counting upward. We shall study this subject more fully in a later lecture.

This is a bare outline of the teachings that we have received on the subjects treated of. The moon comprises another subject, which will merit in due time very particular study, indeed.

First a nebula, then a comet, then a planet; but the above sketch outlines the state of a solar system in the first era of the *solar* manvantara. Now let us take any one planet and shortly, briefly, touch upon the nature of a *planetary* manvantara. The sun, of course, remains throughout the solar manvantara. It began with it, and when the solar system comes to an end, the sun's pralaya will also come. But the planets are different in certain respects. They have their manvantara also, each one of them, lasting usually many billions of years; and when a planetary chain or body has reached its term, when its hour strikes for going into rest, or into pralaya or dissolution, the manvantara ends and pralaya begins, but in this case it is not a prākritika-pralaya which, you remember, signifies or means the dissolution of nature. The planetary body remains dead, as is now the moon itself, but it sends its principles (precisely as the former solar system did) into a laya-center in space, and they remain there for "innumerable ages." Meanwhile the other planets of that solar system go through their cycles; but the planet which we have picked out for illustration, when its time comes again to descend into manvantara, follows its line of development in precisely the same way as outlined before. It descends again into manifestation through the inner divine planetary thirst for active life and is directed to the same solar system, and to the same spot, relatively speaking, that its predecessor (its *former self*) had, attracted thither by magnetic and other forces on the lower planes. It forms, in the beginning of its course or journey downwards, a planetary nebula; after many aeons it becomes a comet, following ultimately an elliptic orbit around the sun of our solar system, thus being "captured," as our scientists wrongly say, by the sun; and finally condenses into a planet in its earliest physical condition. The comets of short periodic time are on their way to rebecoming planets in our solar system, provided they successfully elude the many dangers that beset such ethereal bodies *before* condensation and hardening of their matter shield them from destruction.

SIX

(a) The hierarchy of Creative Powers is divided into seven (or 4 and 3) esoteric, within the twelve great Orders, recorded in the twelve signs of the Zodiac; the seven of the manifesting scale being connected, moreover, with the Seven Planets. All this is subdivided into numberless groups of divine Spiritual, semi-Spiritual, and ethereal Beings.

The Chief Hierarchies among these are hinted at in the great Quaternary, or the "four bodies and the three faculties" of Brahmâ exoterically, and the Panchâsyam, the five Brahmâs, or the five Dhyani-Buddhas in the Buddhist system. — *The Secret Doctrine, I, 213*

The refusal to admit in the whole Solar system of any other reasonable and intellectual beings on the human plane, than ourselves, is the greatest conceit of our age. All that science has a right to affirm, is that there are no invisible Intelligences living under the same conditions as we do. It cannot deny point-blank the possibility of there being worlds within worlds, under totally different conditions to those that constitute the nature of our world; nor can it deny that there may be a certain limited communication between some of those worlds and our own. To the highest, we are taught, belong the seven orders of the purely divine Spirits; to the six lower ones belong hierarchies that can occasionally be seen and heard by men, and who do communicate with their progeny of the Earth; which progeny is indissolubly linked with them, each principle in man having its direct source in the nature of those great Beings, who furnish us with the respective invisible elements in us. — *Ibid., I, 133*

W E OPEN our study this evening by reading from *The Secret Doctrine,* volume I, page 258:

"Whatsoever quits the Laya State, becomes active life; it is drawn into the vortex of MOTION (the alchemical solvent of Life); Spirit and Matter are the two States of the ONE, which is neither Spirit nor Matter, both being the absolute life, latent." (*Book of Dzyan,* Comm. iii, par.

18).... "Spirit is the first differentiation of (and in) SPACE; and Matter the first differentiation of Spirit. That, which is neither Spirit nor matter — that is IT — the Causeless CAUSE of Spirit and Matter, which are the Cause of Kosmos. And THAT we call the ONE LIFE or the Intra-Cosmic Breath."

In our study of a week ago we embarked upon a brief discussion, or rather a short excursus, with regard to certain astronomical factors which enter very largely into the occult or esoteric teaching which leads to a proper comprehension of cosmogony or world building, and also of theogony or the genesis of the gods or divine intelligences who initiate and direct cosmogony, as these are outlined in *The Secret Doctrine.* Within the time at our disposal we shortly reviewed the esoteric formulae in which the ancient wisdom is imbodied, and the *effectual* agencies which act at the dawn of manifestation; and this evening we shall undertake briefly to review the *causal* agencies or aspects of the same subject.

The dawn of manifestation, as *The Secret Doctrine* tells us, begins in and with the awakening of a laya-center. The Sanskrit word laya, as we saw before, signifies in esotericism that point or spot — any point or any spot — in space which, owing to karmic law, suddenly becomes the center of active life, first on a higher plane and later descending into manifestation through and by the lower planes. In one sense such a laya-center may be conceived of as a canal, a channel, through which the vitality of the superior spheres is pouring down into, and inspiring, inbreathing into, the lower planes or states of matter, or rather of substance. But behind all this vitality there is a driving force. There are mechanics in the universe, mechanics of many degrees of consciousness and power. But behind the pure mechanic stands the spiritual mechanician.

It would seem absolutely necessary first to soak our minds through and through with the thought that everything in our cosmical universe, i.e., the stellar universe, is *alive,* is directed by will and governed by intelligence. Behind every cosmic body that we see, there is a directing intelligence and a guiding will.

If theosophy has one natural enemy against which it has fought and will always fight it is the materialistic view of life, the view that nothing exists except dead unconscious matter, and that the phenomena of life and thought and consciousness spring from it. This is not merely unnatural and therefore impossible; it is absurd as a hypothesis.

On the contrary, as we may read in *The Secret Doctrine*, the main, fundamental, and basic postulate of being is that the universe is driven by will and consciousness, guided by will and consciousness, and is spiritually purposive. When a laya-center is fired into action by the touch of these two on their downward way, becoming the imbodying life of a solar system, or of a planet of a solar system, the center manifests first on its highest plane. The skandhas (which we described in a former study) are awakened into life one after another: first the highest ones, next the intermediate ones, and lastly the inferior ones, cosmically and qualitatively speaking.

In such laya-centers the imbodying life shows itself first to our physical human eyes as a luminous nebula — matter which we may describe as being of course on the fourth plane of nature or prakriti, but nevertheless in the second (counting downwards) of the seven principles or states of the material universe. It is a manifestation in that universe of daivī-prakriti, i.e., "shining" prakriti or "divine" prakriti. As the aeons pass this laya-center, now manifesting as a nebula, remains in space steadily though slowly developing and condensing (following the impulses of the forces that have awakened it into action on this plane). As the aeons pass, I say, it is drawn towards that part or locality in space, if we are speaking of a solar system, or towards that sun, if we are describing the coming into being of a planet, with which it has karmic — skandhic — affinities or magnetic attraction, and eventually manifests in the latter case as a comet. The matter of a comet, by the way, is entirely different from the matter we have any knowledge of on earth, and which it is impossible to reproduce under any physical conditions in our laboratories, because this matter, while on the fourth plane of manifestation (otherwise we should not sense it with our fourth-plane eyes), is matter in another state than any known to us — probably in the sixth state, counting from below, or the second state counting from above.

Of such matter is the sun, or rather the solar body, in its *outward form* composed. It is physical matter in the sixth state, counting upwards, or in the second state counting downwards or outward; and its nucleus which, as H. P. Blavatsky tells us in *The Secret Doctrine,* is a particle or a solar atom of primal matter-stuff, or spirit-stuff, is matter in the seventh state counting upwards, or the first or highest counting downwards.

This comet in time, if it succeed in pursuing its way towards becoming what it is destined to be, becomes finally a planet; it so becomes unless it meet with some disaster, as when it is swallowed up by one or another of the suns which it may pass in its far-flung orbit. Some comets have already in our solar system so nearly reached the planetary state in its first stages, on the way to becoming a full-grown planet of the solar system, that their orbits lie within the confines or limits of this system. Such, for instance, is Encke's comet, having an elliptical orbit, and moving around the sun in a closed curve in the space of a little over three years. Another one is Biela's which, I believe, has not been seen again, after it appeared to break into two, I think in the 'fifties of last century. Another one was Faye's, having the largest orbit of all these three. Two others are de Vico's and Brorsen's.

It would seem as if all those comets which are drawn into elliptical orbits around our sun, were so drawn because they were karmically destined ultimately to become planets of our system; but others, again, suffer another fate. They perish, absorbed or torn to pieces by the inexpressibly active influences which surround not merely our own but all other suns, because each sun, while being the center of its own system of planets, and their life-giver, from another aspect is a cosmical vampire. There is much more on this subject that must be said, but it is very doubtful whether, at the present stage of our study, it would be wise to embark upon a wider exposition now.

We desire this evening to take up again the same thread of thought, continuing with a study of the beginning of things as outlined in Genesis, and as illustrated more particularly by the Jewish theosophy called the Qabbālāh. If the time allotted to us be insufficient to do so this evening, we hope to begin that study at our next meeting.

Nothing in the universe is separate from any other thing. All things hang together not merely sympathetically and magnetically but because all beings are fundamentally one. We have one *self*, one self of selves, manifesting in the Inmost of the Inmost being of all. But we have many egos, and the study of the ego in that branch of our thought which is embraced under the head of psychology is one of the most inherently necessary and one of the most interesting and important that can be undertaken.

Around the ego, so far as we humans are concerned, center some of the most important teachings of the esoteric wisdom. Without going into this study at some length, it is impossible for us to understand certain of the teachings in *The Secret Doctrine*. The ancient Stoics (the very wonderful philosophy originating with some of the Greek philosophers, and which became so deservedly popular among the deeper thinkers of Rome) taught that everything in the universe is intermingled or interwoven, not by fundamentally distinct essences or entities interpenetrating each other, nor in what theosophists today call "planes of being," merely, but by various aspects or differentiations of one common substance, the root of all, and they expressed the principle through the three Greek words, *krasis di' holou*, "a mingling through everything," an *intermingling* of all the essences in the cosmos, arising out of, and differentiated from, the root-substance common to all. This is also the teaching of the esoteric wisdom. It is the manifestation, in other words, of all beings: of all thinking, unthinking, and senseless beings, and of all the gods giving direction and purpose to the complex universe which we see around us today; and in this varied life was placed the primal cause of all the beauty, the concord, as well as the strife and discord that do exist in nature, and which is the cause of the so-called mistakes that nature makes. The origin of what many people call the "insolvable riddle" of the "origin of evil." What is the "origin of evil"? The ancient wisdom says that it is merely the *conflict of wills* of evolving beings — an inevitable and *necessary* phase of evolution.

Properly to understand this intermingling involves another important subject of study which we shall take up at a later date, and this is the doctrine of hierarchies. Hierarchy, of course, merely means that a scheme or system or state of delegated directive power and authority exists in a self-contained body, directed, guided, and taught by one having supreme authority, called the hierarch. The name is used in theosophy, by extension of meaning, as signifying the innumerable degrees, grades, and steps of evolving entities in the kosmos, and as applying to all parts of the universe; and rightly so, because every different part of the universe — and their number is simply countless — is under the vital governance of a divine being, of a god, of a spiritual essence, and all material manifestations are simply the appearances on our plane of the workings and actions of these spiritual beings behind it. The series of hierarchies extends infinitely in both directions. Man may, if he so choose for purposes of thought, consider himself at the middle point, from which extends above him an unending series of steps upon steps of higher beings of all grades — growing constantly less material and more spiritual, and greater in all senses — towards an ineffable point, and there the imagination stops; not because the series itself stops, but because our thought can reach no farther out or in. And similar to this series, an infinitely great series of beings and states of beings descends downwards (to use human terms) — downwards and downwards, until there again the imagination stops merely because our thought can go no farther.

The eternal action and interaction, or what the Stoics also called the intermingling, of these beings produce eternally the various so-called planes of being, and the action of the will of these beings on matter or substances is the manifestation of what we call the laws of nature. This is a very inaccurate and misleading phrase; but it seems justifiable in a metaphorical sense, because as a human legislator or a human lawgiver will set forth or set down certain rules of conduct, certain schemes of action, which are to be obeyed, so the intelligences behind the actions of nature do the same thing, *not* in a legislative way, but by the action of their own spiritual economy. So man himself, in similar fashion, lays down the "laws" for the less lives which compose his essences — the principles under the center which he governs — and which comprise even the physical body, and the lives building it. Each one of these lives is a microcosmic universe or cosmos, that is to say, an ordered entity, an entity ruled by inescapable or ineluctable habit, which our scientists, applying the rule to universal cosmical action, call the laws of nature.

And they in turn, these less lives, have similar universes under them. It is unthinkable that the series can stop or have an end because, if it did, we should have an infinity that ends, an unthinkable proposition. It is merely the paucity of our ideas and the feebleness of our imagination which make us to suppose that there may be a stop at certain points; and it is this feebleness of thought which has given birth to and promoted the rise of the different religious systems; in one case the monotheism of the Christian Church, and in another case the monotheism of the Mohammedan peoples, and in another case still the monotheism of the Jewish people. Of these three, the Jews have had the longest history and the wisest history, for the Jews originally were never a monotheistic people. In their early history they were convinced polytheists — using the term in the philosophical sense, lest people imagine when they hear of polytheism that it means our absurd modern Western misconception of what we think the cultured Romans and Greeks thought about their gods and goddesses, or what we think they ought to have believed, which is conceited nonsense.

The popular mythology of the Greeks and Romans, as also that of ancient Egypt or of Babylonia, and that of the Germanic or Celtic tribes of Europe, was understood in a different way from our gross misconception of it; and conceived of in a different way by the wise men in those days, who understood perfectly well all the usual symbols and allegories by which the esoteric teachings were outlined and taught in the popular mythologies. And we must remember that "exoteric" does not necessarily mean false. It means only that in exoteric teachings the keys to the esoteric teachings have not been given out.

We often hear the claim made by monotheistic believers that the great "prophets" of Israel, the so-called wise men of that people, knew better than their ancient predecessors what their people ought to know and believe. These prophets taught monotheism, we are assured, and redirected the thoughts of the people away from the ancient beliefs — indeed, the multiplicity of beliefs — towards one tribal God whom they called Jehovah, a word, by the way, which the later orthodox Jewish religionists held, and still hold, so sacred that they would not even pronounce it aloud, but in reading aloud substituted for it another word when this word Jehovah occurred in a sentence in the Jewish Bible. Now this substitute word is *Adonai,* and means "my lords" — in itself a true confession of polytheistic thought. Judaism is replete in its Law or Bible, at least, with polytheism; and so prone is the human heart to follow the instincts of its spirit that when the Christian Church in its blindness overthrew philosophical polytheism as an error in religion, the reaction, fully to be expected as a consequence, very soon set in, and that Church answered the cry of the human heart by substituting "saints" for the injured and banished gods and goddesses, thus inaugurating a cultural adoration of dead men and women for powers, intelligences, in nature! They had to give them saints in order to supply the places of the forgotten deities; and even gave to these saints more or less the same powers that the ancient gods and goddesses were reputed to have exercised and to have had. They had a saint as a patron or protector of city, state, or country: St. George for England, St. James for Spain, St. Denis for France, and so on. The same thought, the same function, the same desire satisfied — the instincts of the human heart cannot be ignored or violated with impunity. But how greatly different was the initiate view of the wise men in pagan times!

When the ancients spoke of the multiplicity of gods they did so with wisdom, understanding, and reverence. Is it conceivable that the great men of the ancient days who then discovered and established the canons of belief followed by us — usually ignorant of our great debt to them — even today in all our lines of thought, and which we value like little children and have valued since the rebirth of literature in our Western world — is it conceivable, I say, that they had no conception of cosmical or of divine unity, something which even the average man of intelligence today will come to? How absurd! No! They could think, and they knew as well as we do, but they also knew, yea, even the degenerated thinkers in the early ages of the Christian era, that if "God" made the world, being a perfect and infinite Being, his work (or its work) could be only a perfect and infinite work, worthy of its perfect and infinite Maker, free from vanity, free from limitations, free from sin, free from decrepitude and ceaseless, gnawing change. Yet, as we see and consider the things around us, as we know that the world, being an exemplar of change and hence of limitations and decay, therefore cannot be and is not infinite, we know — the instincts of our being tell us — that it is the work of less beings, of minor and limited powers, however exalted spiritually. And as we penetrate into our own thoughts and study the life of the beings and of the nature around us, we see also that there is life *within* life, wheel *within* wheel, purpose *within* purpose, and that behind the outward manifestations or action (the "laws of nature") of the so-called gods, there are still more subtil powers, still more exalted intelligences at work — verily, wheels within wheels, lives within lives, and so on forever — an unending and boundless unity in multiplicity, and multiplicity limitless and unbounded in unity. So, as said before, when we speak of the unity of life, or of the "divine unity," we merely mean that here our penetrating spirit has reached the limit of its present powers, a point at which human thought can go no farther. It has run to its utmost limits, and from the feebleness of it we are bound in truth to say: here is as far as our thought can go. It is our present "Ring called 'Pass Not!'" But this honest confession of human limitation does *not* mean that there is "nothing" beyond. On the contrary, it is a proof that life and space are endless.

Now the Neoplatonists who came into prominence in the early centuries of the Christian era — and who, with the Stoics, provided Christianity with most of what it had that was philosophically good and spiritual and true — taught that the summit, the acme, the flower, the highest point (that they called the hyparxis) of any series of animate and "inanimate" beings, whether we enumerate the stages or degrees of the series as seven or ten or twelve, was the "divine unity" *for that series or hierarchy*, and that this hyparxis or flower or summit or beginning or highest being was again in its turn the *lowest being of the hierarchy above it*, and so extending onwards for ever.

Change within change, wheel within wheel, each hierarchy manifesting one facet of the divine cosmic life, each hierarchy showing forth one thought, as it were, of the divine thinkers. Good and evil are relative, and rigidly offset and equilibrate each other. There is no *absolute* good, there is no *absolute* evil; these are mere human terms only. "Evil" in any sphere of life is *imperfection*, for *it*. "Good" in any sphere of life is *perfection*, for *it*. But the good of one is the evil of another, because the latter is the shadow of something higher above it.

Just as light and darkness are not absolute but relative things. What is darkness? Darkness is absence of light, and the light that we know is itself the manifestation of life in matter — hence a material phenomenon. Each is (physically) a form of vibration, each is, therefore, a form of life.

Various names were given to these hierarchies considered as series of beings. For instance, let us take the standard and generalized Greek hierarchy as shown by writers in periods preceding the rise of Christianity, though the Neoplatonists, as we have seen, had their own hierarchies, and gave the stages or degrees thereof special names. It is often asserted by those people who know everything — I mean the bigwigs of the modern day, who even believe that they know better what the ancients believed than the ancients did themselves — that Neoplatonism was evolved merely to oppose and overthrow, and to take the place of the wonderful, soul-saving, spiritual doctrines of Christianity, forgetting that from Neoplatonism and Neopythagoreanism, and Stoicism, early Christianity drew nearly everything of religious and philosophic good that it had in it. But the Neoplatonic doctrine was, in sober fact, actually the setting forth to a *certain degree only* of the esoteric doctrine of the Platonic school and was, in its esoteric reach, the teaching which Plato and the early Pythagoreans taught secretly to their disciples.

We now resume our thread. The hyparxis, as we showed, means the summit or beginning of a hierarchy. The scheme started with the divine, the highest point of the series or its divinity:

(1) Divine; (2) Gods, or the spiritual; (3) Demigods, sometimes called divine heroes, involving a very mystical doctrine; (4) Heroes proper; (5) Men; (6) Beasts or animals; (7) Vegetable world; (8) Mineral world; (9) Elemental world, or what was called the realm of Hades. As said, the divinity (or aggregate divine lives) itself was the hyparxis of this series of hierarchies,

because each of these nine stages was itself a subordinate hierarchy. The names mean little, you may give them other names; the important thing is to get the thought. Now, as said before, remember that this esoteric wisdom taught that this (or any other) hierarchy of nine, hangs like a pendant jewel from the lowest hierarchy above it, which made the tenth counting upwards, which we can call, if you like, the superdivine, the hyper-heavenly, and that this tenth was the lowest stage (or the ninth, counting downwards) of still another hierarchy extending upwards; and so on, indefinitely.

Now when the Christians finally overthrew the ancient religion, when the karmic cycle had brought about an era of what Plato called spiritual barrenness — and we remember to divide the work of evolution into two parts, epochs of barrenness and epochs of fertility — when the Christian religion came in as part of an epoch of barrenness, the Christians took over very much of this ancient thought, as was only to be expected: history merely repeated itself. And they derived it, as was said before, mainly from the Stoics and the Neopythagoreans and the Neoplatonists, but mostly from the Neoplatonists. This was done in very large part at Alexandria, the great center of Greek or Hellenistic culture at that time; the chiefest thinkers of the Neoplatonists also lived in Alexandria. This Neoplatonic stream of beautiful thought in the Christian religion entered into it with special force around the fifth century, through the writings of a man who was called Dionysius the Areopagite, from the "Hill of Ares" or Mars at Athens. The Christian legend runs that when Paul preached at Athens, he did so on Mars Hill or the Areopagus, and that one of his first converts was a Greek called Dionysius; and Christian tradition goes on to say that he was, later, the first Christian Bishop of Athens. Now this may all be fable. However, the Christians claimed it as a fact.

In the fifth or sixth century, five hundred years more or less after Paul is supposed to have preached in Athens, there appeared in the Greek world a work calling itself the writings of Dionysius the Areopagite — claiming authorship from this same man. It is evidently the work of a Neoplatonist-Christian. That is to say, of a Christian who, for reasons of his own, perhaps policy (social or financial), remained within the Christian Church, but was more or less a Greek pagan, a Neoplatonist at heart. This work, by coming out under the *name* of the first (alleged) Bishop of Athens, Dionysius, almost immediately began to have immense vogue in the Christian Church; and it remains to this day, not indeed one of the canonical works, but one of the works which the Christians consider among the greatest they have on mystical lines, and perhaps their most spiritual work. It very deeply affected Christian theological thought from the time of its appearance.

One of the works comprised in this book, attributed by the Christians themselves to Dionysius, Paul's first convert in Athens, is a treatise on the Divine Hierarchies, in which the teaching is that God is infinite and therefore did the work of creation through less abstract and spiritual beings; and a scheme of hierarchies is here set forth, one lower than another, one derived from the other — which is exactly the teaching in the Qabbālāh; which also is exactly the teaching of the Neoplatonists and essentially that of the Stoics, and of the old Greek mythology. It is a pagan teaching throughout, and merely became Christianized because adapted to the new religion, and because Christian names are used: instead of saying and enumerating gods, divine heroes, demigods or heroes, men, and animals, etc., the names are God, Archangels, Thrones, Powers, etc. But the schematic or essential thought is the same. Furthermore, there are actually passages in the works of this Dionysius which are taken word for word, wholesale, from the writings of the Neoplatonist Plotinus, who lived and flourished and wrote voluminously on Neoplatonic subjects in the third century.

Now this work, particularly in the field of dogmatic ecclesiastical thought, formed the basis of much of the theology of the Greek and Roman Churches; we may even say that on it their medieval theology was actually based. It formed the main source of the studies and writings of the Italian Thomas Aquinas (13th century), one of the greatest medieval doctors of the Christian religion, and of Johannes Scotus, called Erigena, an Irishman (9th century), and probably of Duns Scotus (13th century), a remarkable Scot; and of many more. Spenser, Shakespeare, and Milton, to speak only of English literature, are full of the spirit of these writings. They provided much of the mystical thought of the Dark Ages, and ultimately in a degenerate form helped to give rise to the hairsplitting and quibbling and squabbles of the quasi-religious writers known as the Schoolmen. But these men had lost the inner sense or heart of the thing through the ecclesiastical growth and political power of the Christian Church, and they began to argue about things of no spiritual consequence whatever, such as: which came first, the hen or the egg? or, how many angels can dance on the point of a needle? or, if an irresistible force meets an immovable obstacle, what then happens? These most pragmatical and useful diversions and intellectual vagaries lasted for a certain time, and then, with the renaissance of thought in Europe, due largely to the labors of the devotees of science and natural philosophy, the European world gradually began to pull out of this mental slough, and brought in an era which is now in full and strong current, and which has inaugurated and continued for good or for ill (perhaps both) the streams of human thinking as we see it today.

In conclusion, we may call attention to the fact that just about the time when the first 5,000 years of the Hindu cycle called the kali yuga (lasting 432,000) came to an end, there also came to an end a certain "Messianic" cycle of twenty-one hundred years — (actually, if we come to exact figures, 2,160), which is, note well, just one half of the Hindu-Babylonian root-cycle of 4,320 years.

SEVEN

HIERARCHIES: ONE OF THE LOST KEYS OF THE ESOTERIC PHILOSOPHY.
THE PYTHAGOREAN SACRED TETRAKTYS. THE LADDER OF LIFE:
THE LEGEND OF PADMAPĀNI.

Theophilosophy proceeds on broader lines. From the very beginning of Æons — in time and space in our Round and Globe — the Mysteries of Nature (at any rate, those which it is lawful for our races to know) were recorded by the pupils of those same now invisible "heavenly men," in geometrical figures and symbols. The keys thereto passed from one generation of "wise men" to the other. Some of the symbols, thus passed from the east to the west, were brought therefrom by Pythagoras, who was not the inventor of his famous "Triangle." The latter figure, along with the plane cube and circle, are more eloquent and scientific descriptions of the order of the evolution of the Universe, spiritual and psychic, as well as physical, than volumes of descriptive Cosmogonies and revealed "*Geneses*." The *ten points* inscribed within that "Pythagorean *triangle*" are worth all the theogonies and angelologies ever emanated from the theological brain. For he who interprets them — on their very face, and in the order given — will find in these seventeen points (the seven Mathematical Points hidden) the uninterrupted series of the genealogies from the first *Heavenly* to *terrestrial* man. And, as they give the order of Beings, so they reveal the order in which were evolved the Kosmos, our earth, and the primordial elements by which the latter was generated. Begotten in the invisible *Depths*, and in the womb of the same "Mother" as its fellow-globes — he who will master the mysteries of our Earth, will have mastered those of all others.

— The Secret Doctrine, I, 612–13

"*It is that* LIGHT *which condenses into the forms of the 'Lords of Being' — the first and the highest of which are, collectively,* JIVÂTMA, *or Pratyagâtma* (said figuratively to issue from Paramâtma. It is the Logos of the Greek philosophers — appearing at the beginning of every new Manvantara). *From these downwards — formed from the ever-consolidating waves of that light, which becomes on the objective plane gross matter — proceed the numerous hierarchies of the Creative Forces, some formless, others having their own distinctive form, others, again, the lowest (Elementals), having no form of their own, but assuming every form according to the surrounding conditions.*"

— Ibid., II, 33–4

W E OPEN our study this evening by reading from *The Secret Doctrine*, volume I, page 274:

> The whole Kosmos is guided, controlled, and animated by almost endless series of Hierarchies of sentient Beings, each having a mission to perform, and who — whether we give to them one name or another, and call them Dhyan-Chohans or Angels — are "messengers" in the sense only that they are the agents of Karmic and Cosmic Laws. They vary infinitely in their respective degrees of consciousness and intelligence; and to call them all pure Spirits without any of the earthly alloy "which time is wont to prey upon" is only to indulge in poetical fancy. For each of these Beings either *was,* or prepares to become, a man, if not in the present, then in a past or a coming cycle (Manvantara).

When we ended our study last week, we left unmentioned a number of very important things, which we shall have to take up this evening. First, a few words more concerning the nebular theory or hypothesis and the planetary theory deriving from it, as considered from the theosophical standpoint, and consequently a further explanation or rather development of the doctrine of hierarchies, which will lead us to the study towards which we have aimed, that is to say, the consideration of cosmogony or the beginning of worlds as outlined in the Jewish Book of Genesis or Beginnings.

About one hundred years ago, more or less within a few years of each other, there died three remarkable men, namely Kant, perhaps the greatest philosopher that Europe has produced; Sir William Herschel, the astronomer; and the Marquis de Laplace; the first a German, the second an Anglo-German, and the third a Frenchman. All these three men in some degree were responsible for the enunciation and the development of the theory of world-beginning which eventuated in the nebular hypothesis of Laplace. It is interesting also to note that all three men were of humble birth, and by the force of their own intelligence and character became, all three of them, remarkable men. Kant was, I believe, the son of a saddler; Sir William Herschel was also of humble origin, and was in youth an oboist in the Hanoverian Guards; and Pierre Simon Laplace was the son of a farmer; Laplace was ennobled, and upon him was conferred the nobiliary title of marquis.

Now the nebular theory really originated with Kant; he it was who laid down the basic lines, the fundamental ground, as it were, upon which the theory was later developed mathematically by Laplace. Coincident with Kant's work and writings was the astronomical work of Herschel in England, and those two men were responsible for the fundamentals of the nebular theory. Laplace took it up after they had more or less laid down the main lines, developed it into what is called the nebular hypothesis or theory of Laplace, and on account of its explaining in mathematical form the mechanism of the universe, that is to say, of the solar system and the planets and their satellites, it has been called a "magnificently audacious" hypothesis. It was Laplace who carried the theory a good deal farther than the work of Kant and Herschel; and, in a sense, Laplace materialized it. As H. P. Blavatsky tells us, if the nebular theory had remained at the point where Kant and Herschel had left it, there would be little for the theosophical writers and thinkers to do except to develop it and explain it in accordance with the esoteric philosophy.

It is very interesting to note that another great man, Swedenborg in Sweden, also worked upon the same theory and apparently had very nearly the same ideas that Kant and Herschel had as regards a nebular genesis of cosmical systems. Now these two latter men had a spiritual idea back of the theory which they enunciated, and it was the abandonment of that spiritual idea by Laplace, and the substitution by him of a mechanico-mathematical theory in its place, which furnished those influences which directed the nebular hypothesis away from the line and thought and teachings as laid down in the esoteric philosophy, as taught by the ancient teachers.

The nebular hypothesis has in some respects been much changed since the day of Laplace; scientists have thought more about it, a fact which was also true in 1887 or 1888 when H. P. Blavatsky wrote *The Secret Doctrine*. There has been an attempt by later astronomers of our own day, Sir Norman Lockyer and the American astronomer and mathematician See, to replace a nebular origin of cosmical bodies, at least in part, with what has been called a planetesimal hypothesis or a planetesimal origin — that is to say, that the bodies of the solar system have been built up of and by cosmic dust and tiny planets drawn together by the force of gravitation. Now this theory is, philosophically speaking, at an immense distance from the teachings of the esoteric philosophy, although this philosophy does admit and teach that at a later stage in the evolution of cosmical bodies collection and concretion of stellar dust is, actually, one of the phases in the growth of worlds.

Theosophy admits that a planet or a solar system, in the course of its formation, does gather to itself stardust and vagrant bodies dispersed in space; but this factor in its growth is not its origin. The origin of a sun, of a solar system and of the planets in it, and consequently of the entire universe within the encircling zone of the Milky Way, has a spiritual background, has spiritual essences or gods behind it, who form such a system and direct it, and are the mechanicians in it and of it. Their work is carried on (more or less) along the main lines of the nebular theory as enunciated by Kant and Herschel: that is to say, space is eternally filled with matter in a certain state or condition of being, and when this matter, as Kant and Herschel would have said, receives the divine impulse, it is concreted and becomes luminous, and this concretion is further (and later) strengthened by its drawing into itself, from the immense spacial expanse in which it is, material stardust and larger bodies.

When we look up at the sky we see material bodies, fourth-plane bodies seen with our fourth-plane eyes, but behind these fourth-plane bodies there are spiritual intelligences, which are called in the esoteric philosophy, *dhyān-chohans*, or "lords of meditation." As the ancients put it, every celestial body is an "animal." Now the word animal comes from the Latin, and means a living being. Commonly, in speech, we speak of animals when we should say beasts or brutes; that is, a brute is an entity which has not yet been raised to the level of a *self-conscious* entity; it is *brute* in the original Latin sense, i.e., "heavy," "gross," hence irrational and incomplete; it is not yet finished. But an *animal* really means a living being, and in that sense the word applies to human beings.

Likewise, in the view of the ancients, it applies to the stellar, solar, and planetary bodies — they are animals in the sense of being living things, with a physical corpus or body, but nevertheless animate or insouled: in the mystical teachings of the esoteric philosophy they are insouled things, as indeed every atom is, every tiny universe, or tiny cosmos.

Now this insouling is done by (or is the action of) what is commonly called hierarchies. There is not for every individual entity in kosmos, whether atom, beast, man, god, planet, or sun, one concreted soul, as it were, derived from the universal world-soul, with nothing — no connecting links — above it and nothing below it; not at all. There are no true vacancies in nature, physical, astral, or spiritual; there are no vacuums. Everything is linked on to everything else, by literally countless bonds of union, which is another master key to the teachings of the esoteric philosophy. As in man, so in every other unit of being, in every other entity, the universal life manifests through a hierarchy; the multiform and varied qualities of beings are but the life-rays of a hierarchy, that is to say, grades or steps of consciousness and matter, ascending from below upward or, if you like, coming downwards from above, through all of which the center of consciousness — call it soul or ego for the moment — must pass in its evolution towards godhood.

This teaching of hierarchies is fundamental. It is one of the present-day "lost keys" of the esoteric philosophy. Nothing can be understood adequately without a clear comprehension of it. As man is in our ordinary psychology considered to be a triad or a triform entity — body, soul, and spirit — so he may be considered from another point of view as a fourfold entity, or as a fivefold, a sixfold, or a sevenfold, or (the most esoteric of all) as a tenfold entity. Why *ten?* Because ten is the key number which explains the compound fabric of the universe. The universe is built on a denary scale, that is, on a scale counting by tens. In a few moments we shall develop in outline the philosophical import of seven and ten. Let us say now that man is septenary in our view only because we reckon in, as principles, two elements of his being which are not, strictly speaking, *human* principles: one, the physical body which really is not a "principle" at all; it is merely a house, his "carrier" in another sense, and no more belongs to man — except that he has excreted it, thrown it out from himself — than does the house in which his body lives. He is a complete human being without it.

The second strictly nonhuman principle is the highest of all the seven, the higher self, the ātman, the seventh — nonhuman because it is *universal*. The *self* no more belongs to me than to you or to anyone else. Selfhood is the same in all beings. But beyond the ātman, there is the Paramātman, which we have briefly studied before, the supreme self. The ātman is, as it were, the star of our own self-issue, the root of our selfhood, the point where we cling, as it were, to the Highest. If we can conceive of an ocean of superspiritual ether, so to speak, and in that ocean — call it consciousness — a vortex, a laya-center, a point, a Primordial Point, whence the six principles below it flow forth into concrete manifestation through its vehicles — the souls or egos — we obtain a very crude conception of the root of our being. It is the ātman, the channel or spiritual point where the superspiritual breaks, as it were, from and through a barrier downwards into individualized life. This process we shall more fully explain later, and shall then illustrate it by diagram.

Now this matter of hierarchies is dealt with in the different world religions virtually in the same manner but under different names and in different paradigmatic schemes. For instance, you can think of the ten parts or grades or steps of a hierarchy as one under the other, like the floors in a house or like the flats in an apartment house, a very gross simile, it is true, but having the advantage of suggesting steps or planes, and of suggesting high and low. We can think of a hierarchy in another, more subtil, manner, as consisting in triads of spheres, or living centers, three triads hanging from the tenth or highest point; and that highest center is, as already explained, the point beyond which our thought and imagination can soar no higher, and we merely say that this center is the highest that the human intellect can reach. But we know that beyond this tenth which is our highest there is also the lowest center or plane of another hierarchy still higher from which our hierarchy hangs as a pendant; and so on endlessly. We cannot say of infinity that it begins here and ends there: if this were so, it would not be infinite, it would not be boundless. Our doctrine of universal life, of universal consciousness, of one

universal "law" working everywhere, means that that "law" manifests in every atom, and in every part of universal being, and in
all directions, and for all duration, and in the same manner everywhere, because it cannot manifest in radically diverse ways; if
so, it would be many fundamental "laws" and not one "law."

For instance, in our last study we considered the hierarchy of
the Neoplatonic philosophy, which is really the esoteric teaching
of ancient Greece in the form that Plato gave to it. And there
were nine stages, nine degrees, hanging, as it were, from the
topmost, the spiritual sun or the central sun. We can conceive
of these hierarchies as seven concentric circles around and deriving from a central point, the highest triad, which we can call the
infinite or the Primordial Point; or, again, we can call this Primordial Point the ātman or self of the thinking entity, man, and then
the other spheres or circles of being around him will stand for his
six other principles, somewhat in this fashion:

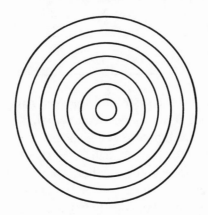

This is one way of representing a human individual hierarchy,
the different spheres or concentric circles, six of them, all flowing
forth from the center, or seventh element, the self. All hierarchies
are divided into seven, nine, or ten. The reason for this is a
question that we shall have to go into by and by. There is no
need to represent all these methods or paradigmatic schemes,
but the idea is the same in all. Another way of representing a
hierarchy by paradigm is by like lines, ten of them, in this way:

——————————————————————— 1
——————————————————————— 2
——————————————————————— 3
——————————————————————— 4
——————————————————————— 5
——————————————————————— 6
——————————————————————— 7
——————————————————————— 8
——————————————————————— 9
——————————————————————— 10

or by representing the nine stages or spheres as three triads on three planes, and the tenth on its own fourth plane:

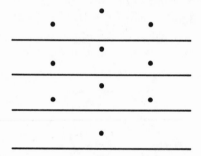

We have studied the system of the Neoplatonic hierarchies in brief outline; and, if we have time, we shall take up this evening two other paradigmatic schemes by which hierarchies are variously represented. Let us call earnest attention here to the important fact, before going farther, that these schemes, these paradigmatic representations on a flat surface, do *not* mean that the grades or steps or planes of being are either flat surfaces, or are like nests of boxes; they merely show by analogy, by hints, the relations and the functions of the grades among themselves.

It is obvious to any thinking man that the hierarchies of being do not rise one above another like the floors of a house. It is perhaps true that all over the world they are so represented by different systems; but this is merely to show that there is a high and a low, a *series* of conditions or states of spirit and matter. Just as we would teach children, so the ancient teachers taught us, in simple ways. Nor are we to imagine that the hierarchies actually extend somewhere in space in the form of triangles or circles. We represent them in this way in order to show their intermingling relations and their interpenetrating functions among each other. Why, however, do we separate the grades into triads? Because certain ones of these grades or planes are more nearly related, intermingle more easily, function more easily together, since their conditions or states are more closely akin. (1) The first triad, the highest; (2) the intermediate; (3) the lowest triad; and all overshadowing the corpus, the physical body. Or we can take another scheme, and have the three lowest centers forming the bottom triad; the three intermediate centers next; and then the three highest; all the three triads hanging from a point, the Primordial Point, "God," if you like.

Now let us consider the question: Have the Christians a hierarchy in their theology? They have; and by this I mean that the Christians had one, apparently from the earliest times, till the natural resiliency of the human mind began to exert itself in rebellion against the dogmatism and materialization of the Christian teaching which reached its climax in the epoch preceding the renaissance of thought, when the discoveries of science freed the human mind from its dogmatic shackles. Nevertheless, up till that time this teaching of hierarchies controlling living beings flourished in the Christian Church, and it originated in the form it then had, as we pointed out in our last study, in the writings of Dionysius the Areopagite. One of his works was called *On the Celestial Hierarchy,* and it showed how all spiritual being was divided into a hierarchy of ten degrees or stages, the tenth or highest being God. This mystic writer followed this work with another called *On the Ecclesiastical Hierarchy,* and he claimed as a good Christian, or in order to please his good Christian friends — there is every reason to believe that he copied the hierarchical scheme of the Neoplatonic philosophy, which was purely pagan, of course — that on earth the celestial hierarchy was reenacted or reflected or repeated in an ecclesiastical hierarchy, which was the Christian Church, topped by Jesus as the highest representative thereof and as the "Logos of God."

What were the names that Dionysius gave to the grades or stages of his hierarchy? First, God, as the summit, the Divine

Spirit; then came the Seraphim; then the Cherubim; then the
Thrones, forming the first triad. Then Dominations, Virtues,
Powers, forming the second triad. Then Principalities, then Arch-
angels, then Angels, the third triad counting downward.

It is interesting to note that this hierarchy is syncretistic,
that is, composite, taken from different sources and built up into
a unity. Seraphim and Cherubim are from the Hebrew. This
plural word *Seraphim* comes from a Hebrew root meaning to
"burn with fire," hence, to be inflamed with love. *Cherubim*
is a curious word, but scholars generally think that it means
"forms." The Seraphim are mystically believed to be red in color,
and the Cherubim dark blue. The Thrones, the Dominations,
the Virtues, the Powers, the Principalities, are all taken from
the Christian teachings of Paul in the Epistles, Ephesians 1:21,
and Colossians 1:16, and are distinctly mystic. The two last,
the Archangels and the Angels, are not at all Christian in their
origin, but are derived in indirect and tortuous descent from the
ancient Greek and Asiatic — especially old Persian — system of
thought which recognized messengers or ministers or transmitters
between man and the spiritual world; the Greek word *angelos*
(angel) originally meant "messenger," and the highest type of
these were called Archangels, or Angels of the highest degree.

The fault, or rather inadequacy, of this Christian system
is that its highest point reached no higher than this God here,
a modification on Greek lines of the Jewish Jehovah; and it went
no farther below in reach or extent than man himself. The Ineffable, Unthinkable, on the one hand, and the immeasurable
spheres of beings below man, on the other hand, are ignored. It
was merely a chapter torn out of the ancient wisdom and taken
over into Christianity; but small and imperfect as it was, it
provided Christianity with all the mysticism and spiritualizing
thought that saved it from utter materialism in religion during
the Middle Ages.

Let us now take up another hierarchy, the Jewish scheme of
the Qabbālāh. You see that there are nine degrees here, nine
degrees all pendant from the supreme self or God. Now the
Jewish Qabbalistic hierarchy, or hierarchies, or system of hierarchies, is an outgrowth of the teachings and thinkings of the

Jewish doctors or rabbis from a time very far back, and is actually a reflection of esoteric Babylonian teachings.

As the Book of Genesis (the first few chapters of it at least) is very largely taken from the Babylonians, so the Jews derived their angelology, or system of angels or angelical hierarchies, from that same source. Now this teaching found its finest expression in the Jewish theosophy called the Qabbālāh (this word, as said before, meaning "to receive" — i.e., traditionary lore handed down from teacher to teacher), and the teaching of the hierarchies in the Qabbālāh is fundamental, the whole system being based on it: it implies the intermingling and the interchange of all life and all beings, between low and high. Hence the Qabbālāh is, so far as it goes, a faithful reflection of the esoteric philosophy. The Qabbālāh as outlined in the book *Zohar,* a word meaning "splendor" — this book is often called the Bible of the Qabbalists — is in large part exoteric from the theosophical viewpoint, because all our teachings, *with regard to certain things,* are in the *Zohar,* but not all the explanations are there, and this fact makes the book exoteric, in so far as the keys are lacking.

The teaching in the Qabbālāh with regard to the hierarchies and the ladder of life is that from the Boundless, or Eyn Sōph, down to infinity below, the ladder of life consists of steps, or degrees, or grades, of consciousness and of consciousnesses, and of being and of beings, and that there is a constant interchange, an interflow of communication, between these innumerable grades of the various hierarchies or worlds. Precisely our teaching — naturally. The Qabbalistic hierarchy consists of, or more accurately is typified by, nine grades or planes or spheres hanging from a tenth (or a first, if you like), all together making ten. They bore the following names. The first is called the Crown, the Primordial Point, the first and highest of the Sephīrōth (sometimes spelt Sefīrōth) or the grades, steps, planes, or spheres, before spoken of. The next Sephīra is called Wisdom. (We have no time now to give the Hebrew words here; they may be found in any book on the Qabbālāh.)* The next, the third, is called Understanding or, perhaps better, Intelligence. These form the

---

*See *Isis Unveiled,* II, 213; and *Theosophical Glossary.*

head and two shoulders of the Ādām Qadmōn, or Archetypal Man, or Ideal Man. According to the thinking of the Qabbalists, as these hierarchies are particularly and sympathetically related to certain respective parts of the human body, so these three just spoken of have each its respective relation: certain parts about the crown of the head, or in or from the head, or belonging to the head, for the first Sephīra; the right shoulder to Wisdom; the left to Understanding. The right arm is called Greatness, or sometimes Love; the left arm is called Power, or sometimes Justice, and is considered a feminine quality; the breast or region of the chest or heart is called Beauty. The right leg (remember I am speaking generally of the Archetypal Man) is called Subtility; the left leg is called Majesty, and is considered a feminine quality. The generative organs are called Foundation.

Now these make nine. Each of these grades is assumed to emanate from the one above it. First the Crown; from the Crown, Wisdom; from the Crown and Wisdom, Understanding; from the three — Crown, Wisdom, and Understanding — comes the fourth; from the four all together comes the fifth; from the five all together comes the sixth; and so on down to the ninth; and the ninth, with all the forces and qualities of the others behind it, produces this round being, an egg-shaped container or "carrier" or vehicle, an auric egg; and this auric egg, as the tenth, is called Kingdom, or sometimes Dwelling Place, because it is the fruit or result or emanation or field of action of all the others, manifesting through these different planes of being.

Why should the hierarchies sometimes be numbered or reckoned as seven, and sometimes as ten? Because ten is the most sacred fundamental number in occultism. It is that upon which the universe is built. The fabric of being is built along the lines of the decad or ten. The Pythagoreans, members of one of the most mystic of the ancient Greek schools of thinking, had what they called the sacred *Tetraktys*, a word referring to the number four; and how did they represent the Tetraktys? In this fashion: first a point above and alone, the Monad; then two points below that, or the Dyad; then three points below these, or the Triad; and then four points below these, or the Tetrad — ten points altogether. They had an oath which they considered the most sacred adjuration of the Pythagorean School, which they uttered when they swore by the "Holy Tetraktys." What is this oath? It is worth remembering: "Yea, by the Tetraktys, which has supplied to our soul the fountain containing the roots of everflowing nature." This is just full of profound thought. Finally, the Tetraktys emblematized (among other things) the procession of beings into manifestation. First the Primordial Point, then the line, then the superficies, then the cube: $1+2+3+4=10$.

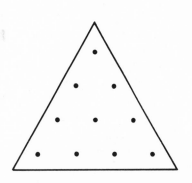

What, finally, is the difference between the system of seven and that of ten? The seven is the fundamental number of the *manifested* universe; but over the seven hovers eternally the infinite and immortal triad, the *Unmanifest*. This is the key. Some religions specialize in sevens; but all religions have the ten, also, in their various numerical schemes.

As H. P. Blavatsky says, the number ten is the secret or sephirical principle of the universe, because on and through this denary system the universe is formed and built. Man (as a *whole*) is tenfold, the universe (as a *whole*) is tenfold, but both are septenary *in manifestation*. Every atom, every living being, and every universe is a complete hierarchy of ten degrees: three highest considered as the root, and seven lower in active manifestation. This root, or highest triad, is a Mystery-teaching, concerning which very little open explanation is to be found even in the ancient literatures.

In *The Secret Doctrine*, volume I, page 98, H. P. Blavatsky first enumerates certain things in the Stanza there printed, to wit: "The Voice of the Word, Svabhavat, the Numbers, for he is One and Nine," to which she joins the following as a footnote:

Which makes ten, or the perfect number applied to the "Creator," the name given to the totality of the Creators blended by the Monotheists into

One, as the "Elohim," Adam Kadmon or Sephira — the Crown — are the androgyne synthesis of the 10 Sephiroth, who stand for the symbol of the manifested Universe in the popularised Kabala. The esoteric Kabalists, however, following the Eastern Occultists, divide the upper Sephirothal triangle from the rest (or Sephira, Chochmah and Binah [that is, the Crown, Wisdom and Understanding]), which leaves seven Sephiroth. . . .

Then on page 360 she says in relation to other matters: "The 10, being the sacred number of the universe, was secret and esoteric . . ."; and on page 362: ". . . the whole astronomical and geometrical portion of the secret sacerdotal language was built upon the number 10, . . ."

It may be interesting and well worth while to point out here that these quotations give the reason why the numerical computations of the esoteric philosophy have not yet been satisfactorily solved by students with a mathematical turn of mind — because they will persist in working with the number seven, alone, in spite of Madame Blavatsky's open hints to the contrary, for she says openly that the number seven must be used in calculations in a manner hitherto unknown to Western mathematics. The hint ought to be sufficient in itself alone, because the seven, considered as a basis for computation, is a very unwieldy and awkward number with which to calculate. The subject is alluded to in veiled manner in her esoteric *Instructions*, number I, page 9, in speaking of Padmapāni, or the "Lotus-handed" — one of the names in Tibetan mysticism of the bodhisattva Avalokiteśvara. H. P. Blavatsky says, after narrating a legend concerning this character:

He vowed to perform the feat before the end of the Kalpa, adding that in case of failure he wished that his head would split into numberless fragments. The Kalpa closed; but Humanity felt him not within its cold, evil heart. Then Padmapāni's head split and was shattered into a thousand fragments. Moved with compassion, the Deity re-formed the pieces into *ten* heads, three white and seven of various colors. And since that day man has become a perfect number, or TEN.

In this allegory the potency of SOUND, COLOR AND NUMBER is so ingeniously introduced as to veil the real esoteric meaning. To the outsider it reads like one of the many meaningless fairy-tales of creation; but it is pregnant with spiritual and divine, physical and magical, meaning. From Amitâbha — *no color* or the *white glory* — are born the seven differentiated colors of the prism. These each emit a corresponding sound, forming the seven of the *musical scale*. As Geometry among the Mathematical Sciences is specially related to Architecture, and also — proceeding to Universals — to Cosmogony, so the ten Jods of the Pythagorean Tetrad, or Tetraktys, being made to symbolize the Macrocosm, the Microcosm, or man, its image, had also to be divided into ten points. For this Nature herself has provided, as will be seen.

One more citation, in order to finish the subject. On page 15, H. P. Blavatsky writes shortly as follows:

As the Universe, the Macrocosm and the Microcosm, are *ten*, why should we divide Man into *seven* "principles"? This is the reason why the perfect number ten is divided into two, a reason which cannot be given out publicly: In their completeness, *i.e.*, super-spiritually and physically, the forces are TEN: to-wit, three on the subjective and inconceivable, and seven on the objective plane. Bear in mind that I am now giving you the description of the two opposite poles: (*a*) the primordial triangle, which as soon as it has reflected itself in the "Heavenly Man," the highest of the lower seven — disappears, returning into "Silence and Darkness"; and (*b*) the astral paradigmatic man, whose Monad (Ātmâ) is also represented by a triangle, as it has to become a ternary in conscious Devachanic interludes.

EIGHT

TRACES OF THE ESOTERIC PHILOSOPHY IN GENESIS.

The oldest religions of the world — exoterically, for the esoteric root or foundation is one — are the Indian, the Mazdean, and the Egyptian. Then comes the Chaldean, the outcome of these — entirely lost to the world now, except in its disfigured Sabeanism as at present rendered by the archaeologists; then, passing over a number of religions that will be mentioned later, comes the Jewish, esoterically, as in the Kabala, following in the line of Babylonian Magism; exoterically, as in Genesis and the Pentateuch, a collection of allegorical legends. Read by the light of the Zohar, the initial four chapters of Genesis are the fragment of a highly philosophical page in the World's Cosmogony. — *The Secret Doctrine*, I, 10–11

The first lesson taught in Esoteric philosophy is, that the incognizable Cause does not put forth evolution, whether consciously or unconsciously, but only exhibits periodically *different aspects of itself* to the perception of *finite* Minds. Now the collective Mind — the Universal — composed of various and numberless Hosts of Creative Powers, however infinite in manifested Time, is still finite when contrasted with the unborn and undecaying Space in its supreme essential aspect. That which is finite cannot be perfect. . . .

The Hebrew Elohim, called in the translations "God," and who create "light," are identical with the Aryan Asuras. They are also referred to as the "Sons of Darkness" as a philosophical and logical contrast to light immutable and eternal. . . . The Zoroastrian Amshaspends create the world in six days or periods also, and rest on the Seventh; whereas that *Seventh* is the *first* period or "day," in esoteric philosophy, (*Primary* creation in the Aryan cosmogony). It is that intermediate Aeon which is the *Prologue* to creation, and which stands on the borderland between the uncreated eternal Causation and the produced finite effects; a state of *nascent* activity and energy as the first aspect of the eternal immutable Quiescence. In *Genesis*, on which no metaphysical energy has been spent, but only an extraordinary acuteness and ingenuity to veil the esoteric Truth, "Creation" begins at the third stage of manifestation. "God" or the *Elohim* are the "Seven Regents" of Pymander. They are identical with all the other Creators. — Ibid., II, 487–8

THIS evening we commence our study with the following citation from the first volume of *The Secret Doctrine*, page 224:

Mankind in its first prototypal, shadowy form, is the offspring of the Elohim of Life (or Pitris); in its qualitative and physical aspect it is the direct progeny of the "Ancestors," the lowest Dhyanis, or Spirits of the Earth; for its moral, psychic, and spiritual nature, it is indebted to a group of divine Beings, the name and characteristics of which will be given in Book II. Collectively, men are the handiwork of hosts of various spirits; distributively, the tabernacles of those hosts; and occasionally and singly, the vehicles of some of them.

And on page 225, second paragraph:

Man is not, nor could he ever be, the complete product of the "Lord God"; but he *is* the child of the *Elohim,* so arbitrarily changed into the singular masculine gender. The first Dhyanis, commissioned to "create" man in their image, could only throw off their shadows, like a delicate model for the Nature Spirits of matter to work upon. (See Book II.) Man is, beyond any doubt, formed physically out of the dust of the Earth, but his creators and fashioners were many.

It seems advisable first to speak of two things, a less thing and a greater thing; we take the less thing first. As has been seen from the beginning of our studies, we have been bringing forward for our consideration at every one of our meetings teachings found in the great religions of the world, mostly of the past, which are similar to or identical with our own. This has been done in order to join all these teachings, as found in the old religions, with the teachings as given by H. P. Blavatsky, that is, with theosophy. This shows the universality of thought in religions and thereby induces a spirit of kindliness and brotherhood, and leads to the accentuation of the moral sense which so greatly lacks in the comparative religious study of the doctrines of the predominant ancient religions by the mass of scholars in the Occident today. It does away at one sweep with the egoistic opinion that "we are more perfect and morally better than you are," with the idea that we Occidentals are a superior people, and with the idea that a certain race and a certain religion are, by the fiat of the Deity, the chosen receptacles or vehicles for the only truth: that all the other religions are false, and that those who professed them in ancient times were merely brands prepared for the burning!

The second thing and the greater is this. We have constantly been bringing forward certain religious or philosophical analogies and certain points of view thereupon which are veritable doctrinal touchstones; our aim being that those who may read these studies shall be enabled to have at hand, and — through the thoughts therein expressed — to have clear-set in their own minds, *keys* by which to test the truth and reality of the essential or fundamental doctrines of these ancient religions, because all *these* doctrines in their *essence* and in their *inner meaning*, in those old religions, are true. In this sense Brahmanism is true, in this sense Buddhism is true, likewise Confucianism, and the doctrines of Lao-tse called Taoism. They are all true in that sense.

But all of them have been, in greater or less degree, subject to the influences of certain creations of human fancy; and for one who has not been trained in these studies, it is often difficult to separate the merely human fancies from the nature-true teachings of the ancient wisdom-religion. All the ancient religions sprang from that same source — theosophy, as it is called today. But it is, as said before, sometimes difficult to know what is the original teaching and what the merely human accretion or creation. These creations of human phantasy and irreligious fear are very evident in the two modern monotheistic religions which have sprung from Judaism, that is to say, in Christianity and in Islam. In these two the human accretions of phantasy are very marked; but in both of them there exists a solid substratum of mystical thought based on the ancient teachings of the wisdom-religion.

In Christianity it is particularly in the Neopythagorean and the Neoplatonic forms, as Christianized somewhat and as manifested in the teachings of Dionysius, called the Areopagite; and in the later Mohammedan religion it is manifested somewhat more distantly in the borrowings from Greek thought mainly, though also from other sources, as we find them outlined by the Mohammedan doctors and thinkers, such as Ibn Sina, commonly called Avicenna in Europe, a Persian, who lived and wrote at the end of the tenth century; by Averroes in Córdova, Spain, properly called Roshd, who flourished during the twelfth century; and by another eminent Mohammedan scholar (mentioning these three out of many) Al Farabi, of the tenth century, by descent a Turk. The ancient wisdom also affected the teachings of Mohammed in a highly mystical form, though greatly changed, as shown in the Sufi doctrines, which are particularly and manifestly of Persian origin, owing their rise to that spiritual-minded and subtil people, the Persians. These doctrines are a very welcome contrast with the hard and mechanical religious beliefs which arose out of the egoism of the crude Arabian tribes of that period.

The main theme of our study this evening is the consideration of the opening verses of the Book of Beginnings called Genesis — the first book in the Law of the Jews. We shall first read the English translation of these verses as found in the "authorized version," and of the same chapters we shall make a translation ourselves, in which you will be enabled to see the difference from the former; and we will explain what the difference is, and how it comes to be, and for this purpose we shall have to go into a brief exposition of certain peculiarities of the ancient Hebrew tongue.

In the authorized version of the English Bible, called the version of King James, the Book of Genesis opens as follows:

1. In the beginning God created the heaven and the earth.

2. And the earth was without form, and void; and darkness was upon the face of the deep. And the Spirit of God moved upon the face of the waters.

3. And God said, Let there be light: and there was light.

4. And God saw the light, that it was good: and God divided the light from the darkness.

5. And God called the light Day, and the darkness he called Night. And the evening and the morning were the first day.

6. And God said, Let there be a firmament in the midst of the waters, and let it divide the waters from the waters.

7. And God made the firmament and divided the waters which were under the firmament from the waters which were above the firmament: and it was so.

8. And God called the firmament Heaven. And the evening and the morning were the second day.

9. And God said, Let the waters under the heaven be gathered together unto one place, and let the dry land appear: and it was so.

10. And God called the dry land Earth; and the gathering together of the waters called he Seas: and God saw that it was good.

26. And God said, Let us make man in our image, after our likeness: and let them have dominion over the fish of the sea, and over the fowl of the air, and over the cattle, and over all the earth, and over every creeping thing that creepeth upon the earth.

27. So God created man in his own image, in the image of God created he him; male and female created he them.

In the first place, Hebrew is a Semitic tongue, one of the company of languages of which Arabic and Ethiopic and Aramaean (or Aramaic) and Phoenician and Assyrian are other members. The Hebrew in which the Bible is written is called the Biblical Hebrew. It is ancient Hebrew. The language spoken in Palestine at the time when Jesus is supposed to have lived upon the earth in Jerusalem and around that district was Aramaean, and not Hebrew, which was then extinct as a spoken language, and of course when he spoke to his disciples he spoke to them in Aramaean.

The Hebrew language as found in the ancient manuscripts of the Bible — none earlier, probably, than the ninth century of the Christian era — is written with "points," taking the place of vowels, because Hebrew writing is a consonantal system; its alphabet is wholly consonantal. It has the aleph or *a*, which is nevertheless reckoned as a consonant. It has the waw or *w*, and it also is reckoned as a consonant; and it has the yod or *y*, also reckoned as a consonant, but it has no vowel signs proper.

Thus, the language is written without true vowels. Furthermore, in the most ancient manuscripts — and certainly it was so in the original or pre-Christian era texts — the letters are all run together, following one after another, without separation of words. There were some marks possibly, by which certain things in the text were pointed out as of particular importance; but the letters followed one another interminably, with no separation into words, and without vowels. So, you see, there is an open field for many kinds of speculation, even for very able Hebrew scholars, as to what any certain combination of letters found in this endless stream may have originally meant. This way of writing was universal, practically, in ancient times; the earliest Greek and Latin manuscripts of the New Testament are written in this fashion, which merely followed the ancient custom, as may still be seen on the ruins of public buildings in Greece and Rome. Obviously, interpretation, or correct reading, was often dubious: the reader might be very doubtful of the original sense of a passage in a manuscript so written.

So much was this the case that there arose in Palestine at an undetermined date — but we know that it may go back to about the time of the fall of Jerusalem before Titus or, say, about the beginning of the Christian era — a school of interpreters, who interpreted by what they were pleased to call "tradition," *māsōrāh*, that is to say, "traditional" knowledge, how the Hebrew Bible should be read, how these streams of consonants should be divided up in reading into words, and what vowel points should be put there in order to fix the pronunciation in accordance therewith. This system of "points" was probably not introduced *into the text* till the seventh century. This school was called the School of the Māsōrāh, and its expounders and followers were called Masoretes.

This School of the Māsōrāh reached its fullest development and completion probably in the ninth century of the Christian era. But while this school depended upon what it called tradition, there is no certainty of proof that their interpretations of their own combinations of letters into words were always correct. They seemed to have got, however, and to have passed down to posterity, *some* knowledge of the general original sense.

In order to illustrate this matter, let us take the first five English words of Genesis: we drop all the vowels, retaining only the consonants, and we have this: nthbgnnnggdcrtd. You could here insert vowels almost ad libitum in seeking a meaning. "In the beginning God created," and now imagine endless lines of such consonants!

Add to it the fact that Hebrew writing begins at the right hand and runs to the left. Furthermore, it begins at what we would call the end of the book, and runs to the front, as writings in other Semitic tongues do. This fashion of writing was not uncommon with other peoples in ancient days. Greek and Latin writing in ancient times sometimes followed this system, but later, as you can see today if you have been in Greece or in Rome, in the old inscriptions on the temples and elsewhere, it usually began at the left and went to the right, usually with no breaks for words. In the very old Greek writings (and elsewhere too) they also had what they called *boustrophedon*, from two Greek words meaning "ox-turning," taken from the path followed by the plowing ox: when it starts, let us say, from one end of a field it goes to the other end and then turns and goes back in the opposite direction, parallel with the other line, in plowing its furrows. This method is not followed in the Hebrew manuscripts of the Bible that we possess.

Now, in beginning our translation of the first verses of Genesis, we are met in the very first two words by a difficulty. These words can be translated in two or three different ways. The translation as given in the European Bibles, and as found in the authorized English version, is a fairly correct rendering so far as mere words go; but anyone who has undertaken translations from a foreign language and particularly from a dead one, and more especially again from a religious tongue and one evidently written more or less in cipher, can realize the difficulties there lie in picking out the various meanings which any one word may have, in choosing which is the word that is best for the translation, which word carries the meaning nearest to the intention of the writer. The first two words as usually read are *be* and *rēshīth;* and so divided, their meanings are as here follow: *be* means "in," *rēshīth* means "beginning," this second word being a feminine form and coming originally from the masculine word *rēsh,* or *rōsh,* meaning (among several other things) "head," "chief part," "first part." Hence we may translate *be rēshīth* as "in first part," or "in highest part," etc.

But this same combination of letters — *brashīth* — could also be translated (by dividing differently) as *bōrē,* one word, a verb, and *shīth,* another word, a noun: *bōrē* meaning "forming," and *shīth,* an "institution," "establishment," "arrangement." "Forming the establishment (or arrangement)" — of what? The text goes on to say what is arranged or established — by arranging "formed the Elohīm heaven and earth."

Furthermore, the word *rēsh,* or *rōsh,* above selected, may also mean "head" as before said, signifying "wisdom," or "knowledge": hence, "in wisdom the Elohīm formed heavens and earth." Remember, it is permissible to put in vowels almost at choice, because vowels do not exist in the original text of the book, in the Bible, itself; hence the opening for more than merely one interpretation.

Rēsh, or *rōsh*, then, also means "head"; it also means "wisdom"; it also means "host" or "multitude." So here we may select still another — a fourth — translation: *berēsh*, "in multitude," or "by multitude." *Yithbārē* would then be the next word, "formed Elohīm." Here comes again another remarkable change in meaning — and I am making these remarks in order to point out how the Hebrew text of the Bible may bear many translations. Supposing then that we divide the first fourteen Hebrew letters of the text into the following word-combinations: *be-rēsh yithbārē elohīm*, we get (by using *yithbārē*, which is one of the forms of the Hebrew verb, called the reflexive form, meaning action upon oneself) the following translation: "by multitude," "through multitude, the gods formed themselves." What follows in the text? "into the heavens and the earth"; that is, "in a host (or multitude) the gods formed (made) themselves into the heavens and the earth." See the vast difference in meaning from the authorized version. This last translation we believe is the best; it shows at once the identity of thought with all other ancient cosmogonic systems.

"By multitude formed" (or "evolved": this word *bārā* means "to fatten," "to shape," "to become heavy or gross," "to cut," "to form," "to be born," "to evolve") — "by (or in) multitude" or "through (or in) multitude evolved Elohīm themselves into the heavens and the earth."

Now the fourth word, *elohīm:* this is a very curious word. The first part of it alone is *el*, meaning "god," divinity, from which comes the second, a feminine form, *elōh*, "goddess"; *īm* is merely the masculine plural. So, if we translate every element in this single word it would mean, "god, goddess, plural" — showing the androgynous essence of the divinities, as it were: the polar opposites of the hierarchy, the essential duality in life.

Verse 2: "And the earth became ethereal." Now the second word, a verb, in the Hebrew text of the second verse answers to two Latin verbs: *esse*, "to be," and *fieri*, "to become"; but almost always its original sense is *fieri*, "to become," like the Greek *gignomai*, meaning "to become," to grow into a new state of something. "And the earth became" or "grew into ethereality." The two next words (*tohū* and *bohū*) of the text, which we here translate "ethereality," are very difficult words rightly to interpret. They both mean "emptiness," "waste," "immateriality," hence "dissolution"; the fundamental idea means something *unsubstantial*, not materially gross. We continue our translation: "And darkness upon the face of the ethers. And the rūahh (the spirit-soul) of the gods (of Elohīm) (fluttered, hovered) brooding." The word we translate "brooding" is derived from and means the action of a hen which flutters and hovers and broods over the eggs in its nest. How graphic, how significant is this figure of speech!

You see the same thought here that you see in practically all the ancient teachings: the figure or symbol of the cosmic soul brooding over the waters of space, preparing the world egg, that of the cosmic egg and the divine bird laying the cosmic egg. "And the spirit-soul of Elohīm brooding upon the face of the waters," says the Hebrew text. Now "waters," as we have shown before, was a common expression or symbol for space, the ethereal expansion, as it were. We continue our translation:

And said (the) Elohīm (the gods) — light, come-into-being! and light came-into-being. And saw (the) gods the light, that (it was) good. And divided Elohīm between the light and between the darkness. And called Elohīm the light day, and the darkness called they night. And (there) came-into-being eve, and (there) came-into-being morn. Day one. And said Elohīm, (let there) come-into-being an expanse in (the) midst of the waters, and let it be a separator (divider) between waters and waters. And made Elohīm (or the gods) the expanse, and they separated between the waters which (were) below the expanse, and between the waters which (were) above the expanse, and (it) came-to-be so. And called Elohīm (the gods) the expanse heavens, and (there) came-into-being eve, and (there) came-into-being morn. Day second. And said Elohīm (the gods), (let there) be-gathered-together [i.e., solidified, condensed] the waters above the heavens into one place, and (let there) be-seen the dry-part [the solidified or manifested part — the word means "dry," in opposition to humidity; humidity means water, standing for space, therefore, the collected matter of a planet to be, of a solar system to be, or a universe to be], and (it) came-to-be so. And called the gods the dry-part earth, and the solidification (gathering-together) of the waters called they seas. And saw Elohīm (the gods) that (it was) good.

Now turn to verses 26, 27, 28 of the same, the first, chapter:

And said (the gods) Elohīm, Let us make humanity [the word is *Ādām*] in our shadowy image [in our shadow, in our phantom; the word is *tselem*], according to our pattern (or model). And let them descend into the fish of the sea and into the flying creatures of the heavens, and into the beast, and into all the earth, and into all moving creatures which move upon the earth. And formed [or shaped or evolved, the same verb as above, *bārā*] Elohīm (the gods) humanity in their phantom, in the shadowy image of Elohīm, formed (or evolved) they him.

Now come two very interesting words, usually translated "male and female," which are two of the meanings respectively found in the dictionaries; but the root-meanings of these words are "thinker and receiver" (or receptacle): "thinker and receptacle evolved they them. And blessed them the Elohīm," that is, the Elohīm blessed them, "and said to them the Elohīm, be fruitful, increase, and fill the earth," and so forth.

You see, therefore, that here, merely by using other words than those usually chosen by Christian translators, or later Jewish translators, and yet recognized dictionary words, and by forcing no meanings, we have found the identical meanings of the eso- teric teachings as outlined in *The Secret Doctrine* when treating of these subjects. First the hierarchy and its manifested divinities evolving the universe or kosmos *out of themselves,* using the reflexive form of the Hebrew verb *bārā,* as shown above. Further- more, a study of the first verse of Genesis will show us that the evolution treated in it has no relation solely and especially to the creation of this earth or of any other particular earth, but is a general doctrine having reference rather to the first manifes- tation of material being in ethereal space, and that the fowls of the air and the fish of the sea and the beasts, which are spoken of, do not necessarily refer (although they could) to the particular animals which we know under those names on earth, but do also refer (in accord with a well-known fact of ancient mythology) to the "animals of the heavens," of which we spoke in our last study, i.e., to every globe of the starry spheres, to every nebula and to every comet, each such being considered in the ancient teachings to be a living being, an "animal," having its physical corpus or body, and having behind it its director, or governor, or divine essence, or spirit.

Furthermore, we see that the Elohīm evolved man, humanity, *out of themselves,* and told them to become, then to enter into and inform these other creatures. Indeed, these sons of the Elohīm are, in our teachings, the children of light, the sons of light, *which are we ourselves,* and yet different from ourselves, because higher, yet they are our own very selves inwardly. In fact, the Elohīm became, evolved into, their own offspring, remaining in a sense still always the inspiring light within, or rather *above,* according to the interpretation authorized by the very words chosen from the dictionary and flouting no rule of Hebrew grammar. For, following the ancient teachings of the esoteric philosophy, and strengthened by exactly similar thought in the Babylonian religious teachings from which these Hebrew teachings originally came, we see that the Elohīm *projected themselves* into the nascent forms of the then "humanity," which thenceforward were "men," however imperfect their development still was.

What were these Elohīm, these divinities, these gods? In the hierarchical system of the Qabbālāh they are the sixth in derivation from above, from the first or the Crown, and thus are by no means the highest. They were, cosmogonically, the *manifested* formers or weavers of the web of the universe. Jehovah, spoken of in the second chapter of Genesis, is the third angelic potency, counting downwards from the Crown — the summit of the hierarchy of the Qabbālāh.

In chapter five of Genesis, verses 1 and 2, there is an interesting expression. We translate:

This (the) book of the generations of humanity (Ādām). In the day of Elohīm (of the gods) evolving humanity, in the pattern (or model) of the Elohīm, made they him. Thinker-and-receptacle made they them, and blessed them and called their name humanity (or Ādām) in the day of their making.

Evidently, it is not here a question of a single human pair, of a man and a woman in our sense, but of nascent androgynous humanity, and *they had one name,* Ādām, and their attributes were thinker and casket (or receptacle): ethereal beings — children of the Elohīm, who are themselves — capable of thinking and of receiving and understanding and developing under the lessons which were to follow from their incarnations in the lower fleshly beings they themselves evolved, and signified under the terms as set forth here: the "fowls" of the "air," and the "fish" of the "sea," and every living thing which moveth upon the face of the earth.

These ancient writings have more than one mystical or esoteric application or, as H. P. Blavatsky says, they have more than one key. But, again, what or who were these Elohīm? *They were our monads* — as the term is used in theosophy. It is curious, by the way, that Leibniz, the great Slavic-German philosopher, evolved a theory of monadic evolution which is singularly like our own in some respects. For him, the universe was replete with progressing entities, which he called monads, spiritual beings which evolved through the forces innate in themselves, yet acting and reacting upon each other — a faithful echo, in so far as it goes, of the ancient wisdom-religion.

Again, what do we mean when we speak respectively of emanation, evolution, and creation? Emanation and evolution are closely similar in meaning. *Emanation* is from a Latin word meaning "flowing out," and in all the ancient teachings of importance the idea was that the gods actively, transitively, "flowed out" from themselves their offspring or children. *Evolution* is also a Latin word and means "rolling out," "unfolding," something which is unfolded; and obviously a thing which is "flowed out," using the words transitively, is also unrolled out, unfolded out.

Now *creation* originally in its Latin sense meant practically the same as does this Hebrew word *bārā*. It meant "making," "shaping," "carving," "cutting" — of course out of preexisting material or matter, and the Christian theory (which was more or less that of the Jews in their later days) that God made the world "out of nothing" is preposterous, absurd, both historically and linguistically. It is founded on no ancient teaching whatever, and it arose naturally enough, in a sense, from the monotheistic mania which endeavored to make God extra-cosmic, apart from the universe, and above it, a pure spirit, having no relation of ineluctable union with his creatures, God the "Father and Maker" of them, and yet an absolute personal nonentity — having no "body, parts, or passions," yet a *Person* withal! Of course the two concepts are contradictory and mutually destructive, and had we the time it would be easy to dilate further on the preposterous absurdity of which we speak.

We can see, therefore, in closing our study this evening, that it is very difficult to say which of these three, emanation, evolution, creation, is first in the order of procession. Was it emanation, followed by evolution, followed by creation; or was it evolution, followed by emanation, followed by creation? Certainly, creation — in its original sense of shaping, forming — comes the last of the three, as is easily shown. The difficulty lies in the fact that in every cosmic act of emanation we immediately perceive an act of evolution or unfolding; and in every act of evolution we immediately perceive an act of emanation. Every monad *pari passu* passes from one into the other, just as all mankind evolved *pari passu* from one into the other. We should, probably, say that emanation, evolution, creation, work simultaneously and coordinately, *during manifestation.*

But taking the question from a purely philosophical standpoint, it is probably accurate and best to say that the first step from what we call the Unmanifest into the manifest is emanation, a flowing out from its source of a monad or rather a host of monads which, as they in turn follow the pattern set for them by their source and their karmic past, grow darker, and more material, proportionately as they recede from their central fount of life; and, again, as they emanate, they also evolve, bringing out from within that which they innately are or have, and they do this in accordance with the karmic lines or patterns upon which we have faintly touched in previous studies, when speaking of the skandhas, because every act of emanation and of evolution begins a new life cycle following the pralaya or rest period of a former life period or manvantara. Then finally, when the period of self-consciousness is reached in the cyclical progression of evolution, comes a period of will, conscious choice, when man begins to "create" or fashion *voluntarily;* that is, through the exercise of his will and his intuition and his intellect he carves his own destiny and likewise affects the world *creationally* which exists around him.

NINE

OUTLINE OF ESOTERIC COSMOGONY. GLOBES, ROUNDS AND RACES:
COSMIC TIME PERIODS.

Can one fail to recognise in Creuzer great powers of intuition, when, being almost unacquainted with the Aryan Hindu philosophies, little known in his day, he wrote: —

"We modern Europeans feel surprised when hearing talk of the Spirits of the Sun, Moon, etc. But we repeat again, the *natural good sense and the upright judgment* of the ancient peoples, quite foreign to our *entirely material* ideas upon celestial mechanics and physical sciences . . . could not see in the stars and planets only that which we see: namely, simple masses of light, or opaque bodies moving in circuits in sidereal space, merely according to the laws of attraction or repulsion; but they saw in them *living* bodies, *animated* by spirits as they saw the same in every kingdom of nature. . . . *This doctrine of spirits, so consistent and conformable to nature,* from which it was derived, formed a grand and unique conception, wherein the physical, the moral, and the political aspects were all blended together . . ." (*"Egypte,"* pp. 450 *to* 455.)

It is such a conception only that can lead man to form a correct conclusion about his origin and the genesis of everything in the universe — of Heaven and Earth, between which he is a living link. Without such a psychological link, and the feeling of its presence, no science can ever progress, and the realm of knowledge must be limited to the analysis of physical matter only. — *The Secret Doctrine*, II, 369–70

W E OPEN our study tonight by reading once again from pages 224 and 225 of *The Secret Doctrine*, volume I, as follows:

Mankind in its first prototypal, shadowy form, is the offspring of the Elohim of Life (or Pitris); in its qualitative and physical aspect it is the direct progeny of the "Ancestors," the lowest Dhyanis, or Spirits of the Earth; for its moral, psychic, and spiritual nature, it is indebted to a group of divine Beings, the name and characteristics of which will be given in Book II. Collectively, men are the handiwork of hosts of various spirits; distributively, the tabernacles of those hosts; and occasionally and singly, the vehicles of some of them.

And the second paragraph on page 225:

Man is not, nor could he ever be, the complete product of the "Lord God"; but he *is* the child of the *Elohim,* so arbitrarily changed into the singular masculine gender. The first Dhyanis, commissioned to "create" man in their image, could only throw off their shadows, like a delicate model for the Nature Spirits of matter to work upon. (See Book II.) Man is, beyond any doubt, formed physically out of the dust of the Earth, but his creators and fashioners were many.

In continuation of our study of the esoteric sense underlying the first chapter of Genesis, we must point out that this chapter does not deal with man as we now know him. The "man" spoken of therein is the spiritual being which descended into matter in the first round of this manvantara, as a spiritual, or rather ethereal, being; and consequently, when in verse 27 we translated the peculiar phrase, "thinker and receiver formed (or evolved) they them," we must understand that this allusion does not refer to sexual man and woman of the present time. These words, *thinker* and *receiver,* refer to the spiritual nature of the then ethereal vehicles of humanity, not to our present-day man or woman; and the word receiver can also be translated *receptacle,* the vehicle or house of the higher nature. Also, at the period dealt with in this verse 27, man in the general sense — humanity — was of double sex, or androgyne; hence, obviously, there was no "woman" then. This first chapter practically ignores the first, purely sexless, state of ethereal Adam, and enters upon its description of "man" when the latter was already sinking into material existence as a semi-self-conscious ethereal androgyne. In other words, the first chapter does not detail the separation of the sexes, which occurred far later. This general statement is plainly shown by even the exoteric rendering of the teaching; but let us read from another chapter of Genesis, verse 5 of chapter 2:

And every plant of the field *before it was in the earth,* and every herb of the field *before it grew:* for the Lord God had not caused it to rain upon the earth, and there *was not a man* to till the ground [italics ours].

"Man" had not yet come. Let me preface future explanations

by saying that this second chapter of Genesis deals with the third and the fourth rounds of our manvantara, the latter or fourth being our present round, and more particularly with the third root-race of our fourth round; whereas chapter first is a highly generalized and succinct Jewish epitome of early cosmogony, and ends with a similarly brief allusion to rounds first and second.

And in verses 19, 20, 21, and 22, we find the following:

19. And out of the ground the Lord God formed every beast of the field, and every fowl of the air; and brought them unto Adam to see what he would call them: and whatsoever Adam called every living creature, that was the name thereof.

20. And Adam gave names to all cattle, and to the fowl of the air, and to every beast of the field; but for Adam there was not found an help meet for him.

21. And the Lord God caused a deep sleep to fall upon Adam, and he slept: and he took one of his ribs, and closed up the flesh instead thereof;

22. And the rib, which the Lord God had taken from man, made he a woman, and brought her unto the man.

As in verse 5 above, I use here the ordinary English translation of the so-called authorized version, although, as a matter of fact, a very luminously different translation could be made of these verses. It would lead us too far from our main point to do so now.

In the first place, this second chapter records a different method from that recorded in chapter 1, and a change as regards the evolving of the ethereal being from the Elohīm, having reference to the making of physical humanity, or "man," from the "dust of the ground" (verse 7). In the second place, this English word *rib* of verses 21 and 22 should be translated "side," the allusion being to the *separation* of the androgyne or dual-sexed humanity of race the third of our fourth round into sexed humanity as now existent.

Now Plato in his *Banquet* (§190), alludes to this same historical physiological fact of prehistory, and says that (one of) the early races of mankind was bisexually formed; that they had great and terrible powers, and that their wickedness and ambition waxed very great, so that Zeus grew angry at their wickedness and decided to cut them in two, as one would divide an egg with a hair. This Zeus did; and bade Apollo to render the two halves

more shapely, etc. Apollo so did, and he closed up the flesh of the
two halves. Since then all mankind was man and woman. A typically Platonic tale, imbodying actual facts of forgotten history.
This deals with the earliest portion of the fourth root-race, and
much more especially with the middle period of the third root-
race of the fourth — or present — round on this planet.

We will now leave for the present, with a few more words of
explanation, the outline of emanation and evolution as found in
the Jewish Bible; but before leaving it, it will be well to say a few
words on the question of the Elohīm.

Elohīm is a word frequently found in the Jewish Bible and is,
as stated in our last lecture, in itself an evidence of the polytheistic
bias, teachings, and beliefs, of the ancient Jewish people. The
Bible itself shows it. Usually this word — a plural common noun —
is to be translated as "gods." But in most places where it occurs
in the Hebrew text it is translated in the English authorized
version as "God." There is no true or solid reason for such a translation; the proper rendering is gods. But the monotheistic and
Christian tendencies of the translators made them set the translation for what they considered to be the best interests of the
Christian Church, and their God Almighty; so they translated it
in various places by various names, as, for instance, "judges" in
Exodus 21:6, 22:8–9, and in many other places; but the essential,
intrinsic meaning is always gods, or beings having divine standing.

We now approach in our studies very difficult and, indeed,
highly esoteric matters. In the first place, let us never forget that
the Elohīm, the gods, who are spoken of under various names in
the various religions of the ancient world as the creators or rather
evolvers or parents of mankind, are spiritual beings — *who are
ourselves*. And the key to this apparent riddle is found in the
doctrine and exposition of the hierarchies of individualized life.

A hierarchy can be considered as an aggregate unit, as a
collective entity in the same sense that an army is; nevertheless,
an army is composed of units; and yet, again, this army of beings
in any one hierarchy is indeed from another aspect more than
a mere collective entity, because it is united in its apex, in what is
actually the fount of that hierarchy. This fount is the hyparxis
or spiritual sun from which all the other nine planes or classes

of the hierarchy emanate and evolve down to the lowest, thence beginning a new hierarchy; even as the hyparxis of any one hierarchy is the lowest class or plane of a superior hierarchy, and so practically ad infinitum.

Man is a spiritual being throughout, through and through and through. Matter itself is but one manifestation of spirit. We live in a universe of spirit and, although matter exists, it exists as māyā, illusion; not as a mere illusionary nothing, but as something, as a modality, so to say, of spirit. But as we grow higher into the upper planes of the hierarchical scale, the māyā, for the sphere of life embraced by that hierarchy, fades away from before our eyes, and we see truth in greater degree and progressively more widely the higher we go.

With regard to the descent into matter, or falling into matter, of mankind, that is to say, the descent into manifested being of the spiritual entities, the spiritual hierarchy which man actually and properly is, we must remember that we cannot understand this profound subject very well without undertaking an outline or sketch, more or less complete, of what are the rounds and races; yet before doing this, we must clear away from our minds certain scientific conceptions, or rather misconceptions, which have been implanted in us by intensive teaching from childhood, and which have for that reason become a part of our mental life.

Two main pillars of our modern science are the following: first, the doctrine of the conservation of energy, that the amount of force or of energy in the universe is constant, and no increase can be created to add unto it, and no amount can be taken away from it. The second great pillar is the doctrine of the correlation, or the convertibility, of forces, that any force can, at least theoretically, be converted into some other force, as mechanical motion into electrical and electrical into mechanical, and so forth as regards the other forces working in matter.

Now these two theories or doctrines of science do make an approach in certain respects to the esoteric conception of the wonderful element back of and causative of all the changes in nature, but nevertheless the conception of the esoteric philosophy cannot accept either of these two doctrinal pillars of science as thus conceived. First, the doctrine of the conservation of energy:

it is perfectly true that no "new" force can be "created," and it
is likewise perfectly true that no energy or force can ever be
utterly lost. *Forces are not converted or transformed,* as the twin
doctrine of science has it; it is possible, however, for a force to
pass from one plane of being into another — to come into one
plane from a higher or, indeed, from a lower. In other words, it
is possible for a force- or energy-element outside of some plane
to enter into being and manifestation upon it. Hence, the
materialistic doctrine of a universe of dead, lifeless, nonvital
matter — nothing above it or beyond it or below it or through it —
cannot be accepted by students of the esoteric philosophy.

As regards the correlation or convertibility of energy: it is
true, in one sense, that all the forces in the universe are correlated.
It is a fundamental axiom of theosophy that the universe, our
universe, any universe, is a living organism, and hence that its
energies or forces, and all of them, are correlated; but this does
not mean that one force can *become another.* The idea offends
the very essence, the very foundation of the esoteric teaching
with regard to manifestation, its hierarchies, and individual lives
— all offspring of the ONE LIFE. What happens is rather this:
that one force is not *turned into* or *converted into* another, but
evokes or calls forth or arouses into active life or manifestation
a "force" which was not "latent" — a curious contradiction of
sense — but *which was in equilibrium.* When the modern scientist
speaks of latent or potential energy, it is to the occultist a con-
summate logical absurdity, the very name energy or force meaning activity, and to talk about a "latent force" is like talking about
"latent activity" or "dead life," or a square triangle, or a flat
sphere. It is impossible as long as we base our conception on the
scientific postulates. But — and note this well, please — an occultist could use this phrase "latent force," because in his mouth the
phrase has a meaning and sense.

For instance, a spiritual — hence latent or nonmaterial — force
is not "converted" into matter; a material force is not "converted"
into spirit. Why? Because spirit and matter, or force and matter,
are not two, but fundamentally and essentially ONE. Throughout
the long period of manvantaric time there is a gradual evolution
of one thing into another, but this procession of life is not accom-

plished along the lines or by the methods of the scientific theories which apply in the doctrine called the convertibility of material energy. The latter is a dream; it does not exist.

This is, in fact, a subject which we shall have to develop more fully at a later period of our study, but we come now to the question of the descent of spiritual and then ethereal man into matter, down the ten steps of the hierarchical scale. We saw in a former study that this descent was begun by the entrance through a laya-center of the spiritual entities seeking manifestation on lower planes, the time having struck for them to open their great mahā-manvantara or the world period which was to follow. As soon as the spiritual essences touched the highest degree of the lower plane, our fourth-matter plane, it stirred the particular laya-center therein, to which they were directed by karmic energy, into corresponding activity or sympathetic life. This first manifestation thereof as seen from the same plane was the nebula, a cloudy nebula; the second stage, aeons later, was a spiral nebula; and the third, aeons still later, was an annular nucleated nebula, like a ring with a globe in the center; the latest stage, before the evolving body settled into life as a planet, was a comet, directed or drawn to that particular solar system or sun to which it was karmically related in the former planetary manvantara.

Now the life cycle or manvantara of a planet consists objectively of seven rounds, or smaller manvantaras, around seven globes; but this is preceded by three elemental cycles — ten in all. The first three stages or cycles, call them the three elemental rounds, if you will, are on the three archetypal planes above the seven. This period is not yet really *ethereal* manifestation: it is the first descent of the arūpa (or bodiless) beings of spiritual nature into subspiritual manifestation; but when the third or lowest of the three archetypal planes has been traversed, by that time the life-wave or life-essence has consolidated sufficiently in ethereal matter to form an airy shape or ethereal globe. This globe thence starts on the manvantaric cycle down into matter, a cycle which proceeds in several stages, actually seven, and upon and in seven globes, as already stated.

During the *first* round, upon the first globe, the life-wave has to complete a ring consisting of seven root-races on that globe; after, or rather at, the end of the evolution of each root-race, respectively, the root-race's surplus energy is thereupon exploded or protruded into the sphere lower and there forms the first, second, third, etc., element of the second globe of the first round. The life-energy or life-wave has to run a ring of seven root-races in and upon that second globe, and when each such root-race has reached its end there, its surplus energy is thereupon exploded or protruded exactly as before into a magnetic center below it, and the seven there, after all have arrived, form the third globe, and so on till the seven globes are formed. This is the first round. Beginning with the second round on the seven globes, the process is altered in important particulars, because all the seven globes are already formed, as globes.

At the end of the first round there is a planetary obscuration or rest period, when the entities leave the last globe, the seventh, and enter into a (lower) nirvanic period of manvantaric repose, answering to the devachanic or between-life states of the human entity between its respective lives. And so also at the end of the second round, and of the third, when we reach the fourth, which is our present round.

As the life-wave cycles down into matter, it grows with every yuga (or age) grosser and more material, until the middle of the fourth round (ours), when it begins to ascend. Every round is grosser than its preceding one until the present, our fourth, the most material, is reached. This descent is called the shadowy arc, or cycle of darkness. We have, already, passed the lowest or middle period of the fourth round, and in consequence now have begun the ascending arc, or the luminous arc. We have three and a half more rounds to run before we reach the end of the kalpa, or planetary manvantara, when the great nirvana or para-nirvana of the entire septenary planetary chain of the seven globes takes place.

Now as regards the geometrical outline of the course followed by this descent into matter, we may consider it to be in the form of an epicycloid. Let me try to explain diagrammatically what is here meant by an epicycloid. An epicycloid is formed when a point on a small circle, which runs around and upon the convex

side of the circumference of a larger circle, traces a curve which
touches the circumference of the larger circle at the beginning
and end of each revolution of the smaller circle thereupon, as at
A and B in the figure. The curve
AB is the epicycloid. For instance,
this figure shows the two circles: we
will say that the point on the smaller
circle begins its curve at A, rolling
upwards to the left; at B the point
on the smaller circle has completed
a full revolution; the curve AB is the
epicycloid.

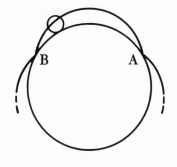

   Any point on this smaller circle
as the latter rolls along the outside
of the circumference of the larger circle will describe or generate
a curve, which is an epicycloid. There is a geometrical relation
between the commensurable radii of any two circles: for instance,
if the radius of this smaller circle is *one* and the radius of the
larger circle is *seven,* the proportion being 1 : 7, the rolling point
will describe or generate seven arcs or cusps around and upon
the circumference of the larger circle.

   Each one of these seven arcs represents here, geometrically, a
globe of a round. (Equally well does it represent geometrically
one of the seven root-races on each globe during any round.)
In the first round, the life-wave, starting from the seventh or
highest plane, *after* its third full elemental cycle of and in the
arūpa world, begins to form the rūpa or form world; and as the
smaller circle rolls along the circumference of the greater cycle,
so to say, the life-wave (or globe) progressively grows more
material, each one of these arcs which the cycling smaller circle
makes on the circumference of the greater, representing a sphere
of being, and also *geometrically* represents the life-wave of the
planet beginning the evolution of material existence, "rising
upward" or increasing in material density until it reaches its
maximum of materiality, and then "descending" or decreasing
in materiality until it again touches the plane of departure, the
circumference of the greater circle (or cycle).

   The process by which the spirit descends into matter is called in Sanskrit *pravritti* (which we may paraphrase into English as "earth-birth," or "earth-day"), practically the same word as evolution or emanation in our modern tongues; and the process of entering upon or ascending along the luminous arc, ultimately to find itself home again in the spiritual world, is called *nivritti*. Both words are from the Sanskrit root *vrit*, meaning "to revolve" or "to roll." The prefix *pra* answers to the preposition "forth" or "forward," and the prefix *ni* to the prepositional phrases "out of," "away from," hence backwards, or reverse action. Pravritti is therefore used to mean the evolution or emanation of matter, which is equivalent to the involution of spirit; nivritti, the evolution of spirit — the reverse process.

What are the durations of the time periods during which the life-wave manifests in the manvantara of seven rounds, and in the seven respective planets of *each* round? As H. P. Blavatsky has told us, the doctrines concerning the time periods have been from immemorial time considered too esoteric to be given to the outward world in anything at all approaching fullness of teaching or detail, but throughout the teachings that have been openly given there are many hints of immense value. For instance, the time required for one round — that is, the cycle from globe A to the last globe of the seven (we will call it Z), starting from the root-Manu or collective "humanity" of globe A and ending with the seed-Manu or collective "humanity" of globe Z — is called a round-manvantara, and its period is 306,720,000 years. It is called manvantara because it is the "reign of one Manu" — say, a certain *quality* of humanity. Now this word *manvantara* is Sanskrit and means "between Manus," i.e., between a root-Manu on globe A and the seed-Manu on globe Z, for a *round*-manvantara. Now to this period of 306,720,000 years must be added the length of the *sandhi*, meaning "connection," or "junction," or interval, according to a certain method of calculation, necessary in order fully to complete the evolution of the planet for the round; this sandhi is of the length of a krita yuga, or 1,728,000 years, which brings the complete period or term of a *round*-manvantara to 308,448,000 years of mortals. As has already been stated, there is, after the end of every round, an obscuration which also lasts for a certain period which we do not here specify.

But how long a period do the *seven* rounds take for their course? What is the period of a mahā-manvantara, or great man-vantara, sometimes called a kalpa, after which the globes no longer go into mere obscuration or repose, but die utterly? The period of the mahā-manvantara or kalpa is also called a Day of Brahmā, and its length is 4,320,000,000; and the Night of Brahmā, the planetary rest period, which is also called the paranirvanic period, is of equal length. Seven rounds, as said, form a Day of Brahmā.

These figures are the Brahmanical figures, and they are also the figures of esoteric Buddhism (for we insist that Buddhism *has* an esoteric doctrine). The root-number 432, as any student knows, is also found in the chronological doctrines of ancient Babylonia; it is likewise the real meaning in the chronological line of the Pythagorean Tetraktys, 1–2–3–4, the 432 springing from the unity or monad, a subject of which we spoke in our last study.

We are also told that the duration of a planet's life, i.e., of a planetary chain of seven globes, is one of 360 *divine* Days, corresponding to a *divine* Year, and that Brahmā's Life (or the life of the universal system) is one hundred of those divine Years — expressed in 15 figures of years of mortals. A planetary manvantara is also related to the duration of life of a solar system; a planetary manvantara (or seven rounds) is a Day of Brahmā, as already said; each of these Days lasting 4,320,000,000 years of mortals, which really means the *lifetime of a planet during its seven rounds*, and corresponding to one incarnation of a human life on earth.

How long, then, does Brahmā live in any one of his manifested universes, which we know are called the "outbreathings of the Self-Existent"? We can calculate it — 4,320,000,000 times 100, times 360, or in other words, 36,000, lives has any planet to live before the prākritika-pralaya (or the *elemental* pralaya) sets in, the end of *that* life (or pravritti) of the universal system.

What happens when comes the end of a solar system? At a former meeting we spoke of the "bells of pralaya." It was with no intention of attempting to be rhetorical, or of employing ora-torical phraseology that we used this phrase. We have no such

ambition. We chose the words because the teachings are that
when the great (or mahā-) pralaya comes upon the planets of
any system and their sun, then strange noises of various kinds are
heard in the air of a planet belonging to such a solar system; and
these noises are repeated in miniature, so to say, not only at the
end of the planetary manvantara (or the lifetime of the planet),
but also in still smaller miniature at the end of every round.
These phenomena are also alluded to in other religions than the
Indian, as for instance in the Christian and Jewish: in Revelation, 6:14; and in Isaiah, 34:4. The Christian writers speak of the
time, 2 Peter, 3:10, 12–13, when the "elements shall melt with
fervent heat," and "the heavens shall pass away with a great
noise," but they "look for new heavens and a new earth" — or
a new planetary manvantara — and allude to pralaya as the time
when "the heaven departed as a scroll when it is rolled together,"
etc. These allusions to pralayic disintegration are figurative to
a certain extent, but are sufficiently along the lines of the ancient
Eastern thought to show us whence they came — from the archaic
wisdom-religion (theosophy) of the Orient. We are told that some
of the strange noises that will occur towards the end of the
prākritika-manvantara, before the cosmic or prākritika-pralaya
sets in, are strange hollow boomings, strange cracklings as of
musketry fire, strange bell-like ringings as of the snapping of
immense metallic belts.

Now the sun is both the heart and the brain of our solar
system, and sends seven-faceted life into every atom of its universe, the solar universe of which we and our planet Terra are
a part. The sun itself is in some respects a vampire, but it is also
preeminently and essentially a life-giver. It is, cosmogonically,
our elder brother, and not at all our physical parent as modern
scientific wiseacres would have it. It is also in a vital sense our
father-mother, because through it, from planes superior to our
own, come down the life-streams from worlds (systems) above
ours — yet our planet, as all the other planets, also in a relative
degree receives these life-streams, as every individual atom and
every human being, in the smallest miniature thereof, receives the
same individually from the Inmost of the Inmost within itself or
himself. This is, as you will remember was stated in former

studies, the same spiritual life; but *cosmically*, that is to say, with regard to the universe, the sun is the brain and heart of our system, vitalizing and informing the endless hosts of beings under its systemic sway.

We do not see the (true) sun. The sun is not burning, or incandescent. Heat exists around the sun, but it is not from burning gases or incandescence. We see the sun's robes, or reflection, but we do not see the sun itself. It is, in very truth, a spiritual thing, and we think we receive our entire supply of heat and light from it because the *forces* flowing from the sun act in conjunction and reactively with the forces on our own earth — forces working in the universal nature around us. If most of our *light* is due to the sun, this is *not* the case with 75 percent of the *heat* which we receive, which comes — most of it — from our own globe and its forces, and especially from the immensely thick clouds of cosmic dust which fills all space. The electromagnetic forces at work between this cosmic dust and our earth furnish most of the terrestrial heat.

I wish this evening before closing to call your attention to the fact that the ancient initiate-astronomers, when speaking of the seven sacred spheres of our universe — the seven or nine in which the bodies of the solar system and the stars were set, beyond which was the Empyrean or the fiery sphere — desired to convey a meaning which is now lost, for the masses. There was a meaning of deep and wide significance also in their *geocentric* teachings. They knew as well as do we (and we have proofs of it), that the earth and the other planets whirl around the sun in elliptical orbits, but they had a reason for teaching the geocentric doctrines in public, and some day we shall have need to go into an analysis and proof of this assertion.

Let us close our evening's study in calling attention to the fact that theosophy is a doctrine of hope; it is a doctrine of spirituality; it is a doctrine which refines and elevates man; it is a doctrine in which there is room for the humblest to understand something and for the brightest and highest and most spiritual of us to put our feet on the lowest steps of that spiritual stair along which we may climb in hierarchical ascendings up to the highest, not only in our own planet, hand in hand with the great

Buddhas of former times and of the times to come, but beyond our planet and beyond our own solar system into those illimitable spiritual spheres in which the solar system now exists, and through which we derive our life — spiritual, mental, psychical, prānic, and physical.

TEN

THE DOCTRINE OF SWABHĀVA — SELF-BECOMING — CHARACTERISTIC
INDIVIDUALITY. MAN, SELF-EVOLVED, HIS OWN CREATOR.
"MONADOLOGIE" OF LEIBNIZ CONTRASTED WITH
TEACHINGS OF THE ESOTERIC PHILOSOPHY.

The MONAD emerges from its state of spiritual and intellectual unconsciousness; and, skipping the first two planes — too near the ABSOLUTE to
permit of any correlation with anything on a lower plane — it gets direct into
the plane of Mentality. But there is no plane in the whole universe with
a wider margin, or a wider field of action in its almost endless gradations of
perceptive and apperceptive qualities, than this plane, which has in its turn
an appropriate smaller plane for every "form," from the "mineral" monad up
to the time when that monad blossoms forth by evolution into the DIVINE
MONAD. But all the time it is still one and the same Monad, differing only
in its incarnations, throughout its ever succeeding cycles of partial or total
obscuration of spirit, or the partial or total obscuration of matter — two
polar antitheses — as it ascends into the realms of mental spirituality, or
descends into the depths of materiality.   — *The Secret Doctrine*, I, 175

In other words, no purely spiritual Buddhi (divine Soul) can have an independent (conscious) existence before the spark which issued from the pure
Essence of the Universal Sixth principle, — or the OVER-SOUL, — has (a)
passed through every elemental form of the phenomenal world of that
Manvantara, and (b) acquired individuality, first by natural impulse, and
then by self-induced and self-devised efforts (checked by its Karma), thus
ascending through all the degrees of intelligence, from the lowest to the
highest Manas, from mineral and plant, up to the holiest archangel (Dhyani-
Buddha). The pivotal doctrine of the Esoteric philosophy admits no
privileges or special gifts in man, save those won by his own Ego through
personal effort and merit throughout a long series of metempsychoses and
reincarnations.   — *Ibid.*, I, 17

THE GENERAL TEXT of our study this evening is found
in *The Secret Doctrine*, volume I, page 83, stanza 3,
verse 10:

10. FATHER-MOTHER SPIN A WEB WHOSE UPPER END IS FASTENED TO SPIRIT (*Purusha*), THE LIGHT OF THE ONE DARKNESS, AND THE LOWER ONE TO MATTER (*Prakriti*) ITS (*the Spirit's*) SHADOWY END; AND THIS WEB IS THE UNIVERSE SPUN OUT OF THE TWO SUBSTANCES MADE IN ONE, WHICH IS SWÂBHÂVAT (*a*).

(*a*) In the Mandukya (Mundaka) Upanishad it is written, "As a spider throws out and retracts its web, as herbs spring up in the ground . . . so is the Universe derived from the undecaying one" (I. 1. 7). Brahmâ, as "the germ of unknown Darkness," is the material from which all evolves and develops "as the web from the spider, as foam from the water," etc. This is only graphic and true, if Brahmâ the "creator" is, as a term, derived from the root *brih*, to increase or expand. Brahmâ "expands" and becomes the Universe woven out of his own substance.

The same idea has been beautifully expressed by Goethe, who says:

"Thus at the roaring loom of Time I ply,
And weave for God the garment thou see'st Him by."

In the course of our studies we have been advancing stage by stage, step by step, from general principles, and our course has been always towards that point of emanation and evolution which finds itself at the dawn of manifestation, or the opening of man-vantara. We have touched upon many subjects but lightly, be-cause the intricacy of the theme did not at the time permit us to go into and to follow side-avenues of thought, however attractive and important they might be; but these avenues we shall have to explore as time and opportunity bring once more before us, in the course of our study, the portals which we have passed and perhaps have merely glanced into.

We have brought to the attention of those who will read these studies certain fundamental natural principles, as fundamental and important in their respective bearings as the two foundation stones of popular theosophy today, called reincarnation and karma. One of these principles is the doctrine of hierarchies, upon which much more could be said, and will be said in due time.

Another such fundamental principle or doctrine — a true key opening the very heart of being and, besides other things, reach-ing into the root-meaning of the so-called origin of evil and of the inner urge towards right and righteousness, which man calls his moral sense — is that which flows forth from the philosophical conceptions behind the word *swabhāva*, meaning, generally, the essential characteristic of anything. The medieval scholastics spoke of this essentiality of things as their *quidditas*, or *quiddity*, — the "whatness" of anything: that which is its heart, its essential nature, its characteristic essentiality. The word *swabhāva* (a noun) itself is derived from the Sanskrit root *bhū*, meaning "to become," or "to be," and the prefix *sva* (or *swa*) is also Sanskrit and means "self." The word thus translated means "self-becomingness," a technical term, a key word, in which philosophical conceptions of immense and wide-reaching import inhere. We shall develop some of these more fully as we proceed with our studies.

In the quotation from the stanzas which we have read this evening, you will have noticed the word *swabhavat*, from the same elements as is swabhāva, from the same Sanskrit root. *Swabhavat* is the present participle of the verb *bhū*, meaning "that which becomes itself," or *develops from within outwardly its essential self* by emanation, evolution; in other words, that which by *self-urge develops the potencies latent in its nature*, in its *self*, in its *being of being*. We have often spoken of the Inmost of the Inmost as implying that inmost link or root by which we (and all other things) flow forth from the very essence of the heart of things, which is our UTTER SELF, and we have spoken of it sometimes with the hand placed upon the breast; but we must be exceedingly careful not to think that this Inmost of the Inmost is *in* the physical body. Let me explain just what I mean. The Qabbalists divide the planes of nature into which the ten Sephīrōth became — queer English this, but very accurately and correctly expressing the thought — into four during manifestation, and they were called the four ʿōlām, a word having originally the meaning of "concealed" or "hid" or "secret," but also used for "time," likewise used almost exactly in the sense of the Gnostic teaching of "aions" (aeons) as spheres, lokas in Sanskrit. The highest of the Qabbalistic ʿōlāms, or spheres, was ʿōlām atsīlōth, meaning the "aeon" or "age" or the "loka" of "condensation." The second was called ʿōlām hab-berīāh, meaning the aeon or age or loka of "creation." The third in descent and increasing materiality was called ʿōlām ha-yetsīrāh or loka of "form." The fourth, last, most material and grossest, was called 'ōlām ha-'aśīāh, meaning the aeon or world of "action" or "causes." This last plane or sphere or world is the lowest of the four, and is sometimes called the world of matter or, again, of "shells," man (and other physical entities) sometimes being considered a shell in the sense of being the garment or the vehicle or corpus of the indwelling spirit.

Now *psychologically* these four spheres were considered as being copied, or reflected, or as having a locus (place) in the human body; and in order to correspond with the four basic principles into which the Jewish Qabbalistic philosophers divided man, neshāmāh (or spirit) was supposed to have its locus in the head, or rather hovering thereover; the second, rūahh (or soul), was supposed to have its locus or center in the breast or chest; the third, the lowest of the active principles, called nephesh (or the animal-astral soul), was supposed to have its locus or center in the abdomen. The fourth vehicle was gūph, or the inclosing shell of the physical body. The neshāmāh, the highest of all, from which the others emanated stage by stage — the rūahh from neshāmāh, the nephesh from rūahh, and the gūph from nephesh (the gūph actually is the linga-śarīra, esoterically, and *secretes* the human physical body) — should not be considered so much *in* the head as *overshadowing*, as it were, the head and body. It may be likened to a solar ray, or to an electric ray, or again to the so-called Golden Chain of the great Greek poet Homer and the far later Neoplatonic philosophers, which connects Zeus and all lower entities; or to the chain of beings in a hierarchy linked by their hyparxis with the lowest plane of the next *higher* hierarchy.

This Inmost of the Inmost is in that part of us which overshadows us, which is *above* us physically, rather than *in* us. And it really is our spiritual monad. Therefore, before we can know what we mean by swabhāva, and the wonderful doctrine fundamentally emanating therefrom, we must understand what we mean by monad and the sense in which the word monad is used. Those who were students of H. P. Blavatsky while she was alive with us, and who have studied under W. Q. Judge and Katherine Tingley, will realize the necessity of making our sense clear by choosing words which shall convey clearly and sensibly, and without possibility of misconception, the thoughts which lie behind the words. In European philosophy, monad, as a philosophical word, seems to have been first employed by the great Italian philosopher, the noted Giordano Bruno, in thought a Neoplatonist, who derived his inspiration from the philosophy of Greece now called Neoplatonism. A more modern use of the word monad, in a spiritual-philosophical sense, was that of the Slavic-German philosopher, Leibniz. Monadism formed the heart of all his teachings, and he said that the universe was composed, built up, of monads: that is to say, he conceived them to be spiritual centers having no extension, but having an inner and inherent energy of development, the respective hosts of monads being of various degrees and each one achieving its own development by an *innate characteristic nature* (or swabhāva). The essential meaning of this, as it is at once seen, is *characteristic individuality,* which is *self,* pursuing its own unfoldment and growing by stages higher and higher through *self-unfolding* or *self-becoming* (or swabhāva). Leibniz taught that these monads were connected, spiritually, psychically, and physically, by a "law of harmony," as he expressed it, which is our swabhavat — the "Self-Existent," developing during manifestation into the hosts of monads, or monadic centers.

Leibniz seems to have taken (at least in part) the main philosophical conception as regards his monads, as developed in his philosophy — in his *Monadologie* — from the Flemish mystic, Van Helmont. This man Van Helmont, however, took it from Bruno or, perhaps, directly, as Bruno did, from the Neoplatonic philosophers. As far as the basic ideas of Bruno, Van Helmont, and Leibniz go, they very much resemble each other; they resemble also the teaching on this subject of the esoteric wisdom, esoteric theosophy, but only in so far as we consider *manifestation,* because the monads themselves, in their ultimate, enter into the "silence and darkness," as Pythagoras would have put it, when the great mahā-pralaya or cosmical dissolution begins. A monad in the ancient teachings now called theosophy — remember that "theosophy" really means the wisdom which the gods or divine beings study, a truly divine thing — means a spiritual atom (we are compelled here to use popular language), and a spiritual atom is equivalent to saying pure individuality, the selfness of the self, the essential nature or characteristic or swābhāvic core of every spiritual being, the *self* of itself. This esoteric wisdom derives this self — not its ego, which is an entirely different and lower and inferior thing — it derives this *divine* monad, this divine substance-consciousness, from the Paramātman, the so-called supreme self, not that this supreme self is God in the curiously contradictory Christian sense, but supreme in the sense of absolute, unconditioned, and all-pervading universality for and in a single cosmical aggregation of hierarchies, for it is the summit, acme, pinnacle, and *source* thereof.

If we remember what we have studied in this connection, and the conceptions that we figurated on the blackboard by means of diagrams, we shall recollect that we represented the highest that we could intellectually conceive of as a triangle, figuring it thus in our minds. Not that this highest actually *is* a triangle, which would be ludicrous, but we represented it diagrammatically to ourselves in that fashion; and the highest sphere — in the mathematical sense of being without physical extension as *we* conceive of such — from which all the succeeding ten steps, planes, degrees of any hierarchy radiated, we called the Boundless, the Without Bounds, the *Eyn Sōph* as the Qabbalists said; and the two aspects of the Boundless formed, so to speak, the two sides of this divine triangle, one of these two aspects being Parabrahman (beyond Brahman), and the other being Mūlaprakriti (or root-nature). It must be remembered, in this connection, that any diagrammatic representation may and often does figurate different conceptions when the premises differ. And next, that from this divine triangle there was a reflection, as it were, an emanation, into the lower shadow, into the substance or matter below, the rays of the upper sun shining into the lower atmosphere, so to say, and illuminating it, and that this lower illuminated atmosphere or substance was called the lower monad, and the upper was called the higher monad; and that, as the energy or life-waves swept downwards through the second monad or the lower monad, the square or manifested nature came into being as the third stage of evolution. With the premises before stated, therefore, this upper triangle, which may be considered as one, or a trinity in unity, is the upper monad, or the Inmost of the Inmost, the self of the self; and the lower triangle is its emanation, its three lines representing Father, Mother, and Son. The Father, again, may be considered as the primal point of the second or lower triangle, that is to say, the point forming the apex of the triangle, which is a laya-center through which stream down into our sphere the manifesting forces which *themselves become* the universe.

Herein we may see an example of the philosophical value of the hierarchical system considered as a representation of nature's symmetrical architecture, because each stage of the downward progress, each step or plane downwards, is informed, insouled, by the upper parts which *remain* above; while the lower planes or parts are spiritually and ethereally and physically secreted and excreted step by step, plane after plane, and cast forth like foam on the substratal waves of life. The physical nature as we see it even on this our own plane is, so to speak, concreted divinity, and it actually is concreted light, because light is ethereal matter or substance.

Some day we shall have to study this question of spirit and substance, force and matter, and their relations and interactions,

more thoroughly than we have been able to do thus far in our
lectures.

Now, from the highest of the highest, from what is to us the
unknown of the unknown, the Inmost of the Inmost, through all
these planes, there streams down, as it were, the divine ray, passing from one hierarchy to another hierarchy below it, and then
to another still lower, and then to a third yet more material, and so
on till the limit of the cosmical aggregate is reached, when it begins to ascend along the stupendous round, returning towards its
primal source. Note carefully that as it descends it *evolves these
various hierarchies from itself;* and on its ascending round draws
them back into itself again. Surrounding this immense spiritual
aggregate, we are taught to conceive an aura, as it were, taking
the shape of an egg, which we can call, following the example of
the Qabbalists, the *Shechīnāh,* a Hebrew word meaning "dwelling" or "vehicle," or what the esoteric philosophy calls the auric
egg in the case of man, and representing in this paradigmatic
scheme the universe which we see around us in its highest aspects,
for this aura is the very outgrowth of Mūlaprakriti; while this
mystical line which we draw in the figure as running down through
all the various grades of the hierarchy is the stream of the self,
the Unconditioned Consciousness, welling up in the inmost of
everything.

To come back to the word *swabhavat,* the "self-becoming," the
"self-existing": it is, in the superspiritual, following the above
paradigm, the second *divine* monad or second *divine* Logos; or,
looking at it in another and lower way, it is the first *cosmic*
monad, the reflection of the primeval or primal divine monad
above it, and is the first manifestation or quiver of cosmic life
when, the end of universal pralaya having come, the cry goes
forth, so to say, on the watchtower of eternity, "Let there be
manifestation and light!"

The Elohīm in a former stage were monads; and you remember
that we made our own translation of verses 25, 26, and 27 of the
first chapter of Genesis, and we saw that these Elohīm said, "Let
us make man in our own shadow or phantom (in our own shadow-
selves or matter-selves), and in our own pattern," that is, they
made man by *becoming* him; stated in other words, humanity

is the lower principles of the Elohīm themselves as monads.

So the monad is the inmost of ourselves, not as a soul, as a "gift of God," but as the highest part of ourselves; and our very bodies are concreted spirit, which is on *this plane* the lowest, the shadowy end, the matter-end, of the self-hierarchy which each one of us is.

Let us remember again that each hierarchy has its swabhāva or specific characteristic. To exemplify it by colors, one hierarchy is predominantly blue, another is predominantly red, another green, another yellow or golden, and so on; but each one has its own forty-nine roots or divisions, forty-nine aspects of the one underlying root-substance *common to all,* so that of necessity each one of these forty-nine in its turn develops one of the other colors. So that, if we could perceive it spiritually, we should see all nature around us everywhere flashing and coruscating in a most marvelous interplay of colors — a wonderful picture! This is sheer fact, not a metaphor. And, furthermore, there is for every kosmos a cosmic hierarchy which includes all the lesser hierarchies thereof, and each hierarchy, large or small, is linked on, above and below (or outward and inward), to other hierarchies, higher and lower, and each separate, individual hierarchy consists of nine (or ten) planes or degrees. Seven of these are, throughout, on the manifesting planes. Hence, a hierarchy, strictly speaking, consists of ten planes housing ten states of matter and ten forces, but seven thereof are *manifesting* forces; the seven in manifestation run from the arūpa (or formless) to the rūpa (or form) worlds, and they are all linked together, coordinated together, combined together, beyond present human conception or understanding.

It is along these lines of spiritual thought that the dogmatic religious or scientific system quarrels, if we may use this expression, with the esoteric philosophy, because that system is based — at least as regards the scientific view — upon purely mechanical and materialistic hypotheses invented by the scientists of the last century concerning the nature and action of what is called matter and force, as if there could in reason be a true definition or explanation of these two on a basis of fortuitous mechanicalism arising out of utterly lifeless "matter."

Let us say now, although it is departing a little from our main theme, that force is simply matter on a higher plane — ethereal matter, if you will; and that physical matter is simply force on our plane. Matter actually is naught but concreted force; or, to reverse the idea, force is nothing but sublimated or etherealized matter, because the two, matter and spirit, are one. It is best and truest to say that matter is concreted or compacted force, just as nature (matter as we know it) is equilibrated spirit.

We may once more return to this wonderful teaching of swabhāva, after this rather long but necessary explanation or introduction. The monad is our inmost self; each man has his own, or rather *is* his own, monad. Each being of whatever degree or kind has its particular characteristic nature — not merely the outer or vehicular characteristics that change from incarnation to incarnation, and from manvantara to manvantara — but every entity, high or low, has, so to say, a keynote of its being. This is its swabhāva: the selfhood of the self, the essential characteristic of the self, by the urge of which the self becomes the many selves, producing and manifesting the hosts of varied qualities and types and degrees. Now note carefully: the *urge behind* evolution or development is not external to the evolving entity but *within itself;* and the future results to be achieved in evolution — *that which the evolving entity becomes* — lie in germ or seed *in itself;* both this urge and this germ or seed arise out of one thing, and THIS IS ITS SWABHĀVA.

Remember what we said in our former study about the nature and evolution of the universe. What is a — or any — universe? It is a *self-contained* and *self-sustained* and *self-sufficient entity in manifestation,* but is merely one of countless hosts of other universes, all children of the Boundless. There is, for instance, an atomic universe, and a terrestrial or planetary universe, and a human universe, and a solar universe, and so on indefinitely; yet all hang together, interpenetrate each other, and form any cosmical aggregate. And how and why? Because each universe, great or small, is a hierarchy, and each hierarchy represents and is the development of and is a part of the spiritual urge and evolving germ arising out of the self thereof, of the self of each, each developing and evolving its own particular essential characteristic;

and all these forces taken together are the swabhāva of any entity. Swabhāva, in short, may be called the essential individuality of any monad, expressing its own characteristics, qualities, and type, by *self-urged evolution.*

We should note also in passing that perhaps the most mystic school in Buddhism, which H. P. Blavatsky says has practically kept most faithfully to this one of the esoteric teachings of Gautama Buddha, is a school still extant in Nepal, which is called the Swābhāvika school, a Sanskrit adjective derived from the noun swabhāva; this school comprises those who follow the doctrine of swabhāva, or the doctrine which teaches the becoming or unfolding of the self by inner impulse — the *self*-becoming. We do not, according to it, become "through the grace of a God." We *become* whatever we are or are to be through our own selves; we make ourselves, derive ourselves from ourselves, become our own children; have always done so, and will forever do so. This applies not only to man, but to all beings everywhere. Herein we see the root, the force, the meaning, of morals. Responsible for every act we do, for every thought we think, responsible to the uttermost farthing, never anything "forgiven," never anything "wiped out," except when we ourselves turn the evil we have done into good. We shall have to discuss more fully, some time, the question of the origin of evil which is involved herein. We may note in passing that this school is called "atheistic" and "materialistic," simply because of two reasons: first, the profound thought of this doctrine is misinterpreted by Occidental scholars; second, many of its followers have, in fact, degenerated.

You see immediately the ethical force of such a doctrine as this of swabhāva, when it is properly understood. We become what we are in germ in our inmost essence; we also follow and make a part of, likewise, the type and the course of evolution of the particular planetary chain to which we belong by affinity. We first follow along the shadowy arc down into matter, and when we have reached the lowest point of that arc, then, *through the inner impulses of our nature*, through self-directed evolution — which is the very heart of this doctrine of swabhāva, one of the most fundamental doctrines in the esoteric philosophy — when we have reached the bottom, I repeat, then the same inner impulse carries us (provided that we have passed the *danger point* of being attracted into the lower sphere of matter) up the luminous arc, up and back into the higher spiritual spheres, but beyond the point of departure whence we first started downward on our cyclical journey into material experience for that manvantara.

We make our own bodies, we make our own lives, we make our own destinies, and we are responsible for it all, spiritually, morally, intellectually, psychically, and even physically. It is a manly doctrine; there is no room in it for moral cowardice, no room in it for casting our responsibility upon the shoulders of another — God, angel, man, or demon. We can become gods, because we are gods in the germ even now, inwardly. We start upon our evolutionary journey as an unself-conscious god-spark, and we return to our primal source of being, following the great cycle of the mahā-manvantara, a self-conscious god.

Let us say here that we have come at this point to what is a great puzzle for most of our Occidental orientalists. They cannot understand the distinctions that the wonderful old philosophers of the Orient make as regards the various classes of the devas. They say, in substance: "What funny contradictions there are in these teachings, which in many respects are profound and seem so wonderful. Some of these devas (or divine beings) are said to be *less* than man; some of these writings even say that a good man is nobler than any god. And yet other parts of these teachings declare that there are gods higher even than the devas, and yet are called devas. What does this mean?"

The devas or divine beings, one class of them, are the unself-conscious sparks of divinity, cycling down into matter in order to bring out from within themselves and to unfold or evolve *self*-consciousness, the swabhāva of divinity within. They begin their reascent always on the luminous arc, which never ends, in a sense; and they are gods, *self*-conscious gods, henceforth, taking a definite and divine part in the "great work," as the mystics have said, of being builders, evolvers, leaders, of hierarchies; in other words, they are monads *which have become their own innermost selves;* which have passed the Ring-pass-not separating the spiritual from the divine. Remember and reflect upon these old sayings in our books — every one of them is pregnant with meaning, full of thought.

This, therefore, is the doctrine of swabhāva: the doctrine of inner development, of bringing out that particular essential characteristic or individuality which is within, of self-directed evolution; and you must perforce see the immense reach that it has in the moral world, in the theological world, in the philosophical world, yea, even in the scientific world as regards the knotty problems of evolution, such as the evolution of species, inheritance, development of root types, and many more.

We shall one day have to study more carefully than the mere sketch we have given here these divine, very divine, doctrines, especially in their bearing on questions of human psychology; for upon these doctrines depends the further (and a better) comprehension of the very tenets which we have outlined this evening and at former meetings. We cannot understand the universe or the working and interplay of the forces therein until we have mastered at least to some degree, and followed out, the injunction of the Delphic Oracle, "Man, Know Thyself!" A man who knows himself truly, knows all, because he is, fundamentally, all. He is every hierarchy; he is gods and demons and worlds and spheres and forces, and matter and consciousness and spirit — everything is in him. He is in one sense built of the roots of everything, and he is the fruit of everything; he has endless time behind him and endless time before him. What a gospel of hope, what a gospel of wonder, is this; how it raises the human soul; how the inmost part of us aspires when we reflect upon this teaching! No wonder that it is called the "teaching (or wisdom) of the gods," *theosophia* — that is to say, the teaching which the gods themselves study. How does a man become a *mahātman* or "great self"? Through self-directed evolution, through *becoming that which he is in himself*, in his innermost. This is the doctrine of swabhāva.

And here we should at least allude to the mystery of individuality. Remember that personality is the "mask" (*persona*, as the Latins said) or reflection in matter of the individuality; but being a material thing it can lead us downward, although it is in essence a reflection of the highest. It is an old saying that those things are most dangerous which have reality or truth in them; not those things which are truly unreal or false, because they of themselves fall to pieces and evanish away in time.

Monads, psychologically (we have the four monads, the divine, intellectual, psychical, and astral, corresponding to the four basic planes of matter, but all four monads deriving from the highest) from the standpoint of generalization, are spiritual atoms, buddhic atoms, being universal principles so far as are concerned the planes below, the buddhi being perhaps the most mysterious of the seven principles of man and, from our present viewpoint, the most important. But the human monad as contrasted with the divine monad above it, the potentially immortal man, comprises the three principles, ātman, buddhi, and the higher manas. These three principles are required in order to make a self-conscious god. Ātman and buddhi alone cannot make a *self*-conscious god; they are a god-spark, an undeveloped or unevolved god-spark. We have to use in this connection human terms; we have not the terms in English or in any other European language properly to express these subtil thoughts.

In conclusion, let us remember that while each man has the Christ within himself, and can be "saved" only by that Christ, he can be saved by that inner Christ only when he *chooses* to *save himself;* the initiative must come from below, from himself. And while some people, through misunderstanding of this wonderful doctrine of swabhāva, may speak of fatalism, we can do no more this evening than to say emphatically that this doctrine is not fatalism. It is absolutely the contrary of the fatalistic hypothesis, which asserts that there is a blind or unknown or conscious or unconscious force outside of man, directing him, driving him, in his choice, acts, and evolution, to annihilation or heaven or hell. That is not the doctrine of swabhāva and it is *not* taught in the esoteric philosophy.

ELEVEN

THE COSMIC PILGRIMAGE. FROM UNSELF-CONSCIOUS GOD-SPARK
TO FULLY SELF-CONSCIOUS GOD.

Unveil, O Thou that givest sustenance to the Universe, from whom all proceeds, to whom all must return, the face of the True Sun, now hidden by a vase of Golden Light, that we may see the Truth and do our whole duty on our journey towards thy Sacred Seat. — Paraphrase of *The Gāyatrī*

ON PAGE 605 of the first volume of *The Secret Doctrine* we find the following:

But one has to understand the phraseology of Occultism before criticising what it asserts. For example, the Doctrine refuses (as Science does, in one sense) to use the words "above" and "below," "higher" and "lower," in reference to *invisible* spheres, as being without meaning. Even the terms "East" and "West" are merely conventional, necessary only to aid our human perceptions. For, though the Earth has its two fixed points in the poles, North and South, yet both East and West are variable relatively to our own position on the Earth's surface, and in consequence of its rotation from West to East. Hence, when "*other* worlds" are mentioned — whether better or worse, more spiritual or still more material, though both invisible — the Occultist does not locate *these spheres* either *outside* or *inside* our Earth, as the theologians and the poets do; for their location is nowhere in the space *known* to, and conceived by, the profane. They are, as it were, blended with our world — interpenetrating it and interpenetrated by it. There are millions and millions of worlds and firmaments visible to us; there still greater numbers beyond those visible to the telescopes, and many of the latter kind do not belong to our *objective* sphere of existence. Although as invisible as if they were millions of miles beyond our solar system, they are yet with us, near us, *within* our own world, as objective and material to their respective inhabitants as ours is to us. But, again, the relation of these worlds to ours is not that of a series of egg-shaped boxes enclosed one within the other, like the toys called Chinese nests; each is entirely under its own special laws and conditions, having no direct relation to our sphere. The inhabitants of these, as already said, may be, for all we know, or feel, passing *through* and *around* us as if through empty space, their very habitations and countries being interblended with ours, though not disturbing our vision, because we have not yet the faculties necessary for discerning them.

This seems to be a very appropriate general text for us to choose in closing our sketch of the hierarchies, and more particularly our development of the doctrine of swabhāva, upon which we touched in our last meeting: the doctrine of the characteristic nature, of the individuality, or type-essentiality, of each individual monad, growing and manifesting and becoming itself in the manifested world in which it is itself the seed of its own individuality. The bearing of this concept on the doctrine of evolution — "rolling out or unfolding of what is within" — and especially on the mooted and knotty problem of the so-called origin of species, is simply immense, for it is the key thereof.

We can use the word *individuality* for the meaning of swabhāva, provided that we do not use it in contradistinction to *personality*. It is individuality in the sense of signifying the being and the unfolding of that particular quality or essential characteristic which distinguishes one monad, one human entity, one cosmos, one atom, from another of the same kind. Fundamental as is the doctrine of hierarchies, and illuminating as is the light that it throws upon other problems, it itself cannot be properly understood without its complementary doctrine of swabhāva; and, vice versa, we cannot properly understand the doctrine of swabhāva without understanding the doctrine of hierarchies.

We hope this evening to develop the true meaning of swabhāva, and thus to finish this part of our study, having now reached the frontiers, as it were, of cosmical manifestation; and in beginning our study of it in detail, we are obliged to touch upon a very essential aspect of the doctrine, another aspect of it which is fundamental for the proper understanding of this portion of the teaching of the ancient wisdom; it is a portion which pertains to psychology. Indeed, this doctrine of hierarchies and this its complementary doctrine of swabhāva, are both in a very large measure fundamentally psychological.

Swabhāva is a Sanskrit term, a noun derived from the root *bhū*, meaning "to become," and hence "to be," a psychological concord which is found also in several other languages, as in both Greek and English for instance. In Greek the word is *gignomai;* and in English it is *be.* In old Anglo-Saxon we have this word with the essential future sense completely retained and psychologically distinctly felt, to wit: *ic beo, thu bist* or *byst, he bith* or *biath,* etc., meaning "I, thou, he will be," in the future sense of "become." It is obvious that the psychological force of this means that *being* is essentially a *becoming* — a growth or evolution or unfolding of inner faculty.

English, as a matter of fact, had originally and still has only the two natural grammatical tenses — the imperfect tense, or the tense of imperfect or incomplete action, commonly called the present; and the perfect tense of perfected or completed action, or the past.

Now what constitutes one hierarchy as different in essence — or swabhāva — from another hierarchy? It is its swabhāva, or the seed of individuality which *is* it and is in it. It is that seed which, developing, makes *a* hierarchy, and that seed in developing follows the laws (or rather nature) of its own essential being, and this is its swabhāva. In *The Secret Doctrine,* H. P. Blavatsky often speaks of one particular quality or plane of universal being, which she calls *swabhavat,* the neuter present participle of the same root *bhū,* and used as a noun. Like swabhāva, it is derived from the same root, with the same prefix, and means that particular thing which *exists and becomes of and in its own essential essence;* call it the "Self-Existent," if you like. It is, though a Sanskrit word, a Buddhistic term, and its Brahmanical equivalent in the Vedanta would probably be the cosmical side of Paramātman, supreme self, the individualized aspect of Parabrahman-Mūlaprakriti: superspirit–root-matter.

Swabhavat is the spiritual essence, the fundamental root or spirit-substance, the Father-Mother of the beginning of manifestation, and from it grow or *become* all things. It can be conceived of as did Spinoza, the Netherlandish Jewish philosopher, as God, as the one underlying being or substance; though in our studies we have eschewed the use of the term "God," for a reason hereinafter to be set forth. Or it can be conceived of as Leibniz did, as a collective unity of an infinitude of emanated monads or "entelechies," to use Aristotle's term. Spinoza was an absolute idealist, while Leibniz was an objective idealist, which we also are, by the way. Swabhāva is the characteristic nature, the type-essence, the individuality, of swabhavat — of any swabhavat, each such swabhavat having its own swabhāva.

The main and essential meaning of the doctrine of swabhāva is the following — and it is so fundamental, so important in order properly to understand what follows, that we are going emphatically to urge it upon the attention of everyone. When cosmical manifestation begins or opens, it does not open helter-skelter, in disordered confusion, or by chance; it begins in conformity with the *characteristic seeds* of life, called, commonly, laws, which have been in latent existence through the period of the mahā-pralaya preceding the beginning of the new manvantara, and these laws — we use the term under strong protest — are really the intrinsic and ineluctable *karmic habits* of nature to be *this* or *that*, its swabhāvas, in short, its hosts of innumerable entities or essential natures; and these laws are actually impressed, stamped, upon ethereal and physical matter by the monadic essences or the monads. The swabhāvas of the monads give their swābhāvic natures to nature! The monads are individuals, and conceiving them as collected together in a unity and forming a body of a still greater monad, Leibniz gave to this greatest monad the Latin term *Monas monadum* — the "Monad of monads." This monad is, in short, our hierarchical summit, of which we have several times spoken before. But where is there any need to call this "Monad of monads," this hierarchical apex or summit, God? We can conceive of something still higher, and so forth almost at will. To stop at any point and call it God would simply be *creating* a deity — a God man-made, truly!

However, a man must pause somewhere in thought. So we begin with swabhāva which, being an abstract term, is not a limit or boundary in itself. It is pure individuality working in spirit-matter of which it is the highest part or summit. Now this essential nature (or swabhāva) of a monad develops and *becomes* in matter a hierarchy, whether that hierarchy be an atom, a man, a planet, a sun, a solar system, or a cosmical universe (or a universal cosmos) such as we find within the encircling zone of the Milky Way. The monad does so following the driving essential urge of its own inner essence, its individuality, its swa-bhāva. Hence it is that as the monads are individuals, so are the resultant hierarchies individualized. And generalizing, as the monad grows into or becomes the hierarchy, descending the shadowy arc — that is, descending into matter — as it *becomes matter in its lower parts* (the upper portion of the monad remaining always in its own pure unadulterated state) it reaches a certain point which is the end of its cyclical development for that period of evolution or manvantara, and then it begins cycling upward and back again, and this part of its journey is called the luminous arc, because its tendency is towards light, or spirit, following the phraseology of the ancient sages.

We studied some time ago in the Hebrew Bible, chapter 1, verses 25 and 26, how the Elohīm said: "Let us make 'man' in our own shadowy image (in our own shadow), and in our archetypal pattern." These Elohīm who so "spoke" were monads, together forming a hierarchy, each one of them, again, a hierarchy by itself. As each individual man is a subordinate hierarchy of the greater hierarchy of humanity, so humanity is a subordinate hierarchy of the still greater hierarchy of the planet, and the planet Terra a subordinate hierarchy of the still greater hierarchy of the solar system; and so forth, as long as you care to follow the thought. Man is himself composed of less beings; he himself is a microcosm or little universe; he to these less beings is as a god — he to them is the *Monas monadum*, the Monad of monads. We shall later see reasons of great force why we have sedulously eschewed using this word God. It is a colored word, spoiled with the thoughts which have been tacked on to it; colored by them all, and it is for these reasons a dangerous word to use, because both misleading and inadequate.

As this monad in the beginning of manifestation in cosmos breaks through the laya-center, that is to say, through the neutral point, the vanishing-point where spirit becomes matter, or vice versa (you can call it the ātman of the six lower degrees or principles which are to follow in sequential evolution) — as the descending monad breaks through the encircling matter of the cosmos around it, it follows in its course its own inner urge or,

rather, is driven thereby; it is *self-expressive,* but still self-uncon-
scious. But when any particular "atomic" part of this cosmic monad reaches self-consciousness and becomes a man, the path that
its evolution follows thenceforward is *consciously self-directed.*
Up to the time of the entrance of the *self-*conscious mind into
man, the evolving entity is under the impulse, the propulsion, of
dire and implacable necessity which, however, is most emphatically *not fate;* and this is because, up to this critical point in
evolution, the evolving entity is an imperfect being still: it is not
a *self-*conscious thing, but an unself-conscious god-spark. It cannot as yet direct its own destiny on the planes of manifestation,
but automatically follows the course of the hierarchy to which
it belongs. This spiritual-mental impotency ceases when the
self-conscious state has been reached, which is in man. From
this moment, in growing degree, man becomes himself a creator
— a creator, self-consciously, of himself; he reaches upward or
inward or outward (the adverb matters not) and *becomes that
which he essentially is within,* continually aspiring toward the
Inmost of the Inmost; and he finally reaches the point, at the end
of this Day of Brahmā — after seven planetary rounds — where
he blossoms forth into a self-conscious god, not yet "God," or the
summit of the hierarchy to which he belongs by karmic descent,
but *a* god. No longer is he a nonself-conscious monad, but a
self-conscious monad, a planetary spirit, a dhyān-chohan, to use
a beautiful Buddhistic term, a "lord of meditation," one of that
wondrous host of spiritual beings who are the full-blown flowers
of former world periods or manvantaras. This wondrous host are
the perfect men of those former world periods; and they guide
the evolution of this planet in its present manvantara. They are
our own spiritual lords, leaders, and saviors. They supervise us
now in our evolution here, and we follow the path of the general
evolution outlined by them in our present cyclic pilgrimage.

When we first started on this pilgrimage as unself-conscious
god-sparks, destined to become self-conscious men in this our
manvantara, it was these dhyān-chohans — flowers of the former
manvantara — who opened the path for us, who guided our uncertain steps as we became men, incarnations of our higher selves.
But when we became self-conscious entities or men, we began to

guide ourselves; and to work consciously with them according to our evolution, to "work with nature," as H. P. Blavatsky nobly expressed it, is our highest duty and our brightest hope. It is our future destiny to become such godlike beings ourselves, thereafter in our turn to inform, inspire, and guide less evolved entities in future manvantaras, as we have been informed, inspired, and guided by them; and finally, after many kalpas, after many Days of Brahmā — each one of such Days a period of seven planetary rounds — we shall become a conscious part of the cosmical Logos, the Brāhmic Logos, using the phrase Brāhmic Logos as meaning the highest conscious entitative intelligence of the solar system; thence upward and upward forever.

We return to our main theme. When the monad has reached the first point of cosmic manifestation, it has already descended through the first three of the ten planes or degrees or steps, i.e., through the three planes or degrees or steps forming the upper triangle or triad of the ten planes in and on which the universe is built. It now begins definitely to cycle downward, and its entrance into cosmic manifestation, as already said, is the laya-center which is the ātman or universal spirit, no more belonging to any particular entity or man than does the ātman of any entity or man in any other planet of any other solar system. Ātman is ourselves merely because it is the link which connects us with the higher. As a matter of fact, the human being or man consists of five principles, because the ātman is not his except as a "plank of salvation"; and his gross physical body is not really a principle at all. This matter of component principles in man we shall have to go into more fully when we take up our study of human psychological composition.

Now the upper triangle of the ten above alluded to actually is *extended or developed out from the monad itself,* as the petals and leaves of a flower are extended or evolved out of its seed: it draws its life and being from within itself. It is the elemental world, *spiritually* speaking; as the three worlds below our mineral kingdom are the elemental worlds of ourselves, *materially* speaking, forming an elemental world, "spiritually" speaking, of the hierarchy below our own.

This inner urge driving the monad to express itself in manifestation and form is the will of higher beings, working through itself, of which higher beings it forms an integral part — just as our brain, or our body, follows the implacable law of necessity which we impose upon brain or body by our thoughts and our will, yet both brain and body are parts of ourself in matter. The monad must reach self-consciousness in order to "free" itself and thus become a self-conscious, self-directed god.

These things are so important for properly understanding our future study that we feel necessitated again and again to return to them. They are basically fundamental, lying at the very root of all our teaching. Understand clearly and well that this is *not* *fatalism*. That doctrine runs directly contrary to the doctrine of swabhāva, the doctrine of *self*-expression.

As an egg unfolds within itself the germ which is to become the future chick; or the human egg, the ovum, unfolds the germ within it which is to become the future child of man, similarly does the universe develop, similarly does an atom develop, thus also does a monad develop. It is unfolded within the auric egg. The human ovum, the seed of the plant, each is nothing but an egg. The shape may differ, the life form may differ, but this has nothing to do with the principle of unfoldment of which we are speaking. The encasement within the auric egg envelops the germ of individuality — or swabhāva — which is destined to follow its course along its own characteristic line of unfoldment: what is in the egg or seed comes out, each species according to its own kind, and this is its swabhāva. The Greek Stoic school taught the existence, both cosmically and infinitesimally, of *spermatic logoi,* "seed-logoi," each such spermatic logos producing creatures after its kind and according to its own essence — like the Hebrew Biblical Elohīm — and this is again swabhāva.

We saw in our study of the Qabbālāh how the highest world unfolded itself and *from itself* emanated or evolved the second world, thus actually *becoming* the second world: being thus both parent and child. The second world was thus the child of the first; the third was the child of the first *and* the second; and the fourth, the "world of shells" — or of beings living in gross bodies, or "shells" — was the child of the first, the second, and the third, all working together in order to produce this fourth. Note well, however, that each superior sphere or world *remains intact on its own plane,* though evolving from itself the next succeeding inferior world.

The Stoics had a doctrine of development which in its essence is the pure teaching of our own philosophy, though expressed in different form and under different names. They expressed it in this wise, following the mechanical mode so agreeable and dear to the Greek mind. It is curious, by the way, that the Oriental mind has always preferred to follow the psychological and spiritual lines of thought, rather than the mechanical or, as we would now say, the scientific. But the Stoics taught in Greece, and later in Rome, that the mechanism of the essential nature of the Deity — and this essential nature is our swabhāva, what we would call Father-Mother — was *tension,* and *slackening* of this tension, this slackening of tension being the first act of world-building. They took as an analogy in illustration of the idea the well-known fact that when a metal grows hot it then expands, and finally is vaporized; and using this simple matter-of-fact analogy they said that the "natural" state of *pneuma* ("spirit" = the Deity) is fire — not physical fire, but the seed of that cosmic element from which physical fire springs. The slackening of this tension produced the first differentiation of the primal substance (or pneuma = "God"), and this differentiation then awoke to active life the life-seeds, slumbering or latent, which came over from the previous period of manifested life; the life-seeds, or seed-lives — their spermatic logoi — thus awaking, proceeded to build and guide the forthcoming world period and all the entities in it, each such seed-life bringing forth from itself its essential species, or characteristic essence, i.e., swabhāva. This is the teaching in miniature, but as the Stoics gave it, of the esoteric philosophy.

Now when the universe was to come forth *from its own being,* taught the Stoics, the tension of the primal substance or divine fire slackened, or contracted as it were, and this contraction, by condensation, gave birth to the aether; next, as the tension slackened in the aether, this gave birth to air; and it, next, to water; and it, finally, to earth. We are not speaking of the material fire, air, water, earth, that we see around us, but we refer to the *elements* or *seeds* of these, the earth and the water and the air and the fire that we see around us being merely material samples or the last progeny, as it were, of the elemental seeds from which these respectively sprang. "Fire" gave birth to the "aether," the latter being its shadow, the shadow of itself. The "aether" gave birth to *its* shadow, or "air," its encasement or body; and the "air" to "water"; and the "water" to "earth." The Stoics taught further that all these things can be respectively transformed one into the other — the dream of the alchemist, and also the dream, psychologically, of initiates who aim and strive to transform the base into the pure, the material into the spiritual.

Returning once more to our main theme, it is to be noted that naturally, as the monad — the root or the individuality of a hierarchy of any kind — cycles down into matter, it produces from itself, it expands outwardly from itself, its own shadows (or lower vehicles) which grow constantly more dense in direct proportion to the greater descent of the monad. In this connection the question arises, that as there are certainly worlds of happiness, worlds of peace, in the higher spheres, how about those nether worlds; how about those lowest states of being of which H. P. Blavatsky speaks as the *avīchi?* There is no hell in the Christian sense. Such a hell is a vague bogey of the imagination; but there are, in very truth, lower spheres: just as there are higher, so there must be lower. There cannot be good without evil, for the one is the shadow of the other and balances it in nature. These lowest spheres have a well-defined part to play in the great cosmic drama. They are the cleansing houses, so to say, of the souls of those who persist in evildoing. Like attracts like. These lower spheres are *necessarily* entered into by those who willfully, through a prolonged series of incarnations, refuse to follow the spiritual light within themselves. Like attracts like, we repeat it. As a matter of fact, such souls, so stained and weighted with evil, are actually pursuing their own cyclical pilgrimage, drawn by *attraction* to like spheres and dwellings. During the cyclic pilgrimage of the atom-souls down into matter, many millions and millions have failed to pass the danger point and, instead of thereupon beginning their journey homeward up the luminous arc, are swept into the terrible maelstrom of the current that goes downward farther into matter! Therefore, into relatively greater suffering. These must wait until their time comes again in the next manvantara, and another chance in the future kalpa of the earth. For *this* Day of Brahmā, for *this* manvantara of seven rounds, all is ended for them as regards their *conscious* journey back to their divine source.

These are doctrines (such as that of the avīchi-nirvana, just hinted at in the preceding few sentences) which were taught in the ancient esoteric schools. From them, by misunderstanding and corruption of them, have been derived the bogey doctrines of a fiery, material hell in which are, for eternity, to burn the ethereal souls of willful sinners! These souls are said to be of an asbestos-like nature, forever burning fiercely yet never consumed, like pitch burning for utter eternity in utterly endless fire! What frightful nightmares of a gross and materialistic "religious" teaching! It is amazing how the mind of man will invent things to torture itself with. But it also shows that back of all these fearful, nightmare doctrines and dogmas there is some fundamental fact which the untaught mind sees through thick clouds darkly and falsely, and distorts; some element of truth which needs only proper explanation for understanding.

And how the human heart must melt in pity! Do we realize how real these doctrines were to our ancestors of only a few score years ago? And that in some backward-looking churches today these same horrible doctrines are still taught as actualities, though more or less secretly as if in utter shame, and that there are misguided and unhappy men who believe them, and on their deathbeds suffer in anticipation the tortures of the damned, tortures worse, certainly, than any which nature has prepared for them as guerdon for their mistakes and sins? Think of the horror of it! Think of the duty that we owe to our fellow men to teach them the proper explanation and meaning of these distorted and tortured doctrines in all their sanity, in all their beautiful hope! There is a moral element involved in it for us. People sometimes ask what is the use of studying *The Secret Doctrine?* What is the use of spending so much time in studying the rounds and races? Here is one of the uses. Essentially you cannot change men until you have changed their minds. *Teach men properly and nobly to think, and you teach them properly and nobly to live, and properly and nobly to die.* There is nothing like a noble thought to lift a man. It is sheer folly and egoism that says, "What is the use of these so-called noble thoughts? My thoughts are good enough for me."

After all that has previously been said, nevertheless, we have just begun our exposition of swabhāva. We shall not have this evening the time and opportunity to touch upon the very important psychological aspects of it which we had hoped to do. We have still a few moments of time, however. Let us then try to illustrate more clearly this doctrine of swabhāva on the line of it chosen before. Imagine an individual monad sending its ray, or descending, through that sphere which becomes the spiritual-atomic* plane of the six planes below it. This ray forms it itself into respective principles and planes as time passes, and it gathers and gleans the experiences of each separate plane. Leaving that spiritual-atomic* or ātmanic plane, it evolves out of itself its shadow, which is like an encasement, an aura, thus forming its auric egg there, and this second plane or principle we call our buddhi, and as the monadic life or ray passes still farther down into that shadowy life, this buddhic plane and principle become to it the real and the true. As cycles of time pass on, the descending monadic ray (or seed) evolves another shadow, another encasement, another subtil body, another aura, another auric egg, *out of itself,* and this is our manas. Each of these three principles — as indeed have all the seven — has seven degrees, seven stages, from the "atomic"* of any one of the three down to its lowest, which is its corpus or body. And so on with the remaining four lower planes and principles of man. Each one of these principles is "fully" developed on our globe in the respective and similar one of the rounds of the seven of the Day of Brahmā. Further, on each one of the seven globes of the planetary chain, one of the seven principles especially is developed. Again, as just shown, at the end of each round, one plane and one principle of the seven is developed, preparatory to evolving the succeeding one in another round. It takes fully two rounds, for instance, to bring out two planes and two principles in full; but

---

*[ātmic?]

during the first and the second rounds, for example, the other planes and principles have been coming up by degrees, evolving little by little, developing step by step. The chick does not grow in a day; the child does not become a man in a week; his soul does not develop within him in a fortnight. If a man lived the life he should, he would be at his best and noblest at the time when he thinks it is time for him to draw up his legs in bed and die. The physical body may be then ready to die, but the man within, that which is the real being, should be growing greater and nobler and grander. It is for this that we really live.

And so runs the course of evolution to the end of the seven rounds, each round bringing out one principle and one plane, as said; in each round, each one of the remaining principles is brought out or evolved in less degree, there being thus, to use Ezekiel's figure, "wheels within wheels." At the midpoint of the fourth round, which is the middle round, there comes a time when the monadic ray reaches the very acme of materiality — when the life-wave reaches a point where it branches both downward and upward, and then, in the words of Ezekiel, chapter 18, "the soul that sinneth, it shall die," meaning that the monadic ray courses downward and loses all chance for ascent back homeward along the luminous arc, for *that manvantara*. It follows the downward path. But those others that can and *do* follow on, they indeed pass the danger point.

A Day of Brahmā is composed of seven rounds, a period of 4,320 million solar or rather terrestrial years. Seven of these Days, again, are required to make a solar manvantara, which is a term used in the esoteric philosophy in a peculiar sense, because seven times seven rounds are needed in order to bring out to their fullest each of the seven principles and seven planes of which the manifesting hierarchy is composed. Of the Life of Brahmā, we are told one half is already passed, one half of 311,040,000,000,000, plus some few more billions of our years! I refer to the *Sūrya-Siddhānta*, an ancient Sanskrit cosmogonical and astronomical work which, from the statements and facts given within it, claims an age of somewhat more than two million years, according to popular interpretation. I think our modern orientalists give its origin as occurring more or less around the beginning of the

Christian era or later, simply on the one ground that the Greeks brought to northwestern India certain forms of computation which are found in the *Sūrya-Siddhānta,* a theory which is purely arbitrary, and based upon no certainly ascertained fact except the self-evolved or "swābhāvic" theories of the orientalists themselves!

TWELVE

PSYCHOLOGY: ACCORDING TO THE ESOTERIC PHILOSOPHY.
IMMORTALITY IS CONDITIONAL: THE LOSS OF THE SOUL.

> Stoop not down, for a precipice lies below the earth,
> Drawing under a descent of seven steps, beneath which
> Is the throne of dire necessity.
> — PSELLUS, 6 (Cory, *Ancient Fragments*, p. 278)

> Devilish (*asurya*) are those worlds called,
> With blind darkness (*tamas*) covered o'er!
> Unto them, on deceasing, go
> Whatever folk are slayers of the Self.
> — *Īśā-Upanishad*, 3 (Hume, trans.)

IN OPENING our study of the holy science which we are privileged here again tonight to investigate, let us begin by reading from H. P. Blavatsky's *Secret Doctrine*, volume I, the last paragraph on page 272:

(1) The Secret Doctrine is the accumulated Wisdom of the Ages, . . .

Next page, second paragraph:

(2) The fundamental Law in that system, the central point from which all emerged, around and toward which all gravitates, and upon which is hung the philosophy of the rest, is the One homogeneous divine SUBSTANCE-PRINCIPLE, the one radical cause.

Last paragraph:

(3) The Universe is the periodical manifestation of this unknown Absolute Essence.

Next page, second paragraph:

(4) The Universe is called, with everything in it, MAYA, because all is temporary therein, from the ephemeral life of a fire-fly to that of the Sun.

Last paragraph:

(6) The Universe is worked and *guided* from *within outwards*. As above so it is below, as in heaven so on earth; and man — the microcosm and miniature copy of the macrocosm — is the living witness to this Universal Law and to the mode of its action. We see that every *external* motion, act, gesture, whether voluntary or mechanical, organic or mental, is produced and preceded by *internal* feeling or emotion, will or volition, and thought or mind. As no outward motion or change, when normal, in man's external body can take place unless provoked by an inward impulse, given through one of the three functions named, so with the external or manifested Universe. The whole Kosmos is guided, controlled, and animated by almost endless series of Hierarchies of sentient Beings, each having a mission to perform, and who — whether we give to them one name or another, and call them Dhyan-Chohans or Angels — are "messengers" in the sense only that they are the agents of Karmic and Cosmic Laws. They vary infinitely in their respective degrees of consciousness and intelligence; and to call them all pure Spirits without any of the earthly alloy "which time is wont to prey upon" is only to indulge in poetical fancy. For each of these Beings either *was,* or prepares to become, a man, if not in the present, then in a past or a coming cycle (Manvantara). They are *perfected,* when not *incipient,* men; and differ morally from the terrestrial human beings on their higher (less material) spheres, only in that they are devoid of the feeling of personality and of the *human* emotional nature — two purely earthly characteristics.

And on pages 21 and 22, beginning in the middle of the sentence:

. . . the differentiation of the "Germ" of the Universe into the septenary hierarchy of conscious Divine Powers, who are the active manifestations of the One Supreme Energy. They are the framers, shapers, and ultimately the creators of all the manifested Universe, in the only sense in which the name "Creator" is intelligible; they inform and guide it; they are the intelligent Beings who adjust and control evolution, embodying in themselves those manifestations of the ONE LAW, which we know as "The Laws of Nature."

Resuming our thought from our last study of two weeks ago, we shall take up this evening an outline of the psychological nature of man, because if man understands *himself*, he understands that *from which he came,* and *which he is* — he understands the universe proportionately with his own development of spirit and of mind and of the percipient faculties that go with the development of spirit and of mind in man. In order to enable us more easily to understand and more clearly to set forth the essential characteristics of man's psychological economy, we shall endeavor

to show how closely these are related to two fundamental theorems, or principles, or doctrines, of the wisdom-religion; and these
two are (1) the law or rather the *fact* of hierarchies; and (2) the
law (we use the term again under strong protest) of the essential
nature of things called swabhāva, meaning, as said before, *self*-
evolution, *self*-formation, *self*-development, *self-becoming*. In it
inheres the foundation of the law of morals. As is obvious, man
is responsible to himself and, because man is a part of other
things, he is therefore responsible to other things also. Likewise,
as a corollary of the foregoing, after death man does not "meet
his Creator," but verily he has to meet and to reckon with his
creature, that which he has built up in himself during his life —
his astral self.

What makes a rose bring forth a rose always? Why does the
seed of an apple invariably bring forth apples? Why does it not
bring forth thistles, or daisies, or pansies? The answer is very
simple; very profound, however. It is because of the swabhāva,
the essential nature in and of the seed. Its swabhāva can bring
forth only that which itself is, its essential characteristic, its own
inner nature. The Stoics of Greece and Rome expressed this fact
of evolution by saying that in the opening of a period of manifestation, it is the *pneuma* — "spirit" — which relaxes its tension,
condensation or concretion thereupon ensuing of the said pneuma
or spirit, and evolution begins, emanation and evolution both
begin, following the causes set up and active in the preceding
period of manifestation. There spring into life coordinately with
the opening of the new period the spermatic logoi, the seed-logoi,
an expression translated from the Greek *spermatikoi logoi*, "spermatic reasons," "seed-reasons," *logos* meaning "reason," hence
"cause," among other things. It was these seed-logoi which were
the fruits or results, the karmas, of former periods of activity.
Having attained a certain stage of evolution or development,
or quality, or characteristic, or individuality in the preceding
manvantara, when the next period of evolution came, they could
produce nothing else but *that which they were themselves*, their
own inner natures, as seeds do. The seed can produce nothing
but what it itself is, what is in it; and this is the heart and essence
of the doctrine of swabhāva. The philosophical, scientific, and

religious reach of this doctrine is simply immense; it is of the first importance.

The habit or, if you like the word, the "law" of swabhāva can work only in that which is itself, because only its own vehicle, its own self, is appropriate for the manifestation of itself — obviously! Hence, the manner of evolution and emanation, and the progress of the hierarchies, are as set forth before; that is, that from the highest, evolution and emanation proceed downward into the more material, and so on down the line of the shadowy arc into matter, until the turning point of the descent is attained, whereupon begins the ascent along the luminous arc.

We must note well, however, that the higher does not leave its own sphere in this process; the higher does not wholly become the lower, and the lower wholly become the still lower, leaving a vacuum or an emptiness above. The higher spheres remain always. It is like the flame of a candle laid at the wick of another candle; and from that one candle you can light all the candles of the universe, without diminution of its energy or of its force or of its characteristic essence. The highest remains always the highest; it is that part of itself, as it were, that is the developing energy acting from within; its skandhas it is which produce, as the Stoics would have said, this "relaxation of tension," this condensation or concretion of parts of itself. A perfect analogy is found in the intrauterine development of man and his descent into incarnation. His spiritual nature does not come down and become his actual body; it remains always his spiritual nature. But from it, it throws out parts of itself, its lower aspects or principles — if we may so put the idea — and each one of these, as the manvantaric cycle proceeds, in its turn secretes, protrudes, and excretes something lower. So that the physical man, the body, is in very truth the "temple of the living God," which is itself the glory thereof, hence a part of the temple; the temple, verily, is the lowest manifestation of the living God within.

Now swabhāva works through the hierarchies. We have returned to these two capital matters time after time, because it is all-important from the philosophic, from the spiritual, and from the ethical aspects that these things should be as clear as possible in our minds. Take, for instance, the cosmogonical relation. We are not created by an extracosmic God; karma, on the other hand, is not an extracosmic entity which said, "I create," and the world sprang into being. The highest essence, the inmost of the essence of every hierarchy, of the practical infinitudes of hierarchies, interlocked and co-related and working together and forming the universal cosmos in which we live — the highest part of each one of these hierarchies is a superdivine monad, which we can call Parabrahman-Mūlaprakriti. And its first manifestation or downward-looking energy, its first breaking-forth into the plane below, is Brahman acting in turn through its cosmic veil, Pradhāna, as you will remember we have before studied; and then comes Brahmā-Prakriti, otherwise called Purusha-Prakriti, which is the cosmic soul or individual, and the nature or the vehicle in which it manifests; the Logos and its universe; the monad and its sheaths, and so on.

Having these things clearly in mind, we can now take up directly and more easily, more comprehensibly, the study of what we mean by the psychology of man. The word is ordinarily used to signify in our days and in the seats of learning in the Occident a study more or less cloudy, mostly beclouded with doubts and hypotheses, actual guesswork, meaning little more than a kind of mental physiology, practically nothing more than the working of the brain-mind in the lowest astral-psychical apparatus of the human mind. But in our philosophy the word psychology is used to mean something very different, and of a nobler character: we might call it pneumatology, or the science or the study of spirit, because all the inner faculties and powers of man ultimately spring from his spirit. But as this word pneumatology is an unusual one and might cause confusion, let us retain the word psychology. We mean by it the study of the inner economy of man, the interconnection of his principles, so to speak, or centers of energy or force — what the man really is inwardly.

Man, like everything else in the universe, is founded upon the decadic skeleton or numerical framework of being — the number ten. Three of these ten elements or planes or principles belong to the arūpa or formless world, and seven belong to the world of manifestation and form. These seven latter principles produce each other on a downward scale in the process of manifestation, exactly as the hierarchies do, each one emanating or evolving a lower, and this lower evolving or emanating a still lower one, and so down to the seventh or lowest.

Man can be considered as a being composed of three essential bases; the Sanskrit term is *upādhi*. The meaning of the word is that which "stands forth" following a model or pattern, as a canvas, so to say, upon which the light from a projecting lantern plays. It is a play of shadow and form, compared with the ultimate reality. These three bases or upādhis are, first, the monadic or spiritual; second, that which is supplied by the lords of light, the so-called mānasa-dhyānis, meaning the intellectual and intuitive side of man, the element-principle that makes man man; and the third basis or upādhi we can call the vital-astral-physical, if you please.

These three bases spring from three different lines of evolution, from three different and separate hierarchies of being. Remember that each hierarchy possesses in itself in embryo everything that the entire universe is and has, the least as the greatest, if we can say "least" and "greatest" of that which is endless — at any rate the least and greatest of any period of manifestation. This is the reason why man is composite. He is not one sole and unmixed entity; he is a composite entity, he is a thing built up of various elements, and hence his principles are, to a certain extent, separable. Any one of these three bases can be temporarily separated from the two others, without bringing about the death of the man physically. But the elements, so to say, that go to form any one of these bases cannot be separated without bringing about physical dissolution or inner dissolution.

Now these three lines of evolution, these three aspects or qualities of man, as said, come from three different hierarchies, or states, often spoken of as three different planes of being. The lowest comes from the earth, ultimately from the moon, our cosmogonic mother; the middle, the mānasic or intellectual-intuitional, from the sun; the monadic from the Monad of monads, the supreme flower, or acme, or rather the supreme seed of the universal hierarchy which forms our cosmical universe or universal cosmos.

It depends upon a correct understanding of the general inter-connection or the interworking of these three separate parts of the economy of the inner man, whether we shall obtain a proper grasp of our future studies. We meet, as we have seen, at every step new ideas, new thoughts, new links with the universe of light and being around us, and of which we also are children. How terrible it would be if we were to reach the limit of all that it was possible to know! On the contrary, endless vistas of growing knowledge are always before us, and we cannot attain them otherwise than by mounting the steps of knowledge one by one.

We have heard it said that immortality is conditional. This is a certain truth. Immortality is not unconditional, and why? For the reasons just pointed out. Man is a composite being and, as the Buddha said in the closing words of his life, "Brothers, all that is, is composite and transitory. Therefore work out your own salvation." This contains the core of the whole philosophy of evolution, and occultly designates ultimate immortality or annihilation for any one manvantara for man as a thinking entity.

Immortality is assured if the central principles which compose the intellectual-intuitional man have succeeded in rising to the monadic plane where they become one with the monad, shining upon them as a spiritual sun. And the loss of a soul for the manvantara is assured if its swabhāva, its essential, characteristic energies are directed downwards into brute matter.

However, the loss of the soul cannot ensue as long as even one sole, single, spiritual aspiration remains functionally active. Only when the unhappy entity has arrived at the point where it can say, "Evil, be thou my God!" when not one single, quivering aspiration spiritward remains, is it "lost" for the manvantara, when its essence, as it were, is inverted, and its tendency is downwards, downwards into the avīchi, where circumstances may bring about an almost immediate annihilation of it or, perhaps, a manvantara of avīchi-nirvana, a fearful state indeed contrasted with the wondrous nirvana of the dhyān-chohans or lords of meditation.

On the one hand we may raise ourselves to become a god, yea, even while dwelling in the flesh. On the other hand we may allow ourselves to sink to the Eighth Sphere, where we pass into

the yawning portals of the Planet of Death. Has it ever occurred
to any one of us to ask: Why are we here? Why, having had an
infinity in which to evolve, are we not higher than we are now?
Has it ever occurred to any one of us to ask whether we may not
be the "fallen angels," those very spiritual "athletes" who in a
former great manvantara failed to win onwards to the goal, failed
to rise, failed to make the goal intended for them, and were "cast
down" to work our weary way upward again?

Again, what do we mean by soul as contrasted with spirit?
We speak of the *human* soul and the *spiritual* soul, and we speak
of the *astral* soul, and we speak of the *animal* soul. But we do not
use those terms in connection with the word spirit. Does it not
teach us that the meaning of *soul* is that of a *vehicle*, an upādhi,
in general; that vehicle, or any vehicle, in which the monad, in
any sphere of manifestation, is working out its destiny? But these
vehicles are *conscious* vehicles, they are living and sentient vehicles having each one its own consciousness and its own thinking
faculty; even these gross physical bodies of ours are not merely
insensible stocks. The physical body has its avenues of dull
consciousness and life; it can feel and, after its own poor dull
manner, it can think.

So, then, the loss of the soul is the loss of that which we,
through interminable ages, very, very laboriously have built up
as our inner temple, our home, in which we should rise to meet
the gods, to become one with them; and more, it is the vehicle
through which we should carry up with us entities below us at
present, but through us approaching our own dignity of humanity
— entities of which the soul is actually composed, even as the
atoms in our physical bodies are infant-souls, physical entities,
embryonic things which we are informing and inspiring, if, indeed, we are not sentencing them to a cycle of woe.

With knowledge comes responsibility. The moral law will not
be thwarted. It cannot be played with. At every step, with
every morn, at every turn, at every choice, we face the right-
or the left-hand path, and we are forced to choose. We must
see to it, every time, whether our feet are to be set upon the luminous arc, or upon the path of shadows leading us downwards.

THIRTEEN

THE PROCESS OF EVOLUTION. SELF, EGO, AND SOUL:
"I AM" AND "I AM I."

Nothing in nature springs into existence suddenly all being subjected to the same law of gradual evolution. Realize but once the process of the *maha* cycle, of one sphere, and you have realized them all. One man is born like another man, one race evolves, develops, and declines like another and all other races. Nature follows the same groove from the "creation" of a universe down to that of a moskito. In studying esoteric cosmogony, keep a spiritual eye upon the physiological process of human birth; proceed from cause to effect establishing . . . analogies between the . . . man and that of a world. . . . Cosmology is the physiology of the universe spiritualized, for there is but one law.
— *The Mahatma Letters to A. P. Sinnett*, pp. 70–71

WE OPEN our study this evening by reading from page 178, and a small portion from page 179, of the first volume of *The Secret Doctrine*, as follows:

Now the Monadic, or rather Cosmic, Essence (if such a term be permitted) in the mineral, vegetable, and animal, though the same throughout the series of cycles from the lowest elemental up to the Deva Kingdom, yet differs in the scale of progression. It would be very misleading to imagine a Monad as a separate Entity trailing its slow way in a distinct path through the lower Kingdoms, and after an incalculable series of transformations flowering into a human being; in short, that the Monad of a Humboldt dates back to the Monad of an atom of horneblende. Instead of saying a "Mineral Monad," the more correct phraseology in physical Science, which differentiates every atom, would of course have been to call it "the Monad manifesting in that form of Prakriti called the Mineral Kingdom.". . . As the Monads are uncompounded things, as correctly defined by Leibnitz, it is the spiritual essence which vivifies them in their degrees of differentiation, which properly constitutes the Monad — not the atomic aggregation, which is only the vehicle and the substance through which thrill the lower and the higher degrees of intelligence.

It will perhaps be well to preface our remarks by reminding ourselves of the two general desires which Katherine Tingley had in mind in inaugurating our studies; first, the elucidation of the teachings contained in H. P. Blavatsky's wonderful work; and secondly, the providing of tests, doctrinal tests, as it were, not tests in a dogmatic sense, but doctrinal or mental tests which each one of us may have in mind to remember and to apply when he takes up some book treating of the ancient religions of the world, or of the modern theories concerning those religions as given out by some modern thinker.

The world at the present day is simply overwhelmed with books of various sorts treating of quasi-spiritual, and of so-called psychic and quasi-psychic matters, and to one who does not know the key doctrines of theosophy, who has not, as H. P. Blavatsky had, at his mental elbow, so to say, the teachings of the ancient wisdom-religion by which all these various matters may be tested and proved, there is place for much mental confusion, indecision, and doubt as to what the real sense or meaning thereof may be, because many of these books are written very ably. But ability in writing well is no sign or proof that an author understands properly the ancient thought; such ability is merely the capacity of presenting certain thoughts — the writer's own views — clearly and often very praiseworthily; but merely praiseworthy writing is certainly no proof that a writer possesses an adequate and sufficient criterion of the ancient truth itself.

Having therefore these doctrines of the ancient wisdom-religion (theosophy) in mind, and properly understanding them, we have tests by which we may prove to ourselves whether such and such a doctrine of any religion, ancient or modern, or such and such a teaching of any thinker, ancient or modern, is in accord with that primeval spiritual and natural revelation granted to the first members of the first human and truly thinking race by the spiritual beings from whom we likewise derived our inner essence and life, and who are, really, our own present spiritual selves. Not being tests in a dogmatic religious sense at all, they are not "necessary to salvation." Heavens and hells do not depend for their reality upon their acceptance or rejection by men, for instance; but we mean that theosophy provides us with tests

which are tests in the same way as are the facts which an expert
in mathematics, or in chemistry, or in any other branch of science
or natural philosophy, is enabled to employ in order to ascertain
when something new comes under his eye, or under his hand,
whether this new thing agrees with the truths already established
by himself and his collaborators in work.

At our last meeting we treated perforce only vaguely, and in a
mere sketch, of the difference existing between the *spirit* and the
soul. The spirit is the immortal element in us, the deathless flame
within us which dies never, which never was born, and which
retains throughout the entire mahā-manvantara its own quality,
essence, and life, sending down into our own being and into our
various planes, certain of its rays or garments or souls *which we
are;* and furthermore, that these rays, in descending, constituted
the life-essences of a hierarchy, whether we treat of our own
selves as individual human beings, or whether we think of the
atom, or of the solar system, or of the universal cosmos.

We have this evening to consider more particularly the nature
and differences of *self* and *ego;* and if we have time we shall
have need to remark at some length upon a doctrine which is
very strange to Western ears, and yet which contains in itself the
core, the very heart of what emanational evolution is, and which
also shows to us what our destiny is. It is that destiny which
leads us both downwards and then upwards, back to our spiritual
source, but possessing — rather being — something more than we
possessed — or rather were — when we began our great evolutionary pilgrimage.

Now before we start upon a sketch of the nature of, and the
difference between, self and ego, let us undertake very briefly
an analysis of what we mean when we speak of karma, for it is
necessary here. As we all know, *karma* is a Sanskrit word, and
it is derived from the Sanskrit root *kri,* a verb meaning "to make"
or "to do"; by adding the suffix *ma* to the root *kri* or the stem
kar, which comes through one of the rules of Sanskrit grammar
from the root *kri,* we have the abstract noun, *karma.* Literally it
means "doing," "making," hence "action." It is a technical term,
that is to say, it is a term from which hangs a whole series of
philosophical doctrines.

We can consider it best from the standpoint of translating it by the word results, because this word "results," or "fruits," seems to be its most general application in the technical sense of the esoteric philosophy. Now karma is not a law; no God made it. A human law, let us remember, is a maxim of conduct or order of right laid down by a lawgiver, forbidding what is wrong and inculcating and commanding what is right. Karma is not that. Karma is the *habit* of universal and eternal nature, a habit inveterate, primordial, which so works that an act is necessarily, by destiny, followed by an ineluctable result, a *reaction from the nature in which we live.* It was called by Mr. A. P. Sinnett, one of H. P. Blavatsky's early helpers, the "law of ethical causation," an inadequate and misleading term, because first, karma is more than ethical, it is both spiritual and material and all between. It has its application on the spiritual, mental, psychical, and physical planes. To call it the "law of cause and effect" is much better, because more general, but even this does not describe it adequately at all. The very essence of the meaning of this doctrine is that when anything acts in any state of imbodied consciousness, it sets up an immediate chain of causation, acting on every plane to which that chain of causation reaches, to which the force extends.

Human karma is born within man himself. We are its creators and generators, and also do we suffer from it or are clarified through it by our own previous actions. But what is this habit in itself, *das Ding an sich,* as Kant would have said, this inveterate, primordial habit of nature, which makes it react to an arousing cause? That is a question which we shall, at some future time, have to go into more fully than we can do it this evening, but we may say this much: that it is the *will of the spiritual beings who have preceded us in bygone kalpas or great manvantaras, and who now stand as gods, and whose will and thought direct and protect the mechanism and the type and quality of the universe in which we live.* These great beings were once men in some former great manvantara. It is our destiny ultimately to become like unto them, and to be of their number, if we run the race of kalpic evolution successfully.

Man, as H. P. Blavatsky has set it forth, weaves around himself from birth to death a web of action and of thought — each one of them producing results, some immediately, some later. Each act is a seed. And that seed inevitably, by the doctrine of swabhāva, will produce the results which belong to it, and none other.

Swabhāva, as we remember, is the doctrine of the essential characteristic of anything, that which makes it what it is, and not something else: that which makes the lily a lily, and not a rose or a violet; that which makes one being a horse, and another a fly, and another a blade of grass, and so on — its essential nature.

In our study of hierarchies in former meetings, we noticed that each hierarchy proceeded from its own seed, its own seed-logos or the highest part of it, its crown or pinnacle; and that everything rolled down from it, rolled out from the seed into being. So the human body grows from a microscopic seed, as it were, into the man we know, partaking of the nature around it, because it is a composite being. All composite things are temporary and transitory. If they were not composite, they could not manifest in any manner whatever. It is the compositeness, the compound nature of them, which enables them to learn and to mingle with and to be one in the manifested sense with all the manifested universe around us.

We mentioned in former studies the wonderful doctrine of the ancient Stoics of Greece and Rome, called the *krasis di' holou*, the "mingling through everything," the "intermingling of all"; when this doctrine was applied to the gods, the ancient Stoics called it theocrasy — not theocracy, which means something else entirely. Theocrasy means the "intermingling of the gods," even as human thoughts mingle on earth.

Now the self remains eternally itself on its own plane, but in manifestation it intermingles, if we may use that term, with the spheres of matter by raying itself, as does the sun; by communicating itself as the divine ray. It shoots down into the spiritual world, and thence into the intellectual world, and thence into the psychic world, and thence into the astral world, and thence into the physical. It creates at each one of these stages, at each plane of the hierarchy, a vehicle, a sheath, a clothing, a garment, and *these*, just expressed by various names, on the *higher plane* are called *souls,* and on the *lower plane, bodies,* and it is the destiny of these souls — garments or vehicles or sheaths of the spirit — ultimately to be raised upwards to divinity.

There is an immense difference between purely *unconscious* spirit-life, and fully self-developed, *self-conscious* spirituality. The monad starts out on its cyclic journey as an unself-conscious god-spark, and ends it as a self-conscious god, but it does this through assimilation of manifested life and by carrying up with itself the various souls which it has created in its cyclic pilgrimage, in them developing its inner essence and through them understanding and coming into relation with other monads and other *soul*-selves. It is the raising of the soul (or rather the souls) through the self, to divinity, that constitutes the process of evolution, the unfolding of the potentialities and capacities of the divine seed.

We may now ask: What is the difference between the *self* and the *ego?* The *individual* self, we know, is a spiritual or rather monadic "atom." It is that which in all things says "I am," and hence is pure consciousness, direct consciousness, not reflected consciousness. The ego is that which says "I am I" — indirect or reflected consciousness, consciousness reflected back upon itself, as it were, recognizing its own māyāvi existence as a "separate" entity. See how marvelous these teachings are, for if we understand this doctrine aright, it means spiritual salvation for us; and if we understand it wrongly, it means our going downwards! For instance, intensity of egoism is the understanding of it wrongly; and, paradox of paradoxes, impersonality is the understanding of it rightly. As Jesus said in the first three Gospels, Matthew, Mark, and Luke, voicing one of the teachings of the ancient wisdom: "He who saves his life shall lose it, but he who gives up his life for my sake, shall find it."

Here we have the real meaning imbodied in a "dark saying" of a matter that we studied somewhat at our last meeting: the doctrine of the loss of the soul. There, in words ascribed to Jesus and thrice repeated, we have the inner meaning of this mystery: the *because*, the *why*, and the *how* of it.

We return to the strange doctrine mentioned before, strange to Western ears, strange to Western thought. You will remember that H. P. Blavatsky frequently describes the processes of evolution and of development as the starting out of the spiritual essence down the shadowy arc into matter, and its growing more and more dense, compact, and heavy the deeper it goes into the ocean of the material world, until it passes a certain point — the turning point of the forces which *arising in itself* urge it forward in that mahā-manvantara; and that then it begins to rise again along the upward cycle, the luminous arc, back towards the divinity from which it emanated as a ray or rays. This monadic essence, this monadic stream, passing into evolution is, like an army or host, composed of a quasi-infinitude of individual monads. We may call them spiritual atoms, unself-conscious god-sparks. They gather to themselves as they descend into matter — which is eternally there from the infinitude of evolving beings in all stages of development which had preceded them — or, rather, they *derive* reflected or indirect consciousness (*self*-consciousness) from that contact and intermingling. They begin to have more than the mere feeling or rather simple cognition of "I am," or pure consciousness; they begin to feel themselves self-consciously at one with all that is. The unself-conscious god-spark is beginning self-consciously to recognize its own essential and inherent divinity. It is developing *self*-consciousness, and this *self*-consciousness is what we call the ego, the recognition that "I am *I*," a part or ray of the All *recognizing* that wondrous truth.

Now consider the hierarchy of the human being growing from the self as its seed — ten stages: three on the arūpa or immaterial plane, and seven (or perhaps better, six) on the plane of matter or manifestation. On each one of these seven planes (or six planes), the self or Paramātman develops a sheath or garment, the upper ones spun of spirit, or light if you will; and the lower ones spun of shadow or matter; and *each such sheath or garment is a soul;* and between the self and a soul — any soul — is the ego. First in order is the self, the divine entity or thing, or monad, behind all; and growing from within it, like a sun developing from within its own essence, along the karmic lines or paths of the memories or "results" or "fruits" brought over from the preceding great manvantara, thus developing strictly according to the skandhas in its own nature, is the ego, contacting and intermingling with matter and the other hosts of intelligences of *this*

mahā-manvantara. The ego throws out from itself — as the seed
will throw out its green blade, developing into the tree with its
branches and its twigs and its numberless leaves — it throws out
from itself its garment or sheath or vehicle spun of light or spun
of shadow, according to the plane or point upon which it is; and
this ethereal or spiritual or astral garment of the ego is the soul —
that is, any soul.

There are many souls in man. There are likewise many egos
in man; but back of them all, both egos and souls, is the deathless flame, the self. Remember that the ancient Egyptians also
taught of the various souls of man, of the manifold selves of man,
of the several egos of man. We have not spoken often as yet
of the ancient Egyptian teachings, because they are exceedingly
difficult on account of being inwrapped in complicate symbol
and allegory; they are the most hid, perhaps, the most inshrouded
with tropes and figures of speech of any ancient system. But the
old truths are there; they are the same age-old teachings.

Now evolution is the unfolding, the developing, the bringing
out from the divine seed within of all its latent capacities, its swabhāva in short; its individual characteristics or the essence of its
being. The whole effort of evolution, however, is not merely to
bring out that which is within each individual seed, but also that
each individual monad, and each ego, and each soul, shall gather
up from the matter in which it works other less progressed
entities which become parts of itself, and shall carry them along
with it on the arc of the evolutionary journey upwards.

Each one of us is therefore a potential Christ, a potential
Christos, because while we are, each one of us, a Christos within,
intrinsically, each one of us is, or should be, a "savior" of his
fellow men likewise, and of all the lower beings under him, under
his guidance and sway. If a man or woman ill-treats or treats
nobly the atoms of his or her body, he or she is held responsible
at the hands of karma, so to say, before the divine tribunal of
his own self; yea, to the very last farthing he shall be held to
a strict accounting. Look at the dignity with which this noble
teaching endows and crowns our human species! What a sublime
meaning do the doctrines of our Teachers have in this light! Man
is responsible; because when he has achieved self-consciousness

even in minor degree he becomes a creator thereby, and becomes therefore responsible to a coordinate extent. He becomes a collaborator and co-worker with the gods whom he is destined to join as one of themselves.

If the life-stream, if the stream of monads, if any individual monad has passed the lowest point of its manvantaric cycles safely, has safely swung past the path leading downward at the midpoint of the fourth round, and successfully starts out on the upward way, along the luminous arc, it is safe to a certain extent, but not yet wholly so, because that same test comes again at the midpoint in each round. But the midpoint of the fourth round is the most critical. We all know what a round is, and the seven through which we must pass before we complete our evolutionary pilgrimage on this planet. But if the monadic spark passes safely through each of the three rounds to come, then in the last round, on the last or seventh globe, in the last race of that globe, he shall blossom out as a dhyān-chohan, a "lord of meditation" — already almost a god. And those of us who shall have made the race successfully shall, after the long nirvana that awaits us after the seven rounds are completed, which nirvana is a period of unspeakable bliss corresponding to the devachan between two earth lives — those of us, I say, who shall have become these lords of meditation, shall become the forerunners, the makers, the developers, the gods of the future planet which shall be the child of this, as this globe, Terra, was the child of our mother, the moon; and so on forever, but always advancing higher and higher up the rungs of the wondrous ladder of cosmic life.

This is the strange and wonderful doctrine, strange and wonderful to Western ears. Endless are the ramifications of thought which spring from it. Think of the destiny before us! Yes, and it is also wise to look at the other side. Let us turn our faces from the morning sunlight occasionally, and look in the other direction. Remember that we have innate and ineluctable moral responsibilities where ethical problems are involved. We have, to a certain extent, knowledge; hence power, hence responsibility. Behind us, trailing upwards, are infinitudes of beings who are less than we. Each one of them is on the same path whereon we have trodden ourselves; each one of them having to go over that same path, stained with the blood from our own feet. And shall they fail for lack of our help? They shall have to pass the danger point, even as we have done; because the teaching is that at the middle point of every evolution there is a downward path, leading into spheres of being grosser and more material than ours.

When our planet first started, or rather first was started, on its course of emanational evolution, the propelling agents in that were the dhyān-chohans from the lunar chain, i.e., those who had run the evolutionary race successfully there; and behind them, trailing after them, we came, seven classes of us, the most evolved, the less, the less, the less, the less, the animals, the vegetables, and the minerals.

Our time is drawing to a close this evening, but there is one point which it seems incumbent upon us to touch upon at least slightly. When Leibniz spoke of the inherent urge in every monad propelling it into manifestation, he spoke from the ancient books, from the Pythagorean and the Neoplatonic teachings, of which he was a student, and he meant what we do when we speak of the swabhāva, the essential nature of a thing. There is, however, one point of his teaching to which we must allude, where he says in substance that our world is the best possible world in the universe. Those of you who are acquainted with the great French philosopher, Voltaire, may remember his book, *Candide*, or "Optimism," in which Voltaire evidently is tilting at the optimistic theories of Leibniz, and in which two of his characters are the inveterately irrational optimist, Dr. Pangloss, and the young man, Candide, Dr. Pangloss's pupil, a young philosopher, a thorough-going selfish optimist, who accepted all the rebuffs of life with great indifference and calmness, and with a smile at human misery. And Voltaire has a passage commenting upon these two characters (*Candide*, ch. vi), where he says, with all that pungent, aphoristic point which is so great an ornament of the French genius, *Si c'est ici le meilleur des mondes possibles, que sont donc les autres?* — "If this is the best of all possible worlds, how about the others?" A very comprehensive remark indeed, and a very true one. It is not the best possible of all worlds. Far from it. It were indeed a weary and hopeless outlook for our human kind, if it were! Yet the great German philosopher was right in this sense, that it is the best possible world which the world's karma has enabled it to be or to produce; and if it is not better, we ourselves are largely responsible for it.

We see in this amusing reference to the theories of Leibniz and Voltaire the true meaning of the word optimism. Our own majestic philosophy gives us a far wider vision, a more penetrating insight into things, a profounder understanding of the so-called riddle of life. *Everything is relative*, one of the greatest teachings of the esoteric philosophy. There are no absolutes (in the usual European sense of that word) anywhere. Everything is relative, because everything is interlinked and intermingles with every other thing. If there were an absolute, in the European sense, there could be nothing but the barren silence and immutability of complete and utter perfection, which is impossible, for there would be in such case, there could be, no growth, no future growth, no past development, spiritually, mentally, or in any other wise.

We now close. At our next meeting we shall take up the study of the so-called hells and heavens, for this branch of our investigation is a very necessary part of the psychological side of our study which we began at our last meeting. We say this evening only this, that all the doctrines and dogmas and teachings and tenets of the great world religions are based fundamentally upon some more or less obscure truth, usually very much obscured by ignorance or fanaticism, or by both. And, in conclusion, let us note well that there are no hells, and there are no heavens, as these are commonly supposed to be, but spheres of life and experience corresponding to each class of the myriad degrees of entities in being. As Jesus is said to have stated in the Christian Gospels: "In my Father's house are many mansions." There are in the endless kosmos innumerable appropriate places of retributive bliss or retributive woe for all grades of souls, and in these karmically appropriate spheres, the countless hosts of evolving entities of all classes find their properly and exactly adjusted places.

FOURTEEN

The devachan ["heaven"] merges from its highest into its lowest degree — by insensible gradations; while from the last step of *devachan* [downwards], the Ego will often find itself in *Avitcha's* ["hell's"] faintest state, which, towards the end of the "spiritual selection" of events may become a *bona fide* "Avitcha." — *The Mahatma Letters*, p. 188

From Kama Loka then . . . the newly translated "Souls" go all (*but the shells*) according to their attractions, either to Devachan or Avitchi. — Ibid., p. 199

Ye suffer from yourselves. None else compels, . . . — Sir Edwin Arnold, *The Light of Asia*, bk. 8

WE OPEN our studies this evening by reading from *The Secret Doctrine*, volume II, page 273, the following:

For the evolution of Spirit into matter could never have been achieved; nor would it have received its first impulse, had not the bright spirits sacrificed their own respective super-ethereal essences to animate the man of clay, by endowing each of his inner principles with a portion, or rather, a reflection of that essence. The Dhyanis of the Seven Heavens (the seven planes of Being) are the NOUMENOI of the actual and the future Elements, just as the Angels of the Seven Powers of nature — the grosser effects of which are perceived by us in what Science is pleased to call the "modes of motion" — the imponderable forces and what not — are the still higher noumenoi of still higher Hierarchies.

This is an exceedingly interesting paragraph. It contains, in small compass, the entire outline of the studies that we have been pursuing for some weeks past.

In taking up this evening the study of the so-called heavens and hells, it may be well first of all to repeat that there are no heavens and there are no hells, *as these are outlined in the exoteric religions.* Those conceptions are based, however, upon teachings which actually came from the Mystery-doctrines and they contain in themselves the outline of a truth, indeed, of a great truth, when properly understood. But while we do not accept the Christian heaven and the Christian hell, nor the Mohammedan heavens nor the Mohammedan hells, nor the literal exoteric teachings concerning them as found among the Buddhists and the ancient Greeks and the Romans, nevertheless there actually are in nature certain spheres of being in which those portions of man's constitution which survive the death of the physical body find *appropriate* dwelling places; they are, in fact, retributive realms or spheres of being, to which are magnetically attracted those parts of his constitution which in him are of similar or identical quality.

Jesus, in the Gospel "according to John," 14th chapter, the second verse, says the following: "In my Father's house are many mansions: if it were not so, I would have told you. I go to prepare a place for you." He said this in the long final address which he gave to his disciples before his arrest and appearance before the authorities, according to the Christian legends.

There is no great religion of the ancient time which does not teach in more or less clear and definite form the existence of certain forces of reward or of retribution, acting after man's death in appropriate spheres in which the so-called soul of man meets with retribution or, as some say, "punishment" or "reward" after physical death. Those spheres in which the soul shall receive appropriate retributive purgation or punishment are called hells in the English tongue; and those in which the soul shall receive appropriate retributive repose and reward are commonly called heavens; and because these words are familiar to Europeans, and represent with fair accuracy the general idea of postmortem retribution prevalent in all great religions, it may be best for us to use them. But we must positively clear out of our minds, wash our minds clean of, all ideas that have been put into them by the miseducation of the dogmatic theologies, if we are to gain a correct idea of what the esoteric philosophy teaches on these lines.

We must remember that we are studying the occultism of the

archaic ages. Now this word occultism meant originally only the science of things hid; even in the Middle Ages of Europe, those philosophers who were the forerunners of the modern scientists, those who then studied physical nature, called their science *occultism,* and their studies *occult,* meaning the things that were "hid," or not known to the common run of mankind. Such a medieval philosopher was Albertus Magnus, a German; and so also was Roger Bacon, an Englishman; both of the thirteenth century of the Christian era.

Therefore, occultism as we use the term, and as it should be used, means the study of the hid things of being, the science of life or universal nature. In one sense this word can be used to mean the study of unusual "phenomena," which meaning it usually has today among people who do not think, or who will not think, of the vastly larger field of *causes* which occultism, properly speaking, investigates. Doubtless mere phenomena have their place in study, but they are on the frontier, as it were, on the outskirts — and they are the superficialities — of occultism. In studying true occultism we must penetrate deep into the *causal* mysteries of being; and, in very truth, we have been doing this in these studies: step by step have we been going deeper into the realm of causes.

Now in order fully to comprehend the destiny of the soul, post-mortem, and before its next rebirth in a physical body on this plane, it is incumbent upon us first to say that there is a vast field of teachings with regard to death upon which we do not feel at present privileged to roam. The reason for our necessary reticence and silence is this, that the teachings with regard to the deeper mysteries of death give keys to mysteries of still greater magnitude and scope, and in ancient days were communicated only to a chosen few, at any time. Any one of you who chooses to look into the religious mystical literatures of the world can prove this fact for himself.

In former studies we have traced the peregrination of the monad from the state of latency into manifestation, *as viewed from below.* Now the monad is a spiritual "atom," so to say; let us call it this evening a spiritual *radical* (radicle), using this word radical in precisely the double sense in which H. P. Blavatsky used it when she spoke of comets as "those long-haired sidereal radicals" — with a touch of real humor in one sense, but also hinting, by the use of the word, at a great truth of the esoteric philosophy with regard to comets in calling them radicals. You know what *radical* originally meant. It meant a (little) "root," from the Latin *radix*, hence its application to a comet as the *root* or the *germ* of a future world. So, also, a monad is a radical, a radical in both the senses in which she used the word: an "aggressive" (in the sense of self-acting, self-developing) entity, and also a root, a germ of a future god.

Now this radical, in order to attain self-consciousness, and conscious self-consciousness, must pass down the arc of shadows until it reaches the *turning point* of the great cycle in that manvantara, and as an integral part of and belonging to the hierarchy evolving in that manvantara. By that time, if its karma is so, it has reached conscious self-consciousness, and is manifesting on our plane as a man. Thereupon it starts upwards along the luminous arc or the arc of ascension, and if it is successful in its cyclic pilgrimage, it finally blossoms forth into a god. We must remember this general outline if we wish to understand clearly what we mean by heavens and hells.

The whole aim of evolution, the entire destiny of the spiritual radical, is the elevating of the consciously personal into the consciously impersonal — so important a thought that we are obliged to say that it lies as the very first conception and as the root of the whole esoteric philosophy. A self-conscious god can be such only because it has a *vehicle of self* to work through; and this is what the spiritual radical lacks when it starts out on its cyclic pilgrimage. Manhood must be raised to godhood.

We may begin to see here the meaning of what H. P. Blavatsky spoke of as the loss of the soul. At every step downward, as its self-consciousness is slowly and gradually evolved in any manvantara, the monad fabricates into itself, or secretes from itself, and excretes from itself, vehicles proper for its cognizing the forces and matter on the various planes through which it passes, and in which it manifests. Those on the higher planes are egos, and each ego secretes its own appropriate vehicle called a soul. Consequently, there is an ego and a soul for each step downward:

a dual vehicle for manifesting the monadic essence on every plane. Through the whole, as a golden cord, runs the self, the innermost consciousness, the spiritual "I am." The ego-soul gives to the monad the consciousness "I am I." The self, however, is the same in all of us. "I am I" is the quality only of the ego. Therefore the important thing is to "save" the ego. The higher egos are saved because of previous salvation gained in former manvantaras. But the lower egos and their souls are built up out of the matter and consciousness of *this* manvantara, and they must be "saved." The state of human consciousness in which we — mankind — now live in this epoch and in this manvantara is called in the individual the human soul, the human ego; and this human soul and this human ego must be "saved," because our self-consciousness is centered therein. We use the word saved, because none better occurs to us; at least the word is familiar. This saving means that the ego-soul must be rescued from the magnetic attraction of matter.

But what happens if its education is incomplete when at the bottom of the arc, before beginning the ascent along the luminous arc, it becomes unable to run the race and fails? Suppose that the pull of matter is too strong and that its attraction is downward. Slowly, in that case, the links with the higher self are broken, the golden chain is ruptured, and the whole effort of the monad in that manvantara is lost. The entity cycling downward is what is called a lost soul.

Now a lost soul has naught to do with the heavens and the hells. The state of nirvana, again, has nothing to do with the heavens and the hells. The heavens and the hells concern only the truly *human* entity: that is, the human ego and the human soul; only this grade of consciousness, for to it belong those consciousnesses which can partake of the conception of, and can experience, felicity or misery. Nirvana is beyond felicity; it is, of course, beyond misery. Its opposite pole is nirvana-avichi, which is the utter contrast of nirvana; it is the lowest point, the nether pole of conscious being.

When the body breaks up at physical death the astral elements remain in the "shadow-world" with the same conscious center, as in life, clinging within them, still vitalizing them; and certain processes there go on, but there is no need for us to take time this evening in discussing what kāma-loka is or devachan is, particularly. When the "second death," after that of the physical body, takes place — and there are many deaths, that is to say, many changes of the vehicles of the ego — when the *second* death takes place, what becomes of the human center, the truly human entity? We have been told that the higher part of it withdraws into itself all that aspires towards it, and takes that "all" with it into the devachan; and that the ātman, with the buddhi, and with the higher part of the manas — which is the so-called human soul, or the mind — becomes thereupon the spiritual monad of man. Strictly speaking, this is the divine monad within its vehicle — ātman and buddhi — combined with the human ego in its higher mānasic element; but they are joined into one after death, and are hence spoken of as the spiritual monad.

The human monad "goes" to devachan. Devachan is a Tibetan word and may be translated as "god-land," "god-country," "god-region." There are many degrees in devachan: the highest, the intermediate, and the lowest. What becomes of the entity, on the other hand, the lower human soul, that is so befouled with earth-thought and the lower instincts that it cannot rise? There may be enough in it of the spirit-nature to hold it together as an entity and enable it to become a reincarnating entity, but it is foul, it is heavy; its tendency is consequently downwards. Can it therefore rise into a heavenly felicity? Can it go even into the lower realms of devachan and there enjoy its modicum of the beatitude, bliss, of everything that is noble and beautiful? No. There is an appropriate sphere, a sphere appropriate for every degree of development of the ego-soul, and it gravitates to that sphere and remains there until it is thoroughly purged, until the sin has been washed out, so to say.

These are the so-called hells, beneath even the lowest parts of devachan; and the arūpa heavens are the highest parts of the devachan. Nirvana is a very different thing from the heavens. Nirvana is a state of utter bliss and complete, untrammeled consciousness, a state of absorption in pure being, and is the wondrous destiny of those who have reached superhuman knowledge and purity and spiritual illumination. It really is *personal* absorption into or identification with the self — the highest SELF. It is also the state of the monadic entities in the period that intervenes between minor manvantaras or rounds of a planetary chain; and more fully so between each seven-round period or Day of Brahmā and the succeeding Day or new kalpa of a planetary chain. At these last times, starting forth from the seventh sphere in the seventh round, the monadic entities have passed far beyond even the highest state of devachan. Too pure and too far advanced even for such a condition as the devachanic felicity, they go to their appropriate sphere and condition, which latter is the nirvana following the end of the seventh round.

Now what do the ancients say in their exoteric religions about these so-called heavens and hells? Every such ancient religion taught that the so-called heavens are divided into steps or grades of ascending bliss and purity; and the so-called hells into steps or grades of increasing purgation or suffering. The esoteric doctrine, or occultism, teaches that the one is not a punishment; nor is the other, strictly speaking, a reward. The teaching is, simply, that each entity after physical death is drawn to the appropriate sphere to which the karmic destiny of the entity magnetically attracts it. As a man works, as a man sows, in his life, that and that only shall he reap after death. Good seed produces good fruit; bad seed, tares — and perhaps even nothing of value or of spiritual use follows a negative and colorless life. There is no "law" of karma; we repeat, there is no "law" of karma. There are no "laws" of nature; we repeat, there are no "laws" of nature. What is a natural "law"? Is a natural "law" a god? Is it a being? Is it an entity? Is it a force? Is it an energy? If so, what god produces it? The word *law*, however, is convenient enough *provided we understand what we mean by it*. Perhaps no better word, in our day, could be found for ordinary usage in writing popularly or in conversation. But do not let us make the mistake of taking abstractions for realities.

In this study of the marvelous doctrines of occultism we shall never move a step forward towards a proper understanding of nature, if we do make this mistake. We must wash our minds clean of Occidental scientific and theological miseducation. The so-called laws of nature and the law of karma are simply the various workings of consciousnesses in nature: truly and actually, they are *habits, habits of beings*. We replace the abstractions of Occidental science and theology with the action and the ineluctable results thereof of consciousnesses and wills in the spheres of being of the hierarchies of life. We are simply abusing our intelligence, stultifying our intellects, when we go around and around the vicious circles of materialistic theory and think we have satisfied our inquiring minds by replacing the work of endless hosts of beings in and of nature with an abstraction called law or laws. Think of it! Do we realize that not one single great thinker of the ancients, until the Christian era, ever talked about laws of nature, as if these laws were living beings, as if these abstractions were actual entities which did things? Did the *laws* of navigation ever navigate a ship? Does the *law* of gravity pull the planets together? Does it unite or pull the atoms together? Nonsense. This word law is simply an abstraction, an expression for the *action of entities in nature*. The ancients put realities, *living beings*, in the place of laws which, as we use the term, are only abstractions; they did not cheat themselves so easily with words. They called them gods. Very good; call them, then, gods. They called them spiritual entities. Very good, then; call them so. Call them dhyānis, or by any other name you please. But pin your faith, direct your intellects, to actual, living beings, to realities, not to nothingnesses, not to abstractions, which have no reality except as modes of speech.

Let us take for example the ancient Brahmanical teachings. There we find many divisions of heavens and hells; but the common one is the division into seven lower spheres or lokas, or hells, or infernal halls, and the seven superior lokas, which we may call heavens. The Buddhist teaching usually gives the number as 21 hells, for which the common word is *nārakas;* and the Buddhists also used the word lokas for the higher spheres; but note well that in all ancient systems, these higher and lower spheres or grades were in ascending and descending steps. There was the highest, and all the others which followed, decreasing in felicity and purity by degrees, each one growing more material and less happy with each step downward, until they passed insensibly into the higher hells, and here again still further increasing in materiality downward until the end of the hierarchy of these stages was reached.

Among the very lowest of these hells the Buddhists placed *avīchi*. This is a Sanskrit word, and its general meaning is "waveless," having no waves or movement, suggesting the stagnation of life and being in immobility; it also means "without happiness," or "without repose"; and below that another hierarchy begins, a new world. What endless realms for speculation open to us here!

We can here but sketch — our remaining time this evening is so short — an outline of the doctrines concerning the heavens and the hells. In beginning with a general outline, we are pursuing the general plan of our studies here. First, we try to give the general sketch, the general view, later filling in the necessary details as we pursue our subject, although frequently alluding to another teaching connected with it, purposely doing so; and in this way we are following the ancient system or method of teaching these different subjects. In our modern Occidental institutions of learning, it is customary, perhaps a rigorous requirement, that the lecturer shall pursue to the end all details of a subject embarked upon: opening one line of investigation and not deviating from it until everything in theory and practice, or supposed to be there, is known, or thought to be known; and when that one line of study is fully exhausted, and when the intellect is completely crystallized in that form, and weary, then opening a new line of investigation. This method is positively contrary to nature. Neither child nor adult learns life's lessons in such artificial fashion. The ancients knew better the psychology of teaching and learning. They built up, first, the general view, such as has a man on a mountaintop with the general topographical view before his vision, whence he constructs a topographical survey which he retains in his mind; and when he goes down into the valley, he is enabled easily to fill in all necessary details. This is nature's method, if we may so speak of it; and it is what is called the Platonic method: first the general, then the particular. In logic, this is called the deductive system, as opposed to the Aristotelian or inductive method, on which modern Western teaching is based.

Now the Egyptians, as we know from their papyri, taught the

existence of many spheres after death, the many planes of felicity
and beatitude and the many planes of suffering or purgation,
spheres which the defunct entity had to pass through before
it reached one or the other of the goals of postmortem life: heaven
or hell. The teachers of ancient times had a way, an allegorical
way, of expressing the course of life after death, and in this
manner kept the intuition alive and active without touching upon
forbidden matters, secrets or mysteries of the sanctuaries. Let
us take in this connection, as illustration, the teaching of the
Mithraic religion, which came very close at one time to ousting
completely the Christian doctrine. The Mithraists taught the
existence of seven (and nine) heavens, each one preceded and
followed by another one, inferior or superior, respectively; and
each one was to be attained by a "ladder," which was only a
graphic, a neat, way of speaking. Of course they meant only that
the ladder was a representation of the steps, grades, or degrees,
which the soul had to climb in order to attain the goal; and the
ladder was likewise a figure of the degrees of the hierarchy — the
steps, the planes, the spheres, of which it is composed. They had
also their seven degrees of initiation, based upon the rising scale
existent in nature; and two other degrees which were held as too
sacred to speak of openly; and this makes nine degrees in all.

How about the ancient Scandinavians? Take the case of their
Niflheim, a word meaning "cloudy (or misty) dwelling place,"
"home," or "mansion." This nebulous region was the ninth, the
lowest, in their system, and itself was composed of nine minor
worlds or spheres. Very careful indeed were the writers of the
Eddas in the way they taught; but they give us enough to show
us the same identical teachings as found elsewhere over the
world. I am speaking here more particularly of the Prose Edda,
which is more open in its esoteric allusions than is the Poetic
Edda, the Edda of verse. Now the Prose Edda tells us that on one
side, the northern, of the cosmic space, were cold and gloom, and
it gives to this sphere the name *Nifl,* "nebulous region," which is a
generalizing of the meaning of the name. Nifl had nine divisions
or degrees, but more particularly Nifl was the name of the lowest
of the nine; still, the Edda gave that name to the entire series of
nine spheres on the north. A middle region was the *Ginnungagap,*

an Old Norse word which can be translated perhaps as "yawning abyss," or abyss (or gap) of abysses; this was the middle or inter- mediate sphere. And then came *Muspellheim* to the south, a place of fire and flame and warmth, not necessarily anything like the Christian hell, for, as a matter of fact, it was nearer like a heaven than a hell; elemental or divine beings lived there, a natural thought to the cold-enduring Scandinavians. Their hell was cold, and the hells of Southrons were hot — these words being merely appropriate ways of expressing things to be easily appre- hended by the people.

What did the early Christians or the medieval Christians believe as regards heaven and hell? Let us choose the descrip- tions of Dante, the great Italian poet, for instance, for he echoes the ancient pagan teaching remarkably in some ways; always in a distorted manner, it is true, but you can see the ancient truth under all that he wrote. How significant it is that he made Vergil, the great Latin poet, his conductor through his Infernos, or Hells, and through his Purgatory; but in due deference to his Christian teachers and the Christian age in which he lived, when he came to the Heavens, which he describes, he has a Christian guide, his Beatrice, and of course he had to follow his Christian doctrines. Dante divides his Hells into nine circles. He divides his Purgatory into seven circles, preceded by the Ante-purgatory, and followed by the Terrestrial Paradise, which make again nine. In each of these Hells, and in each of these divisions of Purgatory — places of purification — he shows the lowest as the most terrible; the second above it is not quite so fearful, and the third less so than the second; and so on up through the eighteen circles or degrees of Hells and Purgatory to the topmost one of the Purgatory, which is scarcely, if at all, unpleasant. Finally, Dante divides his Heavens into nine, and these are topped by the Empyrean, the dwelling place of God and his Angels! ! Thus, there are nine Hells; seven divisions of Purgatory, with the Ante-purgatory and the Terrestrial Paradise — again nine; nine Heavens; the Empyrean: $9+9+9+1 = 28$, divisions of nonphysical life, each one appropriated to punish certain vices or reward certain virtues after death. A curiously faithful, curiously distorted, and often grotesque, parody of the archaic doctrine.

FIFTEEN

THE EVOLUTION OF THE "ABSOLUTE." GENERALIZED PLAN OF
EVOLUTION ON ALL PLANES. SEVEN KEYS TO WISDOM
AND FUTURE INITIATIONS.

Containing all things in the one summit of his own hyparxis, he himself
subsists wholly beyond.   — PROCLUS, *The Theology of Plato*, p. 212

You will not understand it, as when understanding some particular thing.
— DAMASCIUS (Cory, *Ancient Fragments*, p. 281)

Things divine are not attainable by mortals who understand body,
But only as many as are lightly armed arrive at the summit.
— PROCLUS, *Commentary on the "Cratylus" of Plato*

IN OPENING our study this evening we read first from
The Secret Doctrine, volume I, page 570, the first paragraph:

While the Christian is taught that the human soul is a breath of God —
being created by him for sempiternal existence, *i.e.*, having a beginning, *but
no end* (and therefore never to be called eternal) — the Occult teaching
says, "*Nothing is created, but is only transformed.* Nothing can manifest
itself in this universe — from a globe down to a vague, rapid thought — that
was not in the universe already; everything on the subjective plane is an
eternal IS; as everything on the objective plane is an *ever becoming* — because transitory."

You will remember that at our last meeting we were obliged
to confine ourselves to a short review of the subject of the heavens
and hells as doctrinally held by various exoteric religions; and in
considering several theological or philosophical or mythological
teachings about them, we had reached the viewpoint of the medieval Christian theology, as represented in the *Divina Commedia*
of the great Italian poet, Dante; and we found in that really noble
poem once again, as we found in the other systems that we have

mentioned, the wonderful number nine as the root-number of division.

We also touched briefly upon the ancient Scandinavian beliefs in regard to this subject as found in the Younger or Prose Edda, and merely vaguely alluded to the teachings therein contained. We also spoke of the beliefs of the Greek and Latin Stoics; and we might also have pointed out that in an important so-called Hermetic work, supposed to have had its origin in Egypt, but which has been greatly altered by later Christian hands — the work I refer to being called *The Divine Poemandres* — there are seven spheres or stages of being spoken of, as also vague allusions to an eighth, while a ninth is merely hinted at also.

Now turning to ancient Greece again, we find that the great poet Homer, in the eighth book of the *Iliad*, makes his Zeus speak, in addressing the gods and goddesses, of the Golden Chain. Zeus tells the other divinities in very masterful language of his supreme power, and that if they all, the gods and goddesses of high Olympus, were to drag downward at one end of that Chain, and he were to hold the other, he Zeus himself, alone, could drag it upwards with all the gods and goddesses, all the seas and the earths, and hang that Golden Chain, with them all at the nether end, to one of the pinnacles of heaven. What is the meaning of this curious tale? The following:

This Golden Chain represents the concatenation of the living hierarchies which we have studied before — the Golden Chain of all being, inward and outward. In the same address to the assembly of the divinities of Olympus, Zeus speaks as follows: "Any one of you who despises my words and will, I shall cast down into gloomy Tartarus . . . which is as far below Hades as Earth is below Olympus." This shows us somewhat of Homer's representation of the framework of kosmos, which was somewhat as follows: Earth, or rather the universe, was represented as a sphere; Olympus was placed at the upper or northern side or pole; what was called Earth was the next part below; below Earth was Hades; and at the nether pole from Olympus was placed Tartarus. Homer, through his Zeus, tells us that as far below Olympus as Earth is, so far below Hades is Tartarus.

The Greek poet Hesiod, in his *Theogony*, beginning with verse

721, also tells us that if a brazen anvil were allowed to fall from Olympus to Earth it would take nine days to fall, and would reach the Earth on the tenth; and if that same brazen anvil, in continuing its course, were to fall from Earth to Tartarus, it would again take nine days to fall, and would reach Tartarus on the tenth. So the Latin poet Vergil (*Aeneid*, 6, 577–9) has the same general idea.

We see therefore in Greek and Latin mystical thought the same principle of hierarchies and scales of nines and tens that we have met with before. The theory calls for a continuous succession of planes or spheres of being, ranging from higher to lower; repeated uninterruptedly throughout the range of any general hierarchical system of worlds. For instance, beginning at Tartarus, there follows a new subhierarchy, a new sphere, a new egg, of being; just as the Olympus of any one such system is the nether pole of a still higher hierarchy than itself. And so on throughout the universe.

Now this "nine days' falling" of Hesiod's "brazen anvil," and any other similar figure, is simply the well-known mythologic way of speaking, rendering in an easily understood form for the general public, with their sleeping minds, the esoteric doctrines, the doctrines of occultism, that is to say, the facts of inner being, as those are found in all the mystical teachings of all the ancient nations.

This subject of the hells and heavens rests upon several fundamental esoteric factors which we have been studying continuously since these meetings were inaugurated last January. As said at our last meeting, there are in very truth no hells and no heavens, in the ordinary Christian sense at all. But there are spheres of retribution, spheres of probation, which are particular spheres of being; and some of these hells, as described for instance in the Brahmanical and in the Buddhist religions, are actually spheres of near-pleasure, rather agreeable than otherwise; they are described as really very pleasant and interesting places! But they are still lower than the heavens, so called.

We might consider the description of some of the so-called heavens, on the other hand, as not so exceedingly pleasant; the idea being that just as are the conditions among men on earth, so it is among appropriate spheres of retribution or probation or purgatorial cleansing: when the compass of man's life on earth has been brought to its end, everything then moves according to strict analogy and according to strict gravitational attraction. *Nothing can go to any sphere or go into any state for which it is unfit. Everything finds its exactly appropriate and similar goal, or home, or sphere.*

These heavens and hells are *states*, of course; so is earth life a state. But if a thing is a state, it is also the state of a thing; and if it is a thing, it must have place, or position, or locality. That is obvious. So, therefore, while these heavens and hells are states, they are likewise localities, places. The ancient wisdom speaks of them in general by the Sanskrit word meaning "the three worlds" — *tri-bhuvana*, i.e., three briefly generalized abodes or mansions or dwelling places; as Jesus says in the Christian scriptures: "In my Father's house are many mansions." They are states of mind for the entities who dwell therein, and it is through these states of mind that the purgatorial cleansing of the soul-nature is accomplished.

Why does a man go to hell? Because he *wants* to go to hell. Why does a man go to heaven? Because he *desires* to go to heaven. A man goes *wherever he wills to go*. If during his life he has lived an evil existence, it is because the impulses and attractions of his being were such; and can such a soul, inwrapped with earthly attractions, ascend into spiritual spheres? Can the operations of spiritual beings, of the so-called higher laws of nature, attract a man whose soul is absorbed in heavenly aspirations into one of the lower and pain-racked spheres of purgation? Never. Think of the meaning involved in this thought. We must therefore take warning therefrom, and live in accordance therewith. Let us hearken to these doctrines, sublime in their grandeur. Every word of them is pregnant with profound meanings.

Let us go a little farther. You may remember that some months ago we pointed out that in the ancient wisdom, in the ancient occultism, there was a teaching which actually had originated a modern scientific doctrine, born nevertheless in a distorted form of materialism, regarding the operations of nature, the so-called conservation of energy, which is one of the great pillars of modern materialistic science; and also its twin dogma, the so-called correlation of forces. Those two scientific doctrines were born of the supposition that there is nothing in existence but inert, lifeless, soulless matter, impelled by strange and unknown and perhaps undiscoverable impulses, which were called forces, springing forth in some unknown and perhaps undiscoverable way. Science is changing its viewpoints in many directions, it is quite true, but yet some materialistic ideas still remain. Now, in our time, everything is supposed to be fundamentally force; matter itself is supposed to be force. The ideas, as you readily see, still are the same; the words alone are changing. It is, however, a step ahead, but we should not let ourselves be carried away by mere words, providing the thought behind the words is the same and as fully materialistic as ever.

But there are signs that other changes also are rapidly taking place in scientific realms. Within three weeks [1924], the present speaker read the report of an address by an eminent English physicist, an honor and credit to his country, intuitional in some ways, who tells us what the latest discoveries are demonstrating to the scientists of the time. What is this new light? Just what we pointed out some months ago as a fundamental teaching of the ancient occultism, that force is simply matter in an ethereal state; or, to put it in another and a truer way, matter is simply crystallized force, so to say, force and matter being in essence one. This scientist further tells us that modern thinkers are now beginning to believe that matter is not eternal. Of course, we also believe that, *provided that by "matter" we mean merely physical matter*, the basic māyā — or illusion — of physical being. But if we mean by "matter" the substratum, the essential *substance of being*, we differ instantly, for indeed *that is eternal*. IT is Mūlaprakriti, root-substance, the garment of Parabrahman.

Again, what do we mean when we speak of Parabrahman and Mūlaprakriti, essential consciousness and essential nature — or essential substance or "matter"? We mean this: that Parabrahman-Mūlaprakriti can be for any human intellect merely the absolute state of the hierarchy, the highest portion, its flower, its principle, its root, its seed — that from which the rest evolves, or goes out and becomes the manifested universe we live in and know and are a part of. As Paul says in the Christian Gospels, "In him [that is, in It — the Greek allows this translation] we live and move and have our being," i.e., we *are It,* in the sense of being essentially a part of the flower of our hierarchy, the highest *to us,* for It is the root of consciousness of and in *our* kosmical universe or universal kosmos, which latter is all that is comprehended within the zone of the Milky Way, that is, the universal kosmos that we know of. The summit of it is this root from which all these numberless inferior worlds or universes inside it have come forth, have evolved forth; its children the solar systems, the suns, the stars, the planets — all the living beings, all the atoms, all the worlds or universes, in short, the kosmos — all come forth from It. It is the summit, the flower, the acme, as also the seed; it is the absolute Paramātman, supreme self.

What do we mean by the word Absolute? Do we mean God — if you like that word, if you really wish to call it God? But do you know anything about God? Don't we see that the instant in which we stultify our intellects, cripple our intuition, limit the soaring of our interior faculties by speaking of bounds, whether inferred in thought or word, then we reach ends and halt? Remember always in this connection, that beyond and beyond and beyond the kosmical universe, beyond our ken, beyond our imagination, there is always endless life, endless being, for there is no end anywhere; and this thought is what was meant in the ancient occultism when its teachers spoke of that "circle whose circumference is nowhere and whose center is everywhere," the "boundless," the "without bounds." This word Absolute, misused as it is in modern philosophy and even among our own selves, is the exact translation of the Sanskrit *mukti,* or *moksha,* which I will allude to in a moment. Absolute is the modern English form of the past participle passive of the Latin word *absolvere,* meaning "to loosen," "to set free," "to release," and hence "perfected." Not utter, limitless perfection like the immortal gods in some religions were supposed to have, which is always impossible. But the relative perfection, i.e. the summit, the acme, the flower, the root, the seed, of any hierarchy; and particularly for *us* of that hierarchy which is for *us* the highest — our kosmical universe.

Now the Sanskrit words *mukti* or *moksha:* the former comes from the Sanskrit root *much,* meaning "to release," "to set free,"

as said; *moksha* from the Sanskrit *moksh,* with an almost identical
meaning, and probably a desiderative of the same root *much.*
The meaning is that when a spirit, a monad, or a spiritual radical,
has so grown in manifestation that it has first become a man, and
is set free interiorly, inwardly, and from a man has become a
planetary spirit or dhyān-chohan or lord of meditation, and has
gone still higher to become *interiorly* a brahman, and from a
brahman the Parabrahman for its hierarchy, then it is absolutely
perfected, free, released: perfected for that great period of time
which to us seems almost an eternity, so long is it, virtually
incomputable by the human intellect. This is the Absolute: limited in comparison with things still more immense, still more
sublime; but, so far as we can think of it, "released" or "freed"
from the chains or bonds of material existence.

When the great period of the universal kosmic pralaya occurs,
and the universe is indrawn (following the Oriental metaphor)
into the bosom of Parabrahman, what then happens? The spiritual
entities then enter into their paranirvana, which means exactly
for them what is meant for us when we speak of the death of the
human being. They are drawn by their spiritual gravitational
attractions into still higher hierarchies of being, into still higher
spiritual realms, therein still higher rising and growing and learning and living; while the lower elements of the kosmos, the body
of the universe (even as does our physical body when the change
called death comes — death, the twin sister of life), follow their
own particular gravitational attractions: the physical body to
dust; the vital breath to the vital breath of the kosmos; dust to
dust, breath to breath. So with the other kosmic principles, as
with man's principles at his decease: the kāma of our nature to
the universal reservoir of the kāmic organism; our manas into its
dhyān-chohanic rest; our monads into their own higher life.
Then when the clock of eternity points once again for the kosmos
to the hour of "coming forth into light" — which is "death" for the
spiritual being, as death for *us* is *life for the inner man* — when
the manvantara of material life comes around again (the period
of spiritual death for the kosmos is the material life of manifestation), then in the distant abysms of space and time the kosmic
life-centers are aroused into activity once more: first the stage

of the nebular fiery cloud; then the whirling nebula; then the spiral nebula; then the ringed nebula; then the sun and the planets, and finally the human and other beings that grow on the last; each one of these planets having its seven rounds to fulfill in the forthcoming planetary periods, time after time, during endless life. Endless hope and experience lie in this marvelous scheme, but always at every step on the path there is a dividing of the ways for those entities which have attained moral responsibility, an up and a down, for the "moment of choice" is really continuous.

At the present period we have lived somewhat more than half of the mahā-manvantaric cycle; we are, for the mahā-manvantara of our kosmical solar system, at the point where matter has already reached its ultimate degree of development *in our hierarchy*. We have lived, according to the ancient numerical teaching, 155 trillion, 520 odd billion solar years. One half of our mahā-manvantara is gone; and there still remain nearly 155 trillion, 520 billion solar years. More accurately, we have slowly passed the actual lowest point of the great universal kosmical cycle. That lowest point, where matter reached its greatest degree of physical manifestation for us, for our great wave of life, was when the moon had reached the middle point of its fourth round, which was ages and aeons before it became our physical satellite. The ancient teachings are that as the great Parabrahman of our hierarchical system has 100 divine Years of life to live, each Year having 360 Days, and each Year being divided into 12 Months, and as 50 divine Years have passed, therefore on this planet Terra, on this earth, we have attained to or reached the first divine Day of the first divine Month of the ascending cycle of the second period of 50 divine Years. We have, then, come down the cycles for the last 155 trillion, 520 odd billion years, cycling down, in and through our hierarchy, to the lowest point of it on the moon; and have, since that point was reached ages agone, slowly and painfully begun our climb upwards again towards the Ineffable, the summit of our hierarchical system, our "Absolute." Please remember very carefully that we use this word Absolute only in the sense and meaning hereinbefore explained.

How did the Absolute become the Absolute? By chance? There is no chance. There is nothing but endless life and endless consciousness and endless duration, working according to the principles and elements of *inherent nature,* which is called swabhāva in our Sanskrit works. The root-meaning of this word swabhāva is "self-generation," "self-becoming." *We generate ourselves throughout all times:* give ourselves our own bodies; climb our own ladders, step by step; seek our own hells and find our own heavens. And, the whole purpose, the whole effort, of universal evolution, according to the teaching of this ancient wisdom, is this: raising personality into individuality, substance into divinity, matter into spirit, grossness into purity.

Whence then came the Absolute, the supreme self or spirit, or Paramātman, of which we are sparks? By growth from within outwards; and from without inwards. It was once, in incalculable aeons gone by, a man. Think of the sublimity involved in this teaching; consider the almost endless aeons of the past; and that what in its far, faraway origin was a spark of divinity, a spark of another and former Absolute, is now our "God," our Paramātman, our supreme self, of which we are verily the children, and in which we move and live and have our being. What is the main lesson that we may draw from this? What was the psychological mystery hinted at by us in our last meeting? It is this, and we touch but lightly upon it: our human souls are gods in embryo; our human souls were formerly animal souls; our present animal souls will in a future manvantara become human souls. Our human souls in a future manvantara will become monads. Man, if he make the manvantaric race successfully, is destined to be the composite logos of a forthcoming hierarchy; as he now in fact is, in the inferior hierarchy of himself, the logos of the quasi-infinitude of less beings composing his personal nature. Reflect long over this mystery, wonderful, sublime!

Are these teachings not thought-compelling? No wonder they have been held secret and sacred in the ancient wisdom. Why? For many reasons. First, because they *could not be understood* without the necessary spiritual and intellectual training; and yet it is remarkable, it is truly astonishing, how often and how, in so many ways, we see allusions to them in the ancient exoteric teachings of the various religions. Remember that "exoteric," in the ancient religions, does not mean "false." The word merely means those teachings for which the key has not been openly given.

I have noticed and read in some of the translations from the Welsh made for us by our Welsh scholar, Professor Kenneth Morris, teachings that I believe to be taken from the ancient Welsh books, which have caused me to gasp in amazement, that these teachings of the ancient wisdom, so sacred and occult, should have been so boldly put forth by the ancient bards in open language. But I looked again, and I saw how a Master-hand had worked, disguising and hiding while openly teaching. The arrangement, the very beauty, of the imagery used, misled the too inquiring and the too clever mind. But for him who has the key, it is easy to follow. Likewise have I found the same method not only in the wonderful Celtic teachings, but also in the teachings of ancient Egypt, and of other countries.

At a former meeting I touched, perhaps, too slightly upon the much vexed question, as some people call it, of good and evil. That is a subject which properly comes at the close of the studies concerning purgatory, hells and heavens. Christian thinkers have found it impossible to solve this problem satisfactorily to any thinking and reflective mind. But though it is to them and others a much vexed question, to a student of the ancient wisdom it is really very simple. How can a Christian who believes that his God, that his Creator of *all that is*, One who therefore must be likewise the creator of *evil* — how can he reconcile this necessary conclusion with his other teachings concerning his Deity, for instance that God is all good, and from Him proceeds necessarily therefore nothing but good? Is evil then the work of the Devil? What child would not then ask, whence then the Devil and the evil proceeding from him? From God? But is God not all good? Hence the inevitable deduction that God is either not all-good or not all-powerful. Evil would not be, could not be, by their theory, unless a fruit of God's wisdom, because if the case were otherwise, it would exist without the divine permission, i.e., contrary to God's will, which *ex hypothesi* is impossible, since God is all-powerful. The logical difficulty under their theory is complete and unanswerable by it.

What, then, really is the origin of what is called good and evil?

Good and evil arise out of the conflicting action of the multimyriad wills in manifestation. *Good is relative;* there is *no absolute good. Evil is relative;* there is *no absolute evil.* If good were absolute, its opposite, its shadow, or nether pole, evil, must also be absolute. Both, however, are relative things. They offset and balance in nature the one the other, like all other pairs of opposites, such as heat and cold, high and low, day and night, north and south, etc. They arise, as just said, out of the conflict of wills, conscious and unconscious. All the innumerable, multitudinous beings in manifestation are, each one of them, more or less "selfish," more or less seeking its own, hungering and thirsting for sensation of various kinds. Even spiritual evil exists; and there are high agents of "spiritual wickedness," of which the Christian Apostle Paul has spoken, forming the opposite agencies to the high agents of good. The agents of spiritual wickedness are called by us the Brothers of the Shadow, and the others are called by us the Brothers of the Light. The Brothers of the Shadow work in and with matter, for material and selfish purposes. The Brothers of the Light work in and with nature for spirit, for impersonal purposes. They contrast one with another.

These two bodies represent two fundamental paths in nature, the one the right-hand path, the other the left, and are so called in the ancient occultism. The Sanskrit name for one, the left-hand path, is *pratyeka-yāna. Yāna* means "path" or "road," and also "vehicle"; and we can translate *pratyeka* in this connection by the paraphrase "every one for himself." H. P. Blavatsky, as you will well remember, has spoken of the Pratyeka Buddhas, high and in one sense holy beings indeed, but craving spiritual wisdom, spiritual enlightenment, for themselves alone, selfishly, in indifference to the sorrow and pain of the world, yet so pure withal that they are actually buddhas of a kind.

The other body follow the path which in Sanskrit is called *amrita-yāna,* the "immortal vehicle" or "path of immortality."

The one, the former, is the path of the personality; the other, the latter, is the path of the individuality. The one is the path of matter; the other is the path of spirit; the one leads downward, the other path loses itself in the ineffable glories of conscious immortality in "eternity."

Now these are the two bodies of entities representing the two sides of nature, and the conflicts or oppositions of these two sides of nature, together with the battles of will with will, of the hosts of beings in manifested existence, produce the so-called evil in the world, arising out of the selfish activities of the inferior or less developed or evolved entities. Selfishness, therefore, is the root of all evil. The old teaching is true, and that is all there is to it. On the highest planes of being, there is neither good nor evil; there is neither life in our sense, nor death; there is neither beginning nor end of personal action of any kind. But there is what is called in the wonderful ancient Brahmanical teachings, *sat, chit, ānanda; sat* meaning "pure being"; *chit,* "pure thought"; *ānanda,* "bliss"; and this is the state of what one may call the Absolute.

In closing our study this evening, let us remember that the kosmic work of the monad, the *spiritual radical,* is so important that we refer to it again here. It itself can evolve only by raising inferior souls and psychological vehicles into *self-conscious entities,* which thus in turn themselves become monads. THIS IS THE GENERALIZED AND ENTIRE PLAN OF EVOLUTION ON ALL PLANES. This is our great work. This is our high destiny. Our supreme self, our Paramātman, our supreme monad, our highest self, the summit of our hierarchy, is doing that work consciously; we as self-conscious humans are doing it in our smaller way; and this is the whole plan of manifested being, the generalized outline of kosmic evolution, as said just now. No man can live unto himself alone; no man can rise to spirit alone. It is of the very essence of nature that he must, willy-nilly, carry with him, up or down, innumerable other entities and inferior selves, along the upward or the downward path.

A few words more on a very important subject. The ancient wisdom tells us that there are seven doctrinal keys to wisdom and future initiations. During our study of those seven keys we have briefly alluded to five. What are they? These seven keys we may call *sapta-ratnāni,* the "seven jewels" or "gems," or "treasures," and they are as follows. First, that operation of nature — using nature in the sense of the absolute, total aggregation of all that is, inside and outside, backwards and forwards, up and down, right and left, everything, everywhere — which in man manifests as *reimbodiment,* or *reincarnation,* can be briefly expressed as the change of his vehicle or body when his inner state or condition changes; for by the operations of nature he is finally called to gravitate towards, or must go to, another state or condition and place. This is called death, but it is another form of life. There is the first key. Apply it to our teachings in its many and various reaches.

The second key is the doctrine of action and reaction, called *karma.* These first two keys we have but briefly touched upon in these preparatory studies. In future studies we shall find it necessary to go into them more in detail.

The third key is the doctrine of interpenetrating beings or existences, otherwise called the doctrine of hierarchies, which are also inseparable and universally interpenetrating planes or spheres. *Everything exists in everything else.* There are, in strict truth, no absolute divisions anywhere, neither high nor low, neither within nor without, neither right nor wrong, nor up nor down. Fundamentally, there is naught but an eternal Is and an eternal Now. As the ancient Stoics said so finely, "Everything interpenetrates everything else." The very atmosphere we breathe, for instance, is vibrant and living with the multitudinous lives; the monadic essences or lives are in the air we breathe, in our bones, in our blood, in our flesh, in everything. Think of it, then; let your thought go free, release yourself inwardly. Let your imagination carry you into the wonders that these keys open up to our minds. Conscientious study of the ancient wisdom and a pure and unselfish life will be your unfailing guides.

The fourth key is the doctrine of swabhāva, the doctrine of the essential characteristic of any entity, of any spiritual radical; the doctrine also of self-generation or self-becoming in manifestation, thus affirming one's responsibility in and for oneself. This is the most abstruse, the most mystic, of the four keys, hitherto mentioned, for actually it is the key to the other three keys.

The fifth is the key to self-conscious being and existence, a subject to which we have alluded this evening and also in our last study; for the entire aim, method, and operation of universal being is the raising of the inferior to the superior; and this great work cannot ever be achieved by following the "path for oneself," the *pratyeka-yāna,* but by following the *amrita-yāna,* the "immortal vehicle," or the path of self-consciousness in immortality. Make your thought free, I repeat; let it go out released!

As regards the other two keys, I ought to say, perhaps, that they belong to high degrees of initiation. I know but very little of the seventh; my studies have taught me very little about it, so closely is it hid. I know this, however, that understanding and use of this seventh key can be reached by very few men on this earth. As regards the sixth key, we are taught that it can be reached by great effort in the higher degrees of initiation.

This evening closes the last of our preparatory studies. We shall go to higher themes in the future.

SIXTEEN

ĀTMA-VIDYĀ: HOW THE ONE BECOMES THE MANY. "LOST SOULS"
AND "SOULLESS BEINGS." MAN, A COMPOSITE BEING: NO
ABIDING PRINCIPLE IN MAN.

Thus, therefore, the doctrine of the Egyptians concerning principles, proceeding from on high as far as to the last of things, begins from one principle,
and descends to a multitude which is governed by this one; and every where
an indefinite nature is under the dominion of a certain definite measure, and
of the supreme unical cause of all things.

— IAMBLICHUS, *On The Mysteries*, section 8, 3
(Thomas Taylor, trans.)

But at the close of the minor cycle, after the completion of all the seven
Rounds, there awaits *us no other* mercy but the cup of good deeds, of *merit*,
outweighing that of *evil* deeds and *demerit* in the scales of Retributive Justice. Bad, irretrievably bad must be that *Ego* that yields no mite from its
fifth Principle, and *has* to be annihilated, to disappear in the *Eighth Sphere*.
A mite, as I say, collected from the Personal Ego suffices to save him from
the dreary Fate. Not so after the completion of the great cycle: either a
long Nirvana of Bliss (unconscious though it be in the, and according to,
your crude conceptions); after which — life as a Dhyan Chohan for a whole
Manvantara, or else "*Avitchi Nirvana*" and a Manvantara of misery and
Horror as a —— you *must not* hear the word nor I — pronounce or write it.
But "those" have nought to do with the mortals who pass through the seven
spheres. The *collective* Karma of a future Planetary is as lovely as the collective Karma of a —— is terrible. Enough. I have said too much already.

— *The Mahatma Letters*, p. 171

WE OPEN our studies, taking them up tonight at the point
where we left them last summer, by reading extracts
from *The Secret Doctrine*, volume I, pages 206–8:

There are four grades of initiation mentioned in exoteric works, . . .
Three further higher grades have to be conquered by the Arhan who would
reach the apex of the ladder of Arhatship. . . . The *Arhats* of the "fire-mist"
of the 7th rung are but one remove from the Root-Base of their Hierarchy —
the highest on Earth, and our Terrestrial chain. This "Root-Base" has a
name which can only be translated by several compound words into English

— "the ever-living-human-Banyan." This "Wondrous Being" descended from a "high region," they say, in the early part of the Third Age, before the separation of the sexes of the Third Race.

. . . It was not a Race, this progeny. It was at first a wondrous Being, called the "Initiator," and after him a group of semi-divine and semi-human beings. *"Set apart"* in Archaic *genesis* for certain purposes, they are those in whom are said to have incarnated the highest Dhyanis, . . . *to form the nursery for future human adepts,* on this earth and during the present cycle. These "Sons of Will and Yoga" born, so to speak, in an immaculate way, remained, it is explained, entirely apart from the rest of mankind.

The "BEING" just referred to, which has to remain nameless, is the *Tree* from which, in subsequent ages, àll the great *historically* known Sages and Hierophants . . . have branched off. As objective *man,* he is the mysterious (to the profane — the ever invisible) yet ever-present Personage about whom legends are rife in the East, especially among the Occultists and the students of the Sacred Science. It is he who changes form, yet remains ever the same. And it is he again who holds spiritual sway over the *initiated* Adepts throughout the whole world. He is, as said, the "Nameless One" who has so many names, and yet whose names and whose very nature are unknown. He is *the* "Initiator," called the "GREAT SACRIFICE." For, sitting at the threshold of LIGHT, he looks into it from within the circle of Darkness, which he will not cross; nor will he quit his post till the last day of this life-cycle. Why does the solitary Watcher remain at his self-chosen post? Why does he sit by the fountain of primeval Wisdom, of which he drinks no longer, as he has naught to learn which he does not know — aye, neither on this Earth, nor in its heaven? Because the lonely, sore-footed pilgrims on their way back to their *home* are never sure to the last moment of not losing their way in this limitless desert of illusion and matter called Earth-Life. Because he would fain show the way to that region of freedom and light, from which he is a voluntary exile himself, to every prisoner who has succeeded in liberating himself from the bonds of flesh and illusion. Because, in short, he has sacrificed himself for the sake of mankind, though but a few Elect may profit by the GREAT SACRIFICE.

We have here read one of the most sublime passages in this wonderful book; and it is hoped to comment upon and illustrate, if possible, the matters spoken of in what we have just read. We cannot do this altogether directly; the subject is too profound and no sufficient preparatory study has been made; but we can do so indirectly to some extent. It is necessary to do so to some degree because this sublime subject is the seventh of the seven jewels (counting upwards). You will remember that these seven jewels or gems or treasures were given as follows: the first or lowest is rebirth, or rather reimbodiment, better still, perhaps, regeneration. In Sanskrit it is called *punarjanman,* and in Greek *palingenesis,* both words representing practically the same thought: the first element in each word meaning "again" or "anew," and the second element in each meaning "generation" or "birth," "coming into being."

The second jewel, counting upwards, is the doctrine or fact in nature called karma, the doctrine of results. The third jewel is the doctrine of hierarchies, of which the Sanskrit term is *lokas.* The fourth is the doctrine of swabhāva, which we have studied somewhat in former meetings, this Sanskrit word having two general philosophical meanings: first, self-begetting, self-generation, self-becoming, the general idea being that there is no merely mechanical or soulless activity of nature in bringing us into being for *we brought ourselves forth,* in and through and by nature, of which we are a part of the conscious forces, and *are our own children.* The second meaning is that each and every entity that exists is the result of what he actually is in his own higher nature; he brings forth that which he is in himself interiorly, nothing else. A particular race, for instance, remains and is that race as long as the particular race-swabhāva remains in the racial seed and manifests thus, and so forth. Likewise is the case the same with a man, a tree, a star, a god — whatnot!

The fifth jewel, counting still upwards, is the doctrine of evolution, which we have already very briefly studied in the theosophical sense. This esoteric teaching is not the doctrine of transformism, which is, properly speaking, the correct name for the materialistic doctrine of Darwin and of the Frenchman Lamarck from whom, doubtless, he drew the idea. Rather it is the theosophical idea of unfolding, or unwrapping, a doctrine — with its corollary, involution — that is expressed by two Sanskrit words, these being first, *pravritti,* meaning the "unfolding forth" of the spirit-entity into matter, or of matter-lives into spirit-entities, as the case may be; and second, *nivritti,* meaning the "infolding" of spirit-entities into matter, or of matter-lives into spirit-entities, as the case may be.

The sixth and the seventh treasures, or jewels, were touched upon very slightly at one of our recent meetings. We venture now to add a few more ideas to what was said before. The sixth jewel is the doctrine expressed here also by two compound words of contrasted sense: first *amrita-yāna,* a Sanskrit word meaning "immortality-vehicle," "carriage or bearer, or rather path, of immortality," and referring to the individual man; and the other word is *pratyeka-yāna,* a Sanskrit word meaning (in paraphrase) the "path of each one for himself." It is impossible to translate this latter compound word into English by a single word. Both the idea and the vocable do not exist in English. It may perhaps be approached by the theosophic idea latent in the word *personality;* and the mysterious relation of individuality to personality is included in these two compound catchwords or technical terms; and therefrom hangs an entire doctrine or department of thought of the wonderful philosophy of occultism, the esoteric doctrine. With it — as also with the seventh jewel — are connected closely the doctrines of the ancient wisdom relating to the monads of the various classes: whence they came, how they came, yes, and why they came.

We are touching upon all these profound subjects very lightly at present, because they will all recur again and again in future studies, and will in due course be more fully illustrated and explained more clearly.

Now, the last or the seventh jewel, counting upwards, is called *ātma-vidyā,* literally meaning the "knowledge of the self"; this compound is only a catchword as are the others, but it imbodies and hides a doctrine which is truly sublime. You will remember that the present speaker, in connection with this seventh jewel, stated that he knew little or almost nothing of it. This phrase was badly chosen, and perhaps produced a misleading impression. It is well understood that any earnest and devoted student of the Esoteric School can understand at least appropriate parts of this mysterious doctrine — something at least — the degree of his apprehension thereof depending upon his inner state of enlightenment, his fidelity to the Teachers, his loyalty to the principles of the School, and his ability in understanding and penetrating somewhat into the depth of its teachings.

But while this is the case with the students, each one according to his capacity, others higher than we are can understand more of it; naturally, the Teachers understand more of it than we do.

Probably, however, there are not ten men today on earth who can understand this doctrine in its fullness. It is a wonder-teaching that even the Masters have probably not solved utterly. The Masters of the Masters know more of it than the latter do, i.e., the Chohans, as they are called — *chohan*, a Tibetan word meaning "lord," used in the sense of preceptor, or teacher. But the main and essential meaning of this wondrous doctrine, running all through it, is this, which is its keynote: HOW THE ONE BECOMES THE MANY; and this is the most difficult problem that the human spirit has ever attempted to solve.

Take as an analogy, for instance, the monad. To speak of the monad as "descending" into matter is to speak wrongly, though constantly this phrase is used, because it is a convenient method of expression; and if this fact is understood, it is probably permissible as a phrase. But actually, when we come to study the facts, very soon we see and we know that the monad does not "descend" into matter. Similarly, the One, though it is appropriate and convenient to speak of it as "becoming the many," never becomes many, remains eternally itself, the summit of the hierarchy, its root-base, which is this Wondrous Being, the supreme Initiator, on whatever plane it may be placed. Yet the many flow forth from It; and It is their supreme self, their Paramātman.

This, then, is the general theme of our discourse this evening; but because we have no time now to make a complete résumé of our studies during the course of last spring and winter, this evening we shall go over very shortly a few doctrines which were touched upon in former studies, for the sake of brushing up our recollection of them. The first one that we turn back to, then, is the doctrine of swabhāva, as contrasted in meaning with the ideas involved in the kin-expression, swabhavat. This difference in meaning, which is very great, is not generally understood, and the two words often have been sadly confused by students. They are very different in meaning, though both come from the same Sanskrit root *bhū:* swabhāva; swabhavat. (Let me tell you here that the Sanskrit sound represented in English as *a* is pronounced like the *u* in *but* or *tub;* but when the *a* is written as *â* or *ā*, it is pronounced *ah,* as in *father.*)

As just said, these two words are both nouns derived from the same Sanskrit word *bhū,* meaning "to become" — not "to be" in the passive sense so much, but "to become," to "grow into" something. The quasi-pronominal prefix *swa* means "self"; hence the noun means "self-becoming," "self-generation," "self-growing" into something. Yet the essential or fundamental or integral *self,* as said before, does not do so. Like the monads, like the One, the self fundamental sends down a ray from itself, as the sun sends a ray from itself into the darkness of matter; and it is this spiritual ray which "descends" into matter, *self-generating or self-becoming a self-conscious entity in its turn* — the solar light, the sun itself, remaining ever in its own integrity or *ens,* never descending, never commingling integrally as an entity with the multitudinous hosts of matter-lives, its own children.

Now swabhavat is called by H. P. Blavatsky, Father-Mother. It is a state or condition of kosmic consciousness-substance, where spirit and matter, which you know are *fundamentally* one, no longer are dual as in manifestation, but one: that which is neither manifested matter, nor manifested spirit, alone, but both are the primeval unity; spiritual ākāśa; where matter merges into spirit, and both now being really one, are called Father-Mother, the spiritualization, so to say, of spirit-substance. See how we have to hunt for adequately expressive words in our wretchedly imperfect European languages! The Sanskrit word expresses the idea, if you understand it, instantly.

These two nouns, then, as you see, are from the same root, and the two words are closely connected in origin, but they are not the same in meaning at all. Swabhāva is the self-generation of anything, of any entity, of any monad. Swabhavat is the Father-Mother, the kalpic ākāśic spirit-substance, never descending from its own state or condition, or from its own plane, but the quasi-infinite reservoir of being, of consciousness, of light, of life, and the source of what science, in our day, so ridiculously calls the "forces" of nature universal.

These deeply mystical and very profound themes we shall have to go into more fully in the future; but for the present it will suffice to remember that swabhavat is kosmical spirit-substance, the reservoir of being and of beings. The Northern Buddhists call

it swabhavat, more mystically *ādi-buddhi* — "primeval buddhi";
the Brahmanical scriptures call it ākāśa; and the Hebrew Old
Testament refers to it as the kosmic "waters."

Now the next subject which needed a little illustration was the
very solemn question of "lost souls," as contrasted with "soulless
beings." It may be well to say that these three or four subjects
are briefly again touched upon this evening because it has come
to attention that these matters have been mistaken by some of
our hearers. There is an immense difference between "lost souls"
and "soulless beings." A lost soul is one in whom the "golden
thread" uniting the lower thinking entity with its higher self is
completely ruptured, broken off from its higher essence or root,
its true self. The case here is hopeless, virtually; there can be no
more union for that lower self which, at the moment of final
rupture, commences sinking immediately into the Eighth Sphere,
the so-called Planet of Death. A soulless being, a soulless man, is
one in whom the thread has been worn, so to speak, very thin; or,
rather, where the spiritual and impersonal aspirations in this life
and in other lives have been so few, the attempts to unite with the
higher part of the self have been so weak, that slowly the spiritual
ray has been withdrawing itself from the lower part; but it is not
yet ruptured completely. It still remains; and even *one single
holy and impersonal aspiration* may cause reunion. It is not a
lost soul; but so far as the human entity is practically concerned,
it is properly called a soulless being, for the entity lives almost
wholly in his lower principles. Soulless beings furnish those cases
which are popularly spoken of as "men and women *without
conscience.*" They seem to have no moral sense, although their
mental and psychical faculties may still be strong and keen.

These are the worst cases of soulless human beings. Other
cases are those of men and women who merely do not seem to
care for anything that is good and beautiful and true, noble and
high and lofty; their desires are of the earth, earthly; their passions
are strong and their intuitions are weak. These cases are very
common indeed; so much so that H. P. Blavatsky says in her *Isis
Unveiled* that we "shoulder soulless men" every day of our lives.
Look into the faces of the men and the women whom you see on
the streets. Go to town; go anywhere; the situation actually is

a terrible one. There is a full possibility that a weak-souled human being, perhaps beginning merely in giving way to the lusts of the will, and to the passions of the mind, and to the instincts of the lower nature, may, little by little, but inevitably and surely, starve out, or wear away by attrition, all the attachments of the higher ray which bind it into the lower nature, and which, if they were fully strong and active, would make the man (or woman) a walking god among us; verily, a god in the flesh. Instead of this, in the worst cases of the soulless being, you would have before you little more than a human shell (alive, but *spiritually almost dead*) in the man or the woman, as the case may be. A soulless being was once an insouled man or woman who, before the former state, had the same chance successfully to run the race that we all have. This is indeed a solemn verity, and one which H. P. Blavatsky has told us should be taught and reiterated in our teaching, because it is truly helpful as a warning. Not one of us is absolutely safe at this midway stage of our evolutionary journey; for not one of us knows what he is capable of, either for good or ill.

There is the truth; and it is no trifling matter. Is there any reason for wonder that all our teachers have told us repeatedly that every teaching that is given in the School is founded upon what men commonly call ethical principles of conduct, and must be studied in that light? It is the only thing that, put into sincere practice, will save us surely; for these principles come first and in the middle and at the end of our studies.

In future studies we shall have to trace to the end the destiny of these two classes of beings; but it may be well to say a few words now of the fate of the lost soul. There are two general classes of these: the lower, but not the worse; and the higher, the worse. In order to make the meaning of this very difficult subject more clear, I shall have to go into a new but collateral thought, which is the key: *man is a composite being.* On this fact of human nature reposes a most wonderful truth which is at the foundation of the marvelous psychological doctrines of the Lord Gautama Buddha. It is as follows: there is no abiding principle whatsoever in "man." Fix this like steel into the core of your minds. It will save you from myriad dangers if rightly understood. "Man" is not his higher nature; "man" is that which is called the "human nature." Do you realize how greatly men and women live in what the Hebrews call the nephesh, i.e., live in their astral souls? To a certain extent such unison with our lower principles is necessary; but to follow the beautiful old simile of the ancient philosophers, the astral soul should be our vehicle, our bearer; so to say, it should be made a horse to carry us on our journey; or, to change the figure, a chariot in which we should ride; a horse which we must drive. We, the inner self, should govern and drive our astral steed, but should never allow it to control us.

In order to make this more clear, examine the diagram below:

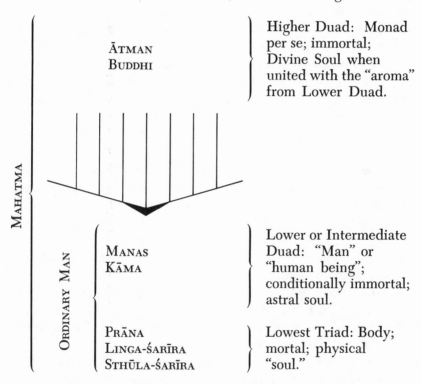

ĀTMAN
BUDDHI

Higher Duad: Monad per se; immortal; Divine Soul when united with the "aroma" from Lower Duad.

MAHATMA

ORDINARY MAN

MANAS
KĀMA

Lower or Intermediate Duad: "Man" or "human being"; conditionally immortal; astral soul.

PRĀNA
LINGA-ŚARĪRA
STHŪLA-ŚARĪRA

Lowest Triad: Body; mortal; physical "soul."

You will notice that man's seven principles and elements are divided into three separate parts: a lowest triad, purely mortal and perishable; an intermediate duad, psychical, composite, and mostly mortal, kāma-manas, the "man" proper, or "human nature"; and a higher duad, ātma-buddhi, immortal, imperishable, the monad. At the death of the human being, this higher duad carries away with it all the spiritual essence, the aroma, of the lower or intermediate duad; and then the higher duad is the higher self, the reincarnating individuality, or egoic monad. Man's ordinary consciousness in life at this stage of evolution is almost wholly in the lower or intermediate duad; when he raises his consciousness to become one with the higher duad, he becomes a Mahatma, a Master.

Now this lower part of the nature is composite. There is nothing permanent per se in it whatever; as an entity, nothing abides. It is ordinary man as he is today, and in him there is no abiding *self-principle* whatsoever. If you fasten your thoughts and your affections to the things of the lower nature, you will de facto, of necessity, follow it, and *become* it, as outlined and shown in and by the doctrine of swabhāva. *As a man thinks, so is he!* The Hebrew words in this old saying, which is taken from Proverbs, chapter 23, verse 7, are Englished: "As he thinketh in his heart *(nephesh)*, so is he," but the Hebrew word nephesh used here really means "As he thinks in his *lower nature, that he is (becomes)*." A Sanskrit commentator, Yāska (*Nirukta*, 10, 17), in his glossary on a certain Vedic text, has the following remark, exactly to the point on the same subject: *Yad yad rūpam kāmayate devatā, tat tad devatā bhavati* — "Whatever body (or form, or shape) a divine being (divinity) longs for (wants, desires, i.e., gives himself up to), that very thing the divine being becomes." Here is the secret of the whole thing. We *are what we make ourselves,* our own children. Nothing but that. And, if our thoughts are upwards, we come finally into the companionship of the divinities; and, before reaching them, come into the companionship of the holy Teachers, because *we make ourselves such, we become like them;* and they, in turn, answer the call.

But if, on the contrary, our thoughts are running downwards, and we wear away the silver thread or the golden thread which binds us to our higher nature, we then naturally gravitate or go downwards: down, down, down, until at last the final rupture of the golden chain or thread comes, and the soul becomes a lost soul, a lost astral soul; and its destiny is as follows. There are two classes of this kind of soul, as remarked before. The first class is the lower but not the worse; it consists of those human beings on this planet (or on any other planet which possesses a humanity similar to ours) who, through native weaknesses of soul and from lack of spiritual attraction upwards, go to pieces after a certain interval of time, *long or short as the case may be:* the lower part of the nature, being composite and impermanent and nonenduring, following natural laws finally simply breaks up and vanishes much as the human body dies and decays. That is the end of it; it is finally annihilated.

The monad of such a soul, meanwhile, there being nothing, no aroma of aspiration or yearning upwards, to take away from that life or from those lives — because, mind you, it is perfectly true that lost souls as well as soul-beings can reincarnate; they can indeed; there are children born lost souls; as a fact it is very rare, perhaps, but the fact can and does take place — the monad, I say, of such a lost soul, in due course of time "reincarnates" again; and the lost soul episode is like a blank page in its "book of lives."

The second class, and the worse by far, are those in which the soul is vitally strong. They are those who are *spiritually* evil, paradoxical as it may sound; those which the Christian teachers have spoken of in the New Testament as beings of spiritual wickedness and iniquity. One may wonder how it can come to pass that a being which has ruptured the golden thread can still have spiritual qualities or parts. That is one of the dark and solemn mysteries which we may have to go into in more detail later. We have no time this evening to do so, beyond pointing out that the explanation lies in an understanding of esoteric psychology, and of the nature of high astral matter. But let me point out this: if a soul can receive an impress, can receive an impulse, and it most certainly does, that impress or impulse will carry it on until its initial strength is exhausted, until the impulse no longer exists, until the impulse has worked itself out. Through many, many, lives of spiritual evildoing, these beings who have eventuated as lost souls have built up through the intensity of their will a bank account, so to speak, of certain forces of nature, impulses of evil, of pure matter, running hot and strong. And when I say hot I do not mean in the ordinary emotional sense, as when one speaks of the "heat of passion." All such passion is dead. Nay, but running hot like the fires of hell: revenge, hatred, and antagonism to anything that is highly good or nobly beautiful, and all such things. These impulses here exist, and they have a spiritual source, for *they are degraded spiritual energies,* spirit fallen and crystallized into matter, so to speak. Very difficult to explain, indeed, is this abstruse subject; but this is the gist of it. Lastly, I might add that these beings can (and do), under certain conditions, go far lower: they enter the lower path, and go still farther down; and if the evil be strong enough in certain rare cases, their terrible destiny is what the Teachers have called an avīchi-nirvana (avīchi being a generalized term for what is popularly called hell), aeons of unspeakable misery, self-imposed, until final dissolution ensues — and nature knows them no more.

Of course you remember that we have studied the subject of hells and heavens, but as yet we have had no time to go into this matter at length. Avīchi is a generalized term for places of evil realizations (but not of punishment in the Christian sense), where the will for evil, and the unsatisfied evil longings for pure selfishness, find their chance for expansion — and final extinction of the entity itself. Avīchi has many degrees, or grades. Nature has all things in her; if she has heavens where good men and true men find rest and peace and bliss, so has she other spheres and states, where go or gravitate those who must find an outlet for the evil passions burning within. They, at the end of their avīchi-nirvana, go to pieces and are ground over and over, and vanish away finally like a shadow before the sunlight in the air — ground over in nature's laboratory.

Now you remember it was pointed out in other studies that in our esoteric teachings there are no "laws" of nature, and this for two reasons: first, because there is no such thing as "nature." Nature is not an entity; it is an abstraction. Nature is not a goddess or a god; it is not a being or a planet; it is not a sphere or a universe. Nature is the abstract aggregate, so to speak, the immense aggregate, of all beings and things, interblending and acting and interacting upon each other: spiritual, intermediate, and lower; and their interblending and interconnection produce what we call nature. The beings here referred to, of course, are of all grades, from the most material, the most degraded, up to the highest, of any hierarchy. And the second reason is that these aggregated beings that we call very conveniently by the term of nature are not "ruled" by "law." Who or what makes any laws that nature shall or must follow or does follow? No one, neither devil nor god. But the query may and ought to arise: does not nature follow certain courses, and when the circumstances and conditions are identical, are not those courses always the same, which are what we call *laws?* Of course, yes; nobody denies a fact. We deny the explanation. Explanations are important. If a man comes to you and says something to you and you find that he is merely talking, giving you words when you want the bread of life, are you going to take what he says for truth? Are you going to take the words only, and be satisfied with husks? Or are you going to think, and say: "My dear sir, I have looked into what you tell me; what you say is merely words; nobody denies the facts that are, but I want an explanation of those words and of those facts. I want something that will feed my soul." Do you get any food for your soul when you hear mere talk about mechanical, incomprehensible laws of nature? Do you realize that no great thinker in antiquity at any time ever used such empty language as laws of nature with the concomitant ideas — or lack of ideas? Never. The expression containing the notion "laws of nature" is a modern product derived from two sources: first from the Christian religion; and second from modern scientific materialism. Men, during all the ages, have been fully aware that nature pursued certain very regular courses, modernly called laws, and always followed the same courses; but our forebears had other and wiser explanations of these regular courses in natural phenomena, for they knew more of the inner mysteries of being, because they had true religion behind and within themselves; they had a universal philosophy; and last but not least they had what were called initiates who personally could go behind and into nature, enter into her and know her at first hand.

Now what causes nature to act as she does? The modern scientist will tell you that he means by the laws of nature those sequences of events which always happen in the same way when the circumstances and conditions are the same; the regular order of phenomena and forces. The Christian theologian tells you what he means by the laws of nature probably somewhat as follows: "Well, brother, it is probably the Will of God Almighty who, it is true, has not vouchsafed to us a full explanation of these difficult problems; but it is fundamentally the Divine Will which has once and for all time created the machine of nature and has set it to running." About two or five or six hundred years ago these gentlemen had another explanation, somewhat different from the above, because modern science had not yet begun to be aggressively vocal with views or a view of its own; and this other theological explanation was that it was God Almighty Himself who personally and actively guided and ordered these things which nature produces. "He sent his rain upon the just and the unjust; He caused the sun to shine, and the rain to fall," and much more to the same tune. But then came along certain skeptical thinkers and they said, "Ha, ha, God the Creator! Then He created diseases; He creates the evils in men's hearts. It must be so, not otherwise, because He created man and all things else and, being all-wise, He must have known what He was doing. Therefore, why punish a man for doing what he cannot avoid doing, because God created man and his mind and his heart and his will?"

So the theologians' later idea, apparently, was that God manufactured the world with His own Almighty Hand, and set it to spinning, and set the various elements thereof each to running in its own way, and let it go forth with a primal impress of the Divine Intelligence upon it.

I think that I am quoting correctly the early modern theological idea.

Now the initiates, knowing nature's arcana, had words fitted to express exactly what they desired to say; words which are impressive and which are not mere abstractions, although when convenient they too used abstractions; they used such words as principles and elements of nature. It is quite true that such words are catchwords, technical words; but they knew precisely what they meant by them. They also spoke mystically and theologically of the "gods." It is one of the most lamentable things for scholars today, that owing to the deliberate and willful suppression by the Christian Church of so many of the truths of antiquity, the average scholar or student has no more idea of what the ancients meant by the gods and their actions than he has of what is taking place at this moment on the star Sirius. Yet, when understood and properly explained, polytheism is seen to be a wonderful and a sublime teaching. It does not mean, for instance, that *each god* is as great and as single as, or omnipotent and omniscient like, the Christian theological notion of their God. Not at all. The gods, i.e., spiritual entities, are the higher inhabitants of nature. They are an intrinsic part of nature itself, for they are its informing principles; they are as much subject to the *wills* of still higher beings — call these wills the laws of higher beings, if you will — as we are, and as are the animals below us. We are gods to the beings composing our bodies. The atoms in our body are, in their way, conscious, and we are like gods to them. And what they might call the laws of nature are *what we think* and *what we will*. Nature is conscious from beginning to end, in varying degrees; although in reality there is no beginning and no end, which are vain dreams.

Furthermore, nature has two aspects, a positive aspect and a negative aspect. Please understand that I am using the word nature, with the meaning pointed out before, because the ordinary expression is convenient, the term is understood. If a speaker has to spend some three minutes or more in order to explain each time anew an already explained use of a word, he will never arrive at the end of what he wishes to say; so, once having made an explanation of what we mean by nature and laws, we may use these or other common words because they are convenient. H. P. Blavatsky also constantly speaks of the laws of nature, and the fundamental law of karma; so again does Katherine Tingley constantly speak of the higher law. Who has not heard highly educated people say that the sun "rises in the east"? Of course they and we know that the sun does not rise in the east. Men very frequently find it useful and convenient to use ordinary language in order intelligently to voice a thought. But this does not mean that they should be held to rigid literal account for what every sane man should know perfectly well is merely a convenient mode of expression.

The so-called laws of nature, therefore, are the *action and interaction and interplay of consciousnesses and wills* — in the kosmos — not so much considered as personalized consciousnesses and wills, but by us those words are used more as abstractions, meaning the combined and aggregate action-results of all consciousnesses and wills in the kosmos. Yet actually, when *traced to causes*, to their sources, these laws are the consciousnesses and wills in action of the multimyriad hosts of beings that *compose and are "nature" itself,* working through, in, and by, "matter," their vehicles — abstractly called nature. Nature has these two poles or sides: the positive pole or side and the negative pole or side. Examine yourself closely, and you will find that even your mind is dual, like everything else, for it mirrors nature. It has its passive side, its unconscious reflexes, just as the body has, just as nature has. It has also its positive or active side. There is a great difference between the conscious will and the unconscious will. Take the body as an instance of what I am trying to say; e.g., the beating of the heart, the automatic winking of the eyes, the processes of digestion. These are unconsciously performed acts, under the control of unconscious or semiconscious elemental entities; when normally functioning, man's will has nothing self-consciously to do with them. They represent the passive side of his will as expressed through those elemental minds. But he also has an active or positive side in which he wills and thinks, and acts accordingly, and for these latter things he is held responsible, he incurs karmic responsibility.

So is it exactly the same in nature, as is illustrated by this example of the passive and active wills in man's own mind and body. The laws of physical nature are the action-results of the passive side of the beings and consciousnesses who and which compose what is called nature; and *the higher those beings are, the less is their active or positive side manifest* on the lower planes.

Work therefore with nature, and not against her; violate none of her laws, if you desire health and happiness. Remember what H. P. Blavatsky says in *The Voice of the Silence* — let us paraphrase it: work with nature and follow her; become one with her, and she will make obeisance unto you as an active, *self-conscious* co-worker — a master. Happiness can be found only in obedience to this fundamental truth of inseparable unity. There is no happiness in unbrotherhood, in acting solely for yourself, in trying to impose your personal will on others. *It is by giving* that life is found in all its beauty, by giving the self to the All. There is no happiness like it; there is no way for inner development to come so quickly and so surely and so safely to the student as that which lies in giving up the personal self to nobly impersonal aims. It is the way to peace and power.

Let us occupy the few more minutes of time that we have in referring to an interesting phenomenon of nature that took place during this last summer. I refer to the near approach of the planet Mars to Earth; and I speak of this with intent, because it is going to illustrate a point in the substance of our theme.

You will doubtless have heard how our scientists have concluded — they say that their theory is true, but it is absolutely false according to theosophy — that the planet Mars is older than the Earth; and the sole reason for their saying this is because when they examine what they can see of the surface of Mars through their telescopes, they see no sign, certain and convincing to all, of even vegetable life. Apparently, they see no particular organic activity of any kind on that ruddy sphere; and they at once jump to the conclusion that Mars is dead, in a state something like that of the moon, and that therefore it is very much older than our planet Earth. In the first place, to the student of the ancient wisdom, the "age" of a planet may be of two kinds. Does it mean *older in spiritual experience* — because, remember, a planet is an "animal" in the Greco-Latin sense, and "animal" means "living being," for it is a hierarchy of lives — or does it merely mean that the physical sphere is older than ours?

Now the teaching of the ancient wisdom is that Mars is *younger* than the Earth. Its body, its physical sphere, is younger; but, at the present time, it is in a state of "obscuration." It is what we may call asleep; it is more than merely asleep, actually, for the vastly larger part of its hosts of lives, of its living entities, have left it in order to go to higher spheres or globes of the Martian planetary chain. But this again does *not mean* — one has to be very careful in the use of expressions in our studies — that there is *no life* on Mars. When our own physical body is asleep, does it mean that it is in decay, that it is dead? Are there no vital processes going on in the sleeping human body? Of course there are, many: recuperation, reinforcing of the bonds of the inner nature; not of the inner nature itself, but there is the strengthening of the bonds connecting the vital astral entity with it.

There are — and this will illustrate another point — on the planet Mars in its present state of obscuration certain beings left there by the receding life-wave of Mars when that planet went into obscuration; and these beings are called in the Sanskrit language *śishtas,* meaning "remainders" or "remains," i.e., those whose duty it is to keep the seeds of life on that planet until the incoming flow of the returning life-wave in the new manvantara to come shall find these bodies ready for them and in all ways appropriate. Now these śishtas are of seven kinds: three elemental; the mineral; the "plant"; the "beast"-type there, which represented the human on Mars; and one other. There are certain ones of these śishtas which are not at all of the lower types; they *must have been* higher than the average of its humanity when that planet went into obscuration, in order to provide for the more evolved humanity coming down on its succeeding round fit and appropriate vehicles for the new life cycle, or manvantara, there. Generally, then, the śishtas are those superior classes — each of its own kind and kingdom — left behind on a planet when it goes into obscuration, in order to serve as the *seeds of life* for the inflow of the next incoming life-wave when the dawn of the new manvantara takes place on that planet.

Venus, on the contrary, is now actively engaged in its last round. The planet Mercury, on the other hand, is just beginning its last round. Both these planets are far older than the Earth. Mars is younger — I am not here talking of the *spiritual age;* I am talking only of the age of the physical body, the sphere. You will find it generally the law (and I am using this term law, remember, because it is convenient), you will find it, generally speaking, a physical fact of nature in our solar system that the farther a sphere (or planet) is from the sun, the *physically* younger it is. Mars, as a matter of fact, has ended its third round. We of the Earth are in our fourth; Venus is in its seventh and last; and Mercury is just beginning its seventh.

I have brought up this matter, because there are some who have misunderstood H. P. Blavatsky's teaching in *The Secret*

Doctrine regarding the six companion-globes of the planetary earth-chain, saying that we came to Earth from the planet Mars which is thus made one of the globes of the planetary earth-chain; that we are now on Earth; and that we shall in the future (next) manvantara go to Mercury, which is also made one of the planetary earth-chain.

This is utterly wrong. As we have just said, Mercury is in its *seventh* round; we are in our *fourth*, and our next round will be our fifth. It is true that Mars has ended its third round; but while the planets farther from the sun generally are the younger, physically, than those nearer it, this does *not mean that they are necessarily the younger spiritually.* For instance, you may take the planet Saturn. The planet Saturn, spiritually, is farther advanced than is the planet Mars, or than is our planet Terra.

If you take up a book of astronomy and compare the varying density of the planets as there given in the tables, you will have a rough-and-ready, and very generally accurate, rule by which to go in order to find out which of the physical planets are *physically* older than others. But then this does not refer to spiritual age or evolution; and this fact shows the complexity that confronts the student in his study of these doctrines, which really are very simple, but seem complex to us because our minds are matter-minds and not spirit-minds. It is difficult to think about such things with the minds we have, because they are matter-built. They go to pieces at our death; and these subjects are based on spiritual facts. Hence the confusion under which Mr. Sinnett and others who followed his lead have labored — even to the extent of denying their own teachers!

The planet Saturn is surrounded with belts and — I am in very deep water here and I wish to speak slowly so as not to give a mistaken impression — the planet Saturn is the last, counting outwards from the sun, of the seven sacred planets of the ancients. As regards our solar system, Uranus and Neptune, certainly not the latter, really do not belong to it. Actually, physically, they do, because they are under that system's influence, somewhat like visitors entertained in a home; but they do not belong to or form a part of the septenary of the seven sacred planets of antiquity of which you all doubtless have read. Those seven sacred planets *provisionally* may be named as follows: Saturn, Jupiter, Mars, Sun, Venus, Mercury, and Moon. I say provisionally, because there is much more behind this matter of the seven sacred planets than appears openly. For instance, the sun and the moon are reckoned in the above list as *two substitutes* for the two real planets; and Mars — to a certain extent — is in the same category. We can say no more of this here.

Shall we say that the sun and moon *represent* two other planets?   Let us take provisionally the list as usually given, including the sun and the moon: each one of these seven globes is a body like our own earth in that each is a septenary chain, sevenfold in composition — six other superior globes of finer matter above the physical sphere or globe, just as we humans have our six principles above this bearer or carrier miscalled a principle, which we call our body. This does not apply in toto to the moon, because the moon is dead; yet even the moon has its six companion-globes. The mysteries concerning the moon, I may remark in passing, are more than interesting, and we shall sometime go into them as far as we can properly do so; but excepting the moons, all the other globes and planets of the solar system have, each one, six companion-globes of finer matter, all fully alive, unless in obscuration; and in the planetary life these form a peculiar analogy with man's seven principles, for if we could see our own principles, could see what the plan of each principle is, we should find that it is an actual rūpa or form. Yet let me here enter a caveat: the six companion-globes of any planet or other sidereal body are *not*, really, the six principles of such a body, *for each one of these seven globes forming part of a chain has its own individual seven principles and elements.* So each planet or sidereal body has its six companion-globes, forming together a planetary chain, and *only those globes which are on the same kosmic plane* of nature or being are physically visible to each other. For instance, we can see only the fourth (planetary) plane globes of each of the other planetary or sidereal chains, because we are on the fourth planetary plane, as they are. If we were on the kosmic plane above us, we should see two Jupiters, two Saturns, and so forth.

The sun also is septenary, as said just now. A wonderful

teaching lies here in that connection. The moon, dead as it is, has also six companion-globes; and when we leave this earth in obscuration at the close of this earth-round, and go to the globe above this, we shall see then the two lunar bodies belonging to that plane, and also two suns.

We now close our evening's study, and express the hope that at the next meeting we shall have more opportunity and a clearer field to go at some length into the truly sublime subject which H. P. Blavatsky has set down for us in *The Secret Doctrine* in the extracts first read this evening.

SEVENTEEN

THE SILENT WATCHER.

For countless generations hath the adept builded a fane of imperishable rocks, a giant's Tower of INFINITE THOUGHT, wherein the Titan dwelt, and will yet, if need be, dwell alone, emerging from it but at the end of every cycle, to invite the elect of mankind to co-operate with him and help in his turn enlighten superstitious man. And we will go on in that periodical work of ours; we will not allow ourselves to be baffled in our philanthropic attempts until that day when the foundations of a new continent of thought are so firmly built that no amount of opposition and ignorant malice guided by the Brethren of the Shadow will be found to prevail.

But until that day of final triumph someone has to be sacrificed — though we accept but voluntary victims. The ungrateful task did lay her [H.P.B.] low and desolate in the ruins of misery, misapprehension, and isolation: but she will have her reward in the hereafter for we never were ungrateful. As regards the Adept — not *one of my kind*, good friend, but far higher — you might have closed your book with those lines of Tennyson's "Wakeful Dreamer" — you knew him not —

> "How could ye know him? Ye were yet within
> The narrower circle: he had wellnigh reached
> The last, which with a region of white flame,
> Pure without heat, into a larger air
> Upburning, and an ether of black blue,
> Investeth and ingirds all other lives. . . ."
> — *The Mahatma Letters*, p. 51

WE OPEN our study by reading a part of the passages of *The Secret Doctrine* that were read at our last meeting, that is to say, from volume I, pages 207 and 208:

The *Arhats* of the "fire-mist" of the 7th rung are but one remove from the Root-Base of their Hierarchy — the highest on Earth, and our Terrestrial chain. This "Root-Base" has a name which can only be translated by several compound words into English — "the ever-living-human-Banyan." This "Wondrous Being" descended from a "high region," they say, in the early part of the Third Age, before the separation of the sexes of the Third Race.

And then we read the last paragraph on page 208:

It is under the direct, silent guidance of this MAHA — (great) — GURU
that all the other less divine Teachers and instructors of mankind became,
from the first awakening of human consciousness, the guides of early
Humanity. It is through these "Sons of God" that infant humanity got its
first notions of all the arts and sciences, as well as of spiritual knowledge;
and it is they who have laid the first foundation-stone of those ancient
civilizations that puzzle so sorely our modern generation of students and
scholars.

As we noted at our last meeting, we are approaching a part of
our studies where, to use the words of the old thinkers, we feel
almost that we should remove our footgear, because we stand on
holy ground. These sublime passages contain, in fact, the outline
of the meaning of the seventh of the seven jewels or treasures
of wisdom, which has the technical name of *ātma-vidyā*. This
phrase literally signifies "self-knowledge."

Now this Sanskrit word *ātman* is exceedingly difficult to translate, but the English word "self" seems to come nearest to an
adequate rendering of it. Ātma-vidyā means much more than
ordinarily we might understand by the words "knowledge of the
self"; yet, were we to know the self in its fullness, we should know
all knowledge that it is possible for man to know. Hence, that
technical name is given to it as descriptive of the entire branch
of the esoteric philosophy which this seventh jewel contains. As
it is, we can know only parts of this branch of the esoteric
philosophy. We are told that it is hinted in the ancient writings,
particularly in the Sanskrit, that even the most spiritual beings
on earth in this our age know not fully all that is contained in this
treasure. There are possibly not a dozen thinking beings on earth
today, who of course would comprise the very highest and holiest
men that the earth has brought forth up to the present period of
evolution, who can in any sense fully understand it. But we can
have and understand appropriate parts of this sublime wisdom-
mystery; and it is these that we are going to attempt to elucidate
to the best of our capacity this evening.

We stated at our last meeting that this seventh treasure or
jewel can be considered as a study of the problem of how the
One becomes the many; but it was also said that, as a matter of

fact, the One essentially never becomes the many. One might as well say that the sun which gives us our light comes down to earth in order to do it; but it does not. It sends out its rays, emanations from itself, which illuminate, vitalize, and quicken our world of matter; and similar is the case with the One.

Further, what do we mean by the One? Obviously, we do not mean the personal God of any exoteric theology. No matter how great, how vast in compass spiritually, we may consider this One to be, it is still a unity, a being, and therefore it is finite. Therefore, in order to elucidate our problem, we turn to another one of these seven treasures, and we find an illustration of this particular branch of our problem in the lokas — a technical word for hierarchies, as is also *brahmānda,* or "egg of Brahmā" — of which the One is the root-base if we consider it as the *origin* of all the beings and things in that hierarchy; or the flower or summit or acme if we consider it as the aim and end of our evolution. This, therefore, is the One. But there are other Ones, Ones innumerable, in the kosmical universe; some higher than our highest, or lower than our lowest degree.

You doubtless remember that in studying the doctrine of hierarchies we showed that these hierarchies are endless in number. They themselves, each one of them, can be considered as a unit; and there are many above us and many below us: innumerable ones above us and innumerable ones below us; innumerable ones within and innumerable ones without our kosmical hierarchy. They are endless in number in all directions. From this One of *our* hierarchy, however, and we mean in this instance the universal kosmos or the kosmical universe, comes all our life, all our being, all that we are without and within. It is the source and origin of everything that we can be and know, working in and upon that background of the Boundless which comprises the limitless aggregate of all other hierarchies whatsoever.

The most extended, the vastest, and the most immense hierarchy of our unfettered imagination is but as a mote of dust, as a single atom, in comparison with the Boundless. The Boundless cannot ever or in any sense be considered as *one,* as a mere unity. *One* implies the finite, the beginning of computation or enumeration; and we must think of the Boundless as a zero, signifying endless and limitless infinitude, with no qualifications whatsoever that belong to all that is manifested or limited; and, on the other side of the illustration, signifying the all-encompassing, endless, boundless Fullness of the All. This is Space, which is either the unlimited Fullness of the All, or the unlimited Emptiness of the All, according as we view it. The latter view is the profoundly spiritual śūnyatā of the Buddhist philosopher.

Let us turn for a moment to another kindred subject. Have we ever considered and pondered over the meaning of the word *immutable* when people use it as sometimes happens when speaking of such subjects as Space, the Boundless, etc.? Has it ever occurred to us to try to realize that if the Boundless were immutable even for the minutest fraction of a second, the entire fabric of universal kosmical being would vanish away in the twinkling of an eye, like a shadow on a wall! All that we can know or mentally figurate of so limitlessly vast a subject as the Boundless, is such thoughts as we vaguely express in words or phrases like "boundless life," which is *motion:* endless and beginningless activity. Immutability is a phantom of the imagination, a mere reflection in our minds of finite pause. There is ceaseless motion, ceaseless and endless and beginningless life in the horizonless fields of the Boundless.

But when we consider the One, the summit, or the root-base of our own hierarchy — or of any other hierarchy — we can by spiritual intuitions grasp the truth concerning it; but if we go beyond that hierarchy, going up step by step from lower to higher spheres, we shall always, we must always, reach a point where our understanding and imagination fall powerless before the immensity of the *(to us)* nonunderstandable, because we can in nowise encompass or comprehend it; only can we see that in It and from It is the infinite life, which *in its ceaseless unending motion* is immutably the same always. *Only in this paradoxical sense is the word immutable permissible.* So much, then, for the Boundless. But as regards the One, it is analogically immutable *only for its own period of activity as source of a hierarchy, and only for those below it;* and hence you will find our books occasionally speaking of the "immutable law," that which for the "seven eternities" during which our period of manifestation endures "varies not, and knows no shadow of turning." And why? Because that highest summit, that One, is the supreme Silent Watcher, the supreme Life-giver, the great supreme Sacrifice, to use H. P. Blavatsky's terms, of our own great kosmic hierarchy, which is the highest that our imagination can attain to. But do not confuse *this* supreme Silent Watcher with the Silent Watcher of the less hierarchy of the Teachers.

When our hierarchy goes into pralaya — which means the release of its entirety of lives and life for higher and spiritual things of greater value and of nobler compass than those we now have or can even conceive of — when that happens, I say, it is but as the passing, as it were, of a cloud hitherto over the "face of the Boundless," and hosts of other universes are then coming equally into manifested life as ours will then be passing out of it for its pralayic rest. Try and form some simple concept of the meaning of endless and beginningless eternity and of the Boundless, and drop it there: unceasing life, endless activity, never-ending life and consciousness in unceasing motion everywhere. It is only "parts" — which, as compared with the totality which is the Boundless, are as nothing — only such parts, so to say, this, that, or another part which, in its māyā of manifested life and unmanifested repose, alternately is active or passive, which passes away and then returns again. The wise ancients never bothered their heads much about any foolish attempt to fathom the Boundless or the limitless Eternal. They recognized the reality of being, and let it go at that, knowing well that an ever-growing knowledge of the universal life was and is all that human intelligence could ever attain to by an ever-expanding consciousness.

This alternate appearing and disappearing of worlds or hierarchies is the teaching imbodied in the first of the seven jewels or treasures of wisdom. As the human spirit sends down its ray and reincarnates by means of that ray into a human being of astral matter and of mind-matter and of flesh, so similarly, when the time comes for a hierarchy to reimbody itself, to undertake its task anew of palingenesis or repeated self-generation, the same relative course is run. Never let us forget the ancient axiom of the esoteric wisdom which the Hermetists so beautifully expressed: *As above, so below.* What happens in heaven is mirrored on earth, *mutatis mutandis*. Man's palingenesis, as a microcosm, is but a faithful copy of the palingenesis of worlds, of his own kosmic hierarchy as the macrocosm.

Let us now turn to our main theme for tonight. As the summit of our hierarchy is One, the root of our *ens*, in which we move and live and have our being, as the Christian Apostle Paul puts it; *so similarly in the spiritual-psychological hierarchy there is a One in whom we are all rooted, in whom psychologically and mystically and religiously, yea and aspirationally, we live.* This One is the Great Initiator, the Great Sacrifice, the Wondrous Being referred to by H. P. Blavatsky; the supreme Head of the hierarchy of the Teachers. From it originally come our noblest impulses through our own higher selves; from it come the life and aspiration we feel, stirring oft in our minds and hearts; from it, through our higher natures, come the urge to betterment, the sense of loyalty and troth, all the things which make life holy and bright and high and well worth living.

It was during the third race of humanity of this fourth round on this globe, when the incarnate ray in each of the units of the then mankind had evolved forth its vehicle (by *generating from within itself* this vehicle, fit for the expression of itself, of the divine spirit within); and then that vehicle, or soul, was become self-conscious. Then, as time passed, there came a period when an interpreter, a guide, a teacher, of the race of mankind was needed, because the race was rapidly sinking with every subcycle of the Great Age more totally into matter and consequent illusion and spiritual defilement, for such is produced by the evolving of matter. The dhyān-chohans, the lords of meditation, who were men from a former great period of activity of our planet Terra, beings from a former manvantara, were then leaving or withdrawing from this earth. They had already done their cyclical work, done all they could, in informing, inspiring, and illuminating the then mankind; but they now needed successors more like the sinking men of the period. By reason of a mystery which we cannot elucidate here, the noblest representatives of the then humanity became the direct and willing vehicles of self-conscious rays from these dhyān-chohans, lords of meditation. It was *not exactly* what is called in Brahmanism an *avatāra* — a "descent"

which means the *overshadowing* incarnation of a *portion* of a high
spirit in a high human being; but it was the actual *indwelling*
(fully conscious on both sides, and relatively complete) of a
portion of the essence of a dhyān-chohan in a fully conscious,
willing, and utterly self-sacrificing, man of high degree. Now,
please mark well: the highest one of these incarnations, the
noblest man-fruit of human evolution produced up to that time,
became the head of this spiritual-psychological hierarchy literally,
and in very truth, in his case, was a man infilled with a dhyān-
chohan: what might actually be called an incarnate god. This
was — and still *is* — the Silent Watcher, the Initiator, the Wondrous Being, the Great Sacrifice — "sacrifice" for a reason which
I explain elsewhere.

Pause a moment. Let us think away for a moment from the
thread of our theme. Let us consider the immense hope, the
profound intellectual splendor, and the spiritual beauty which
we find in these teachings. They are well worth thinking over,
indeed! If anything, theosophy, the esoteric wisdom, is a vast
doctrine of hope, not of mere optimism as the word is ordinarily
understood, but a doctrine of vitalizing hope and interior illumination. There, in these wonder-teachings, is the path along which
we may ascend. More particularly, it depends on ourselves
whether our ascent along the stairway of that ray which is living
and working in each one of us is achieved or not; and — pray listen
carefully — whether or not we ascend by our being *consciously*
linked through that Being with the Highest. That Being, that
Wondrous Being, does not "come down" and "descend" into us,
because for it this would be pollution of a sort not to be tolerated;
yet we are linked with it by and through the ray within us. As
the sun sends forth innumerable rays, yet remains ever the sun,
so through this Being pours, as the root-base of our spiritual-
psychological hierarchy, a ray which is instinct and alive in every
normal child that comes into the world.

Now it depends upon us whether we follow along that ray
upwards or, as pointed out at our last meeting, abandon our
divine birthright, and follow the lure of chaos and the Pit —
respond to the exhalations from "hell." There are people, perhaps,
who may not have understood the meaning of the word annihila-

tion as we use it. Let us understand that annihilation, strictly speaking, exemplifies what Katherine Tingley calls the "infinite mercy of the higher law." There is no such nightmare as "eternal suffering." Those human beings who have forfeited their divine birthright go to pieces; they lose their *personal entity;* but when that has happened, there remains but an empty psychic shell. When we lay our body down at death and it goes to pieces and its atoms are returned to the earth which gave it birth, is there anything very dreadful in that? Take the same rule and apply it to the case of the lost souls, of which we were speaking at a former meeting.

If anyone desires to get a masterly outline of this subject, let him turn to *The Key to Theosophy,* pages 92–3 and 113–14, and he will there find what H. P. Blavatsky tells her readers of annihilation, and more particularly in connection with the Buddhist teaching as taught by the Lord Gautama the Buddha. Why I say the "Lord" Buddha will be explained in a moment.

This Wondrous Being is the Chief, the Master-Initiate, the Head and Leader of the spiritual-psychological hierarchy of which the Masters form a part. He is the "ever-living-human-Banyan" Tree from which they hang as leaves and fruits, spiritually speaking. So also do we, spiritually speaking. On every globe, on every man-bearing planet of every sun in the infinitudes of space, we are taught that, as far as great spiritual seers know, the same thing exists there. There is over each one a Master-Teacher, and in each case he merits the term which H. P. Blavatsky gives him, taking it from her own Teachers, of the "GREAT SACRIFICE." Why is he so called? Because, from boundless compassion for those lower in the scale of evolution than he is, he has renounced all hope and opportunity in this manvantara of himself going higher, out of this sorrow-laden world, and remains behind among us as our great Inspirer and Teacher. He himself can learn nothing more of this hierarchy, for all knowledge pertaining to it or possible in it is his already. He has *sacrificed* himself for all below him.

There are some people who talk of sacrifice of that sort as if it were something gruesome or evil! Why, is there anything more sublimely beautiful than the giving of self in noble service to others — to *all?* Is there anything which actually can lead man higher? Is there anything which opens the heart more? Is there anything which opens more the doors of inspiration? And, on the other hand, is there anything which more quickly closes these doors, or more fully belittles man, which more quickly shrivels the self, than does its opposite: personality, selfishness, egoism? Ay, there is a joy, an unspeakable joy, in self-sacrifice of this high kind. The Wondrous Being is technically called the Great Sacrifice because, having reached the pinnacle of evolution in this our hierarchy, he can learn nothing more in or from that hierarchy. He has deliberately renounced further progress for himself in our manvantara, and this truly is the greatest of sacrifices; and he has renounced it in order to live for those less beings who are weary, and who stumble on the upward way; following the dictates inherent in that noble cry: "How can I live in heaven when one single being on earth must suffer?" We are reminded of the old story of the Scotsman who, when told by his Dominie that his dog could not go to heaven with him, answered instantly: "Oh, Dominie, if my dog cannot go to heaven with me, then shall I stay here on earth with my faithful dog; for he never would abandon *me!*" That is a touch of the same spirit of devotion.

In the great Indian epic, the *Mahābhārata,* we find a closely similar tale of one of the great heroes of that work who, having met with severe trials of many kinds on his way to *swarga* or heaven, successfully passed them all; but when he finally reached the confines of heaven he was met by the devas, who told him: "Brother, your faithful dog enters not here." And he said: "Oh, then shall I go back with my dog, my faithful companion who loved me and who has followed me everywhere. Shall I abandon him and leave him outside?" And the devas, according to the beautiful legend, then opened wide the gates of heaven, and the heavenly choristers began to sing a paean of welcome and praise to the faithful hero-heart, who would have renounced his own unspeakable bliss for the sake of a loving and faithful creature less evolved than he.

This is the spirit of renunciation of self for others, as exemplified in legend and story. Is there anything more beautiful than it?

Now let us go a step farther. Let us leave our theme for a few moments and take up again a matter which we feel was not fully understood, perhaps, due to our insufficient exposition of it at our last meeting. We spoke then of there being two classes of lost souls. That is quite correct. But we must also point out that there are likewise two subdivisions in the second of these two classes, and these two subdivisions of the second class are those who fully merit the old Christian term "workers of spiritual iniquity." The first subdivision comprises those who are commonly called conscious sorcerers; and the second comprises the same type of beings but includes those who have reached such a point of inner power, yea, of *evil* spiritual strength, that they are able even to defeat nature's call to dissolution for the entire term of the manvantara. They merit truly the old mystic saying, "workers of spiritual evil."

In order to make this difficult subject somewhat clearer, consult and reflect over the subjoined diagram, which gives a brief outline of the various consciousnesses in a hierarchy:

Dhyān-chohans ⎫
Buddhas   ⎪
Mahatmas   ⎬   . . . . The "Awakened," of various
Chelas   ⎪   degrees.
Good Men   ⎭

Soulless Men   . . . . Very numerous; the "Living
                              Dead."

Class 1 Men thoroughly evil; very few. ⎫ Lost Souls: actually,
         ⎧ Spiritual Sorcerers   ⎪ or to be. Destined,
         ⎪   Subdivision 1   ⎬ all, for annihilation.
Class 2 ⎨   ⎪ Class 2 are extreme-
         ⎪ Chohans of Conscious Evil   ⎪ ly few.
         ⎩   Subdivision 2   ⎭

The entire system hangs like a chain from the primeval seed, the root-base of the hierarchy.

The first subdivision comprises those who are annihilated when this globe goes into its obscuration. But to the second subdivision belong they who are almost human incarnations of what the Tibetans called the *lhamayin;* or sometimes they may even be overshadowed by the *māmo-chohans* which preside at the pralayas. These last, however, are not exactly "devils" or evil entities, but rather beings whose destiny it is for the time in view to carry on the work of destruction, of desolation. As regards the higher spiritual sorcerers and workers of evil, the second sub-division, their final destiny is truly terrible, for there awaits them at the close of the manvantara the avīchi-nirvana, the absolute contrast and nether pole of the nirvana of spirit; and then a manvantara of unparalleled misery. They are the polar opposites of the dhyān-chohans. Final and utter annihilation is their end. Nature is bipolar; and as is the action, so is the reaction.

Now annihilation, as it is used in the esoteric philosophy, does not mean what people commonly imagine it to be. It means the breaking up, the dissolution, of a personal entity, but never of the immortal individuality, which is impossible. We speak, and speak correctly, of the dissolution or the annihilation of an army, or of the annihilation of a flock of sheep. When the separate entities are gone, killed, or whatever it may be, the *flock* of sheep is no more, the *flock* is dissolved. It is annihilated as a flock, as an entity. And similarly, annihilation in its psychological sense does not mean that it is the immortal spirit which is annihilated. That idea is perfectly ludicrous. An immortal spirit cannot be anni-hilated. Its residence, its dwelling place, is infinite space; and its time is eternity. But as our body dissolves, is annihilated as a body, is resolved and dissolved into its component elements, so with the lost soul which is at first a mere psychic shell, when the impulses which came to it in the time when it was linked with an incarnate spirit have spent their force; then its term comes, it is dissolved, it is annihilated, it ceases, it passes out of being. There is nothing left of it, for like a dead physical body it is resolved into its component elements. But in the first stages it becomes spiritually dead, though mentally alive. It is a psychic corpse, from which the immortal element has fled. That is what a lost soul is.

Students of the esoteric philosophy know what happens to the kāma-rūpa of a man after the death of the physical body. It is finally dissolved, or annihilated. It is in nature's course that it must be so. I tell you that when we spoke at our last meeting of the ancient wisdom-teachings of the Lord Buddha, to the effect that there is "no abiding principle in man" — using the words of Rhys Davids, the eminent Welsh scholar, who is a bright literary honor to his country despite the mistakes that he makes in misunderstanding much of the inner sense of the Buddhist teaching — we mean simply this: that *the only abiding thing in man's nature is from and in his higher self*, his higher nature. His body; his vital force; his astral double, the linga-śarīra; the kāmic principle; the manas; all these pass away at death. Nothing of an abiding principle in the combination of these five; yet while these five component parts of man's psychology hang together in physical life, they form the "man." Is there any one of you so egoistic as to think that this poor being of clay now speaking before you is the immortal spirit? Or the life which informs it? Or this poor mind of matter, which I am using as an instrument wherewith to speak to you? No!

The thought just expressed is commonly supposed — and rightly supposed — to be a Buddhist teaching; it is also the teaching of the ancient wisdom; it was likewise the teaching of the Stoics, and also of Plato. Why, it is likewise the teaching of the scriptures of Judaism and of Christianity. You doubt it? Turn to the Book of Ecclesiastes, one of the so-called sacred canonical works of the latter two religions. We have made our own translation of the following passages, for we trust not the translation of the theological scribes. They are too harsh on the one hand, and insufficiently clear on the other. We find, then, in Ecclesiastes, chapter 3, verses 18–21, the following — and please remember that this book is supposed to have been written by the so-called "wisest man in the world," Solomon. Whatever we may think of that notion, those who accept this book believe it. It is old-fashioned and popular theology.

Said I in my heart, concerning the nature of the sons of man (*Ādām*) (it is) that the Elohīm may form them, and to show that they are beasts, they themselves. For the destiny of the sons of man (*Ādām*) and the destiny of the beast is one destiny to them: as dies the one, so dies the other; and the thinking faculty [the Hebrew word is *rūahh*, very extraordinary indeed!] is one for all; and the superiority of man over the beast is nothing, because all are illusion. All go to one place. All are from the dust, and all return to the dust.

But now listen to the following, showing that the writer of this, although he certainly was not that mythical figure Solomon, was nevertheless a man who *knew*. Listen!

Who knows the thinking faculty of the sons of man which, herself, ascends above; and the thinking faculty of the beast which, herself, descends under the earth?

There we have the age-old teaching regarding psychology, and when properly understood, it will easily be seen that every word of it is true. And when the key-wisdom behind this brief exposition is understood, it will be seen to be unutterably beautiful. What vain illusions did those misguided men of the early sects of Christendom foist upon the early western European world; what irreligious folly, to teach that the physical body of man is such a permanent and necessary thing that it will be resurrected and, if the life of the indwelling soul was good, shall sit with multitudes on the "right hand of God Almighty." What unbelievably crass materialism! More spiritual harm was done to the European races by teachings such as this than anything, perhaps, that history records. Like many other teachings of early Christianity, this one was a horribly mistaken and distorted tenet of the ancient wisdom concerning the regeneration of the personality into an immortal individuality — one of the ancient Mystery-doctrines which we explain briefly elsewhere. On the other hand, it is necessary to teach a man of his *dual nature;* to teach him that he is in his higher nature really an essential spirit, verily, an incarnate god, and that he can become consciously that god in the flesh if he will. And teach him that if he chooses to follow the beast-nature he becomes as a beast, for the inner self tolerates not this latter course. The silver thread (which is golden above) is in that case broken; and instead of the man we have the man-beast, for from the man-beast the soul departs, nature's merciful liberation of the self-conscious indwelling individuality.

There is no "endless torture" or punishment anywhere.

Now my time for this evening is drawing to a close. I have not said one-tenth part concerning this subject of the seventh treasure in its connection with the Wondrous Being; yet I wish to add a few more words tonight before ending. First, as to my reason for using the term the "Lord Buddha." This Wondrous Being overshadowed about twenty-five hundred years ago a pure and noble-minded youth born in the north of India. The vehicle, this youth, was in all ways receptive, and the wisdom-teaching coming from him was given to the world. This chosen vehicle was called Siddhārtha as his personal name; his clan name was Gautama; and he was later given the title Śākyamuni — meaning the Śākya-sage; he was also later called the Buddha. This word *buddha* is a title meaning the "awakened," just as the word *christos* or *christ* means the "anointed." The Wondrous Being overshadowed, and partly entered into, this young man who had come strictly in accordance with the law of cycles, at the cyclically appointed time in the world's course; for an Awakened One, a full Christ, that is to say, a Buddha, was cyclically destined to come at that time. He was in the line of the successively-coming Buddhas, and he was the noblest, he was the highest, of the mystic hierarchy of his period, as also he was then the nearest to this Wondrous Initiator, of any of our race. We know that the Teachers themselves speak of the Lord Buddha as their Teacher. That young man, we are taught, came directly from the Lodge: not his body, but the holy entity infilling it. He was one of their greater ones. Concerning all these profound and wonderful doctrines there is vastly more that simply cannot be uttered here, for obvious reasons; there is an entire department of the esoteric philosophy involved which treats of some of the most carefully guarded secrets of nature and being. We merely, then, hint, and pass on.

H. P. Blavatsky herself, you may remember, took *pansil,* a Pali word meaning the "five qualities or vows" (in Sanskrit, *Pancha-śīla*), and thereby became a *formal* Buddhist. Why? Because, as the messenger from the Lodge, she knew perfectly well that back of the outward teachings, behind the exoteric doctrines of Gautama Buddha, there is the inner truth, there is the esoteric *Buddhism,* as well as the esoteric *Budhism:* the former word spelled with two *ds,* meaning the teachings of Gautama the Buddha; and the other word spelled with one *d,* and meaning "wisdom." And they are truly one when Buddhism is properly explained and understood. She knew exactly what she was about. Look, for instance, at the way in which she writes of the Buddha.

But, while all the above is strict and accurate truth, I must enter here another caveat. Are we Buddhists? No. Not more so than we are Christians, except perhaps in this sense, that the religious philosophy of the Buddha-Śākyamuni is incomparably nearer to the ancient wisdom, the esoteric philosophy. Its main fault today is that its later teachers carried its doctrines too far along merely formal or exoteric lines; and yet with all that, and to this day, it remains the purest and holiest of the exoteric religions on earth, and its teachings even exoterically are true. They need but the esoteric key in interpretation of them. As a matter of fact, the same may be said of all the great ancient world-religions. Christianity, Brahmanism, and others, all have the same esoteric wisdom behind the outward veil of the exoteric formal faith.

You will remember that H. P. Blavatsky says somewhere that of the two branches of Buddhism, i.e., the Southern and the Northern, the Southern still retains the teachings of the "Buddha's brain," the "eye doctrine," that is to say his outer philosophy for the general world; and that the Northern still retains his "heart doctrine."

Now understand those two expressions. They are Buddhist terms: eye doctrine and heart doctrine are real Buddhist terms. They are also esoteric wisdom terms. The eye doctrine is that which is seen; it may be false and it may be true; but in the technical sense it is a true exotericism lacking only the key. The eye doctrine is sometimes called the doctrine of forms and ceremonies, that is, the formal outward presentation. Whereas the heart doctrine is that which is hid, but which is the inner life, the heart-blood, of the religion. As the eye is seen and also sees, so, conversely, the heart is unseen, but is the life-giver, and applied to religion the expression means the doctrine of the inner heart of the teaching. As a secondary thought, it also gives the idea that it contains the nobler part of human conduct, what people call kindliness, humanity, compassion, pity.

EIGHTEEN

THE SPIRITUAL-PSYCHOLOGICAL HIERARCHY OF ADEPTS. THE WON-
DROUS BEING, THE BUDDHAS, NIRMĀNAKĀYAS, DHYĀN-CHOHANS.

Then the Blessed One spake, and said:
'Know, Vâsettha, that (from time to time) a Tathâgata is born into the
world, a fully Enlightened One, blessed and worthy, abounding in wisdom
and goodness, happy, with knowledge of the world, unsurpassed as a guide
to erring mortals, a teacher of gods and men, a Blessed Buddha. He, by
himself, thoroughly understands, and sees, as it were, face to face this universe
— the world below with all its spirits, and the worlds above, of Mâra and of
Brahmâ — and all creatures, Samanas and Brâhmans, gods and men, and he
then makes his knowledge known to others. The truth doth he proclaim
both in its letter and in its spirit, lovely in its origin, lovely in its progress,
lovely in its consummation: the higher life doth he make known, in all its
purity and in all its perfectness.'
— *Tevijja Sutta*, pp. 186–7 (The Sacred Books of the East, vol. xi)

O UR STUDY this evening begins with reading once more
a part of the matter from the first volume of *The Secret
Doctrine*, which was read at our last meeting, namely,
on page 207:

The *Arhats* of the "fire-mist" of the 7th rung are but one remove from the
Root-Base of their Hierarchy — the highest on Earth, and our Terrestrial
chain. This "Root-Base" has a name which can only be translated by several compound words into English — "the ever-living-human-Banyan." This
"Wondrous Being" descended from a "high region," they say, in the early
part of the Third Age, before the separation of the sexes of the Third Race.

This evening we are going to make a step forward, in some
respects, far and away beyond any distance that we have traveled
on a similar occasion. Our preceding two studies have been for
the purpose, mainly, of illustrating some of the preliminary ideas
connected with this wonderful doctrine of the Wondrous Being.

First, then, let us note that the key word of this teaching is the word *banyan*. Doubtless you all know what a banyan tree is, a well-known tree in India, and called the *Ficus bengalensis*, the "Bengal Fig," because it is a relative of the fig tree. It grows rapidly, and soon attains to very respectable dimensions. From its branches there hang down tendrils which, when they reach the soil, strike into the ground and become roots there. And the tendril which grew down and rooted itself in the ground becomes another tree trunk, in its turn sending forth branches, these branches anew sending forth other tendrils, becoming in their turn new roots, which again become new trunks, sending forth other branches, developing in their turn new tendrils, and so on. It is a wonderful figure of speech to have been chosen for this subject.

Now this Wondrous Being is a spiritual banyan. To say that it is our higher self would be using a misleading phrase; it would be doing violence to the facts. Notwithstanding this, however, in one sense it is our higher self, our Paramātman. From it we spiritually spring; and when, in the course of the cycles, the life-wave shall have run its rounds on this planetary chain, into the *hierarchical* banyan again we shall be withdrawn. It is in very truth, so far as this planet is concerned, and so far as its thinking entities more particularly are concerned, our Father in Heaven. The Wondrous Being referred to here must not be confused with its lower copy, the supreme Initiator, the Great Sacrifice, the Head of the spiritual-psychological hierarchy of Adepts, the more immediate subject of our present study.

You will remember that in our former studies we pointed out that the course of the evolution of man, more particularly of his psychological nature, was a copy in miniature of the development not merely of worlds of the macrocosmic scale, but also of various high spiritual beings who form the directing intelligences of the kosmos, and of their vehicles in the universe. First, when the time comes for manifestation, for the sending forth of a life-wave, it begins, rounds out, and then completes its evolutionary course on the first "plane" of its downward and forward journey. Then, passing from that plane, to use the ordinary term, and going to a lower one, it leaves on the plane or sphere to and into which it had first penetrated, vehicles of various sorts, remaining more or less active, though the main vigor of the life-wave has passed on. And so through and in all of the seven planes or spheres of manifestation — first in the spiritual world; then in the psychical; then in the astral; and lastly in the physical; thus reaching the limit which the active impulse or force of the evolutionary wave attains in that particular manvantara, which is what we call absolute matter for that particular life-wave: four planes from its beginning, counting downwards. Three more planes upwards round out the manvantaric cycle.

Remember here that our teaching allows of no such things as "absolutes" in the ordinary sense, for actually all absolutes are relative. The absolute self, our Father in Heaven, is but the Absolute of our hierarchy, its crown, its summit, its glory; or, considering it as the beginning of manifested beings, the root or the seed thereof. And, as all nature works in bipolar phases, "absolute matter," therefore, is *the ultimate depth to which a spiritual impulse can reach in that particular manvantaric cycle.* Below it are other complete hierarchies; while above our hierarchical (not individual) Father in Heaven is the lowest plane of another but superior hierarchy, one of innumerable multitudes of hierarchies, which in their aggregate comprise the universal kosmos.

In our last study we spoke of the care that we should have when we speak of the One; the reason is that there are infinite multitudes of such Ones, a necessary implication of what we have said this evening and elsewhere.

Now, as the monad descends into matter, or rather as its ray — one of other innumerable rays proceeding from it — is propelled into matter, it secretes from itself and then excretes on each one of the seven planes through which it passes its various vehicles, all overshadowed by the self, the same self in you and in me, in plants and in animals, in fact in all that is and belongs to that hierarchy. It is the one self, the supreme self or Paramātman of the hierarchy. It illumines and follows each individual monad and all the latter's hosts of rays. Each such monad is a spiritual seed from the previous manvantara, which manifests as a monad in this manvantara; and this monad through its rays throws out from itself by secretion and then excretion all its vehicles; and these vehicles are, first, the spiritual ego, the reflection or copy in miniature of the monad itself, but *individualized* through the manvantaric evolution, bearing or carrying as a vehicle the monadic ray. The latter cannot directly contact the lower planes, because it is the monadic essence itself, the latter *a still higher ray* of the infinite Boundless composed of infinite multiplicity in unity.

The next vehicle is the spiritual soul, the bearer of the spiritual ego. On its own higher plane, this vehicle is, as it were, a sheaf or pillar of light. Similarly with the various egos and their related vehicle-souls on the inferior planes, all growing constantly more dense, as the planes of matter, into which the monadic ray penetrates, gradually thicken downwards and become more dense until the final "soul." The final soul is the physical body, the general vehicle or bearer or carrier of them all. Soul, as the term is here used, is seen to be a general expression for any bearer or carrier of an egoic center, or ego.

When we call this hierarchical Wondrous Being our highest self, we mean that it is the primeval or originating seed from which we grow and develop into composite entities, the immortal divine part of our nature and being. We can consider it, *in one aspect,* as a sheaf of divine light separating into innumerable individuals or entities (monads and monadic rays) in a manvantara; and when the pralaya comes, again withdrawing and drawn back into itself, enriched and ennobled, however, *through its countless hosts of manifested monads and monadic rays,* with the individualizing experience that these latter have gained, because, though at first unself-conscious god-sparks, they are now *self-conscious* divinities. The innumerably various individual consciousnesses increase in power and glory and self-cognition by means of the life and lives through which it (and they) have passed. Hence the wonder-teaching flowing forth from this.

Listen carefully: last spring we pointed out that the one end and aim of all manvantaric evolution is the *raising of the mortal into immortality;* and we mentioned as an illustration of the idea the beautiful Invocation of Katherine Tingley, "that from the corruptible I may become incorruptible; that from darkness

I may go forth in light." That, indeed, is the aim and end of kosmic evolution. Have we reached as yet such a state, you and I? We have not; and our immortality as men is nonexistent or rather conditional, and will so be until we have "raised the corruptible into incorruptibility."

In order to make things more clear, please note the following: no student of these studies should feel discouraged at what may seem to him to be the confusion caused by using such words as spiritual, divine, Wondrous Being, the One, hierarchy, and many more, in various places which seem different from other places or conditions. The fact is that such usage is really unavoidable. No European language has evolved terms or expressions suitable to these majestic and often (to us) complex doctrines; and hence a speaker is obliged to do the best he can in this respect. But please mark this well: there need be no confusion whatsoever, and in time there will be none, if the student or reader will constantly bear in mind the following facts. The entire framework of kosmos, or nature, is builded throughout in scalar fashion, and on correspondences and repetitives, so that, actually, the same descriptive words are properly applied to any theme of a repetitive character, for the reason that there are no absolutes anywhere, and everything is strictly relative to everything else. The only differences are those of evolutionary development, and the relative and varying greater or less degree in which spirit or matter is evolved or manifesting. The divine of one hierarchy is actually grossest matter to another far superior hierarchy; but within one and the other the repetitive rules apply very strictly, because kosmos or nature follows *one general course and one law,* and has one general and *throughout-repeated* course of action, which applies as strictly and fully to a kosmos as to the less kosmos, the atom.

Hence, the Wondrous Being of our own planetary spiritual-psychological hierarchy of Adepts, etc., is a correspondence in small of the kosmical One of the universal kosmical hierarchy of the solar system, etc.

Bearing this rule ever in mind, confusion will gradually fade away into dazzling light of illumination. It is well worth trying!

Some perhaps may think it a remarkable thing that in our last two studies we contrasted the case of the lost soul with the case of the children of this Wondrous Being — the buddhas. Naturally the former are the other or nether pole of the buddhas, as these lost souls are, like the buddhas, cases of extreme rarity of occurrence. In our present state of evolution, in which these lost souls occur, equally rare is the other occurrence: the raising of the mortal into immortality, of the corruptible into incorruptibility.

Let us go into this a little farther. What is it that is "lost"? It is the soul. Now what is soul? As I have explained before, by our use it is a vehicle on the higher planes manifesting as a sheaf or pillar of light; and on the lower planes, depending upon the spirituality of the plane, or its materiality, a more or less physically corporeal body. These souls in all cases are living, more (or less) conscious, sentient entities; living beings, composite: each one of them composed of innumerable multitudes of less (inferior) entities, as our body itself is composed of quasi-infinite numbers of atomic cosmoi, tiny cosmoses, minute universes.

Now such a soul becomes lost, *annihilated* truly, when it has lost its touch or rather union with that which gives it immortality — *or the promise of it.* For, if and when the impulse, all impulses or aspirations, towards the indwelling divinity, towards its closer union therewith, have faded out or ceased completely, then there is nothing left in it to hold it together, for it is wholly a compounded thing, as said before, and it then disintegrates, falls to pieces, as the physical body will disintegrate in the fire or in the earth. What then happens to the immortal monad which had informed it? Its career in that vehicle is violently checked. The course of nature, of destiny, in that particular instance, has been violated and interrupted. Yet all the previous spiritual gleanings from the former lives of that monad in other former vehicles still remain; and, after a certain period, the monad shoots forth another ray, another ego, although the page of the lost soul remains blank, so to say — it is, as it were, nonexistent, completely wiped out. Immortality has no record of it. It is truly a terrible thing, not only spiritually, but for the higher soul, the spiritual ego, itself (see diagram p. 240).

On the contrary, on the other side, when once in many, many generations the flower of spirituality blooms full in a soul, and mortality is raised into immortality, we have the opposite case:

a Master is born, consciously immortal, linked for ever with his higher individual self. As the one case is one pole, so is the other case the other pole of nature's course.

But when the former soul is lost, there is then for it no more pain, no more sorrow; it is wiped out, and vanishes, even as a shadow which passes along a wall and is gone.

Now listen: modern science tells us in its hypotheses built upon its recent discoveries, that every physical atom is composed, first, of a central nucleus which is called a proton; and, second, that around it go circling, cycling, revolving — precisely as the planets and many comets in the solar system do around the sun — other corpuscular bodies called electrons. We will use these facts as illustrative of our theme because the conception is so closely similar in outline to that of the ancient wisdom. The next idea to grasp is that mere bulk, mere magnitude, is no proof or criterion of greatness, either in spiritual grandeur or in physical power. The fact is that every atom in the manifested universe is a bearer and a carrier of *lives*. Our bodies are actually composed and builded up of innumerable hosts of such atoms, every one a miniature cosmos or solar system, every one of them carrying its hosts of astral-psychic and even spiritual infinitesimals. Over all, through all, permeating all, controlling all, giving connected and inhering life to all, are the predominant life, power, and characteristic of our own personality, of our own personal ego as man; the Paramātman, the spiritual self, the Father in Heaven, of these infinitesimal beings. We are not necessarily greater *in essence* than any one unit of these innumerable hosts of infinitesimals which live, and move, and have their being, in one or another or another or another atom of our body. There may be entities among them very much farther advanced than we are, paradoxical as the statement may sound; and therefore I repeat: "Break the molds of your minds; let in the light!" Because a thing may be strange to the mind and because it may sound new, is it therefore necessarily untrue? How dare you or I or anyone say: "This or that is the *only* truth, the *only* thing that can be"? What is the criterion of truth here? What, indeed, *is* truth, as judged by such standards?

Let us go a step farther. Take our body or, for instance, its organs — the heart, the liver, the brain, and others, each one receiving from the predominant personal ego of the man certain particular rays of force, and each one a kosmical universe or a universal kosmos for the hosts of atomic infinitesimals composing it — in this connection, I say, has it ever struck you, has it ever occurred to you, that our solar system is such an atomic infinitesimal as compared with the universal kosmos; formed of its proton the sun, and of its electrons the planets, each planet bearing its hosts of lives, and forming a part of the vehicle or body, if you will, of some immense titanic entity utterly beyond our sphere of comprehension? "God"? But why God? What assurance have we that such a titanic entity is better than you or I, as God is supposed to be? Mere magnitude or bulk, mere material magnitude, is absolutely no criterion of anything. Our picture may or it may not be true. But the point to get here is this, that as our body is held together by the forces driving through it, and coming from us, secreted and excreted by you and by me; so does the One of the universal kosmos — or of any hierarchy inferior to it — send forth and control the many. Thus, then, the universal kosmical Wondrous Being is our highest self; which in no way whatever contradicts or interferes with the other fact, *that each one of us has his own monadic higher self, a spark thereof, destined in its turn to become in future manvantaras the highest self of a kosmos.* Profound, sublime thought! And the Wondrous Being of inferior scope and splendor, who is the root-base of our own planetary spiritual-psychological hierarchy of Adepts, a miniature as it were of the kosmical, is the one spoken of in the passage from *The Secret Doctrine* which forms our present theme.

Now, the hierarchical Wondrous Being has been deliberately spoken of in our last two studies, and also in this our present study, as an *entity* because, generalizing the conception, it *is* an entity. But there are three forms in which, or planes upon which, this entity manifests; and for the sake of perspicuity and convenience, just here, we are going to use the Buddhist phraseology, the phraseology of Buddhism and Tibet, as expressed in the Sanskrit language. The highest aspect, or the highest sub-entity of the Wondrous Being is called *ādi-buddha*, *ādi* meaning "primeval" (or the highest). This ādi-buddha is in the *dharma-*

kāya state: a Sanskrit compound of two words meaning the "continuance-body," sometimes translated equally well — or ill — the "body of the law," both very inadequate expressions, for the difficulty in translating these extremely mystical terms is very great. A mere correct dictionary translation misses the esoteric meaning entirely; and just there is where Occidental scholars make such ludicrous errors at times. The first word comes from the root *dhri*, meaning "to support," "to sustain," "to carry," "to bear," hence "to continue"; also human laws are the agencies supposed to carry, support, sustain, civilization; the second element, *kāya*, means "body"; the noun thus formed may be rendered the "body of the law," but this phrase does not give the idea at all. It is that spiritual body or state of a high spiritual being in which the sense of soulship and egoity has vanished into a universal (hierarchical) sense, and remains only in the seed, i.e., latent — if even so much. It is pure consciousness, pure bliss, pure intelligence, freed from all personalizing thought.

The second aspect or subentity is called the *dhyāni-buddha*, "contemplation-buddha," a great descent from the former, so far as mere impersonal spirituality goes. This is carried by the *sambhoga-kāya*, two Sanskrit words meaning "enjoyment-body," or rather "participation-body," because the buddha in the sambhoga-kāya state still participates in, still retains, its consciousness as an individual, its egoship and its soul, though it is still too far above material or personal concerns to care about or to meddle with them; and therefore it would be powerless here on our material earth. As H. P. Blavatsky once said, a god from the spheres celestial, living solely in its own nature, and without a material body to manifest in material spheres, would be utterly powerless there.

The third, and lowest, yet in one sense the highest aspect or subentity (highest on account of the immense, willing, *self-sacrifice* involved in its incarnation in human flesh) is the *mānusha-buddha*, meaning "human buddha," because born in a human body for compassionate work among men. The mānusha-buddha at will or need lives and works in the *nirmānakāya*, "form-body," about which a very wonderful doctrine exists, to be explained later.

The dhyāni-buddhas are one of the ten classes of beings which came to our globe from the preceding planetary manvantara. We will recite them, as follows: three elemental kingdoms, the lowest; the mineral kingdom; the plant kingdom; the beast kingdom. I pause a moment in order to make a remark. Please do not say "animal" in this connection. We must have precision here. Animal means any being which has an *anima*, or "vital soul." Man is an animal in that sense, but he is not a beast. His vital-astral-physical body is a beast, and he works in and with a human soul through a vital or beast soul, enlightened by a spiritual soul. We hope to have time later to illustrate this point more fully this evening.

Then another kingdom after the beast kingdom: the mānusha-kingdom or human kingdom. So far, then, we have three elemental kingdoms, 3; then the mineral, 4; plant, 5; beast, 6; human, 7. Then begin the dhyān-chohans of three classes. Man in his higher nature is an embryo dhyān-chohan, an embryo lord of meditation. It is his destiny, if he run the race successfully, to blossom forth at the end of the seventh round as a lord of meditation; if you like, as a spiritual planetary, or a planetary spirit, when this planetary manvantaric kalpa is ended, this Day of Brahmā, which is the seven rounds in seven stages each. But there are three classes of dhyān-chohans, as said; these three classes in their turn are each divided into seven, as you know. Now of these three the lowest class being divided into seven, of these seven the fourth is that dhyān-chohan who is *our* "God in Heaven," *for this fourth round.* Its spiritual primary is the ādi-buddha of the fourth round. It itself is a dhyāni-buddha.

Let us try to make this clearer. On each planet or globe of the seven globes forming the planetary chain, as the life-wave touches it in a round — and similarly through all the seven rounds — there is evolved, or rather appears, a buddha, it might be better to say a mahā-buddha: one at the commencement of a globe's awakening to life again, and another mahā-buddha when the life-wave leaves the planet after completing its round there. Likewise, for each race during such a globe-round there appears another buddha who, so to say, is a ray from the mahā-buddha of the planet, and is called the race-buddha; and he in his turn, at the

middle of the race, or when the central point of the race is nearing, overshadows a chosen human vessel of purity and nobility,
or spiritual grandeur, this last becoming the buddha preparing
the spiritual way for the great race-buddha of the succeeding
root-race, who appears shortly before the close of the preceding
root-race. Such a one (as this last) was the Lord Śākyamuni,
Gautama Buddha, who is now living on earth, as the Teachers tell
us, a nirmāṇakāya. A nirmāṇakāya is the lowest of the three
mystical vehicles, as we explained a little while ago. It exists in
seven degrees or kinds, the lowest being the case where the entity,
the spiritual entity, retains all his human principles except the
physical body — all. He is a man in every respect, except for the
physical body, which he has discarded.

Now all these buddhas — and we have no time this evening to
illustrate the wonderful mysteries connected with this doctrine
— all these buddhas *of a round* derive from the dhyāni-buddha
of that round. They form part of the spiritual-psychological hierarchy of that round. It is this dhyāni-buddha of our fourth round,
our Father in Heaven, who is the Wondrous Being, the Great
Initiator, the Sacrifice, spoken of before. The name and titles
are sometimes likewise applied to that spiritual entity, the race-
buddha, who comes shortly before or at the beginning of a root-
race; and who at certain epochs during the course of that race
chooses a fit human vehicle, usually one of the Great Lodge,
overshadows this chosen vessel or incarnates in it, as the case may
be — depending upon the materiality of the race and round and
many other factors — and so overshadowed, the chosen vessel
becomes the mānusha or human buddha. Strictly speaking, the
race-buddha himself is a mānusha or human buddha also. As
remarked before, probably none of these titles or names are hard
and fast as limited to one sole entity; they are often applied,
mutatis mutandis, to more than one sole entity or class. This is
extremely suggestive.

It is in this manner that this subject of the Wondrous Being,
which seems so intricate, but which is actually so simple, is explained. It seems intricate on account of its subtility, but it is
very simple indeed. It is our brain-minds of matter which prevent
us from seeing it easily and clearly. The ray running through all

our individual being, from which we draw our *spiritual* life and *spiritual* sustenance, comes direct to us from this hierarchical Wondrous Being *in whom we all are rooted.* He to us, psychologically and spiritually, holds exactly the same place that the human ego, the man-ego, holds to the innumerable multitudes of elemental entities which compose his body — atomic infinitesimals, before referred to, are *not* meant here.

But listen: the analogy is correct also in this respect, that if we made it universal, kosmic, we would say that that inexpressible One — which is the Utmost of the Utmost, and the Inmost of the Inmost, *of our kosmical universe,* comprising the greatest boundaries of the Milky Way — corresponds to all within the Milky Way as our human ego corresponds to the infinitesimal atomic universes which compose its own physical body. The symbology is there; the correspondence is there; and it is by the correspondence that we are striving to explain somewhat of the mystery, how the One becomes the many; not because the One "descends into matter" or becomes "many" materially and literally. Not at all. But in the same way that the sun is an immense and exhaustless reservoir of vital, psychic, and spiritual rays, sending them out through billions of years, exhaustlessly; in the same way this hierarchical Wondrous Being of kosmic magnitude, *through its inferior but high Wondrous Beings of various degrees,* enlightens us and uplifts us and inspires us, and leads us onward and upward towards immortality, for aye doing its best, through its own spiritual ray within us, to illumine and lighten our material corruptibility, in order to make it incorruptible; that from personality we may enter individuality; "that from darkness, we may go forth in light!" And the time will come when we shall do this work and become incorruptible *consciously,* working with nature and becoming one with her; for, just as this Wondrous Being is the foundation-force back of and behind all that we call nature, so that same Wondrous Being in far-gone former manvantaras was then a man, even as you and I now are. *Such we shall also become, if we run the cosmic race successfully.* Wonderful, inspiring thought!

Now I wish to read a citation from Katherine Tingley, taken from one of her recent lectures, because it is so appropriate to our present studies on this point, that if we come here with pure hearts and a sincere motive, learning from each other in the spirit of true comradeship and brotherly love, we shall all get something high and fine, something to urge us upward and onward. It will be a holy thing, a benediction. Listen:

> A man gets what he works for, and if he does not work for it, he does not get it. But when one wants truth so much that he is actually hungry for it, he gets it. It is the wine of life, so to speak, the revelation of the book of life. No language can describe it.
>
> Those who desire the truth, those who have the courage to enter the new life, those who have the desire to be reborn in a sense, must throw overboard everything that has held them down in their limitations, in their doubts, in their fears, their dislikes, and their passions. Man is a majestic being if he knows his own spiritual nature, and works assiduously to become that which he was intended to be.

We are cutting brief our lecture tonight; it is already very long; we have still more to say, and our time for closing is drawing near.

Another thought that must be hinted at tonight is that H. P. Blavatsky's *Secret Doctrine* is both an exoteric and an esoteric book. It contains doctrines which were esoteric before this book was printed. Now they are "exoteric." But if anyone thinks — I never did, thank the immortal gods — that he knows *The Secret Doctrine* by reading it once or even a dozen times, or a score of times, he mistakes greatly the situation. It must be read not only between the lines, but within the words. I have found the value of the following rule: never take a single statement in it and allow your mind to mold itself around it, never let a single idea crystallize; break the molds, let in the light. It is an excellent rule. As soon as a man says: "I have the truth," look out for him, for he is probably blind. The molds of his mind are crystallized, and he cannot see the light.

These things, these thoughts that we study, are serious, there is no playing with them; it means *going up* or *going down;* and we have the choice of paths daily, momently, instantly. I do not mean this as a preachment. I speak from my heart, for I have found the truth of what I say, and its great value.

Now to illustrate by a diagram this question of souls and egos alluded to this evening:

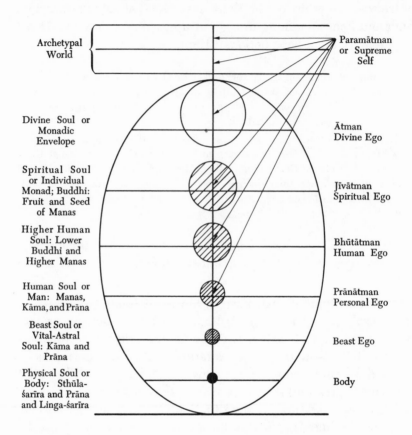

Archetypal World	Paramātman or Supreme Self
Divine Soul or Monadic Envelope	Ātman Divine Ego
Spiritual Soul or Individual Monad; Buddhi: Fruit and Seed of Manas	Jīvātman Spiritual Ego
Higher Human Soul: Lower Buddhi and Higher Manas	Bhūtātman Human Ego
Human Soul or Man: Manas, Kāma, and Prāna	Prānātman Personal Ego
Beast Soul or Vital-Astral Soul: Kāma and Prāna	Beast Ego
Physical Soul or Body: Sthūla-śarīra and Prāna and Linga-śarīra	Body

Please note here what is intended to be an egg-shaped design. It is not a graphic representation, that is, a *picture;* it is a paradigm. A paradigm is a graphic symbol, but not a picture of a thing.

Let the three parallel lines drawn above the egg represent, if you will, the arūpa world, the formless world; and the seven planes comprised within the egg, the rūpa world, seven being the number of the principles always in manifestation, held in union as an individual by the higher triad, the arūpa triad, its root above.

The three higher of the seven within the egg are also called arūpa, formless, but only relatively so. Please remember one of the first lessons of the esoteric wisdom: *there are no absolutes.*

We speak indeed of absolutes, but only as relative absolutes. The popular, ordinary sense of this word as "limitless or endless *completions*" is utterly inadmissible, for *there are no absolutes* of that kind, for *every thing* is relative in quality and space and time to *some thing else*, and it must be so unless we cast logic and common sense to the winds.

Just think of it: if any thing were absolute in the old popular sense, it would be everything, and there could be nothing but that in manifestation, hence no change for betterment, no progress, no evolution. Relativity — which means universally occurring relationships in space and time — is the very heart of the conception of the kosmos as an aggregate of evolving entities, the offspring of infinite motion, infinite life, infinite progress always.

To continue our discussion of the paradigm: through this egg-shaped paradigm falls the ray from the arūpa world, represented by the vertical line signifying the self universally manifesting in every atom it touches in this kosmos — and it permeates them all — as the self individual, the self egoic, the human self, the astral self, etc. These three highest divisions, the arūpa triad, collectively are likewise called the Paramātman, the supreme self, the summit or flower of the hierarchy, the root-base or source of that self.

Please always keep in mind that there is another hierarchy above our highest division, this division beginning with the lowest, the "absolute matter," of that higher hierarchy. *Everything is relative.* Absolute matter even of our own hierarchy would be intangible, invisible, to us. Why? Because our present physical senses do not belong to its plane, and therefore have not been trained by evolution to take cognizance of it; our senses, eyesight, smelling, tasting, hearing, touching, can cognize only those things, and all those things, which they have been built to cognize through experience in and through ourselves. We have not descended in this manvantara into the absolute matter of any other hierarchy than our own; we have gone down only as far as the stages of this hierarchy would let us go. I do not here mean our kosmical hierarchy. Rather, I mean our planetary hierarchy. Do not be absolute in the application of terminology, for the reasons already set forth. We must, when we hear a "hierarchy" spoken of, immediately question *which one*. When we hear the "self" spoken of, we must immediately question *which one*. When we hear the "soul" spoken of, let us immediately ask ourselves *which soul*. This is a safe rule and guide to follow in interpretation of any and all passages.

Now, as just said, these three highest planes represented by the three horizontal lines paradigmatically represent the Paramātman or supreme self of the hierarchy, in the archetypal world. If you please, let this topmost circle inside the egg represent the monadic envelope or the divine soul, which is called, from another standpoint, the ātman or divine ego. The circle on the horizontal plane below the monadic envelope let us call the spiritual soul or the individual monad. The self corresponding to it is the jīvātman. Next comes the third circle in this egg, and corresponding to it is the higher human soul, composed of the lower buddhi and the higher manas; and the self corresponding to it is the bhūtātman, meaning the "self of that which has been," or the reincarnating *ego*. The fourth is the lower human soul or man, manas and kāma; and the self corresponding to it is prānātman, or personal ego. The next circle, still lower — growing progressively darker like all the others, which I have attempted to illustrate by increasing the shading — is the beast soul, kāma-prāna. And the self corresponding to it may be simply called the beast ego. Finally, the lowest "soul" of all is the physical body. Remember that the word *soul*, in our ancient wisdom, means vehicle; and, of course, this lowest vehicle, the physical body, also comprehends the prāna, and the linga-śarīra or model-body which is its background and seed and root. These three are inseparable.

Please notice in this diagram the role played by the self, represented roughly by the line dropped from the highest and running through and permeating all the planes below its archetypal origin. I wish to call to your attention the fact that not merely Plato, but the entire Greek school of mystic philosophies, spoke of the self as immanent in kosmos, and as a sacrifice, which Christian mystics call sometimes the "Christ crucified in matter"; and, if we care to make the application to the exoteric Christian religion of the doctrine of the Wondrous Being which we have been studying, we shall discover that the whole Christian mythos or story was actually drawn from it, the entire thing, and distortedly called the "incarnation of the Logos." In old Greek philosophy, the word *logos* was used in many ways, which the Christians sadly misunderstood. The dhyān-chohan, of which we have spoken this evening, is our spiritual logos, the planetary logos, *so far as this fourth round is concerned.* The spiritual entity behind the sun is the solar logos of our solar system. Small or great as every solar system may be, each has its own logos, the source or fountainhead of almost innumerable logoi of less degree in that system. Every man has his own spiritual logos; every atom has its own logos; every atom has its own Paramātman and Mūlaprakriti, for every entity everywhere has its own highest. These things and the words which express them are relative. Bulk and magnitude have nothing whatsoever to do with it; it is quality, *spiritual quality,* which is the true criterion. This is a great and useful thing to remember. I have found inestimable help in that one rule.

We have only a few minutes more of time this evening. I have been asked briefly to speak of another matter, and that is in connection with the recurring cycles of the year, and especially as regards the New Year. H. P. Blavatsky somewhere, I think it was in an old issue of her magazine *Lucifer* at the beginning of the year of 1890, says, among other things in a very interesting article, that theosophists and esotericists particularly should hold the 4th day of January as the beginning of the new year. Now that is an extremely interesting statement; and in general connection with it, I wish to call your attention to one very important fact, which is that the esoteric wisdom is based entirely on nature and her fundamental operations. Nature, as we understand that word, does not mean only the physical, visible universe. That is merely the shell or body of nature the real. Nature, with us, means *the entire aggregate of everything that is,* inwards and outwards, of all planes in all spheres throughout the Boundless.

The significance of this in the present connection is that the esoteric method of reckoning time is a natural method, based wholly on recondite operations of nature. It is not an artificial method. You will find that none of the real anniversaries is based on man-made ideas or on chance, such as the artificial scheme used by the French during the French Revolution; or dating from the founding of a city, like Rome; or from the death of some great man, like Jesus. Such methods, as a matter of fact, are unknown in the esoteric chronology, though parallels do exist, but these are based on natural cycles. The ancient wisdom bases all its chronological reckonings upon the kosmic clock which nature gives us, and which is majestic, infallible, and a perfect timekeeper. That clock is the heavenly vault; and the sun, the moon, the seven planets (as the ancients reckoned them), and the stars, are the "hands" marking time cycles. The year mostly used in reckoning time by the ancients is what astronomers call the tropical year, so called from the change of the seasons. Winter, spring, summer, autumn; winter, spring, summer, autumn; recurring regularly; and recurring regularly because based on the movement of the earth around the sun, like a hand on the dial of the kosmical clock. The so-called anomalistic year and the sidereal year were both known to ancient astronomy, but were not used except for purely astronomical (not astrological) calculations, or only rarely for astrological reckoning.

Mark the difference between *astrology* and *astronomy*. Astronomy is the science of the movements, and the relations to each other, of the stars and planets. That is all. It simply tells us what they are made of, where they move, and when they move, and how long it takes them to move along certain orbits or paths, and is purely exoteric. But *astrology*, mind you, means the "*science* of the stars" (while *astronomy* proudly calls itself the "*law* of the stars"), just as *geology* means the "*science* of the earth." Ancient astrology — not the pasteboard-science which passes under that name today, but the ancient spiritual-astral astrology, a true and profound wisdom about the evolution of divinity into and through matter, and about the human soul and the human spirit — taught the science of the relations of the parts of kosmic nature among themselves, and more particularly as that science applied to man and his destiny as timed by the celestial orbs. From that great and noble science sprang up, as said, an exoteric pseudoscience, derived from the Mediterranean and Asian practice, eventuating in the modern schemes of so-called astrology — a poor, degraded, and worn-out remnant of ancient wisdom.

All nations had ways of reckoning the year and fixing the

beginning of the year. Not all nations put the opening of the year at the same date; some nations reckoned from the winter solstice, that is when the sun has attained its southernmost point, before beginning its slow course northwards again. I am speaking as an inhabitant of the northern hemisphere. Of course, in South America and in other lands below the equator, the conditions are reversed. But now we are speaking of the northern hemisphere. Other nations reckoned the beginning of the year at the summer solstice, about June 21st or 22nd; while the winter solstice takes place on or about December 21st. Other nations again reckoned the opening of the year at the spring equinox, March 21st or 22nd. Other nations began the reckoning of the year at the autumnal equinox, six months later, on September 22nd or 23rd. The Jews, for instance, had two years: a civil year, beginning in September at the autumnal equinox, and a religious year, beginning with the spring equinox. The ancient Germanic nations of northern Europe before the time of Caesar began the year at the winter solstice on December 21st; the ancient Greeks began their year at different times of the annual cycle, but most often, probably, in the autumn; and the ancient Romans began it in the spring. The ancient Egyptians began it in the summer; and the ancient Persians, and the Syrians, and other nations, had each its own period for opening the year.

The Mediterranean civilizations were already on the downward path for many centuries before what in Europe is popularly called the year 1 A.D. They were slowly losing a great deal of the ancient wisdom, and an understanding of its great secrets, and it was shown not merely in the manner in which the Eleusinian Mysteries were modified and changed, but also in the constant shifting and remodeling of their calendars, and in their methods of computing time, of calculating chronological periods, the beginnings and ends of various cycles, etc. The Romans were particularly blameworthy in this regard. They were perhaps worse in that respect than any other nation known to us. If some dictator or political chieftain wished to have a few days more of power, or to prevent or to postpone an election, he would begin to meddle with the calendar, a course of conduct carried on with the connivance or through the ignorance or negligence of the pontiffs. And so finally it came about that on account of the disorder of the calendar at the time of Julius Caesar — to be exact in the year 46–47 B.C. — the calends of January, that is the first day of January, fell on the day of the season which now corresponds to the 13th of October; and if the confusion had continued indefinitely, the first of January would in due course have taken place in all the months of the year, wandering through them, and finally completing its course around the year somewhere in March, having completed the cycle. It should be added that the old standard Roman year was lunar, consisting of about 354 days.

Julius Caesar deserves credit for having stopped this confusion by his reformation of the Roman calendar. I do not mean to say that Caesar did it all himself. He did not; for though he was a clever man and an amateur astronomer, yet he had the services of an Egyptian — or Alexandrian Greek — astronomer, a man of great ability, called Sosigenes. In the year 47 B.C., when the first day of January fell on what would now be the 13th of October — just exactly as if our own first of January this year had occurred two or three months before in the late autumn, on the *season-day* properly belonging to the 13th of October — these two eminent gentlemen, or perhaps three, if we include M. Flavius, put their heads together and shuffled the calendar into conformity with the seasons again. Caesar was Pontifex Maximus at that time, and it was his duty to take charge of or oversee the correct computing of chronological periods, etc. This he did, inserting two extra months (one to have 33 days and the second 34 days) between November and December of that year, 47, and adding an intercalary period or "month" of 23 days to the preceding February, making an addition of 90 days to that year in order to harmonize the calendar with the seasons. That year, then, was 445 days long; and because it was such a long year, and ordinary people were so puzzled as to the way in which business, etc., was going to be done, it was called the Year of Confusion, but Macrobius neatly calls it the "*last* year of confusion"! Then Caesar fixed the new calendar to have a mean year of 365 days, with a leap year each fourth year of 366 days; an arrangement that has lasted to our own time in the West, but slightly modified. This arrangement of the calendar, of course, abolished the old Roman lunar year. But, if he had only begun the year as he should have done, according to the ancient reckonings, the old reckoning of the ancient wisdom, at the beginning of one of the four *seasons* of the year and when the moon was new — at the winter solstice, or, if you please, at the spring equinox, or the autumnal, or the summer solstice — if he had taken the old beginning of the year of his own people, the Romans, as it had been before in the early days, that is to say, on December 21st or 22nd at the winter solstice, or at the spring equinox in March, of Numa, everything would have been "all right."

But now mark what happened. He had Sosigenes whispering in his ear, and Sosigenes knew more than Caesar, but he forgot one little thing. He said — this is an imaginary conversation, but something like it, I think, must have taken place — "Brother Caesar, Imperator! According to the old way, the way of our noble ancestors, the year ought to begin not merely at the winter solstice but also at new moon. Now the new moon this year does not fall on the day when the winter solstice takes place, but it falls seven days later, for the solstice this year falls on December 24th." "That is right," said Caesar. "We will begin the year seven days later than the solstice. We will call that day the calends of January" — or, as we should say, the first of January. Caesar made December to have 30 days; later changed to 31 days. And that is how our habit of putting the beginning of the year on the first of January instead of on the day of the solstice, December 21, arose. Had Caesar (he had it in his power to do so as Pontifex Maximus) proclaimed in his edict that the calendar as reformed by him would commence running on the first occasion when the winter solstice and a new moon coincided; or at one of the other three beginnings of a season which coincided with a new moon, it would have been exactly right, according to the ancient wisdom; — because, mark you, all these ancient methods of chronological reckoning were not based merely on the fact of somebody founding a city, or on the fact of somebody happening to die on a certain day, but on coordinated astronomical and terrestrial events. The ancient methods were based on the time dial of the kosmos. Caesar should have waited till a new moon coincided with one of the two solstices, or with one of the two equinoxes, beginning the new year at the moment the moon was new on that night. Evidently, Caesar felt that he could not wait; or, perhaps, did not desire to wait; or did not *know*.

Now, then, as time went on and Christianity in later years came into vogue, people naturally kept the beginning of the year as on January first, the month-day established in the Julian calendar. But finally the Christians began to think that they ought to have their own day for beginning the new year in a religious sense, connected with the supposed birth of Jesus; and so, early in the history of Christianity, eastern Christians took the 12th day after December 25, the 6th of January, in celebration of the mystical epiphany and birth (and baptism) of Jesus. It was, in a religious sense, the beginning of their year. The English call this festival Twelfth Day, as being the twelfth day after December 25th. What a curiously confused mess of ancient ideas and new dogmas! His "birth day" was later transferred to December 25.

Why was the 6th of January chosen, instead of the 4th? For this reason. The winter solstice, when Caesar and Sosigenes made their corrections of the calendar, was made to fall on the 24th of December. The *next new moon* fell, then, on the first of January, which was why Caesar said the new year was to begin on that day, the calends of January. Then, many years later, 14 days after the day which the Christians thought was the solstice in their time, December 23–24 (December then having 31 days and not 30 days, as arranged by Caesar), was the sixth of January, which the Christians called the Epiphany, copying an ancient pagan word and idea. *Epiphany* is a Christian word which originally belonged to the Mysteries of the old pagan Greek religion and to the ancient wisdom; it means "appearance" of a god, and was adopted by and adapted to the Christos-mythos.

Let us return to H. P. Blavatsky and her article in *Lucifer*. We see that calendars can be changed; that calendars can be made by men; that the Roman calendar was also changed and was made by men; and that the Julian calendar, with modifications, has come down to us, and is the one used in Europe and America today. It is no proper calendar for esotericists to use in order to compute the esoteric cycles or the beginning of the true esoteric year.

Why did H. P. Blavatsky choose the 4th of January of the

current calendar for the beginning of the esoteric year? The true esoteric year should begin on the 14th day after the winter solstice, provided that the winter solstice coincide with a new moon. The 14th day thereafter, would, of course, be a full-moon day. The day of the winter solstice could be used as a beginning of the civil year, if so desired; and the 14th day thereafter as the beginning of the esoteric year. Caesar, had he wished or, rather, had he known more, could have so arranged his calendar to fit, either for the new moon at a winter solstice or a summer one, or at one of the equinoxes. But H. P. Blavatsky chose January 4, because it was the 14th day after the winter solstice — not because it was the 4th, or any other month-day.

Now January 4th is 14 days after the winter solstice on December 21st, and when coinciding with a full moon it is an *astrological date*. It is not a man-made date. It does not depend upon a man-made calendar. It falls fourteen days after the festival of the true winter solstice; and when the winter solstice also coincides with a new moon, *a secret cycle opens*. Put the winter solstice where it belongs, and ten days will bring you to the first of January by our present calendar. Notice the number ten. H. P. Blavatsky also says in her article that the celebration of the new year by esotericists should be in connection with the Budha-wisdom, a word coming from the same root from which Buddha, the Lord Gautama's title, was taken, the root meaning "to awaken." Now, again, what is Budha, from the same root? Budha is the Sanskrit name for the planet Mercury, which the Greeks called Hermes, and the Latins Mercurius, and which we, adopting the Latin name, call Mercury. Hermes has always been the particular overseer of mystics in many, perhaps all, nations. In ancient Greece, he was given the titles of *psychagog* and *psychopomp*, meaning "conductor of souls" to the nether world, likewise the Mysteries. No matter what form the interpretation of the ancient wisdom may have taken in ancient times, one invariably finds the planet Hermes, or Mercury, associated closely with the teachings of the Mysteries dealing with the afterworld. In India, Hermes was named Budha, as just said; and he was called the son of Soma, or the Moon.

For instance, in Homer's *Odyssey*, you read how Hermes led

the souls of the dead suitors, "gibbering like bats," to the "meads of asphodel" (book 24). This allusion to the work of Hermes the psychopomp, the "helper," is a "mystery" which was taken directly from the Eleusinian Mysteries or, perhaps, from still earlier Mysteries.

Mark then, that our new year should begin 14 days after the winter solstice, *provided that day is a Mercury-day.* Now how are we going to know whether it is a Mercury-day or not? There is the rub. Have you any idea how the days of the week came to be named in the order that they now have, and have had for ages, in many parts of the world widely separated from each other? Why one day is called Sun's day, and another Moon's day, and another Tuesday — Tiw's (Mars's) day? Do you know the old Anglo-Saxon names for these, by the way? Wodnesdaeg, Wednesday, for Mercury-day; and Frigedaeg, Friday, or Venus-day; Thunresdaeg, Thursday, or Jupiter-day; Saeternesdaeg, Saturday for Saturn's day, and so forth. The system was as follows: the first hour of a day beginning when the central point of the sun is on the eastern horizon of that day, according to the ancient system, was said to be under the direct rule of one of the seven sacred planets. Now if the planet Mercury, for instance, was the one in control of that first hour, the whole day which followed that first hour was called Mercury-day. Every succeeding hour of that same day was said to be under the control of one or the other of the seven planets, following each other in a certain order, as follows: Saturn, Jupiter, Mars, Sun, Venus, Mercury, Moon — the Sun and the Moon, however, being substitutes for two secret planets. The day has 24 hours: beginning with Mercury, for instance, and counting the seven planets in the order just given through all the 24 hours, would bring in the 25th hour, which is the first hour of the next day, with Jupiter in control, and that day would then be Thursday; and so on throughout till we come to Mercury again — one week of seven days. You can easily prove this for yourself. As regards the real esoteric Budha-day, or Wednesday, or Mercury-day, I say here only this: if the winter solstice is coincident with a new moon, *plus something else, that day is a real astrological Budha-day;* and, of course, 14 days later, or two weeks, is likewise a Budha-day, *but at full moon.* Verb. sap.!

Now let us go another step farther. The 4th of January, 1890, fell on a Saturday, although H. P. Blavatsky in that article had been speaking of Hermes. But that was merely because she of necessity used the week-names and month-days of the current calendar, spoiled and ungeared as it is. So it is perfectly obvious that the year she is alluding to was the esoteric astrological year, and not the popular one of the current calendar. This manner, above given, of computing cycles of time, following the hour of the kosmical clock, is the one that was always followed in the ancient wisdom. They rejected any other way, because it is the method or the way in which nature herself works in the rounds, in the races, in the kalpas, etc.

NINETEEN

THE SEVEN JEWELS AND THE SEVEN STAGES OF INITIATION.

These Portals lead the aspirant across the waters on "to the other shore."
Each Portal hath a golden key that openeth its gate; and these keys are: —
1. Dâna, the key of charity and love immortal.
2. Shîla, the key of Harmony in word and act, the key that counterbalances the cause and the effect, and leaves no further room for Karmic action.
3. Kshanti, patience sweet, that nought can ruffle.
4. Virag', indifference to pleasure and to pain, illusion conquered, truth alone perceived.
5. Virya, the dauntless energy that fights its way to the supernal TRUTH, out of the mire of lies terrestrial.
6. Dhyâna, whose golden gate once opened leads the Narjol [Naljor] toward the realm of Sat eternal and its ceaseless contemplation.
7. Prajna, the key to which makes of a man a god, creating him a Bôdhisattva, son of the Dhyânis.
Such to the Portals are the golden keys.
— H. P. Blavatsky, *The Voice of the Silence*, pp. 47–8

THE MAIN text that we shall have to consider this evening is that on page 207 of volume I of *The Secret Doctrine*, which has already been read twice, the part dealing with the "ever-living-human-Banyan." As our studies will also include a paragraph on page 424 of the same volume, this latter I shall read. It opens section xii, "The Theogony of the Creative Gods":

To thoroughly comprehend the idea underlying every ancient cosmology necessitates the study, in a comparative analysis, of all the great religions of antiquity; as it is only by this method that the root idea will be made plain. Exact science — could the latter soar so high, while tracing the operations of nature to their ultimate and original sources — would call this idea the hierarchy of Forces. The original, transcendental and philosophical conception was one. But as systems began to reflect with every age more and more the idiosyncrasies of nations; and as the latter, after separating, settled into distinct groups, each evolving along its own national or tribal groove, the main idea gradually became veiled with the overgrowth of human fancy. While in some countries the Forces, or rather the intelligent Powers of nature, received divine honours they were hardly entitled to, in others — as now in Europe and the *civilized* lands — the very thought of any such Force being endowed with intelligence seems absurd, and is proclaimed *unscientific*.

Now then, first, has it ever occurred to us to consider, to ask, why the doctrines which we have been studying for the past months have always been held so secret? There are three general reasons for this, two rather, the third being a corollary of the second. The first is that these teachings have from time immemorial been considered the noble reward, the sublime reward, for those who give themselves heart and soul and irretrievably to the Teachers and to the terrestrial-celestial body that they represent. That is the less reason for the silence. The greater is the following, that these doctrines from their very nature being so abstruse, so subtil that our poor minds of matter find difficulty in comprehending them, would almost of necessity be misunderstood without a preliminary training and education. It requires literally years of study and training to bring the mind into such a state that it can receive these glorious teachings, these sublime doctrines that we have been studying, with some modicum at least of intelligent comprehension. If they were given out to the world indiscriminately, what would be the consequence? Intuitive but otherwise untrained minds would worship the Teachers, Masters, as gods; or the stupid heads in the multitudes would persecute them and try to do them to death as "devils," were they to appear publicly and openly live among men. And a third party of the public, the skeptics, would deride, would mock, not only the Teachers themselves but their holy message.

These rules of secrecy are based on natural law, and on a keen understanding of the workings of the human mind. These doctrines were formulated in the dawn of time by giant intellects, and by godlike minds. He indeed must be blind and perverse of will who can look upon them after study and close examination as speculations or as mere theorizings. What a compliment was paid to H. P. Blavatsky by those who in their blind ignorance said that she had invented them! Think of what that means, what a wonderful woman, according to them, she must have been! And obviously, the truth is the direct contrary. Did she ever claim that they were originated and formulated by her? No; from the beginning she said: "I am but a voice speaking for Those who sent me."

These reservations of secrecy, caution, and prudence, are not the singular and otherwise unknown rule of the trans-Himalayan school to which we belong. They were the invariable rule of all the great Mystery Schools of past times. Even in the latest of the exoteric faiths, in the Christian religion, you find the same thing, and conceived in words, by the way, which are as unkind as it is possible to put them in — almost cruel in the haughty reserve that they signify. Yet they are not so when properly understood. I refer to certain warnings uttered by the mythical Jesus in the Sermon on the Mount; and remember, that Sermon is prefaced by the words of explanation that he went up onto a hill in order to escape from the crowds thronging and pressing him, when he then called his disciples and delivered unto them the so-called Sermon on the Mount, *evidently a Mystery-teaching.* More of this hid meaning we shall point out this evening. But here are the words:

> Give not that which is holy unto the dogs, neither cast ye your pearls before the swine, lest haply they trample them under their feet, and turn again and rend you.
> Ask, and it shall be given you; seek, and ye shall find; knock, and it shall be opened unto you: For every one that asketh receiveth; and he that seeketh findeth; and to him that knocketh it shall be opened.
> — Matthew, 7:6–8

It is extremely doubtful if the real Jesus, the center around whom were collected the legends of the Mystery-figure Jesus, ever used language of that kind; but it represents the spirit of esotericism and is a true echo of the esoteric methods of the Near East, leaving the framework of the words aside. It shows the immense prudence and caution that always surrounded the giving out of any part of the ancient Mystery-teachings. From immemorial time was it always so.

And, another thing. The penalty for betrayal of the Mysteries, in later times, was death. Never in any circumstances has the power or the force of the Lodge, has the hand of a Teacher, been raised in violence or in hatred against a betrayer, against the unfaithful, no matter how grave the crime might have been. Their punishment was in this: they were *left strictly to themselves;* and the inner penalty *was the withdrawal of the Deathless Watcher,* the *higher self within,* which had been consciously and successfully invoked upon entrance into the Mysteries, and in the higher degrees of initiation had been faced, literally face to face. The early and automatic penalty was inner death by the soul-loss. *The betrayer lost his soul.* Let me tell you further, in passing, that practically all the civil institutions of ancient times, punishments among others, were based upon what took place in the Mystery Schools. Such, for instance, was the crucifixion of the Romans, taken direct from one of the ceremonies of initiation, the "mystic death"; taken from it, stolen from it, and made an instrument of legal murder by the State in later, degenerate times. Another instance, also taken from the ceremony of the mystic death was the "cup," in India the Soma draft. In Greece we find Socrates punished by drinking from the cup of hemlock; and we are reminded of Jesus, praying that the "cup" might pass from him. Numerous other very different instances could be cited.

Similarly in Egypt and in other countries, when the periods of spiritual barrenness, of which Plato tells us, had succeeded the periods of spiritual fertility; when those periods came upon the world the State then undertook to punish in its own name the betrayal of the Mysteries, which by those times had become merely a State institution and nothing much else, merely a part of the religious establishment. Two or three instances have come down to us so far as Athens in Greece alone is concerned. One was Socrates, 5th–4th century B.C., who unwittingly betrayed some of the secrets of the Mysteries; and despite his innocence of conscious wrongdoing, they unwillingly killed that great man. Another was the philosopher-poet Diagoras, 5th century B.C., who was accused of impiety, of so-called atheism, and who fled from Athens. A third was the dramatist-poet Aeschylus, 5th century B.C., who had to flee to Italy in order to escape death. He was accused on the same grounds, of what was called profanation or impiety.

Another instance which we might mention, of a quite different type, is that of the wearing of a crown or a diadem by civil rulers, formally enacted in the coronation of a king — a ceremony adopted from the Mysteries. Some of the earliest crowns which they wore had outstanding spikes, reminding one of the crown of thorns of Jesus; or it may have been in the form of the Greek diadem, representing, in Greece, the crown of the central and west and northwest parts of Europe. As just hinted, this also was a symbol

of one of the ceremonies of one of the stages of initiations, a
ceremony signifying what occurred when the one undergoing
trial was in a state of *samādhi*, as the Hindus say, and his head
was surrounded with a glory or aura radiating from the brain like
the spikes of the early crown, in which state, also, a nimbus or
aura surrounded the body as well as the head, but far less strongly.

Now we embark more particularly upon our main theme. It
will be recalled that we have been studying from the time these
meetings were inaugurated about a year ago the so-called seven
treasures or jewels, and we are now studying certain aspects of
the seventh or highest, more especially in its relation to the Wondrous Being, called the Great Initiator, the Lonely Watcher, the
Silent Witness, and by other such names. And we called attention
last week to certain of the analogies which our own human life
bore to the kosmic Wondrous Being — for instance, particularly
the analogy of the infinitesimals, the lives infinitesimal, living in
and upon the kosmoi or universes comprised in our own physical
body, the atomic infinitesimals, and how our personal self was
the supreme self of that host of those almost innumerable atoms;
that it was the self which held that infinitesimally immense
kosmos together, and permeated all in it, and reached through all
in it, like a mystic fire. And we also pointed out how, nevertheless,
each one of those atoms, being a universe in itself, had its own
entire hierarchy, its own series of ten degrees or stages, counting
from its own supreme, its own Parabrahman and Mūlaprakriti,
down to its own "absolute matter."

Similarly, our own universal kosmos can be considered as an
imbodied soul or rather self, made up of almost innumerable
kosmic atoms or solar and planetary bodies, living with numberless companions on the face of the Boundless. We began to have
some intelligent comprehension from this study of the self, how,
in a sense, the One might become the many, yet remaining forever
the One, merely calling it the One because it is the summit or
SELF of that most great hierarchy which our imaginations can
attain to. But beyond its boundaries there are innumerable other
such Ones, and beyond all such Ones, there are innumerable hosts
of infinitely greater Ones; and so ad infinitum! The best way by
which to represent the Boundless, in which they all move and live

and have their being, is by the age-old symbol of the zero — limitless boundlessness.

That symbol is remarkable also in another respect, that it so clearly and beautifully exemplifies the teaching of the Void, the Emptiness, called in Buddhism *śūnyatā,* meaning the "empty," the "void." It is really extraordinary how our Western scholars will misunderstand and therefore misrepresent these things. They are such literalists that they will take a word and drive that word to literal death. They take the form of the thought, the body, and see little or nothing of the soul behind it. They seem to have no realization of the mystic meaning behind this wondrous thought, the Void, the Emptiness.

Do you remember that in a former study we spoke of a medieval mystic, Bernard of Clairvaux in France, who said that the state a student of mysticism should aspire to was that of *emptying* himself, utterly casting out everything that was personal or limiting, everything that was bound and finite? Such a state of mind lets the free winds of infinity blow through one, as it were!

Let us pause a moment over this. The Void is a symbol of the Boundless; hence, it is everything *because* it is *no thing.* "Nothing," if you like. Not "nothing" in the Christian theological sense, but *no thing,* no manifestation. It is not a consciousness, because it is *all consciousness,* which is unconsciousness in every personal and limited sense; consciousness is a human term. Yet it is not unconsciousness, because it is all unconsciousness of any personal or limited sense, and unconsciousness is a human term. It is both the limited and the illimitable time, and eternity; everything and therefore no thing. Call it by anything and you limit it. It is that which is and was and in the utter eternity ever shall be. And because it is nothing finite, because it is not a thing, because it is not one, or two, or three, but beyond all numeration; because it is beyond all human thought and similitude and comparison and expression, it is called that which the human mind reaches when it opens to its utmost for an abstraction, the Void, which is likewise utter Fullness.

Our study this evening calls to us to move forward. Each one of our studies lately has been dealing with very difficult subjects; and each one, if properly understood, means a great stride forward for us along the esoteric path. Tonight, let us be more particular in our remarks.

These seven treasures, then, represent in doctrinal form the seven stages of initiation. We are told that there are ten stages or degrees of initiation, which means that there are three more than the above named seven of these treasures. But we need not consider these three others. They are utterly beyond our capacity. They belong, we are told, to beings who have advanced so far beyond us that they can no longer truly be called human entities, although they do belong to our planetary chain by reason of past evolutionary karma.

Each stage or degree of initiation after the third of the seven, we are taught, is marked by something more than teaching. The first three initiations, or stages or degrees in initiation, are composed of teachings. With the fourth degree, there begins another method. What is this method?

It is one of the fundamental teachings of occultism that nothing can be *truly known* which is not *experienced, lived through.* As a matter of fact, we all know this, as it is common experience. One of the so-called laws of our being, one of the fundamental conditions of our human nature is this, that thoroughly to know a thing, thoroughly to enter into it, thoroughly to understand it, you must *be it,* you must *become it.* You cannot tread the Path until you become and are that Path. Thus, therefore, the different stages or degrees of initiation are really a kind of forcing-process for certain chosen spirits, certain chosen souls, who have proved themselves worthy: a "forcing" or developing-process enabling them through actual experience, individual experience, to pass through and realize the hid secrets of being which the slow processes of evolutionary development would have brought to them as the ages rolled by. It is, in fact, a quickening or awakening of the man to inner knowledge and power. These different stages or degrees of initiation are marked by preparatory purifications, first. Then came the "death," a mystic death. The body and lower principles, so to say, are paralyzed, and the soul is temporarily freed. And, to a certain extent, the freed inner man is guided and directed and helped by the initiators while it passes into other spheres and to other planes and learns the nature of these *by becoming them,* which is the only way by which knowledge thereof roots itself into the soul, into the ego: by *becoming the thing.*

The initiant is one undergoing initiation — and remember that initiation means "beginning"; an initiant is a "beginner," while a person initiated, an initiate, is one who has begun an undertaking. Please also note that adept means one who is "skilled"; hence, even in our ordinary life, a chemist, a physician, a theologian, a mechanic, an engineer, a teacher of languages, an astronomer, are all "adepts," persons who are skilled, each in his own profession. Those two words have, generally speaking, the same meaning also in the Esoteric School: an Adept is one who is skilled in the esoteric wisdom, in the teachings of life; and an initiant is one who is beginning to learn them. To say that you and I are beginners, i.e., initiants, is merely stating the obvious truth. It is likewise a convenient word, for it tells you nothing definite as to degree or stage; it is a generalization. Hence one could properly ask: "beginning where and what?" I may be at the bottom rung of the ladder of initiation, and you may be at the top; yet each one of us is *beginning,* for progress is endless.

Let us then closely examine all these or any other similar statements, for our own sakes. We are taught strictly to examine, strictly to search into, everything that is told us; to awaken ourselves to the *realization of things,* to *live the life,* to *be it,* to *become it;* for such is the old teaching of uncounted ages gone by.

Now the passage from *The Secret Doctrine* to which we have alluded this evening and which forms our main theme at present, in which H. P. Blavatsky speaks of the "ever-living-human-Banyan," refers also to the *arhats* (a Sanskrit word meaning "worthies") who belong to the seventh rung of the spiritual-psychological hierarchy, being only one remove from the root-base of their hierarchy, which is the Wondrous Being of our present study, therefore on the eighth plane of the ten composing that hierarchy. There is a still greater and more Wondrous Being on the ninth plane; the highest of all, the summit of all, is on the tenth.

Let us make a step still farther forward. We are taught that at the fifth initiation, part of the wonderful experience that the initiant of that degree must go through is that, after due and sufficient preparation and purification of the lower self and of the soul within, the one under trial in the mystic path meets his higher self, his own inner god, face to face for "a passing moment." Woe unto him if there be anything in him which cannot support the trial! The warnings given to us in this respect are solemn indeed. The Deathless Watcher knows all, and accepts no excuses. Those who fail have indeed another chance in another life, or in other lives; but no base metal either now or then can be accepted in this dread test. The inner nature must be pure gold tried in the fire, nothing counterfeit, nothing that is weak and will break or fail when the test comes upon it. You must then be fully ready to take your place in the Guardian Wall; no weakling can stand there.

We are further told that in the sixth degree, instead of one's own higher self, the initiant meets another One, a matter which we will tonight pass over in silence. And in the seventh degree, the same proceeding takes place as part of the mystic death, and the aspirant — can we say "meets face to face"? no, *he becomes for a passing moment the Wondrous Watcher himself;* and either returns among men as a ————, or vanishes and is seen no more. In the former case, he *knows*, because he has *become!*

We have spoken tonight of the Christian mythos. We deliberately have chosen this term, for truly it is a mythos. The entire story of Jesus as it is given in the so-called Gospels is a Mystery-story. No such man or being as the Jesus of the Gospels ever lived. Remember what a mythos is. It is a tale or allegory imbodying some secret truth. In this case, it is the story of the Mysteries partly told in symbol and allegory, partly told with some degree of later ignorant embroidery; but, as a whole, representing almost, as it were picturing, what took place in the Mysteries of Asia Minor. The manner and style of narrative, in all such cases, depended upon the national custom of celebrating them, and on the cast of mind of the peoples among whom such or another scheme or system of initiation prevailed. But the Jesus of the Gospels is a Mystery-figure only: a composite figure based on mystical teaching. Undoubtedly there did exist a young Syrian initiate of that time, around whom were grouped these various tales and stories taken more or less bodily from the Mystery Schools of Asia Minor and especially of Alexandria; because Alexandrian mysticism is the main origin of theological Christianity, for in that city it had its rise theologically. This Syrian initiate, probably a young Jewish rabbi, was possibly actually called Yeshua, Iesous in Greek, Jesus in Latin. The Hebrew word *yēshūaʿ* itself means "savior," and the later Christians of course seized upon this name — or later conferred it upon their supposed founder — and wove a mystical tale about his name, thus symbolizing his mission on earth as a "savior." We all know the Christian tale. But from the very beginning of it as the Gospels give it: from the story of the Magi following the star, to the *mystical death by crucifixion,* and the *rising again on the third day from the tomb,* it is nothing but a copy, more or less denatured and faded and poorly woven together, of great actual Mysteries, the Mysteries of *some* of the ceremonies of initiation, of which the earliest Christians certainly had some knowledge (see Origen and Clement of Alexandria, for instance). But the story in its various imperfections shows clearly that it is only a feebly constructed allegory, or mythos, of actual initiatory occurrences.

Apollonius of Tyana, the Greek, was probably as noble a character as was the Syrian Yeshua, or Jesus. Jesus is merely the Roman form of the name. We read of the marvels of Apollonius of Tyana, of his works and life, in the mystic "Life" written by Philostratus. But Apollonius is a *historical* character, and Jesus is not. The story of Apollonius is an interesting one. We read of his "vanishing away" before Domitian, when he was on trial before that eccentric and severe monarch; and much more. Why was it that Jesus was said to have been "crucified"? But he was not actually crucified. It is a Mystery-story, as I have said; and not necessarily a Jewish Mystery-story, nor a Greek Mystery-story. Each nation had its own Mysteries, greatly resembling one another, but varying in detail; but in all, there was always the "mystical death"; there was always the "descent into hades" or "hell"; there was always the "resurrection," the rising, usually after "three days"; and the "glorification" at the end of the trial.

Very many of the things that occurred in the Mysteries were taken over into civil functions of the State, and they thus formed the types of many institutions in civil life in ancient times. The king and his ministers or servants, as officers or functionaries of the State, were taken over from the ancient Mysteries, as copies of the teacher and his disciples or officials. This is one reason (of two reasons) why the ancients wrote of their divine dynasties of primeval times; and on this also was originally founded the idea of the "divine right of kings" — in later ages so greatly misunderstood and abused. Why, the very calendars of the ancient nations were based upon the same thing: they were derived, taken over, from the Mysteries. Originally, they were based on actual astrological truths, real knowledge of time periods; and later were misunderstood and misapplied.

For instance, have you realized that the Christian commemorative holy days of Good Friday, and Easter three days later, are practically the same thing as the winter solstice of December 21–22, and Christmas, December 25, three days later? Both are based on the same original idea of the mystic death, and the birth or resurrection three days later of the "unconquered Sun," exemplified in the "death" and "resurrection" of the successful neophyte in the Mysteries three days later! Why was it, I ask you, that the Christians adopted both the ancient pagan festival of the winter solstice, and the ancient pagan resurrection-mythos, and made an Easter out of the latter — one being the *alleged* anniversary of their Jesus' birth (Christmas), and the latter the anniversary of his "resurrection"? Because they wanted very much to connect and bind together their newfangled religion with the personality of the great Jewish prophet or initiate later called Jesus; and, at the same time, to connect him with the archaic Mystery-teachings of the School of Wisdom. Now, as the Jewish or rather Syrian festival took place in the month of the spring equinox, or rather *on the day of the full moon* following the spring equinox, they copied the ancient Mysteries again here, as follows: they, as it were, severed the symbol into two parts, and called one Christmas, commemorating the birth of the physical body of their supposed Jesus; and the other part they called resurrection, or Easter, commemorating the "birth" of the transcending Christos. It was a curious *tour de force*, as the French say, a curious feat of "mystical gymnastics," as Katherine Tingley so neatly puts it. But, and please mark this, these two dates were actually in very truth closely connected in the ancient Mysteries, and very much in the line the Christians followed!

Now, if you take the mystic calendar that guardedly we spoke of last week, it is remarkable how it fits in with the Mystery-teachings connected with this Wondrous Being, the Great Initiator. As to the article in *Lucifer* (January 1890) referred to, in which H. P. Blavatsky speaks of the date which the esotericists should call the New Year, i.e., January 4th — does anyone really think that she meant that January 4th per se has any especially magical or mystical properties or influences? No; she did not. Our calendar-day for January 4th is a date of a purely mechanical calendar, with nothing mystical or hid in it at all. If we were to fall into a period of universal ignorance such as the Mediterranean nations fell into after Christianity became powerful, we should forget even how to take care of our merely mechanical calendar, and find ourselves unable to make it conform to the changing seasons. We should then be in the same troubled case as the European peoples were in, in the sixteenth century, when Pope Gregory XIII had certain contemporary mathematicians reform the old Julian calendar because of the disorder it had fallen into through the pure ignorance of Gregory's predecessors. They did not know how to intercalate the necessary days at the proper time, and in February 1582, when the Julian calendar was reformed by Papal Bull or Edict, they were eleven to twelve days behind the true year. Similar was the case when Julius Caesar reformed the calendar in the year 47 B.C., only much worse, for owing to political machinations, doubtless, of the different Pontifices Maximi, the calendar of the Romans, as I remarked last week, had fallen so far behind the natural year of the seasons that the calendar January the first fell on what was really October 13th, according to nature; and the calendar winter solstice, December 21st or 22nd, fell on October 3rd, or thereabouts; and if Caesar had not corrected the growing disorder and confusion, the constant loss of the days through wrong or omitted intercalations would have let the calendar year fall continually backwards all through the natural year, perhaps. So you see that when speaking of H. P. Blavatsky and the astrological calendar, most certainly we do not mean merely the mechanical calendar of common use; nor did H. P. Blavatsky mean it. But she meant a date depending upon real astrological facts.

Remember that astronomy is merely the mechanical aspect of true, ancient astrology and, for that reason, astronomy deals only with the positions, movements, and physical conceptions of planetary and solar and stellar bodies. It is in real fact merely one branch of the ancient astrology, a sublime science of the celestial bodies, and we do *not mean* what modern writers mis-call astrology — a paper-science at best. We have spoken suffi-ciently strongly against such a misconception at other meetings.

Now our real year, our mystic year, is quite a different one from the civil or ordinary chronological year. The civil chronological year could begin on the true date of the winter solstice, that is to say, on the day and moment when the sun is farthest south, and just as it begins its journey northwards again. That is one of the natural periods of time and season division; and it is also an astrological time period, if we wish to form a time cycle, but with one important change. Now what would be that astro-logical cycle? We could start our civil year at the winter solstice *when the moon is new*. But *fourteen days after the true solstice* or on what is now January 4th, according to our present calendar, *the moon is full;* and that day opens under the control of the planet Mercury or Hermes, the particular leader, guide, and director, of initiations and the Teachers. This is the case, mark well, when that planet is in inferior conjunction at sunrise; or more particularly when Sun, Mercury, Earth, and Moon are all in syzygy — all along a straight line — Mercury being between Sun and Earth, and the Moon *full*. The planet Mercury then controls the first hour of the 14th day after the winter solstice; but that solstice must concur with the new moon, and Mercury on that 14th day afterwards must be in inferior conjunction at sunrise. The 14th day (January 4th) is then a true "Wednesday" or Mercury-day. Thus opens the cycle. How long that cycle lasts, I have not had opportunity to investigate. Our astronomers here can work it out. But thus we should have two years: one for what we may call the civil year (fundamentally an astrologi-cal year) for the purposes of civil chronology, by which ordinary time would be reckoned; and the Budhic-cycle year. The civil year would then begin with the day of the winter solstice, let us say December 21–22, in the night between December 21st and

22nd. The next day therefore would be the first day of the first
month of the new civil year; but our mystic year, our Budhic
year, would begin fourteen days after that *at full moon*, on a
true Wednesday or Budha-day.

We turn now to another matter, which is of real importance.
I refer to the diagram which was discussed somewhat at our last
meeting, and which we then had no time to explain in detail.

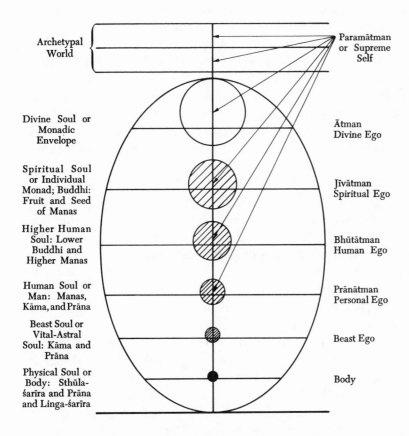

This paradigm, this symbol, can refer either to man, or *mutatis
mutandis* to the universe of any full hierarchy, it matters not
which hierarchy. Note then, first, that we have at the top of the
diagram the archetypal world, which is the root or seed, if we

look upon it as the origin or commencement of things, as the locus of the initiation of kosmic evolution and progress; or which is the flower, the end, the consummation of things, if we look upon it as the full-blown flower of the kosmic evolutionary cycle. It may be divided into three planes, so to say, forming the highest triad or divine triad; the second of these planes is called the Paramātman or supreme self. The first plane represents the Parabrahman, with its field of Mūlaprakriti; this highest triad, as represented, applies to any hierarchy — this hierarchy, that hierarchy, any hierarchy, as this paradigm is representative of all. The Paramātman likewise represents the First or Unmanifested Logos. The third plane, or lowest of the triad, represents the Third or Manifested Logos, or Brahmā-Purusha-Prakriti. Then, following the diagram downwards, we reach the seven principles and elements in manifestation, formed of the three quasi-arūpa or formless planes, and of the four rūpa planes, or planes of form. The egg-shaped envelope of the hierarchy is divided into these seven planes, if you please, and six centers of consciousness with their inseparable six vehicles or "souls." The vertical line running up and down through the egg represents the indwelling self: that self which in you and me and in all is One; that which in all of us says "I am." It does not differ in you or in me, for it is One, the universal self of the hierarchy. But what is it in you and me or in anyone which says "I am *I*, not *you*" — that which is *self*-consciousness? That is the ego, the "I," but not the self, for the self is beyond and outside of all such limitation of consciousness. It recognizes no distinction between Thee and Me.

You remember the beautiful Sufi legend, how the Soul, wandering in search of truth, came finally to the House of God and knocked at the portal. Then in answer to the knock, thunder reverberated through the spaces of Heaven, and God called out: "Who art thou?" And the Soul replied: "I." And God answered: "I know not *I*." Then the Soul wandered again for many ages in tribulation and sorrow, and finally it came anew, and once more knocked at the portal of the House of God. And the voice of God called out and said: "Who art thou?" And the Soul replied: "*Thou*." And the voice of God then answered and said: "Enter into thine own, for we are One." No distinction there between I and Thou — a beautiful legend imbodying one of the profoundest concepts of the ancient wisdom.

Further, we have attempted to represent paradigmatically the decreasing consciousness, understanding, power, potency, force, expansion, comprehension, by the six circles gradually decreasing in size downwards, along the central line representing the self. It is impossible to represent adequately on a flat surface a purely metaphysical subject; but our wish in so doing is to show that the higher the circle or sphere is, the more spiritual the sphere or center is; the larger and the more comprehending it is in both quality and potency, not necessarily in magnitude. Further, we have attempted to show the increasing materiality in these centers or spheres as they go farther downwards, by thicker and thicker shading of these centers in the diagram. The highest center is the divine soul or monadic envelope. It is the first or highest vehicle of the ātman; and as an egoic center it is the divine ego. The next one downwards is the spiritual soul or the individual monad. This, and the one above it, combined, are the inner Christ; and corresponding to the spiritual soul or individual monad is the jīvātman or spiritual ego. It is that portion of our spiritual economy which is deathless as an individualized ego; deathless until the end of the mahā-manvantara of the solar system. When the solar pralaya arrives in the grand fullness of time, there comes a moment, a final instant which is the utter completion or consummation of all things in that system; and in the twinkling of an eye, literally, and instantly, all the planets and the sun itself are "blown out," as it were. The last one of all manifested beings has at that instant gone to higher planes; and there being nothing whatsoever left to hold physical matter together anywhere within the solar system, that system immediately falls to pieces and vanishes away (as I have said before) like an instantaneous shadow passing over a wall.

The second center is comprised of buddhi, both the fruit and the seed of manas. This is the center or seed or root or base of the reincarnating ego. Then below it comes in our diagram the higher human soul, composed of the lower buddhi and the higher manas, with the self permeating it, as said above. Corresponding to it as egoic center is the bhūtātman, explained at our last meeting, otherwise the human ego. Next comes the human soul or man: this is formed of manas, kāma, prāna, and the egoic center corresponding to it is the prānātman, or the personal ego, which is mortal. There is no abiding principle from and including this, downwards; no abiding principle in "man" whatsoever. The next below is the beast soul, or the vital-astral soul, the kāma-prāna; its quasi-egoic center being the beast ego, if you like: that elementary principle of egoship in the beast which holds it together during its existence. Our teachings do give to every animate thing a soul; not a human soul or a divine soul or a spiritual soul, but a *soul corresponding to its type*. What it is, what its type is, *comes from its soul;* hence we properly may speak of the different beasts as having, one or the other, a duck soul, an ostrich soul, a bull or a cow soul, a chicken soul, or a nightingale soul, and so on. The lower entities, considered as a kingdom, are differentiated into these different families of animate beings by the different souls within each; and of course behind the soul from which it springs, there are in each individual entity all the other principles that likewise inform man. *But all the higher principles are latent in the beast.* That is why man belongs to another — the human kingdom, for there is in him the buddhi principle more or less active. Manas springs forth from the buddhi as the fruit from the flower; but manas itself is mortal, goes to pieces at death. All of it that lives after death is only what is spiritual in it, and that can be squeezed out of it, so to say. H.P.B. calls it the aroma of the manas, much as the chemist takes from the rose the attar or essence of roses.

The last is the physical "soul" or body: the sthūla-śarīra, the gross body, prāna, and the linga-śarīra.

We have spoken before of the lost soul as being at one pole, and of the Master at the other pole, of consciousness. It is between the higher human soul and the human soul (or man proper) that lies the psychological frontier over which one must pass forwards or upwards, backwards or downwards; into regeneration or degeneration. If you go upwards and continue to go upwards or rather inwards — please remember that we are obliged to use human language in all such descriptions; we actually do not go up in space; it is *quality* that we are speaking of, the refining of the quality of the human ego, the penetrating, the breaking into, as it were, of the final sheaths of our inner being that makes the distinction — if we continue to go upwards or inwards, we attain finally to Masterhood. But, contrariwise, if we go downwards, if our egoic soul-quality wholly deteriorates, then at last we lose the ego-center, the soul-center which, divorced from its upper life-thread, is dissipated and, as said, is at last annihilated. There is the case of a lost soul at one pole of consciousness, and of the Master at the other pole. When mortality becomes immortality, when the corruptible becomes the incorruptible, then do we attain to full and complete conscious Masterhood — a lord of life.

As said before, when the conscious center which we now are is given over to full attraction or gravitation towards matter, the momentum increases with time and use and, through attrition as it were, that part of us where our egoic consciousness then resides, called soul, is worn away and finally vanishes. It is wiped out, annihilated; nothing is left of it. It sinks into the Eighth Sphere, the Planet of Death, where it meets finally its fearful fate. As to the monadic (the spiritual) essence of our being, it then has to evolve a new conscious center or egoic vehicle for future reincarnations. That is where the seriousness of this thing comes in. It has to develop or evolve the new soul-center, the new egoic center, in order to take up again the link in the series of lives; and it may be that in certain circumstances ages upon ages may pass before the newly evolved vehicle of monadic consciousness is able to make up the lost time and opportunities. In the meanwhile, the racial life-wave has swept far along the pathway of destiny; leaving the "failures" far in the rear.

TWENTY

THE HIGHER ASPECT OF HUMAN PSYCHOLOGY. INITIATION AND THE
MYSTERIES: AVATĀRAS, BUDDHAS, AND BODHISATTVAS. THEIR
RELATION TO GLOBES, ROUNDS, AND RACES.

Truly, "for the salvation of the good and the destruction of wickedness,"
the personalities known as Gautama, Śankara, Jesus and a few others were
born each in his age, as declared — "I am born in every Yuga" — and they
were all born through the same Power.

There is a great mystery in such incarnations and they are outside and
beyond the cycle of general re-births. Rebirths may be divided into three
classes: the divine incarnations called Avatāras; those of Adepts who give
up Nirvâna for the sake of helping on humanity — the Nirmânakâyas; and
the natural succession of rebirths for all — the common law. The Avatâra is
an appearance, one which may be termed a special illusion within the natural illusion that reigns on the planes under the sway of that power, Mâyâ;
the Adept is re-born consciously, at his will and pleasure;* the units of the
common herd unconsciously follow the great law of dual evolution.

What *is* an Avatâra? for the term before being used ought to be well
understood. It is a descent of the manifested Deity — whether under the
specific name of Shiva, Vishnu, or Âdi-Buddha — into an illusive form of
individuality, an appearance which to men on this illusive plane is objective,
but it is not so in sober fact. That illusive form having neither past nor
future, because it had neither previous incarnation nor will have subsequent
rebirths, has naught to do with Karma, which has therefore no hold on it.

---

*A genuine initiated Adept will retain his Adeptship, though there may
be for our world of illusion numberless incarnations of him. The propelling
power that lies at the root of a series of such incarnations is *not* Karma, as
ordinarily understood, but a still more inscrutable power. During the period
of his lives the Adept does not lose his Adeptship, though he cannot rise in
it to a higher degree.

— H. P. Blavatsky, "The Doctrine of Avatâras," "*S.D. III*," p. 364

P LUNGING directly into our subject this evening, it will be
remembered that we have been studying the nature of
the Wondrous Being of whom H. P. Blavatsky writes in
the first volume of *The Secret Doctrine;* and that the key words
by which we may gain some appreciation of the way this Won-

drous Being works in humanity, and more particularly in the psychological hierarchy, through the cycles of the Mysteries and of initiation — these key words were the "human Banyan."

Also we read on page 424 of the same volume, under section the 12th, "The Theogony of the Creative Gods," H. P. Blavatsky's words concerning the hierarchy of forces, where she points out how these forces were originally understood in their proper sense as intelligences and consciousnesses working in nature; but that each nation, as the cycles of time passed by, understood these forces and intelligences in the same way indeed, but gave to them different names, and developed a philosophical understanding of the machinery, so to say, of the kosmos in slightly differing manners or forms, and that these different philosophical forms were the various schools of the Mysteries; for instance, in Samothrace and Eleusis in Greece, and similar schools in other countries.

Now up to the present time we have been talking in more or less generalizing terms regarding this Wondrous Being; but tonight we are going to try to particularize, asking ourselves definitely who and what this Wondrous Being is.

To do that, we are undertaking an extremely difficult task, on account of the subtil nature of the subjects which in their entirety expose the truth about this Wondrous Being. We cannot understand who and what this Wondrous Being is without understanding something of the initiations of the Mystery Schools; and to understand those we must understand something of the higher aspect of human psychology; and again, to understand that, we must understand the other doctrines which we have been studying, such as that of hierarchies, and the doctrine of swabhāva, and so forth.

Please understand that these seven jewels, these seven treasuries of wisdom, comprehend in small compass all possible human knowledge during this kalpa; that is to say, the key teachings which form those seven treasuries. They comprise everything that man has known, that humanity now knows, and that humanity can know, in this kalpa. They are, really, a short synopsis in the form of philosophical principles — these seven jewels — of all possible human knowledge; and it depends upon each one of us how much of that knowledge we can understand.

You probably also have noticed that not one of these jewels can be fully understood if considered alone. They complement each other and explain each other. Every one of them is explained by the other six; each one of them explains the other six and complements them. Please do not imagine for a moment that they are separate and distinct compartments of knowledge in the materialistic sense. There is but one knowledge, one truth, as there is but one life, and one ultimate being; but these various jewels, these seven jewels, are different facets, so to say, of that truth, different pillars, to change the figure, in the temple of divine wisdom.

It will be remembered that at our last study we spoke of two main reasons why the Teachers have kept these and other doctrines so secret, and why the penalties for betrayal of this knowledge were so great. First, because these teachings that we have been studying, and many others, derivatives from them, are the sublime reward of those who have proved themselves worthy of them and of going farther in behind the veil of life. But the greater reason is that they could not be understood by the untrained mind even were they told; they simply could not be understood. Great minds would understand more than would little minds, of course; but on account of the imperfect spiritual development of men's minds so far in this fourth round, men simply cannot understand them without at least some training, and the result of unlawful exposure of them would be degradation of the teachings which originally were given to men by the gods in the early ages of the human race.

This statement is no vain remark. These teachings have been betrayed in some degree at different times, and they have always resulted in what we call black magic, the natural result of a misunderstanding and of a misapplication of them and of the principles of truth which are in them. Even today we find men and women, although they know nothing whatever of these secret doctrines, going up and down the land, charging for their teachings on what they call spiritual realities, and professing to know everything in heaven and on earth. Note well that no true spiritual teacher ever charges money, or any other fee, for spiritual truths.

We all know what H. P. Blavatsky said about such action. "I

would liefer starve in the gutter than take a penny for teaching spiritual truths." That is the test by which one may know, one of the tests at least, the true teacher from the false. That is one way in which a teaching may be degraded. Our Teachers have no desire to have these glorious doctrines misunderstood and degraded and, perhaps, human souls in relatively large numbers misled and their feet set upon the path which leads downward.

Now in Greece — we will take this case first as an example — there were two bodies of the Mysteries, the Less and the Greater. The Less, in Attica, were celebrated in the springtime; and the Greater were celebrated at about the period of the autumnal equinox, in September, at Eleusis. The Less consisted, first, of purifications of the soul and mind outwards and inwards, mostly inwards, for that is the real purification; and, second, of dramatizations of that which was to take place in actuality later in the Greater Mysteries. They represented in dramatic, pictorial form that which the Greater Mysteries were to bring to the candidates.

The Mysteries of Samothrace, also a Greek institution, and like those of Attica a State institution in the later days, were probably the oldest in Greece. But these two schools of the Mysteries, while teaching the same fundamental verities and the same ultimate truths, did not teach the same things. For instance, the Mysteries of Samothrace were what we today would rather call scientific. They dealt with the nature and operations of the Kabeiroi, who belonged to the class of spiritual entities called "builders," the lower septenary; whereas at Eleusis — and this name *Eleusis* means the "Advent" or the "Coming," and the *Eleusinia* "things that are to come" — at Eleusis the more theological and mystical doctrines were taught, more particularly that which will happen to man after death. Hence the name of the place, Eleusis, where they were celebrated, and the name of the Mysteries themselves, the Eleusinia, i.e., the things which shall be or shall come.

Each country had its own mystical jargon or dialect or manner of speaking of and in the various Mysteries; and with regard to the Mysteries in Greece and in Syria and in Palestine, these jargons or technical words nearly resembled each other. For instance, in Syria, outsiders were called swine and dogs; betrayers were called wolves. Those of you who remember your New Testament will probably remember the instances in which swine and dogs and, I think, also wolves are spoken of. Foxes was a term for those who tried to enter the Mysteries unlawfully. All these terms are taken from the attributes of certain animals, which man in unlawful action copied: the fox on account of its cunning; the wolf on account of its bold cruelty and lack of conscience — that is the reputation it has, at least; swine and dogs on account of the reputation that these beasts have always had in the Orient.

But while these terms were a part of the jargon of the Mysteries of those countries in those days, as was pointed out at our last meeting, it is not the language used in our School. I do not believe, as said, that Jesus ever called those who were not initiates in the Mysteries of his time "swine and dogs." If he did this, the presumption becomes a certainty that he did not belong to our School; but as he did so belong, we must conclude that such language came from his disciples living probably in Alexandria, where the Gospels were almost certainly composed and written in the form in which we now have them.

Next — and now we turn to the direct subject of our study, to our main theme, our main thought. Open wide your hearts; cast out for a short time from your minds all thoughts which are personal and unworthy of the atmosphere into which we are now entering. At our last study we took four technical words in order to explain somewhat by them our present great subject, talking around it rather than talking of it, four words used in the trans-Himalayan Buddhism because, first, they are the words which H. P. Blavatsky used; secondly, because they are the words which are in the esoteric books of the East belonging to our School. Three of these are, *ādi-buddha,* the "primal wisdom," or Logos, as a Greek would say; then the *dhyāni-buddha,* the "buddha of meditation or contemplation," of which buddhas there are seven; then the *mānushya,* the "human buddha." But these three are all connected: the ādi-buddha as the Logos, the dhyāni-buddha as the causal buddha, the mānushya-buddha as the agent on our plane of the celestial hierarchy. These buddhas belong to the celestial hierarchy as contrasted with the kosmic hierarchy or builders. The fourth word is *bodhisattva.*

At former meetings we have spoken of the planetary spirits, using this term in a general sense as equivalent to dhyāni-chohans or lords of meditation. Now this evening we go a step farther. The planetaries are the builders of the astral-material world, and they draw their plan, and they draw their higher life, and they draw their wisdom (outside of that which they themselves have won) from the celestial hierarchy, the upper septenary; and this celestial hierarchy originates in ādi-buddha, primordial buddha, or the Logos.

Now for each round of our septenary planetary cycle (that is of this kalpa, or Day of Brahmā comprising all the seven rounds) there is a presiding dhyāni-buddha, a buddha of contemplation, a causal buddha; and all the events of all the seven globes of our planetary chain are under the overseeing or supervision of the particular dhyāni-chohan of that round. Our present round, being the fourth, is under the supervision of the dhyāni-buddha belonging to the fourth degree of the celestial hierarchy. For each globe of the planetary chain there is what the Buddhists call a *bodhisattva*, a Sanskrit word meaning "he whose essence is wisdom."

This bodhisattva is a mind-born son, so to say, of the dhyāni-buddha of that round. There is a dhyāni-bodhisattva for this globe, and also one for each one of the three globes which precede this globe on the downward arc, and likewise a bodhisattva for each of the three globes which follow this globe on the upward arc — one bodhisattva for each. This dhyāni-bodhisattva is the spiritual head of the spiritual-psychological hierarchy of each globe. Take our globe, for instance. Our dhyāni-bodhisattva is the Wondrous Being, the Great Initiator, the Silent Watcher of our globe; in one sense an emanation from the dhyāni-buddha overseeing all the round, but not merely an exudation or prolongation, if you will, of the dhyāni-buddha. Each bodhisattva is an entity in himself. He is as a ray of that dhyāni-buddha.

Next, during evolution on our earth (and on the other seven globes correspondentially) the life-wave runs through seven stages called root-races. Each one of these root-races is ushered in by a mānushya-buddha, a human buddha, who is the "son" of the globe-bodhisattva in the same way as the globe-bodhisattva is a "son" of the dhyāni-buddha of the round. Each one of these seven root-races is furthermore divided at its middle point, so to speak. When half of its cycle is run, then the racial cataclysm ensues, for that is the way in which nature operates; and preceding that cataclysm there is another human buddha, or mānushya-buddha, of less degree.

Is this Wondrous Being a man? He is. Is he more than a man? He is. Is he a septenary entity? He is. How is the influence of this Wondrous Being communicated to his agents, the human buddhas and the human bodhisattvas?

Let us study for a moment an allied subject, a psychological one, before we go farther. We cannot understand what comes to our theme farther on until we have at least sketched out this psychological subject. Man, as you know, is sevenfold. Man may be divided in a triform way: a spiritual man, an intermediate or highly ethereal man, and an astral-physical man. In other words and in "psychological" terms: (1) divine man, (2) spiritual man, (3) personal man. Now, then, what is an avatāra? An avatāra, as commonly supposed, is the descent of a god into a human form. That idea is exoteric. It is not false, but simply put in that way and with nothing more added in explanation it is very misleading.

You remember what Krishna says in the *Bhagavad-Gītā:* "I incarnate in period after period in order to destroy wickedness and reestablish righteousness." Krishna there represents the Logos, or rather, perhaps, the logoic ray; and the Logos — or its ray or influence — on our plane would be utterly helpless, inactive, and have no possible means of communication with us and our sphere, because that logoic ray lacks an intermediate and *fully conscious* vehicle or carrier, i.e., it lacks the intermediate or highly ethereal mechanism, the spiritual-human in us, which in ordinary man *is but slightly active.* An avatāra takes place when a direct ray from the Logos enters into, fully inspires, and illuminates, a human being, through the intermediary of a bodhisattva who has incarnated in that human being, thereby supplying the fit, ready, and fully conscious intermediate vehicle or carrier. This "human being" has no karmic ego of its own. The egoity, the ego, the intermediate part, the highly ethereal and fully conscious intermediary, the spiritual-human element, is supplied by the incarnating bodhisattva; that is to say, the highly evolved personal principles of a buddha, otherwise a nirmānakāya — not the highest element of that buddha, which is in nirvana, but the spiritual-personal element of the buddha, glorious, pure, and great, the spiritual-personal ego — enters into the body of that utterly pure human being before or shortly after its birth, and thus supplies the intermediate vehicle appropriate for the incarnation of the logoic ray. That is an avatāra.

For instance, a child is born. That child has an inner psycho-astral nature of transparent purity and beauty and it attracts magnetically, if you like, but spiritually, actually, a ray from the Logos. Its own higher self is fully active, of course, and the logoic ray — which is ITSELF — manifests in it. Furthermore, a bodhisattva, under the conditions which prevail when an avatāra is required on earth, enters that body also, thus supplying the egoic element. So, then, we have this marvelous thing: a pure human body with its prāna and astral model-body, but with no true karmic ego incarnating, a bodhisattva supplying that egoic element of still greater purity than possible to ordinary men, and evolved to the degree required for the incarnation of the logoic or ātmic ray, that logoic ray and the higher self of the born child really being one. But this mystery in life is a very exceptional circumstance.

Let us turn to another facet of the same psychological subject. Take the case of the Lord Buddha. Please notice that we here speak of the Lord Buddha, although we speak of the great man as Siddhārtha, his personal name, and of the sage Gautama, or Gautama-Śākyamuni. Gautama was his family name; Śākya, his clan name; Śākyamuni, the Śākya sage, was the title given to him in later life and after. When Śākyamuni entered nirvana during life, he is then exoterically said to have "died" at the age of eighty years; but our teachings show him actually to have lived to one hundred years before he gave up his physical body and remained on earth as a nirmānakāya. We all know what a nirmānakāya is; it is a complete man minus the physical body only. But is that all there is of this wondrous mystery? It is not. The higher portions of the Buddha were in nirvana; yet the spiritual-personal ego remained on earth, active, an active entity, a force for spiritual good as a nirmānakāya, overshadowed by the nirvanic element, and this nirmānakāya was, please note carefully, a human bodhisattva. It is the teaching that this bodhisattva, the egoic element of the Buddha Gautama, as was the case with previous buddhas, was a spiritual-human ray from the globe dhyāni-bodhisattva.

You perceive the difficulty, the extreme difficulty, in making these subtil and highly spiritual subjects clear to minds untrained in our metaphysic. Actually they require years of deep thought. Let us look at it from another aspect again. Who was Jesus? What was Jesus? Who was Apollonius of Tyana? What was he? The teaching is that both were incarnations of a nirmānakāya, and both had the same mysterious connection with the bodhisattva of the Buddha Gautama. Apollonius was not an avatāra, though Jesus was. There are close psychological similarities between these two wonder-cases of history; but they are not identically the same mystery. I merely note here in passing that mystically a buddha stands higher than an avatāra, for reasons which will be explained in due course of our study.

Let us go a step farther. You all have read of the incarnations of the buddhas in Tibet. We are now speaking in exoteric language, such as you will read in Sven Hedin or various others of the European explorers. Some of them have seen these so-called incarnations of the Buddha. Please understand once for all that our School is not Lamaism; our School is representative of the archaic, esoteric, wisdom of the world, although it is true on the other hand that the esoteric side of Tibetan Lamaism, properly understood, is the nearest doctrinal approach to the doctrines, in large degree, of our School. With all the faults that the Tibetans may have, with all the various drawbacks that we Westerners may consider them as having in one way or another, nevertheless the esoteric teaching in Tibet is nearer to that of our School than any other.

But how did this very curious and interesting doctrine of the continued reincarnations of the Buddha in the Tibetan Tashi-Lama and the Dalai-Lama, and in various others of the Buddhist hierarchy in various monasteries in Tibet, originate? It originated in the mother-doctrine that we are now studying. You will remember that H. P. Blavatsky speaks in the passage in *The Secret Doctrine* that we are now studying of an event that happened before the separation of the sexes in the third root-race, when a certain "spiritual being" incarnated in men; and she says that this was not a race but, after this Wondrous Being, became a succession of great spiritual entities. It is actually the *passing on* of the inner self, the ego if you like, the ethereal man, of that original Wondrous Being that came to humankind from superior spheres in order to enlighten and to save mankind, beginning with the third root-race — passing on down through the ages thereafter in vehicles of human flesh and mentality even to our present time. You will remember how she speaks of this Wondrous Being as a man, and yet not a man, one concerning whom legends are rife in the Orient. In all ages there have been mysterious allusions to the Master-Initiate, to the Great One, to the Head of all Teachers, to the Silent Watcher, to the Great Initiator, and so forth and so forth. Tibetan Lamaism drew this teaching of the continued reincarnations of the Buddha from that fact. This is an interesting question, and perhaps some day we shall investigate it more fully; but we cannot touch upon Tibetan Lamaism at greater length this evening.

It is necessary, however, to understand that the difference between the transmission of an egoic element as in the buddhaic line in Tibet, and those exceptional incarnations called the avatāras, is in one sense great; and in another sense they are very much alike. They are very much alike in this, that in both cases the upādhi (or vehicle) chosen for the manifestation of the superior entity is a human being. Also in both cases the psycho-ethereal upādhi is a bodhisattva; that is to say, in the case of an avatāra, the bodhisattva is the glorified personal man of a buddha, of a mānushya-buddha; the lamaic succession is also bodhisattvic, but of inferior intensity, so to say — a bodhisattvic *influence* rather than a full incarnation of a bodhisattva, as in the case of an avatāra.

The doctrines that students of Buddhism set forth in the books which they publish on Buddhism, in the West, are of course those that they derive from the Buddhist books themselves, usually with very inadequate understanding of the subtil points of that most spiritual of all religions; and unquestionably these scholars strive to understand and truthfully and honestly to set forth that which they believe to be the real meaning of Buddhist teachings. But it is an amazing thing that they do not succeed better; and the reason is that they come to their study with materialistic Western minds, materialistic Western preconceptions and prejudices. They come to their study in an attitude of mind which they themselves do not recognize as existing, and hence talk sagely — when they fail to grasp meanings — of the "superstitious extravagances of Oriental imagery," etc., etc. Now how is it possible to understand the real nature or the real essence of anything if you begin your study with the prepossessing idea that you know better and more than did the persons who wrote the things which you are studying? Such egoism destroys sympathy and obscures true vision; and if your study be of religious subjects, inevitably you will look upon all statements made or doctrines formulated as "monkish vagaries." But, as was pointed out in other studies, there is no exoteric doctrine belonging to the great *ancient* world religions which is intrinsically false. The fact is that the exoteric teaching *is* the truth, but it needs a key in order to explain it; and without the key it actually can be, and usually is, misunderstood and misinterpreted, and degraded in a manner very similar to that of which we spoke upon opening our study this evening.

Let us now turn to another subject connected with this, collateral, and showing another facet of the jewel. They tell us that the human buddha, the mānushya-buddha Gautama-Śākyamuni, was born 643 years before the first year of the accepted beginning of the Christian era. Our doctrine tells us further that a human racial buddha comes at the beginning of, and a minor one preceding the middle point of, a root-race. I call your attention to the fact that we are now approaching the middle point of our fifth root-race. We are in the fourth subrace of that fifth root-race, not in the fifth subrace thereof. Please get this point clear in your minds. It will be between sixteen thousand and twenty thousand years yet before the racial cataclysm will ensue which will cut our fifth root-race in two, exactly as happened to the fourth-race Atlanteans and to the third-race Lemurians who preceded them; and as it will happen to the two root-races which will follow ours, the sixth and seventh.

Now the reason why some students have supposed that racially we are now in the *fifth* subrace is on account of a misinterpretation, very pardonable, it is true, because we all know that the subject of cycles and numbers is always closely veiled. This misinterpretation or misconception appears to have arisen from what H. P. Blavatsky writes in volume II of *The Secret Doctrine* on pages 435 and 445; and I desire to call your attention to the fact that one of the commonest "blinds" that a teacher is obligated to make when writing of esoteric matters in a public work is *using the same word in varying senses.* There is an esoteric obligation to do so when it is necessary, in order to tell the truth for those who can and who may read, and yet to hide it from the "dogs" and "swine" and "foxes," if you will forgive my use here of the New Testament or Syrian jargon. I call your attention in the above connection to *The Secret Doctrine,* volume I, page xliii: ". . . each Round being composed of the Yugas [Ages] of the seven periods [root-races] of Humanity; four of which are now passed in *our* life cycle, the middle point of the 5th being nearly reached." I call your attention also to page 610 of this same volume where H. P. Blavatsky says: "But as we are in the mid-point of our *sub-race* of the Fifth Root Race — the acme of materiality in each — therefore the animal propensities, though more refined," etc. The "acme of materiality in each" means only one thing — *the middle point of the fourth of any cyclical series:* for instance, *the fourth primary subrace;* the *fourth subrace* of the *fourth primary subrace* of the fifth root-race, and so forth.

Suppose that for convenience' sake we divide the races in the following way: *root-*race really meaning the first or root- or originating primary subrace, but commonly applied to all the seven successive primary subraces of a root-race and all the many other smaller subraces included in those seven. The first *root-*race then is the first primary subrace, of which primary subraces there are seven in the great racial cycle; then the secondary subrace, seven of them in each primary subrace; then seven family races in each secondary subrace; then seven national races in each family race. We need go no farther. A few steps more in the series and you will come to the unit-entity, or individual man. But please also examine page 147 and page 710 of volume II, for they will well repay your close study of them.

In another part of *The Secret Doctrine* you will remember that H. P. Blavatsky, in speaking of the precessional cycle of 25,920 years, here giving the ancient figures, calls it the cycle of a family race, that is to say, the race including seven national races. The European race is a family race; and hence when she speaks of the lifetime of this family race she says it has about 16,000 more years to run. So you see that from our ordinary human viewpoint we are not yet very near the great racial cataclysm; but from the standpoint of the cycles of the age of a root-race so short a period as 16,000 years is like saying tomorrow, or even the next hour. A short period of 16,000 or 20,000 years is insignificant in duration in the drama of the soul.

And H. P. Blavatsky somewhere — I think it was in her magazine *Lucifer* in 1887 or 1888 — alludes very graphically to the earthquakes then reported in the newspapers as occurring, and she calls them the *forerunners* of that which is going to happen to us *as a race*. But is America the home *to be* of the 6th subrace? Yes. *Which* subrace? Subrace is vague enough! Is it to be a sixth *family* race? But if America is then to be in about 16,000 years, or the latter part of a precessional cycle of 25,920 years from now, the home of the sixth family race, H. P. Blavatsky goes on immediately, in a masterly way, just as any initiate would, to lead the mind on, and she says that America is also to be the *seed-land,* the *nursery,* of the sixth root-race, a statement also true, but including a vast period of years between the two points! When that latter far-distant day dawns America will then no longer be. Much of the land of the Americas that is now above the waters will then be under them, and new land, now forming the sea bottom, will have arisen above its surface. For all we know, North and South America may be more widely united. New land will rise out of the present Pacific, thus raising the old Lemurian beds again, to be joined to us here on our western coasts.

So when we read of subraces let us beware, let us be careful, lest the molds of our minds, misleading us, lead us astray after mere words which are blinds. Break the molds of your minds at all costs! Free your minds, keep them plastic! Refuse to take as the sole truth any isolated statement whatsoever, wherever you may find it. *Take it,* but not alone; contrast it, compare it, study it, and analyze it if you want the truth. Especially is this necessary when it is a question of cycles, and of the words dealing with cycles. Watch carefully when you see the word subrace, watch carefully when you read of the Buddha. Which buddha? Or of the bodhisattva — which one?

So we postpone for a later and more extended study the subjects which we have attempted this evening to outline. Much more should and will be said about this Wondrous Being. But, in closing, do not misconstrue my words about this Wondrous Being. Remember the series: first, the Logos, the ādi-buddha; then the seven dhyānis, each one of the seven inspiring and overseeing one of the seven rounds, who is the causal buddha, the sun, if you like, emanating out innumerable inferior beings. Then the dhyāni-bodhisattvas, for each globe of the planetary chain, seven of them; and seven mānushya-buddhas, one such for each one of the seven root-races on each globe during each round. There are probably almost numberless cases where a bodhisattva, a buddhic ray, as the cycles of time pass, reaches out from the Lodge of the Masters, where the Great Initiator, the Highest One, is, the Man-Emanation of the Wondrous Being, and inspires and instills the ancient wisdom into the soul of some great and pure human being, such as was Jesus of Nazareth, and Apollonius of Tyana, and many, many others whose names are not familiar to us Westerners.

And in the initiations there are three things that take place. They are directly connected with the subject of the Wondrous Being and the bodhisattvas. Remember that initiation is the quickening or enlivening of the soul of one who is prepared. It is a quickening process of evolution, for producing a more rapid evolving of the inner man, which otherwise an ordinary man would achieve only after many ages. In these initiations, and in the fifth, to particularize, there occurs what is called the *theophany*. The Christians use that word and also *epiphany*, which is a minor form of the same thing, and they say it should be celebrated on the 4th–6th of January, the matter having direct relation with the calendar of the solar year of which we spoke in our last study. *Theophany* originally meant the "appearance of a god." It actually is the following mystery: in the fifth initiation, the human being under trial, the chela under trial, *meets his own god-self face to face,* and for a longer or shorter time *becomes one with it.* He then knows truth. You will remember that the only way of really understanding a thing is *to become that thing*. And that is the real meaning of what takes place in the true, real initiations, and the *epiphany* is a minor manifestation of the *theophany*. It is a Greek word meaning "shining upon," or illuminating; whereas *theophany* means the "shining forth visibly of a god" — *the man's own inner higher self*.

If the theophany is more or less complete upon the ending of the initiation or the trial, the chela then has *theopneusty*, meaning "divine inspiration." He is consciously united with his inner god, his higher self. Literally, the inner god of the candidate breathes down into him, for a longer or shorter time, depending upon his advancement, the wisdom and the knowledge of all the universe, so to say, in degree greater or less, depending upon the candidate's advancement and receptivity.

The highest of all the ancient initiation achievements in Greece was called the *theopathy*, meaning "suffering a god" — not a god who suffers, but one who suffers the conscious entrance into him of a god. This is not, of course, an avatāra, which is something else entirely, as we have shown above; but it means that at initiation and for a less or greater time afterwards, according to the spiritual power and receptivity of the initiate, he becomes, through that holy presence in him, a walking, living god, *his own* inner self. Finally, in some rare cases the theophany, the theopneusty, and the theopathy last as long as does the life on earth of the initiate.

TWENTY-ONE

INITIATIONS AND THE ANCIENT MYSTERIES. ROOT-RACES AND THEIR SUBDIVISIONS. GLOBE ROUNDS. PLANETARY ROUNDS. SOLAR KALPAS: HOW CALCULATED. RACIAL CATACLYSMS.

"As to the Philosophy, by whose assistance the Mysteries were developed (and which, we may say, they were designed to teach), it is coeval with the Universe itself; and, however its continuity may be broken by opposing systems, it will make its appearance at different periods of time, as long as the sun himself shall continue to illuminate the world. It has, indeed, and may hereafter be violently assailed by delusive opinions; but the opposition will be just as imbecile as that of the waves of the sea against a temple built on a rock, which majestically pours them back, broken and vanquished, foaming to the main. However it may be involved in oblivion in barbarous and derided in impious ages, it will again flourish — through all the infinite revolutions of time."
— THOMAS TAYLOR, *Eleusinian and Bacchic Mysteries*

Hence in the *Smaragdine Tablet*, disfigured by Christian hands: —
"The Superior agrees with the Inferior; and the Inferior with the Superior; to effect that one truly wonderful Work" — which is MAN. For the secret work of Chiram, or King Hiram in the Kabala, "one in Essence, but three in Aspect," is the Universal Agent or *Lapis Philosophorum*. The culmination of the Secret Work is Spiritual Perfect Man, at one end of the line; the union of the three elements is the Occult Solvent in the "Soul of the World," the *Cosmic* Soul or Astral Light, at the other; . . .
— *The Secret Doctrine*, II, 113

The intention of all mystic ceremonies is to conjoin us with the world of the Gods. — SALLUST

The design of the Mysteries is to lead us back to the perfection from which, as a Principle, we first made our descent. — PLATO

Blessed are the pure in heart: for they shall see God [their own inner god]. — JESUS

I have heard of thee by the hearing of the ear, but now mine eye seeth thee. — JOB

THIS evening we are going to speak of another matter collateral with our main theme yet very important; and at our next meeting we shall endeavor to take up the scattered threads which we have unloosened, both in generalization and in particular, and gather them together and weave them into a consistent whole, making as nearly as possible a clearer picture for our brain-minds of what we can understand at present of the seventh treasury of wisdom. Also, if we have time this evening, we shall endeavor very briefly to treat of a matter left incomplete at our last meeting, that is to say, the question of the seven root-races of mankind through which the human wave of life passes during the present fourth round on our globe.

We open our study in reading from volume I of *The Secret Doctrine,* page 424, the extract which we have read before:

To thoroughly comprehend the idea underlying every ancient cosmology necessitates the study, in a comparative analysis, of all the great religions of antiquity; as it is only by this method that the root idea will be made plain. Exact science — could the latter soar so high, while tracing the operations of nature to their ultimate and original sources — would call this idea the hierarchy of Forces. The original, transcendental and philosophical conception was one. But as systems began to reflect with every age more and more the idiosyncrasies of nations; and as the latter, after separating, settled into distinct groups, each evolving along its own national or tribal groove, the main idea gradually became veiled with the overgrowth of human fancy. While in some countries the FORCES, or rather the intelligent Powers of nature, received divine honours they were hardly entitled to, in others — as now in Europe and the *civilized* lands — the very thought of any such Force being endowed with intelligence seems absurd, and is proclaimed *unscientific.*

Note the calm but trenchant irony in this extract. I merely call attention to it before passing on. Now this extract, though dealing with the various aspects which the ancient religions took as the ages passed, leading to their differentiations into the so-called great religions of the world, nevertheless fits in very well by analogy and by comparison with the subject which we are going to treat in particular, although briefly, this evening, that is to say, the question of initiations and the ancient Mysteries, and also a much misunderstood fact in nature closely connected with the ancient Mysteries, which was evolved into a doctrine by the ancients and called by them the "succession of teachers" — *guru-paramparā* in Sanskrit, and distortedly and faintly reflected in the Apostolic Succession in the Christian scheme.

The Christian Church very early took over that doctrine of the succession of teachers, with much other theological timber, from the old religions of the countries bordering the Mediterranean Sea; and the doctrine which it took over became for that Church the so-called Apostolic Succession of the Church of Rome, the popes succeeding one another and claiming to be the successors of the fisherman-apostle of Galilee, Simon Peter. We do not care to go into this aspect of the matter for it is useless for our present purpose, and no benefit can be gained by it; but wherever we look and whatever line of human social or religious activity we may choose to take for our study, we shall always find that there is a passing on of authority or a passing on of teachings, or of both. The various heads of even our political bodies succeed one another, and usually carry on a political tradition. Big businesses succeed one another, and usually pass on, from man to man, a tradition of commercial policy and expansion, and so forth. It is simply an exemplification in ordinary practical life of a rule of nature; that is to say, that man, being a mortal being, having to die, but being an entity of thought and of heart, does not want to see that which he feels to be good, or which he believes to be good, lost; and so he transfers either authority or teaching, or both, to another whom he considers fit and capable to carry on his teaching or authority, or both.

It is in the religious field of human activity that this system is most marked, and where the feeling is the strongest. A succession of "prophets" succeeding each other in the ancient Mysteries, a succession of hierophants succeeding each other therein, is a fact well known to us, even ordinary knowledge such as you may find in an encyclopedia or in school books.

In Greece, for instance, in taking the Eleusinian Mysteries as an example, we know that the hierophants were drawn from one family, the Eumolpidae, living in Athens, and the torchbearers were drawn from another family, the Lycomidae, living in Athens; and we have reason to believe that the Mysteries of Samothrace, the seat of an older rite, and which were, like the Mysteries of Eleusis, a State function, were also conducted in the same manner by the passing on of the tradition held sacred and incommunicable to outsiders; and the bond of union between the initiates of these so-called Mysteries was considered indissoluble, impossible of dissolution, for death merely strengthened the tie.

Now outside of the fact that men like to pass on what they think and believe to be good, whence arose throughout the various countries of the world of which we have some knowledge the remarkable mystic similarities we know of, whence came to them all the closely similar knowledge and authority which were passed on from one head to another? It must have come from somewhere. Men no longer believe in the empty philosophico-scientific theory or fallacy of fifty years ago, to the effect that, for instance, six men, living in six different isles, will inevitably and infallibly tread six more or less identical paths of mental and physical thought and ceremony. It was once a scientific heresy to doubt that theory. It was called a fact, though there were no facts to prove it; it was a theory merely, having no other foundation than imagination overworked in order to find an explanation of similarities and identities such as the above.

Let us say here that we look with respect and reverence upon the discoveries of the many great and noble-minded men who have given us brighter views into the shell of nature, the outward physical shell, and whose lives often are models of self-sacrifice; but while we recognize that every new light shed into our minds, showing us new views into the heart of nature, is good for us, nevertheless we draw a sharp line of distinction between *science*, the noble knowledge of classified truth, and the *theories of scientists*. We accept a theory if it is good, but only as a theory; and it must be corroborated by nature herself before we will accept it as a fact, as a part of science per se.

So, then, we receive the following bit of knowledge from our Teachers that this particular doctrine, which in the Church of Rome is called the Apostolic Succession, and in the ancient Mysteries was called the Passing of the Word, the Passing of the Knowledge, the Passing of the Authority, or by some similar expression, originated in our Order, but obviously not in our lifetime. We are merely a generation, one of many, carrying on the tradition of the knowledge which originated in the final ages of that vanished continent Lemuria and was more particularly developed in Atlantis, where were first established the ancient Mysteries.

As in the highest of the Lodges, we are taught, the truth is

passed from the great Master-Initiator to his successor to the truth
and the authority, so in the inferior Lodges, the same system is
followed; and we in our work merely carry on the same tradition.
It is saddening to see how learned ignoramuses with high-sounding
names, or possibly with an alphabetical string of academic titles
after their names, sometimes talk about the Mysteries of which
they can really know nothing outside of the scattered data found
imbodied in old literature. They are mere bookmen, readers, and
not understanders. It is also truly pathetic to hear some folk talk
about the non-necessity of having a leader, because they believe
that one man is as good as another, and that no man can be very
much better than another, and to see their opinion that all this
talk about spiritual, inner light and illumination passed on from
initiate to initiate is just thingumbobbery!

Are they wise? But ask them for proof of their theory, and
they can give you none. No proof whatsoever; it is pure speculation. On the contrary, we may point out to them even such facts
as we know, or the things of which history has left certain records
in her annals, where invariably you will find the same old tradition
coming down the ages of the passing down of the knowledge and
of the authority and of the doctrine.

Now when we speak of Mysteries and initiations we use those
words in a sense which to us is sacred, and with no wish or desire,
far less with any attempt, to create a false and mischievous atmosphere of emotionalism. We speak of facts. You know that every
member of the School is more or less a scientist, i.e., a "knower"
and researcher. We are taught to use our brains and our minds
and our wills first of all for self-conquest, and then to analyze
properly ourself and the world we live in. Have we not been told
again and again that we must consult our consciences before we
accept anything? In order to do that, we have to think; we also
know that even if in doing so we should, *through our own blindness or incapacity,* reject a truth offered to us, we shall nevertheless have done aright, because we have been faithful to ourselves
and to our consciences, and that the karma of that rejection will
be merely temporary, because the inner man understands, and the
truth in time will dawn in faithful hearts.

We are taught that the Mysteries — we take those of Greece

for an example — were divided into two parts. Let us particularize and take those of Eleusis: you will remember that Eleusis as a word means "advent," "the coming," that which is coming, the promise. As the Mysteries of Samothrace were rather what we would call scientific, dealing more with the operations of nature, and the origin of those operations and the method of controlling them, and teaching what they led to — in other words, what we would today call science; so the teachings at Eleusis were rather those religious and philosophic doctrines of esotericism giving to men what the great Roman orator, Cicero, called a brighter view of life and a livelier hope as regards death, because they taught of the things which are to be, more particularly the so-called, and thoughtlessly so-called, "dark mysteries of death." These Eleusinia were divided into two parts, as said above, the Less Mysteries and the Greater Mysteries. The Less Mysteries were celebrated in the early springtime, more or less about the time of the Anthesteria, the Flower Festival, and the celebrations took place at a small town called Agrae. Those Mysteries were mainly dramatic in form, with this one object in view: to prepare him or her who was initiated into these Less Mysteries better to understand, more quickly to apprehend, and more easily to seize with the mind, that which he was to go through in the Greater Mysteries of Eleusis, providing that in the interim and during the time of trial he proved himself true and fit and clean.

Even in the days when early Christianity had superseded the degenerate and corrupt religions of the Mediterranean countries, even then, fallen as the Eleusinia were from their former high state, yet they were considered so highly that initiations still took place in them. They were actually finally stopped on the initiative of the pagans themselves, the school closed by an order of the Christian Emperor Justinian in Constantinople, but closed on the petition of the better of the so-called pagans themselves. The truth is that the Mysteries were not overcome by Christianity, but fell because of intrinsic degeneracy. Can we imagine what those men must have felt in the day when they saw that which was dearer to them than life closed and ended by their own will, invaded and degraded by degenerate rites and beliefs and, doubtless, also by the Christian fanatics?

Now the dramatizations in the Less Mysteries were not what we would call plays exactly; they were plays in one sense because they were dramas. But they were enacted in the form of spectacles in which the would-be disciple, the initiant or the one to be initiated, had to take the main part himself or herself. Let us give a concrete example, which at least will be interesting and perhaps illuminating, remembering that there were various kinds of styles of initiations and of Mysteries existing in the different countries, although fundamentally they were all one and still today are one in the great secret sodalities; but in each country the initiations and Mysteries took on different aspects, as it were, as for instance in Hindustan as compared with Greece. The initiator and the neophyte might use a different language, and wear different clothing, etc., and perhaps go through a different rite, and so on and so on. But fundamentally the idea was the same the world over. It must be remembered that the Smaller Mysteries were preparations for the Greater. In the former, the candidate was *taught*, and enacted as a drama what he would have to experience psychically and spiritually in the Greater Initiations.

One of these rites was the drama, or the trial rather, that the neophyte would have to pass through in actuality later, in the Greater Initiation, and it was the meeting with his inner self, his own inner self, not in the vague and abstract way in which we today speak of a man as having "found his true self"; but in the Less Initiation the neophyte was actually put through training and purification in order to fit him to undergo the real test, in which he met his own inner self face to face, as another individual apparently, at first, but at a still higher initiation to be blended with that other self, his own self, his higher self.

This rite is one of the Smaller Mysteries, those of purification and training, and was enacted at the town of Agrae, not far from Athens, where the Less Mysteries were held, and it was enacted dramatically. The neophyte was then and there taught to anticipate and understand what was coming to him if he was successful later in the Greater Rite. He was frankly and openly told at the last what he was there to meet if he desired to go to the end of the path. And similarly with the other stages or degrees of initiation.

Now it is not certainly known how many degrees or secret stages there were of the Eleusinia, but we know that there were several; and we know that to the very end, before they were finally closed on account of their degeneration, they were so carefully guarded, so faithfully kept hid, that to this day scholars are mentally running around in bewilderment, in an endeavor to find out what really was taught in the Eleusinia, in these Mysteries which aroused the admiration of the greatest men of antiquity. In those of Samothrace likewise the circumstances of secrecy and degree were very similar.

Take Egypt: the pyramids, we are taught, were simply — the Great Pyramid especially — majestic initiation-temples. There too the Mysteries and the initiations were most sacredly guarded and kept secret. They were kept only for those who had proved themselves worthy, not by talk but by act, and who had been tried and tested in many different ways. And why? Because it was a dangerous matter for unprepared minds. Our Teachers tell us plainly that there were three results of an initiation: one success; another failure, which often meant death; and the third (a partial failure) often meant madness. But success meant glory unspeakable. Why was it that madness and death sometimes ensued? Through any outward punishment? No. The results were wholly from within the candidates themselves. They were plainly told, these neophytes: "Come with a clean heart, and glory unspeakable and knowledge of the gods shall be yours; but come with a perverse and wicked heart, with your mind untrained and with your will unset, and you will never be able to face that which you will have to meet in the other world." Because that is what the Greater Mysteries were, a passing behind the veil of this physical shell. No wonder that the training was severe, arduous! Those ancient men had high hearts in their bodies and wise old minds.

Now those Mysteries are not dead today. We are taught distinctly that the same ancient truths, the same entrance into glory, the same beautiful realization of the highest hopes that man bears in the secret recesses of his heart, the same surpassing knowledge of life and being: all can be had by him who *wills* and who *dares* and who *knows how to keep silent*. That is what the Masters have taught us. They also have taught us another great truth, that it is not a *sine qua non* for success to have a mighty brain-mind, for they have told us plainly that even some of their own Brothers, some of the Masters themselves, are such by virtue of their spiritual grandeur, and not by virtue of any brain-mind eminence alone nor of any particular mental power; and further that such of the Masters, spiritual sons of glory, may stand high even among themselves. We are further taught that this brain-mind of ours is very often a hindrance to us; it is indeed a most useful servant if we keep it a servant, but it is a master which will inevitably put our feet upon the left-hand path unless illumined and guided by the spiritual nature, because all its thoughts are thoughts of self, and all its thinking is for gratification of its own desires; its horizons are limited, and its outlook is short; its self-born inspirations are few and far between; and it is mortal and dies with the body. It depends upon ourselves as to which side of our nature, the higher or the lower, we shall, as William Quan Judge used to say, nail our faith, pin it there and keep it there.

The other matter mentioned at the beginning of our study this evening is that of the races through which mankind, as a life-wave, passes in its journey from the beginning of evolution on this globe to its end. You will remember that there are seven such root-races which form the evolutionary cycle, in this fourth round, which is what we call one globe-round; and we are at the present time, as said before, in the fourth subrace of our present fifth root-race. There is confusion about these races in the minds of some students, because H. P. Blavatsky, as was pointed out at our last meeting, was under the necessity when she wrote of keeping quiet, or rather hid, certain teachings which she was not then empowered publicly to give out. Had there been the proper appeal from her students, perhaps she would have done so then. At any rate, we shall give a short outline in an attempt to illustrate this rather difficult subject.

Let each line of the following diagram represent a root-race. There are seven lines (or root-races), and you will notice that the junction-line, beginning one root-race out of the preceding root-race, is at the middle point of the former, that is, at the fourth subrace of the preceding or mother-race. It is so in all the lines (or root-races). Now we are at present in the fifth

root-race, two races short of the completion of our globe-cycle
or globe-round, and our present fifth root-race is almost at the
point, the middle of our fifth root-race, where the sixth root-race

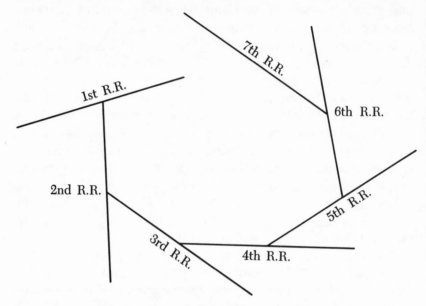

to come will branch off. Each root-race, each of the seven, is
divided in our teachings into seven minor races as follows. Notice
the recurrence of the number seven:

	1. Primary Subrace	(7 minor divisions of it)
	2. Secondary Subrace	(7 ” ”)
One	3. Family Race	(7 ” ”)
Root-	4. National Race	(7 ” ”)
Race.	5. Tribal* Race	(7 ” ”)
	6. Tribal Generation	(7 ” ”)
	7. Individual Man	(say 72 years)

We say 72 years, because the average man, barring accidents
and malignant diseases which may carry him off before his time,
usually lives about 72 years. Some human beings live much
longer, of course. If we took count of all human deaths — of the

---

*Another name may be suggested which is better for this and the fol-
lowing.

babies who die in such numbers in infancy, and of all who die in shipwreck, and of all the men killed in wars, and of all the murders and of all the diseases, and of the train and automobile wrecks, and of all such accidents — probably the *average* length of human life today would not be more than 15 or 20 years; but those cases, after all, are exceptional. Man lives today, on a natural average, about 72 years, barring all accidents, etc., as above suggested.

The following is an interesting calculation, offered only as a suggestive thing. Suppose that you desire to calculate the length of time of a root-race, and please understand that what we are saying now is only a rough approximation. Take then 72 years, the famous three score years and ten in the Bible — a mystery-figure, a round number for 72 — and multiply it by seven: we get one tribal generation; multiply it by seven again, we get one tribal race; multiply that by seven and we get one national race, and your figure will come to about 25,920 years, the length of the precessional cycle; multiply that by seven again, and you get one family race; multiply that again by seven and you get a secondary subrace; and multiply that by seven once more and you get a figure which is really the entire time period of a root-race. This calculation is very rough numerically, and is so intended to be; but it is suggestive.

You see we do not count the root-race as one of the seven here, but make it the all-inclusive one, and why? Because if we did so count it, we should be counting the primary subrace twice. A *root*-race really ought to mean the race which originates a thing, or is its "root." It is therefore, strictly speaking, from the first primary subrace that all the others of the series grow, exactly as the root of a tree sends up its trunk, and the trunk its branches, the branches their smaller branchlets, the smaller branchlets still smaller branchings, they the twigs, which bear the leaves. Therefore, according to the above series, it is the primary subrace which really is the *root*-race.

Now there are seven (please mark again, seven) root-races in one globe-round, that is to say, a planetary round as it passes through our globe. Seven globe-rounds equal one planetary round; seven planetary rounds equal one kalpa or manvantara

or Day of Brahmā, and seven kalpas plus seven planetary pralayas (or seven periods of planetary rest) equal one solar kalpa.

7 Root-Races = 1 Globe-Round
7 Globe-Rounds = 1 Planetary Round
7 Planetary Rounds = 1 Kalpa = 4,320,000 of our years
  (plus several more ciphers)   + 000
7 Kalpas + 7 Planetary Pralayas = 1 Solar Kalpa

These figures are given because they are fundamental. They
are accurate as far as they go. We shall have to deal with them
in future studies.

Please note in conclusion that the drawing on page 294, illustrating the birth of root-races from each other at the middle point
of each, equally well can represent a primary subrace or a secondary subrace, or a national race, or a tribal race, etc., and the
reason is obvious, because there are no perfectly unique and
singular things in nature anywhere. Nature does nothing but
repeat itself, and the man who said that nature never repeats
itself uttered a titanic fallacy. Nature does nothing but repeat
itself. Did you ever see a thing perfectly unique — utterly different in all respects from everything else? On the contrary, you see
everything everywhere repeating itself: the seasons year in and
year out; day and night year in and year out; the planets circling
around the sun continually; their satellites circling around their
primaries in more or less the same way; and so forth. There is
constant repetition everywhere. A tree in putting forth its foliage,
puts forth its own leaves; it does not put forth something unique
and unheard of — pumpkin pies or chairs or temples or houses; it
puts forth that which belongs to it, as all trees do.

Cycles can be found in every branch of life; for instance,
children are born on the average at the end of ten lunar months
or nine solar months. A child can live and be perfectly healthy
and successful, if born at seven months after conception, but it
is often a child of great sensitiveness, high-strung, of nervous
temperament, and it needs the most anxious and loving care,
because it has to finish its growth in the cold outside, and nature
takes two other months to do it normally.

Now, as said before, we shall endeavor at our next study to link together the various threads of thought which we have gathered up and weave them into a whole so consistent, so coherent, that even our brain-minds can grasp at least some notion of the sublime theme that we have been studying within the last few weeks.

TWENTY-TWO

Know that the stream of superhuman knowledge and the Deva-Wisdom thou hast won, must, from thyself, the channel of Alaya, be poured forth into another bed.

Know, O Narjol [Naljor], thou of the Secret Path, its pure fresh waters must be used to sweeter make the Ocean's bitter waves — that mighty sea of sorrow formed of the tears of men.

Now bend thy head and listen well, O Bôdhisattva — Compassion speaks and saith: "Can there be bliss when all that lives must suffer? Shalt thou be saved and hear the whole world cry?"

— *The Voice of the Silence*, pp. 67, 71

IN OPENING our study this evening let us read from The *Secret Doctrine*, volume II, pages 281–2:

As the "coats of skin" of men thickened, and they fell more and more into physical sin, the intercourse between physical and ethereal *divine* man was stopped. The veil of matter between the two planes became too dense for even the inner man to penetrate. The mysteries of Heaven and Earth, revealed to the Third Race by their celestial teachers in the days of their purity, became a great focus of light, the rays from which became necessarily weakened as they were diffused and shed upon an uncongenial, because too material soil. With the masses they degenerated into Sorcery, taking later on the shape of exoteric religions, of idolatry full of superstitions, and man-, or hero-worship. Alone a handful of primitive men — in whom the spark of divine Wisdom burnt bright, and only strengthened in its intensity as it got dimmer and dimmer with every age in those who turned it to bad purposes — remained the elect custodians of the Mysteries revealed to mankind by the divine Teachers. There were those among them, who remained in their *Kumâric* condition from the beginning; and tradition whispers, what the secret teachings affirm, namely, that these Elect were the germ of a Hierarchy *which never died since that period:* —

*"The inner man of the first * * * only changes his body from time to time; he is ever the same, knowing neither rest nor Nirvana, spurning Devachan and remaining constantly on Earth for the salvation of man-*

THE BEACON

120 WALL STREET, 24TH FLOOR - NEW YORK, NEW YORK 10005 - USA

Please make check or money order payable to THE BEACON. Residents of Canada & other countries please pay in US funds with international or postal money order, or check drawn on a US bank. Please allow four to six weeks for delivery of first issue.

Name_____

Address_____

_____

Subscription Form

[ ] 1 year $17.00   (6 issues)

[ ] 2 years $32.00   (12 issues)

[ ] 3 years $48.00   (18 issues)

Please start with ....issue

[ ] Single issue $3.00.......................

.......................(OVER)

PLEASE ENTER THE FOLLOWING GIFT SUBSCRIPTIONS:

[ ] 1 year - [ ] 2 years - [ ] 3 years

[ ] 1 year - [ ] 2 years - [ ] 3 years

_____

_____

_____

_____

_____

_____

PLEASE SEND A COMPLEMENTARY BACK ISSUE OF THE BEACON TO THE FOLLOWING:

_____

_____

_____

kind. . . ." "Out of the seven virgin-men (Kumâra) *four sacrificed themselves for the sins of the world and the instruction of the ignorant, to remain till the end of the present Manvantara. Though unseen, they are ever present. When people say of one of them, "He is dead"; behold, he is alive and under another form. These are the Head, the Heart, the Soul, and the Seed of undying knowledge . . ."*

. . . Higher than the "Four" is only ONE on Earth as in Heavens — that still more mysterious and solitary Being described in Book I.

— the Wondrous Being of whom we have spoken before.

Plunging then directly into our study, let us first ask ourselves one question. Whither are we as a race, as men, as thinking entities, traveling, in what direction? The ancient wisdom tells us that we are traveling *inwards,* not up, not down, not to right or to left, not forward or backward, but *inwards,* leaving the realms of matter, taking them with us in fact by spiritualizing the inferior coatings: traveling inwards on that path which began with our descent (if you like the term) into matter, into manifestation, and henceforward raising matter towards spirit, its real source or root, following the path *which we ourselves inwardly are,* and marching inwards, ever more inwardly, until at the consummation of all things we shall attain a goal, an end, even more supernal than that which we left in commencing our peregrination downwards into experience.

The next thought that occurs is: Are our higher natures separate from ourselves, paradoxical as it may sound? Are they ourselves? What are they? We all know, as students, the teachings concerning the seven principles of man; but when we stop to ask ourselves what are these seven principles really — do they form a unity, or is each one of them an entity in itself? — then we enter upon very difficult subjects indeed. Let us say first that the four lower principles are borrowed or rather, perhaps, *evolved out of ourselves* in combination with elements drawn from the common storehouse of nature, as man takes into his body for his nutrition his food formed of atoms, yet each one of those atoms in itself is the vehicle of a monad, manifesting in that sphere or plane of life. But our three higher principles are each one a separate entity but conjoined into an inseparable unity during the manvantaric cycle. And we see the reason why this is so in studying the seventh of the seven treasuries of wisdom, which seventh is the supreme key of all the other six.

We begin to form some conception of what lies before us in this study: how unity becomes multiplicity and how multiplicity resolves itself back into unity. Note first the difference between *one, unity,* and *union. Union* is an assemblage of things straitly united together; *unity* is an assemblage of things but with a common head or source, the summit of a hierarchy, for instance; whereas *one* is a monad, an individual, and therefore indivisible. Now we are a *union* in our four lower principles; we are a *unity* in our three higher principles, our upper triad; and we are *one* in the three highest, the highest triad, so called for easy comprehension.

The three principles forming the upper triad exist each on its own plane, and we feel their influence, because we are in spiritual rapport with them. Nevertheless each one exists on its own plane in consciousness and power. We know of each only what we have so far evolved; all we know, for instance, of the third principle (counting from the top), the manas, is what we have so far assimilated of it in this fourth round. It will not be fully developed until the end of the next round. What we call our manas is a generalizing term for the reincarnating ego — I am now speaking of the higher manas.

Turning a moment to a collateral subject, we must realize that all our consciousness, i.e., the consciousness of the ordinary man, pertains to this our present plane, but that there are innumerable other planes of the kosmos surrounding us, interpenetrating us, and of these other planes each has its own entities, its own beings, thinking and unthinking, as our plane has, each class appropriate to its own sphere or plane, and that our very earth interpenetrates them as they interpenetrate us, and that the reason we do not see their habitations and them, and their dwellings, and the lower creatures living there, is because our senses are not yet fitted to cognize them, have not been evolved or trained to know them or see them, for our physical senses have but a very limited perception of things. But there indeed they are. Some of these planes belong to our own hierarchy, and some do not. Those which do not, belong to other hierarchies each having its own series of planes or worlds. As in a chord of music each note may be distinctly heard, each being separate from the other, but together they form a chord, a musical harmony, so it is with these planes. It is, if you like, all a matter of differing vibrations, this word being used here in its scientific sense. If the vibrations are such that our senses can cognize them, we see them then, or hear them, or touch them, or taste them, or smell them, as sense perceptions; and if our senses are incognizant of them, we know nothing of them. Yet they are there!

Similarly with our three higher principles, the upper triad. The ego exists with its own consciousness, and its own forces, and its own dwelling which is a "soul," and we feel its effects, we feel its flux, which to us is an influx; and similarly with the buddhic principle, and with the ātmic ray. We say that the ātman is universal, and so it is; but it belongs *(so far as we are concerned in our present stage in evolution)* to the fourth kosmic plane, though it is our seventh principle.

What I am trying to say is that the destiny of man is to raise his focus of consciousness from the lower to the higher; and with each step that he makes upwards, or more properly inwards, *he finds a new world,* with its own inhabitants, as said above, with its own conditions and "laws," with the "habitations" of its inhabitants. And following the ancient axiom of the Hermetists, "As above, so below," we can see the perfect truth, the perfect fidelity to fact, in stating that these various planes or rather worlds — some of which are immensely higher than ours, some only a little higher, some immensely lower than ours, some only a little lower — that each one of these planes or worlds, I repeat, has its own life and thinking beings, its own trees, and its own stones, and its own storms, and its own fire, its own inhabitants, and its own animals, and all the rest of the manifold and various things and entities, similar to but not identical with the beings we see around us on our plane. Think of the vastness of the spaces of consciousness and being which this thought brings home to us, the illimitability of life, its utter and perfect endlessness, promising endless evolution before us, as there have been endless experiences and evolution behind us! The reflection is an ennobling one.

Now the summit of every hierarchy, as so often said, is *one:* and may be considered as one in three or three in one, a philosophical conception of the ancients whence the Christians got their dogma of the Trinity. This is the uppermost triad. Next comes a unity of what we call our upper triad, three separate principles per se, yet bound together in a compact unity in the seventh or highest principle, the ātman, which is the self, the "universal selfhood," not our ego, but that feeling or consciousness of selfhood which is the same in you and in me and in every human being, and even in all the inferior beings of the hierarchy, yea, even in those of the beast kingdom under us, and dimly perceptible even in the plant world, and which is latent even in the minerals. This is the pure cognition, the abstract idea of *self*. It differs not at all throughout the hierarchy, except in degree of self-recognition. When you say *self*, you mean the same thing that I do; but when you say *myself, I am I and not another*, that is the consciousness of your *ego*, and it is not the same as when I say *I am I*. When this ego is raised from the lower planes to the higher, it comes naturally in touch with higher things. From the inferior consciousness we become by evolution conscious of our-self as a man, or *self*-conscious; and from the man we become a Buddha or a Christ, reaching full expanded *self*-consciousness. And there are thereafter other planes still higher than this, of which we now say no more. Finally, the four lowest principles form a *union*, nonpermanent, transitory, and dissoluble at death.

Remember that these planes or worlds extend as such in both directions, inwards and outwards — one reaching ever into greater superiority to us, from our standpoint; and the other direction going downwards or, as it is sometimes expressed, along the path of the left hand.

Now let us read another extract, as our next subject, from *The Secret Doctrine*, volume I, page 572:

Esoterically the teaching differs: The divine, purely Adi-Buddhic *monad* manifests as the universal Buddhi (the *Mahâ-buddhi* or Mahat in Hindu philosophies) the spiritual, omniscient and omnipotent root of divine intelligence, the highest *anima mundi* or the Logos. *This* descends "like a flame spreading from the eternal Fire, immoveable, without increase or decrease, ever the same to the end" of the cycle of existence, and becomes universal life on the Mundane Plane. From this Plane of *conscious* Life shoot out, like seven fiery tongues, the Sons of Light (the *logoi* of Life); then the

Dhyani-Buddhas of contemplation: the concrete forms of their formless Fathers — the Seven Sons of Light, *still themselves*, to whom may be applied the Brahmanical mystic phrase: "Thou art 'THAT' — *Brahm.*" It is from these Dhyani-Buddhas that emanate their *chhayas* (Shadows) the Bodhisattvas of the celestial realms, the prototypes of the *super*-terrestrial Bodhisattvas, and of the terrestrial Buddhas, and finally of men. The "Seven Sons of Light" are also called "Stars."

Sublime beyond ordinary human comprehension are the truths of life and the mysteries of being! We are taught that there exists a Hierarchy of Compassion, which H. P. Blavatsky sometimes called the Hierarchy of Mercy or of Pity. This is the light-side of nature as contrasted with its matter-side or shadow-side, its night-side. It is from this Hierarchy of Compassion that came those semidivine entities about the middle period of the third root-race of this round, and incarnated in the semiconscious, quasi-senseless men of that period, those advanced entities otherwise known as the solar Lhas, as the Tibetans call them, the solar spirits, who were the men of a former kalpa who during the third root-race thus sacrificed themselves in order to give us intellectual light; incarnating in those senseless psychophysical shells in order to awaken into a divine flame of egoity and self-consciousness the sleeping egos which we then were. They are ourselves because belonging to the same spirit-ray that we do; yet we, more strictly speaking, were those half-unconscious, half-awakened egos whom they touched with the divine fire of their own being. This our "awakening" was called by H. P. Blavatsky the incarnation of the *mānasaputras*, or "sons of mind" or light. Had that incarnation not taken place, we indeed should have continued our evolution by merely "natural" causes, but it would have been slow almost beyond comprehension, almost interminable; but that act of self-sacrifice, through their immense pity, their immense love, though, indeed, acting under karmic impulse, awakened the divine fire in our own selves, gave us light and comprehension and understanding. So from that time we ourselves became the "Sons of the Gods"; the faculty of self-consciousness in us was awakened, our eyes were opened, responsibility became ours, and our feet were set then definitely upon the path, that inner path, quiet, leading inwards back to our spiritual home.

In speaking of initiations at our last meeting, you remember it was pointed out that initiation is in fact a quickening process, but it is also something else; it is a copy, an endeavor to copy, what was done by the incarnation of those lords of understanding, sons of light. It is an attempt to stimulate, to awaken into activity, the inner spiritual self, to enliven us more quickly, to enable us to see and understand, saving those who successfully pass through the tests aeons and aeons of suffering and strife and, noblest of all, enabling those whose minds have become enlightened, themselves to do the same for their brothers who are less progressed than they.

Why is it that from the very beginning all the Teachers who have appeared among men continually teach us the duty as well as the need of self-control, and of pity and of compassion and of spiritual understanding? Why? Because these things verily are the keys, these are the open sesames, these are the things which unlock the portals, not merely to let in the light, but when the light is seen, to give it again to others, for who is the man who would not follow it?

Let us write down the following names, cited in the above extract from *The Secret Doctrine*, and reduce them to hierarchical form so that they will more easily remain in the memory:

1. Ādi-buddhi.

2. The second is mahā-buddhi, which is in fact mahat. It is likewise the First Logos, adopting the Greek method of nomenclature.

3. The third is universal light which is also life, also called in the Sanskrit, divine matter, divine nature, daivīprakriti; the Second Logos.

4. The sons of light, called the logoi of life, the Third Logos.

5. The dhyāni-buddhas, the buddhas of contemplation or meditation.

6. The celestial bodhisattvas, a Sanskrit word meaning "he whose nature is essentially celestial wisdom or bodhi."

7. The superterrestrial or superhuman bodhisattvas.

8. The mānushya-buddhas, or the human buddhas.

9. Men.

This is the Hierarchy of Compassion, emanating or evolving from the supernal regions, and they are the flowers of the evolutionary course; and these regions themselves form the first (or the tenth) or the root, if you like, of the Hierarchy of Compassion, counting upwards or downwards.

Now the essential aim of this hierarchy, the whole purpose and strife, if you like the word, of evolution, is to raise the corruptible into incorruptibility, to raise imperfection to perfection, to raise the mortal so that it shall put on immortality or, in other words, to raise the personal man to be the individual man, to make of the human a divine being. The average man has of course not yet reached that sublime stage, and hence, as was pointed out before, there is no abiding principle whatsoever in *personal* man, because he is composed only of the five lower principles; and when we say personal man we mean the man of this period, of this epoch, the evolving entity of the present time, the *person*. But overshadowing this person, incarnating in this person (if we can use the term incarnating) there is the divine flame, there is the divine seed, there is the constant impulse from the god within, telling us always *"Come up higher, come to me; be the path and walk it; I am the way, the truth, and the life"* — in the heart of each one of us. It is there; and as soon as the personal man *consciously* allies himself with this divine spark, he becomes thereby impersonal and immortal in his inner consciousness and therefore incorruptible, at least until the end of this mahā-kalpa; and then his sublime destiny is to enter into that ineffable nirvana where he will remain in indescribable bliss and universal understanding until the next kalpa begins, whence he starts out anew but on a far more elevated plane. He starts out as a leader of that new humanity. He then finds it his turn to become one of that band or company or body of sons of mind or light, himself in his turn to endow with self-consciousness and future spiritual immortality the semiconscious beings of that cycle to come.

Bodhisattva: this is a keyword. You will remember it was pointed out at a former study that the dhyāni-buddhas, who are fifth in the enumeration of this Hierarchy of Compassion, these lords of contemplation, are seven in number, and each one of them has governance or rather has the overseeing of one of our rounds.

(Remember that there are seven rounds in a kalpa.) He is its head, the constant stimulator behind that force in nature which we feel always within us. That "force" is the divine urge, as philosophers might call it. It is not, however, yet truly divine; because noble, great, as these spiritual beings truly are, they have not yet reached the summit of their own hierarchy; but their great work is what we may call the divine urge, the push, behind the evolutionary process. Further, each of these dhyāni-buddhas in himself is a hierarchy, just as we pointed out that every atom is a hierarchy, every man is a hierarchy and, indeed, every entity is a hierarchy of greater or of inferior degree, because everything that is composite is necessarily divisible into degrees of spiritual and intellectual excellence.

How else could the evolving beings learn? If man existed in nothing but the pristine purity of his divine essence, what would there be for him to learn, how could he learn? Each one of these dhyānis has, or gives birth to, so to say, or emanates or evolves from himself, seven "sons," called celestial bodhisattvas, and each celestial bodhisattva has charge of one of the globes of our planetary chain, so that not only each planetary round, but each globe also has its spiritual head. It is a hierarchy in that sense again, as well.

Furthermore, let us take our earth, the fourth globe, as a further example. The celestial bodhisattva of our globe in his turn gives birth to seven superhuman bodhisattvas, and these superhuman bodhisattvas or superterrestrial bodhisattvas have, each one, charge of one race of the seven root-races in each round and give birth by a wonderful process, which we shall shortly describe, to seven human buddhas — each one, each superhuman bodhisattva, to a race-buddha. A bodhisattva, as explained exoterically, means one who in another incarnation or in a few more incarnations will become a buddha. That is true, but it is an exoteric teaching, that is to say, it is incomplete, and therefore misleading. A bodhisattva from the standpoint of our occult teachings, our esoteric teachings, is more than that. When a man, a human being, has reached the point where his ego becomes conscious, fully so, of its inner divinity, becomes clothed with the buddhic ray; where, so to say, the personal man has put on the garments of inner immortality in actuality, on this earth, here and now, that man is a bodhisattva. His higher principles have nearly reached nirvana. When they do so finally, such a man is a buddha, a human buddha, a mānushya-buddha. Obviously, if such a bodhisattva were to reincarnate, in the next incarnation or in a very few future incarnations thereafter, he would be a mānushya-buddha. A buddha, in the esoteric teaching, is one whose higher principles can learn nothing more; they have reached nirvana and remain there; but the spiritually awakened personal man, the bodhisattva, the person made semidivine, to use popular language, instead of choosing his reward in the nirvana of a less degree, remains on earth out of pity and compassion for inferior beings, and becomes what is called a nirmānakāya. A nirmāna-kāya is a bodhisattva, a personal man made semidivine. He clothes himself in a nirmānakāyic vesture. The nirmānakāya, you will remember, is one who is a complete, thinking, spiritual entity, minus the physical body only.

Let us take an example of how this works. Remember, please, apropos of our subject, that we are studying the nature of the Wondrous Being only incidentally at present, as being an illustration truly sublime of the seventh treasury of wisdom, the ātma-vidyā, the knowledge of self. Now let us take our illustration. Some time after Gautama Buddha died, there was born in the south of India a man who made a great mark in the Indian world thereafter. His name was Śankarāchārya. Āchārya is a Sanskrit word meaning "teacher" or "master"; and the name of the man himself was Śankara; the two words joined together make Śankarāchārya, "Śankara the teacher," as the Hindu Vedantists of the Adwaita or nondualistic school put it. Now here again is a very interesting thing, briefly alluded to before. Śankarāchārya was an avatāra, which means an incarnation of a "god," and yet he stood less high than the Buddha (Gautama) who had preceded him, although the latter was a man. How shall we explain that wonder? Easily. The Buddha Gautama became a buddha *through his own efforts*, throughout innumerable ages; whereas Śankarāchārya was in one mystical sense what may truly be called an illusion from the standpoint of esoteric manhood. Śankara was a man, there was a physical body, there was the great spiritual

essence within; *but there had been no previous Śankarāchārya.*
Śankarāchārya per se, spiritually, was a divine ray. The ātman
and the buddhi, born in the body of this Brahmana, were there,
also the kāma, the prāna, the astral model-body, and the physical
body — but no illuminated personal ego; and in order that that
avatāra at that time in history might do its work, the bodhisattva
of the Buddha entered into that body and gave it light, provided
the illuminating ego, thus repeating the aeon-old mystery of self-
sacrifice, taking on the "sins" (or karmic heritage from parents)
such as they may have been, if any, of that body, thus giving the
chance for that divine ray, that avatāra, to work in the world: providing the vehicle through which the divine ray might manifest
to and in the world of man.

That is the secret of an avatāra; but not *every* bodhisattva is
necessarily the vehicle of an avatāra, for the avatāras come at
particular and specified periods. Buddhas also come at particular
and specified periods, but leave behind them a bodhisattva, their
ego, their illuminated thinking part, the nirmānakāya, devoted to
the work of saving the race, for of such is the conscious part of
the Hierarchy of Compassion on our globe.

This was one of the ancient Mystery-teachings in the old
Mystery Schools.

But that is not all there is to this true and wondrous mystery.
This same bodhisattva, we are taught, also provided some centuries later the conscious vehicle, the egoic power, in the person
called Jesus, in Palestine. These are subjects, however, which we
cannot go into more deeply tonight. They are only an illustration
how this Hierarchy of Compassion works on earth in its sublime
overseeing and protective work of and for the human race.

We turn now to some questions which have been handed in,
five of them in number which, before we close this evening, we
shall read and do our best to answer. I mention this now before
continuing our subject, because the very theme upon which we
have touched in connection with the Buddha Gautama and Jesus
is mentioned in these questions, questions which all of us probably
have asked ourselves, and have hunted for answers to them.

We have now gained some idea of what we mean by self-
knowledge, of our unity with all, of how our individuality was

born, as it were, of heaven and of earth: the inner divine ray and the lower personal man, the latter raised upwards until he becomes one with that divine ray, thus becoming a fit and purified vehicle for it. We have also seen that the study of the Wondrous Being is a most sublime illustration of the exalted spiritual state to which we should attain, and shall attain, run we successfully the race.

Now let us go a little farther in our thought in connection with this Wondrous Being. We have seen that he or it is both — as H. P. Blavatsky said, using popular language — of heaven and of earth. His roots are the dhyāni-buddha of this round, and the ray reaches him as a man through the celestial bodhisattva emanated by the dhyāni-buddha, and also through the superterrestrial or superhuman bodhisattva in ultimate charge of our root-race. The Wondrous Being is here considered in his (or its) racial aspect. Note well, however, that there is also a Wondrous Being for our globe; also one for the entire planetary chain, etc.

There is a tradition, and our Teachers tell us that it is a tradition founded on truth, that even unto this day there exists in Central Asia a certain mystical and mysterious land, or district if you like. It is called Śambhala. This is a word known in Sanskrit literature, but because the sayings and legends regarding it are connected with what our self-sufficient European Sanskritists and Orientalists call "pagan superstition" and the "love of the Orientals for imagery," and so forth, our European scholars say that it is a myth. Blind men! It is an actual district on earth, in a certain part of Tibetan territory, and has been for ages the subject of much mystical speculation, and remains so to this day. It is the "home" of our exalted Teachers. It is likewise the "home" of the Wondrous Being considered as man, or in his racial aspect. This Wondrous Being incarnates himself from age to age at will and at pleasure, but never leaves the duty he has taken upon himself, nor will he ever drop it until his work is done. He is the spiritual bond and link of the various bodhisattvas and buddhas of the Hierarchy of Compassion with superior worlds and with us and the lower beings of our round. This land of Śambhala is described as a place of great beauty, surrounded by a high range of mountains. It is said that no human eye will ever see it unless permitted to see it. It is said that to this land of Śambhala go those who are "called" there, sometimes to return and sometimes to remain; and that there, supreme over all the Masters, reigns the human aspect of this Wondrous Being, the Great Initiator, the Great Sacrifice.

These are the teachings; and it is further said that from this land, spiritually, continually, and also in actual physical shape at cyclical critical periods, go forth Masters into the world. Can any thoughtful and spiritual mind read H. P. Blavatsky's story and history, what she says and what she did, without reading between the lines and behind the words? Have we ever taken it into our hearts how much it meant for her, and to her, when she spoke of her "going home"? Have we ever considered what might have been incarnate in that woman-body? The saviors take up bodies, sometimes, in this manner, as they please from age to age, and sex itself matters little, though usually man-bodies are selected. Such physical body-instruments as are most appropriate for the work to be accomplished are the ones chosen.

We are further told that these four kumāras of whom we have read this evening — "higher than the 'Four' is only ONE" — are spiritually and originally the four celestial bodhisattvas of the four globes of our round, and by correspondence of the four completed root-races of our earth, higher than whom there is none on earth except this ONE. Let us take these wonderful teachings into our hearts and make them a part of us! There is infinite beauty in them, hope unspeakable; there is spiritual life, there is intellectual health.

What is the matter with men's minds? Does not every one of us know that the average human being won't take truth when he sees it, unless it accord with his preconceptions? And why is this? Because his mind is so full of and so confused with his own brain-mind ideas, with his own opinions, which he thinks are so much superior to anything that comes to him from any other source, especially if from an impersonal source. We are all in the same mental condition; we are all cursed with these molds of mind which blind us. Every one of us, in different degrees, doubtless, some less than others; but we are all cursed with it by our own will, and all we need to do is to exercise our will and break these molds of mind, in order to let in the light, and the spiritual life, and the understanding, yea, and holy compassion. What keeps all these out of our minds and hearts as an active force except these molds of mind? "Give up your life if ye would find it."

Sometimes men may accuse you and say that you are atheists because you do not believe in a personal God. Let me read just here what a great Greek thinker said on that subject when he was accused of "atheism." And let me say, before reading: *atheist* meant among the Greeks one who did not accept the gods of the multitude, the mythologic gods of the State. It was no such term of opprobrium and hatred as it has become under the Christian theological dispensation. It meant rather, "You are a radical!" — not much if anything more. But the Christians have turned that perfectly legitimate word — which meant one who accepted not the gods of the State — into an expression of hatred, signifying moral degradation. Remember that the Christians themselves were called atheists by the pagans, simply because they did not accept the mythologic gods of the State; and the Christians, when they became powerful, retaliated in kind, and called the pagans atheists, because they refused to accept the Jewish-Christian God, Jehovah.

But what said Epicurus, called by later ages than his own an atheist, and a sensationalist, and possibly by every other evil-sounding epithet which men in hatred can heap upon one whom they dislike? "The gods are, yet they are not what the multitude imagine them to be. The man who denies the existence of the gods worshiped by the multitude is neither an infidel nor an atheist; but he who thinks the gods are what the multitude hold, is an atheist and impious."

Now our time for this evening is drawing to a close. We take up the questions above spoken of. These questions may have occurred, doubtless have occurred, to each one of us; and perhaps we have searched for answers. I will give them as if they had been asked from the floor here:

I understood you to say in the Thursday meeting, one week ago, that Jesus and Apollonius were nirmānakāyas. In *Isis Unveiled*, volume II, page 159, H. P. B. says that while Jesus and others were united to their spirits permanently, Apollonius and others of his class were so united only at intervals. I should think a nirmānakāya would be permanently united to his spirit, when working on this earth.

This question has been largely answered by what we have already explained to be the meaning of a bodhisattva. A nirmāna-kāya is a *state* assumed by or entered into by a bodhisattva. When that state is ended the nirmānakāya ends. *Kāya* means "body," "vehicle." Therefore, Śankarāchārya, Krishna, Lao-tse, Jesus, were avatāras in differing degrees. There was a divine ray which came at the cyclic time of each such incarnation, and the connecting link, the flame of mind, was provided in each such case by a member of the Hierarchy of Compassion. But these avatāras were not all equally great. Apollonius, while not an avatāra, was a nirmāna-kāya — a bodhisattva. As said before, the bodhisattva stands actually, in the Hierarchy of Compassion, higher than an avatāra, in the same way as a man who has gained divinity through his own efforts, and remains behind in the world of men out of compassion for it, and in order to help it spiritually, really stands higher than the devas or gods in their crystallized cold purity.

Jesus, and others such as Krishna and Lao-tse, were united to their spirits permanently. Obviously this means not the physical bodies of those great men, but that the particular ātma-buddhic ray which was called on earth Jesus, or Krishna, or Lao-tse, informed men who naturally were *always* united to their spirits, though each manifested through a bodhisattva-nirmānakāya. They could be nothing else. They could not be an avatāra through a being inferior to a bodhisattva. Apollonius and the Bodhisattva Gautama and others of his noble type, were not permanently allied to their spirits, or rather were not merely, solely, ātma-buddhic rays, because they were men made perfect through experience: personal men become semidivine, and actually, as said, such a being stands far higher than a spiritual ray or monad per se, because such as the bodhisattvas are the fine flowers of evolution.

Next question:

At one Thursday evening meeting, it was declared that the words of the Sermon on the Mount were not the words of Jesus, but gatherings of ancient wisdom compiled by some later writer. I don't understand just how in Katherine Tingley's addresses, etc., this Sermon and Jesus are always placed together as one being the author of the other. I got the impression at this meeting that Jesus was merely an Initiate Jew, but not nearly of such grand stature as to command the adoration of all Christians. However, perhaps I did not hear correctly.

Our question is here framed in a most careful manner. In the first place, then, it is not to be said, and it was not said, that the Sermon on the Mount was not the *logia* or "words" of Jesus. What was said, inadequately doubtless on account of the shortness of time, was that the Sermon on the Mount, as we now have it in the New Testament, was in all probability composed in much the same manner as the four canonical Gospels were composed. Doubtless it is based on the *logia* and sayings of the Master, Jesus. Unquestionably a man, Jesus, lived. Unquestionably he had a school. Unquestionably he had his disciples. Unquestionably he taught them and his sayings were treasured by his disciples; but, as time went on, much was forgotten, and they were revised and edited, and we now have them in the form in which they appear in the New Testament. This was rendered easy enough by the fact that a good deal in those writings was on matters of more or less common philosophical, or even esoteric, knowledge, more or less current in the thought of the day, and it required but little skill to weave together these ideas into a more or less logical whole. The very fact that the well-known contradictions and incongruities in the four Gospels, when compared, prove various redactions by different writers shows that they were compiled from differing bases of theory. For the theosophist, certain expressions used therein show him that the esotericism of Syria played a large part in their compilation, as was natural enough. Jesus taught universal truths; his half-instructed followers misunderstood much. Those expressions and terms were used in the Mystery Schools of the eastern Mediterranean world of that period, but do not belong to our School; and as Jesus certainly belonged to our School, the presumption is, as said, that his sayings had been "touched up" and with extraneous matter formed into the four Gospels. Somebody or rather somebodies doubtless thought the scattered sayings of the Teacher could be improved upon — made "more clear and easy."

Such seems to be the fate of nearly all great teachings. There is absolutely no preventive of it except the faithful hearts of men and women who stand to the death for the pure teachings of the one who gave them light and an awakened inner life. Let us never forget it!

Our questioner was correct in the impression he received that Jesus was stated to be an Initiate Syrian — a Jew if you like. We speak now of Jesus the man; but I do not think that we ever said that he should command, in any circumstances, the "adoration" of the Christians or of anybody else, because such worship is a thing precisely forbidden to all followers of the truth — impersonal and ineffable. That idea is a misunderstanding of our meaning by the questioner.

Here is another question:

Another perplexing thing to me is the many different ways in which the 7, 9, and 10 principles of man and the universe are enumerated. In *Instructions* Nos. I and II by H. P. Blavatsky, it is said that ātman is not really a principle of man at all, but that the auric envelope makes up the seventh. Yet in our esoteric meetings, ātman is often spoken of as belonging to man. The esoteric and exoteric enumeration of these principles differs, and often manas is called but one principle, then again divided into two and the lower manas joined with the kāma principle, etc.

These well-taken points, of course, are something that each one must solve for himself, by studying the literature which we already have, so ably written by our older students. Of necessity the seven principles are subject to different methods of enumeration, because each method of enumeration or presentation in diagrammatic or paradigmatic form merely shows another vista of the truth, shows another facet or way of looking at the one jewel. So a man, if he were in India, who desired to study that wonderful monument of beauty, the Taj Mahal, would not merely look at it from the front and then go away, but would go inside and study it in detail; and go to the back of it, and to the right and to the left, thus seeing all sides of it, meanwhile gathering all information possible from authorities. In much the same way the seven principles, or the ten, are subject to different methods of presentation. As a matter of fact, ātman is put as the seventh principle, because it is the permanent root of our being; but if we knew the kāma principle were that root, then it should be called the seventh, or rather the first or highest, as being the root of our being; or the manas, under similar conditions, should be called the seventh. The ātman is put as the first or highest because the seven principles of man are considered in a generalizing way, and the ātman or self being the root or the highest element of being is considered as one of the seven principles, though in reality it is a *universal* principle.

Our fourth question shows how deeply our questioner has thought:

The doctrine of cycles, and the exact number of years the human race will take in one manvantara or a Day and Night of Brahmā to reach the 7th race and 7th round, taken in conjunction with the doctrine of free will, always somewhat puzzles me. Why does not man's free will and failures continually keep upsetting the exact number of years it takes him to reach to certain future rounds and races? In *Theosophy: The Path of the Mystic*, Katherine Tingley says that humanity has passed the worst point, the crucial point, in its evolution, and that no powers in heaven and hell can stay its progress, but yet she keeps on talking to humanity as if it were on the brink of destruction.

In the first place, in the large sweep of things, taking the seven rounds as a kalpa or as a whole, and even more strongly so as regards the solar kalpa, that is, the cycle of the solar system, the exact number of years of even a human's many incarnations is definite and set, in much the same way as the number of turns (or days and nights) which our globe, the earth, makes in one year, or one revolution around the sun. In other words, the number of days is set and determined in a year, or the number of days in a lunar cycle or month. But while that is so in the general sweep of things, the doctrine of free will which man has is a very real truth, and man's failures or successes do work to retard or to hasten the number of a human being's incarnations, for instance — which briefly covers the question our questioner has asked.

The total number is set; but just as the bodies of the solar system, the planets, as is known to astronomers, sometimes due to their perturbations are occasionally a little behind or a little ahead in time, nevertheless in the long run they "arrive on time," as if they were endowed with consciousness, and had to arrive at the goal at the time when the hour is set therefor. So man's free will can alter the course or time periods of his incarnations, but not their number. In any round, in any root-race, he can change them in that respect, but he will have to pay for it by karmic retribution, for a reaction sets in; and there will be an adverse current running the other way. Shall we say, finally, that man has no free will because he is bound to a globe which he cannot voluntarily leave? Of course not, although he is, *nolens volens,* carried around the sun by our globe's annual course. There is much more that might be said to clarify this point, but it is too strictly esoteric to speak of here.

As regards Katherine Tingley's words, permit me to point out that our questioner has quoted her exactly, as far as the sense goes. It is a fact that we have passed the worst point, the crucial point, in our evolution. It was the middle of the fourth race of this fourth round. Things could not have been worse from the spiritual viewpoint in our entire manvantara. It was the midmost or lowest point of several cycles. We, as a racial body, passed through it successfully, but many, many entities fell and took the downward path. "But yet she keeps on talking to humanity as if we were on the brink of destruction" — do not you know that even in this fifth root-race we have not yet reached the middle point of the fourth primary subrace thereof — its middle and therefore dangerous point? And that the great racial catastrophe due for our fifth root-race has therefore not yet come upon us? As H. P. Blavatsky pointed out in 1887 or 1888, the great tidal waves and earthquakes occurring in the last few thousand years seem to be premonitions of what a few more thousands of years will bring upon us with augmented force.

The last question is:

The names given to the Absolute in its different manifestations are confusing to me (or perhaps just hard to remember). In Patañjali's *Yoga Aphorisms* man's higher self is called Īśwara, in the *Bhagavad-Gītā,* Purusha; again it is often called ātman. In Chapter viii of the *Bhagavad-Gītā* the names adhyātman, adhibhūta, adhidaivata, adhiyajña, brahman, and so forth, are all used with very subtle differences of meanings.

They are; but the meanings are also explained in the first part of *Bhagavad-Gītā,* chapter 8. We may here point out that even as in the arrangements of the seven principles in the various books, these names are attempts to show other or different views of the one thing.

In conclusion, we will translate these five Sanskrit names: *adhyātman* means the "original ātman or self," equivalent to Paramātman, or supreme ātman, the highest of the hierarchy. *Adhibhūta* means that supreme thing, or the higher egoic principle or "original element," in us coming over from other manvantaras; it is, so to say, the incarnating essence of the element. *Adhidaivata* means "more divine," the highest part of all from the serial standpoint, the hierarchical standpoint, considering various stages. *Adhiyajña* means the greater, the "superior sacrifice."

Krishna in the high spiritual sense was the greater sacrifice, the primal sacrifice, the first initiator on the part of the Hierarchy of Compassion, a sacrifice through pure love and compassion, than which, in men, there is nothing more sublime, because it makes us as one of the gods. *Brahman*, the last word, is, as we all know, a Sanskrit word of which the essential root means "expansion"; it is that part of the celestial economy which first initiates manifestation, the expansion of the One into the many.

TWENTY-THREE

THE SUN AND THE PLANETS. THEIR ROLE IN THE EVOLUTIONARY DRAMA.

The most mystic of discourses inform us, that the wholeness of him (the sun) is in the supermundane orders: for there a solar world and a total light subsist, as the oracles of the Chaldaeans affirm. . . .

Unwearied nature rules over the worlds and works,
That heaven drawing downward might run an eternal course,
And that the other periods of the sun, moon, seasons, night, and day, might be accomplished.

— PROCLUS, *Commentary on the "Timaeus" of Plato*
(CORY, *Ancient Fragments,* pp. 274–5)

T HE SECRET DOCTRINE, volume I, pages 279 and 280:

Whatever may be the destiny of these actual writings in a remote future, we hope to have proven so far the following facts:

(1) The Secret Doctrine teaches no *Atheism,* except in the Hindu sense of the word *nastika,* or the rejection of *idols,* including every anthropomorphic god. In this sense every Occultist is a *Nastika.*

(2) It admits a Logos or a collective "Creator" of the Universe; a *Demi-urgos* — in the sense implied when one speaks of an "Architect" as the "Creator" of an edifice, whereas that Architect has never touched one stone of it, but, while furnishing the plan, left all the manual labor to the masons; in our case the plan was furnished by the Ideation of the Universe, and the constructive labour was left to the Hosts of intelligent Powers and Forces. But that *Demiurgos* is no *personal* deity, — *i.e.,* an imperfect *extra-cosmic god,* — but only the aggregate of the Dhyan-Chohans and the other forces.

As to the latter —

(3) They are dual in their character; being composed of (*a*) the irrational *brute energy,* inherent in matter, and (*b*) the intelligent soul or cosmic consciousness which directs and guides that energy, and which is the *Dhyan-*

Chohanic thought reflecting the Ideation of the Universal mind. This results in a perpetual series of physical manifestations and *moral effects* on Earth, during manvantaric periods, the whole being subservient to Karma. As that process is not always perfect; and since, however many proofs it may exhibit of a guiding intelligence behind the veil, it still shows gaps and flaws, and even results very often in evident failures — therefore, neither the collective Host (Demiurgos), nor any of the working powers individually, are proper subjects for divine honours or worship. All are entitled to the grateful reverence of Humanity, however, and man ought to be ever striving to help the divine evolution of *Ideas*, by becoming to the best of his ability a *co-worker with nature* in the cyclic task. The ever unknowable and incognizable *Karana* alone, the *Causeless* Cause of all causes, should have its shrine and altar on the holy and ever untrodden ground of our heart — invisible, intangible, unmentioned, save through "the still small voice" of our spiritual consciousness. Those who worship before it, ought to do so in the silence and the sanctified solitude of their Souls; making their spirit the sole mediator between them and the *Universal Spirit,* their good actions the only priests, and their sinful intentions the only visible and objective sacrificial victims to the *Presence.*

We proceed to gather up this evening more of the scattered threads left over from our former studies. First, let us look a little more closely into what is meant by a bodhisattva. It will be remembered that a bodhisattva was spoken of as the personal man relatively perfected; the case where the personal entity had become an impersonal entity, where mortality had put upon itself the vesture of immortality; in other words, a case where the personal man has become an Awakened One or a Buddha short of Buddhahood complete by only one stage; or, to use the Christian (early Christian-Greek) mystical expression, a Christ on earth.

Now a bodhisattva, being such, practically means what we might call the higher manas, the higher self (not the highest self, but the higher self) fully developed and in the full radiance of the dual monad ātma-buddhi, and thus forms a fit vehicle, a fit medium, between the divine and the lower selves of man; and thus provides an appropriate channel of communication in cases where an avatāra is due for manifestation on earth. There could be no such thing as an avatāra among men were it not for this medium supplying the necessary psychospiritual link. Pure spirit, in endeavoring to act upon earth, can have neither effect upon, nor chance of communication with, men, because it is the actual divine essence, so to say, of the kosmos and needs the two spiritual qualities or vehicles buddhi and manas-taijasa in order so to manifest, and the bodhisattva, in supplying the spiritual egoic quality, the intermediate quality, furnishes that necessary medium or vehicle. The bodhisattva, furthermore, who, instead of pursuing its own natural karmic higher course in the nirvanic state, chooses by virtue of the compassion inherent in itself to remain on earth, as a helper of mankind, in that case becomes a nirmānakāya, a fully conscious thinking entity upon this our human plane, minus only the physical body. It is stated in the esoteric philosophy that Gautama the Buddha made that sublime choice, and furnished the intermediate principle for the Hindu avatāra, Sankarāchārya, of whom we spoke at our last meeting. There is a tradition and a record among us likewise that the same bodhisattva furnished the intermediate principle of the avatāric manifestation called Jesus, as also in two other cases which we here leave unnamed, the reason being that each race and each subrace, as well as every smaller racial cycle of importance, as we know, is under the particular guidance of a buddha, or of minor incarnations or over-shadowings by him.

Gautama the Buddha was himself an avatāra *plus*, i.e., in a larger sense; that is to say, instead of furnishing an intermediate vehicle from himself, in a minor cycle, he was that intermediate vehicle himself in his psychospiritual totality, inspired by his own divine nature, and with his own physical body as the "temple" thereof, differing in that respect from an avatāra per se, in which the intermediate vehicle is furnished by the bodhisattva-nirmāna-kāya of the buddha under whose governance, or rather overseeing, the particular race in which the avatāra appears runs its course as a minor cycle of the greater racial cycle of that buddha himself. An avatāra, therefore, requires the bodhisattva of the racial buddha as a vehicle in order to manifest upon earth at the time he is due to appear. A buddha does not, because, although an avatāra in the sense of being under the direct and fully actual illumination of his own divine self (which is a superterrestrial bodhisattva, studied at our last meeting), *he has karma behind him*. It is the direct and actual reincarnation of a divine man, which an avatāra is not. An avatāra is, in a sense, an illusion or māyā, because the intermediate or egoic quality — the offspring metaphysically of karma — is lacking there and has to be furnished by the bodhisattva-quality or vehicle.

An avatāra, formally only, stands higher than a bodhisattva, but it is a higher stage merely of form of and in a hierarchy, and not from the evolutionary viewpoint. A buddha becomes such by *self-directed evolution,* the great truth that Katherine Tingley so often tells us of. An avatāra comes by karmic *racial* necessity at certain epochs in the world's history; a buddha does so likewise, but also by *personal choice* out of an immense compassion for his inferior fellow beings still involved in the toils of material existence. There is the difference, and a very important one it is to remember for our future studies.

We might say in passing that at about our present period, what is called a Messianic cycle is ending and, naturally, a new one is opening — a Messianic cycle running 2,160 years, in definite, exact figures. These cycles succeed one another continuously. So if we choose to count backwards, we can say, if we like, that the European Messianic cycle which is ending, or out of which we are emerging, is that inaugurated for Europe by Jesus, the Avatāra. Interesting thoughts come up in this connection which we may safely leave for consideration at another time.

So much for those threads.

Please remember that evolution comprises two lines of action, as it were, two forces running collaterally, that is to say, the spirit or the developed side of existence on the one hand, and that of the undeveloped side on the other hand: otherwise, darkness and light, or the selfish and the compassionate, which, you will remember, is a subject that we alluded to somewhat in studying the fifth of the seven treasuries of wisdom of the Hierarchy of Compassion which is the unselfish or immortal side of existence.

Now the action and interaction of these two lines of energy supply the motive forces behind evolution, behind progress; and the course which evolution takes really arises in, springs out from, and is inaugurated by, the impulses at the opening of the manvantaric cycle given to the dark or matter-side of existence by the dhyāni-chohans, I mean by the higher parts or entities of this Hierarchy of Compassion. It is the *keynotes* furnished by them, *the primal and original impulses* depending of course upon destiny (or karma) which give the originating plan and the driving power behind everything that happens in that manvantara throughout its cycle of evolution until its close; and while free will exists in man as soon as he has learned to obey the spiritual statutes of self-consciousness, this free will itself, being a divine energy and in a sense springing itself from the general dhyān-chohanic impulse, can in no circumstances militate against, be contrary to, or adversely affect, the general evolutionary current which bears the manifold hosts of entities in manifestation always towards the ultimate goal, signalized by H. P. Blavatsky in the ancient saying, "The Day Be With Us" — the end of a manvantara or the opening of pralaya.

Thus, then, these two lines of energy are eternally coactive — using the word eternally in the sense of lasting throughout the solar kalpa — on one side, the "dark," undeveloped forces of matter; and, on the other side, the Hierarchy of Compassion with its innumerable units urging the hosts of evolving beings forward in one direction, the whole effort of the Hierarchy of Compassion being to raise other less developed beings or units from the matter-side up into the "light-side." The entities of the Hierarchy of Compassion in past manvantaras were themselves thus so raised by other Hierarchies of Compassion, now by this time far, far ahead of us in evolution; and it is our sublime destiny in the future kalpa ourselves so to guide the entities behind us now, a process called the "Passing on of the Light," as the Greek and Latin poets put it.

Furthermore, as briefly alluded to at our last study, please remember that the ancient initiations, and the Mystery Schools in which those initiations took place, were established solely for the purpose of "forcing" or quickening the evolution of fit and proper candidates. They were established from the same motives of compassion that presided over the acts of the great actors of the primal drama, the opening acts of our manvantara. They copied, as it were in miniature, what took place in those primordial times, and what took place in actual life in the Hierarchy of Compassion on our earth, or that section, rather, of the Hierarchy of Compassion which we call the Great White Lodge.

Let us turn a moment to another collateral and very important matter upon which we have touched but lightly, because the questions involved are so profound that it was impossible in treating of one subject adequately to make the meaning clear without temporarily dropping our main theme. But it is likewise necessary not to go too far ahead and leave these loose threads behind; we must gather them in also and weave them into the fabric, into the picture, which we are endeavoring to make.

We refer more particularly to the role which the sun and the planets of our solar system play in the evolutionary drama. There are great mysteries connected with this, and we are told very plainly that not merely the ultimate word but even specifying explanations in no circumstances are given out except to those who have pledged themselves irretrievably and irrevocably to the Lodge. And even then they are given out only with "mouth to ear," and "at low breath"; and, furthermore, only to those, says H. P. Blavatsky, who have passed successfully their fourth initiation, which consists very largely in *the personal and individual experiencing of the teachings given in the three preceding stages* — three stages of preliminary teaching and training, leading to actual personal experience thereof in the fourth initiation, in which, we are told, the candidate must leave the body of flesh, yea, even the brain-mind, behind, and *become* that of which he was taught, because only by *being* can he *know*. Nevertheless a great deal has been openly said that is, to the student, very illuminating as regards these subjects.

First, at various times we have spoken of the sun, of our solar orb, as the central locus of our solar system. So it is, not merely physically but also in other ways. The sun, paradoxically but truly, supplies most of our material, vital powers; and it is interesting to note that the nearer the planets are to the sun, as a general rule, the more dense they are. Mark well that Mercury, the planet of bodha or of wisdom, the particular guardian and initiator in the Mysteries, is the nearest to the sun (but one) of *our* seven planets, i.e., the seven Mystery-planets. Note the words "but one." You will remember that the ancients spoke of seven Mystery-planets: Saturn, Jupiter, Mars — I give them in the old order — Sun, Venus, Mercury, and Moon. This matter we shall develop somewhat in diagrammatic form later this evening if we have the time.

The intra-Mercurial planet, as it is called, according to our teaching became practically invisible to the physical eye during the third root-race, after the fall of man into physical generation. On March 26, 1859, a body was seen crossing the solar disk, making what astronomers call a transit. That body has not been seen again; but there are other reasons which have induced some astronomers to believe that there actually is an intra-Mercurial planet (although they cannot find it again despite the search for it), such as the perturbations of Mercury. An attempt at explanation of these perturbations has been recently made, based on the relativity doctrines of Einstein, and that explanation is now in fashion. Nevertheless, our Teachers say that there is an intra-Mercurial planet; we may call it Vulcan, as the astronomers so called it.

Even if Vulcan became invisible during the third root-race, it could yet become visible in transit, that is, in crossing the sun's disk, as this body was actually in 1859 seen to do, because although invisible to our unaided sight, yet through the lens of a telescope when turned upon the unsurpassed illumination of the sun's disk, its body could probably be seen against the great brilliance of the solar orb. The immensely great illumination provided by the sun would readily throw into shadow, or make appear as a shadow, any body of less brilliance, or any body normally too ethereal to be seen otherwise.

The seventh planet, our teaching is, is a planet which under proper conditions is sometimes seen apparently near the moon. It is said that it has a retrograde motion, and that it is slowly dying. It has reached the end of its cycle. I think it erroneous to say that the moon "hides" it. That may be a good way, perhaps, of expressing a certain appearance, but I think it is a misleading one. Let us keep the facts just as they were given us, that it is sometimes "seen apparently near the moon," that it has a retrograde motion, and that it is slowly dying.

Vulcan is in one mystic sense the highest of the seven sacred planets; perhaps not the least dense, but in one sense the highest psychologically; and we have reason to believe that the other planet sometimes seen apparently near the moon is perhaps the lowest of the seven sacred planets. This does not mean that our teaching limits the number of the planets of the solar system to seven. On the contrary, we are taught that there are many more planets in the solar system than are known to astronomers, some perfectly invisible, because they are on planes both higher and lower than our plane. There are planets in our system higher than ours, higher than any planet visible to us; there are also planets in our system much lower than ours, much lower than any planet visible to us.

These seven especial planets were called sacred for a reason most difficult openly to explain; but we may say this, that the seven planets which we *on earth* (please note the qualification) call sacred, are those planets (and the earth is not one of them) which are the *upādhis* — a Sanskrit word meaning "bearers" or "carriers" — (to us) of the seven solar forces. They are all "higher" in that sense, or from that point of view, than is the earth; and they are all intimately connected with this earth, and provide this earth, not with its principles, but with spiritual and intellectual and psychical and astral and vital powers, so to say. These seven sacred planets, moreover, are our "makers," and oversee our destiny.

This is a bit of the genuine ancient astrology. It is not merely to the physical body of the seven planets that we allude; doubtless each physical planet or rather globe has its own *astronomical* forces, such as gravitation and magnetism, and so forth; but we are here speaking of the inner or occult action of them. Each of the globes of our planetary chain, moreover, each of the seven globes thereof, is under the particular watchfulness or care of one of these seven Mystery-planets. Furthermore, each round is under the particular overseeing of one of these seven sacred planets. Furthermore, each race on any one of the globes is under the particular care and overseeing of one of these seven sacred planets. For these reasons, as well as for others still more important and intimate on account of their strait connection with our planetary chain, were they called the seven sacred planets.

The sun and moon are not two of the seven, although for purposes of esoteric astrology they were substituted for the real two, because one is apparently near the moon, and one is so near the sun. Yet, for all that, the sun and moon are both closely in interaction respectively with those two.

With regard to the sun: What is the sun? Is the sun a physical body only? It is not. It is not really a physical body, for it is not gas, it is not gaseous. It is not solid, nor is it liquid or gaseous. *The sun is a reflection.* What do we mean when we say a reflection? We do not mean the word in the full, complete, and exclusive sense in which it is commonly employed, as when we speak of the reflection of an image in a mirror. We mean it in this sense, that the *true* sun is a body — strange as it may seem to our present-day scientists — of energy or force. Modern science is beginning to understand now that force and matter are fundamentally one thing. Some years ago everything in the scientific imagination was *matter*. Now everything has become *force* to it. Marvelous, that these scientific gentlemen do not see how easily they change the bases of their thought, and how dogmatic they so often are as regards each new series of bases that they assume! But there the fact is. Science today tells us that matter is simply force, which is true. But it is matter all the same. There is no need of running to one extreme in trying to pull ourselves out of another. No need of incurring the perils of Scylla in trying to evade those of Charybdis. Matter exists, it is; it is the upādhi or carrier of force, and force is also the intrinsic life of matter. Nevertheless matter exists; it is a māyā, an illusion indeed, but it *exists*. Māyā does not mean illusion in the exclusive and full sense of nonentity. Not at all. Māyā actually implies that something exists to produce it, but that the seer of it does not know what the reality is behind; in other words, *our senses do not tell us the truth about the thing behind the manifestation.* That is what māyā means, not that the thing itself is nonentity. That view is an absurdity.

If you examine photographs of sunspots, if you look at the sun through a good telescope and center your gaze upon a sunspot when it is near a limb of the sun, near an edge, you will see that as the spot crosses the solar disk, it seems to be black. Now why does it appear black? We know that it is not black in color. Our scientists have proved that fact, but the visible disk of the sun is so intensely brilliant that the less brilliance of the part within the spot, though very brilliant itself, seems dark to our eyes.

Suppose that we were to say that the sun we see is simply like the glow around some electrical machines, merely a "reflection" of the electrical current, as it were, a māyāvi manifestation on our plane of a force so immense that we can form no proper conception of it. Suppose that we were to think of the sun as occupying no space (or dimension) at all, and that what we see, that immense apparent body of light, were like an electrical spark, apparently a body, apparently occupying space. Suppose that we go a step further and say that the visible sun which we see is matter in its sixth state of ethereality, and that what is behind that tremendously brilliant veil or reflection is an atom, so to say, an infinitesimal part of matter-substance, matter in its seventh state. It is easy to follow this thought. The sun is a mass of force; as even the medieval philosophers might have said: "Brother, when a man tells you that he has seen the sun, laugh at him. He has not. The sun is invisible. The true sun, the origin and center of these high forces, is on higher planes, and we merely see on the sixth subplane of our kosmic plane this intense brilliance covering so vast a space as the apparent sun does."

Furthermore, while the sun gives us our light on earth, it probably does not furnish us with 30 percent of the heat that we have, and then not by direct physical radiation, but in somewhat the same way in which the electric current furnishes us with heat, or in a similar way — in the *same way* would be, perhaps, too strong a manner of putting the fact. Forces emanate from the solar heart or center and reach the meteoric veils encircling the earth, and arouse electromagnetic currents, producing thus a part of the meteorological phenomena which we experience in storms and fair weather and rain and snow and ice. The earth itself produces probably 70 percent or more of the heat which we know; and such things as storms are caused mostly by electromagnetic action and reaction, if I may use that expression, between the innate prāna, or vital forces of the earth, and the meteoric continent which surrounds our globe like a veil. For we are encircled during our manvantara, and every other planet of the solar system is similarly encircled during *its* manvantara, with a thick veil of meteoric dust, most of it very fine, some of it of more or less large bodies.

Take Venus, for instance, or Mercury. They are surrounded each one with its own veil of meteoric or kosmic dust: each one veils her face, or his face. This meteoric veil acts in one sense as does a cushion, thus forming a protection to its planet. We do not see for that reason the real face of the planet. But Mars has no such veil. Why? Because the vital essence of that planetary chain has left Mars' physical globe for its other globes.

We shall have to reserve until next week the diagram which was to have been shown to you this evening, at which point of study we have now arrived. Let us briefly point out that the diagram in question is taken from the mystical Syrian thought in vogue before the Christian era, and represents the exoteric astrological ideas that the Syrians then had of the relationship of the planes of being, and necessarily therefore of the planets and the mystical positions occupied by each of them in the evolutionary drama. They put it this wise. First and highest was the Milky Way, which to them was the utmost limit of this hierarchy or universe. Then came the Nebulae and Comets, which were represented in the spiritual hierarchy by the Seraphim. The third grade still lower were the Fixed Stars, and they were represented by the Cherubim. Then taking a leap over the immensities of the space of our universe, these old thinkers of Babylonia, Assyria, Media, and doubtless Persia, and of course Phoenicia, and all the other countries of Asia Minor, began the inferior series with the planets of our solar system. First, Saturn, the seat of the Thrones; then Jupiter, the seat of the Dominations; then Mars, the seat of the Virtues; then the Sun, the seat of the Powers; then Venus, the seat of the Principalities; then Mercury, of the Archangels; then the Moon, of the Angels; then our Earth. They also enumerated five elements — an enumeration which is exoteric, but it is the same as the esoteric as far as it goes. Our Earth, as well as interplanetary space, comprises these five elements, and when we say our Earth we mean not merely our physical planetary body of this element upon which we move, but the entire sphere comprehended between the Moon and the Earth. These five elements were named Ether, Fire, Air, Water, gross matter or Earth. Outside of this hierarchy or universe or kosmos they placed the Celestial Waters, even as the first chapter of the Hebrew book of Genesis speaks of the "spirit of the Elohim moving over the waters." "Celestial Waters" was a name frequently given by the ancients to what the Greeks called Chaos, undeveloped matter or, as we today would say, spacial deeps.

Our time of study this evening is drawing to a close. Let us, however, point out the interesting fact that this same series of the planets shows us clearly that the ancients must have understood perfectly well the mechanism of the framework of the visible solar system, and that, if their thought was geocentric, making the earth the center of the kosmos, it was a natural thought; and that as man is instinctively anthropocentric, he cannot naturally think from another standpoint. So, naturally, the ancient astrologers and astronomers, with their feet on earth, calculated from the earth, and saw from the earth, and placed man, looking up towards the spheres of the solar system, on earth as the center of observation even as we do today, not meaning at all that they knew nothing of the heliocentric system, which we know they did know.

What can this mean? This cannot mean anything but one thing, and that is, that these planets were so placed on account of and because of the relative time occupied by each in making the circuit of its orbit, to wit: Saturn, about thirty years; Jupiter, the next "lowest," practically twelve; Mars, the next lowest, practically two; the Sun (or the Mystery-planet, the Sun supplying its place), one year; Venus, the next one, seven months; Mercury, three months; the Moon, one month. We would like to point out also that the days of our own common week are based upon this series, and then we shall close for this evening.

Why, in putting the planets in the order Saturn, Jupiter, Mars, Sun, Venus, Mercury, Moon, did they not make their week of seven days follow that order? Because, dividing the day and night into 24 hours, each day, beginning at sunrise, opens with its first hour under the governance of some particular planet. If you calculate through the 24 hours, beginning with Saturn (there being seven sacred planets), during the 24 hours they go into 24 three times, with three over. Three times seven is 21 hours, with three over: 22, 23, 24, the 25th hour being the first hour of the *next day*. Three times seven running through the 24 hours, we find that if the first hour began with Saturn as presiding planet, the 8th hour would also be under Saturn, the 15th would be under Saturn, the 22nd would be under Saturn, the 23rd then would be under Jupiter, the 24th under Mars, and the 25th hour, the first of the next day, would be Sun or Sunday. By taking this list and counting each fourth, beginning with the one just ended, as the first (or adding three more to the hour just ended), gives you the days of the week. Thus: Saturn, Jupiter, Mars, Sun, SUNDAY; Sun, Venus, Mercury, Moon, MONDAY; Moon, Saturn, Jupiter, Mars, TUESDAY (Mars' day); Mars, Sun, Venus, Mercury, WEDNESDAY, being the Anglo-Saxon *Woden*, corresponding to the Latin and Greek terms; Mercury, Moon, Saturn, Jupiter, THURSDAY (Thor's day); Jupiter, Mars, Sun, Venus, FRIDAY; Venus, Mercury, Moon, Saturn, SATURDAY, again beginning the second or following week.

So the order and names of the days of our week are ultimately based upon a very interesting and occult reason — ancient astrology explained and given to the world only in the Mysteries as we know them. The order and names of the days of the week were the same in India and in Northern Europe, and in some parts of Asia, a matter which has never yet been satisfactorily explained by our calendarists and astronomers. The reason is found in the fundamentally identical astrological system common to the entire ancient world.

PART TWO

TWENTY-FOUR

THE TEN STAGES OF BEING ACCORDING TO THE SYRIAN SYSTEM.
ESOTERIC METHOD OF TEACHING: PARADOXES, INTUITION.

Their writings also [i.e., of the Pythagoreans], and all the books which they published, *most of which have been preserved even to our time* [i.e., to the time of Iamblichus], were not composed by them in a popular and vulgar diction, and in a manner usual with all other writers, so as to be immediately understood, but in such a way as not to be easily apprehended by those that read them. For they adopted that taciturnity which was instituted by Pythagoras as a law, in concealing after an arcane mode, divine mysteries from the uninitiated, and obscuring their writings and conferences with each other.   — IAMBLICHUS, *Life of Pythagoras*, p. 56

Philosophy, according to his [Plato's] acceptation, being not merely a set of doctrines but the perfecting of the whole spiritual life; . . .
        — EDUARD ZELLER, *Plato and the Older Academy*, p. 160

> It moves. It moves not.
> It is far, and It is near.
> It is within all this,
> And It is outside of all this.
>   — *Īśā-Upanishad*, 5 (Hume, trans.)

LET US OPEN our study this evening by reading from *The Secret Doctrine*, volume I, pages 435–6, as follows:

Mor Isaac . . . shows the ancient Syrians defining their world of the "Rulers" and "active gods" in the same way as the Chaldeans. The lowest world was the SUBLUNARY — our own — watched by the "Angels" of the first or lower order; the one that came next in rank, was Mercury, ruled by the "ARCHANGELS"; then came Venus, whose gods were the PRINCIPAL-ITIES; the fourth was that of the SUN, the domain and region of the highest and mightiest gods of our system, the solar gods of all nations; the fifth was Mars, ruled by the "VIRTUES"; the sixth — that of *Bel* or Jupiter — was governed by the DOMINIONS; the seventh — the world of Saturn — by the THRONES. These are the worlds of form. Above come the four higher ones, making seven again, since the three *highest* are "unmentionable and un-pronounceable." The eighth, composed of 1,122 stars, is the domain of the

Cherubs; the ninth, belonging to the *walking* and numberless stars on account of their distance, has the seraphs; as to the tenth — Kircher, quoting Mor Isaac, says that it is composed "of invisible stars that could be taken, they said, for clouds — so massed are they in the zone that we call *Via Straminis*, the Milky Way;". . . That which comes after and beyond the tenth world (our Quaternary, or the *Arupa* world), the Syrians could not tell. "All they knew was that it is there that begins the vast and incomprehensible ocean of the infinite, the abode of the true divinity without boundary or end."

Champollion shows the same belief among the Egyptians.

The main thought this evening that seems to call first for further illustration is the subject of the bipolar nature of being, that is to say, that there are two interacting energy-substance lines in the kosmos, which together comprise the totality of all evolutionary processes: first, the lower, the kosmokratores, or world builders; and second, the higher, the intelligences impelling the former into action and overseeing their evolutionary ways. The second class is of course the higher, and comprises what we, following H. P. Blavatsky, have called the Hierarchy of Compassion.

Now these two lines of action, or classes, may also be called (a) the left-hand or matter-side, and (b) the right-hand or spirit-side, i.e., (a) the builders, the kosmokratores, who are in fact (in one sense) the lower principles of (b) the dhyāni-buddhas, who are the right-hand, or spirit-side, of being, which latter are of the inner kosmos, as the kosmokratores or builders, also called planetary spirits or dhyāni-chohans of a lower grade, are of the outer or material kosmos, that is, as said above, the left-hand side, the matter-side, the night-side, the dark side.

From the interaction of these two quasi-opposing forces (or elements) in nature come into self-consciousness the innumerable monads of inner and outer space, because this night-side or matter-side is made up of the lower principles of the light-side, as it were; and these lower principles are composite, formed of simply innumerable numbers of monads in almost infinitely varying degrees of development. The higher monads form the vehicles of the dhyāni-buddhas, the Hierarchy of Compassion; but there are monads, hosts of them, of intermediate and lower degrees, and of still lower and of the lowest degree; and the lowest form the material world, which we see around us. As said above, from the interaction of the indwelling force and of the vehicle in which it works or, in other words, from the informing spiritual powers impelling and urging these monads in various states of evolution towards further progress, spring the various degrees of consciousnesses in nature. We are some of these monads, both our higher egos and our personal egos. We ourselves are monads in the particular state of evolution in which we find ourselves; and we are on our way to becoming conscious co-workers with nature or, in other words, slowly evolving out (or into) the dhyāni-chohans or lords of contemplation, the mānasaputras, of future manvantaras. We were, in former kalpas, or manvantaras, monads in a still lower state of evolution than that in which we are now, forming then the vehicles of those who are still ahead of us, and who now still work through us, through our higher and our personal egos, and who thus inspire us to progress upwards, and who are, in fact, our inner gods: our very selves, yet different!

The work of evolution is, in fact, the raising of the personal into the impersonal; the raising of the mortal to put on the garments of immortality; the raising of the beast to become a man; the raising of a man to become a god; and the raising of a god to become still more largely divine. When we say "raising a beast to become a man," we do not, however, thereby mean the scientific hypothesis miscalled evolution and properly called transformism. The theosophic doctrine of evolution is immensely greater, infinitely (if we can use that expression) more profound, than those scientific theories. A beast never becomes a self-conscious, thinking man according to the scientific merely mechanical doctrine of materialistic transformism, any more so than a pile of mortar and bricks self-develops into a mansion, or a rough block of marble into a noble statue. It is the inner monad, the indwelling fire, which continually urges or brings forth into action the latent lives and forces in the atoms. Each atom in itself is a sleeping soul, and this, awakened, is what evolves or develops, not the merely physical body. Remember the threefold category that H. P. Blavatsky gives us: *gods*, first; *monads*, second; *atoms*, third — gods, the divine or highest triad; monads, the upper triad of the septenary; and the atoms, the lower quaternary of the septenary. Each one of those atoms, which are simply incalculably great in numbers, forming the lower quaternary, as already said, is a sleeping god, an embryo god rather. Its inner nature must be brought out, and that bringing out is evolution, the bringing out of inner capacities, each atom-entity making, as it does so, its own vehicles. This is the doctrine of self-directed evolution, following the urge, the primordial impress, of the dhyāni-chohans. All this has been set forth by us before.

In past studies we have spoken of the initiations (and of the doctrine of evolution taught anciently therein) as being a forcing-school. This word forcing is ambiguous. The word is subject to misinterpretation. Let us then put in its place the word quickening, or awakening, the word quickening meaning "life" in contrast with what is inert or dead; therefore, it is the quickening, the enlivening, the bringing out of that which is within. This idea is the key thought of the theosophical doctrine of evolution.

A beast no more develops mechanically into a man than do pieces of ivory, and cupfuls of polish, and pieces of wood and rolls of wire, naturally fall together and take proper form and "transform" themselves into a piano. Impossible! What makes a piano is the architect of it, the man, the thinker; so evolution is the working upon and in matter of the spiritual entity which takes and forms and urges onwards the material vehicles in which it is.

When we speak of the incarnation of the mānasaputras, the thinking entities, the sons of mind, it is of course understood that they are parts of, or entities from, the Hierarchy of Compassion, from the light-side of nature; and while evolution, the natural evolving (with the primordial spiritual or dhyāni-chohanic impress behind it) of nature into higher beings, would take place and *actually takes place continuously,* that process would be almost interminable in length of time were it not for the higher beings who give us of their light and their life, and thereby much more quickly lead us on. That is what is meant by the mānasaputras' "descent into incarnation." They are our higher natures and, paradoxical as it is, are more largely evolved beings than we are; they were the spiritual entities who quickened our personal egos, which were thus evolved into self-consciousness, relatively small though that yet be. One, and yet many! As you can light an infinite number of candles from one lighted candle, so can you, from a spark of consciousness, quicken and enliven innumerable other consciousnesses lying, so to speak, in sleep, or latent, in the atoms.

This brings us directly to another matter. We all possibly have heard of "contradictions" in *The Secret Doctrine,* or in our esoteric teachings. There are no contradictions there; there are *apparent* contradictions, if you like, but an apparent contradiction is really the figure of speech called a paradox. It is the famous old way of the ancient schools of occultism, to teach by paradoxes or by parables, as Jesus is said to have done. There is manifest a profound knowledge of human psychology in basing teachings on this principle. The aim is deliberately to arouse the mind, to astonish, to make the hearer *think for himself.* You cannot teach a child to eat or to walk by walking for it or by feeding yourself for it. It must learn to feed itself. It must itself learn to walk.

Similarly, students, neophytes, must learn to think for themselves, to stand upon their own feet. It is, I repeat, a very profound knowledge of psychology, of human thinking, which made the ancient Teachers, and makes the Masters of wisdom today, follow the same old principles, a method which we have followed since these studies were begun. You will have noticed that in no case has any subject been at first openly and fully stated or followed to its ultimate: first, because it is impossible; second, because it was obviously necessary to say certain things first, trying to arouse attention, trying to arouse *honest* objections — not merely criticisms — but honest objections in your *own* mind which you yourselves must solve; and then later other aspects of the subject were brought out and other sides of the teachings were given. Some of you know this fact, of course; but I am speaking more particularly of our younger and newer members. This method is a system of teaching diametrically opposite to that pursued in the Western world since the downfall of the Mediterranean civilizations. The popular method today is that of the pure brain-mind, of that mind which is mortal and goes to pieces with the death of the body. Its forte is the mere memorizing of times, places, names, dates, etc., in short, everything that can be memorized from books or daily occurrences, and stuffed into the brain; and this mind dies. That is one reason why we do not remember our past incarnations, because our minds were puny and dealt with little and evanescent things. But the memory of our past incarnations nevertheless inheres and remains in our higher natures, for this nature deals only with principles and generals; and some day, when we shall have passed out of and beyond our planet, we shall remember those past lives, unless indeed they be those cases of incarnations of a lost soul, in which cases there remain only blank pages, as it were, in the spiritual volume of life.

Let us illustrate some of these so-called contradictions by a few examples: *the moon is older than the sun; the sun is older than the moon.* No contradiction is here, but there is a paradox. Again, *the sun is older than any of its planets; the planets are older than their sun.* No contradiction again, but a paradox. Let us explain these paradoxes at once. Tracing the evolution of the solar system according to the esoteric philosophy, we point out first that the Milky Way is the storehouse of celestial bodies to be; as it were, the nursery from which seeds of future suns go forth to begin their manvantaric courses. When the time comes for such an event to happen, a comet, in its primordial ethereal robes, starts forth to enter upon its peregrinations, and after circling around and passing through what is to us illimitable space for long aeons of time, it, driven or drawn by karma, or under the guidance of karma, if you will, reaches that particular region in space which was actually the spot or region occupied by itself in a former imbodiment as a sun, and it settles there, and awakens and enlivens and quickens the solar dust around it (for space is full of it), and we then have a nebula. Further, it also gathers around itself larger ethereal remnants of its former self when it was a sun; and these then accrete to themselves other particles wandering in space, as we can say, and in due course these other bodies, with their accretions, become the planets of the new solar system.

What is a planet? What its origin? A sun runs through its kalpic course, its manvantaric period, which is a solar manvantara; and when its time comes to go into pralaya, into its rest, its internal force is weakened and — it dies. This is not an event of a day, but an event requiring much time; and what was its lowest principle (corresponding to *our* physical body) disintegrates into literally innumerable particles. Call them atoms, if you like. Remember, please, that the sun is neither solid — nor will it be then, when it dies — nor is it liquid, nor is it gaseous. After its death, it dissolves into innumerable atoms or particles, and these particles begin their long peregrinations through the fields of space, wandering in the immense solitudes for long, long aeons, until that indwelling entity of the former sun, which has its own inspiring inner presence, comes again under the form of a comet and reawakens what is now the solar dust of its former vehicle-self in the space where it formerly was — that dust being the remnants of its own former body. And these particles of the sun that was, are attracted to it again and form its suite of planets. Thus, in a sense, the planets of a sun are its "moons."

So, you see, as an entity, the sun is older than any one of its planetary system, remnants of its former body; but the planets are older than the sun that now is, because they actually are particles of the former sun that was of this plane. Where is the contradiction? A paradox, truly, which we had to solve; for the solving quickens our intuition, and that is one of the main aims and purposes of this system of teaching, the quickening of the intuition. Our brain-mind is a most admirable servant when under direction, but it should never be our master. It is not even a good servant; it has no self-respect. It has no discrimination, judgment, intuition, or understanding.

And similar to the above is the paradox concerning the moon. Perhaps at some future study we may have time to explain it. Also similar is the case of the planetoids, or the so-called asteroids, of which there are so many between the planets Jupiter and Mars. They are remnants of a former solar manvantara.

Further, all the planets not in obscuration or sleeping (as Mars is) are surrounded with thick and often greatly condensed clouds of the kosmic dust which they have accreted unto themselves; it actually is the former solar dust of now disintegrated moons and planets. For over our own heads and over and around every one of the nonsleeping planets of our solar system, there is a continent, literally a continent, of this kosmic dust, so thick is that solar dust and so numerous are the bodies or particles of various sizes which compose it. It acts as a veil protecting us from the terrific energy of the sun, acting not merely as a veil of protection against his rays alone, but also against other accidents that might happen to us were there no such protecting veil surrounding our globe in thick folds.

Mars has at present none or very little of such a protecting veil, simply because its life-energies have gone to another globe of the Martian planetary system — the Martian planetary chain — and the attractive magnetic force which holds together such a veil therefore is largely absent. But Venus and Mercury, for instance, have, as we have, such a protecting veil, although much thinner in Mercury's case than in that of Venus, because Mercury is just emerging from obscuration, and it is what the astronomers see when they look at those planets through their telescopes, when they see the "clouds," and note that they cannot see the face of the planet itself. They really see the veil. We are not conscious of the veil protecting us. Somewhat like a man in a room with one of those white net curtains over his window — he can see outwards, and discern what passes in the street beyond; but the man in the street cannot easily see him.

As a final example this evening of the use of the paradox in our study, I take the following. At a former study we said that nature never repeats herself. We repeat it this evening: nature never repeats herself. In a later study we stated that nature does nothing but repeat herself. We repeat it this evening: nature does nothing but repeat herself. Contradiction? No. Paradox? Yes. Let us see if we can make this apparent contradiction a little clearer. What are cycles? Repetitions. What are hierarchies? Repetitions. What are the main repetitions of a general type? Principles, forces, planets, suns, orbs, atoms, monads, gods — all are manifold repetitions of primal spiritual impresses. Nature works in no other way than by repeating herself — repetitions on inferior planes of primordial principles or root-types.

Now, what mean we in saying that nature never repeats herself? Let us here use our common sense. We are not here to amuse each other with folly. Nature likewise never repeats herself, because you will never find two principles identical, no two cycles are identical, no two men are identical, no two monads, no two suns, no two planets, no two souls, no two egos are identical. Our paradox then is solved by remembering that nature's method is *unity in endless diversity*.

We return now to our main theme. The Syrians had the following method or system of describing the stages of being which we represent in the accompanying diagram: (1) the Milky Way, or the first principle; (2) Nebulae and Comets, or Seraphim,

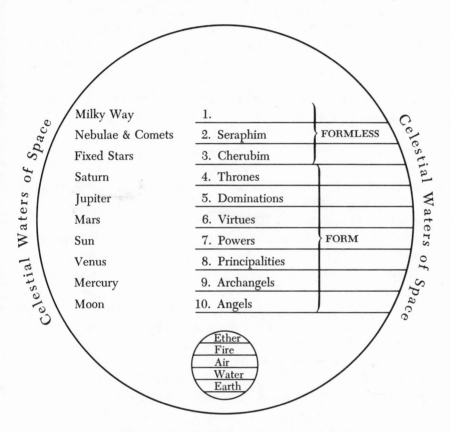

sphere two, counting downwards; (3) the Fixed Stars, or Cherubim. These three were the Formless World. Then the planets: (4) Saturn, Thrones; (5) Jupiter, Dominations; (6) Mars, Virtues; (7) Sun, Powers; (8) Venus, Principalities; (9) Mercury, Archangels; (10) Moon, Angels. These eight, including Earth, Men, were the World of Form.

Then we will draw, if you please, a circle which will represent a sphere, and let it be our Earth; and we will divide this Earth into five zones, the topmost one being that of ether; the one underneath it being fire; the one underneath that being air; the one underneath that being water; and the lowest one being earth.

Please understand also that the Syrians conceived of this world-system as a sphere, as a kosmos; hence, our design must have a circle surrounding it — a conventional figure, it is true, and not implying any particular limitations, but signifying the bounding circle of that particular kosmos or hierarchy. The Syrians further said that outside of this hierarchy, of this kosmos, there were the Celestial Waters, meaning thereby what the Greeks called Chaos, or kosmic matter undeveloped for us, the waters of space, in other words. As regards this metaphor, Celestial Waters, you will remember what the Hebrew Bible also says about the "spirit of the Elohīm" or gods moving on the face of the "waters."

The three highest planes are what we call arūpa, or formless; and the other seven (or eight) planes are rūpa, or formed. They taught that in the beginning of things, i.e., when kosmic evolution began, the primordial essence evolved forth the most subtil and the most spiritual element, and this naturally was the highest, the Milky Way, where all things begin in this system; and that the next step in evolution downwards was the comets and the nebulae; and then the "1,122 fixed stars"; and then the various solar systems — our own solar system, as an example, bringing us thus to the first of the seven planetary regions. Any other solar system would have answered, but ours naturally was chosen, being ours. Each of these steps downwards represents the stage that the evolving wave of life had to pass through before it finally culminated in material existence as on our earth, for instance; finally passing through the last seven stages, the surrounding planes of the globe. First of these last seven was what we may call the Nameless Element; then the superether; then the ether; and then the fire; and then the air; and then the water; and then the earth — these elements not being the material things familiar to us, but the spirits of the elements, the primordial matter of which our elements are merely the material representation.

You will notice that the Christian Apostle, Paul, speaks of several of these powers or elements pertaining or belonging to the various planets as above described in the Syrian system, such as the Dominions, and the Virtues, the Thrones, the Principalities, the Archangels, and the Angels. You will also remember that in a former study we pointed out that really all Christian mysticism was founded by Dionysius, the so-called Areopagite, who also used these same names; so that in addition to the thoughts which Christianity drew from Neoplatonism and Neopythagoreanism, it also drew from (through Paul himself who was a Syrian) these ancient Mystery-teachings as exoterically expressed in the hierarchy as shown in the diagram. But behind this outward expression there was the same exposition, there was the same esoteric system and truth, that we have been studying for some months past.

TWENTY-FIVE

THE MYSTERIES OF SEPTENARY NATURE. CORRESPONDENCES: GLOBES,
ELEMENTS, HUMAN PRINCIPLES. THE SEVEN SACRED PLANETS OF
THE ANCIENTS. RACIAL TIME PERIODS AND CATASTROPHES.

But upon this one of those more antient priests [of Egypt] exclaimed, O Solon, Solon, you Greeks are always children, nor is there any such thing as an aged Grecian among you! But Solon, when he heard this — What (says he) is the motive of your exclamation? To whom the priest: — Because all your souls are juvenile; neither containing any antient opinion derived from re-mote tradition, nor any discipline hoary from its existence in former periods of time. But the reason of this is the multitude and variety of destructions of the human race, which formerly have been, and again will be: the greatest of these indeed arising from fire and water; but the lesser from ten thousand other contingencies. . . . But whatever has been transacted either by us, or by you, or in any other place, beautiful or great, or containing any thing uncommon of which we have heard the report, every thing of this kind is to be found described in our temples, and preserved to the present day.
— PLATO, *Timaeus,* pp. 466–7 (Thomas Taylor, trans.)

LET US OPEN our study this evening by reading from the first volume of *The Secret Doctrine,* pages 611–12, section 15, entitled "Gods, Monads, and Atoms":

The exact extent, depth, breadth, and length of the mysteries of Nature are to be found only in Eastern esoteric sciences. So vast and so profound are these that hardly a few, a very few of the highest Initiates — those *whose very existence is known but to a small number of Adepts* — are capable of assimilating the knowledge. Yet it is all there, and one by one facts and processes in Nature's workshops are permitted to find their way into the exact Sciences, while mysterious help is given to rare individuals in unravel-ling its arcana. It is at the close of great Cycles, in connection with racial development, that such events generally take place. We are at the very close of the cycle of 5,000 years of the present Aryan Kaliyuga; and between this time and 1897 there will be a large rent made in the Veil of Nature, and materialistic science will receive a death-blow. . . .

. . . From the very beginning of Æons — in time and space in our Round and Globe — the Mysteries of Nature (at any rate, those which it is lawful for our races to know) were recorded by the pupils of those same now invisible "heavenly men," in geometrical figures and symbols. The keys thereto passed from one generation of "wise men" to the other.

At our last meeting we discussed a diagram showing the Syrian views, from an exoteric standpoint, of the external and internal structure of the kosmos; and some of you, who perhaps observed carefully, will have noticed that this diagrammatic hierarchy seemed to be represented as all on one plane. Now that is true, in a certain sense; but there is much in connection with that fact that we could not then and now cannot speak of, for the simple reason that we have not as yet laid the foundations for properly understanding it. Let it then suffice this evening to say that, as a matter of real fact, the hierarchies interact and intermingle — cross each other in all directions, as it were.

As remarked in a former study, the direction of our evolution is "outwards" at first, and "inwards" secondly. On descending the shadowy arc or the arc of matter in the beginning of the manvantara of this our planetary chain, the direction which we followed, as members of our planetary life-wave, was from within outwards, i.e., from inner planes, from inner worlds, constantly proceeding "downwards" — that is, into ever-increasing materiality; and when we reached the middle of the fourth round on this our globe, which is the central or turning point of the manvantara of this planetary chain, the impulse slackened and finally reached its close in what we call the fourth root-race, the Atlantean race. Thereafter the reverse process began its action, and progress, advancement, development, retraced its steps, as it were, in a spiral, the direction thenceforward being from without inwards, or an ascent in ever-increasing spirituality. This process of a primal descent into materiality, followed by a reascent into spirituality, is the course followed not merely in the construction, development, and consummation of the destiny of a planetary chain, and of all planetary chains, but also is the course followed in the larger cycles of evolution, such as the solar kalpas, for instance, which comprise, each one, seven of the planetary manvantaras. Seven planetary manvantaras make one solar kalpa; in other words, seven Days of Brahmā or seven planetary cycles, each cycle consisting of seven rounds, form one solar kalpa (or manvantara).

In order to assist our minds in understanding our study this evening, in order to help us in conceiving the idea, let us draw seven circles representing seven globes: three on the downward cycle or shadowy arc, one at the bottom or turning point, and three on the ascending or luminous arc or cycle. We may number with the letters of the alphabet.

Now these circles represent, if you will, the globes of the planetary chain, and the evolution of the life-wave beginning on

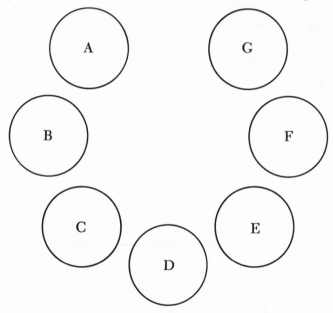

globe A and running there through its appointed cycles, completing them, and then entering B; after completing its course on B, then entering C; and then, on ending its course for the round on C, entering D, where we are now, and also in the fourth round. We are thus halfway around the course for our round, the fourth, and somewhat more, because we are the fifth root-race of our globe D, on which seven root-races must run their course.

Each of these globes, furthermore, is builded out of, and has its correspondence with, what the ancients called the elements, that is to say, the bases of the seven principles of nature. They are furthermore called "rudiments," not in the sense of something incomplete, but in the original sense of root-things, originants. The Sanskrit word for the principles is *tattwa*, meaning "a reality," not the uttermost reality, the Absolute of any hierarchy, but its root-differentiations in manifestation; and the word for the elements is *bhūta*, each element springing from its predecessor or superior and giving life and birth to another, its inferior. The ancients always reckoned four elements, and sometimes five; our School reckons seven in all. The usual enumeration of the ancients is as follows: aether, fire, air, water and, lastly, earth. The last two principles to be enumerated, and the last two elements, the bases of the former two, have been given no names exoterically, because they are not yet known by our present senses. Human consciousness does not yet recognize them, but they are recognized, taught of, and named, in the esoteric philosophy nevertheless; and they are called, for the second, *anupapādaka-tattwa*, a Sanskrit word very difficult to explain in English. The general meaning is that it does not proceed from anything else, i.e., "parentless." It proceeds from itself. Finally, the first of all the seven, the uppermost on the descending arc of nature, is called *ādi-tattwa* or "original tattwa," for the principle; and *ādi-bhūta* for the corresponding element, because it belongs to the same plane of being of the kosmos as the principle ādi-tattwa, but in a somewhat lower degree, being the base or vehicle of the former, the principle.

These elements, of course, are not the familiar things which we know under these names — fire, water, air, or earth — but these familiar things are their correspondences on our earth, in a mystic sense. Now, although the seven globes of the planetary chain are *not* the seven elements respectively, each to each, yet each globe is builded up out of them all and, furthermore, one of the seven elements predominates in each one of the globes respectively. All this will be elucidated in our future studies, when we come to study the lokas and talas. For instance, on globe A: the fire-quality would not be our material earth-fire; it would there be the *spirit of fire*, so to say, the root of fire, because in the esoteric philosophy "fire" is not merely the result of combustion, according to modern scientific ideas, but is an actual element, a rudiment, a base. And similarly with air, proceeding from fire, born from fire; and similarly with the element water, proceeding from air, born from it; and again earth born from water, i.e., the element water.

It is likewise the old Stoic doctrine, that the elements give birth one to another. Manifestation begins on the spiritual plane, and as the life impulses reach forth into grosser forms, into matter (to use the popular expression), the succeeding elements (bases, rudiments) are born, each one from the preceding one, and from *all preceding ones*. For instance, earth is born not merely from the element water, but likewise from fire, and air. Furthermore, the seven rounds of a planetary chain, the seven globes of a planetary chain, and the seven root-races of any globe thereof, has each its predominating correspondence with one of these seven elements. Please understand that we mean not at all the familiar things we know on our earth by those names, but the bases, the originants, the "spirits" of them: the causes, the tattwas, the real things which produce what we see here on our earth.

Furthermore, the seven sacred planets are, each one of them, a manifestation, an incorporealization, of the powers of one of the seven solar logoi, or spiritual forces of our solar kosmos, of which force-elements we may see a faint manifestation or, if you will, an adumbration, in the seven colors of the solar spectrum. We reserve further clearer explanation of this for future studies.

Please note also that our own human seven principles correspond each one, respectively and relatively, with one of these elements. The seven principles and elements of man are a duplication in him of the seven principles and elements of the kosmos. The seven elements, or bases, or rudiments, are the seven vehicles of the seven principles of the kosmos. These elements are at the same time substance and energy or force, because energy and substance fundamentally are the same thing. Matter and force are fundamentally the same thing. It is, as it were, the upper and the lower side, the inward and outward, the impulse and its results or fruits.

And furthermore, with regard to the seven sacred planets mentioned above: when the esoteric science of the ancients spoke of seven *sacred* planets, certain ones especially were designated because, as a matter of fact, each of the planets known to us is itself connected with seven other planets which are to it *its* seven sacred planets. Our earth is not one of the seven sacred planets of the ancients. Those seven sacred planets were Saturn; Jupiter; Venus; Mercury; the planet very near to the sun, at present invisible but suspected, and called by some modern astronomers Vulcan; a sixth which we merely mention, at present; and a seventh sometimes seen near the moon — by those who "have eyes to see"!

It will be recollected that it was remarked at a former study that the Vulcan-planet was first discovered, or supposed to be discovered, on March 26th, 1859, when it was seen in transit across the solar disk, and astronomers since then have searched for it and have not been able to find it. The teaching with reference to that planet, the highest (in one sense) of our seven sacred planets, is this, that it became invisible to our physical senses at about the middle point of the third root-race; but as we have now reached again, on the upward arc, the plane corresponding to the degree of plane-development of the third root-race, in a relatively short cyclic period it should begin again to show itself; but even today, while it might be generally invisible on account of what we may call its ethereality, if searched for by telescope it might nevertheless be seen, under favorable conditions, crossing the solar disk. And why? Because the truly indescribable brilliance of the sun throws anything that appears before it into visibility, so to speak, as a darker body, and it could thus be seen as such a shadowy body crossing the solar disk. At least that is one reason, probably, why astronomers have searched for this planet and have — or have not yet — found it.

With regard to the seventh mentioned above, which is the "lowest" of our seven sacred planets, the one esoterically spoken of as near the moon, that planet is in its last or seventh round, and is therefore dying. The probability is that it also, to our present physical senses, is more or less ethereal, and therefore practically invisible, except under certain very favorable conditions. Before our planet shall have reached its last or seventh round, our moon will have disintegrated into stellar dust, but by that time this secret or Mystery-planet near the moon and now dying will be dead, and will be to us as a moon; not a true moon in the sense of our lunar mother, but rather a satellite. It will *appear* to us as a moon; and, indeed, will be a "moon," because it will be a dead body.

There is a great deal that simply cannot be said — at least not yet — about these seven sacred or Mystery-planets. But we have pointed out before that the seven principal dhyāni-chohans, or lords of meditation, are very intimately connected, each to each, respectively, with the seven Mystery-planets or sacred planets, that is, the seven which are the sacred planets for the earth. There are many other planets in our solar system, but only seven of that number are our seven sacred planets.

Each other planet, Jupiter, let us say for instance, has its own seven sacred planets, and all belonging to our solar system, but not all of them would necessarily be *our* seven sacred planets. Yet each one, by the interconnection or intermingling of the elements of kosmic construction, each one of them, I say, is a solar locus. Here again is something that we must touch upon before we pass on farther.

Man is higher than the globe he lives on. Man is higher than the sun. You and I sitting here, occupy a status spiritually higher than the sun, although it is the spiritual and vital locus of the solar system. The sun we see is not the true sun. The sun we see is merely the focus of the titanic forces playing on the other side, through it. And man is higher than it, and yet comes from it, from the inner side of it, so to say. Further, as pointed out in another study, do not be carried away by scientific theories, for science is absolutely no criterion of spiritual knowledge, which is, as yet, far beyond its scope or reach. Our physical bodies, i.e., the body of each one of us, is a kosmos, even, relatively speaking, a universal kosmos. Modern science is beginning to suspect this truth, and the scientists now speak of the atom, formed of its electrons and protons, as composing a miniature solar system. There is no particle of substance or matter which is free from life, barren of intelligent life and lives; and there are beings in and on the electrons of the atoms of our body which are higher than the *personal* self of us is. A sublime thought to think about! We have, indeed, higher responsibilities inherent in us than we dream of. Our body, in very truth, is a temple of life.

I have received a letter from a friend which is well worth reading at this point. I cite a portion of it with an included quotation concerning the planet Vulcan:

"Seeliger has conclusively shown that there is enough of the cosmic dust which forms the Zodiacal Light to account for all the discrepancies in the movements of Mercury," and so make a Vulcan unnecessary.

This was written about twelve years ago, and was supposed to settle the whole difficulty of Mercury's 42 seconds per century change in perihelion position.

Note first: the perturbations in the movements of Mercury were first explained by an unknown planet called Vulcan. Well, Vulcan could not be found again, so the theorists said that it must be cosmic dust which produces these perturbations. Second theory: I quote again from the letter:

Then comes friend Einstein and starts explaining it in an entirely different way, and "cosmic dust" in its turn is scientifically made away with. Then comes Professor Poor of Columbia University and shows that Einstein's theory about Mercury upsets the positions of the other planets more than it helps Mercury — so there you are!

I admire their wonderful ingenuity in making theories for the marvels they have discovered under the limited conditions at their disposal, but we certainly must keep an open mind on the things which are subject to such various interpretations.

Very well put. It covers the ground very neatly.

We are nearing the conclusion of our study for this evening, but meanwhile there is a matter which requires some treatment before we close, and that is with regard to the root-races of any globe of our planetary chain. Take the races, for instance, of our own globe D of our planetary chain, globe D being the lowest in the chain, as you know. Now these root-races occupy vastly more time in their evolution than is commonly supposed. Time runs into millions of years for any and for each root-race. It is supposed by some who have not read H. P. Blavatsky's *Secret Doctrine* with attention that our root-race, the fifth, is only about one million years old now. That idea is not true, and H. P. Blavatsky says nothing of the sort. In volume II, page 435, she says that our fifth root-race is about one million years old, as a race *sui generis* and *quite free from its parent-stem.* How many more million years did it require to reach even that point, born as a root-race at about the central point of the mother-race? It required millions of years for our race to reach the central point of its career, *where we are now.* Our great racial catastrophe, which will come upon us as their own came in due time upon all other former root-races, and as such a catastrophe will come upon the two races which are to succeed our fifth race, i.e., the sixth and seventh root-races, has not yet reached us, but it is coming.

Another thing: while each root-race is destroyed alternately by fire and by water, let us not forget that the other elements likewise are at work at the same time; but it is fire and water more particularly which affect and cause the displacements of continents or rather their submergence, and the emergence or rising of the new lands. There is an interesting point of our doctrines in this connection, and I now briefly allude to it.

The teaching is that the first, the third, the fifth, and the seventh root-races are what may be called aqueous; and the second, the fourth, and the sixth — those with even numbers — are what we may call the terreous races. In other words, those with uneven numbers, 1, 3, 5, and 7, flourish on our globe at times when the oceans cover more of its surface than does the land; and the conditions are reversed in the second, fourth, and sixth root-races, when there is more land than water on the globe's surface. Fire destroyed the first race, as it destroyed the third race also; water destroyed the second and also the fourth race; and fire will destroy the fifth, water the sixth, and fire again the seventh. Now, geologically speaking, it is this alternation in extent of land or water which brings about this cyclical condition.

Let us try to make this matter a little more clear. The third race perished by fire, which means the action of subterrene earthquakes and of volcanoes, principally, followed by submergence. Now the third race was an aqueous race, that is to say, there was then more water on the face of the earth than land. So today, in our fifth race, at about the middle period of our race's life cycle, there is one-third as much land as water on the surface of the globe, i.e., three times as much water as land. When our root-race shall be drawing towards its end, the coming catastrophe will be shown by immense systemic and minor seismic and volcanic disturbances, announcing the submergence of our continental system and the emergence of new lands for the following sixth root-race, the working of fire. When the Atlantean system fell, when the Atlantean continental system had its catastrophe which slowly overwhelmed it with flood, it was water which caused it. There was then more land than water; nature sought a readjustment, a better balance, and that great system perished by floods. The water came and submerged the land, of course also accompanied by earthquakes and the action of volcanoes. We must not imagine that when a root-race perishes through fire or water as the chief causative agent, that there is then no aqueous or terrene-fire disturbance. On the contrary, fire and water work together, but the one or the other then predominates. The fourth, the Atlantean, was a terreous period, and nature followed her usual course in cases of disturbed equilibrium — "and the waters came and overwhelmed the land." Whence the "waters came" is a most fascinating subject for study, but we have no time to go into it tonight. Ours is an aqueous period; and in due course the waters will slowly tend to disappear, giving place to new lands in the future, the dwelling places to be of the next, the sixth root-race.

Katherine Tingley: I would like to ask Professor de Purucker if he will make an explanation — which I think would be satisfactory to you, and which he could do much better than I — and show what will be the state of civilization, of humanity, at the ending of these different races, when the end comes? How will evolution be marked? Will not those people who will seem to be the "victims" of the terrible catastrophe which comes at the end of every race have the knowledge of the secrets of death, and look upon rebirth as a glorious release?

G. de Purucker: I think certainly so. The end of every race brings with it a perfection of what that race was striving to accomplish. And I dare say that if we could look back and know what took place when the continent of Atlantis sank, we should realize that even those comparatively few, who by death left the physical body during that catastrophe, had the realization that what they had to undergo was no more and no less than merely one form of death inevitable to all men sooner or later. They knew better than we do now, although far more sunken in matter, that life is eternal, for, actually, *there is nothing but life everywhere!* And their physicians could have told them, and did tell them, for they knew, that every disease of our bodies comes about from an excess of life, particularly what we may call the malignant or wasting diseases. In these cases it is life running riot in the body, and that is what causes death. They knew it better than we.

Furthermore, no one should think that in these racial catastrophes everyone is swept away in a moment in a fearful confusion and chaos, and that there is no hope, and that everything is but wild despair. Not at all. These catastrophes come on slowly. The continents sink through the ages. Man migrates and leaves the sinking lands behind, and moves to higher and better ones, new ones, fresh ones, where new races are born out of what we justly may call the death of the old.

Nothing, I suppose, that I might mention, could equal the horror of the catastrophe of Lisbon years ago, when tens of thousands of people perished in an earthquake; or the fearful catastrophe at Messina, in Sicily, only a few years ago; and other earthquakes and tidal waves which you all may remember. We are in our own great cyclical catastrophe now, though it is but beginning. How much worse is the agony of heart, let us say, of one who is at the bedside of one whom he loves! Ah, there you have anguish! But sudden catastrophes, when they do occur, occur mostly on a relatively small scale. When the races near their ends, the continents sink slowly. There are much worse things than merely losing the physical body, for those whose destiny it is to be in a racial catastrophe. They will know the beautiful secrets of death. At the end of our race we shall know it far better than the Atlanteans did. But not one so perishes individually, unless it is his personal karma. How about the tens of thousands who perish yearly in steamer, train, automobile, mine and various other accidents? Pray reflect.

TWENTY-SIX

THE MICROCOSM, A MIRROR OF THE MACROCOSM. ELEMENTS,
PRINCIPLES, MANIFESTATIONS OF THE ONE LIFE. RELATIVITY:
A FUNDAMENTAL CONCEPTION OF THE ANCIENT WISDOM.

"Man," says Van Helmont, "is the mirror of the universe, and his triple
nature stands in relationship to all things."
— H. P. BLAVATSKY, *Isis Unveiled*, I, 213

. . . there is but one element . . . This element then is the — to speak
metaphysically — one sub-stratum or permanent cause of all manifestations
in the phenomenal universe. The ancients speak of the five cognizable elements of ether, air, water, fire, earth, and of the one incognizable element
(to the uninitiates) the 6th principle of the universe — call it Purush Sakti,
while to speak of the seventh outside the sanctuary was punishable with
death. But these five are but the differentiated aspects of the one. As man
is a seven-fold being so is the universe — the septenary microcosm being to
the septenary macrocosm but as the drop of rainwater is to the cloud from
whence it dropped and whither in the course of time it will return. In that
one are embraced or included so many tendencies for the evolution of air,
water, fire, etc. (from the purely abstract down to their concrete condition)
and when those latter are called elements it is to indicate their productive
potentialities for numberless form changes or evolution of being.
— *The Mahatma Letters*, pp. 90–1

L ET US OPEN our study this evening by reading from *The
Secret Doctrine*, volume I, section 16, pages 638–9:

In ancient symbolism it was always the SUN (though the Spiritual,
not the visible, Sun was meant), that was supposed to send forth the chief
Saviours and Avatars. Hence the connecting link between the Buddhas, the
Avatars, and so many other incarnations of the highest SEVEN. The closer
the approach to one's *Prototype*, "in Heaven," the better for the mortal
whose personality was chosen, by his own *personal* deity (the seventh principle), as its terrestrial abode. For, with every effort of will toward purification and unity with that "Self-god," one of the lower rays breaks and the
spiritual entity of man is drawn higher and ever higher to the ray that
supersedes the first, until, from ray to ray, the inner man is drawn into the
one and highest beam of the Parent-SUN.

That is a superb passage. It contains in embryo the substance of our studies for some weeks past. It will be remembered that we have spoken of the Hierarchy of Compassion, the spiritual hierarchy from which we draw our inner life, spiritual and mental, and whose supreme chief is that Wondrous Being who, in his spiritual capacity, is the dhyāni-buddha of this fourth round. His human representative is the chief of what we call the Great White Lodge, he to whom the Masters look up for quickening and enlightenment, he who lights their fires as they light and quicken ours.

How is this quickening and lighting done? How was it that the mānasaputras worked, in their incarnations in the hitherto senseless humanity, to raise man — if we can give to the humanity of that time that name — from spiritually and mentally senseless beings to self-conscious humanhood?

Listen: every one of the seven principles of man, as also every one of the seven elements (corresponding in the kosmos to the seven principles in man), is itself a mirror of the universe, that is, it contains in itself everything that the boundless All contains. Everything is in the microcosm that exists in the macrocosm; the one, the less, mirrors the other, the greater. In other words, each of the elements, each of the principles, each of the rudiments to blossom forth later into divinity, is itself a septenary or sevenfold entity, existing on its own septenary plane, which to it is as palpably certain, real, and substantial as this our physical plane is to us as seen through our physical eyes and heard through our physical ears, or sensed by the media of the other senses, two more of which, by the way, are still to be developed.

Now each one being a septenary, each one of these principles or elements is a copy in miniature, if we may use that word, of the Whole. For instance, the principle of manas is septenary. It has its own ātman, its buddhi, and its manas — the manas-manas, which is its own particular essence or swabhāva; next, its kāma or desire principle; then its vital essence; then its garment, its linga-śarīra, or model-body, so to say, that which gives it its own particular shape and conformation according to the qualities of that plane; and finally its sthūla-śarīra, or lowest portion or vehicle or carrier or bearer.

These mānasaputras or sons of mind, children of mahat, are

said to have quickened and enlightened the manas-manas of the manas-septenary, because they themselves are typically mānasic in their essential characteristic or swabhāva. Their own vibrations, so to say, could cause that essence of manas in ourselves to vibrate in sympathy, much as the sounding of a musical note will cause sympathetic response in something like it, a similar note in other things.

Who are these mānasaputras? They are ourselves in a sense, but we are rather and more particularly those who were quickened and enlivened. They are a mystery; they are at once our higher selves — not our highest selves, but our *higher* selves — and yet different. We have shown in past studies that from the One spring all the manifold differentiations of a kosmic (or any other) hierarchy, and that there is a perfect kinship or unity of being throughout. These sublime thoughts can be very clearly understood if we awaken in ourselves that portion of our nature to which they are native and familiar. We can do it, and it depends upon us to do it. Why is it that the Masters choose, from time to time, a certain one or certain ones, and take him or them to themselves? Because they see in those so selected the inner Master already quickened, enlivened, at least to some extent. Would they take a beast? No. Why not? Because the beast is not quickened. Would they take an ordinary man? No. Why? Because the man is not quickened, he is not awakened, he is not yet conscious in himself of the inner essential Buddha, the Awakened One. There is no question of arbitrary choice about this fact. It is a selection and an election of the fit and proper ones; it is therefore just, it is therefore right.

Let us pursue this thought a little more. Let us take nature and consider her elements. Now this word *element* is from the Latin and it means one of the rudiments of things, the word "rudiment" in its original sense. The Sānkhya especially, one of the six accepted schools of philosophy of India, and also even the Vedanta — perhaps the noblest of those schools — both speak of the six original "producers" or elements of nature as prakritis, the six prakritis derived from the primal Prakriti, or root-Prakriti, the first and highest. The Sānkhya also speaks of them, and so do many students of the Vedanta, as the six tattwas or real elements. Now what is the difference between the six elements or prakritis, and the six tattwas? The prakriti is the vehicular or bearer- or carrier-side, so to say, the substantial side, and the tattwa is the analogic or force-side. And these two fundamentally are one, because, please remember, matter and force, spirit and substance, are both fundamentally one. Matter can be called crystallized spirit. We have to hunt for words in any attempt to describe these things; hence this is an inadequate expression, but it perhaps conveys the meaning. *Parabrahman* and *Mūlaprakriti* — "beyond-Brahman" and "root-nature" — of the Vedanta and the Sānkhya, represent the same thought, and these two fundamentally are one. Root-nature is the veil, as it were, of the primordial energy, the primordial consciousness; and these prakritis in the Sānkhya, these six or seven prakritis, stand for the six or seven elements of nature, corresponding to our human seven or six principles. And these are born, or issue rather, one from the other. That prakriti which is the higher plane is the parent of the prakriti which is the lower plane. First, the primordial one gives birth to the second: ātman, let us say, gives birth to buddhi. And ātman and buddhi combined give birth to manas, issuing from the two former, and containing the qualities of the preceding two as well as its own. And ātman, buddhi, manas then give birth to kāma, the fourth in order; and so on down to the seventh or lowest.

Similarly globe A, the first on the descending arc, gives birth to globe B, and globe B gives birth to globe C; but it does so with the swābhāvic tattwa of globe A also working in it. And globe C gives birth to globe D, our earth, but with the tattwas or intrinsic individualities or swabhāvas of A and B in it also. Globe D thus has the tattwas of globes A, B, and C inherent in it in addition to its own individual characteristic or swabhāva.

When the evolutionary impulse has reached its limit in any one manvantara — and the limits vary in every manvantara, because there is no absolute point or position in space, or any one particular plane where every evolutionary manvantaric impulse in the Boundless must stop, for so many monads, so many hierarchies have so many respective evolutionary impulses and their respective ends — that is, when that outrushing impulse that comes from above, carrying these prakritis and principles down into greater manifestation of matter, has reached the limit possible for that particular manvantara, it then turns, as it were, around the goal and begins the reascent.

We in our planetary chain have passed that goal or turning point *of the rounds.* Furthermore, in each of the races on any globe of the chain; in each of the globes during any round; and for each of the rounds passing through all the seven globes; there is a midpoint in its respective evolutionary course, and that midpoint is its respective goal or turning point, where the respective cycle begins a reascent. Hence, there will then be a sudden rising of the evolving monads or entities; and, correspondentially, senses hitherto latent and undeveloped will be developed, and the principles in nature which we *now* do not cognize will then be cognized and known. Ether, for instance, of which we have a mere presentiment today at the middle point of our fifth race in the fourth round, recognized even by science, will during the fifth *round* become an actuality in what will then be the atmosphere, as palpable and plain to the senses as air is today to us.

So, then, when speaking of the elements or the prakritis, we do not mean that the earth and water and air and fire spoken of by the ancients as elements, are the real elemental prakritis of nature. That is absurd. The ancients used those words symbolically. These four (or five things, including ether) are merely manifestations — four of them so far developed — of four or five out of the seven subprakritis or subprinciples belonging to the lowest prakritic element as manifest at this stage on our fourth globe, corresponding to the seventh or lowest kosmic plane or prakriti.

As each principle is itself a subseptenary and mirrors the Boundless, so does each element mirror all the other elements; and from each element can be drawn the life and nature and characteristic, in minor degree, of course, of all the other six. The above-named qualities of the matter of the seventh or lowest prakriti of our globe, that is to say, *solidity, fluidity, air* (there seems to be no corresponding adjective in English for air, or for the following one), *fire,* are merely the correspondences of the similar subprakritis of the four kosmic elements or prakritis in which our planetary chain exists now. Ether as an element will come next; and in the sixth round will be developed the sixth element; and during the seventh round will be developed the seventh. None of the ancient philosophers of the Mediterranean countries, when speaking of earth, water, air, fire, ether, nor the Hindus, when speaking, for instance, of ākāśa or of ādi-tattwa, meant the material things which we can sense, such as earth and water. They meant the root-elements of nature, of which these four or five things that we sense are, as it were, presentments or symbols.

The Greeks called the elements *stoicheia,* a plural diminutive of the word *stoichos* meaning a "series," in other words, a hierarchy. The singular *stoicheion* would be an entity of a hierarchy, a part of it, one of the composite parts of the hierarchy, although modern scholars can trace no ostensible reason for giving this name to what they recognize as being the ancient conception of the elements of nature. But our philosophy shows why, and explains that the stoicheia are the seven prakritis of the kosmos. Each of the globes of our planetary chain is an imbodiment of all these elements or seven prakritis, but in the manner outlined above, of each element containing *in parvo* all the others. Our earth, for instance, is an imbodiment or representation of the lowest prakriti, but there is water and there is air and there is fire, and we know that there is ether in development. We know four and recognize five, an exemplification of what has just been said. Nevertheless, the seven globes of our planetary chain are not the respective correspondences of the seven kosmic elements. This would be a false analogy.

Each one of the grades of initiation, of which we have spoken before, corresponds to one of these seven kosmic elements; and the trials through which the initiant or candidate must pass, in order to prove his capacity, are regulated and governed by the nature of each one respectively of the seven prakritis. There are, as a matter of fact, ten grades or degrees of initiation and ten kosmic prakritis — seven in manifestation, and three root-prakritis or the highest; but the uppermost three are so far beyond our utmost capacity of understanding now that we can do no more than mention the fact. Always ten: three arūpa or formless (to *us*, please understand) and seven in manifestation; and of these seven the upper triad is, relatively speaking, also arūpa.

Let us here point out something very important — that is, that all the teaching of the ancient wisdom is given from our plane, so that when we say *arūpa* or "formless," it does not mean that in themselves, *an sich,* per se, these higher planes or entities are formless, which would be absurd. But to us they are formless, exactly as ether is formless, because it is not yet (for us) developed. We have as yet but a mere presentiment of it in this fourth round, and only because we are in the fifth root-race, corresponding in element to that fifth element, ether. And as a corollary to that, and it is an important deduction, as regards the beings inhabiting each element, each principle, of the universal kosmos: their habitations, their countries, all that therein exists, to them are as real and palpable as are palpable and material things on our plane to us. Force, to us, is substance in motion. Do you realize that our most dense and rigid matter is force to beings in the hierarchy below us? Do we realize that what we call the density and the rigidity of matter are merely such to *our* senses, and that this very density and this rigidity show and prove that our dense and rigid matter is but a balancing of opposing forces? Why, many modern scientists today, making a right-about-face from what was utter truth to science some fifty years ago, now say that there is no such thing as matter per se, that there is nothing but force. Matter is therefore to it a māyā, an illusion, and so it is. But so is force a māyā, because it is merely matter to something higher than it. *All things are relative,* a statement which is one of the fundamental conceptions of the ancient wisdom.

So when we speak of these various prakritis and principles, let us recognize first that these elements, these tattwas or principles, from whatever viewpoint we may look at them, are all manifestations of the one universal life, which is likewise universal substance in its lower aspect. Spirit and substance, force and matter are fundamentally one, two sides to the same thing.

This, that is so important, we fain would dwell upon much longer and give illustrations of its application to our studies. Let us make a final application tonight. What is the difference between a Master, and me and you? The former has his higher principles awakened and lives in them. And we do not. From the scientific standpoint, that is all there is to it; from the philosophic standpoint, we may say that a Master has become, as far as he can be, more at one with the universal life; and from the religious standpoint or the spiritual standpoint, we may say that a Master has developed an *individual consciousness,* or *recognition,* of his oneness with the Boundless. This is the very foundation of the ethics without which there is nothing worthy of the ancient wisdom. No man can misconduct himself without injecting inharmony, disharmony, into the human hierarchy of which he is a part, and for this he shall pay to the uttermost farthing. But this is no vengeance, no punishment, by nature, which merely readjusts the disturbed equilibrium or disharmony. It arose out of the exercise of free will. And the Masters have learned to govern their wills and to cooperate with nature as a whole; thence they grow in strength of soul, and live in unity with the divine. That is the difference between them and us: they live at one with the spiritual summit of our hierarchy. We can do the same. It is simply a matter of opening our inner eyes, of cleansing our souls, of clearing out from our brains the trash which we eat mentally, the husks which the "swine feed upon," and letting in the pure, clear life, the "wine of life."

It is only the molds of mind that impede us, nothing but the molds of mind; and when we say the molds of mind we do not exactly mean the molds of submental matter in which the mind works. That is, I think, a wrong way to put it. We mean the crystallization of the mind itself, when mental force becomes mental matter. Therefore break these molds; no one can do it for you but yourself. The molds of man's mind are his greatest enemy, his worst foe, his strongest opponent, because these molds are living substance. Your mind is matter, but it is living matter; and every thought you think clings to the mind and inheres in it, and becomes what the ancient wisdom calls an elemental, and it will finally turn and torture you unless you break your mental molds. What man would do otherwise, when there are freedom and light and wisdom and peace and glory and knowledge unspeakable for the having, for the taking, providing that we do indeed take the kingdom of heaven by violence!

TWENTY-SEVEN

THE TWO FUNDAMENTAL KOSMICAL HIERARCHIES: MATTER
AND SPIRIT-CONSCIOUSNESS. CHAOS-THEOS-KOSMOS:
GODS-MONADS-ATOMS.

There are, assuredly, two forms of Brahma: the formed and the formless.
Now, that which is the formed is unreal; that which is the formless is real, is
Brahma, is light.

That light is the same as the sun [the spiritual sun, not our visible sun
which is only a reflection, a veil, a form].

Verily, that came to have *Om* as its soul *(ātman)*. He divided himself
(ātmānam) threefold. *Om* is three prosodial units ($a+u+m$). By means
of these "the whole world is woven, warp and woof, across Him."

— *Maitri-Upanishad,* 6, 3 (Hume, trans.)

An exuberance of power is always present with the highest causes, and at the
same time that this power transcends all things, it is equally present with all
with unimpeded energy. Hence, conformably to this, the first illuminate the
last of things, and immaterial are present with material natures immaterially.
Nor should it be considered by any one as wonderful, if we say that there is
a certain pure and divine matter. For matter being generated by the father
and demiurgus of wholes, receives a perfection adapted to itself, in order to
its becoming the receptacle of the Gods. At the same time nothing prevents
more excellent beings from being able to impart their light to subordinate
natures. Neither, therefore, is matter separated from the participation of
better causes; so that such matter as is perfect, pure, and boniform, is not
unadapted to the reception of the Gods. For, since it is requisite that terrestrial natures should by no means be destitute of divine communion, the earth
also receives a certain divine portion from it, sufficient for the participation
of the Gods.

— IAMBLICHUS, *On the Mysteries,* pp. 265–6 (Thomas Taylor, trans.)

IT IS NEARLY fifty years since H. P. Blavatsky brought
theosophy to us — nearly half a century has passed, and
those of us who have had the opportunity of studying it
during that period, or at least during part of it, realize the great
changes that have taken place in the thought of the world, changes
such that we can only ascribe them to the spiritual impulses given
to the world by H. P. Blavatsky, and those behind her.

At the close of our study this evening we shall point to a number of facts, showing how this great theosophist, penetrating the secrets of the ancient wisdom, foreshadowed, prophesied, if you like, some of the greatest of the scientific discoveries, so called, that have been made during these last fifty years.

These are real revolutions in thought, and it is only just that we should place the merit where the merit is due, for there is no other cause of such revolutions — which are not merely still taking place, but which have hardly yet reached their maximum — than the work done by H. P. Blavatsky, and the spiritual impulse which she brought into the world at that time.

We open our study this evening by reading once again the latter part of what we read at our last study from *The Secret Doctrine*, volume I, pages 638–9, as follows:

The closer the approach to one's *Prototype*, "in Heaven," the better for the mortal whose personality was chosen, by his own *personal* deity (the seventh principle), as its terrestrial abode. For, with every effort of will toward purification and unity with that "Self-god," one of the lower rays breaks and the spiritual entity of man is drawn higher and ever higher to the ray that supersedes the first, until, from ray to ray, the inner man is drawn into the one and highest beam of the Parent-SUN.

Two fundamental lines of thought, we trust, have been brought out in our studies with at least sufficient ·clearness for present purposes. Those lines are respectively the exposition of the nightside, the matter-side, the vehicular side, of nature; and secondly, of the light-side, the spiritual side, the divine side, of nature, the latter also being in our system called the Hierarchy of Compassion. The former hierarchy which pervades and really *is* the space, the matter-space, or the space-matter, in which the second hierarchy works, is composed of the hierarchy of the builders, the masons of the world, the kosmokratores or world makers of mystic Greek philosophy. They are the inferior hierarchy spiritually, but have relative dominion over their subhierarchies from their beginning down to their lowest plane, which forms the mere elemental or nature forces on the lowest plane of their kosmic hierarchy. Such words as *elemental* or *lowest* are mere adjectives describing psychological mysteries. As hinted, the seven grades of them run up to the lowest of the Hierarchy of Compassion, forming the divine side. There is no break between them; actually, they inter-blend and interpenetrate each other. As the spirit works in the soul of man, and the soul of man works in his lower vehicle, so does the Hierarchy of Compassion work in and through the hierarchy of the builders.

This thought is so important for the understanding of the ancient wisdom that we call attention to it again and again, because it provides the philosophical and scientific framework, the structural carpentry, not merely of the universe, but of man's own consciousness, and is the groundwork against which we must place the picture of what takes place in the processes of kosmic evolution and in that of man, as outlined in the ancient initiations and Mystery Schools.

It was said at a former meeting that man is spiritually higher than the sun. So he is; but it was not said *which man* — purposely not said. The sun is the vital locus of his system, and so terrific are the forces of that same inwardly divine entity, even on our plane, that were one of us, a man, to approach within the range of those forces he would be simply annihilated, not merely broken up and dispersed as the physical body is at death, but reduced to nothing, wiped out. Why? Because the first five (counting upwards), i.e., the five lower principles of his psychological economy, would be dissipated into their component atoms, each to each on its own plane, and drawn, sucked, into the stellar body, and only his higher part, the divine part, the spiritual part, belonging to the Hierarchy of Compassion, the Christ part, the Buddha part, would remain intact. Why? Because the latter part itself is of the same substance as the hid sun, of which our physical sun is merely the reflection or the manifestation on this plane of the divine being behind it. Consequently, when we said that man is greater than the sun, we meant that his progress along the path of evolution has proceeded farther than that entity (considered as a reflection) which is the sun. He undoubtedly is farther along the path of evolution than is his solar locus — a paradox, indeed, but true! It was the entry into the senseless "shadows" of his being, i.e., the four lowest of his seven principles, by the manas principle, inferior to the two highest, during the middle of the third root-race in this fourth round, that made of

him the being that he now is, self-conscious; and thereby he
became literally an incarnation of the divine.

It now remains with him to bring into activity those inner
forces, his higher principles, which form his inner spiritual nature,
and which are not indeed inert, but only sleeping, as it were. We
speak of the higher principles as "sleeping" in a man, a form of
speech which is perhaps correct as a manner of expression, but
really it is the lower ones which are asleep spiritually and need
awakening. The very root *budh,* from which we have *buddhi,*
and *buddha,* and *budha* with one *d,* means "to awaken," hence
derivatively "to enlighten." Our higher principles are actual
entities living on their own planes, individual beings, fully conscious and thinking entities. Fix that thought firmly in your minds,
if you please. Our higher parts are not inchoate, uncoordinated,
undeveloped, sleeping things. They are a unity of entities, a
spiritual kosmos in miniature.

The great awakening of the lower elements in third-race man
that was accomplished by the incarnation of these mānasaputras
was repeated, partly dramatically and partly actually, in the
ancient Mysteries and in the initiations, which were thus a copying of what still takes place in nature, and took place in nature
preeminently during the third root-race. And by those initiations
the attempt was still further to stimulate, still more to awaken,
still more greatly to enliven and bring forth that inner and higher
nature of man. That great purpose formed the core, the heart,
and the meaning, of the ancient initiations.

Yet, please mark, *initiation* and *Mystery* do not mean the
same thing exactly. Though very closely similar in purpose and
running on parallel lines, of the two, *initiation* meant teaching,
awakening, opening the mind; the *Mysteries* were the drama-
tized forms of what took place in the higher degrees. There were
three dramatizations, training and educating the neophyte for
what he must be, and go through, in the four higher degrees. He
was directed and helped in those higher degrees as far as was
made permissible by his karma; but the very heart and essence of
the trial was a *test,* and he had to face it alone, and himself to
prove his spirit-power, to prove the soul-nature of him. If he came
through the first trial triumphant, he was granted the privilege,

and he had the inner strength, to undertake the higher degrees. There could, under such conditions, be no full protection, no mollycoddling. Just the contrary of that took place. His teacher watched over his senseless body while his inner nature was out exploring the realms of space, yea, entering into the sun, entering into the planets, and into the moon, and into other things and beings, *becoming, losing his self and becoming,* that which he had to face and conquer, or fail. Glorious were the privileges of victory; and at the end, at the seventh trial, if and when the final triumph came, he rose a glorified Buddha, a glorified Christ, truly a master of men. Then he *knew,* because he had *been.* This was no mere sensual experience, sensual in the sense of being an experience of the senses — hearing, seeing, touching, feeling, smelling, tasting — but it was *being* the things and beings of which he had been taught, i.e., complete knowledge of life in this hierarchy.

Such was the meaning of the higher initiation, of those higher degrees which went beyond the scope and meaning of the Mysteries, which latter were the dramatizations of the processes of kosmical life, the preparation for whatever it was that the candidate had to face in the four higher initiatory degrees.

In order to make the matter more clear, let us write down a symbolic outline of the two lines of growth or development of the two fundamental kosmical hierarchies.

On the left or matter-side:	On the right or divine side, the light-side:
Chaos	Gods
Theos	Monads
Kosmos	Atoms

corresponding each to each; and psychologically, so far as man is concerned, (1) the divine; (2) the spiritual or human; and (3) kosmic-astral.

Chaos is a Greek word, and is usually thought to mean a sort of helter-skelter treasury of original principles and seeds of beings. Well, so it verily is, in one profound sense; only it is most decidedly and emphatically not helter-skelter. It is the kosmic storehouse of all the latent or resting seeds of beings and things from former manvantaras. Of course it is this, simply because it contains everything. It means space, not the highest space, not the Parabrahman-Mūlaprakriti, the Boundless — not that; but the space of any particular hierarchy descending into manifestation, i.e., what space for it is at that particular period of its beginning of development. Remember the principle of relativity. There are no utter absolutes anywhere and never have been and never will be. The directive principles in Chaos are the Gods of the corresponding column.

Theos is a Greek word meaning "god." Corresponding to it are the Monads.

Kosmos is a Greek word meaning "arrangement." Kosmos was also used for a woman's paraphernalia, decoration, and all that kind of thing: cosmetics and robes and jewelry. It meant that which was arranged and kept along the lines and rules of harmony — the arrangement of the universe; and corresponding to it in the other column are the Atoms. Note the three correspondences: Chaos, Gods or divine beings, the kosmic architects; then Theos, for the builders, the kosmokratores, corresponding to the Monads, the spirit-beings; then Kosmos, the universe, arranged as we see it; and the Atoms, or vital-astral seeds, on the divine side.

We do not speak here of chemical atoms, please understand. These belong to the Kosmos. As used in this outline, Gods, Monads, and Atoms, we mean (1) the divine; (2) the spiritual-human; and (3) those ultimate particles of substance which inflame, which inspire, which vitalize, the material kosmos. Each to each: the Gods work in the Chaos; the Monads work in and through the Theos, the theoi, the builders; and the Atoms, as the semiconscious, ultimate entities of matter, work through the Kosmos or the manifested universe, as prepared according to what is popularly called natural law, i.e., the essential and inherent operations of nature, deriving from the Gods and Monads.

Such an atom, according to these parallel columns (which are H. P. Blavatsky's, of course), signifies the ultimate particle of matter, which ultimate particle is matter's seventh principle, its highest principle; and for that reason the sun is called an atom, because it is the seventh or highest degree of matter or prakriti *on this plane.* Prakriti means nature or the developing power, that which has brought forth manifestation. There are seven kosmical prakritis, and we are in the first or lowest; the seventh as you count downwards, the first if you count upwards. Each of these again has seven subplanes. The sun as an entity is the highest entity of the kosmical system, the solar system. But what we see is merely its vehicle, its seventh or lowest or material element or principle, counting downwards. The so-called solar flames are not flames. The sun is not burning; it is not in combustion; it is not hot; what we see is the aura of the sun, the sixth subelement or subprinciple of the first or lowest prakriti. That aura therefore is the sun's material buddhic aura, and looked at from the scientific standpoint it is a globe of kosmic forces. Please remember, as so often said before, that force and matter fundamentally are the same; they are simply different degrees of manifestation of spirit-substance. Matter is crystallized force; or, if you like, though it is not so good a method of describing it, spirit or force or energy is etherealized matter. Much better is it to put it the other way.

Matter on our plane is crystallized light. Light is substance-energy or energy-substance, either will do. Call it force. And light, this force, again is the matter of something still higher than it, the prakriti above it.

Now our time has nearly expired, and we wish to call attention to what was spoken of at the beginning of our study this evening, certain very important and fundamental principles of thought which the scientists call discoveries of our era made by them (or at least in the making by them), but which were anticipated in time by members of this School from the study of theosophical doctrines. Please understand that we look upon science, ordered and coordinated knowledge, as the greatest friend and ally we have. But when it comes to the theories or speculations or dogmas of scientific men, we accept them or reject them exactly in proportion as we think that they contain or do not contain truth — not *my* truth or *your* truth, but as they contain (or do not contain) those fundamental principles which, by their coherency and consistency and appeal to the best in us, announce themselves as facts of being.

Theosophy, indeed, has changed the world's thought. Practice without theory is emptiness of mind; theory without practice is folly. A man who has a beautiful theory, and does no act to carry it into operation or fact, is a drone, for he was not born to be a sloth; but on the contrary, a man who has no theory, whose ideas are not coordinated and directed by principles, is a madman, and acts like a fool. The noblest thing that we can do is so to change the thought of the world that men will realize their oneness with the inner beings on the various planes of life universal, and govern themselves accordingly, not merely in the legislatures, but in their teachings and in their personal conduct of life, and in their care for their brothers, and in their sense of loyalty and fidelity to their teachers, those whom they know and believe to have that truth.

We have drawn up a list of a few such anticipations, and doubtless any one of you could have extended the list to thrice or four times its length. Here they are:

1. That simple materialism, comprising fortuity, chance, and dead matter, producing life and consciousness, as an explanation of life and being, is unscientific, unphilosophical, and impossible, because contrary to nature and reason; therefore absurd.

2. That other planets are inhabited by intelligent beings, or are not so, as the case may be; and that this is denied not from knowledge, but from ignorance only, of such planets; the only planet that we *do* know, our earth, bearing intelligent beings. The denial therefore is irrational, purely speculative and theoretical, and based solely on supposedly true facts concerning atmosphere, cold or heat, etc., as these are known on our planet *only*.

3. The unreal nature of the physical universe, or sphere, i.e., that all we see and know with sensational perceptions is its purely phenomenal appearances.

4. That force is etherealized matter; or, preferably, that matter is equilibrated or crystallized forces.

(These last two have now been fully admitted by exoteric scientists.)

5. That electricity and magnetism are particular, i.e., corpuscular: formed of particles or corpuscles, and therefore matter. They are the phenomenal effects of noumenal causes — matter or rather matters.

6. That the so-called modes of motion, when H. P. Blavatsky first brought her message to the world, i.e., forces, of whilom scientists, as a definition of forces, is a childish effort to explain forces by ticketing them in a new manner which explains nothing at all, all forces being simply moving matters.

7. That all matter is radiant, i.e., radioactive, that is, it *radiates;* some forms or states of matter more than others. Compare the work and discoveries of Becquerel, Röntgen, the Curies, Rutherford, and Soddy, etc., and the work on similar lines of great thinkers in other countries.

8. That light is corpuscular, because a matter, or substance; that is, light is a material radiance, in fact.

9. That transmutation of matters, hence of metals, is a fact in nature, occurring hourly, momently, instantly, and continuously through time.

10. That the atom is a divisible body — i.e., the *chemical* or *physical* atom; it is, so to say, merely a smaller molecule.

(Numbers 6, 7, 8, 9, and 10 have all been admitted by science, or practically admitted; in some cases in full, in other cases verging on full admission.)

11. That the physical atom is a tiny solar system, each member of such a system being in its own turn compounded of physical infinitesimals, or of subatoms, or of infra-atoms.

12. That the nebular hypothesis as commonly accepted was incomplete, insufficient, as a workable hypothesis, although containing certain elements of natural, that is, of occult, truth.

13. That the sun is neither burning, nor even hot, though it is *glowing* in one sense, superficially, i.e., on its "surface"; nor does it recuperate its heat and other forces, as alleged, by shrinkage of volume; nor does radium account for its expenditure of energy, is practically admitted.

14. That storms — rain, hail, snow, wind — and droughts, likewise most of the earth's heat, are not caused by or derived from solar energy, but result from electromagnetic interplay of forces between the earth's mass and the meteoric mass, or "veil," above our atmosphere; such phenomena or effects being accompanied, partly causally, partly effectually, by periodic expansion or dilatation of the atmospheric body and by periodic contraction thereof;

and that the glacial periods, so called, are largely due to the same causes.

(A few months ago, let me interpolate, some eminent scientists in the northern part of California were investigating the upper regions of the atmosphere, and to a certain extent they have come to this conclusion, at least in part and in degree.)

15. That Darwinism and Haeckelism are inadequate to explain and account for the mass of biological phenomena; and neither Darwin's natural selection nor Spencer's survival of the fittest, is other than a minor or secondary operation of nature; that transformism as taught by the modern speculative scientist is not evolution — which is what the ancient wisdom *does* teach — and is both uncertain as a theory because purely speculative, and unscientific because as a theory it is based on data too few; therefore it is incomplete and insufficient.

(We all know what remarkable changes have taken place in the theories of the transformists even since H. P. Blavatsky died.)

16. And lastly, that all things and operations in the kosmos are relative, not absolute, in nature, there being no absolutes except in the sense of relativity of relationships; our teachings thus anticipating the *fundamental* concept of Dr. Albert Einstein on this point.

At our next meeting, we shall take up the study of the atom.

TWENTY-EIGHT

THE ADVENTURE OF AN ATOM. LAYA-CENTERS: SUN, COMETS, AND
PLANETS; SOUL AND MONAD. THE KEYNOTE OF OCCULTISM.

The Occult Science is *not* one, in which secrets can be communicated of a
sudden, by a written or even verbal communication. If so, all the "Brothers"
should have to do, would be to publish a *Hand-book* of the art which might
be taught in schools as grammar is. It is the common mistake of people that
we willingly wrap ourselves and our powers in mystery — that we wish to
keep our knowledge to ourselves, and of our own will refuse — "wantonly and
deliberately" to communicate it. The truth is that till the neophyte attains
to the condition necessary for that degree of Illumination to which, and for
which, he is entitled and fitted, most *if not all* of the Secrets are *incommunicable.* The receptivity must be equal to the desire to instruct. The illumination *must come from within.* Till then no hocus pocus of incantations, or
mummery of appliances, no metaphysical lectures or discussions, no self-
imposed penance can give it. All these are but means to an end, and all we
can do is to direct the use of such means as have been empirically found by
the experience of ages to conduce to the required object. And this was and
has been *no secret* for thousands of years.
— *The Mahatma Letters,* pp. 282–3

L ET US OPEN our study this evening by reading an extract
from volume I of *The Secret Doctrine,* page 567:

As to the "elemental atoms," so called, the Occultists refer to
them by that name with a meaning analogous to that which is given by the
Hindu to Brahmâ when he calls him ANU, the "Atom." Every elemental *atom,*
in search of which more than one Chemist has followed the path indicated by
the Alchemists, is, in their firm belief (when not *knowledge*), a SOUL; not
necessarily a disembodied soul, but a *jiva,* as the Hindus call it, a centre of
POTENTIAL VITALITY, with latent intelligence in it, and, in the case of compound Souls — an intelligent active EXISTENCE, from the highest to the lowest
order, a form composed of more or less differentiations.

Majestic, sublime, are the thoughts involved in the study
which we begin this evening. It ought to be said, perhaps, by
way of preface, that the frequent interruptions of our meetings

necessitated by circumstances have prevented us before from entering upon this new departure in our studies; and we shall not, except by inference, embark upon our present line of thought more fully than we shall do this evening until our studies can be continued more definitely. And why? Because from immemorial time our School has set apart a certain portion of the year, at certain specified times, of never less than three months, in which the studies were pursued daily for hours at a time, with intervals of rest; and these were called periods of initiation. The reason for this method was that frequent interruptions, the inroad or ingress into the thought of daily occupations, so distracted the mind, so tore it away from the higher nature, that it could not successfully meet and understand the things which it was then supposed to undertake and to try to comprehend.

But doing the best we can, we shall begin this evening, very shortly, to undertake a study of the atom, and of what H. P. Blavatsky calls its adventures, by referring to collateral and almost identical subjects: the laya-centers, the sun and planets and comets, and the soul and the monad by contrast with the above.

As we read in *The Secret Doctrine*, an atom is a soul. A soul is an entity which is evolved by experiences; it is not a spirit, it is a vehicle of the spirit. It manifests in matter through and by being a substantial portion of the lower essence of the spirit. Touching another plane below it, or it may be above it, the point of union allowing ingress and egress to the consciousness is a laya-center. A laya-center is, therefore, a center in "homogeneous" substance. It will be remembered that in a former study we derived this word *laya* from the Sanskrit word *lī*, meaning "to dissolve." The word *pralaya* comes from the same root: *laya* is the noun-form from the root *lī*, with a prepositional prefix *pra*, meaning "towards," "forwards," hence "continuous." In other words, *pralaya* means "continuous dissolution." A laya-center is that part of an entity, of an atom which, being relatively homogeneous substance, matter "dissolved" into homogeneity, allows ingress and egress for passing consciousness and consciousnesses.

Let us take the laya-center as manifested in the sun. The sun at its core is a laya-center. Each planet likewise has at its central point, and is in its central point, a laya-center; each comet is in building around a laya-center, its heart or core. Dimensions or positions in space have nothing to do with it, because a laya-center is not of a physical and material nature. It is the disappearing-point for all things below it, and the entering-point for all things above it, for any one particular entity, be it an atom, a sun, a planet, a human being.

The sun, as we see it, is a reflection, as we have often before said. Suppose that we call it a *veil*, which is perhaps a better word, though reflection is just as good, because it actually *is* a reflection — the sun we see, that is. What do we see when we look at the sun? We see a titanic splendor. That is a reflection. The sun itself, its core, could be held in the palm of your hand, and I mean the part of the sun which is behind that splendorous reflection. That part which could be held in the palm of your hand is itself of the seventh or highest stage of the lowest prakriti-stage, a particle of matter-substance of the lowest cosmic grade, the prakriti. The splendor that we see is the aura of that laya-center, its aura or emanations, and these emanations are forces. The sun is a body of unimaginable forces springing from, pouring down through, this laya-center from the true sun which is behind the outer veil. And the golden disk that we see is but the auric manifestation to our physical eyes on this plane of the true sun, pouring through the sun at the center of the visible orb.

So it is in a human being. There is a center in his nature through which pour the forces from above, and through which he himself ascends higher; and that center is the laya-center of his inner nature.

In speaking of the monad, we must not confuse it with the laya-center. A laya-center is the channel, the point, the disappearing-point, the neutral center, in matter or substance, through which consciousness passes — and the center of that consciousness is the monad. For the present moment we need not pause to consider on what plane the monad is acting; on any plane on which it may be acting when it passes from one plane of consciousness to another it does so through a laya-center. It will be remembered that in our last study or two we pointed out the parallelisms running in nature, such as matter and spirit-consciousness. Please remember that these words are used generalizingly, not defining any particular matter or any particular spirit, but only to show the mass of kosmic substance acted upon by the great forces above it, which are the beings of life, the hierarchies of universal nature; and in this kosmic body, in this kosmic substance, there are innumerable laya-centers, because they are really the "critical points," the translation-stages, by which as individuals we gain access to our higher self, and by which the divine and spiritual forces entering into us from above pass.

The sun is the vital focus of its system, outside of other activities far greater still, but the physical sun is that something which we can see with our physical eyes; and further it is a thing of matter, although it is in the sixth degree of our stage of prakriti, counting upwards, the buddhic stage of the lowest prakriti. But the *true* sun, the spiritual sun, is that divine being behind the sun, an entity, a god. The physical sun is its body or garment, just as in ourselves our higher nature is a god, a divine spark, and that divine spark is a *monad.* The soul in contradistinction with the monad is its vehicle for manifestation on any one plane. It really means vehicle. The spirit manifests in seven vehicles, and each one of these vehicles is a soul; and that particular point through which the divine influence passes into the soul is the laya-center, and it is, so to say, the heart of the soul, or rather the summit thereof — homogeneous soul-substance, if you like.

It is very necessary to have these preliminary conceptions clear and definitely outlined in our minds. The mysteries behind these words are sublime, unimaginably beautiful; but we cannot understand them properly without knowing the words, and the implications of thought involved in them when we use them.

All the sectarian departures from the great foundation-religions of antiquity have grown out of the lack of following that one rule. Understand your terms and use them rightly. Disputes have arisen about the meaning of terms, due perhaps to the fact that in the origin of any particular religion those terms were not defined in such clever and appropriate manner that later dogmatists could not fasten upon them in order to misuse them.

It is actually a most difficult problem. We are always between "the devil and the deep sea." On the one hand, we have the people who will insist upon literalisms, such as "Pythagoras, the

Master, said so." A beautiful sense of loyalty to the teacher in some cases, perhaps; but see how it can be misused by the would-be dogmatists, who insist on taking the letter and losing the spirit! And, on the other hand, there are those who think that the letter has no importance, which is likewise wrong; this class think that they have the spirit and they try to force the letter to conform to their conceptions of what the Master or Masters taught, Pythagoras or any other.

So it is necessary that we have these and other similar words clearly outlined in our minds. When we undertake the study of the atom we embark upon new and vast fields of consciousness, and pass in our minds over to other planes; and our only salvation is, as H. P. Blavatsky has told us, to cling like grim death to the fundamental principles of her teachings which are the Masters' teachings. We cannot so cling unless we know exactly to what we should cling. If we were to say that an atom is a god, we would say wrongly. If we were to say that the atom contains a god, we should speak only partly rightly. If we were to say that the atom manifests a god, we approach a step nearer to the truth.

Now comes another thought. What do we mean by *atom?* Do we mean a kosmical atom, an astral atom, a psychical atom, a buddhic atom, an ātmic atom? Our studies of theosophy show us that all these atoms are variously "souls," existent on divers planes, in various degrees of consciousness; and we realize then that the atom *in its essence,* in its inmost of its inmost, is a monad, a divine spark, a being from former manvantaras, which monad has learned its lessons so fully that it needs to learn nothing more in this manvantara. But it is trailed by a train of skandhas, resident in the life-atoms, and which are karmic impressions. These life-atoms are inferior beings, trailing after it, making up its bodies, so to say, as certain elements make up our bodies, beings for which it is responsible because it affected them in former kalpas, former manvantaras, former life cycles: responsible for them because it has soiled them in some instances, and in other instances it has cleansed them from the soil.

What are these inferior things that follow in the track of a monad? They are parts of its being, thoughts of its thought, children of its soul, offspring of its heart. Sublime thought, in which we have the secret of manifestation in the universe, and also the secret of the Hierarchy of Compassion; the secret why one half of nature is what we call matter, crystallized and so-called inert; and why the other half of nature is will and consciousness, intelligence and love, understanding and life. And these two opposites work eternally together during the manvantaras. At every moment in space and time, units of this train of inferior things themselves reach comprehension and understanding, and pass through their particular laya-center into spheres above — themselves having meanwhile developed or evolved other inferior beings trailing after them.

The processes of kosmic life and evolution are outlined in what has just been said. So that when we use H. P. Blavatsky's expression and speak of the "adventures of an atom," we obtain some glimpse of the study now before us. Do you realize that in the studies which we have followed as faithfully as we have been able to do so, there has been laid down the outline, at least the skeleton-framework, of a system of philosophy entire and complete, so majestic in its reaches, so wide in its subject, having such grandeur in its possibilities, such profundity in its inmost nature, that nothing like it is known in the exoteric literature of the world today? Even the magnificent systems of exoteric philosophy of the Orient and the best efforts of European philosophy — which, by the way, are mostly mere verbiage — cannot compare with it. Their light is as a mere rushlight before the blaze of the noonday sun, when we compare them with the esoteric system.

And why is this so? Because we have outlined the teachings of the gods, the teachings formerly taught in the ancient Mystery Schools. Nor have they been more than hinted at. We have not said the one-thousandth part of what remains to be said.

Seven are the keys which open wide the portals of the ancient wisdom. These seven keys we have touched but lightly, of necessity lightly, in our allusions to the seven treasuries of wisdom. In one or another of these seven treasuries, or in one or another of these seven jewels, lies every department of human thought, every thought that human mind can give birth to. These seven treasuries were given and explained to the ancient races by members of the Hierarchy of Compassion, and by their pupils, and they have been passed down to us. But remember that these seven treasuries, as we have already said very plainly, under the names they go by are mere key words, catchwords, reminding-terms.

These sublime ideas make a man feel at home in any part of the universe. This is the very keynote of occultism, the being one with the universal life, at home everywhere. Occultism is the exposition of the essence of life, of the essence of being, and of the essence of living. Let us never confuse it with the so-called occult arts, arts which are strictly forbidden to us as students of this School. The Brothers of the Shadow lead on their helpless victims with the occult arts, enticing them thereby, and their end is nonentity. But the Masters have told us plainly: first learn discipline, first learn the Law. Then the powers which you may crave, you will crave only as spiritual powers, and only to give yourself and them to others. On the path, the so-called occult arts drop away even from the imagination, because their deluding enticements and their allurements are clearly seen. I do not imagine for a moment that any one of us here needs to be reminded of this.

Katherine Tingley has been insistent upon the necessity of first learning the Law — and the learning of the Law means the development of the spiritual nature; and it is the royal road, the royal union. Having it, you have everything in the universe; boundless knowledge, for instance, and the powers commensurate with it then will come naturally. But any attempt to cultivate them prematurely, any mere longing for them, will pull you down as surely as the sun will rise over the eastern horizon tomorrow morning, because it is the personal coloring of the mind, it is the personal wish, it is desire and appetite for power and novelty that want these things. The divine-human entity, the buddha, the member of the Hierarchy of Compassion by divine right, knows these things and wants them not, for he has passed far beyond them. The constant urge with him is to go above matter, to cleanse the heart from soil, to cast off the garments of the mortal man and to put on the robes of immortality which, in fact, inwardly are yours already, awaiting simply for each individual to recognize them, and to become, as the ancient Egyptian expressed it, a "Son of the Sun," a holy initiate.

TWENTY-NINE

SPACE: THE BOUNDLESS ALL. INFILLED WITH INTERLOCKING, INTER-
PENETRATING UNIVERSES. ONE ACTION, ONE HIERARCHICAL
INTELLIGENCE, ONE COURSE OF OPERATION THROUGHOUT
NATURE: ONE ORGANISM, ONE UNIVERSAL LIFE.

Either an ordered universe, or else a welter of confusion. Assuredly then
a world-order. Or think you that order subsisting within yourself is com-
patible with disorder in the All? And that too when all things, however
distributed and diffused, are affected sympathetically.
— *Marcus Aurelius Antoninus to Himself*, 4, 27 (Rendall, trans.)

Constantly regard the universe as one living being, having one substance
and one soul; and observe how all things have reference to one perception,
the perception of this one living being; and how all things act with one
movement; and how all things are the co-operating causes of all things
which exist; observe too the continuous spinning of the thread and the
contexture of the web.   — Ibid., 4, 40 (Long, trans.)

IN CONTINUING our study this evening, let me once more
introduce our subject by calling attention to the fact that
the teachings of occultism are based on a foundation of
ethics and morals; and, as has so often been said, there is the
distinction which marks the division line, as it were, between the
hierarchies on the one side, the ascending or luminous arc, and
those hierarchies on the other side, the shadowy arc, or those
beings and intelligences which are descending into matter for the
experience needed in order to enable them to take their march
on the upward rise.

Ethics is not a subject which is disputable, as between men;
only the forms of ethics are; but the fundamental principles of
right as contrasted with wrong, of duty as contrasted with selfishness, of the joy of renunciation and self-abnegation as contrasted

with the shriveling influence of the opposite theories of being — and there are many in the world — in these lies the distinction between the sons of light and the children of the shadow.

It will be remembered that our subject in closing our last study was the teachings imbodied in the word *atom*. Mark first, please, that this does not mean the atom of science. The atom of science is a more or less clear conception of fundamental material particles which has arisen in the minds of scientists in an attempt to explain the phenomena of physical nature as those phenomena have been studied during the last hundred years or so; and the scientific doctrines concerning the atom are based, furthermore, largely on misunderstood teachings of certain Greek philosophers.

But if we understand the atom as the doctrine concerning it is imbodied in the teachings of the ancient wisdom, we shall find that it is an intelligence and a living being of its kind. Let us then open our studies this evening by reading from *The Secret Doctrine,* volume I, pages 107 and 106; from page 107 first:

. . . every atom in the Universe has the potentiality of self-consciousness in it, and is, like the Monads of Leibnitz, a Universe in itself, and *for* itself. *It is an atom and an angel.*

Not a Christian angel; not a being with wings, etc., but a spiritual intelligence. Then from page 106:

The Doctrine teaches that, in order to become a divine, fully conscious god, — aye, even the highest — the Spiritual primeval INTELLIGENCES must pass through the human stage. And when we say human, this does not apply merely to our terrestrial humanity, but to the mortals that inhabit any world, *i.e.,* to those Intelligences that have reached the appropriate equilibrium between matter and spirit, as *we* have now, since the middle point of the Fourth Root Race of the Fourth Round was passed. Each Entity must have won for itself the right of becoming divine, through self-experience.

These words "self-experience" comprise the thought which Katherine Tingley so frequently emphasizes in her instructions to us — *self-directed evolution,* a doctrine imbodying the necessity of using our spiritual will and our spiritual intelligence for noble and altruistic and impersonal aims. Let us say here again that for man there is always a choice of paths: the right-hand, the luminous arc, upward and upward forever; and the left-hand, the shadowy arc, leading down into those spheres concerning which we have knowledge, of course, and of which we have already several times spoken.

Further, be it noted that this term or word atom is really a catchword. We say atom, but we actually mean a multitude of thoughts connected with cosmogony and evolution. For instance, *gods, monads, souls, atoms,* are words jointly and separately involved in profound doctrines explaining cosmogonical and evolutionary processes. And connected therewith very closely is what is called in occultism the laya-center, to which we have briefly alluded in former studies. In part three of this first volume of *The Secret Doctrine,* H. P. Blavatsky, in section 15, devotes one of the most beautiful parts of her great work to developing the doctrines comprised in what she called "Gods, Monads, and Atoms."

Please understand first, that in these studies, questions of spirituality, ethics, religion, are deeply involved. They go to the very foundation of our being. They are not mere questions of brain-mind disputation, or mere mental exercises in clever speaking. These teachings lead directly to the setting of our feet on the path of the luminous arc; and we who have had the benefit already of these teachings should have some realization, at least, that if there is one primal aim and object towards which we look, it is to become more fully, more heartfeltly, one with that glorious army of which the Masters are the outer vanguard, as it were.

Now what do we mean by space? People generally think of space as a "receptacle of things" — a definition which we reject. They talk about infinite space, and yet at the same time call space a receptacle, a container — a curious commentary upon the loose thinking of our age. Obviously, if it is a *receptacle* it is a *finite thing;* and besides that, the conception entirely misses the heart-meaning of the word space. Understand what *we* mean by space, and we have a key by which to open much of the nobler teachings hid deeply in the elementary studies. Space, as understood in true occultism, means that all that is, is a fullness, perfect and continuous absolutely, endless and beginningless; not a mere receptacle, not a mere container, nothing finite, but the boundless All. Further, space IS; it *is* not merely on or in one plane, but on and in seven planes, the seven kosmic planes of our universe, besides penetrating inwards infinitely, endlessly, and also outwardly endlessly. It is the infinite pleroma of the Greeks, the Greek word *pleroma* meaning "fullness."

Obviously, everything that is, *is a part* of space. Space not being a mere container, an abstraction of the mind, or a mere receptacle, shows why H. P. Blavatsky in her teachings speaks of the only "God" we recognize as That — using the word of the old Vedas — i.e., space, the boundless All. This All obviously contains all things, everything that is, as shown before in our study of that wonderful doctrine of hierarchies, which is the third of the seven jewels or treasuries of wisdom. Space is infilled with an infinite multitude of self-contained universes, interlocking and interpenetrating each other. These universes, again, are themselves infilled with endlessly multitudinous beings of all and various kinds, the high and the low, the inner and the outer. We cannot say the *highest* and the *lowest,* because that form of expression would imply limits or bounds, frontiers, and space is limitless. Only within the confines or boundaries of any one universe or hierarchy may we use the superlative form of these adjectives, and say the *highest* or the *lowest.*

Take any one universe or hierarchy as an instance of the general rule. Any universe is infilled with beings finding their origin and taking their rise in the summit, the acme, the seed in another sense, which is, so to say, the god of that hierarchy; and this god, at the beginning of any period of manifestation, this spiritual, elementary being, casts off from itself, or throws forth from itself, evolves from itself, brings out from itself, a multitudinous series of hierarchies consisting of less or inferior beings, beings less in spirituality and dignity than itself. They are, as it were, the thoughts that the god or kosmic primal thinker thinks. Take the instance of a thinking human being as an analogy. He thinks thoughts. Each thought has its own life, each thought has its own essence, each has its own course to run. Each thought is based on a particular vibration, as it were, using words common to our understanding today. Each has its own particular swabhāva or intrinsic essential nature, which is its individuality.

So this summit of the hierarchy "thinks thoughts." Now I do

not mean to say that this summit is a human being or a god-being, which thinks thoughts as we do. The figure here used is an analogy only. As a man thinks thoughts, and thus fills his atmosphere around him with these living beings, these winged messengers called thoughts, so the primordial elementary being, the summit, the seed, the first to issue forth from the bosom of the infinite Mother, casts forth from itself these parts of itself, these monadic aggregations, these kosmic "thoughts."

And what are these first emanations? They are what the ancient wisdom called the *gods*. And these gods in their turn send forth from themselves other multitudinous series of beings less than they — less in dignity, less in grandeur, less in understanding. And these secondary emanations or evolutions are the *monads*. And these monads, as they pursue their way down the shadowy arc, in the beginning of a manvantara, in their turn cast forth from themselves, in identically the same way and on the same line of action, other entities less than they, forming still more outward hierarchies, more material intelligences; and these tertiary emanations are the *souls*. And the souls, as they pursue their way down, exactly as their higher progenitors did, cast forth from themselves, think forth from themselves, send forth from themselves, evolve forth from themselves, beings still less in wisdom and spirituality and dignity and power than they. And these are the *atoms* — but not the physical atom. Let us cast that idea out of our minds instantly. The atoms of physical science are really molecular aggregations of atomic elements only, existing on the borderland of the astral plane.

The time will come when we shall set forth more clearly than we have time to do tonight, the relation of the atom to the phenomenal physical world. What we need to do this evening in the introductory study now in hand, is to show one action, one hierarchical intelligence, one course of operation, throughout nature. Please remember that these *operations of nature* are what the scientists and Christian theologians, in their ignorance, call the laws of nature. Now there are no laws of nature, as we have set forth and explained before. There are no mechanically acting laws, so called, because there are no law*givers:* consequently there are no such natural laws. But there are *operations of nature,* and these operations of nature are what our thinkers see, and from lack of understanding the ancient wisdom, and perhaps from lack of properly descriptive words, they follow the analogy of human operations and say the "laws of nature."

But they are the spiritually automatic operations of beings in that vast aggregate of entities and intelligences, which is called the universe, which is but one of infinite multitudes of others in space. All that is, is one vast organism. There is no void and no emptiness anywhere — all is infilled and is one boundless fullness. If we can fix that thought in our minds, and think of ourselves as linked in a chain of beings, an endless chain — what Homer called the Golden Chain — we shall realize the force, the philosophical profundity, and the deep meaning of what our teachings set forth when they speak of universal brotherhood, the fundamental unity of all that is. Every one of us has in himself the potentiality of becoming a god, and of advancing from godhood still higher into what are now to us inexpressible spheres of divinity. But it depends upon ourselves. At each instant the choice lies before us: the path to the "right hand," and the path to the "left hand," adopting the old Buddhist nomenclature.

These two arcs, the shadowy arc or the arc of matter, and the luminous arc or the arc of light, or of spirit, exemplify in those two phrases the duality of nature in manifestation; and the beings on the luminous arc are what our Teachers call the dhyāni-buddhas, the buddhas of contemplation, those who once in long past kalpas were men as we are now, human beings. The other arc contains the hierarchies which are descending into matter in order to learn the lessons that we of this kalpa have learned in the past; as the dhyāni-buddhas, the sons of light, did, long, long aeons agone, but who now are the summit of the buddhic hierarchy of which we form a part, if our hearts are sincere and our souls are strong.

The beauty and the splendor of these teachings fill the soul with awe. It needs but the proper comprehension of them, so firmly to fix the mind and the soul to the eternal truth that nothing will ever shake them in future. Ay, if we can but see, there lies unfolded the great mystery of evolution. Those who have advanced along the path have left their records behind them, and there they stand, those glorious entities, armies of them: the lowest are those just beyond us, the chelas, and then higher still are the masters, and the masters of the masters; and then the chohans; and the mahā-chohans; and then the dhyāni-chohans; and then the dhyāni-buddhas; and thus endlessly, on and up, for infinity is limitless and endless. And this process of hierarchical development has been going on from eternity in the past, and will continue into eternity in the future.

The reason why men find it difficult to accept this sublime teaching is the fact that their minds are so full of other thoughts that it is difficult for them to drive in and find place for and fix in their memory these sublime truths. Men will not willingly give up their prejudices; they break not willingly their mind-molds. How many of us come to a meeting like this with minds made up on what we "know to be the truth," because, forsooth, we have so read it somewhere, and our minds are crystallized in that setting. I know how difficult it is for each one of us to keep the mind always free and plastic, always ready to accept the truth, no matter what our own prejudices, religious, philosophic, or scientific, may be. The critic is not the wise man. The critic unconsciously to himself sees his own littleness; the wise man, the man who knows, will say rather, "I will think, I will examine this that the teacher has given me. This is an opportunity; I will not reject it because it seems difficult for me to believe, or because I have read that H. P. Blavatsky in such a passage said so and so." Pray do not take any one passage of H. P. Blavatsky's or Katherine Tingley's or William Q. Judge's, and build an iron wall of prejudice about it, because you think you have understood it. Keep the mind fluid and open and plastic; hold fast to that which your soul, your conscience, tells you is *good;* and, if necessary, *wait!* Thebes was not builded in a day.

Before concluding, there is a question which must have arisen in every thoughtful theosophical mind, and it has been thusly phrased by a student:

If every one is under the guidance of the dhyāni-chohans, how does it happen that, as H. P. Blavatsky says in *The Secret Doctrine,* volume I, page 412, end of the second paragraph, "cruelty, blunders, and but too-evident injustice" are to be found in nature? And she then quotes the saying that nature is a "comely mother but stone cold."

The principles upon which this thoughtful question has been based are very simple indeed. In the first place, the dhyāni-chohans do *not* "guide nature"; not any more than man's inner dhyāni-chohan guides the circulation of his blood, or the processes of his own digestion. Those things belong to the lower spheres of nature. There is a dhyāni-chohan at the head of every department of nature; but direct interference, the old theological idea of an Almighty God interfering with the mess he has himself created, is not accepted in our teachings. The dhyāni-chohans do not "guide" the material processes of nature. They are the summit of the hierarchy and form the "laws" according to which nature works; but every entity, every monad, every atom, every soul, has the power of free will and choice, in more or less limited degree, depending upon its intelligence, and must exercise it or go down. And there is the key, the answer to the question. Man does not control by his thought the beating of his heart or the processes of his digestion, or the time it takes him to grow from babyhood to youth, from youth to manhood, and from manhood to sink into decrepitude. Those things are ruled by what are properly called the nature-forces; and the laws upon which the nature-forces work are those superior operations which represent the automatic spiritual activities of the dhyāni-chohans; but to say that they guide nature is untrue; the idea is a relic of the old theological Christian dogmas which remains in our minds; and we must wash our intellects clean of such thoughts if we wish to understand the heart, the essence, of the ancient teachings, which show one organism, one universal life, in diversified action everywhere. And in this one organism, in this one beating heart, in this one universal life, there are these multitudinous and countless and endless and infinite series of intelligences, each working out its own destiny from inward impulses, controlled by various higher entities in which they move, and live, and have their being.

THIRTY

THE INTERRELATION OF GODS, MONADS, ATOMS — A KEY TO THE
DOCTRINE OF EVOLUTION. SUCCESSIVE EMANATIONS: SHEATHS.
HIGHER BEINGS EMANATING AND CLOTHING THEMSELVES IN
HOSTS OF LOWER BEINGS. MORALITY BASED ON THE
STRUCTURE OF THE UNIVERSE.

But the other medium, which is suspended from the Gods, though it is far
inferior to them, is that of daemons, which is not of a primarily operative
nature, but is subservient to, and follows the beneficent will of the Gods. It
likewise unfolds into energy the invisible good of the Gods, being itself
assimilated to it, and gives completion to its fabrications conformably to it.
For it renders that which is ineffable in the good of the Gods effable, illuminates that which is formless in forms, and produces into visible reasons (or
productive forms) that which in divine good is above all reason. Receiving
also a connascent participation of things beautiful, it imparts and transfers
it, in unenvying abundance, to the genera posterior to itself. These middle
genera, therefore, give completion to the common bond of the Gods and
souls, and cause the connexion of them to be indissoluble. They also bind
together the one continuity of things from on high as far as to the end; make
the communion of wholes to be inseparable; cause all things to have the
best, and a commensurate mixture; in a certain respect, equally transmit the
progression from more excellent to inferior natures, and the elevation from
things posterior to such as are prior; insert in more imperfect beings order
and measures of the communication which descends from more excellent
natures, and of that by which it is received; and make all things to be familiar
and coadapted to all, supernally receiving the causes of all these from the
Gods.   — IAMBLICHUS, *On the Mysteries,* pp. 32–3

TO "KEEP ALIVE in man his spiritual intuitions," describes
very well the work of the Theosophical Society in the
world. But beyond that fine thought we must go if we
are to understand and fully to put the teachings, which have been
given us in trust, into our lives, and thereby to develop the moral,
the ethical, sense which these teachings are first and foremost

meant to develop and to make living in us, if we are to carry out the purpose and aim set before us.

Mere disquisitions on philosophic, religious, and scientific subjects impart nothing of permanent worth, are fruitless, bear no fruit, unless the spirit of the Lodge is behind them; and that Lodge-spirit cannot exist without the spiritual intuitions which exist in the core, in the central part, of every human being. You will notice that the entire tendency of our studies has been to develop the higher nature of us. These teachings of the esoteric philosophy have stood and will stand the test of time and of the human heart. Here is a fact, surely, for which we may give heartfelt thanks.

This evening we are approaching the end of the elementary studies which we have been briefly considering for the last two or three years; and soon it will be our duty to take up more concrete aspects of the ancient wisdom, or wisdom-religion; and, in fact, we have already approached these more detailed doctrines in our present subject — *gods, monads, souls, atoms,* and *bodies.* The necessity for a clear understanding of those former studies, which to some may appear somewhat abstract, is this: their reach into the realms of human thought as represented by religion, philosophy, and science, is immense; they form, as it were, the foundation stones upon which the ancient wisdom rests.

It will be remembered at our last study in *The Secret Doctrine,* volume I, page 107, we read the following: "every atom in the Universe has the potentiality of self-consciousness in it, and is, like the Monads of Leibnitz, a Universe in itself, and *for* itself. *It is an atom and an angel*" — that is, a spiritual being. We are going to speak more plainly on this present subject than we have ever spoken before, and the reason for it is that the proper understanding of the doctrine of evolution — of development and growth — rests upon a correct vision of the real meaning and interrelation of these three: gods, monads, and atoms.

First, it will be remembered that in speaking of space, we rejected the idea that space was merely a container. Now this is not a mere abstraction of thought; it is an absolutely important thing to understand that all being is one immense organism, through which beats one universal heart, so to say. You see there immediately the basis of morals; there is no absolute emptiness, no absolute vacuum, anywhere; all beings are closely related and interchained in the strongest bonds of union: spiritual, divine, intellectual, mental, astral, physical. Nothing can exist without all other things; for the kosmos, deprived of a single atom, would crumble into impalpable dust. No metaphor this; it is an actuality.

Now a monad is often spoken of as descending into matter. This is a fashion of speaking, a method of speech. The monad itself does not "descend," no more than does a god drive our streetcars or blacken our boots. How, then, does the monadic influence extend itself throughout the different planes of nature, so that in ordinary parlance it is in fact correct to speak of the mineral monad, of the animal monad, of the astral monad, of the human monad, of the spiritual monad, of the divine monad? In the following way: but first — as an interpolation — concerning the monad, let me read something that H. P. Blavatsky says (*The Secret Doctrine*, II, 185–6):

The terms "mineral," "vegetable" and "animal" *monad* are meant to create a superficial distinction: there is no such thing as a Monad (jiva) other than divine, and consequently having been, or having to become, human. And the latter term has to remain meaningless unless the difference is well understood. The Monad is a drop out of the shoreless Ocean beyond, or, to be correct, *within* the plane of primeval differentiation. It is divine in its higher and *human* in its lower condition — the adjectives "higher" and "lower" being used for lack of better words — and a monad it remains at all times, save in the Nirvanic state, under whatever conditions, or whatever external forms.

There you have the matter unequivocally stated.

It was pointed out at our last meeting that when the thrill of life in the boundless All first occurs in cyclical duration, the primordial beings issue forth as what are called the gods, and that these gods, as the ages passed, during the progressive manvantaric periods, sent forth from themselves, or cast forth from themselves, or cast out from themselves, or gave birth to, less beings — less meaning inferior, of less divinity, or less sublimity, less grandeur — and these beings are the monads. In exactly the same way the monads sent forth from themselves (or gave birth from themselves to) the souls; and, please understand, just as the monad was in the god, so was the soul in the monad. These entities remained latent in the monads as karmic fruitage from the previous mahā-manvantara. Just as the life remains in the seed when cast forth from the plant, and sends forth its green blade in the springtime; so, when the manvantaric thrill passes over these spaces, after the long pralayic rest, the gods send forth the monads, and the monads send forth the souls, and the souls send forth the atoms. And the atoms similarly send forth from themselves our vehicles, our bearers, our bodies.

Let us see if we can illustrate this by a diagram. Let us take an immense circle to represent the boundless All, which of course is merely a representation for space; then place a point in its center. This point represents the first germ of the kosmic life. This point also has its meaning in the sense of a kosmic seed. Now it is not one point only in the kosmos that springs into activity, but innumerable such points, such seeds. The number is limitless, practically; and each one of such points represents an individuality from the previous mahā-manvantara. But these points as represented in the diagram are symbols; and the one stands diagrammatically for all.  If you please, this point in the quasi-infinitude of a hierarchy, of a universe, is the beginning of that hierarchy, and it represents the god of that hierarchy. This god itself is a synthetic aggregation of multitudinous other gods, as man's body is an aggregation, a synthesis, of multitudinous less or inferior lives.

Now this god clothes itself in its emanations, in its prānic aura, if you like; it sends forth from itself prānic or vital effluvia, and thus it clothes itself in garments, in sheaths of vitality, flowing forth from itself, and these sheaths or garments are its "clothing." Any such god naturally casts its own individuality into its sheath, into its clothing: seven degrees or states of it; its individuality is its swabhāva, an important idea to which we have drawn your attention and on which we have laid emphasis. The swabhāva of an entity is its individuality, the characteristic of it, the essentiality of what it is, as contrasted with some other swabhāva. In ordinary language we may call it individuality. That which makes a rose bring forth always a rose, and not a lily; that which makes a man bring forth always a man and not some other sort of entity; that which makes a god a god and not a monad is its swabhāva. This is a Sanskrit compound meaning *self-generation, self-pouring out*, the pouring out of that which is within and, therefore, derivatively, its individual and own characteristic. Please remember in this connection that always more within, infinitely, boundlessly, more within, are the vast states of consciousness living on the equally vast fields of the spaces of space; the possibilities to be evolved in a man's evolution, and the eternities through which he has passed, and the lives which he has lived through in the past, are endless.

But passing on. This god sends forth its sheaths, and these sheaths consist of less (or inferior) beings. If the god is a primordial entity let us call these latter primal. As man clothes himself in physical flesh, so the god clothes itself in a garment or body, and this garment or body is composed, if you like, of atoms divine. Now these divine atoms are the *monads*. Compared with the god they are the mere clothing of it, just as the synthesis, the aggregation, of physical lives which compose a man's body and which form his physical "coat of skin" or clothing are, as it were, the physical monads or the atoms of the man himself. Similarly, let us, then, advance a point farther. The germ, the seed, the point above mentioned, let us now call a monad — one of the almost infinite number of monads in each god, forming the clothing of each god, the sheaths, the garments of light, that in which a god lives, which it has sent forth from itself, its outpouring of individual life.

Similarly acts the monad as did its father-god; and *its* sheath and *its* clothing are the *souls*, as yet latent, most of them, but some forming the more active part in which it manifests at any one particular time. The same course of action occurs with the soul. The soul clothes itself in *atoms*, the emanations from itself and the outpouring of its own vitality, its own prāna. And then the atoms pour forth from themselves the effluvium of physical-astral life, and these vital effluvia form the physical body of man, his astral body and his physical body.

So you see just what H. P. Blavatsky means by saying that an atom is an "atom and an angel" or a soul. Through all these hosts of beings streams the flow of the self, entering into every one, forming in fact the very root of its being, not however the personalized entity or the ego, but the impersonal self, that which is the same in you and in me; the same in the inhabitants of distant stellar spaces, as it is in us: the one self, limitless, boundless, the ideation of selfhood. Remember that the ego is the sense of "I am I," not "you"; and here immediately the conception of personality enters in. But it is in raising the personality into impersonality, the ego into divinity, the corruptible into the incorruptible, that consists the whole effort and purpose and aim of the divine part of evolution; and that divine part, that particular activity, is that of the higher range of the luminous arc, of the buddhic hierarchy, of which the summit is the dhyāni-buddhas, the buddhas of contemplation; and the material on which they work is these other monads, souls, atoms, which form the matter-side of nature, called the shadowy arc.

You will remember that all these things have been alluded to by us before; but tonight remember this one important point, that the monad does not "descend into matter." It casts forth from itself its life, as the sun pours forth its vitality in rays; and its life manifests first as a monadic entity of inferior grade, as a soul; and the soul in its turn pours forth *its* vitality, manifesting in almost innumerable atoms. The monad itself is but one of innumerable others, emanated, cast forth, breathed forth, if you like to use an Oriental metaphor, from Brahmā, the god, the summit of our hierarchy.

As said, these garments or sheaths of light are those monadic entities which must, during the course of evolutionary progress, become denser, darker, thickened, with the passage of time, until the ultimate result is the last energy, the last expenditure of the divine or monadic force as manifested in the physical body. When equilibrium between matter and spirit is finally reached, when the lowest point in that kalpa, i.e., in that Day of Brahmā, in that period of seven rounds, has been reached, then step in upon the scene the mānasaputras, the sons of mind, entities from the buddhic hierarchy, from the luminous arc of evolving nature, those who had been men before in former kalpas, and who have watched over us, under the guidance of the Silent Watcher, their supreme Head, ever since our present kalpa or manvantara began, aeons ago.

The monad, in one sense, may be called the active god of the hierarchy; or, in man's especial case, man's divine ego, sheathed in its garments of light composed of inferior monadic entities called souls; and the soul may be called an inferior monad, part of the sheaths or the garments of the monad proper. These respective garments are cast forth, somewhat as the tree puts forth its leaves, its branches, its stems, its fruits. Similarly the atoms are born from the prānic or vital essence of the souls, and they form our bodies. So we see that every man, in his inmost essence — that is, inmost for the hierarchy to which he belongs — is a divine being, a god; and his spiritual nature is the monad; and his soul-nature is the ego, that particular entity hovering between the pit and the sun, which must be raised from personality into impersonality, because in the soul resides that particular part of the psychological processes of intellection which makes a man self-conscious, a *self*-conscious being, capable of the ideation of individualized being.

What wonderful thoughts are these! How they do uplift the soul! Man feels his native divinity, his interior spiritual strength; he feels the power of divinity within his own heart, the power for goodness and truth. And how small, how insignificant, how unworthy, seem those things that lie apart from the path of duty, of right!

How many have been hungry for truth, and have searched for it, and yet have found only the husks of a pseudo-esotericism? But *they also should have it.* Human beings, they have a right to it; but they are not going to get it unless they "work for it," for such is the archaic law. These teachings have formed the *reward,* the reward of those who have been faithful.

There is one subject which for certain reasons must now be touched upon briefly. It is a subject which has been deliberately avoided by me hitherto for obvious reasons; I refer to the matter of sex. At our present stage of study, it is necessary then to point out that man at a certain former period of his evolution was without sex, was sexless, and also that in the next coming root-race, the sixth root-race, he will be without sex as we now understand it. Sex is but a passing phase in evolutionary development, and has no more value in one sense, to man, than an evil dream has to a man under certain conditions. Nature has followed that line, as it were, under protest, through the evildoing involved in our past karma, as the only way by which souls can find incarnation at present; but as the race grows in spiritual strength and in spiritual knowledge, and looks with closer self-analysis into its own inner being, children will come into the world without fathers; and from being at first an unheard of phenomenon, and presumably to be called a portent or a prodigy when it first appears, this procedure of generation will become the natural course of things in the sixth root-race. Our present sexually separated men and women, the present method of generation of human beings, of animals, and of some plants, will, in those far distant times of the future, be no more.

In conclusion: you have heard of the ancient Mysteries, and of the doctrine of the "virginal birth." Beginning with the fourth degree or stage of initiation, the future was outlined in the ancient Mysteries to the candidate both by teaching and more especially by causing the candidate himself to *pass through* what was to come to pass in the future ages of racial development; that is to say, the initiant had to *go through*, to *live through*, what the race was to live through for the next two root-races. Previous to the fourth degree, he was taught what the race had already been through, *with allusions to the future*. When we read, therefore, of the "virgin birth" of Christ, for instance, it is true that this has its religious explanation, its philosophical explanation, its mystical explanation, etc.; but it has also its physiological explanation. You will remember what H. P. Blavatsky says about the seven keys which belong to and open each one of these inmost sevenfold mysteries, of which two were held as particularly secret: the physiological, and the spiritual. The physiological key to this aspect of the Mystery-teaching was, as said, that the initiant had to symbolize in his person and had to *pass through* or *live through what was coming;* and he was therefore said, in view of the future racial action along the lines of generation, to have been "born from a virgin."

It is a comforting thing, especially in the present stage of the world when humanity is doing its best to throw off the shackles of Atlantean and Lemurian sin (if we may use this word), i.e., to throw off the horrible karma which holds the world in its evil grip, to know the causes which brought it to be. This gives us knowledge and power to stem this stream of human sin and misery. And, finally, those who will not accept the truth and work with the Law, certainly, as Jesus might have said, will not "sit at my table with me when I partake of the wine of the spirit in the House of my Father." "Those who have ears to hear and to understand, let them hear" — and be *wise!*

THIRTY-ONE

THE BUILDING OF THE KOSMOS. THE SAME FUNDAMENTAL LAW
THROUGHOUT LIFE AND BEING: AN ENDLESS LADDER OF
PROGRESS. ANALOGICAL PROCESSES OF KOSMICAL AND
PSYCHOLOGICAL DEVELOPMENT. THE RIVER OF LIFE.

And by the circulations of the soul being merged in a profound river and
impetuously borne along, we must understand by the river, not the human
body alone, but the whole of generation (with which we are externally surrounded) through its swift and unstable flowing. For thus, says Proclus,
Plato in the Republic calls the whole of generated nature the river of Lethe,
which contains both Lethe and the meadow of Ate, according to Empedocles;
the devouring jaws of matter and the light-hating world, as it is called by the
gods; and the winding rivers under which many are drawn down, as the
oracles assert. But by the circulations of the soul the cogitative and opinia-
tive powers are signified; the former of which, through the soul's conjunction
with the body, is impeded in its energies, and the latter is Titanically torn
in pieces under the irrational life.
— THOMAS TAYLOR, "Introduction to the Timaeus"

In consequence of a reasoning process, therefore, he found that among the
things naturally visible, there was nothing the whole of which if void of
intelligence could ever become more beautiful than the whole of that which
is endued with intellect: and at the same time he discovered, that it was
impossible for intellect to accede to any being, without the intervention of
soul. Hence, as the result of this reasoning, placing intellect in soul and soul
in body, he fabricated the universe; that thus it might be a work naturally
the most beautiful and the best. In this manner, therefore, according to an
assimilative reason, it is necessary to call the world [or universe] an animal,
endued with intellect, and generated through the providence of divinity.
— PLATO, *Timaeus* (Thomas Taylor, trans.)

IN EXPLANATION of what was said in the final part of our
meeting last week: the idea of bringing in the subject,
which was then so lightly touched upon, was to connect
it with the general scheme of evolutionary development that we
shall later have to study more fully, and to show that throughout
the entire universe of beings there runs one general plan.

You all know, of course, that there are seven races all told on
this planet, in this round on globe D, and that each of these races
has its own continent, follows its own course of evolution, has
bodies — that is, the individual units of the race have bodies —
coordinated to and in harmony with the physical surroundings in
which they live. But as regards the question of the division of
the human racial stream, that is, the later third root-race, into the
sexual humanity which has evolved into the men and women of
today, the point to be emphasized at present is that what we call
sex is but a passing phase in racial evolution and, strictly speaking,
is not normal to mankind on globe D of our planetary chain. This
method of procreation actually was copied from the beasts, which
"separated" before "man." Please understand this clearly: sex is
a transitory phase in racial evolution, and has no more importance
than that; and further, as we are now evolving on the ascending
arc, as we have already passed in fact beyond the first steps of the
luminous arc, of the arc of ascent, we shall find as the ages pass
that our present physiological status as men and women is to be
outgrown. As a matter of fact, the Atlantean and Atlanto-Lemurian
karma has weighed so heavily upon us, the fifth race, that we are
actually belated, and have not at the present date, the middle
point of the fifth race, reached that stage as regards the evolving
of the physical body which otherwise we should have reached.

As it stands, however, the teaching tells us that at the end of
our own fifth race, men and women will be disappearing as opposite sexes; and that by the middle of the sixth root-race (the race
to come) men and women as separate sexes shall be no longer.
The race will consist of beings who are physiologically neither
men nor women; and, as hinted just now, the first examples of
parthenogenetic reproduction are already due, and would have
shown themselves already, were it not for our being belated by
the heavy weight of our Atlantean karma, which we have been
carrying, or rather working off.

About the middle of the sixth race humanity — then no longer
"men" and "women," but humanity — will procreate their kind, if
we can here properly use this word, at any rate will evolve or give
birth to their own genus, by a process similar to that which took
place in the early third race, a process called in the esoteric wis-

dom "creating sons by passive yoga"; that is to say, by meditation
and by *unconscious* will, at first, later to be succeeded by *conscious*
will in the seventh or following root-race. The humans of that
period (the sixth root-race) will produce children by meditation
and by will; during the seventh root-race, the last to come on
this globe, during this fourth round — a race which to us now
would seem glorious — the humans of that race will produce their
kind in the same general manner, but by *consciously exercised*
will and meditation, yet still more impersonally and still more
ethereally than the sixth race will do. The sixth will do so, much
as the flowers grow from the plants, almost unconsciously as it
were, hence by "passive yoga"; not so much unconsciously from
the mental standpoint but physiologically almost unconscious of
any "procreative" act, or of any creative act. The seventh will
"create" their offspring with conscious and fully active imagination, a force called *kriyāśakti* in Sanskrit. The difficulty is in
finding words to explain something which to us of the fifth root-
race is nonexistent, almost, and hence speculative or unreal.

The main point then, here, is to realize that this present
physiological state of sex is a passing racial evolutionary phase;
and that every abuse, every misuse, no matter of what kind or
what the world may think about it, is a reaction contrary to the
evolutionary law, to use the popular phraseology; and that while
it is true that the present method is the one which nature has
evolved at the present time, as said before it is not really the
method which primordial humanity might have followed. Even
the Hebrew Bible alludes to this matter in a passage which you
all may recall. We of the fifth race now are on the ascending arc,
and we should at least attempt to lead the race towards a nobler
life as pioneers of nature's forthcoming stages.

Our main theme tonight is the building of the kosmos, the
building of worlds, and the building of man. Throughout the vast
extent of manifested being, there prevail fundamental operations
of nature, which men today call the laws of nature because they
do not understand their origin. Men personify nature, which is
a mere generalizing term; and they use the word law — which is
merely a word adapted from human action — in order to give a
name to those fundamental movements of being. But there *are*

operations of nature, and these fundamental operations of nature are actually the life-currents in the spiritual essence governing our hierarchy, as the life-currents in man are they which govern the atoms, astral and physical, which compose his body.

Remember that *space* is not a vacuum, space is not a mere container; if so, there would have to be a container of that container, and so ad infinitum. But space is the *infinite fullness of everything;* it is the boundless All, without beginning and without end; it is one vast organism; it is a unity; everything is interlocked and interchained with everything else, and through all there runs the one universal life; there is the beating of the one universal heart. This thought is so important for a proper understanding of our philosophy that its repetition surely will be forgiven. There are no vacuum-separations, there is no absolute division anywhere. There is no real vacuum; everything is full, everything is full with and of beings; and these beings with which the boundless All is filled *are space itself.* Therefore, when we speak of space, we mean not merely the vast, boundless extension of any one plane, but more particularly the invisible spheres, the planes within, ascending, as it were, going inwards, and inwards, and inwards forever; and outwards likewise.

The next thought is that through the action and interaction of the gods, monads, souls, and atoms, we conceive a world as springing forth in the beginning of its manvantara, from and through the invisible deeps of space, and extending itself, as it were, casting itself, projecting itself, forward, in its descent down the shadowy arc of matter-manifestation. And how? Not by a something or a somebody which existed before itself was there, but by making itself its own world, evolving out its own kosmos, which thus becomes its garment or body.

The gods — and please do not think of human forms when we speak of the gods; we mean the arūpa, the formless, entities, beings of pure intelligence and of understanding, pure essences, pure spirits, formless as we conceive form — through that impersonal (and may we say inevitable?) energy, at any rate, by reason of the karmic impulses behind them, project from themselves less bodies, inferior bodies, which are the monads; and the monads do precisely likewise and project the souls; and the souls do precisely likewise and project the atoms. Each springs from each. Through all, furthermore, there runs the boundless self, the boundless soul of the upper realms; but each one of these atoms, each one of these souls, each one of these monads, each one of these gods, is its own hierarchy, the supreme part, the head, the seed, from which its own following hierarchy springs. Wheels within wheels, lives within lives, consciousnesses within consciousnesses, beings within beings — a vast and endless congeries of interlocked and interrelated and interliving things. Pray get this thought! It is the very foundation of the ancient wisdom. All questions of theology that have so embarrassed and perplexed the minds of men are solved just by these few simple principles of the ancient wisdom-religion. Think upon them for yourselves, and make your own deductions therefrom.

Now let us briefly follow the evolutionary course of one hierarchy, one solar system. The same law, if you like the word, the same *fundamental operation of nature,* runs through all that which we find done in the case of a solar system, and is also that which takes place in the case of a universe, is that which takes place in the case of a sun, of a planet, and of the beings which overrun that planet. Suppose then that we figurate a god, a divine seven-principled being, starting into activity after its pralayic sleep, bringing with it the karmic seeds, the impulses from the previous mahā-manvantara, every one of those seeds having its karmic swabhāva, its karmic characteristic or essential nature; and starting into immediate activity when the life-wave first arouses the sleeping spheres all comprised within the one immense entity which we have agreed to call a god. We do not exactly mean what the Hindus call a deva, which is something else, but a god. But not *God,* not the Christian God. We mean *a* god, one of the supreme intelligences, each one of which is the head of a hierarchy, the hierarchies themselves being numberless and "filling space," being, in fact, space itself.

We simply must keep several ideas in our heads at once in essaying an exposition of these intricate subjects. There is one of the secrets of understanding the ancient wisdom: to retain in the mind more than one conception at the same time; it is our safeguard against mental biases, and it is easy. Let me illustrate:

a man is driving an automobile; he may be at the same time watching the road, watching for other automobiles, while in the back of his mind there may be forming some plan of work; and he may also be talking to a friend. Let us keep these various thoughts, all that has been spoken of so far this evening, in our mind, as we consider this present matter.

Now this god is seven-principled, as said, and each principle has its own work to do in the building of its kosmos; each one acts according to karmic impulses originating in the previous man-vantara particularly, and in all previous manvantaras in general; and each one of these gods moves into manifestation according to the lines traced out for it by its own past consciousness and actions in former epochs of manvantaric activity. Therefore when these seeds of beings start into active existence, the innumerable monads or divine souls — divine seeds which form the clothing of each one of these seven principles — when all these principles spring into activity, each undertakes its own particular work, a division of labor, as it were, in the divine realms. First, the highest sends forth from itself a host of less beings, inferior beings; and they find their habitat, their habitation and their realm of activity, in the plane next "below," which is that of its second principle. That second principle then begins its own especial activity and does likewise; and thus two of the seven principles and realms of being are now working; and so on down the scale until we reach the lowest, the prithivī-tattwa, of the divine series or scale.

When the astronomer looks into the ethery spaces and sees those starry clouds, those nebulous masses, in some cases — though not in all, for these nebulae are not all the same — in those which are destined for the beginning of worlds, he sees there what has so far taken place in material manifestation of a hierarchy through the activity of the subseven degrees of the lowest or seventh principle of a divine entity or god informing an otherwise invisible life-center, informed by that god's vital essence, which is the fundamental life of that hierarchy, the fundamental impulse, or what men call the fundamental law, the fundamental operation of its nature, the fundamental characteristic, the swabhāva. In such manner, then, the vital essence creates its own dwelling — a sun, a planet, which cycles down, as it were, into visible evolution. But mark: each head of a hierarchy retains its own place, powers, and nature; but its offspring thicken or condense, its offspring thus forming its garments on the several planes of being. Each of these garments is a host of living beings, atoms, souls — the name matters little provided we understand the thought. We must use analogies derived from our human vocabulary, because we have as yet evolved no words which can adequately explain these spiritual things; therefore remember that by the law of analogy such words are applicable, *mutatis mutandis,* as the Latin phrase goes, "making the necessary allowances for circumstances," to various spheres of being.

When this thickening and grossening of the fabric — which takes place from each entity shooting forth from itself, emanating from itself, other less entities, less here meaning inferior — reaches its lowest degree, then we have a sun and planets. Let us take our planet as an instance. When such a planet has reached its lowest point of evolution driven by the karmic impulse inhering in it, which is at the middle point of its fourth round (which we on our planet have passed), then begins the reaction, the reversal of the kosmic operation, and the life-currents begin to withdraw inwards, thenceforth following the luminous arc "upwards": not leaving its garments behind altogether, but as they were sent forth, so are they now withdrawn inwards. This, then, is an outline of the process of the *evolution of spirit,* and the *involution of matter;* just as the processes of projection or casting forth were the *involution of spirit* and the *evolution of matter* on the downward or shadowy arc. Thus is the kosmos built.

Now another thought. Each one of these gods, each one of these monads, each one of these souls, each one of these atoms, is an exhaustless reservoir of consciousness, of force, and of matter. Let us take the ātmic (or seventh or highest) of the god whom we have chosen as example. Such ātmic plane or sphere is a laya-center. A laya-center is a nirvanic center, that part, or place, or condition rather, or state of being, where homogeneity of substance is, where heterogeneity has ceased, or has not yet begun. When such laya-center begins its activity towards evolution, it casts forth from itself ceaselessly, hosts and multitudes of these inferior beings; but its own inner strength is in nowise diminished.

It is, as said, an exhaustless reservoir, a creative center; precisely as the sun — one of the finest analogies that we have — casts forth from itself ceaselessly, during a manvantara, practically illimitable hosts of solar rays, yes, and also of beings. Each one of these beings has its future cyclic course to run; and from being originally an unconscious god-spark, it has to develop into a *self-conscious god,* and do the same kosmic work that its own great progenitor did or is doing.

We ourselves, when we were not men as yet, unevolved rays only, belonged to the lower realms of spiritual being, then pursued our evolutionary course up to self-conscious manhood; and we who are now humans are destined on the future planet which shall follow this our present globe — the offspring of the earth — to attain a development greater than manhood here; and those inferior lives which are now trailing after us on the evolutionary journey, the beasts, the plants, and the minerals, will have then *their* turn to pass through the human stage. Life and being form an endless chain, an endless ladder of progress; yet when manhood has been attained comes moral responsibility: at any moment there lies the path before us — the path to the right, up the luminous arc; or the path to the left, downwards along the arc of shadows.

Our time this evening is drawing to a close, but it is necessary for us to call attention to the following diagram:

	Esoteric Line	Brahmanic Tattwas	Elements	Mystic Greek	
1.	Swabhavat	Ādi-tattwa	The One	First Logos	
2.	Ādi-buddhi (a)	Anupapādaka-tattwa	Spirit	Second Logos	Dhyāni-chohans
3.	Gods	Ākāśa-tattwa	Aether	Gods; Third Logos (Mahat)	
4.	Monads	Taijasa-tattwa	Fire	Daimones	
5.	Souls	Vāyu-tattwa	Air	Heroes	
6.	Atoms	Apas-tattwa	Water	Men	Pitris
7.	Bodies	Prithivī-tattwa	Earth	Beasts	

ELEMENTAL WORLD

8. _____

9. _____

10. _____

Here we have six columns representing analogical cases of cosmical and psychological development. First, we have what we may call the Esoteric Line: to the left of that we have placed the numbers 1, 2, 3, 4, 5, 6, 7, 8, 9, 10, representing the full hierarchy of ten stages or degrees. The next column gives the Brahmanic Tattwas. *Tattwa* is a Sanskrit word, which may be translated as "element," meaning the substantial "reality" back of the phenomenal appearance, upon which the seed-consciousness works; the garment or bearer of the inworking consciousness. Then come in the next column the Elements, as commonly understood everywhere in ancient times. Then comes the Mystic Greek system, as found mostly in the Neoplatonic and Neopythagorean philosophies. And lastly comes the division of the beings composing the evolving life-wave, or river of life, into two generic (general) forms, Dhyāni-Chohans, and Pitris.

1. In the Esoteric Line we have first *swabhavat*, a Sanskrit word meaning, as you know, the "self-evolving," the "self-developing," even translated sometimes as the "self-existent." Corresponding to this is the ādi-tattwa in the next column. *Ādi* is a Sanskrit word meaning "original," "primordial." Corresponding to this among the elements is the One. We have no word for this element. The ancients referred to it in various ways. We will simply call it the One, as it is the seed from which the others spring in descent, that is to say, in thickening and grossening during the evolutionary course. The Mystic Greek has the First Logos to correspond.

2. The planes below are next given, reading from left to right. *Ādi-buddhi*, "original or primordial buddhi"; and when the thought is somewhat changed, and a slightly different hierarchy is to be followed, it is called ādi-buddha, individualizing the hierarchy in tracing the development of the Hierarchy of Compassion, though when we speak of ādi-buddhi, we refer rather to the action of the principles than to the entities imbodying those principles. Corresponding to it in the Tattwas is *anupapādaka-tattwa*, another Sanskrit word meaning "parentless," that which does not follow an individualized progenitor, therefore parentless, not that it has no source or origin, but that it itself is the primal seed of *individuality*, which in this particular hierarchy first springs into

manifestation in it. The case is like the entrance of the manas into man, thereby giving him self-consciousness and individuality, which he does not get from his parents. Among the Elements we may call it spirit. The Mystic Greek has it as the Second Logos.

3. The third plane below is the gods, corresponding of course to the mānasaputras in man, the sons of mind. Its tattwa is ākāśa-tattwa, the word ākāśa meaning "brilliant," "shining," "luminous." Let me point out here parenthetically that, strictly speaking, swabhavat is the proper correspondence of ākāśa; but the way in which this diagram is arranged is an attempt to show corresponding intelligences and activities in the several individual hierarchies here set forth; and therefore ākāśa-tattwa corresponds in it to the gods in the Esoteric Line. Among the Elements it is aether, but not the ether of science. The ether of science is merely one of its lower principles. The Mystic Greek has likewise the gods, otherwise composing the Third Logos. In Brahmanic philosophy this plane is called *mahat*, a word which means "great." Mahat is a technical term in the Brahmanic system, and is the Father-Mother of manas; it is the "mother" of the mānasaputras or sons of mind, if you like, or that element from which they spring, that element which they breathe and of which they are the children.

4. The monads, corresponding to *taijasa-tattwa*, meaning "the shining," "the brilliant," "the fiery," "the sparkling." Among the Elements it is fire. The Mystic Greek has the daimones corresponding to it, beings whom the Christians have turned into demons or devils. It simply means spiritual beings of a certain class; but this thought is too intricate to go into at any length this evening. I may merely point out that the daimones belong to the hierarchy of consciousness, as shown in the diagram, and not to the hierarchy of the shadowy arc. Socrates, as you know, frequently alluded to his *daimonion*, meaning his "guardian angel." As he said: "My daemon told me never what to do, but always what to refrain from doing." It is, as it were, the "conscience" of later thought.

Now these four classes are grouped under the general heading of the Dhyāni-chohans, the chohans of meditation, the lords of meditation. The following three classes belong to the Pitris —

beings of lower degree, whom you will remember as mentioned in *The Secret Doctrine* and there called "Fathers," because they are more particularly the actual progenitors of our lower principles; whereas the dhyāni-chohans are actually in one most important sense our own *selves*. We were born from them; we were the monads, we were the atoms, the souls, projected, sent forth, emanated, by the dhyānis, as pointed out before.

5. Now the fifth degree downward comprises *in this particular diagram* what are called souls in the Esoteric Line. In the Brahmanic Tattwas we see vāyu-tattwa. *Vāyu* means "airy," "aerial." In the Elements, air; in the Mystic Greek, the heroes. These are the highest class of the Pitris.

6. The sixth are the atoms. Please remember, as said before, that atom as here used does not mean the atom of science, but what we may call the astral monad, of which the atoms of the physical world are the emanations, the projections. The atoms, the astral atoms, clothe themselves in the physical world, which is their garment-offspring. The Brahmanic Tattwa is apas-tattwa; the Elements show here water; and the Mystic Greek, men.

7. The seventh is the bodies, vehicles merely, corresponding to prithivī-tattwa. *Prithivī* is a Sanskrit word meaning "extension," i.e., wide, spacious. It is common to speak of prakriti as "matter," but really prithivī is the word better corresponding to what we call matter. Prakriti is rather "nature" and the living garment of spirit. The Element is earth: and the Mystic Greek in this hierarchy of entities shows the beasts.

These last three classes are the Pitris: and below these seven comes the Elemental World, in three planes. One of these elemental planes or worlds we may mention in passing, as it is the "interior realm" which has its locus or habitation at the center of any globe.

Now the evolution of mankind depends upon and follows that of the respective elements in each instance — that is to say, that the human life-wave evolves in each of the seven elements one after the other, from the highest downwards to the last; and then on the turn of the grand cycle, ascending through them all to the highest again. Each globe of the seven of the planetary chain, each of the seven root-races on every globe, partakes of the nature

and qualities of the kosmic element it happens to be evolving in
and through, whether it be what is technically called earth, or
water, or air, or fire, or aether, or spirit, or the Nameless One.
Man's seven principles likewise correspond to and are derived
from the seven kosmic elements, each to each. And mere bulk of
body, or size, has nothing to do with the nature of man and his
powers, with the building of man, or his destiny.

For instance, the first and second root-races were gigantic
beings as far as mere size was concerned, but they were otherwise
mere shells, mere phantom creatures, so to say, the offspring of the
pitris alone, as yet not filled with the divine fires of self-consciousness and intellect. They were ethereal on what was then an
ethereal earth, our present gross planet Terra. They had no physiological organs, properly speaking, and their shapes were different
from ours, although the general human skeletal framework as we
now know it was within them, evolved from the previous round
on this earth.

In races the fifth and the sixth still to come, humanity will
evolve bodies corresponding to the surroundings they will then be
in; and, in very truth, those surroundings themselves will be developed or made by the humanity evolving therein, actually evolving
their own surroundings, which will be their own emanations. We
may conceive of them, if you like, as very small beings, lilliputian
in size, perhaps, but nevertheless of gigantic intellects, and of
immense spiritual powers. If we will only once realize, as even
our scientists are beginning to do, the almost limitless forces
locked up in an atom — a thing so small that it as yet is merely
a figment of the scientific imagination, which no one has ever
seen, or knows anything about except certain deductions which
have been more or less gradually made by studying the workings
of the atoms through the physical phenomena of beings — we can
realize that if even physical matter contains forces or powers as
great as even one atom has, what may not man be or become, upon
evolving that which is within himself, evolving the unspeakable
grandeur of his inner nature, as he is going to do — at least those
who will pass the "critical periods." We may understand, I repeat,
that mere size of body does not mean possession of power or of
knowledge, or of intelligence or of compassion. As a matter of

fact, it is perhaps rather the contrary: mere volume or rather mass weighing the inner spirit rather heavily down.

And it is quite permissible to conceive of gods so small that an atom, one of our physical atoms, would be a cosmical universe to it. And to use the old Brahmanic terms, there sits at the heart of Being a god, thinking divine thoughts, and ruling its universe.

So when we speak of men at the end of the fifth race in future ages as evolving physical vehicles out from themselves, which nevertheless will preserve the same general skeleton outline as at present; when we say that their shape will be neither that of man nor of woman, we simply mean that man himself, through suffering and experience, and through the evolving of that which is lying latent within him, and even now ready to appear, will bring forth into exteriorization from within himself his own inner nature: a sexless being. From that time forwards, men and women will be no more, replaced by far nobler humans.

You will remember that at our last meeting it was said that the time had even now come when children might be produced without fathers; but the race is belated in its evolutionary course, and probably ages will yet pass before this parthenogenetic process begins. Yet even this process is merely the first step to a still more different process to come later, but it will take place before this our fifth root-race ends; it will come to pass partly because men and women *are growing more alike, instead of more unlike.* As long as marriage lasts, however, it ought to be a union of mutual respect and kindness, in which each helps the other to grow morally and intellectually.

At the end of this fifth root-race, man and woman as sexes will have nearly passed away; and in the sixth race, naturally, at certain specified times, without passion, by meditation and by passive will and thought, humans will evolve forth their offspring, much in the "unconscious" way (though the term unconscious is incorrect) that the flowers bring forth their blooms; and in the seventh race of this round on this planet the humans of that splendid time will bring forth from within themselves glorious creations of the active will and of the imagination, their "children"; and there will then be a race of Adepts, of incarnate devas upon earth. This will be in the seventh race on this planet during this present fourth round. It is only because we have sunken morally and are belated that the phenomenon of virginal birth has not yet appeared on earth as a physical fact; though, as pointed out at our last meeting, it has been "prophesied" in religious mysteries, and the initiation ceremonies contained one where the initiant, after certain conditions had been complied with, was said to be "born of a virgin," thus anticipating, or rather forecasting, what was to come to the entire race in the future; this being, as said before, a reward for noble service rendered in behalf of mankind. Here is a wondrous truth, concealed and kept hid for fear of the profanation which would be sure to follow if these divine mysteries, if these divine teachings, fell into unworthy hands directed by scheming brains!

THIRTY-TWO

OUT OF THE INVISIBLE INTO THE VISIBLE. FROM THE
VISIBLE INTO THE INVISIBLE. THE MAGNUM OPUS.

5. This (universe) existed in the shape of Darkness, unperceived, destitute of distinctive marks, unattainable by reasoning, unknowable, wholly
immersed, as it were, in deep sleep.

6. Then the divine Self-existent (Svayambhû, himself) indiscernible,
(but) making (all) this, the great elements and the rest, discernible, appeared with irresistible (creative) power, dispelling the darkness.

. . .

19. But from minute body(-framing) particles of these seven very powerful Purushas springs this (world), the perishable from the imperishable.

20. Among them each succeeding (element) acquires the quality of the
preceding one, and whatever place (in the sequence) each of them occupies,
even so many qualities it is declared to possess.

21. But in the beginning he assigned their several names, actions, and
conditions to all (created beings), even according to the words of the Veda.

22. He, the Lord, also created the class of the gods, who are endowed
with life, and whose nature is action; and the subtile class of the Sâdhyas,
and the eternal sacrifice.

. . .

51. When he whose power is incomprehensible, had thus produced the
universe and me, he disappeared in himself, repeatedly suppressing one
period by means of the other.

52. When that divine one wakes, then this world stirs; when he slumbers
tranquilly, then the universe sinks to sleep.

53. But when he reposes in calm sleep, the corporeal beings whose nature
is action, desist from their actions and mind becomes inert.

54. When they are absorbed all at once in that great soul, then he who is
the soul of all beings sweetly slumbers, free from all care and occupation.

. . .

57. Thus he, the imperishable one, by (alternately) waking and slumbering, incessantly revivifies and destroys this whole movable and immovable
(creation).

— *The Laws of Manu* (The Sacred Books of the East, vol. xxv)

A FAR-SEEING hope and a bright peace abide in the hearts
of all faithful students; in those at least who have
learned to perceive that behind the mask of visible
things there is a splendor of life and consciousness which is theirs

for the taking; and also that it depends upon themselves entirely to what extent they may advance along the pathway which ascends ever upwards and onwards along the luminous arc, upon which we, as a race, have been and are now marching ever since the middle part of the fourth root-race.

The Mystery Schools of antiquity made the one great aim and object of their studies and initiatory ceremonies the bringing forth into actuality in each candidate or initiant of his immortal nature, of that part of him which belongs to, or rather is the offspring of, the inner monad; that which in fact makes him a conscious part of the buddhic hierarchy, of the Hierarchy of Compassion. It is the union of the personal man with these higher principles of his own nature that produces the living Christ, or the fully Awakened One called the Buddha. It was the object of initiation, as said, not merely to make man conscious of this higher life within him, of these splendors within, but also to enable him to become ready and fit to teach others of that life which he himself felt within himself. That was the main object and aim of all the Mystery Schools the world over, however much they may have differed in forms and in the words in which they clothed their thoughts. It was, in other words, to make each initiant or candidate a living follower and example of the Silent Watcher.

Now there are many Silent Watchers, as has been pointed out. The Silent Watcher, in fact, is the hierarch or supreme hierarchical Head of any one particular hierarchy of the numberless hierarchies in the kosmos; the one spoken so inspiringly of by H. P. Blavatsky in *The Secret Doctrine* is the chief of the dhyāni-buddhas governing this fourth round on this planet.

It would seem a curious thing to refer to in this connection; and yet it seems a necessary thing to do, to speak of the different vagaries of thought, quasi-philosophic, quasi-scientific, quasi-religious, which are being spread abroad in the world today.

Many are the teachings of theosophy, which are now so familiar and beautiful, which in the beginning were not easily received by many in the world because they were strange and conflicted with the prejudices — religious, scientific, and other — that men had at the time.

How many people objected to the teaching of reincarnation

when it was first promulgated! What did someone once say to the present speaker: "I do not want to be reborn a cab horse; I do not want to be reborn a flea; I am a man!" Obviously, there was here no objection to the doctrine of reincarnation which teaches no such metempsychosis as that; the objection was to his own prejudices, and he did not know it.

Similar is the case with some of the doctrines which will have to be developed and unfolded in our studies here. I will not say that among ourselves these teachings will meet with misunderstanding; but among others they may meet with objectors; the root-thoughts or bases of them may be misunderstood at first, and the objectors may not wait for time and reflection to confer an understanding of them. Meanwhile, let us remember that the utmost vigorous exercise of the intuitional and of the intellectual powers of each student is absolutely necessary, and is actually demanded. We take nothing on blind faith; but while that is the fact, on the other hand there likewise remains for us the duty to cultivate the spiritual and meditative faculty within our being, the immortal part of our natures.

Let us now take up the study which we temporarily closed at our last meeting — gods, monads, and atoms, as regards their respective work in the building of a world, in the building of a cosmos, and in the building of man. We refer not only to his body of flesh, but this noble doctrine includes also the *why* and the *how*, yea, and the *when* of his descent through spiritual spheres into incarnation and his existences in those spheres. Let us read first from *The Secret Doctrine*, volume II, page 267:

The doctrine teaches that the only difference between animate and inanimate objects on earth, between an animal and a human frame, is that in some the various "fires" are latent, and in others they are active. The *vital fires* are in all things and not an atom is devoid of them. But no animal has the three higher principles awakened in him; they are simply potential, latent, and thus *non-existing*. And so would the animal frames of men be to this day, had they been left as they came out from the bodies of their Progenitors, whose *shadows* they were, to grow, unfolded only by the powers and forces immanent in matter.

Out of the invisible into the visible, from the deeps of inmost space, when the time comes, the life-wave sends forth its flowings into the exterior and into the outer spheres, making for itself as it advances, creating for itself, through the beings which represent that wave, its own garments, which kosmically are its planes, its worlds. These several stages of evolution or progression, as before said, are (1) the gods, whose garments are (2) the monads, whose garments are (3) the souls, whose garments are (4) the atoms, whose garments are (5) bodies. Refer the order to worlds, and the doctrine is true. Refer the order to man, and the doctrine is true. Refer the order to the elemental, mineral, vegetable, beast, and human kingdoms of this earth, and the doctrine is again analogically true. Stage by stage, degree by degree, as the living wave advances, it projects from itself at each stage, it casts forth from itself at each stage, innumerable entities inferior to itself, which form its vehicles, which we may also call its garments, its bodies, or its planes and its worlds. Each god of the great host, for instance, from within itself produces multitudes of monads; each monad produces from within itself multitudes of souls; each soul produces from within itself multitudes of atoms; and these clothe themselves in vehicles of matter, or bodies, and all run through their long evolutionary course. Then, when the lowest point of the great round of life has been reached, the upward cycle begins: there is a reentering of the vital forces, a gathering up, a gathering withinwards, of the hosts of beings; the visible passes back by degrees into the invisible, plus the growth and experiences gained during the journey by each individual entity. Each one has advanced one plane upwards in its evolution; each one has gone so many milestones farther along the path; and, finally, the life-wave enters the divinity from which it went forth, but nobler, higher, in every respect. It began its long evolutionary course after its equally long pralayic sleep, obeying the karmic impulses awakening it to a new life period; and now having completed it, it is once more ready to issue forth again to form a new manvantara, and in order to do this, once again develops from within itself new planes, new elements, new principles, new hosts of beings as it did before, but now nobler, ever new ones going forth, growing ever higher and higher in grandeur and power. Such is a general outline of the evolutionary course.

You know the old saying: "As it is above, so it is below." That

saying is found in an ancient writing said to have been engraved
on an emerald table; according to the legend, it was called the
"Emerald Table of Hermes," and is undoubtedly based on one of
the ancient Hermetic teachings. I will quote the first few lines
of it:

True, without error, certain most true; that which is above is as that
which is below, and that which is below is as that which is above, for
performing the marvels of the Kosmos. As all things are from the [Primordial]
One, by the mediation of One [the Logos — that is to say, the host of Dhyān-
chohans], so all things arose out of this One Thing by evolving . . .

And that "One Thing" is the summit of any hierarchy, the divinity
already spoken of in giving the general outline of the evolutionary
procession.

Turning to the Zoroastrian faith, we find the following verses
in an ancient work (which modern scholars, for reasons best known
to themselves, try to bring down to late times, but which unquestionably contains very archaic thought) called *The Desātīr*, in the
chapter called "The Book of Shet the Prophet Zirtūsht," Zirtūsht
being one of the forms of the name which in English is called
Zoroaster, following the Greco-Latin form:

29. Know, O My Friend! that the essence of the Self-existent is one, and
without limits or conditions.

30. Being is like light; and light becometh visible. [Mark that!]

35. Whatsoever is on earth is the reflection and the shadow of something
that is in the [spiritual] World-Sphere.

36. While that resplendent something remaineth in its native condition,
it is well also with its shadow.

37. When that resplendent thing removeth away from its shadow, life
removeth to a distance.

38. Again, that light [that resplendent thing] is the shadow of something
still more resplendent than itself [note the hierarchical teaching here];

39. And so on up to Me, who am the Light of Lights [the hierarchical
head].

It probably has occurred to every thoughtful mind that if man
has within himself a quasi-divine monad, and seated within that
divine monad a divinity, a god, it is strange that our consciousness

of this unity with the divine through this monadic link is not stronger in us than it is today. The Christians speak of their guardian angel, and so do the Mohammedans; and other peoples, such as the Greeks, spoke as did Socrates of the daimon, the guardian self; but why is it that our conscience is not stronger and more vocal than it is? Why is it that we have to work and struggle inwardly to get this interior illumination consciously, which, even according to the Christian teachings, must be "taken by violence"? Is the reason not here? Man is composite; he is a complex, a compound being, and lives on different planes, and these planes are the seven elements of nature; and the seven elements of nature are its seven principles, and the seven principles of man can otherwise be called man's seven elements.

The monad lives in its own world, in its own logoic activity, with its quasi- or semi-divine powers in full action, far more self-conscious on its own plane than you are or I am on this our plane of consciousness. And similarly with the god within us, seated within the monad.

But further, you will remember that in discussing the teaching referring to the Silent Watcher, we pointed out that it was based on the fact of the many and the One — how man and the universe are both, respectively, many and one, many in the lower nature, and one in the higher. Now, then, please note carefully the following: our consciousness is no higher than it is because we are (each of us) a person; and it is the raising of this person, of this personal self, of this personal soul, into the impersonality and individuality of the monad, that is the great work, the magnum opus, of life. Here is the answer in brief to the question propounded above. The purpose of all initiatory ceremonies — to put the answer in another form, the aim of all initiatory teachings of the ancient Mystery Schools — was *the evocation of the higher self, of this inner being;* and it is possible to do it. A strong and indomitable will is the first requisite. Purity of life is the second, mental purity above everything else. And absolute loyalty and devotion to the teachings of the esoteric wisdom and to the teacher, is the third; and these three principles of life and conduct are true *rāja-yoga;* and this "kingly union" is the union with the god within, our divine self. When this union takes place, then you have what the Greeks called in their ancient Mysteries, *theopneusty*, the breathing into the personal of the impersonal essence.

Yet preceding this stage or degree of initiation, the second or intermediate, there came the first of these initiations, the actual and real meeting *face to face* with the god within, your own higher ego-self; and this degree was called *theophany*, a Greek compound word meaning the "appearance of a god" — i.e., of that god which is within you, your own inner self. Further, when the two preceding unions were achieved, when the high degrees of theopneusty and theophany had been won, there came a third and last stage, which the Greeks called *theopathy*, a Greek compound word meaning "suffering a god," "enduring a god" — a meaning later to be more fully explained. Such an initiate became even in life an evolved Christos, or as the Buddhists call it, an Awakened One, a Buddha, the awakening to the living buddhic entity within the man, the last stage of human knowledge possible on this earth on this round, the fourth. Very few indeed are they who attain to this supreme stage of incarnate wisdom! Such a one was the Lord Buddha, Gautama Śākyamuni, Prince of Kapilavastu. He it is, we are told, who today as a nirmānakāya forms the summit (or Silent Watcher) of the hierarchy of sages forming the Great Brotherhood, living among them invisible to those of lower degree and visible to those of higher degree; in what the Buddhists of the north call the sacred land of Śambhala, that mysterious locality which is placed north of the Himalayas, and not so far from what is called the desert of Gobi or Shamo. And that wondrous thing, that wondrous entity, that wondrous being, which was in H. P. Blavatsky and worked through her, came from Śambhala — came from this hierarchy. I do not here refer merely to the woman, to the physical body; no, nor even to the personality born in Russia; but to that wonderful thing who incarnated in that body, and who left part of "herself" behind there and who went forth into the world crippled psychically, obeying in this respect an archaic law, which was the cause of so much misunderstanding about her. This entity did its work in the world at the proper cyclic time for its appearance among men: the opening of a new Messianic cycle.

You know the warning about "false Christs" which is given in the Christian Gospels: in Matthew, chapter 24, verses 23, 24, and 25, and in Mark, chapter 13, verses 21, 22, and 23. They are practically the same in sense and words, and they evidently are both — Mark and Matthew — taken from a former, earlier, Christian Gospel, possibly the so-called Gospel "according to the Hebrews," of which scholars know, but which they have never yet found. At any rate, the writer of the above warning spoke truly when, using the alleged words of Jesus, he said in substance: "Many shall come after me, teaching false Christs, who will try to lead you astray, saying 'Lo, here he is!' and 'Lo, there he is!' Believe it not." These words are not necessarily of solely Christian application: it is the warning against imposture contained in them that we quote. They could apply equally well to Jews, Hindus, Buddhists, ancient Americans, Scandinavians, to any people living anywhere in the world, for the warning could apply to all. Why? Because there are in fact cyclic crises or periods when real "saviors" of men do appear, as also "false prophets" and "false Christs." They come always whenever the time is ripe. After every period of 2,160 years, the length of the Messianic cycle, there comes a recrudescence of spiritual faith into the world at times of material growth and spiritual decadence; in those times that Plato calls the barren periods, a Messenger "comes" from Śambhala, and gives his doctrine to men and establishes it, and then passes. And instantly copyists, or perhaps false disciples, those who perhaps are seeking prominence for themselves, or who are deceived, or who perhaps are even misled by their own prejudices, by the weaknesses of their own human minds — let us put it in the most charitable way possible — begin making sects, begin preaching "false Christs," begin to make an appeal to the wonder-loving appetite of the people. And a new sect is born, and either dies out or lives on for a time, and the world is priest-ridden and man-hierarchy ridden for another series of centuries, until by his own spiritual vigor and his mental strength man frees himself again; and after turbulence and achings of the heart there comes a new real light, a new real Christos, a new light from the Hierarchy of Compassion. It is the working of the same old appeal to men's spiritual inner fires, by the spiritual dhyānis who incarnated primarily in the third root-race on this planet in this round as the mānasaputras, and who thereby saved us from aeons of animality and unspeakable degradation, and untold ages of light-less wandering.

There is the situation. We must follow either the "right hand" or the "left," as the ancient Buddhists said. "Keeping the link unbroken" means following the right-hand path. Each one of us as individuals has the choice. None other can choose for us. All the teacher can do is to appeal and to teach. Each one of us has his conscience, which he must follow, and with which no inter-ference is ever tolerated. But mark you, be sure that the path you choose is the path of conscience and wisdom. Be sure you are not led along the left-hand path by wiles and guile of many kinds.

These are old and trite sayings, but they have always a proper application. Their truth is not lessened by the fact that we are all familiar with them.

At our next meeting we shall have to undertake more definitely the study of how the life-wave passes into imbodiments, making its own vehicles by projection from itself — by bringing forth from within its own focus of vitality — innumerable inferior entities, giving them forth as man gives forth his thoughts; and then in future studies show how the life-wave passes down the shadowy arc into ever grosser manifestation, until the critical period is reached, when the ascending cycle of the luminous arc begins. We shall have to refer more fully to the old Greek and Roman philosophic school, the Stoic, and show how true were their teachings regarding the evolution of the elements, these elements following each other down into manifestation, each giving form to each. For in this teaching we may find a proper understand-ing of how the kosmos is built, and how man is constructed, and the *why* and the *how* of his evolution, and why he is here on earth now and not elsewhere, either farther along the path or not so far.

All these are matters which are directly connected with the scientific researches of our own day, for modern scientific dis-covery is making great strides forward, and will sooner or later need guidance, or it too will take the left-hand path. H. P. Bla-vatsky has told us plainly that it is through the Theosophical Movement that will come the light which is to enlighten the world and guide the footsteps of man on the path along the luminous arc; and it is our duty to aid in this noble work with all our strength. And if we do not understand our own philosophy properly and rightly, so that we can meet others and talk with them convincingly, we are failing in our duty. But those of us who have an indomitable will and who have awakened the inner Christos within, even to such a small extent that we can see even something of that wonderful light within which gives us far-seeing hope and abiding peace; those of us who have felt it even in slight degree, will realize that in it and nowhere else on this earth, nor in any other sphere, visible or invisible, lies the path, the ancient path, the small, old path of which the Upanishads speak, that leads to the heart of the universe.

THIRTY-THREE

THE LIFE-WAVE AND THE SEVEN ELEMENTS. THE ESOTERIC PHILOSOPHY AS TAUGHT BY THE STOICS.

If, out of the material portion of the ether, by virtue of the inherent restlessness of its particles, the forms of worlds and their species of plants and animals can be evolved, why, out of the spiritual part of the ether, should not successive races of beings, from the stage of monad to that of man, be developed; each lower form unfolding a higher one until the work of evolution is completed on our earth, in the production of immortal man?

— H. P. Blavatsky, *Isis Unveiled,* I, 340

The most positive of materialistic philosophers agree that all that exists was evolved from ether; hence, air, water, earth, and fire, the four primordial elements must also proceed from ether and chaos the first *Duad;* all the imponderables, whether now known or unknown, proceed from the same source. Now, if there is a spiritual essence in matter, and that essence forces it to shape itself into millions of individual forms, why is it illogical to assert that each of these spiritual kingdoms in nature is peopled with beings evolved out of its own material? Chemistry teaches us that in man's body there are air, water, earth, and heat, or fire — *air* is present in its components; *water* in the secretions; *earth* in the inorganic constituents; and *fire* in the animal heat. The Kabalist knows by experience that an elemental spirit contains only one, and that each one of the four kingdoms has its own peculiar elemental spirits; man being higher than they, the law of evolution finds its illustration in the combination of all four in him. — Ibid., I, 343

FOR THOUSANDS of years there has been no such attempt as there is at present, on the part of the Masters, our Elder Brothers, to bring forth to the attention of mankind the doctrines which we have been studying at these meetings for the past few years, as any student of antiquity may assure himself. The reason is that at about the time of the discovery of America there came the end of one of the racial cycles, and the inauguration of another, which has culminated at the present time in the various spiritual, psychical, and physical disturbances both of man and of the earth, such as we have been experiencing in the last ten or twelve years.

You remember what Cicero, the Roman orator, tells us of those who never had had the immense advantages conferred by initiation. He tells us, in the metaphorical language of his day, that those who were initiated lived and died with a brighter hope and a deeper knowledge of man and things; and that those who did not have the supreme advantages of the secret teachings of the ancient wisdom given through initiation, lived, more particularly after death, in what he described as the shades and mud and degradation and sorrow and filth — words which well merit our attention, because Cicero, like most men of his time, had indeed passed through the Eleusinian rites, a fact which we know because he himself so tells us.

Now the main subject which we have to study more fully this evening is the procedure followed by nature in the building of worlds and of the kosmos and of man; and directly connected with this our subject are the different views of the gods, the monads, the souls, the atoms, and the bodies, which we have been studying this winter.

You remember that the ancient Greeks and Romans had a school which they called the Stoic, from the Stoa Poikile or Painted Porch, in Athens, where the Stoic teachers taught. This school was founded by Zeno of Citium, in the island of Cyprus, at about the end of the fourth century before our present era; and it formed at about the time of the downfall of the Roman Empire the religious science or scientific religion of the most advanced thinkers of that era. There is no question that Zeno had been initiated, probably in the Samothracian as well as in the Eleusinian Mysteries; because we know that the doctrines that he taught are not only practically identical *as far as they go* — please note the qualification — with our own, but there are allusions and hints here and there scattered throughout these teachings which show us very plainly that these doctrines of Stoicism did not originate with him, according to the views of the modern scholars, but must have taken their origin in a far past, in an antiquity originating far beyond anything of which history has preserved annals.

Among the doctrines of Stoicism was that of the genesis or birth of the elements of the kosmos. Five were spoken of, and two more were vaguely hinted at. The five were aether, beginning with the highest; then what was called fire; then air; then water; and then earth. Now these kosmical elements are not the familiar things which we know by those names, for they were taken merely to symbolize, through certain appropriate qualities which they possess, the actual elements of kosmical being.

These elements of nature, which the Brahmanical philosophy called the tattwas, may likewise be called the *principles* of kosmos, precisely as man's seven principles may be called the *elements* of his being. We can say the elements of kosmos, or the principles of kosmos, and it means for present purposes the same thing; and we may say the elements of man or the principles of man, and it means for present purposes precisely the same thing. Seven different qualities or states or conditions of prakriti or nature — call it also substance or matter for the present, if you like. The present is not an appropriate time to go into a too detailed distinction of the difference — which does exist — between matter and prakriti. At any rate, the elements are seven different states or conditions or qualities of prakriti, the manifested side of kosmical being.

These seven elements or principles — five, as openly taught — according to the Stoic philosophy were derived one from the other, in order as follows: first, the Nameless One; second, its progeny or offspring or child, which is the second element lower in the scale; the third was aether, the progeny or offspring of the second, combining in itself, at the same time, the qualities or powers of the second, its parent, and of the first, its grand-parent, so to say. Then came fire, containing in itself the elements of the three preceding, and also its own particular swabhāva or essential characteristic. You will remember what swabhāva means: the particularity, the essential nature, the real character-istic, of a thing, which makes it different from some other thing. The swabhāva of a rose makes the rose plant bring forth a rose always, and not a lily or a violet; and the swabhāva of a man brings forth as offspring a man always and not a gooseberry or an acorn. This is swabhāva, or self-nature. Call it the essential individuality, if you like; it is the special or germinal individuality. Then from fire, as a parent, sprang air. We are using these familiar terms, with a warning, as said before, that they do not really mean the familiar material things which we know by those names. However, this element called air contains in itself the qualities of its own nature, likewise those of fire, its parent, and of aether, its grandparent, and the qualities of the second and the first elements as well. Then comes water, containing in itself its own qualities and also the qualities of the five which precede it. Finally comes the seventh or last, gross matter, or concreted substance, containing in itself the qualities of all the six which precede it; each element giving birth to each following one as the life-wave ran its course down the shadowy arc of manifestation, or the building of the framework of the kosmos.

Thus, said the Stoics, is the kosmos built — enunciating an exactly similar doctrine to our own, indeed, identical, as so far outlined. Simply change the names: use gods, monads, souls, atoms, bodies, or bearers, and add life force, and the kosmical self as the first, and our seven kosmical principles are there. Then, said the Stoics (expressing here their doctrine in our own terms), when the impulse of the evolutionary life-wave had reached its ultimate cycle of descent, i.e., had reached its lowest point on the fourth round, then began the period of ascent; and water drew into itself, as the life-wave advanced upward, earth, and mingled it with itself; and air, following in turn, drew within itself the water containing the earth, and mingled it with itself. Then fire drew into itself the air containing the two lower elements in itself; and the aether then in its turn drew into itself the fire, with its elemental containments; and the second element, counting downwards, drew into itself the aether; and finally the first, or Nameless One, then drew into itself the second, containing the elemental qualities of all the others: and then, using the Stoic language, the "tension" of the divine Essence was restored to its own quality and kind, as far as that Essence had emanated a life-wave of innumerable living particles or monads, and there was repose and bliss and utter peace and ineffable rest until the cyclic time came for the next evolutionary outpouring of the innumerable lives.

This is, as seen, a doctrine precisely similar to our own, as shown in the teaching setting forth the evolution of lives during the rounds of a planetary chain. Descending along the shadowy arc into manifestation through matter, the life-wave advances downwards until it reaches its lowest cyclical point, then rises along the luminous arc until all is withdrawn again into the Essence which sent it forth, or rather from which it went forth; individual experience gained, many stages in evolution passed through, by every unit or monad of the life-wave which had come down into matter for the purpose of gaining soul-experience there, and incidentally giving to the circumambient matter itself an upward impulse. For matter is nothing but crystallized spirit; or, if you like, spirit is etherealized matter; though the former statement is the better way by far in which to express the fact.

All this of course happens in what is called space. Space is not a mere container or receptacle of things, as our modern dictionaries define it, for in that case it would be a thing finite in itself; and, as said before, in such case we should have to find or conceive of a container to contain the container, and so ad infinitum. But space is the endless and beginningless *pleroma,* "Fullness," as the Greek philosophers said: the boundless All, the field of action of the universal life, the endless and beginningless Fullness. Space is the vast, truly incalculable, aggregation of the innumerable hierarchies forming manifested being. We live and move and have our being in space, as the beings, living in and upon the atoms which compose our bodies, live in our bodies, which to them are practically endless space, the illimitable pleroma.

Break the molds of your minds; allow your thought to lead you into the vast expanse of the universal consciousness which these sublime ideas must open to you. Imagine, if you will, that life is endless; that throughout all runs the beating of the universal heart; and, furthermore, that there is nothing great, nothing small, except by comparison, except relatively so. We bring forward again here the thought which we have often before expressed, an axiom which is one of the fundamental truths of the esoteric wisdom, the ancient wisdom of the olden times, and this fundamental truth or principle is that of relativity. Everything is relative; there are no absolutes anywhere, except relatively so;

there are no jumping-off places; there are no ultimates; there are no bounds beyond which the evolving spirit may not go. Everything is related to everything else. How can a thinking man talk of infinites, and at the same time speak of absolutes? Why, the very word absolute, as pointed out in a former study, means what the Hindu word *mukta* means, "released," "free." *Absolute* means released, unchained, unbound — freedom.

You remember that when Paul, the apostle of the Christians, during one of his missionary journeys, spoke to the men of Athens from Mars' Hill, i.e., from the Areopagus, he used words which are unquestionably, I think, the finest in the Christian New Testament, for they are purely pagan philosophy. In addressing the men of Athens, he told them that when he disembarked, on coming up to Athens he found an altar dedicated "to the Unknown God" — *agnōstō theō*. Now he must have disembarked at the old port of Phalerum, the port of Athens which was used before (and after) the building of the Piraeus. We know also, from the Greek historian and traveler, Pausanias, in chapter 1, book 1, of his work, that there were altars in that port dedicated to the "Unknown Gods." This word, translated into English as "unknown" (*agnōstos*), means in Greek not so much "unknown" as "unknowable" — unknown in the sense of unknowable; unknown because it was unknowable.

Now Paul, in speaking to the Athenians in his sermon to them, used the following words, as given in the Christian writing, Acts, chapter 17, verse 28: "For in him we live, and move, and have our being; as certain also of your own poets have said, For we are also his offspring." I may point out in passing that the Greek of this passage allows us to translate the Greek word *autō* just as well "it" as "him": "For in *It* we move, and live, and have our being." The Christians of modern days, having in mind their personal, active, monotheistic deity, in translating this passage naturally took the word as of the masculine gender; but the neuter gender is grammatically correct also and philosophically better by far.

Ay, Paul, the "Christian" — shall we so call him? at any rate he was an initiate — Paul, the "wise masterbuilder," as he calls himself, thus hinting at his esoteric affiliations, not only tells us that in It we live and move and have our being, but makes reference constantly to matters of initiation. The many mystical allusions to various matters which occur throughout the writings ascribed to him, show very plainly how far the Christianity of today has wandered from its first founders.

These poets of whom Paul here speaks are unquestionably the two famous Stoic philosophers, Aratus (a countryman of Paul, both he and Aratus being probably natives of Tarsus in Cilicia) and Cleanthes of the Troad, who wrote, by the way, one of the finest examples of Greek religious poems extant, greatly admired even by Christian writers because they believe they see in it what they would probably call a nascent monotheism, in the Christian sense. But it was simply a hymn of reverence to the Stoic divine Essence, the hierarch of the grand hierarchy of our universe, its supreme head, which in the poem Cleanthes called Zeus. Please always remember that though Zeus may be called the supreme hierarch of a universe, or kosmos, or hierarchy, he is but the head of *one* of innumerable other similar hierarchies, hierarchies of the vast aggregate, endless and beginningless, which compose manifested being.

In him — in it — we live, and move, and have our being. And this *it* is what we very rightly call space, which is the vast, endless and beginningless congeries of living beings. There is no vacuum, no vacuity, no emptiness, no "nothing," anywhere. *Everything is full, not merely of life, but of living and conscious things*, and of beings of infinitely varying degrees of consciousness, such as you and I are, for example. Think of it! Open your minds, and let the thoughts which this divine idea gives to you stream in. Let them find a habitation in your souls! They bring endless comfort and peace, and lead to further illumination.

Verily, such is space, sevenfold space, more particularly the vast spaces of space inwards, inwards, inwards, endlessly.

In opening our more particular study for this evening, let us read from *The Secret Doctrine*, volume II, page 492, the second paragraph:

The Secret Doctrine points out, as a self-evident fact, that Mankind, collectively and individually, is, with all manifested nature, the vehicle (*a*) of the breath of One Universal Principle, in its primal differentiation; and (*b*) of the countless "breaths" proceeding from that One BREATH in its secondary and further differentiations, as Nature with its many *mankinds* proceeds downwards toward the planes that are ever increasing in materiality. The primary Breath informs the higher Hierarchies; the secondary — the lower, on the constantly descending planes.

A wonderful passage! Note particularly the reference to the "many mankinds," concerning which matter we shall speak at greater length in a future study.

During our last study we traced very briefly the evolution from a *god* (one of infinite multitudes of divinities or gods), of other multitudes of inferior beings; of *monads* springing from that god and forming its luminous garment, its vehicle, its carrier, its bearer, its body. Each one of those innumerable multitudes of monads, in its turn, sends forth from itself, projects from itself, other innumerable multitudes of *souls*, which form its garment, its bearer, its carrier, its vehicle, its body. Again, every one of such souls in its turn sends forth from itself other innumerable multitudes of *atoms*, prānic-astral entities — not the physical atom of science, please — and these atoms form the garment, the carrier, the vehicle, the bearer, the body of such a soul.

Each one of these atoms, in its turn, concretes around itself, gathers to itself, the life-atoms waiting over for it from previous cycles of activity, which are the skandhas belonging to that plane of manifestation, and thus forms its physical vehicle in which all the other principles (mostly latent) reside.

Now this vast collection of entities — gods, monads, souls, atoms — passed down through the kosmical elements which we have described, using the Stoic formulae rather than the Brahmanic which are not so well known to European readers, but which equally well could have been used; and as these courses of life, as this life-wave, travels downwards into matter, through each element, through each one of the seven elements, it gives birth to one class of these entities which we have been describing. The god lives on the plane of the Nameless One; the monads live on the plane of the second element, likewise unnamed in the literature of the ancients; the souls live on the plane of aether, ākāśa; and the atoms live on the plane of air, the fourth plane, the prānic-astral world.

Thus, the elements of the Stoics, seven in number, but only

five openly named, form the principles of nature; and the life-wave in passing through these elements builds its appropriate habitations in each one of them. At certain appropriate planes, these habitations take the form of globes, and these globes are the seven forming our planetary chain; they are globes built of these innumerable, multitudinous hosts of atoms, of souls, of monads; some "awakened," some partly "awake," some still sleeping in the lower spheres.

Then when the hosts of beings composing the life-wave — the life-wave being composed of the entities derived from a former but now dead planet, in our case the moon — find that the time has arrived for them to enter upon their own particular evolutionary course, they cycle downwards along the planetary chain that has been prepared for them by the three hosts of elementary beings, of the three primordial elementary worlds, the forerunners of the life-wave yet integral parts of it. Remember, a hierarchy consists of ten degrees or states; three, as the Pythagoreans would have said, remaining in the silence and darkness — to us — of divinity, and seven entering into manifestation. This life-wave passes seven times in all around the seven spheres of our planetary chain, at first cycling down the shadowy arc through all the seven elements of the kosmos, gathering experience in each one of them; each particular entity of the life-wave, no matter what its grade or kind, spiritual, psychic, astral, mental, divine, in it, advancing, advancing, advancing downwards, advancing until at the bottom of the arc, when the middle of the fourth round is attained, they feel the end of the downward impulse. Then begins the upward impulse. According to the Stoic doctrine, everything passes by degrees back towards the divine, through the elements again, the lower being withdrawn into the higher, until at last the great cyclic round is finished, and the cycling beings reenter divinity, man being in the front ranks. As so often said before, "man" begins his evolutionary journey an unself-conscious god-spark, and ends it as a self-conscious god.

And when we say "man" of the later stages of that journey, we mean the *thinking entity*. The personal, by that time, will have become the impersonal; the mortal will have been raised into immortality. These two ideas comprise two of the most sublime teachings of the ancient wisdom. The main thing to realize at the present time is that space is a vast, beginningless and endless Fullness; it is the boundless All; and, further, that it is composed of the numberless hierarchies, which actually *are space itself*, the spaces of space; and, still further, that these hierarchies in their turn are composed of incalculable numbers of evolving beings in all the seven stages of development; and that each such being has its own grand cycle to perform: first down the shadowy arc and then, when the end of that particular evolutionary wave or course has been reached, the reascent along the luminous arc upwards, towards the source from which it originally came. Then, finally, the long pralayic sleep. At its end comes the kosmic reawakening, obeying the karmic impulses from the preceding manvantara and manvantaras, the opening of a new evolutionary course through the spheres of life, but on higher and far sublimer levels than before.

THIRTY-FOUR

THE SPACES OF SPACE. THE SECRET DOCTRINE, A UNIFIER: UNIVERSAL
KEYS. DOCTRINES OF THE VOID AND OF THE FULLNESS CONTRASTED.

Mme. Blavatsky, speaking on this subject in her *Secret Doctrine,* quotes from
the old *Book of Dzyan* thus:
"An army of the Sons of Light stands at each angle, the Lipika in the
middle wheel."
The four angles are the four quarters, and the "middle wheel" is the center
of space; and that center is everywhere, because as space is illimitable, the
center of it must be wherever the cognizing consciousness is. And the same
author, using the *Disciple's Catechism,* writes:
"What is it that ever is? Space, the Anupadaka. What is it that ever was?
The germ in the Root. What is it that is ever coming and going? The great
Breath. Then there are three eternals? No, the three are one. That which
ever is is one; that which ever was is one; that which is ever being and becoming is also one; and this is space."
In this parentless and eternal space is the wheel in the center where the
Lipika are, of whom I cannot speak; at the four angles are the Dhyan Chohans,
and doing their will among men on this earth are the Adepts — the Mahâtmas.
The harmony of the spheres is the voice of the Law, and that voice is obeyed
alike by the Dhyan Chohan and the Mahâtma — on their part with willingness,
because they are the law; on the part of men and creatures because they are
bound by the adamantine chains of the law which they do not understand.
— W. Q. JUDGE, *Echoes from the Orient,* p. 15

Thou hast to study the voidness of the seeming full, the fulness of the seeming
void. — *The Voice of the Silence,* pp. 55–6

I N OPENING our study tonight, let us again read the passage
on page 492 of the second volume of *The Secret Doctrine,*
read at our last meeting:

The Secret Doctrine points out, as a self-evident fact, that Mankind,
collectively and individually, is, with all manifested nature, the vehicle (*a*)
of the breath of One Universal Principle, in its primal differentiation; and
(*b*) of the countless "breaths" proceeding from that One BREATH in its
secondary and further differentiations, as Nature with its many *mankinds*

proceeds downwards toward the planes that are ever increasing in materiality. The primary Breath informs the higher Hierarchies; the secondary — the lower, on the constantly descending planes.

We have here in brief compass not only the outline of the hierarchical teaching, but also of the entire building of the kosmos which, repeated in the small, means likewise the building of the microcosm or man.

You will remember that at our last meeting we discussed, more or less briefly on account of the shortness of the time, the question of the nature of space, and what space was, and what space was not. We endeavored to point out that space, in the ordinary conception of things, means a receptacle or a container; in other words, it usually means *place*. Space is used almost synonymously with place; but this is not the use which is authorized or taught in the esoteric teachings, wherein it is shown that space is the illimitable series of hierarchies, which do not merely fill, but which *are* the boundless All, beginningless and endless; and that space, as the old Greeks put it, was an endless Fullness, endless and beginningless, and they called it the pleroma, or the Fullness; one universal life, one heart, so to say, pulsating or beating throughout.

We also spoke of — and please mark this carefully — the spaces of space, the inwards of space, the inward parts, bearing to space the same relation that man's own inner principles bear to his outer vehicle.

Now then, tonight we are going to execute an apparently complete right-about-face; after thus having pointed out in former studies what space was considered to be in certain branches of the ancient wisdom, as among the Stoics, and among the Brahmans, and in other schools of thought alluded to merely, we shall now take up very briefly likewise the manner in which space is looked upon more particularly by our Esoteric School, and especially by the holders of the esoteric doctrines of Gautama the Buddha.

We are now going to say, and prove, that the secret doctrine of the ages is above everything else a unifier; that we are learning, we are beginning to understand, a series of doctrines which give us the keys to the great religions of the past ages; and that these keys are universal in their proper application, each depending solely upon the inner capacities of the individual as to how much he may gain by turning a key once around, or twice, or three times, mayhap even seven times.

There is a doctrine of the Northern Buddhism — and we choose it in order to illustrate the esoteric teachings regarding space — called the doctrine of the Void, the doctrine of the Empty, likewise found in other schools in past times, such as were illustrated by the Greek Atomists, Democritus, Leucippus, and Epicurus, and by the great Roman poet Lucretius; and even spoken of by some of the Stoical philosophers, who otherwise taught the doctrine of the Fullness. We have an illustration here that may be a lesson to us, as will appear later on this evening, that things which may seem to be or form a contradiction in *The Secret Doctrine,* or elsewhere in our teachings, are not really contradictions, though they may be paradoxes. A paradox, please understand, is a statement which appears to be or contain a contradiction, but which actually is not one.

The word used in the Buddhist Sanskrit writings to describe this Emptiness is śūnyatā. *Śūnya* means "empty" or "void." The *tā* is the same grammatical suffix in Sanskrit as *tas* is in the Latin, *unitas, trinitas, vacuitas,* and is found in English as the *ty* in eternity, or unity, or vacuity, and so forth: therefore śūnyatā is to be translated "vacuity."

These Buddhist philosophers teach that the only reality, the only fundamental thing, so to say, of being, is the illimitable Void. From it in the beginning, or in time, springs forth a kosmos, or spring forth the universes; and to it they return when their cycle of manifestation is ended. This doctrine of the Void is of a far more spiritual nature than the doctrine of the Fullness. It is much more difficult to understand than the latter, because our European minds are not trained to the thinking required easily to understand thoughts such as these. We can much more easily, much more quickly, comprehend and understand the Fullness of things, than we can the thought that out from the illimitable and perfect Void spring into life all the infinite manifestations of kosmic being; and that back into the Void they sink again when their life cycle is run. In other words, our minds find it easier to understand the mystical and the religious rather than the truly philosophic and the truly scientific. Yet this doctrine of the Void was taught by the grandest intellect, the most titanic spiritual power, known to mankind in the annals of recorded and unrecorded history; I mean by him whom we call the Lord Buddha, Gautama Śākyamuni.

This does not mean that we are Buddhists, as has been pointed out in former studies; but the doctrines which the Buddha taught are also ours, when we apply to them the key which we have. You will remember that two kinds of doctrine were taught by the Buddha, i.e., the doctrine of the eye, very faithfully preserved by the Southern school of Ceylon, Burma, Siam, and so forth; and what is called the doctrine of the heart, that is, the hid doctrine, the Mystery-doctrine; respectively so called because the eye can see outward or visible things; but the heart is not seen, and in it, according to the old thought, flow the fountains of life. This doctrine of the heart is the esoteric wisdom, the unseen part of the teaching, its core or heart, that which is not given out to all.

Practically all the religions and philosophies of the Occident, even in Greek and Roman times, have preferred to demonstrate their tenets on the background, or on the foundation, of the doctrine of the Fullness; i.e., that the universe is infinitely full, and that this fullness is composed of infinite multitudes of beings. Now *that doctrine is true* — we repeat it emphatically; but likewise is truer still the doctrine of the Void. No contradiction exists here, as will be shown.

What do we mean when we speak of the Void, then? The doctrine of the Void means, or rather can be illustrated by, two things. When we look into what people popularly call the infinitudes of space, what do we see? We see what to us is emptiness. But this so-called ether (these ethery spaces), even according to the theories recently taught by our modern scientists, is more rigid than steel, denser than our densest matter; and the hard and dense material stuff that we know on this earth, the hard rocks, the harder metals, etc., are like floating foam, foamy bubbles, holes, as it were, floating in and on the infinite vast expanses of the kosmic Void.

The other way by which to approach our subject is the following: What is that which is not matter? Spirit. Can you put spirit into a container? Can it be encompassed or measured? No. Why not? Because it cannot be contained, in our sense of the word. It, to us, is emptiness, void. It is that which infills the vast ethery spaces, and it is merely the feebleness of our senses and the weakness of our understanding causing us to live in the external, which make us foolishly to believe that this which we see is the *real*, and that the so-called ethery spaces are unreal or empty in the popular sense.

The Void, then, is the *higher planes* of the boundless All; that which to us is void, and which therefore was so expressed by the ancient philosophers — teaching as they did the usual sort of men, they used simple language so that men could more easily understand, just exactly as in the case of the much misunderstood geocentric system so much mocked at by our wise modern natural philosophers. And yet, is it not true that every point in space is its center? Why, the idea is a common thought among thinking men. Even the rather orthodox French philosopher Pascal, copying an ancient Greek figure of expression, says that space or infinity is that which has its center everywhere, and its circumference nowhere.

Naturally, then, the ancients looked upon our earth as the center of space, and so would the inhabitants of Venus, or of Mars, or of Jupiter, or of the Moon, or of the Sun, or of any other body or point in space. They spoke and taught anthropocentrically, as pointed out in one of our earlier studies, i.e., from the human standpoint of comprehension.

And likewise — and this is a passing thought — when our own ancient esoteric philosophers spoke of the planets, spoke of Venus, or of Mars, for instance, as a "constellation," they knew perfectly well what they were saying, and they did not speak in ignorance. Why did they speak of a planet as a constellation, which in ordinary astronomical terminology or parlance means a collection or a gathering of stars? Because every one of the visible planets we see is but one of seven, six of them invisible to our physical eyes, the seven forming a planetary chain. And, furthermore, these planetary chains are composed of seven distinct and separate globular bodies, forming, to the eye of the seer, a true constellation; and furthermore still, each one of these seven globes has fourteen different lokas (or rather seven lokas and seven talas) or "worlds" attached to it, making thus, counting all the seven globes, 49 worlds or planes or lokas and 49 talas. As hinted at in our former two or three studies, where we spoke of the life-wave coming down and passing through the seven elements of nature, we implied that the life-wave formed and built in each one of the seven elements its appropriate habitat or habitation. Each one of these seven globes or spheres is built for the development of one of the seven principles of man; and each one of these seven globes has its own seven subprinciples or subelements to boot; precisely as the interior nature of man has built corresponding upādhis or vehicles as his own seven subprinciples in each one of his seven greater principles, therefore 49; and as each principle is bipolar, there are $49 \times 2 = 98$ conditions or states all told. Each principle of kosmos or of man must have its chance for manifestation in its own "home" or element, in its own vibratory surroundings, in its own particular magnetic sphere; and a proper understanding of all this can be obtained in no other way than by following the hierarchical evolutionary course of the great titanic intellects and spirits which govern our kosmos.

The doctrine of the Void, then, is actually identic with the doctrine of the Fullness. There is a distinction, however, and this distinction is, as pointed out, that the doctrine of the Void is the more spiritual of the two, and treats of the upper or superior nature of the kosmos, of the inwards and the yet more inwards and of the still more inwards, infinitely, of the spaces of space; whereas the doctrine of the Fullness treats of the kosmoi, the kosmoses, as they are *in manifestation*. But the same thought, precisely the same idea, lies back of both doctrines.

This opens the avenue for a further brief explanation of what was pointed out in our last study or two. Some perhaps may have thought that there was a radical difference between the *principles* of man and the *elements* of man, or the *principles* of space and the *elements* of space. The difference is not radical; it does not go to the root of the case. But there is a distinction. Fundamentally the elements and the principles are one. As explained before, force and matter are essentially one. Spirit and substance are essentially one. Spirit may be called etherealized matter, or matter crystallized spirit, but the latter is the better form of expression. It is permissible to make a distinction between a force and its material vehicle, its material self, so to say.

The seven great elements of the kosmos are the vehicles of the seven great forces of the kosmos, and those seven great forces are the principles of the kosmos; hence, the seven great elements in which they work are the vehicles of the kosmic principles. The principles are the energy-consciousness side, and the elements are the matter-prakriti side of being. There is the sole distinction. But, as said, there is no radical difference between them. It is rather a distinction of states or conditions. A force, however spiritual it may be, is matter to a still higher force. Matter concreted, as we may think it to be, is force to a matter inferior to it. The explanation of the paradox lies in pointing out the relationship of the planes of being each to each, as these work, or are worked upon, in the great kosmic Void-Fullness.

We would like to point out further that in speaking of principles and elements as is here done — the seven principles and elements of man may be instanced — the teaching as above given is accurate in every particular. The point to remember is that these so-called seven principles of man or of the kosmos, considered as descriptive words, are *generalizing* terms. You could not, for instance, separate man into seven naturally distinct pieces and lock each piece into a separate receptacle. And why? Because these seven principles are to be thought of much as if we were to speak of *consciousness* and *force* and *matter* and *energy* and *element*, etc. They are generalizing terms. They are the consciousness-substance, the matter-force, of the boundless All in which man moves, and lives, and has his being. Great intellects of the past have analyzed this matter-force or spirit-substance and have shown that it consists *in manifestation* of seven apparently discrete, seven separate, parts, which yet *essentially are one* — the One Life, universal and boundless. They are, first, the self; then the vehicle of the self, the vehicle or fountain of pure impersonal individuality. Then, third, the capacity for personal or limited thought, egoity; then the principle of "hate and love" or "attraction and repulsion" in the kosmos or in man, called kāma. Then, fifth, the vitality or life principle, derived directly from the first;

and then, sixth and seventh, the astral and physical bodies, vehicles.

Now you see that these are *general* principles of being. But when we undertake to analyze man more particularly, for purposes of accurate esoteric study, we shall find, when we come to that part of our investigations, that we shall have to be far more particular in the terms we use if we are to get a proper understanding of what man is, how he is built, his relationship to other beings in the kosmos, why he evolves as he does, and his final destiny. The greatest questions of the spirit-side of nature, the greatest questions of psychology, the great problem of psychophysical evolution, are bound up in just this thought that we have here enunciated.

Our time is so short at any one of our meetings that we can do little more in that time than briefly hint at certain things, taking them up at later meetings for further consideration. But mark you, it is better so. Such was always the method of the ancient schools. Never did they teach according to our modern boasted system of turning and twisting and hammering at a subject until the life went out of it, and the brains of their pupils wearied and became set in mental molds. This brain-mind method has no element of inspiration in it whatsoever. That method cripples the thinking entity. On the contrary, the ancient teaching was by proper suggestion, making the disciple to do his thinking for himself, on a hint or at an allusion, making his mind to catch the holy fires of inspiration, so that he should lighten up his own inner temple with the thoughts that his own divine monad infused or inspired into him. Parables, hints, suggestions, were the teacher's method; and then always, at a later date, catching up the thought again, opening the door a little wider, raising the veil of Isis a trifle more, rendering help in this manner.

Thus, then, we have seen that the elements and the principles are essentially one, dual only in manifestation. We have seen that the principles of nature and of man are the energy-consciousness side of nature and of man; and that the elements in the kosmos or in man are the matter-prakriti side of nature and of man. But remember always that force and matter, spirit and substance, consciousness and its vehicle or upādhi, are essentially one. As said before, a force or a spiritual energy is concreted matter to another one diviner than it; and the concreted matter of our plane is a whirling cyclone of force to the matter inferior to it. A fact, this, which our scientists are beginning to realize, as shown in their teaching of the whirling electrons, tiny bodies, whirling in the molecular aggregate called the physical atom — a miniature solar system, they say. A true thought that, and inspired.

Remember that śūnyatā, called the doctrine of the Void, refers to the spiritual side of being, and that the doctrine of the pleroma, the doctrine of the Fullness, refers to the matter-prakriti side of being, the side of manifestation, which passes away when the great manvantara is finished.

But remember also, as said several times already this evening, that when we speak of substance or of spirit, of force or of matter, of purusha or of prakriti — to use the Brahmanical Sānkhya terms — it is only by way of voicing the things which we have learned through our various inner faculties and outer senses about the kosmos, and that fundamentally these respective pairs are one. Spirit and substance or matter are one, and both will sink back again into the vast illimitable Void of the unbounded divinity when the time of universal pralaya comes. Remember the ancient mystic saying that the disciple should learn to know the meaning of the statement: the fullness of the seeming void, and the voidness of the seeming full.

Now this "seeming full" of matter is truly śūnya, emptiness, mostly holes, so to say. Śūnya is the ancient Brahmanical doctrine of māyā, a doctrine of the Vedanta, called the "end of the Veda," because it is claimed to be the perfection or end of the teaching concerning the esoteric side of the Vedic poems. *Māyā* means "illusion." Not that the manifested kosmos does not exist; it does exist, or it could not be or provide an illusion. The illusion consists in not properly understanding it. If matter or substance (or nature, prakriti) did not exist, you might as well say that spirit does not exist, because they are fundamentally one. The truth is that matter is not the substantial, infinite element, the *essence of reality*, which our Western minds — untaught and undisciplined in these ideas — think it is, merely because it seems solid to us and therefore "real." It is illusion because it is deceptive; and actually, as the Buddhists taught, thereby teaching the same thought as the Brahmanical Adwaita-Vedanta, śūnyatā is the doctrine of emptiness, of the elemental vacuity of the manifested universe, and hence is the doctrine of māyā, illusion: illusory because *unreal.*

Even the modern natural philosophers, the physicists, the chemists, now are beginning to understand that this so-called apparent universe is mostly vacuity. They have never yet been able to find out what matter really is; it is a figment of the scientific imagination, as commonly explained, and all they know about it is simply what their own intuitions and scientific deductions have told them: that back of the seeming, back of the appearances, there is *something* concerning which they say — "We are learning more about it. What it really is, *we do not know!*"

As a final thought tonight, let me point out that although we have been speaking during recent meetings of the gods, monads, souls, atoms, bodies, which still form our present subject of study, we have not yet finished it by any means; we have barely entered upon it. Using the term gods, we use a term which is familiar. It is a good term, a truthful term; there is no reason to reject it; but yet it is not the term used in our esoteric system. Our esoteric Tibetan teachings use for it the expression dhyāni-buddhas, and the lower side of the god-plane where they belong is occupied by the dhyāni-chohans. *Dhyāni,* a Sanskrit word adopted into the Tibetan terminology, means "meditation" or "contemplation"; therefore the former expression means "buddhas of meditation" or of contemplation; and the latter means "lords of contemplation" or of meditation. The latter term, however, is not infrequently used to include both classes. In the Mystic Greek system, these gods, these dhyāni-buddhas, were called logoi, logoses. The word *logos* is a Greek vocable meaning "word." It also has a derivative meaning given as "reason." Why? Because the Greek philosophers saw that when a man thinks and desires to express his thought, to convey the thought to another, he must use *words.* The word is the carrier of the thought over to another mind: and from this simple illustration the word *logos,* meaning "word," was adopted into the philosophic language and into the religious language (and later into Christianity), to mean that power or energy or entity which carries the divine thought over to lower planes — carried over from the plane above or behind it, from the intellect or mind behind it, from the consciousness behind it, to lower planes. In our case, the monads occupy this second or lower plane.

In conclusion, I desire to translate from the original Greek the first five verses of the Christian Gospel ascribed to the disciple whom Jesus is said to have especially loved, John, called John the Divine, divine meaning here theologian. He was thus called theologian, we must suppose, because he was the only one of the four writers of the four accepted Gospels who wrote anything resembling in style or in matter the fine, lofty, theological teachings belonging to the Neoplatonic or Neopythagorean school — an unintended compliment to the latter. These quasi-pagan teachings are found in the first part only of the Gospel according to John. They are as follows — and I would that I had time more fully to explain them than the necessarily brief commentary on them that I can make this evening:

1. In the beginning was the logos, and the logos was towards god, and the logos was god.
2. This [the logos] was in the beginning towards god.

I am making my own translation; the so-called Authorized Version is a literary farce, translated to suit the monotheistic prejudices of the Christian exegetes; and the Revised Version is no better.

3. All things were generated through it, . . .

The Greek word *egeneto*, here translated "generated," could likewise be translated "came into being." The English word generated itself comes from the same Aryan root. I read again:

3. All things were generated through it, and without it not a single thing was generated [came into being].
4. That which was generated in it was life, and the life was the light of men.
5. And the light shines in the shadow, and the shadow took it not up.

Don't you see our teachings alluded to there; the very words used in the ancient doctrine, ay, even from the Book of Dzyan, the "spirit and its wing," the "wing and its shadow"? *Shadow* is an ancient Mystery-term meaning "vehicle" or "body" as was pointed out in a recent study, in a quotation read from a chapter of *The Desātīr* called "The Book of Shet, the Prophet Zirtūsht," or Zoroaster. There the word shadow was used in exactly the same sense.

Note the thought here: in the beginning of our manifested universe existed the logos, being the first entity or thing brought into manifestation in the beginning; and this logos was *towards* god. The Greek word here translated "towards" is *pros*, meaning motion towards a thing. Of course, the logos sprang from the spirit divine, god, but the attempt here in this Gospel is to emphasize the thought that its natural aspirations were towards its parent-fountain. A great secret of occultism lies in this thought. "As a man thinketh, *so is he*," says in substance a Hebrew writing, Proverbs, thereby uttering a profound truth. Man follows infallibly the bent of his nature, his desire. He is magnetically drawn towards that which his heart longs for, and *that which he wants he gets;* if he wants heaven he will get it; and if he wants hell, he will be magnetically drawn to spheres infernal. This, in brief expression, is an outline of the whole mystery of so-called karmic fruits, of heaven and of hell — and much more which we must here leave unsaid.

"And the logos was towards god" — aspiring towards its own divine source; and this god was swabhavat, Father-Mother; not swabhāva, which is an entirely different thing. As pointed out before, swabhavat is what certain Asiatic and other schools call Father-Mother, the great Vacuity, śūnya, the great Emptiness, ākāśa in Hindu writings, which is the great Void *to us*, but the great Fullness in another sense. What we call the great Fullness is the manifested universe flowing forth in wondrous procession from the Void, or swabhavat, or Father-Mother, or mahāśūnya, or ākāśa, various names for the same thing.

Verse 2. "This was in the beginning towards god." So anxious was the writer of this Gospel to point out that the logos originated in the beginning, and that the aspiration of the logos was towards its parent-source, that he must needs repeat it once again.

Verse 3. "All things were generated through it," that is, *came into being* through it. This shows that it is the demiurgus or world fashioner which was in the writer's mind, and this logos is on the third lower plane only of manifestation, on the third kosmic plane; as we say, the third logos from above, which is the manifest logos or the world maker, the world artificer. The writer continues: "And without it not a single thing was generated." So anxious, so desirous, was he to show that there was no creating of souls or worlds or anything else by an extra-kosmic god, that he has to point out again here that it was the logos, the kosmic word, carrying its force down from its parent, that *from itself* generated things, cast them forth, projected them, evolved them, exactly as we have been pointing out in our recent meetings as being the course or method of manifestation. And these things were the monads, the atoms, the souls, and all the rest.

The writer continues, changing the thought-type somewhat, for fear that it will be thought that this generation of the beings on so high a plane is the mere matter and gross physical things which we see around us: "That which was generated in it [in the logos] was life" — not stones, trees, stars, planets, etc., men, and other things, but *life*. And the life — mark this — "was the light of men," the spiritual light illuminating mankind; in other words, man's higher nature, or verily our own inner logos, our own "inner god," our own inner Christos.

And this logos, the third or manifest logos, is but the vehicle of a logos still higher than itself. During the processes of generating or bringing forth all these things which are less than itself, every single step brings forth *light*, for light is one of the first manifestations of the creative activity — remember, *creation* in its original sense means *formation*. This light of the third kosmic plane is daivīprakriti. We borrow the word from the Vedanta of Hindustan; it means "shining or divine prakriti," of which ākāśa or swabhavat is the "crown." Swabhavat or ākāśa is the first manifest kosmic element or manifestation of prakriti, or essential nature itself. Remember that there are seven natures, one within the other; seven elements; seven kosmic forces. "And the life was the light of mankind" — our own higher nature.

And the last verse: "And the light shines in the shadow" —

which, as regards man, is its vehicles or our higher minds. "And the shadow took it not up," i.e., primordial man had as yet evolved no vehicle or mind fit to "take it up" or in.

This thought here enables the writer of this Gnostic Gospel — Gnostic at least in the first part thereof — to introduce his sectarian teachings: "There was a man who was sent from God, whose name was John," to preach the gospel of Jesus Christ, the human logos, the savior of mankind. He, Jesus Christ, was this light, who "became flesh" (!) and came into the world as the "light of men." Tragic! A beautiful teaching of the ancient Mystery-religion from the beginning of time is here taken and adapted, and applied — as pointed out in a previous study — to a mere Mystery-figure, a mere type-figure of the ancient Mysteries. Not that Jesus did not ever live; a man, a Hebrew rabbi if you like, called Jesus, did live; but the Christos of whom the Christian Gospels write is a type-figure of the Mysteries, but much and sadly distorted.

THIRTY-FIVE

OCCULTISM AND THE MYSTERY SCHOOLS. SEVEN DEGREES OF
INITIATION: MAN BECOMES A GOD. SEVEN KOSMIC PLANES:
OUR PLANETARY CHAIN OF SEVEN GLOBES ON THE FOUR
LOWER PLANES — THE PASSAGE OF THE
LIFE-WAVE THERETHROUGH.

The world — meaning that of individual existences — is full of those latent
meanings and deep purposes which underlie all the phenomena of the Universe, and Occult Sciences — i.e., *reason* elevated to supersensuous Wisdom —
can alone furnish the key wherewith to unlock them to the intellect. Believe
me, there comes a moment in the life of an adept, when the hardships he has
passed through are a thousandfold rewarded. In order to acquire further
knowledge, he has no more to go through a minute and slow process of investigation and comparison of various objects, but is accorded an instantaneous,
implicit insight into every first truth. Having passed that stage of philosophy
which maintains that all fundamental truths have sprung from a blind impulse — . . . ; the adept sees and feels and lives in the very source of all
fundamental truths — the Universal Spiritual Essence of Nature, SHIVA the
Creator, the Destroyer, and the Regenerator.
— *The Mahatma Letters*, p. 241

I say again then. It is he alone who has the love of humanity at heart, who is
capable of grasping thoroughly the idea of a regenerating practical Brotherhood who is entitled to the possession of our secrets. He alone, such a man —
will never misuse his powers, as there will be no fear that he should turn them
to selfish ends. A man who places not the good of mankind above his own good
is not worthy of becoming our *chela* — he is not worthy of becoming higher in
knowledge than his neighbor. — Ibid., p. 252

There is but one general law of life, but innumerable laws qualify and deter-
mine the myriads of forms perceived and of sounds heard. — Ibid., p. 255

THE SEARCH for truth is the noblest aim that man can
pursue. The original principles of being were uncovered
ages upon ages agone, and were coordinated into a complete and marvelous system. Upon that wonderful system as
a basis, the teachers of ancient times laid the foundations of the
superstructures of the various philosophic and religious systems

which have come down to us in the world's literatures as now extant. These systems contain in greater or less degree fundamental truths of being, the study of which in our own time is called occultism — the science of the kosmos and of man as a part thereof; telling us of the origin, the nature, and the destiny of the universe and of man, a part thereof. The Mystery Schools of antiquity formed the inner focus of the ancient thought, and the doctrines there studied were called the heart doctrine, because they represented the doctrines that were hid; and the various philosophies that they expounded in public were called the eye doctrine, because they were the doctrines in exoteric phrasing of the things that were seen and not the things that were hid. The heart doctrine comprised the solutions of the enigmas of being, and these solutions were put forth in exoteric form under the guise of allegory and in mythological treatment, and formed the eye doctrine, or the exoteric religions or philosophies.

But all these ancient philosophies were founded on wonderful and sublime truths, compared with which the philosophies of modern Europe are mere verbiage, little more than fine words. The doctrines comprised in occultism treat, as said, of the real nature, origin, and destiny of the kosmos and man. These Mystery Schools taught *causal things,* and their effects in life; they taught of the most intimate and profound relations of the elementary beings, whatever their degree in the kosmos, to each other. They taught man that the way to a complete understanding of the mysteries of being was by searching within; that no man could understand a truth properly which merely entered his ears, without having developed in himself also first the capacity, the inner faculty, of comprehension; and it was the development of this inner faculty of comprehension or understanding that was the main aim of the schools of initiation.

The whole effort, then, of these initiating schools was to make man *know* himself. Why? Because the inmost essence of man is rooted in the inmost essences of the universe, and by following the small, age-old path, as the Upanishads said, which lies within man himself, and to which Jesus alluded when he said, "I am the way, the truth, and the life" — by following that small, old path inwards, man could climb step by step inwards or "upwards," inwards and inwards forever, constantly expanding into greater fields of consciousness. And this evolving of the inner man is achieved through the evocation of the spiritual powers latent in man's higher nature. It is, in fact, the uniting man's soul to his divine monad, his inner god.

As pointed out in former studies, three were the states, after the fourth degree of initiation, which the initiant or candidate must win: first came the theophanic mystery, which is the appearance at the solemn moment of initiation of man's own inner god to himself; and this holy presence was called by the Greeks *theophany*, "the appearance of a god," i.e., man's own higher self to himself. And while in the average candidate this sublime moment of intellectual ecstasis and high vision lasted but a short time, with further spiritual progress of the candidate the theophanic communion became more enduring and lasting, until finally, ultimately, man knew himself, not merely as the offspring spiritually of his own inner god, but as that inner god itself, in his essential being.

That was the first step, the first realization. The second came in what the Greeks called *theopneusty*, which is a Greek compound word meaning "the inbreathing of a god," and in which man not merely was conscious by inner senses, and outer senses even, of his inner divinity, but he felt the inspiration flowing through his intellectual and spiritual veins, as it were — felt the inbreathing from his own inner god and became, thus, inspired, the very word inspiration meaning "inbreathing." With the passing of time and the greater purification of the soul-vehicle, which is man himself, this inbreathing or inspiration became permanent.

Finally, there came at the seventh initiation the most sublime mystery of all, called *theopathy* by the Greeks, meaning "the suffering a god" — a technical term; that is to say, not that the god suffered, but that the initiant, the candidate, suffered himself to become, abandoned himself fully to be, a truly selfless channel of communication of his own inner god, his own higher self; he became lost as it were in the greater self of his own higher self. This personal self became absorbed, transmuted, and its lower characteristics vanished away like a cloud before the sun; and with the passing of time and the greater cleansing of the vehicle, the soul, the personal man, became blended utterly with his own inner god. And that was theopathy.

Now the various degrees of initiation in the ancient Mystery Schools comprised, first, three degrees, which were those of teaching. With the fourth began the personal experience; that is to say, the teaching was continued, but in addition to that the initiant, the candidate, was made to *be*, to *become*, that which before he was taught of, told about; because the only way utterly to know a thing, the only way utterly to understand a thing, is to become it.

There is vastly more in this thought than appears on the surface, and more than we have time this evening to enter into. But let it remain in your minds. And the teaching was continued with every step higher, up to the seventh, ay, even up to the tenth degree. We stop at the seventh, because the three highest degrees are far beyond our comprehension, and pertain only, we are told, to the highest of the Masters.

Teaching continued even up to the seventh initiation, coordinately with the self-experiencing, the self-becoming; and in this way man not merely knew, but felt himself, realized that he was, one with the kosmos, not merely its offspring and child in a detached manner, but verily, in every sense of the word, it itself. Then came the realization of that kosmic self, the ātman, that which is the same in you and me, in every dweller on this globe, and in every dweller in every one of the planetary or stellar bodies in space; the feeling, the sense, the knowledge, "I am." That which separates us is the feeling of "I am *I*," and "you are *you*"; and this is the action of the ego, egoism.

Yet, mystery of mysteries, know this: it is only through the passing across of egoity into universality that man becomes a god. If there were not the egoic principle enlarged and purified to contain it and to understand it, there could be no such thing as the Hierarchy of Compassion, there could be no such thing as the luminous arc. It remains with each one of us so to live the life, so to purify his inner sheaths of being, so to transmute his soul-essence, that they may become fit channels of communication between his own inner god and himself. When man has accomplished that, he becomes omniscient for our kosmic hierarchy;

omniscient, for all knowledge of it and in it is his. And why? Because his essence of consciousness, the egoic essence, has become united through his own inner god with the universal plane, the ātmic plane; and knowledge and wisdom then stream through him as the sun-rays stream through the atmosphere.

We have read from *The Secret Doctrine* at three or four former meetings a paragraph which we shall repeat tonight, in volume II, on page 492, as follows:

> The Secret Doctrine points out, as a self-evident fact, that Mankind, collectively and individually, is, with all manifested nature, the vehicle (*a*) of the breath of One Universal Principle, in its primal differentiation; and (*b*) of the countless "breaths" proceeding from that One Breath in its secondary and further differentiations, as Nature with its many *mankinds* [please note that] proceeds downwards toward the planes that are ever increasing in materiality. The primary Breath informs the higher Hierarchies; the secondary — the lower, on the constantly descending planes.

We have there, comprised in brief compass as said before, the entire outline of the study which we have been pursuing this winter; and at a later moment this evening, or perhaps at our next meeting, we shall go into this question of the various mankinds spoken of. There is involved in this a great and wondrous mystery. Let me merely say at the present moment that the humanity of which we form a part on earth today, that is to say, the particular life-wave which we call mankind or humanity or human beings, is not the sole and only life-stream of intelligent egos traversing the various rounds of evolution on our planetary chain. There are six others, all evolving contemporaneously with us, some ahead of us, and some behind us; and they are evolving in the various lokas or talas which we shall try further to elucidate this evening. A most difficult subject this, but one which we shall do our best to explain, because it is absolutely necessary, even in small degree, in order properly to understand the fundamental questions of the evolution of the evolving ego. Evolution is a subject which is interesting the world very much at the present time, and which our scientists limit, of course, merely to the physical world, more especially as concerns man and the beasts, which are two stirpes (to use the Latin word) only of the vastly numerous families of evolving beings, some ahead of us and some behind.

Now you will remember that at our last two or three meetings we spoke of the principles and elements of the kosmos. The elements form thereof the vehicular, or bearer, or carrier side; and the principles form the energy-consciousness side; and we shall this evening limit our study (with mere allusions to human elements and principles) to the kosmic planes, because our present endeavor is to get a clear picture, as clear as possible at the present time, of what we mean when we speak of kosmic planes, of the seven globes of the planetary chain, and of the rounds.

It is most interesting to note that these subjects, which so many people have misunderstood to be merely interesting questions for intellectual entertainment, are intimately involved with the moral, and with the spiritual, nature of man; and no man can have a proper comprehension of ethics and morals without understanding his proper place in the universe: his origin, his nature, and his destiny. What morals need in Occidental thought is a foundation based on science and philosophy. Morals are not something which is up in the air; they are not something which man must merely live by — they are that, indeed, but they are much more. The moral sense springs from man's spiritual consciousness, and no man — and we lay it down positively — can really understand a theosophical doctrine from the intellectual standpoint only and without having the spiritual light upon it. And that light, that spiritual light, manifests in man's intellectual realm of thought as his instinctive moral sense, that which the great German philosopher Kant spoke of as the one thing which held him firmly to the belief that our universe was something more than mere force and matter.

Remember first, that, as pointed out in the Upanishads and in the several wonderful Brahmanical philosophies, in ancient Greek thought, in Christianity, and preeminently in our own teachings — throughout the world, in fact, in the various ancient philosophies and religions — when we speak of divine things we must understand that *we also are a part thereof,* and that even the physical world itself, the material world itself, is but the garment of the divine; imperfect, because it is builded by imperfect *because evolving* hierarchies, by imperfect entities, of which we also are examples. Remember what Goethe says, in his *Faust:*

Thus, at the roaring loom of Time I ply,
And weave for God the garment thou see'st Him by.

And as Paul, the Christian, said, "In It we live and move and have our being."

Search into yourselves. The teachings given out in these studies are the keys. Prove them; examine the literatures of the world; search all things; and, as Paul said (speaking as an initiate), retain that which is good, retain that which you *know to be true*.

Seven, then, are the elements of kosmos; seven, then, are its principles, working through those seven elements. From the consciousness-side they are consciousness on the one hand, vehicle on the other. From the substantial side they are force on the one hand, and matter on the other. Let us illustrate this first of all by seven horizontal, parallel lines, to represent the elements and principles of kosmos.

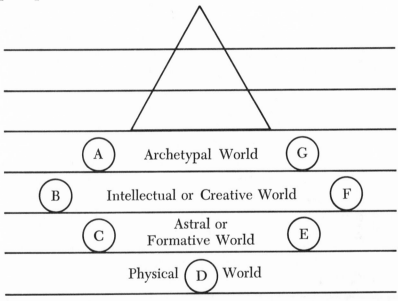

Please remember that this figure is a diagram. The elements, the principles, of the kosmos are not really one above another, like a series of steps, or like the rungs of a ladder. This figure is a diagram only, that is, it is a *symbol*. The elements of the kosmos, the principles of the kosmos, the spheres of the kosmos, are *within* each other, the most spiritual being the inmost. But this being impossible in representation on a plane surface, we have to figurate the idea schematically, diagrammatically, paradigmatically. Therefore this figure merely shows first, that there are seven planes in kosmos. Let us next represent the evolving and originating life forces, the gods and the intelligences of the three higher planes, by a triangle, using the old Platonic and Pythagorean symbol — a beautiful symbol — because it shows and suggests the originating point, the kosmic point, the seed, from which all divine things spring; and which shows the apex of the triangle also vanishing, as it were, through the highest plane, through a laya-center, a neutral center, a nirvana of all things less or lower than it, vanishing more inward into something higher. Exactly as a seed, an acorn, for instance, will bring forth an oak, in its turn shedding its harvest of acorns, so the kosmic seed sends forth from itself these hosts of hierarchies of beings, themselves producing other lower hosts on the downward scale. Let us then represent this process by a triangle.

The four lower planes of the figure, which are the four lower *kosmic* planes, represent all the states that man can reach to in his present period of development. Our own ātmic essence springs forth from the fourth kosmic plane, counting downwards. Further, let us next represent our planetary chain in the following manner, that is to say, by inscribing circles, seven of them, on these planes, two on each plane, with the exception of the lowest plane where we inscribe only one circle, representing our own globe Terra. Then, we number these circles respectively, beginning with the left and going downwards, A, B, C, D; and then going upwards, E, F, and G. Please note that there are two circles or globes on each plane, with the exception of globe D, our own. These seven "planes" are really the seven kosmic elements respectively.

It is extremely tempting to suppose, or to think, that each one of these seven globes has a respective habitat or locus or place on or in each one of the kosmic elements, but it is not so. That idea is what we call a false analogy, a tempting suggestion leading the mind astray.

Now, then, when we speak of the seven elements of the kosmos, we mean by elements exactly what the ancients meant, which they described by verbal symbols. They spoke of four usually, occasionally of five, and they were the same all over the world — earth, water, air, fire; sometimes a fifth, aether, was mentioned; but these were certainly not the material earth, water, air, or fire that we know. These things of earth were chosen because they symbolized, by reason of certain attributes inherent in them, the four planes or rather elements of nature on which the seven globes of our planetary chain live and move and have their being. We can say that *earth* represented kosmic matter, concreted substance, the lowest element of all; and that *water* represented Chaos in the ancient sense — as the Hebrew Bible puts it, the "waters" of space over which brooded the Elohīm, the gods, mistranslated "God." And we can say that *air* is spirit. The very word *spiritus* in Latin means "breath," "wind," "air." And *fire* is the symbol of divine light, the first emanation of the kosmic Logos, which we call, adopting the Sanskrit-Buddhist term, *daivīprakriti*, "divine nature," "divine light," light being one of the first emanations in the beginning of the evolutionary processional period.

Therefore, when we speak of elements, we mean rather what the average European mind understands by "spheres of action," worlds: the world of kosmic matter, the world of Chaos, the spheres of spirit, and the world of the divine light or daivīprakriti.

The logoic world, which is to us the quasi-divine, the fourth kosmic plane, counting downwards, comprising the planetary globes A and G, let us then call the archetypal world, and we so write it in our diagram. The world beneath, comprising globes B and F, we will call the intellectual or creative world. The world below that, comprising globes C and E, we will call, if you please, the astral or formative world. And the lowest element or world of all, on which our sole globe is, our planet Terra, let us call the physical world.

You will here recognize at once what we have stated before in connection with the doctrines of the Qabbālāh — the four worlds that it teaches of. Those of you who have studied the Qabbālāh may remember that its world of emanations or archetypal world is called *atsīlōth;* then comes the second, the world called *berīah,* or creative, following downwards; and then the third world, called the world of formation, *yetsīrāh;* and finally the fourth or material world, which the Qabbalists called the world of shells, *qelippōth,* our world, because it is that of the most concreted matter, the shell holding all the others; like the shell of an egg, or the rind of a fruit, and so on, and also meaning something else in connection with kāma-loka, but we are not treating of that part of the subject tonight and merely mention it in passing. These worlds are, of course, our four kosmic elements.

Furthermore, please remember the next important thought. Each one of these seven kosmic elements, counting from the beginning, i.e., counting downwards, comprises in itself all the others which preceded it, of which it is an emanation. For instance, the first, the highest, emanates the second, below it, in which it reflects itself, to boot; yet this second nevertheless has its own swabhāva, its own essential nature or peculiar character-istic, but it also is the carrier or vehicle of the one above it, as just said. Next, these two emanate and reflect themselves into the third, which yet has its own essential nature, but nevertheless is the carrier or bearer of those above it; and similarly with the fourth or lowest world or element.

Every atom, even of the physical world, has everything in it of the boundless kosmos, latent or developed, as the case may be. Note the optimistic trend of thought in this.

Now, then, these four lower kosmic elements or planes comprise all of us, that is to say, all of us that we have so far developed. The summit of the archetypal or fourth kosmic plane is the element where the laya-center of our ātman is — our universal kosmic self. Through it stream the divine forces from above, which originate or rather are our seven principles, our seven elements of being, manifesting in the four lower kosmic elements which likewise form the seven ranges of prakriti or nature as we cognize them. You will remember that every kosmic element in itself is sub-divided into seven subelements, i.e., seven degrees of prakriti. So far as we are concerned, the seven subdegrees of prakriti or nature on each one of these four lower kosmic planes comprise the only degrees of prakriti of which we can at the present time have cognizance, because we have not yet evolved the faculties within us necessary to cognize the higher ones.

As a concluding thought tonight, you will remember from reading the teachings that H. P. Blavatsky gave us in her wonder work *The Secret Doctrine*, that the life-wave pursues an evolutionary course through these seven globes, passing from globe A, after finishing its evolutionary cycle on it, to globe B, finishing its cycle on B and passing to globe C, finishing its cycle on it and then passing on to globe D, and so around the chain, making what we call one round.

But we must be cautious in these matters and avoid leaping to conclusions. The above does not mean that only when everything is finished or perfected on globe A, we then jump to globe B. Not at all. Seven sublife-waves evolve on globe A. When the lowest (or the mineral) on globe A — remember that though it is a spiritual planet, yet the "mineral" of that spiritual planet is as dense and as gross to its inhabitants as our minerals are to us — has finished its development *for that one round,* it feels the impact or impulse of the incoming vegetable kingdom, and its surplus of life overflows into globe B; and when the beast kingdom in its turn impacts upon the vegetable, and when this latter has run its sevenfold course, the vegetable then in its turn overflows into globe B downwards, and the mineral in B passes on to globe C; and when the human world impulses into globe A, then the beast world begins to come down into globe B, the vegetable to pass into C, the mineral into D, and so on. This is the process during the first round; but beginning with the second round the process changes somewhat its order. But we reserve this for future studies.

There is an overflow of the surplus life forces, as it were, from every kingdom into the next globe; and this complicated process is followed (but changed, beginning with round 2) throughout all the rounds, throughout all the seven globes. When globe G, or the seventh, is reached, there ensues for the life-wave a nirvana, answering to the devachan or heaven period between two human incarnations on earth; and also between any two globes there is a smaller time of rest for the evolving life-wave.

This process alone is enough to set the minds of many people in bewilderment. It seems so complicated; in reality it is very simple. It needs only a little honest thought to understand it — half as much thought as most people give to the material things of life: what shall I eat, what shall I put on, what theater shall I go to, how shall I make money, and so forth.

We have spoken of lokas and talas. We shall touch upon that matter more fully at our next meeting. But remember this fact: each one of these globes is divided into fourteen different "worlds." I do not mean globes; I mean *conditions* or *states of matter*. For instance, water may be ice or steam, and yet may be water. Suppose that you had to explain to a man who had never seen ice, had seen merely water, what ice is; and after trying to do so he said: "The man raves; he is trying to tell me that water, the most fluid of things, under certain conditions may become cold stone."

Secondly, when we say worlds (we have to use words in order to give some idea of the meaning) we do not mean globes. A globe is globe A, or B, or C, or D, or E, or F, or G; but each one of these globes comprises or has seven lokas, or "places," or worlds, or conditions, or states, or kinds, of matter — subworlds, if you like; and also seven talas, making fourteen altogether. Please remember also that these fourteen (or these twice seven) worlds are not above each other like the steps in a stair. They are *within each other*, one more inward than another, not exactly like the skins of an onion, but each inner one is finer, more spiritual, more ethereal, than its next outer; and the most ethereal, the most spiritual of all, is the inmost.

Now these seven lokas on each globe are the fields of action of the ascending subwaves in the racial cycles; likewise, the various kinds of bodies, ethereal or physical or spiritual, or whatever else, that the race uses as it passes along the evolutionary cycles, correspond in texture and senses with the various lokas passed through, and the loka which the evolving entity senses is that particular loka or world correspondent to its bodies. And the talas are the same thing on the downward subwaves of the racial cycles. The lokas and talas are always working together, two by two, one of each, because matter is bipolar in manifestation on the globes; of the two (one loka and one tala), one is spiritually positive, attracting one way, and the other is spiritually negative, attracting the other way.

And, lastly, we point out that we are at the present time in one of these lokas and in one of these talas, and that there are six other humanities or life-waves evolving similarly to our own course: intelligent, thinking beings on our planet — I do not necessarily say on our globe D — evolving through these lokas and talas. How this thought stirs the imagination! If this process of evolution did not so take place, we say in conclusion, there could be no completely logical and satisfactory explanation of the phenomenon that the early writers upon theosophical subjects called "fifth rounders" and "sixth rounders."

THIRTY-SIX

INTERPENETRATING SPHERES OF BEING. LOKAS AND TALAS:
BIPOLAR KOSMICAL PRINCIPLES AND ELEMENTS.
THE "HERESY OF SEPARATENESS."

All things are implicated with one another, and the bond is holy; and there is hardly anything unconnected with any other thing. For things have been co-ordinated, and they combine to form the same universe (order). For there is one universe made up of all things, and one god who pervades all things, and one substance, and one law, (one) common reason in all intelligent animals, and one truth; if indeed there is also one perfection for all animals which are of the same stock and participate in the same reason.
— MARCUS AURELIUS, *Meditations*, 7, 9 (George Long, trans.)

Nature has linked all parts of her Empire together by subtle threads of magnetic sympathy, and, there is a mutual correlation even between a star and a man; . . .   — *The Mahatma Letters*, p. 267

If through the Hall of Wisdom, thou would'st reach the Vale of Bliss, Disciple, close fast thy senses against the great dire heresy of separateness that weans thee from the rest.   — *The Voice of the Silence*, pp. 8–9

IN THE JEWISH Talmud there is a quaint old story, full of the profound wisdom of the ancient teachers, about four candidates for wisdom. It tells how they entered into the Garden of Delights, a name which the Jews used, especially the Qabbalists, to designate the realm of occultism, of the occult sciences; and the names of these four candidates for wisdom were as follows: Ben Asai, Ben Zoma, Ahher, and Rabbi Aqiba. As the story goes, "Ben Asai looked — and lost his sight; Ben Zoma looked — and lost his reason. Ahher went into the Garden of Delights and committed depredations therein; but Rabbi Aqiba entered in peace and left in peace. And the Holy One, whose servants we are — blessed be his name — said: 'This old man is worthy of serving us with glory.'"

Here are the four general types of students of the ancient wisdom. Ben Asai, who lost his sight, was one who was attracted by the doctrines and teachings and, like another case mentioned in the Greek legends, looked upon the face of naked truth and was "blinded." He became, that is, a worse exotericist than he was before. He was unprepared, unready. He had forced his way into the place where he did not belong. And he incurred one of the penalties awaiting those who enter into the holy places with an unpure heart and an unprepared mind.

And Ben Zoma looked and lost his reason; he was one whose nature was so essentially selfish that he looked only for that which he himself might gain therefrom. And his nature being unsteady, weak, self-centered and selfish, he lost his "reason," that is to say, he became the slave instead of the master. You know the old medieval saying that the magician who evokes the so-called "spirits of the vasty deep," and is not in complete control of them, is made away with by them, which is a saying teaching the same doctrine that we teach of the utter necessity of spiritual preparation, moral preparedness. "For the pure in heart see God," and have naught to fear, which is the Christian method of expressing the same idea.

Ahher, who made depredations in the Garden, was one who had will power and daring, but likewise was he one who considered self first of all, and he misused the sacred sciences for self-advancement and personal gain, for position, and all the rest of it. He is the type of the black magician, as it is called. Such a one *destroys himself* by entering into a place for which he is not fitted, that is, Ahher who made "depredations"; and so likewise did Ben Zoma.

But Rabbi Aqiba, who entered in peace, and went out in peace, was the type of the man inwardly fully prepared and ready, whose nature was so purified by discipline, by *self*-discipline, so purified by self-forgetfulness and a recognition of the beauties of self-abnegation in the true sense, that through him could stream the rays coming from the divine heart of Being, from the spiritual sun.

Now, what does this allegory teach us? This parable shows us first, that in order to be faithful disciples, and, second, in order to gain that which we are supposed to gain, the first lesson for us is discipline, *self*-discipline, ethics. We continually recur in our studies to this point, because it is of the first importance. Every man thinks he is ethical and moral. Is he? Ask yourself what you or I would do under real temptation. The French have a rather cynical saying that "every man has his price." Is it true? If it is, then neither you nor I, not one of us, is fit to sit here this evening. Only when we have passed beyond the point where anything on earth can move us or sway our will, or buy us, then only are we fit to enter into the Garden of Delights, like the old man Rabbi Aqiba, who entered in peace and left in peace — a Master.

We open our study tonight by referring once more to the extract from the second volume of *The Secret Doctrine*, page 492, which we have read at several meetings, because around it circles the theme of our present study. Please note every word.

The Secret Doctrine points out, as a self-evident fact, that Mankind, collectively and individually, is, with all manifested nature, the vehicle (*a*) of the breath of One Universal Principle, in its primal differentiation; and (*b*) of the countless "breaths" proceeding from that One BREATH in its secondary and further differentiations, as Nature with its many *mankinds* proceeds downwards toward the planes that are ever increasing in materiality. The primary Breath informs the higher Hierarchies; the secondary — the lower, on the constantly descending planes.

We are going tonight to make a great step forward, to make a leap, as it were, over many things that might have been considered, such as the enormously important problems of death, and of the left-hand path, to mention two subjects only. But we are going to do our best (although we have not laid the foundation fully for it yet) to point out what the ancient wisdom meant when it spoke of *spheres of being*. The common term for such a sphere is "plane," which has its value, because we are accustomed to it; and yet we must remember that this word *plane* is a loose word, because it may mean almost anything as vulgarly used, and it does not carry the fundamental thought that these inner worlds are actually fields of action, spheres of being, actual entitative *worlds*, in fact.

You will remember that at our last study we drew seven parallel lines, diagrammatical, illustrating the seven kosmic elements, in which work the seven kosmic forces or principles —

the energy-consciousness side of being. Please note this evening carefully that these elements, the kosmical elements, are worlds. Call them planes if you like, but really they are worlds. I do not mean globes, necessarily, that is, solid spherical bodies. They are around and in globes, yet they are truly worlds, spheres of action, spheres of consciousness; and each one of these kosmical elements, in addition to being a world, is infilled with its own "humanities," countless, numberless, innumerable, beyond all human computation. The human stirps, the human lineage, race, class, is but one among many of them.

The ancient wisdom tells us that there are seven main classes of such humanities or stirpes on every planetary chain, and that on this earth, globe D of our chain, man stands at the head of the classes below him. These classes are recognized in ordinary parlance, in the parlance of our science, as kingdoms: the human kingdom (which is confused wrongly with the beast kingdom) first; the beast kingdom second; the vegetable kingdom third; the mineral kingdom fourth; and below that the three kingdoms of the elementals — call these last nature spirits, or substirpes or sublineages, subraces, sublife-waves of being. And you will have noticed at our last meeting that in the diagram we figured a triangle, representing the three higher or arūpa or formless worlds which thus, with the seven below, make the ten of a complete hierarchy.

Now these kosmical elements or worlds or spheres are divided more particularly into lokas — a Sanskrit word meaning "places" in the sense of worlds — and into talas. And these are as given below, using the names found in the Brahmanical literature of Hindustan, names which we have adopted for convenience because they are in that literature and are more or less known; but this does not necessarily mean that we accept all the ideas connected therewith in the Brahmanical works. We use these names because they show that there are actually seven worlds or lokas, and seven inferior worlds or talas, which we shall begin to define and briefly to describe this evening.

Note that these seven kosmical principles and elements are in fact these fourteen lokas, or rather lokas and talas, seven of each. Let us first enumerate them, name them in order:

Satya-loka .... 1 .... Atala
Tapar-loka .... 2 .... Vitala
Janar-loka .... 3 .... Sutala
Mahar-loka .... 4 .... Rasātala
Swar-loka .... 5 .... Talātala
Bhuvar-loka .... 6 .... Mahātala
Bhūr-loka .... 7 .... Pātāla

First the lokas. Beginning with the highest, that is, the inmost, we find *satya-loka,* a word meaning "reality-world"; *tapar-loka,* the next, is a Sanskrit compound word meaning "devotion-world" in the sense of "meditation," "contemplation," "introspection"; next, *janar-loka* from the Sanskrit root meaning "birth"; *mahar-loka* meaning "great"; *swar-loka* meaning "heaven"; *bhuvar-loka,* an ancient word coming from the Sanskrit root *bhū,* meaning "to grow" or "develop"; and lastly *bhūr-loka,* the lowest. The corresponding talas are, counting downwards from the higher to the more material, *atala, vitala, sutala, rasātala, talātala, mahātala, pātāla.*

Now the first thought which we must concentrate our attention upon is this, that these lokas and talas are not one above the other like the rungs of a ladder; they interpenetrate, they interblend; they do not merely commingle, but interblend. A man's thought, for instance, is not necessarily perfectly divine or perfectly evil. It is composite, blended, of both qualities, but not merely mixed. There is nothing so mechanical as that about this fact. We are studying ethereal and spiritual matters. These lokas and talas blend together. For instance, electricity, whether we call it matter or force, is bipolar. There is a positive pole and a negative pole. We may call a loka one of the poles and its corresponding tala the other, for these correspond to each other in twos, a loka and a tala, each to each. Satya-loka to atala, tapar-loka to vitala, and so on down the scale, until we come to the lowest, bhūr-loka and pātāla.

It is commonly said in the Brahmanical literature that the lokas are the "heavens" and the talas are the "hells." Now that is one way of expressing a profound truth, but we must beware of these words heavens and hells on account of wrong European religious ideas, associated ideas. The actual, esoteric meaning is that the lokas are the luminous arc, or rather that procession of nature and of beings in which spirit or the luminous arc predominates. And the talas are the arc of shadows, the shadowy arc, or rather that procession of nature and of beings in which matter predominates. Each one of the lokas works with its corresponding one of the talas. Here is a root-thought. You cannot separate them.

Each of the seven kosmical elements corresponds, each to each, with the lokas and, each to each, with the talas. In other words, the seven lokas and the seven talas work correspondentially on each one of the kosmical elements or worlds. Furthermore, each one of the seven globes of our planetary chain has its own seven lokas and seven talas by "reflection." You know the old esoteric principle lying at the basis of all our thought, expressed in the so-called Hermetic axiom, "As above, so below; as below, so above." The meaning is that our universe, and every part of it, is not an anarchical universe. Everything is inchained with everything else, and the higher is reflected or rather reflects itself in the lower, the lower being actually the expression of the higher; or, as expressed in our former three or four meetings, the lower worlds are the garments (or expressions, or reflections) of the higher. Nothing is separate from anything else. You know the greatest heresy in Buddhism (and this is likewise our own teaching) is the so-called separateness, the idea or belief that anything is or can be considered apart from the whole. That is also what the Christians meant when they spoke of the "crime against the Holy Ghost." The few early Christians who were initiated considered this crime as the most heinous of iniquities, and they were right.

Now then, having gone thus far, we may see that these talas or inferior worlds are, each to each, each in each, *actually the kosmical elements*. Is this thought clear? Next, the forces working through these talas or worlds, through these fields of action — forces material, ethereal, psychical, spiritual, divine, and so on — are the *principles of the kosmos*, the consciousnesses which infill space and are, in fact, space itself; and these latter are the lokas.

We have pointed out that these elements may be considered serially somewhat after the fashion of the skins of an onion. This is a far better illustration, as being more suggestive, than the "plane"-system, although this system was used too in ancient times; and we also pointed out that these skins of the earth, these skins of the kosmos, grow more ethereal, grow more spiritual, as they proceed inwards. But we do not mean — please mark this very carefully — that these more spiritual or inner worlds or spheres are smaller, i.e., inferior in volume to the outermost rind. Size has nothing whatsoever to do with ethereal or spiritual bearings. Mere bulk or volume has nothing whatsoever to do with consciousness. How then can we reconcile these two apparently contradictory statements, this paradox: that the more you approach the material center of a thing, the denser it is; the more you approach the spiritual center of a thing the diviner it is? You know that the old Greek philosophers, the Atomistic Philosophers so called, such as Democritus, Leucippus, Epicurus, etc., followed by the great Roman poet, Lucretius, said for instance in their Atomistic theories that heaven was composed of the finer, the more subtil atoms, and that the earth and the planetary and stellar bodies were composed of those which were coarser and heavier and therefore fell together, meaning that they were more strongly attracted together. That is true enough, for it is a statement made from the tala-side, that is to say, the matter-side. But now listen.

We have often spoken of a laya-center, a laya-center being the seventh or highest degree of matter (or the first degree of spirit), the vanishing-point of matter into higher realms, the nirvana of matter, the nirvana of any entity of which it is the heart, the center. Our laya-center as human beings is our ātman, our universal self. Each globe is likewise an atom or a monad, or a god, according to the plane or world which we consider it as being in. Now this laya-center is at the center or heart of our being; it is, in fact, that core of our being, and from it radiate, as the rays from the sun radiate outwards, these forces, these elements, these skins of being; these forces and elements or skins growing grosser, in one sense, as they proceed farther from the center. But the more ethereal the original plane is, or the original world or sphere is, or the original field of action is, the more spiritual the originating center is, and the wider is its outflow of radiation. You catch that thought? The spiritual entity continuously flowing through the laya-center has rays which reach far beyond the more material coatings, and which in the lowest, radiate scarcely more than beyond its own circumscribed limits. To change somewhat the illustration, the spiritual, inner realms of man or of globe are the various "planes" or degrees, or spheres, of the auric egg — one of the most sacred of our teachings, and the one concerning which the least has been said.

Let us illustrate this again by an exoteric statement with regard to the three lowest of the lokas respectively, bhūr-loka, bhuvar-loka, and swar-loka. Bhūr-loka is said to be, in the exoteric, Brahmanical books, our earth. Its field of influence reaches little farther than the atmosphere. Bhuvar-loka, they say, has rays (or an atmosphere) which reach to the sun, although actually it is the world or loka next within the earth — not another physical world within the physical earth, skin-of-onion fashion, but an ethereal world within the physical earth. And swar-loka is a world still more ethereal or spiritual, within bhuvar-loka, that has rays (or an atmosphere) which reach even to Dhruva, or the polar star. This may illustrate the point.

And mark you, as a natural fact deduced from this, we could have no connection with beings outside ourselves, or beyond ourselves, or with other planets, or our sun or others, unless there were these atmospheric bearers or carriers, these auric rays, these atmospheres by which we come into touch with other beings and globes and worlds — both on our plane and on other planes. Is that clear? A magnet has its magnetism or magnetic atmosphere reaching beyond itself, which will illustrate the point. It has its limits of reach, of course; and in the same sense all these lokas and talas have their atmospheres. The inner ones have the atmospheres which reach farther than the outer lokas and talas; and so progressively more so as we go inwards.

Now pātāla, the lowest of the talas, is also said to be our earth. That statement also is correct from the point of view of the kosmical planes. Note also that these lokas and these talas are the bipolar elements of nature, the bipolar worlds of being, the ascending and the descending: the involving or the talas, and the evolving or the lokas. By the action of the talas being dominant over the action of the lokas, we "descend," to use the popular phrase, along the shadowy arc, into manifestation at the beginning of a manvantara, and having reached our earth, which is the turning point, we then ascend along the luminous arc, the lokas then becoming the dominant, and the talas the recessive, to use modern biological phraseology.

Satya-loka could not exist without atala as its vehicle or nether pole. Tapar-loka could not exist without vitala as its nether pole; and so forth down the scale. This is one of the most difficult of things to explain in European words; and yet really it is one of the simplest of conceptions. We must cleanse our minds first of mechanical suggestions. We must understand that we are here dealing with spiritual and psychological and ethereal matters and things. There could be no luminous arc without the lokas, and no shadowy arc without the talas, as bases respectively — and when we say luminous or shadowy arc we do not mean an actual arc, for it is a figure of speech. We mean those worlds and those processes and those processions of beings in nature by which, or in which, or through which we descend into manifestation or, on the other hand, by which we rise and grow into spiritual greatness.

Such are the two arcs respectively. Virtue, purity, kindness, compassion, pity, mercy, etc. — all these things are signs that the entity possessing them is evolving the spirit within, and is rising, ascending, along the luminous arc. And where we see selfishness and impurity and unkindliness and cruelty and deception, hypocrisy, etc., they are the signs that the entity possessing them is under the influence or dominance of the descending or shadowy arc, the talas. Nevertheless, from the very beginning and in either direction, the lokas and talas are interblended and work together, for they are spirit and matter.

These two, lokas and talas, therefore work each within the other. For instance, our earth, our planet Terra, our globe, on and in which we live, has its own particular seven lokas and seven talas. As seen from the kosmical viewpoint, the physical loka and tala to our present physical eyes are bhūr-loka and pātāla, or our earth. It is pātāla if we look at it from the material standpoint; and it is bhūr-loka if we look at it from the energy-consciousness side, from the nobler or better side, towards the rising side. Remember always that lokas and talas work and exist invariably two by two — by twos, one of each, and on every plane.

In addition to the seven kosmical principles being respectively these lokas, as said before, and the kosmical elements the seven talas, all fourteen, seven of each, are reflected in each one of the seven globes of our chain. "As above, so below; as below, so above." The little is as the great; the microcosm is but a representation or copy in small of the macrocosm.

Suppose that we were to ask ourselves with regard to these lokas and talas: Where do we stand in the scale? Where are we in loka and tala? We are in the fourth *globe* of our chain, as we know. Let us then take the fourth loka and the fourth tala, i.e., mahar-loka corresponding in scale with rasātala. But, again, we are in the fourth *round* of our planetary chain. Therefore we have this bipolar principle emphasized by the fourth round quality, i.e., mahar-loka and rasātala again. We are, furthermore, in the fifth *root-race* of the fourth globe on the fourth round. Therefore our root-race, though evolving on that fourth globe and in that fourth round, is represented by the fifth of each column: swar-loka and talātala. "Wheels within wheels," as Ezekiel, the Hebrew prophet, nobly said.

Furthermore, where are we as regards the kosmic elements? We have stated this a few moments ago. H. P. Blavatsky, in her diagram of these in *The Secret Doctrine*, which we reproduced at our last meeting, shows that our globe Terra stands in the lowest of the kosmic elements, the seventh counting downwards. Therefore the kosmical element in which we and this globe are, is bhūr-loka and pātāla, kosmically speaking.

It is these actions and interactions, these interblendings of lokas and talas, of these various elements and forces and principles, which render any exposition of them so complicated. However, it makes knowledge of them precious, for knowledge of these things is not cried from the housetops, but, as said before, is given as the reward of merit to those found worthy and well qualified.

Let us approach these questions from another standpoint. Where are we on the kosmical worlds or planes? We are told that Brahmā lives one hundred of his years. *Brahmā*, remember, is a Sanskrit word standing for the spiritual energy-consciousness side of our solar universe, i.e., our solar system, and the Egg of Brahmā is that solar system. We are further told that his life is half ended, fifty of his years are gone — a figure which we express in fifteen figures of our years, i.e., 155 trillions, 520 billions (155,520,000,000,000) of years have passed away since our solar system, with its sun, first began its manvantaric course. There remain, therefore, fifty more such years to pass before the system sinks into rest, or pralaya. As only half of the evolutionary journey is accomplished, we are, therefore, at the bottom of the kosmic cycle, i.e., on the lowest plane, as the diagram above mentioned shows.

And where are we on this planet? We are on the lowest plane here also, because being in the fourth round, we have run our course only by half. The lowest kosmical plane, as said above, is bhūr-loka and pātāla. As a matter of fact, however, as said at another study, we have advanced a little on the ascending arc, because our planetary chain is the child of the lunar chain, and the lunar chain was on the exact lowest degree.

Now these thoughts are laid before you tonight as suggestive propositions for further consideration. Understand first that the universe, according to the ancient system, is divided into seven grades or degrees of being, which are worlds, lokas and talas, that is, these worlds are polarized into lokas and talas, two by two throughout. Our earth shows them as bipolar, because it is the only planet on this plane, in this kosmic element, or world, in this particular degree or sphere. It is the turning point of our planetary chain where matter-spirit equilibrates, rendering it bipolar. Next, that each one of the seven globes of our chain has its own seven lokas and seven talas. As said before, they are popularly called heavens and hells. Not that they are heavens and hells in the European sense of the word, but they represent the two sides of being, the duality of manifestation, the higher and the lower natures, if you like, as well of the planet as of the human being.

Let us go a little farther. In the seven lokas and seven talas of our world, working together as they do, two by two, one of each, one loka and one tala: in each of these there are innumerable hosts of beings. In the higher ones of the lokas and talas are thinking and conscious entities, as our own human stirps (that is, race, lineage, life-wave) is. These lokas and talas interpenetrate each other. As H. P. Blavatsky says in a very noble passage in *The Secret Doctrine*, they have each one their own "geographical" spheres; the respective inhabitants of the different lokas and talas live in their own world, pursue their own vocations, work out their own karmic destiny, even as we do in our world. It is but human egoism that claims so foolishly that ours is the only race of intelligent beings in the boundless kosmos, and which goes so far as even to deny intelligence and consciousness to beings even on other physical planets. It is a position which is intolerable to the mind of really thinking men, because it is based on nothing but ignorance and folly. Nothing can be said for the claim whatsoever; and everything — logic, intellect, analogy, comparing thought, intuition — all speak loudly to the contrary, and proclaim that there is not an atom of the infinite realms of space which is not fully infilled with its own appropriate and proper lines or races of beings.

I beg you to bear these lokas and talas in mind. Please think of them always by twos, one of each, one loka and one tala, its correspondence in the scale, ever working together, as inseparable as positive and negative are, as inseparable as good and evil are, as inseparable as spirit and matter. They represent and in fact *are* the two sides of being, not necessarily the body-side and the spirit-side, but the two contrasting forces, the two contrasted sides of nature, the night-side and the light-side, the shadowy side and the bright side.

The three diagrams to which I now call attention are of three very ancient symbols coming to us from old Atlantean times, and full of suggestive meaning along the lines of our study tonight. Let us take first this one: a circle divided by the twice curved line. Rising out of the circumference and reentering into the circumference, the line proceeds around, forming a figure, of which one side is shaded and the other is left blank. This is a favorite Buddhist symbol. It is found all over the Orient, but particularly in Buddhist countries, and furnishes one of the favorite motifs of Buddhist art. All Buddhist art is religious art, of course. 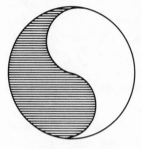Will you please note here that in taking one side, the shaded side, we find the line leaving the circumference at the top, curving around, then recurving itself, and then at the bottom reentering the circumference. And where it reenters the circumference we find the side left blank or void, moving forth in the opposite direction, forming part of the circumference of the circle, ascending until it reaches the summit, and then joining the other line which first went down from that point in the twice curved line to rejoin the point after forming the other side of the circumference. These represent the lokas and talas, or the involution of spirit and the evolution of matter; and, again, the rising one the evolution of spirit, and the involution of matter, joined and inseparable, forming one figure; the circle also suggesting the boundless All; and the shadowy side suggesting the talas, the dark side or the matter-side, and the side left void suggesting the spirit-side, the great illimitable Void of the boundless All, of the boundless Self.

I think that this design, this symbol, is one of the most beautiful, one of the most suggestive, that I have ever known. The more you study it the more it suggests thought. It shows, as said before, our lokas and our talas inseparable and interworking. It shows the descent of spirit, so to say, and the ascent of matter, coordinately and contemporaneously; and it shows the evolution of spirit, and the involution of matter back again into spirit, from which it came and which it fundamentally is.

Let us turn next to another old symbol. It is the swastika, another favorite Buddhist symbol and otherwise found all over the Orient, and even all over the world. It first suggests motion, evolution; the broken arms bent at right angles suggest life, movement, and forward progress, and many other things.

Next, note the cross figure. We have here — and now we come to the symbol-meaning of the cross upon which we must lightly touch tonight — first the vertical line, so called the spirit, and then the horizontal line, the matter which it enters and traverses. The two work together. Take away either arm, or either part of the two lines which make the swastika, and you no longer have a swastika. This also suggests, though less violently, if I may use the expression, the lokas and talas inseparably joined.

And the third of our symbols is what is known to scholars today as the Egyptian tau or ansated or handled cross, also a very old symbol dating from Atlantean times, and found on the backs of some of the statues on Easter Island.

Note the circle at the top of the cross, and the vertical line descending from it, symbolic of the descent of the spirit into matter — the horizontal line — from the sphere of the divine. Its meaning is similar to that of the swastika. The latter, however, emphasizes the movements and circulations of consciousnesses in space, or evolution; while the ansated cross represents a higher plane — the primordial movements and states of kosmic being.

These symbols are really very beautiful. There is no need to sully our thought by adverting to questions of phallic meaning into which they have been degraded. They can bear that interpretation, because you can degrade anything. All life is one, and one general design runs through all. But we shall not speak of this. The main thing we wish to point out now is that in these age-old symbols and particularly in this bipolar, bi-vital, loka-tala Buddhistic figure, the first we discussed, we find the suggested outline, the symbolic or paradigmatic form, of the entire doctrine of the higher and lower spheres of being, kosmical or human, i.e., of the lokas and talas.

There is one more thing to bring to your attention, if you please, and that is to point out at least by suggestion, the perfect coherence of all the limbs of life. How can one otherwise express it, the perfect unity of the mechanism of being? The circulations of the kosmos are carried on not in haphazard form, but from sphere to sphere, from world to world, from plane to plane, by and through consciousnesses, whether they be gods, monads, souls, or atoms, working in the various elements; and more particularly in our solar system this is done through the sun and planets, especially by and through the respective inner atmospheres of their lokas and talas.

In occultism there are seven sacred planets. We recognize many more in our solar system than seven, many more than our scientists do, but only seven planets are held sacred. And why? We can at least say this much, that these seven planets are sacred for us, inhabitants of this globe, because they are the transmitters to us from the sun of the seven primal forces of the kosmos. Our seven principles and our seven elements spring originally from this sevenfold life-flow.

Let us put this matter in another light. On this plane, our physical globe, Terra, is alone, but on the three other planes of being, the globes of our planetary chain, two by two, are not the seven principles of our earth. That would be a false analogy, false analogical reasoning. We must be careful not to be led astray by such false analogies. The seven principles of our globe are the seven lokas and seven talas belonging especially to earth; and the seven principles of each one of the other six globes of our planetary chain are the respective lokas and talas belonging to each one of them. Now these two other globes on each plane of the three planes above ours, making thus the other six globes of our planetary chain, receive their respective life force, receive their respective inflow of intellectual and spiritual energies and beings, from the respective lokas and talas of the sun. There are seven suns, but only one sun on this plane, as our globe is but one on this plane, the lowest of the seven kosmical planes.

THIRTY-SEVEN

THE FRAMEWORK OF THE KOSMOS. LOKAS AND TALAS:
PRINCIPLES AND ELEMENTS, WORLDS — NOT STATES
MERELY. SPACE THE ULTIMATE REALITY.

MAITREYA: The sphere of the whole earth has been described to me, by
you, excellent Brahman; and I am now desirous to hear an account of the
other spheres (above the world), — the Bhuvar-loka and the rest, — and the
situation and the dimensions of the celestial luminaries.

— *Vishnu Purāna*, 2, 7 (Wilson, trans.)

She said: "That, O Yājñavalkya, which is above the sky, that which is
beneath the earth, that which is between these two, sky and earth, that
which people call the past and the present and the future — across what is
that woven, warp and woof?"
He said: "That, O Gārgī, which is above the sky, that which is beneath
the earth, that which is between these two, sky and earth, that which people
call the past and the present and the future — across space alone is that
woven, warp and woof."
"Across what then, pray, is space woven, warp and woof?"
He said: "That, O Gārgī, Brahmans call the Imperishable. . . .

"It consumes nothing soever.
No one soever consumes it. . . .

"Verily, O Gārgī, that Imperishable is the unseen Seer, the unheard
Hearer, the unthought Thinker, the ununderstood Understander. Other than
It there is naught that sees. Other than It there is naught that hears. Other
than It there is naught that thinks. Other than It there is naught that under-
stands. Across this Imperishable, O Gārgī, is space woven, warp and woof
[It is SPACE Itself]."

— *Brihad-Āranyaka Upanishad*, 3, 8, 6–8, 11 (Hume, trans.)

I F BROTHERHOOD is the "lost chord," ethically speaking, in
Occidental thought, may we not say that the loss of the
idea that the universe we sense or know of is but the rind
of things is the cause of the spiritual and intellectual feebleness
of that same Occidental thought? We have lost, as Occidentals,
perhaps the noblest concept of all the ancient world, the concept

which, however, still exists over the larger part of the globe today, and that concept, or knowledge to many, is the fact that the outside world, which our physical senses tell us of, is but the shell of things, of reality, and that the greater part is within, behind the veil of physical existence. Think what that means. We see but the rind, the husk, the shell, the skin of things; but all the great moving forces are from within, all the great circulations of the kosmos are behind the outward seeming, and this verity was the core of the religious and philosophic conceptions of the ancient world, and to a large extent forms even today in the Orient and among the so-called savage peoples — degenerated heirs of a greater wisdom of past time — the philosophic and religious thought which leads them to live and to die in calm peace and hope. And in larger spheres of our thinking we must realize that if we are to understand the great problems of life, the great problems of the various departments of human thought — religion, philosophy, and science — we must go behind this outward veil, we must penetrate more deeply into the heart of things.

The thought is sublime because it contains the fundamentals of the true exposition of life, and because it is a veritable key to the understanding of the ideas which motivated the civilizations of past ages; and our civilization will never reach that which it should be, and indeed which it is destined to be, until this old-world thought is brought back into the consciousness of men. Then indeed it will guide their conduct because it will give a rational explanation of the problems of being; and men and women will live aright, because they will then understand that what human intellect calls justice, that is to say, order, rules the entire universe.

We read again from *The Secret Doctrine,* from volume II, page 492, the same extract that we have read at our previous studies, four or five of them, because it still forms the main theme of what we are here considering and trying to understand:

The Secret Doctrine points out, as a self-evident fact, that Mankind, collectively and individually, is, with all manifested nature, the vehicle (*a*) of the breath of One Universal Principle, in its primal differentiation; and (*b*) of the countless "breaths" proceeding from that One BREATH in its secondary and further differentiations, as Nature with its many *mankinds* proceeds downwards toward the planes that are ever increasing in materiality. The primary Breath informs the higher Hierarchies; the secondary — the lower, on the constantly descending planes.

We continue our study this evening of the framework of the kosmos; and this framework itself is constructed in the manner pointed out in our last study, i.e., by the lokas and talas. And great, unquestionably, was the patience of all here at our last meeting, who listened to our study, to our thought, and realized the immense complexity of a first presentation of these things — who doubtless saw that we were following as closely as possible the methods of study used in the ancient Mystery Schools; and one of these methods was never at the first approach of a new subject, openly and fully, to voice the teaching concerning it, but to begin it first by hint and also by talking around it, about it, never at it or of it. There were several reasons for this, founded on a profound knowledge of human psychology. The whole effort is to enable the hearer or reader to break his own molds of mind; nothing perhaps, knowing human nature as we do, so antagonizes the human mind or renders it more combative than to throw an idea at it, so to say. But let the hearer or reader first feel that he is taken into the thought by indirection, and by an appeal to his own inner spirit — for, indeed, he wants to break his molds of mind himself in the first instance, and to understand of his own initiative; and he is right. Our first duty is to open the way to the hearer *to think for himself.*

This evening, however, having followed the above method at our last meeting, we are going to approach the matter directly, and clear up the apparent confusion.

One of the other methods which we have followed — and you have doubtless noticed it — is the use of the figure of speech called the paradox, for precisely the same reasons outlined above. We must, above all things, prevent the crystallization of the mentality around one thought; and experience has shown that the best way to do this is first to talk around and about a thing; then to present one aspect, and then, if possible, a contrasting aspect, the antithesis or polar opposite of the former aspect; and very soon the mind which undergoes this process, realizes it and says to itself: "I am not going to allow my mind to crystallize about this thought alone; something more is coming, another view. I will await, before judging." This process tends, above everything else, to prevent dogmatism, whether in religion, or philosophy, or science. And mark you, it is the exact opposite of the methods of instruction so dear to the Occidental heart, which likewise is fascinated by the entifying of abstractions. This entification of abstracts, as you know, is the leaning or the attempt mentally to think of abstractions as real entities. It is the exact opposite of the method followed in all ancient civilizations, and even in the Orient today, in dealing with profound psychological or spiritual matters. Their wise old teachers showed them that the entification of abstractions distracts the mind and leads it away from the primal truths of being, for the mind feels temporarily satisfied with phantasms instead of realities, and precious time is lost; while the mind itself is lost in mazes of unrealities. This is another example of the profound knowledge of human psychology that the ancient teachers had.

Even in the Christian scheme of thought, we find Paul following the same line of real entitative instruction by parable and trope, in the old manner, in his Letters, in his Epistles, to the various so-called churches. If the Christian exegetes, the theologians, were students of the ancient wisdom, they would know at least enough not to take the words of Paul literally, because Paul was an initiate, as is shown very clearly by his own writings — not necessarily a high initiate, because this word *initiate* merely means one who has "entered into" a system, and who therefore has some knowledge, has received one aspect at least, has passed through one rite or more of the ancient wisdom.

You know that Paul in his second Epistle to the Corinthians, chapter 12, verses 2, 3, 4, writes as follows: "I know a man in Christ" — note the wording, he does not say "I know a friend of Christ," but "I know a man in Christ" — "fourteen years agone (whether in body I know not, whether out of body I know not, God knoweth). Such a one being caught up to the third heaven. And I know such a man (whether in body, whether out of body I know not, God knoweth), that he was caught up into the Paradise, and heard things not to be divulged, which are not lawful for a man to utter."

Now we have made our own translation of these lines from the Greek original, and while there is no need to repeat the Greek words, I wish to point out that the very words that Paul uses here, "heard things not to be divulged," etc., etc., are the sacramental words, so to speak, the sacred words, used in the mystic ceremonials of the ancient teachings. Further, this shows very clearly that this man was Paul himself, otherwise he would have known nothing of it.

Thirdly, when he shows that this man, he himself, was "caught up to the third heaven," I must point out that if our theologians knew something of the language of the Mysteries, they would at least understand that this expression "third heaven" is an old form or symbol of speech of the initiations.

Remember, we have spoken at other ones of our studies of the fact that beginning with the fourth degree of initiation, in the ancient times, the candidate was made to *be* or to *become* — for the time being — that which he had heretofore been taught of; he was made to go into the different lokas and talas and temporarily *be* the things there in order *to know them.* One of the methods of describing this fact was speaking of being in or of the first heaven, the second heaven, the third heaven, the fourth, and so on. It was another way of saying, by Paul, "In my third initiation I heard things not to be divulged, which it is not lawful for a man to utter."

Now an example of this entification of abstractions, this giving to phantasmal notions both substance and form, is shown clearly in the scientific and philosophic writings of our European thinkers, when they use the word *space* in the sense of a mere concept. Space to them is an abstraction; to us, the ultimate being, reality, all-life. Just think what that means. Space, *ex hypothesi,* is boundless, is what we call infinite; and yet they write of it and talk of it and speak of it as a mere container, a finite thing, and speak of the "dimensions of space." Space, as boundless-all-life, can have no dimensions. You cannot bound or mete or measure the infinite. What they mean is the dimensions of matter, mensuration. They predicate a conceptual abstraction, then proceed to endow it with finite attributes — entifying it, as said above; for to them, space is a mere mental representation.

Some of our Occidental thinkers are even speaking of the "fourth dimension of space," implying that there are others beyond, a fifth, a sixth perhaps. Now we do not admit this idea. Space can have no dimensions. Matter can have three dimensions only, because, as you will readily see, when you express the metes and bounds of manifested substance by length, and breadth, and depth, you have covered the entire field that it presents. But what is it in these minds which induces them to hunt and search for what they so inaccurately call the dimensions of space? It is the intuition, the recognition, of worlds within the outer rind or shell, spoken of before. There is no such thing in nature as "Flatland" or a two-dimensional world, or a one-dimensional world, because each world comprises all "dimensions."

Consider what we mean when we speak of the principles and elements of the kosmos, as pointed out in our last study. The elements are worlds, and the principles are the spiritual forces, entities, spiritual intelligences at the root of them, which work through those worlds or elements. And what do we mean by world? We mean exactly what the English usage of the word "world" is. We go out upon our housetops, or into the roads, or into a field, and see what we call the universe around us, the stars, and the sun, and again the beings on earth; and all this is a world. No, it is not a globe. A globe is merely one of the entities or bodies in a world. So, at our last meeting, when we said that these lokas and talas are not globes but worlds, we meant just that. We may perhaps call them spheres, if you like, but not by using the word "sphere," please, in the physical, geometrical sense. We use it rather in a more abstract sense, as when we speak of the sphere of one's activity, the musical sphere or the musical world, the intellectual or material spheres or worlds. But the word "world" for our present purposes, in order to describe these lokas and talas, is far better. Etymologically it would never do, because this Anglo-Saxon word was originally *weorold*, meaning "man-age," i.e., meaning the age of a man, definitely, in those times, taken as of one hundred years and commonly spoken of in literary usage as an age. It is interesting that this word "world" closely corresponds with the meaning, with the two meanings rather, of the Greek word *aion*, or aeon, which originally meant with the Greek Gnostics both an epoch of time, a period of time, and a spiritual being or world.

Now these lokas and talas, if we refer them to the kosmos, *are respectively the principles and elements of the kosmos.* The lokas are the principles, and the talas are the elements. Loka means "world." The principles, however, are as much worlds as the elements are. The principles of the kosmos are higher kosmic worlds as the elements are lower kosmic worlds. Pause a moment, and see how simple this conception really is. We see the physical world around us, the physical universe. We are taught in our sacred science (in occultism, that is) that the world has seven so-called planes. As remarked before, this word "plane" is an unfortunate term in some ways, because people associate it with its geometrical meaning of a flat surface. It is a loose term, but it is familiar and therefore it is convenient. The elements, the talas, are worlds; so are the lokas; they represent together, in other words, what is popularly called the seven principles of the kosmos. The seven principles of the kosmos correspond in their element-side to the talas; and the seven principles, per se, of the kosmos, that is to say, the spiritual side, correspond to the seven lokas.

The difficulty for us arises, perhaps, because we have been so accustomed to speak of the seven principles of man and, Occidentals as we are, we think of them only as abstractions; accustomed to our habit of entifying abstractions, we do not conceive of them as real, essential things, so that perhaps in our minds we have reduced these principles of man almost to mere words. But, as pointed out in a former study, man has seven principles and also seven elements or vehicles in which those principles work, each principle in its appropriate vehicle, each principle in its corresponding element. Yet we should consider the kosmos in precisely the same manner, because man is but a reflection of the kosmos, he is the microcosm of the macrocosm — "As above, so below; as below, so above."

So then, knowing that our universe has seven planes, that is, seven elements from one viewpoint, and seven principles or the energy-consciousness side from another viewpoint, we may now definitely say that the element-side, the vehicle-side, the matter-

side, the dark side, is the tala-side. The seven talas are the seven
elements or matter-worlds of kosmos; and the seven lokas —
which are worlds also — are the seven principles of the kosmos.

Now if we were able to ascend into any one of the higher
elements and principles of the kosmos, we should find our present
world reduplicated — with modifications, naturally; but each one
of these elements and principles is a kosmic world, a tala or a
loka respectively.

One of the most interesting symbols in use by men of the
ancient world, by which they described these inseparable lokas
and talas, was what is called in Hindustan Vishnu's Sign, and
which for some unknown reason among European mystics is called
Solomon's Seal. This symbol is one of the most widespread,
familiar, and favorite symbols of the Asiatic-European world.

We have here two interlaced triangles, one pointing upwards

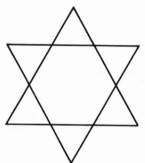 and one pointing downwards, insepa-
rably united in order to form this sym-
bol. Separate them, and this symbol
no longer exists. The triangle with its
point upwards represents the lokas, and
the one with its point downwards, the
talas. This is likewise a symbol of
human and kosmic evolution, of the
duality in nature, and of the interplay
of the spiritual and material forces in
life. If we were to put a point in the center of these interlaced
triangles, we should immediately transfer its symbolic meaning
to incipient kosmic evolution, it then becoming somewhat like the
figure of the circle with the central point. Also, in human matters,
it would then be the symbol of what we call a Master. Sometimes, in the last sense, it is written in more simple shape, as
three dots in triangular form. Sometimes again the three dots
have a fourth in the center, which is but an abbreviated form of
this same figure; but in this case the triangle always points upwards, for it shows that the aspiration of the man symbolized is
upwards, signifying the ascent through the lokas.

This brings us to our next point, and that is that while it is true
that these lokas and talas are "states" in a general sense, it is

only so in the sense in which heavens and hells may be so considered. They are states, of course, but they are also localities, because any entity in or possessing a state must *be* somewhere. Devachan and nirvana are not localities, they are states, states of the beings in those respective spiritual conditions. Devachan is the intermediate state; nirvana is the superspiritual state; and avīchi, popularly called the lowest of the hells, is the nether pole of the spiritual condition. These three are states of beings having habitat in the lokas or talas, i.e., in the worlds of the kosmic egg. And secondly, while the heavens and hells are considered as states, we must remember that hell or heaven is not a condition which exists per se, as does a world. Each is the state of some thing or some entity which is in that state, and which, therefore, being an entity, must have position or place and, according to the invariable rules which govern the kosmos, such states must be likewise correspondential to similar surroundings — in other words, a being in heaven or hell is in a corresponding loka or tala.

So then, before closing tonight, we hope that we have made one thing perfectly clear, that is, to put it briefly, that these lokas and talas are respectively the principles and elements of the kosmos, and also of every globe in that kosmos, each one of which possesses seven lokas and seven talas. These lokas and talas are inseparable, and each one corresponds to a similar one of the other line. That is clear, is it not? The two highest together, the two lowest together, and the intermediate in the same way. Please remember the main thought, that these lokas and talas are *worlds*. They are not mere states only, which means nothing. An entity possesses or is in a state, but a state does not exist per se or "by itself." That idea arises out of the fondness of our minds for entifying abstractions. A state is an abstraction. It must be held or possessed or developed by some entity in order to be anything.

And finally, please remember this, that each one of these lokas and each one of these talas produces the following lower one of the scale from itself, as pointed out before when we studied briefly the elements. The highest of either line projects or sends forth the next lower. It, in addition to its own particular characteristic or swabhāva, contains also within itself the nature of the one above it, its parent, and also sends forth the one lower than it, the third in the line downwards. And so on down the scale. So that each one of the principles or elements is likewise sevenfold, containing in itself the subelements of that or those of which it is the reflection from above.

THIRTY-EIGHT

DEGENERATION AND CLOSING OF THE SCHOOLS OF THE MYSTERIES.
NEOPYTHAGOREAN AND NEOPLATONIC SYSTEMS: MAIN
SOURCES OF CHRISTIAN THEOLOGY. ESOTERIC
AND EXOTERIC TEACHINGS: SYMBOLISM.

There never was, nor can there be more than one universal religion; for there can be but one truth concerning God. Like an immense chain whose upper end, the alpha, remains invisibly emanating from a Deity — in *statu abscondito* with every primitive theology — it encircles our globe in every direction; it leaves not even the darkest corner unvisited, before the other end, the omega, turns back on its way to be again received where it first emanated. On this divine chain was strung the exoteric symbology of every people. Their variety of form is powerless to affect their substance, and under their diverse ideal types of the universe of matter, symbolizing its vivifying principles, the uncorrupted immaterial image of the spirit of being guiding them is the same. . . .

Thus is it that all the religious monuments of old, in whatever land or under whatever climate, are the expression of the same identical thoughts, the key to which is in the esoteric doctrine. — *Isis Unveiled*, I, 560–61

The inference to be drawn from all this is, that the made-up and dogmatic Christianity of the Constantinian period is simply an offspring of the numerous conflicting sects, half-castes themselves, born of Pagan parents.
— Ibid., II, 334

But to assert that Christianity communicated to man moral truths previously unknown, argues, on the part of the assertor, either gross ignorance or else wilful fraud. — H. T. BUCKLE, *History of Civilization in England*, I, 129

PROBABLY there are few things that human beings are so irritable about as the various issues involved in questioning an accepted religion. Outside of the fact that everyone knows that religious wars have always been the bloodiest and bitterest in history, even in ordinary life, if a man's

religious beliefs, or even his vague religious views, are touched
upon adversely, there is aroused in him a feeling of antagonism.
In well-bred men and women this antagonism does not go far,
because they are willing to concede to another a view different
from their own; but, sadly enough, it would seem that there is
very little good breeding in matters of religious feeling. No man
likes to feel that his religion is subject to derision or mockery,
because of course to him his religion is the "true religion." It has
always been so among the adherents of any religion. It is only the
wiser ones who are willing to see a view which a fellow man sees,
and to consider that view honestly, desirous of arriving at some
knowledge of what the critic or the speaker himself believes,
or sees.

Especially is this so in all the various branches of Occidental
religious thought, derived, as we know, from Christianity and
Judaism. The old religions, the religions of the ancient world,
had their popular mythologies which the people believed in; and
some of these old religions are still extant today in the Orient and
elsewhere. But even among those who were not initiated into the
Mysteries, which gave men a wider vision of truth and a deeper
knowledge of human nature, even among those who had nothing
to live by except the various mythologies, and who today have
nothing to live by except the various mythologies, in all these
religions, excepting the Christian, there is a feeling among their
adherents that the other man may know something of value too.
I have often wondered how much in the Theosophical Movement
this spirit of Christian and quasi-Jewish antagonism against another man's belief actually exists among ourselves.

This spirit of religious bigotry, of course, has resulted, as we
all know, in the various religious persecutions, in the various
torturings — physical or other — and inquisitorial actions of the
bigots in temporary power. You find nothing like that in any
of the ancient religions of the globe, neither in present nor in
past times. Why should it have been and even yet be in the
religion of the Occident? As said before, it must certainly lie in
the fact that the adherents thereof have lost the key to the inner
knowledge of their own religious beliefs; and this dates very far
back. We find Gregory Nazianzen, canonized as one of the saints

of the Christian Church, writing to Jerome, another saint of the Church, his friend and confidant, about the way doctrines should be taught, and this is what he says:

Nothing imposes better on people than verbiage, for the less they understand the more they admire. Our Fathers and teachers often have taught, not what they thought, but that which necessity and circumstance obliged them to say.

If we compare this with the spirit which motivated the great religions of past times, we realize that among the initiates of the latter the very expression of a thought which they felt contrary to truth was uttered to the prejudice of a man's own soul; that living as "whited sepulchres," to use the Christian symbol, i.e., living as hypocrites, living a living lie, was considered the one thing that most effectively shriveled the soul of a man, that ate out the core of his being, and rendered him utterly unfit, not merely for an appreciation of the deeper mysteries which lie within nature and within man himself, but likewise utterly unfit to undergo the least of the tests preceding the actual trials of the initiation ceremonies.

Even at the time when the Christian religion is supposed first to have begun its career, although the Mysteries, the initiation systems, had greatly degenerated, they still retained more or less of the ancient spiritual fire and of the ancient truths. So that a Roman emperor, Nero, master of the Western world, was told to his face that he was unfit to pass through the rites at Eleusis, and he dared not go there for that purpose. And Nero was by no means as bad a man as his Christian critics have tried to make him out to have been. We have no wish to whitewash a black character, but he was by no means, and we repeat it, as black in his life or in the things he did, as some men who pass muster as near-canonized saints in the hagiological lists of Christendom.

For one thousand years, beginning from the time of Pythagoras and ending about the time of Justinian, the night of an incoming dark cycle was beginning to settle upon the world; and this period is cut in twain at just about the time when the birth of Jesus is supposed to have occurred. Pythagoras lived in the sixth century before the reputed beginning of our era, i.e., the present era that

is accepted by Occidental peoples; and Justinian lived in the sixth
century after the beginning of that era; and it was in his age, and
by his order, that the last of the Mystery Schools was closed at
Athens, and seven men fled at peril of their lives to Khosru the
Great, King of Persia, and lived there in peace and dignity and
honor at his court until, due to the whirl of the wheel of circumstance, Khosru, victor in his war against Justinian, as one condition of the peace which Justinian purchased with money, laid it
down that these seven philosophers were to be allowed to return
to their own country in peace and to live in peace, and to die in
peace; and so it was.

Compare that noble spirit with the spirit manifest on the other
side, and you have a slight vision of the inspiration which dwelt
in what was called the ancient initiatory life, and of the spirit
which has hovered over the Western world ever since that year
one of our era, so named, the Christian era.

This does not mean that the slightest aspersion is hereby cast
upon the character of the so-called Jesus. Not one word would
a true theosophist ever say against the character of that great and
noble man, or against the teachings supposed to emanate from
him personally. But it is probable that the theosophic effort
which Jesus attempted to initiate did not endure for fifty years
after his death. Almost immediately after his passing, his disciples, all half-instructed, and in some cases almost illiterate, men —
when I say "half-instructed" I mean having very little knowledge
of the teachings which their great Master attempted to give
them — foisted upon the world of their time the forms and beliefs
of early Christianity; and had there been nothing but these, that
religious system had not lived another fifty years. But what
happened? During the oncoming of the dark cycle after Jesus
(which began as before said about the time of Pythagoras), the
last few rays from the setting sun of the ancient light shone feebly
in the minds of certain of these Christian Fathers, Clement of
Alexandria for one, and Origen of Alexandria for another, and in
one or two more like these, who had been initiated at least in the
lowest of some of the then degenerate pagan Mysteries; and these
men entered into the Christian Church and introduced some poor
modicum of that light, some poor rays of it, as it were, which they

still cherished; and these rays they derived mainly from the Neo-pythagorean and the Neoplatonic systems.

People speak of Christianity as if it were wholly derived from Judaism. Very little of it is. It is, in its theology, almost wholly derived from misunderstood Greek thought, mainly, as said, from the Neopythagorean and Neoplatonic systems; and this is obvious to anyone who reads the writings of those who are called the great doctors of Christian theology, such as Dionysius, the so-called Areopagite, whose system is, in essentials, entirely taken from the Neoplatonic philosophy. Mainly derived from him, again, are the present standard theological works of the Church of Rome: I mean the works of Thomas Aquinas. These are today the stand-ard by which the theology of Rome is directed and settled when disputed points are to be adjudicated. And yet, while this is so, and while much of that which was taken over by the early Chris-tian Fathers still remains as factors and words in the Christian theology, it has utterly forgotten the spirit of these early pagan thoughts; and that religion today stands reduced to a system of forms and ceremonies, mostly.

Now this is the situation that we are facing in the Occident, and above everything else it is our duty to bring back the old spiritual life, the old spiritual fire, the holy fire of the ancient days, to our fellow men: not to make the world pagan again — if we can use that term pagan in the sense of reintroducing the old Greek or Roman mythology, not at all; nor to make it Buddhist in the sense of introducing the present Buddhist religion; nor Brahmanical; nor Zoroastrian; because all these in their turn are more or less degenerate — but to bring back the essence of true religion, the living truths, which all the great Masters of the world from immemorial time have taught.

The Christians say that the blood of the saints, the blood of the martyrs, is the "seed of the Church." Let us so live that our lives shall be the seed of the great church or fellowship of the future. Ethics lie at the root of it all; ethics, in the heart and mind of man, are the spiritual light shining through his intellect. They are a guide, a light unto our feet when honestly practiced, unfailing, giving infinite peace to the human heart. When we say ethics and morals we do not mean merely conventional systems of right conduct, though those may be good also. We mean the cultivation of the understanding, of the instinct living in the soul of man, of his intuitional perception, that right is right and wrong is wrong, outside of any conventional systems whatsoever, and that if a man errs, he works, not only to his own undoing, but to the undoing of others with whom he is inseparably linked.

We have been studying at our last few meetings the theme of *Gods, Monads,* and *Atoms,* and we have seen that these are related to and causative of the evolution of the kosmos by their interworking in the lokas and talas — and we have seen that these lokas and talas comprise the structure, the framework, the carpentry, of the universe; that they infill space, and in fact are space itself. There is not, in the absolute sense, a void point anywhere. All being is infilled with swarming multitudes of entities in the various and manifold degrees of development in which they find themselves. But all follow certain general rules of order, certain fundamental operations of the kosmos, which are called in popular parlance, natural laws. We have seen that the energy-consciousness side is the side of the principles; and that the matter-prakriti side, or the element-side, is the side of the talas, as the former — the principles — are of the lokas. And yet these are inseparable, these lokas and talas, each involved with each, the two highest together and the two lowest together, and those between in similar manner, two by two, as inseparable as the two poles of a magnet (you cannot have a magnet with only one pole); as inseparable also as good and evil, as are light and darkness. In fact, these lokas and talas are an expression kosmically of what we call the system of opposites, of contraries, which is another way of expressing duality in nature. They are interlinked from the uppermost or highest down to the lowest; and it is by passing through these principles and elements, through these lokas and talas, that the life-waves, the streams of beings, undergo their evolution, acquire their experience. There are no separations or voids between the hosts of the various hierarchies in the kosmos, which is another way of expressing the same thing. They blend into each other, let us say, if you like; at least as a first suggestion for understanding. They blend together by and through their atmospheres, the outermost atmosphere of one interpenetrating and interblending more particularly with the outermost atmosphere of its superior or of its inferior loka or tala, as the case may be; and the thought here is of "atmospheres" or auras *within each other*, inwardly, not mere mechanical junctions of atmospheres on any one plane.

These innumerable hosts, these swarming multitudes of beings, which infill space and *are space itself*, work downwards along the arc of the shadows in their so-called descent into matter; and then, when they have reached the bottom of the grand cycle in any manvantara, they turn because, having reached the lowest point possible as regards that hierarchy, they cannot go farther down in it. This is a question which we must go into more fully in the future. Please accept it for the moment as a proposition. Thus, having reached that bottom point, that utmost point of materiality, for that particular cycle of evolution of matter and involution of spirit, they turn and begin the homeward course, "ascending" through the lokas and talas as they "came down" through them, and this ascent is the involution of matter and the evolution of spirit or, to put it in other words, matter resolves itself again into the spirit which it fundamentally is.

There is no difference in occultism between force and matter, except in degree of materiality or grossness; there is no difference of kind at all. There is no difference between spirit and substance, except in degree, no difference in kind at all. Both are fundamentally one; and both, when the long ages of the manvantaric cycle shall have ended, shall sink back again into the infinite womb of the great Void, the mahā-śūnyatā, that is to say, back into the illimitable kosmos of the spiritual realms, which is "void" to our lower natures, but actually an ineffable pleroma or Fullness to the divine eye within us.

It is through the working and interaction respectively of the gods and the monads and the souls and the atoms that the various globes of our planetary chain, and of any other planetary chain, and the various lokas and talas pertaining thereto, come into being. These latter are the vehicles of the former: their garments of light, if you like, on the higher planes, and their bodies so called on the lower planes. They are projected, out-thrown, cast forth, emanated, from these gods, monads, souls, and atoms. Please remember that when we say atom we do not mean the chemical atom of modern scientific thought. That atom is, as said before, rather an aggregate of atomic elements. We mean by the term a vital-astral entity. At the heart of it is its monad. At the heart of that monad is its god, and that god is but a ray of the supreme summit of the hierarchy to which it belongs.

Now, any such hierarchy is but one of an endless multitude of others similar to it; yea, there are others so much greater than it, be it as great as your imagination can make it, that it itself seems by comparison but as a grain of sand on the shores of an infinite sea. It is so, even in the outer spaces of astronomy which the instruments of the astronomers can, or at least attempt to, penetrate. There are kosmoi, kosmoses, so much greater than our own universal kosmos (which comprises everything within the zone of the Milky Way) beyond our universe, that our entire universal kosmos could be placed in one of them and lost; and, on the other hand, there is an actual universe at the core of every one of the tiniest atoms of our physical makeup, an actual universe infilled with its own hierarchies, infilled with its own endless hosts of beings.

Remember, please, that bulk, volume, size, have nothing whatsoever to do with consciousness, or with force. And greater than that thought is this: that the worlds we see, the universe we see, are but the rind, the shell, the husk of the greater part which lies within. We see these things around us; they are repeated by reflection from what is within: "As above, so below; as below, so above."

We were speaking of initiations and Mysteries a few moments agone, and perhaps some may have wondered: Are there no records left of these? There are many; but, alas, people do not know how to find them. The ordinary scholar takes such statements as he finds them in his books as simply examples, samples, rather, of what he calls the "unexampled superstition of past ages." He knows everything! Our little mental world of 100 or 150 or 200 years is the *summum bonum*, the *ne plus ultra*, to such minds; everything that preceded that short period was ignorance and superstition; but there are some men and women who have intellects greater than those, intuitions livelier than those, and they have felt and seen at least somewhat of the truth in reading these records of bygone times.

I have personally seen statements in such old records which are amazingly bold and open. For instance, I make mention of things found in articles or poems written by Professor Kenneth Morris, in these cases taken from some of the old Welsh writings, and I have marveled that such things were left open, simply marveled at it; but when you read a little more you find that the allusion is so masterly interwoven with cognate subjects, true but having no direct bearing upon that blazing star of light that springs forth to the eye here and there, that these other cognate subjects actually hide the esoteric star of light, and our modern reader simply reads in such case as he would a fine modern poem, and he sees nothing more.

I will take another instance. Professor Osvald Sirén, in a very interesting lecture he gave on Chinese Buddhist art a few days ago, twice or thrice, perhaps, mentioned two things which are extremely interesting, and they were placed in direct conjunction. You remember he told us in his description of the various postures of these statues of the buddhas and bodhisattvas, that the bodhisattvas wore what he called "crowns"; and he called attention to the headgear, as represented in these statues of the buddhas, and he called it the *ushnīsha*. This is a Sanskrit word, and it comes from the Sanskrit root *ush*, which means "to be warm," "to be hot," "to be flaming," or "fiery." Ushnīsha is also used in the sense of "turban," because this particular headgear somewhat resembles a turban. It is of spiral conical form, somewhat like the spiral shell of some snails.

One of the most interesting and instructive aspects of ancient thought — and it should be of our studies likewise — is that of symbology. It has been very truly said that once an esoteric thought has been vocally expressed or printed, it is exoteric. Of course that is true. That is a fact. But let us not lose sight of another fact, that while a thing, an esoteric truth, may be proclaimed from the housetops, *unless it is understood* it still remains esoteric, although in form, formally, it is exoteric.

I think it was Aristotle who first used these words "esoteric" and "exoteric," meaning that which is inward, and that which is outward and formal. Of course, that distinction is a true one; yet if you examine the literatures, the symbology of the ancient literatures, philosophies, and sciences, with the understanding given to us by the esoteric teachings, you will find that while the symbolism is exoteric because it has been published, it still remains esoteric because it is unexplained, its meaning is still hid.

Now will you please recall to your minds that two years ago, I think it was, we spoke of the fact that practically the entire life of the ancient world in all its branches, religious, scientific, philosophic, social, political, whatnot, was ultimately based on knowledge derived from the Mysteries. This fact is so true and goes so far in reach that, for an example, even the dread crucifixion-punishment of the Persians, Carthaginians, and Romans, a punishment to which only criminals or foreigners were ever subjected, in early times, as a form, arose in the initiatory ceremonies.

To return more directly to the subject of the "crown" and the ushnīsha on the buddhas' heads: the crown, you will remember, was the symbolic sign of one who had passed a certain degree in initiation. He who was "crowned" was an initiate of a certain grade; and this was expressed by saying that he wore a crown. This wearing of crowns has passed into our own European life. The monarchs are crowned, and at their coronations they ignorantly repeat a very, very ancient ceremony, meaning then a great deal, meaning now nothing. And the wearing or use of crowns, at least as a decoration on rings or letter paper, is still retained by European nobility in the form of coronets. Originally it meant that the one so entitled to use the one or the other of these various crowns had passed a certain grade of initiation, and in some cases a high initiation too, if you please. The bodhisattvas were those who were *crowned with the buddhic fire,* which was symbolized by the wearing of a diadem or a crown, or something similar. The crown, actually, if you examine its earliest forms in iconography, you will see evidently originated in two ideas, one of which was the sun, used as a symbol, with its spreading rays — so much so that some of the late studies or artworks of the very last age of the ancient times, that of the Romans, show one or more of the emperors, for instance, with a halo or a nimbus at the back of his head from which spikes spread out, making a crown or representing the solar rays. The solar rite, if you like to call it that, was thus symbolized; and the halo or nimbus back of the heads of the buddha statues, a fact-symbol copied by the Christians likewise, originated from a fact well known to the ancients, and even spoken of in the exoteric literature as it has come down to us. This fact — and this is the second idea or truth mentioned — is that a saint, as the Christians would say, a holy man, as we may say, i.e., one who is in the state of deep samādhi, has his head surrounded with these auric streams, these rays from the vital inner fire, which form a glory around his head, and sometimes even around the entire body. They stream upwards from the back of the head, often symbolically represented in the buddha-iconography as one single, lambent flame soaring upwards from and over the top of the skull. In this case you may perhaps find that the ushnīsha is missing, its place being taken by this flame issuing from the top of the head, a symbolic representation of the fire of the spirit and of the aroused and active buddhic faculty in which the man is at the time.

You see how beautiful these thoughts are, how much there is merely in studying the outward symbology of these old beliefs. How often have I heard this very ushnīsha mocked at by Occidentals, derided with more or less gentle sarcasm. Such mockery comes from a lack of understanding. It pays — even to put it on the personal, selfish plane — it pays to understand and study symbology! There is one more explanation of the ushnīsha, the most secret of all, which we mention but pass over at present. It refers to the popular belief that the ushnīsha is an excrescence or protuberance of the skull itself.

Now, there are a few more things which we ought to inaugurate tonight as a prelude and introduction to the beginning of our study when we next meet. Let me first read from *The Secret Doctrine*, volume I, page 569, the following extract:

> . . . the ancient Initiates, who were followed more or less closely by all profane antiquity, meant by the term "ATOM," a Soul, a Genius or Angel, the first-born of the ever-concealed CAUSE of all causes; and in this sense their teachings become comprehensible. They claimed, as do their successors, the existence of Gods and Genii, angels or "demons," not outside, or

independent of, the Universal *Plenum*, but within it. Only this *Plenum*, during the life-cycles, is infinite.

We have soon to close our study this evening, but let us again point out that in our use of the term *atom*, as H. P. Blavatsky always used it, we employ it as, and give it the same general meaning that, the ancient Greek philosophers did from whom we derive the word. If you remember, it means "that which cannot be divided"; so, then, it was the ultimate particle of substance; and this indivisible atom did not at all mean the atom in our modern, scientific, chemical sense. It meant rather what we called the monad, which was the name given to the spiritual One by Pythagoras, and meant exactly the same thing that atom originally did, the word used by the old Greek Atomists, such as Democritus, Leucippus, Epicurus, and Lucretius of Italy, and by such as they, albeit the Atomistic sense was more materialistic than ours. Furthermore, this word atom is used by us in a general sense, frequently. We have spoken of the sun as an atom, and we have spoken of the earth as an atom, and we have called attention to the fact that the ancient Hindus in their writings called Brahmā (the third hypostasis, so to say, of the divine Brahman) the kosmic atom. The idea is that this kosmic atom is "Brahmā's Egg," from which the universe shall spring into manifested being, as from the egg the chick comes forth, in its turn to lay another egg. Each of these kosmic eggs or universes gives birth, after its rest period has ended, to its own offspring, each of the former derived in similar manner from its own former manvantaric egg.

And a common doctrine among the ancients all over the world, in Hindustan or in Greece or Rome, wherever it may have been, was, as so beautifully expressed in a poem by Cleanthes, the Stoic: "Zeus is all that is. Whate'er you see or know or sense or feel is Zeus. Zeus is all within and all without." Therefore not an atom but is Zeus, as also every potentiality of the infinite kosmos, as of all kosmoi; for every universe or kosmos is but one of the vast and incomputable swarms of living entities which fill the spaces of endless and beginningless SPACE.

THIRTY-NINE

THEOSOPHY AND OCCULTISM. OCCULTISM: THE QUINTESSENCE OF
TRUTH, REALITY; A COMPLETE WHOLE. OCCULTISM
AND MORAL RESPONSIBILITY. OUR SOLAR SYSTEM:
A KOSMIC ATOM, EGG OF BRAHMĀ.

It is easy to become a Theosophist. Any person of average intellectual
capacities, and a leaning toward the meta-physical; of pure, unselfish life, who
finds more joy in helping his neighbour than in receiving help himself; one who
is ever ready to sacrifice his own pleasures for the sake of other people; and
who loves Truth, Goodness and Wisdom for their own sake, not for the benefit
they may confer — is a Theosophist.

But it is quite another matter to put oneself upon the path which leads to
the knowledge of what is good to do, as to the right discrimination of good
from evil; a path which also leads a man to that power through which he can
do the good he desires, often without even apparently lifting a finger.
— H. P. Blavatsky, "Practical Occultism," *Lucifer*, II, 150

Occultism is not the acquirement of powers, whether psychic or intellectual, though both are its servants. Neither is Occultism the pursuit of
happiness, as men understand the word; for the first step is sacrifice, the
second, renunciation. — *Lucifer*, I, 7

Our philosophy of life is one grand whole, every part necessary and fitting
into every other part. Every one of its doctrines can and must be carried to its
ultimate conclusion. Its ethical application must proceed similarly. If it conflict with old opinions those must be cast off. It can never conflict with true
morality. . . . The spirit of Theosophy must be sought for; a sincere application
of its principles to life and act should be made. Thus mechanical Theosophy,
which inevitably leads — as in many cases it already has — to a negation of
brotherhood, will be impossible, and instead there will be a living, actual
Theosophy. — William Q. Judge, *The Path*, X, 235

. . . Tcharaka, a Hindu physician, who is said to have lived 5,000 years B.C., in
his treatise on the origin of things, . . . thus beautifully expresses himself: "Our
Earth is, like all the luminous bodies that surround us, one of the atoms of the
immense Whole of which we show a slight conception by terming it — the
Infinite." — *Isis Unveiled*, I, 560

O CCULTISM, as the Masters and H. P. Blavatsky have told
us, is that sublime wisdom delivered to the early races
of mankind by exalted beings from other lokas; and
while in our modern times to this wisdom has been given the

name of occultism, that is the *science of things which are secret or hid,* and while that name has its correspondence in other languages, as in the Sanskrit *gupta-vidyā,* in the form in which it has been presented to the public in our age, it is called theosophy. One may ask oneself: Is there any intrinsic difference between occultism and theosophy? I think we may say very fairly and justly that there is not, that fundamentally the two are one, two names for one thing. But H. P. Blavatsky very wisely made a distinction, superficial if you like, but convenient, between occultism and theosophy, and this distinction was thought of in connection with the three kinds of members of the Theosophical Movement: first, the members of the Theosophical Society who are neither theosophists nor occultists necessarily, but who are those who so greatly admire our broad and universal platform, who are so much in sympathy with the ideals which theosophy sets forth, that they have thrown in their lot with us, and work with us. The second class comprises those who are more than mere members of the Theosophical Society; they are those who study the particular and certain doctrines which in our time have been called theosophical, and which represent the eye doctrine, as Gautama the Buddha called it; in other words, the publication for the public weal of certain chosen and specified doctrines of occultism, fit for public dissemination in our age. Lastly, those who have given themselves in a larger, in a deeper, and in a more heartful degree than the other two classes have done, to that sublime wisdom which has come down to us from immemorial time as the revelation, if we may use that word, of the truths of the kosmos, and of course of man as a part thereof.

This, then, is the distinction, such as it is, between theosophy and occultism. The theosophical doctrines are more generally for the public, yet they are chosen from the doctrines of occultism; they are the doctrines which are most fit for public dissemination in our age, as already said.

Now the unfortunate part of this matter is the following: everything that is of human nature, or which springs from the heart or brain of mankind, is de facto subject to imitation or even to degeneration; and consequently this name occultism, a truly noble name in its real meaning, is often greatly, even vilely, misused and misunderstood; it is bandied about in the newspapers, and passes from mouth to mouth as signifying little more than the so-called psychistic or wonderment-doctrines on which the public feeds so avidly. That use is a degradation of the original sense. All things which really satisfy the heart and mind of man must be of necessity true in degree, otherwise they could not so satisfy; but, as we all know, men's minds and hearts sometimes feed on mere husks, as it is expressed in the Christian New Testament — feed on husks which the swine eat. You know what the symbolic expression swine means. We have spoken of it before, so we need not now allude to it again. But the point which I wish to impress upon our minds in this connection is, that occultism is the exposition of the very essence, the quintessence, of truth, of reality. It cannot be studied by the higher mind alone, nor can it be studied alone by those other faculties in man which he classes under the generic heading of "feelings." But it must be studied as a complete whole, and it answers fully to all demands of man's entire spiritual and psychological composition, and is therefore entirely and utterly satisfactory. It provides man not merely with a basis for the noblest system of ethics the world knows, but describes to him what those ethics are, and on what they are founded, and what the due and perfect practice of them will lead to. And that leading, we are told, is along that old, small path, of which the Upanishads speak — for those who follow it finally come into direct connection and into confabulation with the all-wise and calm-eyed gods, for that path leads us directly to the heart of the universe — the "heart" in the mystical and esoteric sense: into those places, into those spiritual, superspiritual, and divine, regions where is the core of the being of each one of us.

The various great religions of the present and of the past times have sprung forth from the doctrines of occultism; each one of such religions in its germinal stage, in its beginning, was the spiritual offspring of some great and noble man, one of the Masters, indeed, who taught publicly during the particular period when he appeared among men openly for the salvation of his fellows, giving forth anew, once again, the age-old truths or, perchance, but a newer version of the ancient light to them, elucidating the great problems concerning the kosmos and man, which to those who have not received such light, so harass the human heart and, it may be, the human intellect, with an urgency demanding solution. Such a movement was started in our time by our great-souled Brother, H. P. Blavatsky. It depends upon us almost wholly at the present time, and will in the future so depend very largely, whether that effort is to fail as all religions in the past, save one, have failed, more or less; or whether it is to go forward successfully, doing the work it was intended to do, planting the seeds of right thinking and right action, of human brotherhood, and of universal kindliness, in the hearts of all who follow it; or whether, following the left-hand path, the path of matter, it is to go down and possibly become even an instrument of the Brothers of the Shadows.

Our Teachers have told us plainly that the study of occultism involves a great moral responsibility: that it places such a responsibility upon the shoulders of him or of her who studies it, because *it awakens the inner man;* it awakens his hid powers. And, furthermore, precisely proportionate to a man's earnestness is its study productive of good or, it may be, of the reverse. OCCULTISM CANNOT BE TRIFLED WITH. It deals with direct and original things, if you understand these terms, not with reflected truths. Hence, unless a man's heart be absolutely pure — I mean by that, clean of all personal selfishness — he never is safe. There can be no trifling with it. It calls out of a man all he is inwardly, and brooks no halfway loyalty.

The two paths lie always at our feet; at every step they diverge, one to the right and one to the left; and one single act may induce a habit, which will make a character, in time, by repetition; and that character is you or I, for it is the exercise of knowledge (or half-knowledge) and will.

It is for these reasons that time and again we refer to the necessity of understanding clearly what we mean by morals, and that there is the utmost need for their practice by each one of us, by you and by me, every moment of our lives. Such practice does not mean merely the hypocritical assent of the mentality, with a mental reservation that "finally I shall do as I please." That field of mental reservations is precisely where the Brothers of the Shadows make their conquests of the hearts of men, on just such lines as those. I tell you, with all solemnity, that the warning should be, must be, heeded.

Now, let us open our study tonight by reminding ourselves of the fact that the lokas and the talas of which we have spoken at our several last meetings, as concerns the earth, are its seven principles and its seven elements respectively — and as concerns the kosmos precisely the same may be said; furthermore, that the seven kosmical lokas and seven kosmical talas comprise the entirety, the totality, of all that is in our solar system, which is the kosmic atom. In other words, they comprise the totality of the Egg of Brahmā. You know the meaning of that fine old Brahmanical symbol, the egg, a symbol which is found likewise in other religions, such as the Orphic system in Greece, and the Egyptian system; and we know from the representations we have of the earth-mounds, that anciently it was equally well recognized in North America.

When we speak of the kosmic atom — when we speak of the Egg of Brahmā, which is another way of saying the same thing — when we speak of it as being the solar system, please know that we do not mean the planets together, or the sun alone, or the sun and planets together, which last form merely the outward rind or shell, as it were (or, if we may use a physiological term, the nerve centers, the ganglia, of the physiological operations), of this Egg of Brahmā. When we speak of the kosmic atom, and inferentially of the atom of matter as we know it on this earth, we mean the vital-astral entity behind it, that particular entity considered as a unity, which gives it its life, its swabhāva, that is, its particular or individual characteristic, that which differentiates it from other similar kosmic eggs or kosmic atoms. We may also speak of our earth as Brahmā's Egg, but this is by analogy; the real Egg of Brahmā is the solar system.

We have said before that the lokas and talas are the seven principles and the seven elements of our globe, our globe Terra; but there are other seven lokas and other seven talas which are respectively the seven principles and the seven elements of each one of the other six globes of our planetary chain, *seven of each, to each.* One may ask oneself, if one has not studied occultism, why there should be so much of the sevening process in our studies; why our doctrines should continually run in sevenfold aggregates. The answer of occultism is, because nature has so builded her structures. Outside of such obvious things as the seven principal colors of the light spectrum and the seven rays of the sun (which is almost the same thing), and the seven notes of the diatonic scale in music, and the fact known to students of physiology that many diseases run in cycles of seven days or multiples thereof — leaving these things aside, we find in studying the ancient literatures as showing forth the religions, philosophies, and sciences of the past times, that while they all state the fact under different forms undoubtedly, they all agree more or less unanimously in ascribing to the structural framework of the universe and of man the same system of seven component parts.

This question of numeration is one which we have laid no foundation for at present, and therefore we postpone it for longer consideration to a future time. Suffice it then for the present to accept it as a proposition for study. You yourselves can prove what has been said. The literatures of the world lie open before you. Read them and study them, and you will be convinced as all other sincere students have been convinced who have done it. Study therefore the evidences and prove the facts.

Now the gods, monads, and atoms work through the kosmic egg inwards and outwards, that is, they work through the lokas and talas. As H. P. Blavatsky says in the first volume of *The Secret Doctrine*, on page 619:

"God, Monad, and Atom are the correspondences of Spirit, Mind, and Body (*Atma, Manas, and Sthula Sarira*) in man." In their septenary aggregation they are the "Heavenly Man" (see *Kabala* for the latter term); thus, terrestrial man is the provisional reflection of the Heavenly. . . . "The Monads (*Jivas*) are the Souls of the Atoms, both are the fabric in which the Chohans (Dhyanis, *gods*) clothe themselves when a form is needed."

They so clothe themselves, in order, as pointed out in our former studies of the gods, monads, souls, and atoms, to evolve forth the universe; as the Upanishad puts it, as a spider spins a web. That is a beautiful symbol. From out of themselves, from their own substance, they weave the geometrical pattern of the kosmos and therein work.

The study of the structure or framework of our kosmic atom

is a vast, profound, and intricate subject, and before we can properly do it justice, it would seem better first to undertake at least a cursory examination — for at this point we have now arrived in our studies — of the building of our own globe, as a part of the planetary chain in which it is one of the seven links. Indeed, let us go a little farther than that, and study the working of the life-waves of and in our planetary chain. Our planetary chain, as said before, may itself be considered the Egg of Brahmā, the kosmic egg, the fruit of its parent, i.e., the planetary chain of the preceding manvantara; and it itself is to be the parent of its own future offspring, the planetary chain to come when we in our own chain shall have run our cyclical evolutionary course and sunk into our long and well-earned pralaya, or rest — in other words, after we have rejoined those superspiritual spheres from within which we came in the very beginning of things — to remain there in peace and in bliss ineffable, until the seeds latent in us, the fruitage of our present and future acts and thoughts, shall spring into activity in due time. For all things move in regular courses and according to order, which shall bring us down, in far-distant aeons into the fabrication of the planetary chain to be.

FORTY

DEFINITIONS OF DEITY: ATHEISM; PANTHEISM. IS THERE A SUPREME
PERSONAL GOD? KOSMIC ARCHITECTS AND BUILDERS.
REALLY TO KNOW, ONE MUST BECOME.

"Thus there is but one Absolute Upadhi (basis) *in the spiritual sense,
from, on, and in which, are built for Manvantaric purposes the countless
basic centres on which proceed the Universal, cyclic, and individual Evolutions during the active period."*

*"The informing Intelligences, which animate these various centres of
Being, are referred to indiscriminately by men beyond the Great Range as
the Manus, the Rishis, the Pitris, the Prajâpati, and so on; and as Dhyani
Buddhas, the Chohans, Melhas* (fire-gods), *Bodhisattvas, and others, on
this side. The truly ignorant call them gods; the learned profane, the one
God; and the wise, the Initiates, honour in them only the Manvantaric manifestations of* THAT *which neither our Creators* (the Dhyan Chohans) *nor
their creatures can ever discuss or know anything about. The* ABSOLUTE *is
not to be defined, and no mortal or immortal has ever seen or comprehended
it during the periods of Existence. The mutable cannot know the Immutable,
nor can that which lives perceive Absolute Life."*

"Therefore, man cannot know higher beings than his own "progenitors."
"Nor shall he worship them," but he ought to learn *how* he came into the
world. . . .

There is frequent confusion in the attributes and genealogies of the
gods in their theogonies, as given to the world by the half-initiated writers,
Brahmanical and Biblical, the Alpha and the Omega of the records of that
symbolical science. Yet there could be no such confusion made by the
earliest nations, the descendants and pupils of the divine instructors: for
both the attributes and the genealogies were inseparably linked with cosmogonical symbols, the "gods" being the life and animating "soul-principle" of
the various regions of the Universe. Nowhere and by no people was speculation allowed to range *beyond* those *manifested* gods. The boundless and
infinite UNITY remained with every nation a virgin,forbidden soil, untrodden
by man's thought, untouched by fruitless speculation. The only reference
made to it was the brief conception of its diastolic and systolic property, of
its periodical expansion or dilatation, and contraction. In the Universe with
all its incalculable myriads of systems and worlds disappearing and re-
appearing in eternity, the anthropomorphised powers, or gods, their Souls,
had to disappear from view with their bodies: — "The breath returning to

the eternal bosom which exhales and inhales them," says our Catechism. . . .
In every Cosmogony, behind and higher than the *creative* deity, there is a
superior deity, a planner, an Architect, *of whom* the Creator is but the
executive agent. And still higher, *over* and *around, within* and *without,*
there is the UNKNOWABLE and the *unknown,* the Source and Cause of all
these Emanations. . . .   — *The Secret Doctrine,* II, 34, 42–3

W E APPROACH this evening one aspect of occultism
which has always been held as very sacred and very
carefully guarded, and that is the study of other worlds
than ours, not as those worlds have been set forth in the exoteric
religions, but in accordance with the secret wisdom which has
been handed down to us from immemorial time. We mean the
teaching concerning the superior globes of our own planetary
chain; and on a misunderstanding of the doctrines concerning
the teaching regarding the planetary chain have been based the
exoteric views of the heavens and the hells of the various exoteric
faiths.

One might ask oneself what the proper answer is to give to
those who might ask any one of us: "Is a theosophist an atheist?
Does he believe in God? If not, why not?" Now these questions
are directly connected with the proper understanding of the doctrines about the planetary chain. Let us then first devote a few
moments to answering these questions for ourselves. Are we
atheists? How can we answer that question before we know what
we mean by the term? If we take a modern dictionary, for instance
the *Century Dictionary,* and look up the definition of the term
"atheism," we find three general ones. The first is: "The doctrine
that there is no God." And then follows a quotation from Sir J. R.
Seeley, from his book, *Natural Religion,* page 26: "*Atheism* is a
disbelief in the existence of God — that is, disbelief in any regularity in the universe to which man must conform himself under
penalties." Notice the peculiar limitation of thought involved in
this. If there is no regularity in the universe, therefore there is
no personal supreme God, and therefore if you don't believe in
such a God, the universe is irregular and anarchical, and you
are an atheist!

The second definition is as follows: "The denial of theism,
that is, of the doctrine that the great first cause is a supreme

intelligent, righteous person." The third definition is "godless-ness," with the implied meaning that if you don't accept the God of the one who gives the definition, you are an atheist, and you live a "godless," that is, an evil life. Such, then, are the definitions given in a standard work.

Now any tyro-student of history knows that this question or idea of belief in a god or in no god has varied, or rather has received different treatment in different ages. You will remember doubtless that when the Christian religion first began to run a more or less successful course in Greece and in the Roman Empire, educated Greeks and Romans called the new Christian sect an atheistic sect. They were called "atheists," *atheoi*, merely meaning one, or rather those, who did not accept the established gods of the State, that is, the gods of the State religion; and the term bore with it no particular or necessary implication of evil-doing whatsoever. It was very much as if a European or American were to say today: Such and such a man is a freethinker, or a Confucianist, or a Buddhist, or a scientist, etc.

When the Christians grew more powerful and had in later ages the upper hand of the so-called pagans, they in their turn retaliated by calling the pagans atheists, because the latter did not accept the Jewish-Greek, newfangled Christian God. In other words, the term actually means: "If you accept *my* God you are not an atheist; and if you do not accept my God you are an atheist."

That is just about what atheism has always meant, if we consult the pages of history. But if we think of atheism as containing in itself a necessary implication of evildoing, we lower ourselves to the mental viewpoint of certain very narrow-minded Christians to whom all who do not accept their particular variety of religion, their particular understanding or misunderstanding of Deity, are atheists. We are reminded of course of that Scottish lady of the legend, of whom we have all heard, who with her husband composed a kirk; she and her Jamie alone composed the kirk. But she was "nae sae certain aboot Jamie." Therefore she alone composed the kirk, and her husband Jamie, poor man, came very near to being (in her eyes) an atheist.

Now that is the spirit that has governed Christian thought

practically ever since the death of its founder. So, therefore, when we ask if a man is an atheist, we must be careful first to ascertain what we mean by the term. I have been called an atheist because I do not accept the old orthodox definition of the personal Christian God. I reject the term, if it mean living an immoral life. I reject it with all the indignation of which I am sensible, if the word be so used, for it is an imputation which is grossly unjust. And doubtless any one of you feels exactly as I do. Was it not the author of *The Plough and the Cross*, a very clever Irish writer, who said somewhere that our "forefathers were afraid of ghosts; but we are afraid of names," i.e., of labels and tickets?

Notice the second definition given above, that a man is an atheist if he does not believe in the existence of a supreme, personal, first cause, who is an "intelligent, righteous *person*." I reject such a deity; therefore, according to the dictionary, I am an atheist. But if anyone were to ask me, Are you an atheist? I would say no. And if he were to say, Why? I would say, because to me the boundless All is totally instinct with consciousness and life, an infinitely immense and swarming multitude, endless and beginningless, of beings who form not merely the heart of the pulsating life of all that is, but provide the very consciousnesses which govern and control the innumerable universes of and in the boundless All.

If you turn even to the canonical scripture of the Christian religion and ask what Paul meant when he spoke of Deity, we find there, from him, two definitions worthy of the initiant that the man was, when he said, first: "In It we live, and move, and have our being." This is pure pantheism — not as misunderstood in the grotesque sense which the Christians have misgiven to it, i.e., that every stock and every stone is God, thus showing their profound ignorance of the high and noble philosophical meaning behind the term pantheism; but in the sense that all is life, and that it is impossible to conceive of, nay, even to touch the smallest point of space or being, which lacks that limitless life. For back of A lies B, which is still greater than A; back of B lies C, still greater than B; back of C lies D, yet more grandiose; and so on infinitely, with never an end. What blasphemous ideas have come down through the ages regarding this question of Deity! Here in our Occidental Christianism we have a God, a bundle of contradictions, a misunderstood rendering of Neopythagorean and Neoplatonic, and of some Judaic, thoughts, the curious and contradictory compound called the Christian Deity — I mean the theological definition thereof.

Then another saying of Paul from his Epistle to the Romans, in chapter 11, verse 36: "For out of It, and through It, and back to It are all things." Pantheism this, pure and simple, even as we understand it.

Or, if we turn to the English rendering of John's Gospel, chapter 4, verse 24, we find an affirmation of the opposite thought, which particular translation sprang from the *orthodox* rendering of the text by the later Christians, where this Greek verse is mistranslated as saying "God is *a* Spirit." The Greek original could equally well and even better be translated: "God is Spirit." So be it. They may worship "*a* spirit" if they like, *a* spirit who is a "righteous *person*"; but those whose hearts have expanded under the beneficent influence of the wisdom-religion, and whose minds have opened to somewhat of the understanding which every faithful student of that wisdom should possess, can only reject such a definition of the Deity that he cannot accept, with the indignation which the definition deserves.

No theosophist, H. P. Blavatsky has somewhere said, has ever denied Deity, i.e., limitless life in the boundless All; but this Deity is nothing like, nor in any sense can it be compared with, a finite creator, which such a "person" is supposed to be, however "supreme" and however "righteous" and however great that supposed "person" or that "spirit" may be imagined to be.

Now, if someone were to ask you, Is there a supreme personal God ruling the planetary chain and is it your God? the answer is no. There is a host, a multitude, a hierarchy, of intelligent and of thinking and of highly spiritualized beings, from which the planetary chain sprang forth, but it is not our god, nor do we worship any such. Those beings are our progenitors, our elder brothers in a very exalted sense, for they were men in former manvantaras long since past; but our "god," never, not even when considered as a unity and called the Logos. Our "deity," if it is anything, is that indescribable, boundless life, in its highest aspects, back of everything, forming a background of all manifested being on whatever plane, and in which all is, and from which all is, and to which all is; indescribable, unthinkable, and therefore ineffable.

You remember that when Gautama the Buddha was asked, What is God? and Is there God? that greatest and noblest of Masters was silent. And when asked a second and a third time, What is God? he again was silent. Three times was he asked the question, and three times he preserved his silence.

In our recent studies we have attempted to show that the entire system of beings, the structure or framework of the universe on the background of the Boundless, sprang forth from the action and the intermingling of the gods, the monads, the souls, and the atoms; and that these produced the various planetary chains of our solar system, that is to say, of the kosmic atom or, as the Brahmanical thinkers named it, the Egg of Brahmā. From these gods, monads, souls, and atoms, the manifested being of the solar system came forth.

Let us then turn next to our own planetary chain. You will remember that it is stated to be composed of seven globes, of which our present earth is the fourth and on the lowest plane of the seven; and that this planetary chain is working in four of the planes or worlds of the solar system, in the four lowest worlds thereof, as a matter of fact, our earth occupying the lowest element or world of the seven which compose the solar system. These seven elements are otherwise the kosmical lokas and talas, or kosmical worlds, principles, and elements working together. They are the worlds within the outer seeming, more ethereal than our world, of which ours is a copy, not necessarily a copy in every detail, but a copy on general lines, even as the physical body of man is a copy on general lines of the soul of him; and as his soul is a copy on general lines of the spirit of him; and as the spirit of him is a copy on general lines of his divine root, a god-being or godhead from which he sprang.

You will also remember that there are two general lines or hierarchies of spiritual beings who brought forth our kosmos, of which our planetary chain is one part; and these two are respectively the architects and the builders. The architects form the higher or more spiritual side, and actually form the line of the luminous arc; and the builders or constructors form, on the other hand, the shadowy arc.

In the Buddhist system of Tibet, the general name of dhyāni-chohans, or lords of meditation, is given to both these lines of beings; but more particularly the architects are called the dhyāni-buddhas, the buddhas of contemplation. The Greeks called the world builders, the masons of the world, by the general term of *kosmokratores*, a compound Greek word meaning "world builders." They are those who receive the creative or constructive impress from the beings of the luminous arc, or the dhyāni-buddhas, and carry it out.

In each of these two lines there are seven grades or rather classes: there are seven classes of the dhyāni-buddhas, and seven classes of the dhyāni-chohans; and so far as our own planetary chain is concerned, these seven classes are reflected, repeated, therein.

Furthermore, each one of the seven globes composing our planetary chain is under the particular oversight (I think it would be wrong to use the word direction or guidance, but rather the *over-seeing*), under the particular over-seeing or care — care is perhaps the best word to describe this extremely meta-physical concept — under the care of one class of these dhyāni-buddhas and one class of the builders. That is to say, globe A, for instance, the first, on the descending arc of our planetary chain, is under the care or watchful inspiration or oversight, of one class of these seven of both lines. Globe B is under the care of the second class of each line. Globe C under the same care or inspiration of the third class of each; and our own globe D or fourth has likewise its own dhyāni-buddhas and builders of the fourth class; and the three globes of the ascending arc, similarly.

Do not confuse these two lines, because the distinction is very important if we are to obtain any adequate understanding at all of this branch of the ancient wisdom. The *architects* then, of the luminous arc, provide the model, lay down the plans. They are the architects, the overseers, and their work is carried out by these inferior grades or classes of spiritual beings called the *builders*.

Now with regard to this very question of God, considered

CHAPTER FORTY   509

briefly above, you will remember that the Gnostics, during the time of the beginning of the Christian era, claimed, and we claim with them, that the Christian God, Jehovah, whom the Christians call the Creator, could not for that very reason be a very high god. The very attributes and functions of creation or formation that were given to him show, said these Gnostics, that he was but an inferior deity, a builder, receiving his "orders," so to say, from the divine architects and supernal planners and thinkers of the kosmos, he himself thus being but a builder. As they so well put it, the manifold imperfections and incompletenesses so plainly apparent even to us humans, in the kosmical system, proclaim that it could not be the work of an all-perfect and kosmically omnipotent Deity; from utter perfection could spring forth only a perfect and complete work. The early Christians were unable to understand the deep philosophy behind this unanswerable axiom, and waxed very wroth and indignant indeed against what they called the "blasphemous opinions" of those Gnostics. In common with all thoughtful minds, you will see the deep philosophical and religious implications that lie behind this argument or axiom, but upon them we cannot longer pause at this time. Remember this, though, that in all the ancient faiths you will find two general classes of spiritual beings at work in the kosmos, and they are always divided, as we have already said this evening, into the thinkers or planners or architects, the inspirers; and into the builders. There is, finally, vastly more in this thought than we have time to go into tonight.

Now the Silent Watcher of whom we have spoken at other meetings is the highest of the dhyāni-chohans of our globe; but there is likewise a Silent Watcher for each of the other six globes, and for the planetary chain as a whole. There is likewise a Silent Watcher for the entire kosmical — for the entire solar — system. So when we say Silent Watcher, without further defining, it is like saying spiritual being or hierarchical head. It is a generic term. As remarked at those former meetings, one such Silent Watcher is on our earth today, the supreme head of the Hierarchy of Compassion, the highest link with the spiritual beings of the hierarchy higher than ours upward along the luminous arc. He is, so to say, our supreme Master, our supreme Chief.

You have all studied, of course, in the doctrine concerning our own planetary chain, what are commonly called the seven rounds, meaning that the life cycle or life-wave begins its evolutionary course on globe A, the first of the globes, then, completing its cycles there, runs down to globe B, and then to globe C, and then to globe D, our earth; and then to globe E, on the ascending arc, then to globe F, and then to globe G. This is one planetary round. Then ensues a planetary nirvana, until the second round begins in the same way, but in a more "advanced" degree of evolution than was the first round. Please note that one such round is a *planetary* round. A *globe*-round is one of the passages, one of the seven passages, of that life-wave during its planetary round, on any one and therefore on and through each of the globes: when the life-wave has passed through globe D, for instance, and ends its cycles on globe D, that is the *globe*-round of globe D for that particular planetary round; and so with all the globes respectively. There are seven *globe*-rounds therefore (one globe-round for each of the seven globes) in each *planetary* round. Furthermore, when seven *planetary* rounds have been accomplished, which is as much as saying 49 *globe*-rounds (or globe-manvantaras), then ensues a still higher nirvana than that between globes G and A after each planetary round, which is called a pralaya of that planetary chain, which pralaya lasts until the cycle again returns for the new planetary chain to form, containing the same series of living beings as on the preceding chain and which are now destined to enter upon that new planetary chain, but on a higher series of planes than in the preceding one.

Next, when seven such planetary chains with their various kalpas or manvantaras have passed away, this sevenfold grand cycle is one *solar* manvantara, and then the entire solar system sinks into the solar or kosmic pralaya. Our own sun is then extinguished, suddenly, like a flash of light, or like a shadow passing over a wall. After just a "flickering," finally the light goes out, and the great mass of entities passes into spiritual realms far higher than any of those attained during the highest point of attainment in the period while the solar manvantara lasted, because they are then entering upon their *solar* nirvana.

Let us draw again the same diagram that we copied from H. P.

Blavatsky at a former meeting, from page 200 of volume I of *The Secret Doctrine*. The seven parallel lines represent, if you please, the seven planes or worlds of the solar system. Above or on the

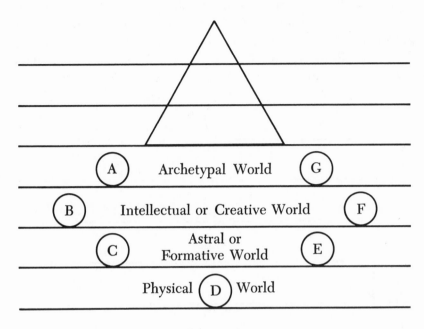

DIAGRAM 1

lowest line of these seven let us place a circle to represent globe D, our earth. On the next plane above we also place two more circles to represent the two globes immediately above our own, called respectively C on the left and E on the right. On the plane above that we place two more globes, and call these respectively B on the left and F on the right. And on the plane above that, the fourth kosmic plane counting upwards, we draw two more circles to represent the two highest globes of our chain, respectively A on the left and G on the right.

Please remember that these kosmic "planes" are merely so called for purposes of convenience. They are actually the seven kosmical lokas and talas of the kosmic system, that is to say, of the solar system. But each one of these is a true world; they are worlds as truly as our own is, which we perceive when we look up and see the stars above us, and look to the earth and see the earth beneath our feet, the trees growing therefrom, the human and other animate beings walking with us, etc. Each one of these kosmic "planes" is a world, but each is again subdivided into septenary divisions, into seven divisions, all of them together making 49 subdivisions of the seven main divisions (or worlds) of the solar system.

Let us illustrate this by another diagram. We draw again seven parallel lines. And let these represent, if you please, the

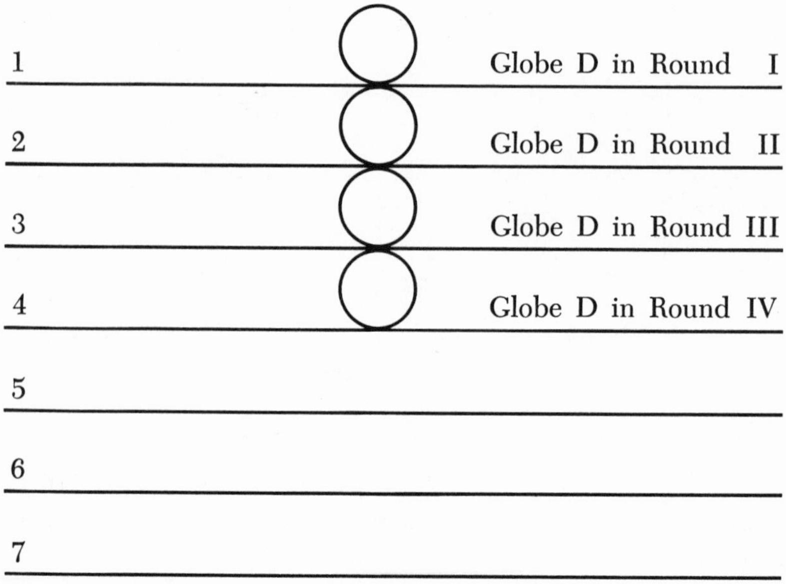

1	Globe D in Round I
2	Globe D in Round II
3	Globe D in Round III
4	Globe D in Round IV
5	
6	
7	

DIAGRAM 2

lowest solar world, or plane, of the seven, the lowest kosmic world, our world, the world we are in now. It, like all the others, is septempartite or divided into seven parts or divisions, representing matter or spirit from the grossest to the highest degree of each in *our* world, from the ethereal (highest) to the most material (lowest); and on one of these planes our globe Terra is at present.

Now what is the manner in which the life-wave in any round works? For the moment, if you will, we shall omit considering the previous three globes, A, B, and C, on the descending turn, and consider only our own globe D, or earth. These seven lines in the diagram are intended to represent respectively the seven grades or materializations of matter in the lowest of the seven kosmic planes, growing more material from the top downwards. Now then, our globe D *in round the first* is in the highest or top-most of these seven subplanes of our own lower kosmic plane, and our own kosmic plane, please remember, is the lowest of the seven of all the kosmic planes. It is the seventh and lowest. The life-wave during round 1 passes through our earth, after evolving it forth, a process which we are to study in detail later; it is a process of evolutionary development which occupies many millions of years; and after finishing its globe-round 1, leaves our globe D and passes to the next higher globe E. All right. As this life-wave is descending into matter for the first three rounds, *our globe* during round first will be on the highest subplane of the lowest kosmic plane or world. The second or next round will find our globe materialized and on subplane the second, counting down-wards; in round the third, still more materialized and on the third subplane downwards; in round 4, that is, where we are now, our globe has reached its grossest state of matter; the downward cycling ceases, and the ascent begins.

What about subplanes 5, 6, and 7? Those planes are related to the destiny of beings who have followed the left-hand path, and who ultimately reach the utmost point of physical materiali-zation in subplane the seventh, or the grossest possible in our solar system, and the last.

We see, thus, that the life-wave in making its first round, round 1, as is illustrated in Diagram 1, passes through (on its descending arc through the lowest four kosmic worlds or planes) the highest subplane or subworld of each one of these lowest four kosmic worlds, forming in each such kosmic world, a globe, one of the then-in-the-making seven globes of the chain. Is this clear? In round 1 the life-wave forms globe A on subplane the highest of the fourth kosmic world or plane. See the diagram. In round 1 the life-wave forms globe B on subplane the highest of the fifth kosmic world or plane. In round 1 the life-wave forms globe C on subplane the highest of the sixth kosmic world or plane; and so with the lowest globe D, our earth; and on the *ascending* scale likewise we see globes E, F, and G, similarly formed, each on the highest subplane of the respective kosmic worlds or planes. Round 2 begins (after the long, long planetary nirvana) on globe A on the *second* subplane of the fourth kosmic world or plane; then the life-wave passes to globe B on the *second* subplane of the fifth kosmic world or plane; then to globe C on the *second* subplane of the sixth kosmic world or plane; then to globe D (our earth) on the *second* subplane of the seventh or lowest kosmic world or plane. Similarly, during this second planetary round, the life-wave passes to all the globes on all the *second* subplanes of the *ascending arc*. Each such passage of the life-wave in and through each globe of the seven globes forms a *globe*-round, as said above.

So with round 3, and again with round 4, where we are now on globe D, on the fourth subplane of the seventh or lowest kosmic plane or world; that is to say, that the life-wave during each planetary round passes through the seven globes of the chain, and from kosmic plane to kosmic plane, but during each one round passes through only one subplane of each kosmic world or plane. The result of this being that during the seven rounds, it passes through 49 subplanes, and the beings composing the life-wave thereby have the chance of working out the destiny for which they came into active manifestation and evolution; for the whole purpose of the evolutionary processes of the kosmos is for the gaining of self-consciousness through individualizing experiences — i.e., experiences which *individualize* (evolve, bring out) the monads. And in order to attain that end, each monad must not merely undergo and mentally experience the various phases and natures of the universal life, but *be them*. As pointed out before in our studies, the initiations of old times, the *real* initiations, the initiations which brought to man's consciousness the knowledge of the spiritual truths of being, were based on this fact: that no man could really know anything merely by being taught about it, but he must *be it*, he must *become it*. In the old Mystery Schools, the system of teaching only during the first three initiations was changed into both teaching and personal experience beginning with the fourth initiation, these personal experiences growing grander and greater with each higher step that the candidate or initiant took; until finally, if he was successful in all the seven degrees, he attained the divine status from which he started forth in the beginning of the kosmic or solar manvantara, *plus divine self-consciousness, self-awakening,* and became thereby a Buddha, an Awakened One; or a Christos, to adopt the old Greek Mystery-term.

During our next few studies we shall continue to investigate the subject of the planetary chain.

FORTY-ONE

THE DOCTRINE OF THE SPHERES. THE UNIVERSAL SOLAR
SYSTEM AND OUR SOLAR SYSTEM. THE SEVEN
SACRED PLANETS: WHY "SACRED"?

But Time was generated together with the universe, that being produced together they might together be dissolved, if any dissolution should ever happen to these. And time was generated according to the exemplar of an eternal nature, that this world might be the most similar possible to such a nature. For its exemplar is permanent being, through the whole of eternity; but the universe alone *was* generated, *is,* and *will be,* through the whole of time. After this manner, therefore, and from such a cogitation of divinity about the generation of time, that he might give birth to its flowing subsistence, he generated the sun and moon, and the five other stars, which are denominated planets, for the purpose of distinguishing and guarding the numbers of time. But the divinity, as soon as he had produced the bodies of these stars, placed them, being seven in number, in the seven circulations formed by the revolution of the nature distinguished by *difference.* . . . But with respect to the other stars, if any one should think proper to investigate their circulations, and through what causes they are established, the labour would be greater than that of the discourse itself, for the sake of which they were introduced. — PLATO, *Timaeus,* pp. 467–8 (Thomas Taylor, trans.)

The lower world is subject to the sway of the upper world.

In the beginning of its revolution the sovereignty over this lower world is committed to one of the slow-moving stars.

Which governeth it alone for the space of a thousand years;

And for other thousands of years each of the heavy-moving stars, and swift-moving stars becometh its partner, each for one thousand years.

Last of all the moon becometh its associate.

After that, the first associate will get the sovereignty.

The second king goeth through the same round as the first king; and the others are in like manner his associates.

Last of all the first king is for a thousand years the partner of the second king.

Then the period of the reign of the second king is also past.

And understand that the same is the course as to all the others.

When the Moon hath been king, and all have been associates along with it, and its reign too is over, one Grand Period is accomplished.

After which the Sovereignty again returneth to the first king, and in this way there is an eternal succession.

And in the beginning of the Grand Period, a new order of things commenceth in the lower world.

And, not indeed the very forms, and knowledge, and events of the Grand Period that hath elapsed, but others precisely similar to them will again be produced.

And every Grand Period that cometh resembleth from beginning to end the Grand Period that is past.
    — *The Desātir*, "The Book of the Prophet, the Great Abad,"
        vv. 102–16 (Mulla Firuz Bin Kaus, trans.)

VAST ARE the reaches of both the space and the time, and profound are the mysteries likewise, connected with and involved in the subjects with which our present cycle of study is opened; for these subjects deal in general with what we may call collectively the *doctrine of the spheres:* that is to say, that particular and fundamental branch of the archaic philosophy and religion of the ancient wisdom which was most especially developed in the countries surrounding the Mediterranean or Inland Sea — a favored study there, even as in the Farther Orient, among the archaic sages of Hindustan, the doctrines regarding the workings of the various monadic states of consciousness were more largely developed and prized.

In our last study we sketched, though briefly, the outline of the theosophical doctrine dealing with the planetary chain of our earth. Now this subject of planetary chains is a special case, as mathematicians would say, of the general doctrine of the spheres; this subject has always been one of the most carefully guarded, considered as one of the most sacred and occult, because it leads us, in its ultimate reaches, directly to the heart of being. In order to reach that heart of being we have to pass through many secret chambers of Mother Nature, chambers which have been held secret from immemorial time, and the arcana of which have been guarded as one of the most sacred possessions of the Guardians of mankind.

You will remember that our studies were originally opened by taking into consideration the general outline of cosmogony and theogony as found in the archaic cosmology and theology of the ancient wisdom. This was sketched in all its general aspects, as an outline only, details being left for filling in at future dates. We passed in review — only in sketch, please bear in mind — how worlds are born, how, like children, they spring from the womb of nature; how, from a germ, they grow into youth, reach maturity, then decline, and finally decay, followed by ultimate death, again to resurrect in cyclic rebirth from that same womb of Mother Nature.

It was shown also that these doctrines of the ancient wisdom, mystic, marvelous, wonderful, leave no query unanswered, leave nothing to be built upon mere faith — blind faith that is; but that each theorem of its philosophy must be, and is, proved, as the study of it progresses. Remember what proof is. Proof consists in bringing conviction to the mind; conviction of its reality, based upon evidence, is the proof of a fact or theorem. Remember that the various circumstantial things which we may bring in production of proof are merely the evidential part, the *evidences* of reality.

Then, as we passed in review, in outline only, these general theorems, we finally arrived at the doctrine concerning the planetary chains, which, as said, is a special case of the general theorem of the wonderful doctrine of the spheres. Henceforth our studies go more into detail. We have sought to conduct our studies together so that the written report of these may help those who are seeking deeper knowledge of the ancient Mysteries and of the ancient wisdom than they can get from the books of the world. One of the reasons for this is that some students have accepted certain statements of Mr. Sinnett on this very question of the planetary chain, to the effect that two of the physical planets of our solar system, Mars and Mercury, were two of the members of our earth's planetary chain, although H. P. Blavatsky in this very volume of *The Secret Doctrine* published several years before her death declared positively that this notion is wrong; for indeed, it is not true.

As our studies proceed, you will see for yourselves that it cannot be true. Let me ask parenthetically: Who was the originator of this idea? You will remember that the earliest teachings were given to two Englishmen in India, Mr. A. O. Hume and Mr. A. P. Sinnett, through H. P. Blavatsky, through Damodar (who later went to Tibet to join the Teachers), and through one or two others. The philosophical, religious, and scientific teachings that Mr. Sinnett received in answer to queries sent by him to the

Masters through H. P. Blavatsky and Damodar were later incorporated by him in two of his works, *The Occult World* and *Esoteric Buddhism,* as he called them. Both were good books for their time, as far as they went, but criticized also by H. P. Blavatsky in *The Secret Doctrine* for their materialistic bias of presentation, and for their overemphasis on certain aspects of the teachings to the neglect of the higher, the more spiritual, the more intellectual, portions, in the attempt by Mr. Sinnett to "reconcile" the teachings of the ancient wisdom with what he obviously thought was the last word of human knowledge, the scientific theories and fads of his day. Those scientific theories and teachings are already out of date now, lost to mind and mostly forgotten. Science has "moved"; but the teachings of the ancient wisdom have remained!

We open our study this evening, after these preliminary observations, by reading from *The Secret Doctrine,* volume II, first on page 699, "On Chains of Planets and their Plurality":

Did the Ancients know of worlds besides their own? What are the data of the Occultists in affirming that every globe is a septenary chain of worlds — of which only one member is visible — and that these are, were, or will be, "man-bearing," just as every visible star or planet is? What do they mean by "a moral and physical influence" of the sidereal worlds on our globes?

Such are the questions often put to us, and they have to be considered from every aspect. To the first of the two queries the answer is: — We believe it because the first law in nature is uniformity in diversity, and the second — analogy. "As above, so below."

And then on page 703:

When, therefore, we find in the Bibles of Humanity "other worlds" spoken of, we may safely conclude that they not only refer to other states of our planetary chain and Earth, but also to other inhabited globes — stars and planets; withal, that the latter were never speculated upon. The whole of antiquity believed in the Universality of life.

In entering upon the present phase of our study, we are obliged to go into detail. But this entering upon a more detailed study is attended naturally with increased difficulties, not only because of the many subjects that we are more or less perforce obliged to meet in following the main theme of our discourse, but also from the fact that not one iota of teaching can be omitted at any one point; it must at least be alluded to if the teaching is to remain complete and whole and not a divided thing. Hence we shall go slowly. It were indeed easy to hurry over this subject, easy to get a general outline, but in such case we could go but little farther than the surface meaning in *The Secret Doctrine;* and our instructions are: simplify by illustration, supporting it by confirmation and proof.

Hence, let us first consider what we mean by the doctrine of the spheres, one of the most archaic of the ancient Mysteries. We mean four things, speaking generally. These four are as follows: first, the *universal* solar system. We mean by this our sun and all the planetary bodies in the solar system, visible or invisible, seen or unseen, known or unknown, owning the sun as their primary. Modern science today recognizes seven, eight, or perhaps nine planets, and a host of planetoids, and no more, as belonging to the solar system. Modern astronomy knows nothing of the great body of the universal solar system except its physical shell, the outer physical clothing of it, the seven, eight, or nine planets which we can see with the physical eye in the heavens, and which are counted as follows: Mercury, Venus, Mars, Jupiter, Saturn, Uranus, Neptune. But the ancient wisdom, the esoteric teaching, tells us that there are actually scores of planets in this universal solar system of ours, and that these scores, excepting those counted by astronomy, are all invisible to us, to our eyes of fourth-plane matter — or seventh-plane matter, according to the way by which we may count.

Neptune is not a member of our universal solar system, according to the ancient wisdom. We will deal with this matter later. Next, Uranus is not a member of *our* solar system, but *is* a member of the *universal* solar system. We shall fully explain what we mean by *our* solar system. Can you blame Mr. Sinnett for not understanding, and therefore thinking that he knew more than the Master did and than H. P. Blavatsky did, and that the archaic teachings contained contradictions, when the man could not get it through his head that the same words may be used with different meanings; and that one of the favorite, sanctified, methods of concealing truth from those not qualified to get it is to say two, three, four, five, six, seven different things with the same words?

First, then, we have the universal solar system, comprising the septenary sun and all the planets of the solar system, visible or invisible, and on seven planes. Then, we have *our* solar system, which is the second of these four aspects of the doctrine of the spheres, and is the group usually called the seven sacred planets of the ancients, as these seven are related to our planetary chain. The third is something to which we shall merely allude as occasion arises, and not go much farther. It is alluded to by H. P. Blavatsky in the first volume (pp. 163-4) of *The Secret Doctrine* in her answer to part of Mr. Sinnett's misunderstanding regarding the earth's planetary chain. You will remember where she speaks of the relation of Mars and Mercury and the four secret planets to our earth; and she explains that they all bear a relation thereto which no initiate will speak of, much less explain. The fourth aspect is our earth's planetary chain per se.

Now Mr. Sinnett asked his question of the Teacher as follows: "What other planets of those known to ordinary science, besides Mercury, belong to our system of worlds?" Please mark those four last words. And he continues: "Are the more spiritual planets — (A, B and Y, Z) — visible bodies in the sky or are all those known to astronomy of the more material sort?" And the answer came as follows: "Mars and four other planets of which astronomy knows yet nothing. Neither A, B, nor Y, Z, are known; nor can they be seen through physical means however perfected." And yet despite that, Mr. Sinnett taught and claimed for years that two of our visible planets, Mars and Mercury, form part of our earth's septenary planetary chain.

You will remember how H. P. Blavatsky alludes to Mr. Sinnett's misunderstanding of the Master's teaching in *The Secret Doctrine*, volume I, especially on pages 162–8 inclusive. Anyone in reading these pages, unless he has a stultified mind or is entirely ignorant of occult doctrines, must instantly sense that she is hinting at more than one thing. Read those pages and ponder them well. At our next meeting we are going into this matter more deeply.

Now then, for a brief review, first, of our universal solar

system: we mean by that expression all bodies and every body belonging to the sun, and revolving around it. The sun is their primary; they circle around the sun as satellites or planets, visible or invisible; that is, the expression *universal solar system* means not only the mere shell of nature — composed of the seven, eight, or nine planets, that the eye sees — but also the great inner core of the solar system, *its seven planes of being*. There are actually scores of planets in our universal solar system, of which we see only seven physical ones, on the same plane as the earth; and if we count our globe as one, there are eight. Neptune, however, as already said, does not belong to it; Uranus does not belong to *our* system of worlds (or *our* solar system), but it does belong to the *universal* solar system, because it is a true planet intimately connected with our sun as regards its origin and destiny.

In order to make this point more clear, let me illustrate what Neptune is by a very fortunate illustration which we can draw from modern science. You know that chemical physics, or physical chemistry, teaches that the atom is composed of a central nucleus, which has been called the proton, answering in the atom to what our sun is in the universal solar system; and that around this central nucleus, revolving with vertiginous rapidity, are other bodies which they call electrons. The chemists theorize — and occultism says that this theory is true, you can find the proof of it in *The Secret Doctrine* — to the effect that if one of these atomic planets or electrons is torn out from that atom, the atom itself is altered or changed; not alone does the electric charge of the atom vary, but the atom itself is de facto altered; and also if, so to say, the atom is electron-hungry, if an electron should pass near — I am using very simple language in order to convey the idea — should pass near that atomic solar system, it may be captured, in which case the atomic electric hunger is satisfied, while the atomic valency is altered.

Neptune, although a "planet" in the sense that it does revolve around the sun, is not a true member of our solar system in any sense. It is a "capture," and its capture changed in one sense the entire nature of our universal solar system; and it will remain captured until the karmic time shall come for it to leave us. It is captured exactly as some of the planets have captured "moons."

Why is it, we may ask, in passing, that Venus and Mercury have no moons; and that Mars is said to have two, and Saturn nine, and Jupiter nine, whereas we know by our teaching that each planet can have but one true moon, the others being mere captures, satellites? Now, suppose we were to say that in the past aeons of time, a comet, nearing the planetary stage, passed sufficiently close to the gravitational attraction of our universal solar system on its own plane of being to be captured, and that due to the interplay of various forces it settled into an orbit around our sun; and that long aeons later our astronomers discovered it and named it Neptune. Please consider that as a theory. We will leave it, if you will, for the time, and call it a theory.

We have said that Uranus is not a member of *our* solar system. We repeat the statement. It is a member, however, of our *universal* solar system.

You see how it was that Mr. Sinnett, through lack of esoteric training, through lack of knowledge of the ancient wisdom, through being absolutely psychologized with the splendid achievements in purely physical discovery of the marvelous scientific advance of his day — the "last word of knowledge," it actually was proclaimed in the scientific periodicals of that day — preferred the scientific theories and fads of the period to the tenets of the ancient wisdom, those tenets which have been proved by generation after generation of titanic intellects, of men, great seers, who had for immemorial ages tested nature, sending their souls into the very womb of matter, into all its seven planes or spheres, and finding out the truth, the reality, of things.

Now, please note: Mr. Sinnett's question referred to "our system of worlds." Do you not see how vague that question was? At least four different aspects of the doctrine of the spheres could be meant by those words. The Teachers had been urging Messrs. Sinnett and Hume to adopt a definite English terminology and nomenclature which, indeed, Mr. Sinnett did adopt, to a certain extent. We owe many of our common terms and expressions to him, and we are duly grateful to him for the good work that he did in this respect; but many of these terms are too vague. For instance, the term "root-race" is a most unfortunate one. At a later date we shall have to show how unfortunate it is. We propose to adopt the Master's own term "stock-race," using the word "stock" in the sense of *body* or *trunk*. We owe to Mr. Sinnett also the expression "round," meaning the passage of the life-wave from globe A, the first of our earth's chain, to globe G, or the seventh at the end; and many more of the words, phrases, and much of the technical vocabulary which is commonly employed by us today are due to Mr. Sinnett and Mr. Hume.

The question about "our system of worlds" asked by Mr. Sinnett provided a perfect opening for the Master to tell him the truth in wholly general terms, and yet to hide from him that which he should not know. Had Mr. Sinnett been definite enough in his question — indeed, to put it in another way, had he been wise enough to ask a perfectly definite question — it would have been much more difficult and embarrassing to the Teacher, in view of necessary secrecy, to give a definite answer. In such case, Mr. Sinnett would have got a definite answer; or he would have been told that his question was one that should not be answered, as indeed happened in several cases. But what was the actual answer that he got? We have read it, and it contains several points of teaching under and in the words. All these four aspects of the general doctrine of the spheres, which we have been alluding to, are contained in the Master's answer in the form of hint and allusion, with especial reference to the most esoteric. "Our system of worlds" was taken at its face value, just as the vague and indefinite question — from the viewpoint of occultism — ought to have been taken. The archaic law is that only those who knock at the door *in the right manner* can enter therein. All depends upon which door you knock at; and this is an old rule, ancient, ancient, ancient, running back into immemorial time, to the very days of the later Atlanteans when the Mysteries were first established in order to segregate the nobler portion of the Atlantean folk from those who were degenerating and rushing to their doom.

So, then, please understand perfectly clearly that our *universal* solar system of worlds means our sun and all the planetary bodies whatsoever in the solar system, of whatever degree or kind, on whatever plane, inner or outer, and in whatever orbits they may be revolving around their primary, the sun. Remember likewise in this connection that our solar system is septenary, that it is composed of seven planes, or worlds, and hence that there are seven suns in it, of which we see but one sun, the lowest in degree.

We might as well say here and now, because it is a part of our study, that the inhabitants of the three globes preceding ours and those of the three globes following ours, in our earth's planetary chain, in each case, see two suns. An illustration of this we have fortunately in modern astronomy, in what are called the star-doubles. There are many kinds of doubles. I do not mean mere optical doubles, but true solar pairs or couples, which is a fact of being closely connected with the very interesting and also mysterious doctrine of obscurations, into which we shall have to go in pursuing this our present study of the earth's planetary chain. But these stellar couples or doubles show that those suns, which are seen as doubles, form a septenary system which, like our own sun, have a lower single sun, or lower fourth-plane sun, just as our own physical sun is. You see here how one key to the ancient wisdom will open the door to nature's secret chambers. Never forget the old Hermetic axiom: analogy is nature's fundamental law, "As above, so below."

Next: the seven sacred planets of the ancients — which ones are they? They are as follows. I am not naming them in their proper esoteric order; I am naming them in the old exoteric Greek way: Moon, Mercury, Venus, Sun, Mars, Jupiter, Saturn. Note, first, that our Earth is not one of these seven sacred or secret planets. Second, that the Moon (the first one in order of enumeration, preceding Mercury) and the Sun, are considered here in exoteric enumeration as planets. Actually, however, they stand for two secret planets which are invisible to us: the Sun for an intra-Mercurial planet which we will, if you like, for purposes of convenience, call Vulcan, a planet visible to the men of the third root-race — or stock-race — in this round, but which now has disappeared from our vision. It will reappear, however, as our own race progresses to higher levels of perception. The Moon, again, as said, stands for another secret planet which is now dying, having nearly reached the end of its septenary life cycle. Before the Earth has reached *its* seventh round, our Moon will have disintegrated into atomic stellar dust; and this present secret planet, being a dying planet, this Mystery-planet for which the Moon is the exoteric substitute, will then be the satellite of the Earth in place of the Moon that was and now is; but that planet-satellite will not be a true *moon*, but a mere satellite. Please note the difference. For instance, the planet Mars has two satellites, Phobos and Deimos. Phobos is not a moon; but Deimos is a true moon, but not of Mars. Phobos is a capture, as we may say, by Mars.

This subject of the seven sacred planets of the ancients is intimately bound up with the doctrine of our own earth's planetary chain, the latter a specific instance of the general doctrine of the spheres; and we shall have to go into this subject as a formal study. But let us point out, before closing tonight, that the sun and moon, as forming two of those seven secret planets in the exoteric enumeration, are substitutes for two secret and invisible planets, briefly spoken of already. Furthermore, with regard to Mars, there is a mystery — i.e., esoteric, secret — connected with this matter which we have not time to go into tonight, but in it lies the reason why H. P. Blavatsky, in alluding to these seven secret planets on a certain page of *The Secret Doctrine* speaks only of four — Saturn, Jupiter, Mercury, and Venus — and hints at three more which she does not mention there as belonging to the group of the seven sacred planets of the ancients.

Note also that every one of the seven globes of our earth's planetary chain is under the guidance, and is actually formed by, one of the seven sacred planets which, for this reason, with other reasons, was called sacred. So, again, each root-race — or stock-race — of every one of the seven globes during each globe-round is under the protection and guidance of one of the seven sacred planets. But the main reason for calling them sacred is this: as our universal solar system is composed of seven planes of being, in other words, is composed of seven worlds, seven planes, seven spheres of life and activity — not globes but spheres in the larger sense, as when a man says spheres of activity — we search for an answer to the question, Why is it so? Here is the answer, and it shows why these planets are called sacred. These seven planets are the houses, each one to each one, of the seven logoi of *our* solar system, thus forming a minor group at the head of which is one of the seven primordial logoi of the universal solar system. When our universal solar system came out of latency as a nebula, later it became a comet, still later separating into sun and planets, each one pursuing its own particular life-path; the separation of the nebular inner life into seven cosmic forces for future life activities was done by the seven primordial logoi.

Put it in this way: the chief Logos of the universal solar system is sevenfold, septenary, i.e., the solar Logos — Brahmā, as the Hindus would put it — is septenary. Then, each of these seven minor logoi, again subdividing into seven forces or powers, form sevenfold groups or minor solar systems, and *our* solar system is one of such groups: seven minor logoi, each one, each to each, is the rector, the guide, of one of the seven sacred planets; if you like, its informing soul. But, mark this: this former subdivision composes the life forces of *our* solar system. Hence *our* solar system forms a group within the universal solar system. We have explained what we mean before. In other words, then, there are forty-nine of these minor logoi in our universal solar system; but our sacred seven which with our earth's planetary chain compose *our* solar system, belong to *our* solar Logos. In still other words, put it in this way: as the sun has its spectrum of seven rays, so each one of these rays again is subdivided into seven minor rays. Please consider that as an illustration. Our planetary chain, you will remember, which will be the subject of our next study, consists of seven globes, collectively the developed sevenfold entity of a former sevenfold chain in another life cycle or manvantara, which chain is now dead, but functioning now as our moon-chain. And remember that when we say our moon in this particular case we mean the sevenfold moon, the entire definite septenary entity. Our present moon, as a matter of fact, is not the *physical* moon that was, which has disappeared, but is its kāma-rūpa, its vampirizing shell, purely and truly in more than one sense vampirizing. It is a phantom of the moon that was, its true shell. Our earth, which grew from it, draws still from it the life-atoms which the karmic destiny of our earth obliges it to gather into itself, for its weal or for its woe, as the case may be.

FORTY-TWO

THE DOCTRINE OF THE SPHERES IN ITS FOUR ASPECTS. THE SEVEN
SACRED PLANETS AND THEIR RECTORS: THEIR RELATION TO OUR
EARTH-CHAIN. THE CIRCULATIONS OF THE KOSMOS: OUTER
ROUNDS AND INNER ROUNDS; ŚISHTAS. ONE UNIVERSAL
BASIC LAW: AS ABOVE, SO BELOW. THE EYE
AND THE HEART DOCTRINES.

The most celebrated of the Babylonians, together with Ostanes and
Zoroaster, very properly call the starry spheres herds; whether because these
alone among corporeal magnitudes, are perfectly carried about a centre, or
in conformity to the oracles, because they are considered by them as in a
certain respect the bonds and collectors of physical reasons, which they
likewise call in their sacred discourses herds [ἀγέλας], and by the insertion
of a gamma [ἀγγέλους], angels. Wherefore the stars which preside over each
of these herds are considered demons similar to the angels, and are called
archangels: and they are seven in number.

> — Anon., *Theologumensis Arithmeticis*
> (Cory, *Ancient Fragments*, p. 276)

The "Doctrine of the Eye" is for the crowd, the "Doctrine of the Heart," for
the elect. The first repeat in pride: "Behold, I know," the last, they who
in humbleness have garnered, low confess, "thus have I heard." . . .
    The Dharma of the "Eye" is the embodiment of the external, and the
nonexisting.
    The Dharma of the "Heart" is the embodiment of Bodhi, the Permanent
and Everlasting.

> — *The Voice of the Silence*, pp. 27, 29

THE TRADITIONS of mankind tell us, and the records of
the ancient wisdom corroborate the traditions, that the
doctrines which we have been studying for the last four
years or so have come down to us unimpaired and in their pristine
purity, in the charge of great minds, great men, great souls. These
traditions as the ages passed, dating from the midpoint of the
fourth stock-race or the Atlantean, took various forms as they

were given out more or less fully at different times; took forms, we say, in the various great world religions; and it is at the back of, behind, under the surface of, these great world religions that we find many, if not all, of the doctrines of the ancient wisdom. We should not include in these religions thus spoken of, the various smaller religions or quasi-religious cults, however large their extent among mankind may have been, because these smaller religions were often the offspring of men who imperfectly understood the ancient wisdom, and who, in some cases, were actually unfaithful to their own teachers. And therein we may find one of the dominating reasons why these archaic teachings have always been held as sacred and secret; because, as was told to Mr. Sinnett and Mr. Hume, the Masters had and have no wish to foist another mere exoteric religion on a world already priest-ridden and creed-burdened.

A source which is polluted at its fountainhead can hardly give forth the pure springs which heal. The best antidote for folly is wisdom; for ignorance, real knowledge; for false and therefore wholly unauthorized theosophy, the archaic teachings of the wisdom-religion.

We take up again tonight the study which was begun at our meeting last week; and the main theme then was what was called the doctrine of the spheres, of which the doctrine of our planetary chain, the planetary chain of our solar system, is a particular case. Let us pass in brief review, at the same time perhaps slightly bettering, the explanation that was then made. The doctrine of the spheres comprises the entirety of the teachings dealing with the origin, the life, and the destiny of the spheres or planets, and of the sun, belonging to and composing our universal solar system. By "universal" solar system we mean all the bodies whatsoever, known and unknown, visible and invisible, that revolve around the sun, which is their primary. There are many such planets, scores of them, most of them invisible to our eyes of flesh.

The second aspect of the doctrine of the spheres is the subsidiary doctrine of the planetary chains. Each one of these planets is a sevenfold body, comprising in a unity seven globes; and one of the seven is visible to our eyes in the cases of the seven or eight or nine planets known to astronomy, because our eyes have been trained through evolution on this planet to see them, for these few cases belong to our own "plane." When we shall be on the globes of our chain to which we shall pass when leaving this earth, our senses will then be trained by nature, by evolution, to cognize, to sense and to see — to know, in other words, other celestial bodies, other planets of our universal solar system. Similarly was it the case with the globes which we left in descending the planetary chain. Each planetary chain, therefore, has seven globes, according to the teachings, existing on four planes: two globes on each one of the three higher planes, and of these seven globes only one is on the lowest plane; our earth is on this lowest or fourth plane of our chain. This doctrine of the planetary chain is our main theme of study at present.

The third aspect of the doctrine of the spheres is what has been called the seven sacred planets of the ancients — likewise a teaching comprising a sevenfold mystery. These planets are respectively Saturn, Jupiter, Mars, Sun (which is a substitute for enumerative reasons for an intra-Mercurial planet), Venus, Mercury, and our Moon which is also a substitute for a planet near our Earth, and which is now dying. These seven sacred planets of the ancients were called sacred for the reasons set forth in our last study. They are the houses of the seven forces of *one* of the seven chief rays of the solar Logos: this one chief ray being our particular logos. This doctrine is really very simple, but because it is a case of seven involved in seven, it sounds very complicated; actually it is not. There are seven main or chief rays or forces which make and which inform the sun; and these seven forces are the seven solar logoi. Each one of these seven main logoi is subdivided in its turn into seven; and these seven subdivisions of one chief ray or logos form the rectors, the genii, the archangels if you will, of which the seven sacred planets are the houses.

Each one of these seven sacred planets was intimately concerned in building one of the globes of our planetary chain. Each one of the stock-races or root-races on any one of our seven globes during the passage through it of the evolving life-wave, is likewise under the direct governance and control of one of these seven sacred planets; and when we say "planet," please note carefully that we do not mean the mere physical body of it, the planet which we see; that is but the house of the sevenfold dhyān-chohan, the rector, the genius, that particular solar force which has builded and which uses that planet as its house — its "nerve center," so to say.

The fourth aspect of the universal solar system deals with the group which is so sacred that, as H. P. Blavatsky says on pages 163-4 of volume I of *The Secret Doctrine:* "As to Mars, Mercury, and 'the four other planets,' they bear a relation to Earth of which no master or high Occultist will ever speak [in public, we should add], much less explain the nature."

This doctrine of the spheres is full of wonder. We have merely sketched an outline of it; and closely connected with it is a twin doctrine, even more sacred and more mysterious, which we may call the *doctrine of the circulations of the kosmos,* of which the circulations of the forces of the universal solar system are a special case. Note here in passing, that the workings of karma and the reincarnation of the human soul on earth are special cases, again, of these two doctrines: the doctrine of the circulations which make the actions of karma to be; and the doctrine of man's successive reimbodiment in houses of flesh, as the doctrine of the spheres shows the building of other globes in houses of physical form, fit for the evolving souls, and providing bodies for them corresponding to each one of those globes. This doctrine of the circulations of the kosmos is one which we approach with a great deal of caution. We should remember that whatever may be said on that subject here at present does not by any means include all that could be said about this recondite subject; no, not one-tenth. This doctrine of the circulations of the kosmos, or of the circulations of the life forces in the universal solar system, among many other things, deals with the passage of the life-wave from globe to globe on our planetary chain; explains to us and elucidates how this is done; while the doctrine of the spheres sets forth to what globes these circulations go, into which globes these circulations enter, and in what states those globes are left when their respective life cycles are completed. This applies also, of course, to us here on earth, and to the life-atoms on our globe here; and, for instance, tells us of such men as we shall be on the next globe following this our earth and such as we were on the globe preceding this earth. And so, on all the globes of our chain the life-wave functions similarly; that is to say, these circulations are related to each globe and to all.

Next, with regard to these planetary rectors or genii or dhyān-chohans — each subsidiary solar logos of the seven minor logoi of one chief Logos forming the presiding genius of each globe — they actually are the builders of our planetary chain, plus the indwelling life or swabhāva belonging to our own planetary chain. The human seed is sown, for example; it grows, becomes an embryo, finally is born, grows into a man. There is the indwelling life, the character, the inward urge, the forward push, the development of the inner faculties; but this is done in a world of surrounding forces which affect it profoundly by action and reaction, or karma. So with the globes; so with our planetary chain as a whole.

Let us also remark in passing that these seven sacred planets are profoundly instrumental in building our planetary chain; but the earth also itself is one of another group or series of seven planets, which build or cooperate in building the planetary chain of certain other ones of our planets — so closely interrelated and interlocked are the functionings of the life forces and life-waves in our solar kosmos, our universal solar system.

Now briefly passing in review questions which we shall study in detail later, please bear in mind that the life-wave in any planetary chain — we will take our own as an instance of the rule — passes once from the first globe to the seventh, through all the seven globes; and when it has thus passed once through the seven globes of the chain it completes what we call one chain-round, *round* being a word which Mr. Sinnett coined for this purpose, and which we still use. Seven such chain-rounds complete a life cycle of our planetary chain. Then what happens?

We now approach another mystery. There are outer rounds and inner rounds. The inner round comprises the passages of the life-wave in any one planetary chain from globe A to globe G (or Z) once around, and this takes place seven times in a planetary manvantara. The outer round — please listen carefully — comprises the passage of the entirety of a planetary chain's life-wave, by the working of the doctrine of the circulations of the solar system, from one of these sacred planets to another, and this for seven times.

Reverting for a moment again to a round in a planetary chain: on our globe, the indwelling egoic force in any one man, or in any one life-entity, evolves for itself bodies correspondential to its surroundings — bodies outer, bodies inner. The higher ones of these inner bodies we may call monadic eggs; and when the life-wave leaves any one such globe of the seven of that planetary chain in order to pass to the next globe, the vehicles correspon- dential and belonging to that particular globe, its own evolutions thereon, remain behind as the *śishtas,* a Sanskrit word meaning "remainders," in order to serve as the first vehicles or bodies for the monads when the same life-wave returns on the succeeding cycle, and after aeons upon aeons of time the monads of the returning life-wave find these "sleeping spheres" or dormant "life-atoms" or vehicles waiting for them. These sleeping spheres or dormant life-atoms are correspondential, each one and all of them, to the particular globe of the planetary chain which had evolved them. Thus the śishtas are the already evolved or *individualized* vehicles or "life-atoms" fit to receive the returning monadic host.

Let us now illustrate this doctrine of our planetary chain by drawing seven circles, each circle to be one of the manifested globes of our planetary chain.

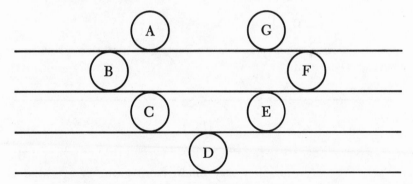

DIAGRAM 1

The life-wave enters globe A, runs through its life cycle there, and then passes on to globe B. Finishing its cycle on globe B, it passes on to globe C; and then to globe D, the lowest of the seven. In our own chain, globe D is our earth. We draw straight lines under the three higher pairs, and one straight line under globe D. These lines represent the four lowest planes or worlds of our solar system, our universal solar system. There are yet three higher planes or worlds, making seven in all; and beyond these higher three planes, there are still three more, thus making the perfect number ten. Of these last three and highest planes or worlds, we shall say nothing more here.

But now let us draw on the three higher planes of the seven, five more circles representing globes as follows: two globes on the lowest plane of these three highest, two more globes on the

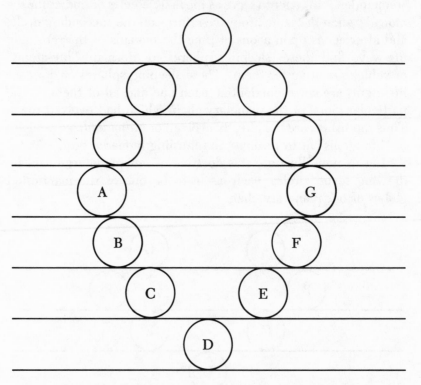

DIAGRAM 2

plane above that; and one globe on the seventh plane from the bottom, thus forming the acme or summit. We then shall have twelve globes in our planetary chain: seven manifest, and five hid; and this is the system of construction (of the solar logoic force) which we are going to study — each one of these twelve globes, by the way, corresponding in the ancient wisdom to one of the twelve signs of the zodiac. You see, then, that there are seven globes in manifestation; one visible to us, the lowest and the fourth; six higher *in abscondito* or hid; and finally five globes on the three higher planes of the seven planes, forming therefore seven plus five, or twelve globes in all. This is just a sketch, at the present time, merely outlining the teachings.

The question naturally arises: What is it that circles from globe to globe of a planetary chain in the inner rounds, and passes from one to the other and each in turn of the seven sacred planets in the outer rounds? We have said that each globe of a chain, when the life-wave leaves it, retains its hosts of monadic eggs as the śishtas. We used the word "monadic" there in a general sense; that is to say, it applies in all cases to that particular part of the entire human spiritual-psychological-physical economy which corresponds to that particular globe — which belongs to it, in short, and which is left behind much as a traveler leaves behind a house or clothing fit for certain climates and weathers when he goes elsewhere; because he is coming back to that his quondam home. But what is it, what is that final ultimate, that monad, that higher monad, which provides and really is the undying seed from which all these others spring forth? That is what H. P. Blavatsky called the spiritual self, the divine soul; the immortal seed, the Father-Mother, the source, the fountainhead — give it any name you like — of the oviform body, the auric egg, which in its essence, not in its shape, contains the divine-spiritual individuality of man or of any other life-entity. That is deathless, birthless; it lasts throughout the entire solar manvantara, and goes into the supreme paranirvana only when the universal solar system in the due course of its cyclic evolution passes finally into pralaya or latency.

Just think a moment, what does all this mean? This means that on any one particular globe — let us take ours, our globe earth, as an illustration, and us men as the examples for the illustration — we evolve here partly from within without by our own inner swābhāvic urge, and partly from without inwards by the reaction of nature around us, certain personalities and certain characters and certain vehicles exactly correspondential to the globe on which we then are. Those characters and personalities and vehicles are utterly unfit for another globe, utterly unfit for another plane. They could no more pass to another plane or live on another globe than, let us say, a rose could live at the bottom of the ocean. They do not belong there; they belong on this earth; they belong in the material and psychological atmospheres of this earth; they belong in and to that particular world of circulation of forces which make this earth and which actually *are* this earth. We do not find roses growing at the North Pole, or glaciers at sea level in the tropics. Everything in nature is fit for and has its own place.

Similarly, on every one of the other globes of our chain, there are bodies or vehicles, etc., evolved, inner bodies and outer bodies, correspondential in each case to those globes, belonging there, which we have made when there, and which we left behind when we left those globes. Similarly, as there is but one fundamental rule, one basic law, to use the popular word, throughout all the kosmos, when man reincarnates he comes back with the same spiritual individuality, indeed, he comes back with the same higher human individuality. But he evolves for himself each time, and on each globe — because the race is different, the karma is different, the circumstances are different, since succeeding evolution has evolved both him and the surrounding globe still more — he evolves personalities, vehicles, etc., out of himself anew from the seeds which at each preceding death had passed into latency in the character, and thus passes into and informs anew the globe monadic eggs of various sorts formerly left behind on the different globes when the life-wave left them to pass onwards.

Those of you who are Oriental classical scholars will readily see how what has been said, little as it is thus far, throws a light which is really dazzling upon the teachings of the greater ones of the ancient religions, such as those of Egypt, and of Greece; preeminently so as regards the doctrines of Brahmanism and Buddhism in India and the Farther Orient. No wonder is it that theosophy has been called the unifying philosophy of the world. It shows the why and the how of all these great ancient religions. It tells us what they were and what they meant.

Now, then, one may ask oneself — and this is a slight digression but apparently necessary — why is there so much talk of seven: seven here and seven there and seven everywhere? Do we live in an anarchical universe, a helter-skelter universe, one without order or well-defined shape? Or do we live in a universe every atom of which is in the grip of forces controlled by forces still higher and more recondite and powerful? Obviously the latter. And these higher forces are in the grip and control of still higher ones. This simply means that there is one consistent life-wave running throughout all being; and being one coherent and consistent will, having one basic direction, it must *act on all planes of the universe* more or less *in the same way*. Hence you see the need, the necessity, the value, to us, yea and the beauty, of the ancient teachings, proclaiming the fundamental operation of nature, commonly called the law of analogy, expressed by the Hermetic axiom, "As above, so below; as below, so above."

The primal kosmic Logos, let us say, has one direction in which its will pours forth in floods of light and life. Those floods pass through their various cycles and formations in descending into matter, and re-arising again towards their source. By doing so they but follow — and cannot do otherwise — the powerful impulses springing from the central heart, that one will. We are tempted to use the words purpose, or design, were it not that these words are so misused in the Christian theological schemes, that it would almost give to listeners an idea of a kosmic personal God, and that blasphemy we do not recognize. Just here is where enter the operations of karma. Karma is not a law made by something or somebody. It is the inherent nature or quality of kosmic being to react against action upon it. It is the doctrine of consequences. Kosmically speaking, it has its flow of action or force in a certain direction, which is the will, the life-flow, of the kosmic Logos, and this life-flow of the Logos, as said before, springing from one heart, the central heart of our solar system, and thus forming the constitution or fundamental operation of universal nature, everything in that nature obeys its direction; and hence we have the doctrine regarding the seven, because it is but the photographing, so to say, on our minds of the facts of the kosmos, the solar Logos being divided into ten parts, of which seven are manifest, and three occult or hid. Everything which owes its life to the Logos, which is part of the Logos, which is subject to the sweep of its energy, and to its "law," is therefore by primal necessity likewise built on a sevenfold plan.

So we can now, with these words of introduction, pass on to consider the first aspect of the doctrine of the spheres, called our earth's planetary chain. This, as illustrated in diagram 2, is composed of seven globes in manifestation, and five hid: the two highest of the lower seven forming the models for the five and last below. The two next globes are grosser and more material; the two following are of still grosser and more material constituency; the series of planes ending with our earth, which is the copy here below of the superspiritual globe forming the last or twelfth — or first — in our entire planetary chain.

Those of you who know your classics will remember how Plato speaks of the fact that the Deity geometrizes according to a twelvefold plan. Why has the zodiac twelve houses or signs? Why were there twelve great gods — seven manifested and five occult — in all the great world religions of ancient times? In these ancient religions, the forms of expression and the words differed, but the heart doctrine was there and the same in them all; not the doctrine of the eye, i.e., the outward things which were seen, the ceremonial ritual and worship which varied, often greatly, the ones from the others. That was the exoteric part — not "false," but unexplained; but the doctrine of the heart, to use our ancient language, our ancient phraseology, meaning the doctrine of that which is *hid and not seen*, and which is the higher expression of truth, is hid, not visible to the physical eye. Therefore the outpourings from man's nobler nature, from his higher soul, spiritual, beautiful, holy, yea and divine, were called collectively the doctrine of the heart also.

Now we said at our last meeting that Mr. Sinnett and Mr. Hume and later others had misunderstood and misinterpreted the Masters' teachings with regard to the globes which compose our own planetary chain; and we referred then to the first volume of *The Secret Doctrine*, and H. P. Blavatsky's kindly but nevertheless mercifully caustic criticisms of Mr. Sinnett's idea that his merely scientifically trained mind knew the secrets of nature really better than his Teacher did, or than did H. P. Blavatsky, his second teacher; and on pages 163-4 of this volume, you will find what she says on the matter. In the first place, she says that in answer to Mr. Sinnett's query the Teacher gave a reply which was more or less vague. This was because the question was very vague. Mr. Sinnett never seemed to realize that he was asking questions, in certain cases, which simply could not be answered by anyone pledged to secrecy. What then was to be done? The Teacher had offered himself to teach. The time had come to teach the world somewhat of the ancient wisdom; a few seeds were to be sown in the world's thought-life. Yet the answer had to be given in a vague way. Had Mr. Sinnett questioned with perfect definiteness, on definite subjects of which he himself had a definite knowledge, he would doubtless have received a definite answer, or would have been told that his question could not be answered for the reasons already set forth. This refusal to answer, indeed, happened several times. His question in this connection was, as read at our last meeting: "What other planets of those known to ordinary science, besides Mercury, belong to our system of worlds?" We have seen that in occultism "our system of worlds" can refer to at least four different things: our universal solar system; our planetary chain; our group of seven sacred planets; and this mystery-group — Earth, Mercury, Mars, and four other secret planets.

Well, the answer came back generalized: "Mars and four other planets of which astronomy knows yet nothing," referring most particularly to the mystery-group. And why? Because Mr. Sinnett had just previously been questioning his informant on a certain aspect of the teachings which could not be fully explained without giving out the doctrine concerning this mystery-group. That is all there was to that. And H. P. Blavatsky says here: "As to Mars, Mercury, and 'the four other planets,' they bear a relation to Earth of which no master or high Occultist will ever speak, much less explain the nature."

Obviously, this sentence does not refer to our planetary chain, because H. P. Blavatsky had already said that Mars and Mercury do not belong to it. Evidently, she is referring to some other group. She also wrote as follows: "For the reply was: 'Mars, etc.

[as a matter of fact the Teacher's answer did not contain the word
etc.], and four other planets of which astronomy knows nothing."
The Teacher's answer contained the word *yet*, "yet nothing."
"Neither A, B, nor Y, Z, are known; nor can they be seen through
physical means however perfected."

Then H. P. Blavatsky continues: "This is plain: (a) Astronomy as yet knows nothing in reality of the planets, neither the
ancient ones, nor those discovered in modern times." Obviously,
she is merely speaking of visible planets; for modern astronomy
did not then admit the existence of other planets on other planes
of the solar system, and does not admit them today. "(b) No
companion planets from A to Z, *i.e.*, no upper globes of any chain
in the Solar System, can be seen." Disproving again what Mr.
Sinnett thought. But also mark you this: the Teacher in his
answer to Mr. Sinnett did not say "companion planets from A to
Z," as H. P. Blavatsky here writes. He said "Neither A, B, nor
Y, Z," specifying *four* planets, two in the beginning, and two at
the end of the mystery-group. You see, then, that there is much
behind all this, much that does not appear on the surface. H. P.
Blavatsky in her turn was faced with precisely the same situation
as the Master was. She could not tell the whole truth, because
pledged to secrecy; yet she had to give some answer; and she
did what Teachers from immemorial time have done in similar
cases. They gave an answer, which was perfectly true, as far as
they could go, but they deliberately, in view of the interlocking
of the nature of the kosmos and also therefore of our teachings,
allowed a hint of something else to come in at the same time,
which served a double purpose: for it was a "blind," and yet
was absolutely responsive and truthful, *as far as it went*.

Then on page 167 (*The Secret Doctrine*, volume I) H. P.
Blavatsky quotes from the Teacher's words again: " '*Let us
imagine* THAT OUR EARTH IS ONE OF A GROUP OF SEVEN PLANETS
OR MAN-BEARING WORLDS. . . .' " Then in parenthesis, and this
parenthesis is H. P. Blavatsky's: "(*The* SEVEN *planets are the
sacred planets of antiquity, and are all septenary.*)." Here still
another, a third, aspect of the doctrine of the spheres is alluded
to. This is a perfect illustration of how such a situation has to
be faced.

As still another example of the policy of secrecy we mention, in another place in *The Secret Doctrine* you will find H. P. Blavatsky's statement that our Earth does not belong to the seven sacred planets of the ancients, and here she says that it does, and the two statements are apparently contradictory. It is a paradox, but it is not contradictory. And fortunately this paradox is easy of explanation. The seven sacred planets of the ancients, as planets of the solar system, are those mentioned in the beginning of our study tonight, i.e., Saturn, Jupiter, Mars, Sun (a substitute), Venus, Mercury, and Moon as a substitute. Our Earth is not included, as you see. But as we also pointed out tonight, each one of the globes of our planetary chain is the child of, in a sense built by, controlled by, and guided by one of these seven sacred planets, that is to say, by the respective genius or rector of each of the seven sacred planets. Hence, the seven globes of our planetary chain were likewise frequently called the seven sacred planets by the ancients, because those seven globes were builded by their cooperative instrumentality, and are under their guidance. The globes were builded by the seven sacred planets, *plus*, as before remarked, the action of the indwelling swābhāvic life of our own planetary chain.

Our time is drawing very near to an end for this evening, but we wish to call attention to two facts only before closing. First, the seven globes of our planetary chain are *not* the seven principles of the earth. The analogy is good and very striking; yet these seven globes of our planetary chain are, each one, a distinct and separate entity; each one of the seven, our earth included, has its own seven principles. Yet the other six globes of our chain are not the other six principles of our earth. The idea is grotesque. It is as much as to say that seven men, seven chelas of the Masters, a group of seven chelas, are the seven principles each of each. Not at all. The seven globes form a single group, but each one is a separate entity and has its own seven principles.

The second thing is this, that these so-called planes, these seven planes, should really and truly be called *worlds*. It is very difficult to find a proper word to describe this fact. These planes, or rather worlds, collectively are the lokas and talas: seven lokas and seven talas, corresponding one to the other, each to each.

This bipolarity of loka and tala, repeated seven times on seven decreasing degrees of materiality counting upwards, or increasing degrees of materiality counting downwards, are the seven planes or rather worlds of the solar system macrocosmically; the seven planes or worlds of our planetary chain are the lokas and talas microcosmically. These lokas and talas, then, are worlds. Look at the world around us: the stars above us, the earth beneath our feet, the winds blowing — in short, all the world we see and feel and know. It is one of the lokas and one of the talas conjointly. And these lokas and talas correspond one to the other, each to each, exactly as in the case of the bipolarity of magnetism or of electricity on our plane. Fundamentally they are one, but they manifest in bipolar character. That particular force or vital current whose tendency is downwards, forms that aspect of the union which is called the tala of any world. And the other, whose aspect is upwards or, technically speaking, north, forms the loka.

At our next study we shall begin a rather detailed investigation of our planetary chain, having now covered the various outlying fields of that which it was necessary briefly to survey before we could adequately understand the teachings regarding the earth's planetary chain.

FORTY-THREE

ANALOGY: THE LIFE OF MAN AND THE LIFE OF A PLANETARY
CHAIN. OCCULTISM AND ETHICS: "LIVE THE LIFE IF
THOU WOULDST KNOW THE DOCTRINE."

Analogy is thus the surest guide to the comprehension of the Occult teachings. . . .

Everything in the Universe follows analogy. "As above, so below"; Man is the microcosm of the Universe. That which takes place on the spiritual plane repeats itself on the Cosmic plane. Concretion follows the lines of abstraction; corresponding to the highest must be the lowest; the material to the spiritual.
— The Secret Doctrine, I, 173, 177

As you may infer by analogy every globe before it reaches its adult period, has to pass through a formation period — also septenary. Law in Nature is uniform and the conception, formation, birth, progress and development of the child differs from those of the globe only in magnitude. The globe has two periods of teething and of capillature — its first rocks which it also sheds to make room for new — and its ferns and mosses before it gets forest. As the atoms in the body change [every] seven years so does the globe renew its strata every seven cycles. . . .

. . . The correspondence between a mother-globe and her child-man may be thus worked out. Both have their seven principles. In the Globe, the elementals (of which there are in all seven species) form (a) a gross body, (b) her fluidic double (*linga* sariram), (c) her life principle (jiva); (d) her fourth principle kama rupa is formed by her creative impulse working from centre to circumference; (e) her fifth principle (animal soul or *Manas*, physical intelligence) is embodied in the vegetable (in germ) and animal kingdoms; (f) her sixth principle (or spiritual soul, Buddhi) is man (g) and her seventh principle (atma) is in a film of spiritualized akasa that surrounds her.
— The Mahatma Letters, pp. 93, 94

Those alone, whom we call adepts, who know how to direct their mental vision and to transfer their consciousness — physical and psychic both — to other planes of being, are able to speak with authority on such subjects. And they tell us plainly: —

"*Lead the life necessary for the acquisition of such knowledge and powers, and Wisdom will come to you naturally. Whenever you are able to attune your consciousness to any of the seven chords of 'Universal Consciousness,' those chords that run along the sounding-board of Kosmos, vibrating from one Eternity to another; when you have studied thoroughly 'the music of the Spheres,' then only will you become quite free to share your knowledge with those with whom it is safe to do so. . . ."*

— The Secret Doctrine, I, 166–7

THESE teachings may seem recondite when first heard, and so indeed they are. But, like all our theosophical teachings, there is one aspect of them which is very simple and contains the principal idea of each thought, i.e., of each doctrine; and it is, in each and every case, this main or principal idea which we illustrate, it remaining for yourselves to fill in the details, and to prove by your own studies the theorems advanced.

But may it not be a good thing to point out that one of the noblest results of these studies is the effect it has on the moral nature of man, of the student? You may tell a man to "be good because it is good to be good," as remarked once before; and this statement is perfectly correct and probably no one will object to it, yet it will not go very deep into the hearer's consciousness and mind. But if you tell a man that he is, in essence, an incarnate god, an incarnate divinity in his essence, and that he has come down into these spheres of matter for purposes of universal work, and that he is failing in his duty, he is failing in his relationship to his own higher self, if that duty be not accomplished, then you put a thought into that man's mind which allows him to think, and makes him think, and gives him a basis for morals, a religious and philosophical basis, which if he has any good in him at all, he himself will follow up to the end.

It is absurd to think that any one of our theosophical doctrines can be divorced from its ethical aspect. They cannot be separated so; and this, perhaps, is the distinction most easily understood between the archaic teachings and those of the various so-called cults or cultuses or quasi-religions which spring up like mushrooms from age to age and from time to time, and have a longer or shorter life, depending on circumstances, causing meanwhile more or less deplorable spiritual injury to the unfortunate people who hear of them and follow them in confidence and misplaced trust.

So far as this question of ethics as connected with our teachings is concerned, pray remember that you cannot understand them adequately unless you "live the life" that they inculcate. Our Teachers have told us so, plainly: "Live the life as it ought to be lived, and knowledge will come to you naturally." There is only one truth in nature, and understanding of it comes naturally to him or her who "obeys the law." Real knowledge brings modesty and compassion and magnanimity and courage in its train, and all the fine, old, noble virtues; and those virtues are the insignia which mark the real disciple — not foolish claims which, in direct proportion as the claims are false, are the more foolishly pretentious. The greater the claims, the less truth is there behind them.

With regard to these doctrines being so difficult: they *are* very difficult, not merely in their elucidation, which we are attempting, but also because they are so intimately interwoven together. Yet this very fact contains the clue, the Ariadne's thread, leading to their solution. The very fact that, just as the forces and principles and planes of nature are so interlocked and are so intimately bound together that *if you really know one you know more or less of all,* just so is it with these doctrines. If you really know one with some fair degree of complete knowledge — some fair degree, I say — you have a more or less perfect key that will fit the locks of all.

Indeed, analogy is the fundamental law or, if you like, the fundamental operation, of our processes of thinking, derived from nature because we are the children of nature; for just as the highest is reflected in the lowest, so is the working of the human mind. If you follow the workings of nature as taught in occultism, you will find that the lowest is but the exemplification or copy of what is above.

These teachings, which we have been studying together here, you will yourselves find in the pages of *The Secret Doctrine*. Search, and you will find them. Yet it may take you years to find them. But that is no real reason for discouragement. Why, in the old times, in India for example, the pupil had to pass ten or twelve years in the study of the sacred Sanskrit language alone before he was even allowed to read the scriptures written in that noble tongue; twelve more years were then passed in study of the scriptures before he was allowed even to speak of, or to give an opinion upon them. Twenty-four years of daily study, from eight to twelve hours a day, so sacred were these ancient teachings then held to be! No one may expect or need think that he or she can have any comprehension of our teachings without some honest effort on his or her own part, to study them, to understand them and, above everything else, to think about them, to reflect on them. That is the greatest help of all, to *reflect*, to ponder them in the mind, to brood over them.

Now, at our last study we passed in brief general review the doctrines concerning the birth, building, growth, maturity, decline, and final death, of our planetary chain. This short general review was made in order that the many and various statements made in *The Secret Doctrine*, here and there, and dealing with all these four aspects of the general doctrine of the spheres, should be separated in our minds. No one can give out any such recondite doctrine in its fullness, in easy language. These doctrines closely interlock; and the more esoteric part is always deliberately hid under the same words which set forth the exoteric presentation. The former must be picked out and studied; the intuition must be developed; the intellect polished; and, above everything else, the spiritual nature must be appealed to and aspired to. This process of study is not so difficult as it sounds, for these higher faculties are innate in us. The spiritual nature is the *real* man. The constant appeals to us by our Teachers to look inwards and to look upwards are not meaningless; they have a most profound practical value for the serious student.

We open, then, our study tonight by reading from the first volume of *The Secret Doctrine* as follows, on pages 158–9:

> Everything in the metaphysical as in the physical Universe is septenary. Hence every sidereal body, every planet, whether visible or invisible, is credited with six companion globes. . . . The evolution of life proceeds on these seven globes or bodies from the 1st to the 7th in Seven ROUNDS or Seven Cycles.

That is, the life-wave circles around the seven globes in seven different courses, each course from globe one to globe the last being called a round. But let us not confuse a general or chain-round from globe A to globe G or the last, with a globe-round, which merely means the passing through or traversing of any one of these seven globes by the life-waves. This latter is a globe-round. Furthermore, these rounds, circling, revolving, from globe A to globe G, in any one planetary chain — ours for instance — is called an inner round. The outer rounds, as pointed out at our last meeting, refer to the seven sacred planets; and these outer rounds we shall not touch upon except very incidentally. But it ought to be pointed out that these seven sacred planets actually build and govern and oversee, *each to each*, all the seven globes of our earth's chain. What are the correspondences here? Let us point them out. We draw a diagram of the twelve globes of our earth's planetary chain once more:

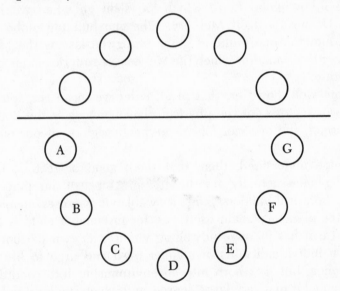

Beginning with the seven globes on our *manifested* planetary chain, below the line which we have drawn in order to separate them from the five which are hid, we will call the first globe A, the next globe B, the next C, the next D, which is our earth. The one above us on the ascending arc is E, the next one above it is F, and the last one of the seven we shall mark as G. There are, furthermore, as shown in this diagram, five hid globes on the three higher planes of the solar kosmos, the universal solar system, which globes we merely mention in passing.

Now the sacred planet which builds and forms globe A, subject of course to the swabhāva of globe A — that is to say, its own indwelling genius or will or spirit, its own individuality, just as a growing child is shaped more or less by its environment, but nevertheless has its own growing individuality and personality — the sacred planet, I say, that builds globe A is the Sun, or rather that planet for which the Sun is an enumerative substitute, and which we will call Vulcan. The sacred planet which builds the second globe, B, is Jupiter. The sacred planet which builds globe C, the one preceding ours on the downward arc, and from which we came during this round before we entered the earth-globe, is Venus. The sacred planet building our own Earth is Saturn. The one building globe E, to which we shall go when we leave globe D, our Earth, is Mercury. The one building globe F is Mars; and the one building globe G, or the last, is the Moon, or rather the planet for which the Moon is an exoteric enumerative substitute.

Note well, however, that in all cases we mean the spiritual genius or rector (not the physical planet) which is the builder, the former, the overseer, of any respective globe of our earth's chain.

Please understand, then, that these genii or rectors, these sacred planets actually are the kosmokratores of our planetary chain, the world builders, *plus* the swabhāvic impulses emanating from the planetary chain itself: as, for instance, a child is born on earth; it has its own indwelling vitality, its own personality, its own individuality, its own inner push and urge to life and experience; but it is born into an environment, into conditions, which mold it in a very large degree, and which similarly in large degree direct the way and manner in which its body and higher principles are builded and work and function.

We merely allude here once more to what was said, I think at our last meeting, that when the last of the seven rounds of our earth's planetary chain is fully completed, the life-waves pass on to one of the outer rounds. Now you know that the moon which we see in our evening skies is but the relic, the kāma-rūpa, of a former planet which lived and completed its life cycle before our earth existed, and which was as full of life and the hosts of lives as our earth is now. It also ran the course of its seven rounds, along seven lunar globes, and when its septenary life cycle was completed, when its seventh round was completed, what then happened? Each globe, as the life-wave left it after completing the last globe-round of the seventh chain-round, passed into invisibility after it had cast forth its energies, a large part of its life-atoms, into a laya-center in space.

Let us take these seven globes, as shown in the diagram, which represent the chain of our earth, and imagine them, if you please, to be the seven globes of our moon during its last round, we mean the seventh or last moon-round. When the globe-round on A is completed, or rather nearly completed, the ten classes of life-entities prepare to leave it. The class which is most advanced projects its energy into space, into another point of the solar system, into what is called a laya-center, which is a Sanskrit word meaning a homogeneous center, a center of homogeneous sub-stance, on a spiritual plane of course, using the word "spiritual" in a general sense. And this process goes on, for all the ten classes of that globe A, each one of these ten families or stocks leaving the globe one by one, until, when the time has come for the last animalcule of the last stock to leave the globe, that globe then suddenly disappears — and is *in abscondito*, invisible. And why? The reason is this: all matter, as our scientists today are beginning to realize, is but another form of kosmic force, for force and matter are one. All matter is built up of atoms; these atoms in turn are built up of electrons and protons; and these in their turn are but tiny substantial entities, *built up of energic matter or force* — force and matter being *fundamentally* one, as spirit and substance are fundamentally one.

Hence, when the life-atoms, when the life, so to say, leaves the globe, it vanishes, because those life-atoms are its ultimate particles. The globe is not annihilated, but it passes into the state which is called *in abscondito*, or invisibility. This is perhaps the most difficult point of all others in our study to explain, because there is nothing known to us at present on earth that we can point to as being analogous to it. At any rate, such is the fact; and, as I have tried to point out, when the life leaves an atom, its sub-atoms, so to speak, are not annihilated, but, as it were, they separate and they become invisible, and the portions of the undeveloped substance which remain behind pass into latency, into dormancy, much like ice crystals hanging in space; pass into latency as tiny globules of force-matter, and remain in that state until the attraction to activity later comes — which is another subject that we shall have to go into some day — to join the new *earth*-globe A, the life-atom returning, after aeons of wandering transmigration, to its own life-source.

Similarly with globe B of the moon-chain, the same process takes place, and it vanishes. And so with all the seven globes. How is it then, it may be asked, if globe D of the moon-chain vanished, that we see our present moon? We have before pointed out that our moon is a phantom, a kāma-rūpa, of the moon's globe D that was, but we of earth happen to be on the plane of what was the astral to the Lunarians. We have gone up a step, and we see with our physical eyes what would have been invisible to us when we lived on the moon. As a man when departing this life leaves his kāma-rūpa in the astral realms behind him, the shade, as the ancients put it, his spook, until it disintegrates — if haply that be the man's fortunate destiny — so does it happen with the globes; because these globes are living things. Can life come from anything but life? Clear your minds of the idea that there is any dead matter. Wipe out all that old scientific trash of fifty or one hundred years ago. There is nothing in it. Already it is ancient and forgotten. The scientists now have new theories. Fifty years ago there was nothing but matter. The forces were only "modes of motion." Forces per se did not exist; nor did anybody know how such "modes of motion" arose out of dead matter. Now, however, they are beginning to tell us that there is no matter, that there is nothing but force; and that what we call the modes of matter are merely quanta of force or energy, certain forms or functions of what these very metaphysical scientists call energy or force or whatnot.

Thus, these various globes of the moon-chain cast their life-substance each into a laya-center; these seven laya-centers forming as it were the planes of rest of these "sleeping spheres." There is more behind this which we cannot now go into; but it would be dishonest to pass over this point without calling to your attention one fact, that the higher nature of a globe, as of a man its child, is deathless, and tastes never of death — during the solar manvantara, at least — sleeps not during these intermediate times of planetary rest, but is in nirvana, for some period of time, at least. Please mark those words.

After long aeons of time, these sleeping spheres reawaken for another period of manifestation, in principle exactly as a man returns to earth incarnation. The thrill of active or to-be-manifested life now runs through these seven laya-centers, and they begin to differentiate. Do you know that the secrets regarding death and human incarnation are bound up in this subject of the planetary spheres, the planetary chain, and also in that marvelous, wonderful doctrine of the circulations of the kosmos?

What do the Christians mean — we make a slight digression which seems necessary and interesting as well — when they speak of the resurrection of the bodies of the dead? A ludicrous doctrine this, if taken at its face value as taught by the old-style theology. Much well-merited criticism by independent thinkers has been directed against this Christian dogma — well-merited criticism, we said; but nevertheless in its pagan origin it was one of the old Mystery-teachings. Here is a part, at least, of the secret of it. The life-atoms which form a man's body, which form a man's astral body, which form a man's psychic nature, which form a man's mental and spiritual nature, are his offspring, the off-throwings of the man in life who now physically is what we call "dead." They are far more "bone of his bone and flesh of his flesh," incomparably more so, than is the son of his parents, because *they are himself, his own dissipated life-atoms,* and they will return to him as inevitably and as infallibly as the strokes of karma for good or ill fall upon a man who has originated them, who has acted upon nature, which automatically reacts, rebounds, against the action. These life-atoms come back to him in the succeeding life, when the attraction pulls them, when the gravitational pull comes from the entity descending again through the various planes of substance into reincarnation. Each plane that he passes through after death in going out, in going up, is again

traversed in coming down into reincarnation; and these life-atoms
flow to him by gravitational attraction, by magnetic pull, and
form anew his various vehicles on the various planes of his being.
They are the life-atoms whose "faces he once dirtied," perhaps,
and which he now again must wash; or, again, those which he
had helped on their upward way. Because, verily, these life-
atoms are themselves germ-souls in their essence, even as we
men in our higher natures are children of the Highest — of the
Logos, whose very essence is in us, *is we ourselves!* These life-
atoms also, even as we ourselves, are building for an immortal
destiny; and this is a really fine illustration of the interlocking
of the hosts of lives of universal being.

Think of the mystery, of the wonder, behind this beautiful
fact. In that way, also, are the worlds builded. This, then, is the
secret meaning of the Christian doctrine of the resurrection of the
body, an old Mystery-teaching ignorantly adopted — not the old
body which Mr. Brown or Mr. Jones or Mr. Smith had, for that is
gone forever; but the life-atoms which builded that former body,
and actually *were* it, collect anew to form the new body of the
reincarnating man. As they were his before, so now they come
back and build him a body more or less closely like to the one he
had left at death in the former life. Can you escape the action of
the law? Think of the moral viewpoints that this action of karma
brings to our eyes. Think of the responsibility, moral and physical
and mental and spiritual, that is ours. We suffer from our own
acts, and we have joy from our own acts; and these little beings,
these embryonic souls, these life-atoms, build the bodies of the
vehicles which once again we live in. Man, each one of us, in
future aeons of time, after ages upon ages in the future, is destined
to be a Logos; and the beings then in his care and charge, his
own life-atoms then more or less "grown-up," will be the archangels, the angels, the prajāpatis, the manus, the human souls, and
all the various smaller entities, less entities such as we now know
of beneath us. The Logos that is now our own Highest, our own
"Father in Heaven," was, aeons upon aeons upon aeons agone, a
man also, of whom our present hosts of beings were then the
life-atoms, marching upwards and onwards. Can you imagine and
see, now, why these doctrines have always been kept so secret

and sacred? Suppose that they were subject to misunderstanding, and misrepresented in cheap advertisement, dropped in the mire, "cast before the swine," as the Syrian Teacher said!

But there is danger in all this. There is always a danger in saying more than should be said about these esoteric and holy doctrines. We have not said more than should be said; we are merely elucidating and explaining what has been said by hint and allusion in *The Secret Doctrine* by H. P. Blavatsky. In future years we may go deeper into these things; but surely enough has been said tonight to show the analogy between and the much that might be said about the life of man and that of a planetary chain.

FORTY-FOUR

PRINCIPLES OF THOUGHT AND STUDY: CAN OCCULTISM BE TAUGHT?
ANCIENT ASTROLOGY A TRUE SCIENCE. OUR EARTH-CHAIN OF
GLOBES, THE SEVEN SACRED PLANETS, AND THE TWELVE
ZODIACAL SIGNS. LIFE-ATOMS: THE BUILDING
BLOCKS OF THE UNIVERSE.

Astrology is a science *as infallible* as astronomy itself, with the condition, however, that its interpreters must be equally infallible; and it is this condition, *sine qua non,* so very difficult of realization, that has always proved a stumbling-block to both. Astrology is to exact astronomy what psychology is to exact physiology. In astrology and psychology one has to step beyond the visible world of matter, and enter into the domain of transcendent spirit.

— *Isis Unveiled,* I, 259

The signs of the Zodiac have more than one meaning. From one point of view they represent the different stages of evolution up to the time the present material universe with the five elements came into phenomenal existence. As the author of *Isis Unveiled* has stated in the second volume of her admirable work, "the key should be turned *seven times*" to understand the whole philosophy underlying these signs.

— T. Subba Row, "The Twelve Signs of the Zodiac"

IT IS AN EGREGIOUS folly to suppose that occultism can be taught in lessons as one would teach a language or a science, and the question arises: How, then, since these meetings are for the purpose of studying together some of the noble doctrines of occultism, how is it that they might seem to be taught in that manner, by lessons in courses? The difference is this: while occultism cannot be taught as one would teach a language, nevertheless, obviously and of necessity, there must be some means and method by which the great sages of olden days communicated from time to time appropriate parts of the esoteric knowledge to the world; and this is done by teaching and elucidating certain doctrinal principles thereof, these principles actually being some of the basic facts of the kosmos. You cannot teach occultism as you would teach a language, for the reason that the facts of being of the kosmos, of inner and of outer nature, are so interlocked that unless one had a thousand tongues, speaking a thousand idioms at the same time, and the hearers were capable of appreciating these thousand idioms at the same instant, one could not convey the ideas, the thoughts, simultaneously into the minds of the hearers. This may illustrate, if poorly, why you cannot teach occultism as you can teach a language, or a mere physical science, or some other ordinary system of exoteric study, such as our universities do teach; for these latter studies or sciences or arts are very simple, dealing with one main line of thought alone.

But the great sages of ancient times laid down certain principles of thought and of study which, they tell us, are, or rather represent, the fundamental operations and characteristic natures of the universe. And not one of those mighty minds ever attempted, because it is de facto impossible, to teach of these operations and natures as one would teach a language or a mere physical science; but by hint, by allusion, by an appeal to the intuition and the innate knowledge of his hearers, and by proper physical illustration, such a teacher leads them on, step by step, until finally the man or the woman sees as in a flash the meaning conveyed as a key, and grasps and applies that key, with greater or less success, depending on the hearer's own spiritual insight. In that way, therefore, are the doctrines of occultism communicated in the first four stages of initiation.

You may take, for instance, the teaching regarding the beginnings of kosmic evolution. We realize from this study that there are seven different principles of and in which the kosmos is builded; which work, each one of the seven, on its own plane — or rather in its own world; and to attempt to describe at the same instant of time the simultaneous operations of these seven principle-elements is physically impossible. But a hint is given, an allusion is made to some one or more facts of universal nature; and the mind of the hearer is opened by an intuitional thought which is aroused in himself by the communication. No child is taught to walk merely by seeing its parents walk, but by itself learning to put leg before leg; and its first feeble and vacillating steps, in time, grow into the assured and confident stride of the man.

So it is with these doctrines. Little by little, step by step, our teachers lead us on to understand, so that we in our turn become teachers to and of ourselves, and are enabled boldly and successfully to apply as keys the doctrines that we have heard to larger doors of learning and knowledge, leading into still more secret chambers of our great Mother Nature. And these chambers are full of wonders and mysteries, mystic and marvelous beyond all comparison with things upon earth. I am thinking, as I speak, of one of the real meanings of that wonderful inscription which Plutarch tells us of in his treatise on *Osiris and Isis*, chapter 9 — Plutarch of Chaeronea, the genial writer, the inimitable biographer, the great-hearted man, initiate, quondam priest of Delphi, of the famous oracle there. One of his most mystic writings it is, and one of the most difficult to understand, so carefully does he veil his real meaning. He says that this inscription, presumably engraved over the portico of the great Temple of Neïth, at Saïs in the delta of Egypt, ran as follows:

> Isis am I, I am all that was, that is, and that shall be,
> and no one of mortals has ever lifted my veil.

And Proclus, the Neoplatonic philosopher, in the course of his commentary on the *Timaeus* of Plato, remarks incidentally as follows with regard to this inscription, that its ending was:

> and the fruit that I brought forth became the Sun.

Neïth is the mystic or occult side of Isis; Isis represented the open side, the obvious or plain side, of the hid goddess Neïth. This veil was the universal nature around us, hiding the mysteries and operations of the great kosmic life. And to this day, no one of mortals, however great, has ever succeeded in raising that veil utterly. But little by little as the aeons of time flow by, our greatest seers, the Masters, and the Masters of the Masters, who also in their spheres of thought and action advance even as we advance, check and prove and try the knowledge communicated by the gods our ancestors to the early races of mankind; prove the truths of being again, modify them in form for presentation to a later age; and in that sense send forth anew to the world, from time to time, some and more of the doctrines of reality. Their work is a very difficult one. There is nothing that men resent so much, nothing that so greatly arouses their ire and their hatred, as to have their cherished beliefs disturbed. Consider how all the world teachers have been received, in whatever age. Look at the great-hearted Socrates who, though not initiated, betrayed parts of the Mysteries to the public ear, from his own intuitional insight — a serious crime in those days. Look at the legends concerning Jesus, legends only, nevertheless representing certain mystic truths; look at Pythagoras; look at every one of those great souls who have attempted to enlighten mankind throughout the different ages: every one of them was persecuted and misunderstood, though every one of them was giving his lifework, his very soul, in order to help his fellows; every one of them was hated; and, in later ages, every one of them, though more or less understood or misunderstood and wronged, was almost — and in one or two cases quite — deified! So has it been today, in our own age.

We enter upon our study tonight by reading again the same extract from volume I of *The Secret Doctrine* that we read at our meeting last week, from pages 158–9:

Everything in the metaphysical as in the physical Universe is septenary. Hence every sidereal body, every planet, whether visible or invisible, is credited with six companion globes. . . . The evolution of life proceeds on these seven globes or bodies from the 1st to the 7th in Seven ROUNDS or Seven Cycles.

You will remember that we passed briefly in review the four aspects of the wonderful doctrine of the spheres; and we merely approached another doctrine still more wonderful, the doctrine of the circulations of the kosmos; and we closed our study for that evening at the point where we saw that each globe of the lunar chain of the sevenfold moon that was — each one of those globes — had perfected its respective series of ten stocks or families and had projected them into a laya-center, one for each globe, in order that these respective ten families or stocks might

have their long pralayic rest; and then that when, after the course
of cyclic aeons, the thrill of waking life returned again to these
sleeping hosts, differentiation set in in these laya-centers as the
life-waves advanced downwards towards them through the various planes of superior matter, quickening and enlivening each
plane, one after the other, as the life-waves went lower and lower
down. Remember that "lower" here does not refer to movement
in space alone, but much more to quality; the life-waves were
descending into grosser and still grosser planes of matter.

The first of the sleeping hosts that felt the inflow of the life
forces as these reached it, coming from the higher spheres, was
that aggregate which was to form globe A of the earth-chain.

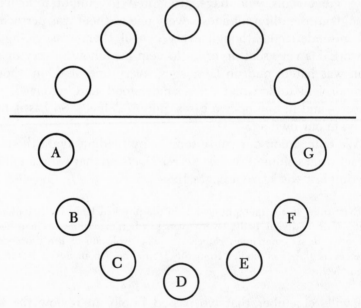

Here, if you will, are twelve globes, representing the planetary
chain of our earth or, inferentially, the planetary chain of any
one of the scores of planetary chains in our universal solar
system. The uppermost five, as shown in the diagram, we shall
say very little of. They are superspiritual worlds. The lower
seven are the worlds in manifestation, and it is these lower seven
that form the main subject of H. P. Blavatsky's outline of the
planetary chains as given by her in *The Secret Doctrine;* and it

is to these seven that we shall restrict very largely our remarks.

These globes of the earth-chain are not yet, as at this point of our study, in existence; but that particular series of ten stocks or families which hitherto has been sleeping — a sleeping sphere coming over from the moon that was, globe A of the moon that was — when it feels the thrill of incoming life, begins to develop into globe A of the earth-chain. This incoming life on each sleeping but now reawaking globe, in the course of the latter's progress to full formation, passes down from the spiritual of its plane to the material of its plane, through seven stages or steps or spaces of evolutionary development. As does globe A of the earth-chain, so do globes B, C, D, E, F, and G; and each in turn, but by a peculiar procedure which we are now going to study.

Now of these ten families, we shall go not much farther with regard to the three highest than a mere allusion to them, and restrict our remarks to the seven manifest stocks or families which form the volumes of the life-waves circling around the seven globes in what are called the chain-rounds. As we saw at our last study, a *chain-round* is the passage of the seven life-waves through the seven globes, once, from globe A to globe G; and a *globe-round* is the passage of these seven life-waves through any one globe — the traversing of any one globe by those seven life-waves — during the course of their chain-round. These rounds are the *inner rounds*. As regards the *outer rounds*, we shall make but little more than an allusion to them at present, and for a very obvious reason. If for some of us, for we are all in the same state in this respect, it is difficult enough to understand even the inner rounds — the passages of the life-waves around the seven globes of our own earth-chain — it would be impracticable, unwise really, at the present time, to overload our minds with the teachings regarding the outer rounds, which we stated as being the passages of the life-waves from, through, and into, in other larger rounds, the seven sacred planets of the ancients.

Before continuing, I would like to make a little digression in order to avoid a later possible misunderstanding. You know that there is a great deal written and taught in the world about astrology, and various so-called astrological teachers print pamphlets and books, and will cast and read your horoscope as best they can.

Occasionally, by a lucky hit, a happy guess, guided more or less by the fragments of ancient knowledge that have come down to us in the books of the ancient peoples, they may tell you something that is true, but how often with the best of goodwill do they mistake. The astrology of the ancients was indeed a great and noble science. Modern astrology is but the tattered and rejected outer coating of real ancient astrology, for that truly sublime science was the doctrine of the origin, of the nature and of the being, and of the destiny, of the solar bodies, of the planetary bodies, and of the beings who dwell on them. This wonderful science was founded on two doctrines mainly, i.e., those two which we have been studying together for the last two or three evenings: the doctrine of the spheres, and the doctrine of the circulations of the kosmos, the latter being microcosmically the doctrine of the circulations of the universal solar system. And the so-called astrology that has come down to us and is with us today, is but a series of sadly incomplete and mutilated fragments of teachings misunderstood by the later Greeks and Romans themselves. Please understand this clearly, because there actually is a vast and noble science which was in the ancient times called astrology, a term which means the "science of the celestial bodies." So great and so noble was it that it was held strictly as a Mystery-teaching. It was always against the law of the Mysteries to tell to the outward world any of these Mystery-teachings — any such divulging of the secret doctrines being held to be a grave crime and, in the later times, was even punished by the State with death.

The ancient nations themselves, the later Greeks and Romans, for instance, forbade the public practice and teaching of astrology, from reasons of sound public policy, because they knew that it could not be taught or practiced honestly in public as a means of private gain. They even went so far in the Roman Empire as to forbid its practice under penalty of banishment or death. Time and again, the Mediterranean nations issued the most drastic laws against it, and against what the Romans commonly called the "Chaldaeans" or "astrologers," because of the much mischief which arose from it. The misleading and unsettling of the minds of the ignorant and thoughtless aroused the legislatures of those times, and they took legislative action in an attempt to curb the growing

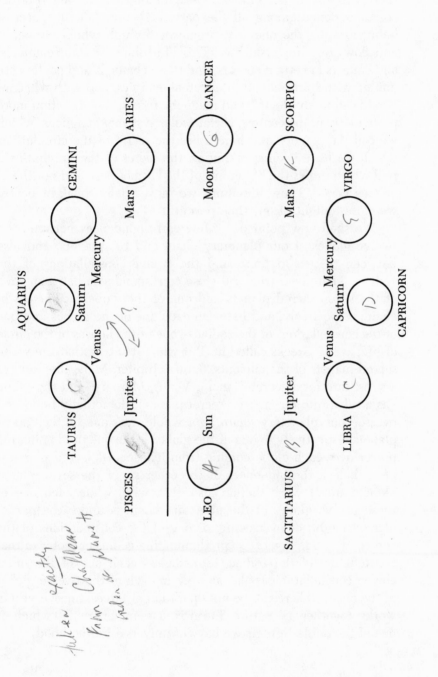

evil. Nevertheless real astrology is a very profound truth, for there actually is a bond of closest union, a strict and perfect correspondence among all the parts of being: all the parts of being forming the one vast organism through which circulates and flows one universal life. This life follows certain channels, and collects in certain centers, and these channels and centers are infilled with spiritual and intellectual energies, and with what we would call today electric and magnetic forces; they function more particularly in the centers, certain solar systemic ganglions, which we call the planets, and herein lies the secret of the circulations which we have been speaking of, the secret of the gravitational pull which draws the life-atoms of the kosmos here and not there, or vice versa. These life-atoms we must briefly speak of before we close tonight, if our time permits.

We shall now point out a few correspondences between the twelve globes of our planetary chain and the planets, and also between these and those and the twelve constellations of the zodiac. There is a strict and close correspondence between each of the seven sacred planets and one of the globes of our earth-chain, respectively; and between each one of the globes and one of the constellations of the zodiac — one of the houses of the circle of life, as the Greeks called it. But while it is true that the seven sacred planets of the ancients, Saturn, Jupiter, Mars, the Sun (as a substitute for a secret planet), Venus, Mercury, and the Moon (as a substitute for another secret planet), do actually build and oversee our planetary chain as a whole, i.e., one of the sacred planets respectively to one of the globes — the one predominating power over each globe coming from its especial sacred planet — nevertheless, the influences of the other six of the seven sacred planets are at work therein also. Likewise, while each one of these twelve globes of the planetary chain is under the particular oversight, or overseeing, of one of the constellations of the zodiac, that is to say, of the predominating genius or rector of that constellation of the zodiac, nevertheless each one of the other eleven constellations is also at work in each of the twelve globes of the chain. There can be no separation of forces, for everything works together in nature towards a common end — which is one of the noblest proofs we have of universal brotherhood.

Let us begin with globe A of the manifest seven. Globe A is under the oversight of the Sun (as a substitute), and its zodiacal house is Leo. Globe B under Jupiter, zodiacal house Sagittarius. Globe C, Venus, zodiacal house Libra. Globe D, our Earth, Saturn, zodiacal house Capricorn. Globe E, Mercury, zodiacal house Virgo. Globe F, Mars, zodiacal house Scorpio. Globe G, Moon (as a substitute for a secret planet), zodiacal house Cancer.

Now going to the five superarchetypal globes, let us take the one at the top, the first (or last) of which, by the way, our poor, material earth is the copy in matter: planet Saturn, zodiacal house Aquarius. Please note that this is the constellation called the Waterman. Continuing to the left, the globe below: the planet is Venus, zodiacal house Taurus. The one below that on the descending arc is under Jupiter, the zodiacal house is Pisces. Crossing along and taking the globe on the same plane as the last mentioned, but on the ascending arc, the planet is Mars, and the zodiacal house is Aries. The one above it and next to the last (or first), the planet is Mercury, and the zodiacal house is Gemini.

If it were possible to do so in the short time we have, we could go into wonderlands of study in following out the various relations of the globes of our chain and of the planets and of the houses of the zodiac, and concerning the beings dwelling on these globes and planets, and concerning the circulations of the life-waves. Let me recall to your mind, before leaving this small detail of our study, a statement made by H. P. Blavatsky in *The Secret Doctrine*, where she says that "if we could only follow the adventures of an atom" — I am quoting in substance — "no romance that has ever been written or imagined, could equal this theme for mystic wonder, and for the profundity of its appeal to the spiritual nature of our soul."

We are now going to pass, if you please, to a much later stage in planetary evolution, possibly returning later to the point where we are now. We have now arrived at the point where we must find out how globe A of the earth-chain, *in the first round,* is builded. These ten families — three of them we will leave without further mention at present — or rather these *seven manifest* families or stocks of the inflowing life-waves, these seven life-waves, are the seven which left the corresponding globe A of the moon at its death, and were its ten or seven principles. They are now reentering into manifestation after their long pralayic rest, clothing themselves with sheaths, or veils, of supersensuous matter as they descend through the three superarchetypal spheres above the manifest four kosmic planes, on the downward arc, until aeons upon aeons later when they have reached this plane — the fourth kosmic plane counting downwards, of the seven kosmic planes, on which fourth plane of the kosmos the forthcoming globe A of an earth planetary chain is to be — they are ready to begin its formation. And how do they proceed? First come the three kingdoms of the elemental world. The first kingdom builds, running the gamut of its seven degrees or stages, and when its work is finished, it goes into obscuration; seven minor steps of building does it build, seven degrees of work has it to do, before its surplus of life can pass to a lower plane on the downward arc, and begin to construct and build the foundation of the *succeeding* globe B to come.

When *its* seven stages of work are finished, the second elemental world then steps in instantly, and follows the same course of seven stages. When *its* seven are finished, it also passes in its turn its surplus of life onwards, down to the foundation prepared for it by the first elemental (or preceding) kingdom, to globe B below. Then follows on globe A the third elemental kingdom. Then, when these three are thus finished, there begins to work on globe A the mineral kingdom, that is to say, the mineral world corresponding to globe A; and when *its* sevenfold work is finished on the basis provided by the three elemental kingdoms, there follows the sevenfold life-wave of the vegetable kingdom; and *it* runs through its seven cycles or stock-races. And when *its* course is finished, its surplus life follows the stream of the already descended entities into the plane below, into globe B, into the work prepared for it by its predecessors.

Then comes the animal kingdom into globe A. Remember, I am speaking of the first round only, so far. When the first round is finished, and the second round begins after the interglobal nirvana between globe G and globe A, the method of procedure is changed. We are now discussing the first round only. When the animal kingdom has run through its seven stock-races (or root-races) on globe A, then comes the seventh and last stock-family or kingdom, or the human, on globe A of our chain.

Now to go back a little. Take the first elemental kingdom on globe A. It is finishing its seventh root-race, its seventh stock-race, its seventh cycle, its seventh ring as Mr. Sinnett called it; and when it has finished this, its life-wave then passes on completely to globe B, where its six preceding stock-races had already gone when they had finished their respective cycles. And what is left behind? Do all the hosts of lives of that first elemental kingdom go there? Do they all pass down to globe B? Please note this detail, for it is very, very important for our future studies. They do not; that first elemental kingdom leaves behind it on globe A the *śishtas* — a Sanskrit word meaning "remainders." This word itself contains a whole doctrine of wonder; and just here is illustrated one of our difficulties in lecturing. Every step that we make forwards opens to view a new avenue, opens a new door, till we are fairly bewildered with the wonder of it all; and we must hold by sheer force of will to our main theme of thought lest we be drawn off into other paths. And this is one of the ways by which the Teachers are enabled to disguise the teachings and hide them from those not entitled to them, as remarked before. They cannot tell all, not even of a single doctrine, for the reason that it simply wouldn't be understood. They tell us as much as they may and can, and give hints and allusions to something else; and this method very conveniently thus acts as a "blind." Hence, sometimes people say, "Why, this doctrine is contradictory!" It is not. Paradoxical, yes; contradictory, no.

Now what are the śishtas of the first elemental kingdom or world that remain on globe A after that life-wave has passed on to form the foundation of globe B? And what are the śishtas of the second elemental world when its life-wave has passed down to globe B and its śishtas remain behind on globe A; and similarly with the third elemental world, and all the other four kingdoms? We will describe what it is by an illustration drawn from our own present mineral kingdom on this earth. The minerals we now have on our earth, today, are the mineral kingdom of our globe D in obscuration here, that is to say, they are the remainders or the śishtas of our mineral kingdom which has passed on forwards to the globes on the upward arc, preparing those globes for our future coming, when we come in our turn on leaving this globe D or earth. Not that they alone work for us, for we work for them too; each kingdom works for each other kingdom, and all work for all. But the real bulk or volume of the mineral kingdom has gone on; and it has left its śishtas behind on this globe earth, its "sleeping spheres," its "sleeping atoms." And so when all the kingdoms of globe A have passed on, each one leaves behind its śishtas, its remainders, its lives representing the very highest point of evolution arrived at by that kingdom in that round, sleeping: sleeping life-atoms, dormant, relatively motionless. Not without life, however; for everything is alive; there is no dead matter anywhere. Is a man dead who is asleep? No; but sleeping, dormant, resting. These śishtas of all the seven kingdoms thus await the incoming of the life-waves on the next round, and then they reawaken to a new cycle of activity.

You know doubtless a beautiful old fairy story, given to us from the French, who got it from the Persians, and the Persians received it from the Hindus; I think that the English version is called "Prince Charming," or "The Sleeping Beauty." The French title of it is *La Belle au Bois Dormant,* "The Beauty in the Sleeping — Enchanted — Wood." Remember the beautiful old tale: the wondrous castle, the enchanted wood, in both of which everything and all is sleeping; even the princess, the castle's châtelaine, is sleeping, waiting, enwrapped in dreamless sleep; and by and by comes along Prince Charming, who sees this enchanted wood and he enters into it. He is a knight-errant, out to achieve deeds of noble doing. He enters this enchanted castle and he sees the Sleeping Beauty, and he bends down and he kisses her forehead; and instantly everything awakens, everything is restored to consciousness, and is set in motion and movement. Thus, verily, is it with the incoming of the life-waves. When the incoming life-waves strike or rather reenter into the dormant life-atoms, they awaken; things are restored to individual activity. Thus, each one of these seven sphere-globes of our chain, when it is in what we call obscuration, is a sleeping sphere, a dormant sphere — full of general life, indeed, as is a sleeping man, but individualized activity is dormant.

Let me say in passing, lest there be a future misunderstanding, that not one of the globes, when in obscuration, remains dormant for the full period of a chain-round. That is to say, when its seven stocks or families have left globe A and passed on forwards to the succeeding globes, globe A does not remain dormant throughout the complete duration of the remaining six-sevenths of the man-vantara of that round until, after the interplanetary nirvana, the life-waves reenter it again. But when a certain period of time has passed, it reawakens and receives another succeeding life-wave. Difficult indeed it is to understand the interworking even of the inner rounds, to say nothing of the outer rounds. And these different life-waves are the seven life-waves passing around the chain, not all together, and not all during the period of one globe-round; but some of these life-waves precede others, because they are more evolved, and run the race more quickly. Hence it is that we have among us what H. P. Blavatsky and the Masters call *fifth rounders* and even, very, very rarely, *sixth rounders.* There again is another one of the many subjects which we must refer for study to future meetings.

So, then, each one of these seven kingdoms, during a globe-round, after the expiration of its seven root-races or stock-races, passes its surplus of life to the globe next following in order around the chain, and itself — its remainders — goes into dormancy or obscuration with the globe that it leaves as a life-wave.

We leave our study tonight at this point to be taken up again at our next meeting. But I would like to add a few general words about the life-atoms before closing. What do we mean when we speak of life-atoms? We do not mean that they are only and merely the atoms of prāna, for those are only one small part of the vast hosts of the life-atoms. The life-atoms in general mean the atoms of life, of the universal life forming our planetary chain. Hence, the expression "life-atoms" is a short and convenient way of saying the *building blocks of the universe,* the bricks, so to say, of the vital kosmos. So many *men* on earth, so many *gods* in heaven. So many *monads* in heaven, so many *life-atoms* on earth, or elsewhere. So many *atoms* on earth, so many equivalent *god-sparks* in heaven. Gods, monads, atoms — you remember the chapter that H. P. Blavatsky has so prefaced in *The Secret*

Doctrine, thus showing the three general classes or degrees of manifested life: the highest, the inner god; the monad, its vehicle, which is man in his essence; and third, himself as a composite being formed of the life-atoms which *he himself has brought forth.* The life-atoms, then, are the vital building bricks of the kosmos. We mean also in one sense that they are the life-atoms of the globe. The globe, all globes, are the life-atoms of a still larger body. Again, there are life-atoms, if you please, on the physical plane; life-atoms on the astral plane; life-atoms on the mental plane; life-atoms on the spiritual plane; life-atoms on every plane or rather world; and, as far as we know, so on forever. Furthermore, each one of these life-atoms, no matter on what plane it may be, is an embryo-soul, growing, evolving, with a sublime destiny before it. Even we are the life-atoms of our own solar Logos, its offspring or children verily, the children of our Highest, of it, the Logos. And in aeons to come, if we run the race successfully as men, and then as dhyān-chohans, we, each one of us, in the infinitudes of matter-space, shall be a Logos; and the life-atoms which *now* compose our bodies and our vehicles, inner and outer, and which are our offspring, our children, shall be in those distant aeons the dhyān-chohans, the archangels, and the angels, and the prajāpatis, and the manus, and the human beings; and all the hosts of the evolving lives now below us and behind us in the grand evolutionary drama of being, shall in their turn also have advanced correspondingly far along the paths of destiny.

Before we close this evening we have been asked to answer the questions: "What proof can you bring to the average man or woman of the truth of these sublime teachings?" "What are the foundations of the teachings of the esoteric philosophy?" The answer to the first question is this: we can bring *proof*, cumulative proof, and you will remember what we have pointed out before as being proof. Proof is the bringing of conviction to the mind, and this conviction is brought by a preponderance of evidence. And if asked the further question, "On what foundation do you bring that proof?" we say, on two foundations, mutually supporting. First, on the innate faculties in the human soul which tell a man that such or another thing is true; he then is satisfied spiritually, intellectually, emotionally. To him it is proved. That is one proof. The other one is perhaps not so strong per se, but to the average man it is perhaps stronger. We can show that the greatest minds of all ages have believed as we believe. They did not use the same words or technical phrases perhaps, did not teach the doctrines in the same form perhaps, but the heart of it all nonetheless was there, the real thing was there, the core of it. You will find all this in the world's literatures; and the only difficulty that it seems to me could be encountered — and I merely make this remark out of prudence — is this: that only too often the ancient literatures are not understood, even by those who translate them and read them. Perhaps to the average inquirer the most convincing evidence is that the finest minds of all times have believed in the theosophical doctrines; and it is to these great intellects that we refer, as to an ultimate court of appeal, much as human beings usually refer disputed questions for solution to the noblest minds that they have among themselves, feeling sure that the questions will be solved in the best way in which good and able men can solve them. I repeat, that we bring proof. But, of course, the inquirer, if honest, must do his own thinking; that we cannot do for him.

The foundations of the esoteric teachings, for the average person rest on exactly the same basis of demonstration that the former question does. If you find that back of the teachings which have come down to us from immemorial times, there are certain facts, certain doctrines, which are the same all over the world, and in all ages, which were not outwardly, not openly expressed, but were kept hid, it is logically necessary to assume that they were looked upon as esoteric, otherwise why hide them? These being the same in substance everywhere, we ask the reason, Why are they the same? The natural — and correct — inference is that they were drawn from the same common source which, now an inference, grows into full conviction as we study them. Really, their best proof is in themselves!

FORTY-FIVE

PHYSIOLOGY, PSYCHOLOGY, AND PNEUMATOLOGY OF THE UNIVERSE.
TEN AND TWELVE PLANES OF THE UNIVERSAL SOLAR SYSTEM:
INTERMEDIATE CRITICAL PLANES. ALL MANIFESTED BEING
A GRADED CONTINUUM OF INTERRELATED, INTERLOCKED
HIERARCHIES: EACH WITH ITS OWN BEGINNING
AND END. ŚISHTAS AND THE SURPLUS OF LIFE.

"*The Sun is the heart of the Solar World (System) and its brain is hidden behind the (visible) Sun. From thence, sensation is radiated into every nerve-centre of the great body, and the waves of the life-essence flow into each artery and vein. . . . The planets are its limbs and pulses. . . .*" (*Commentary.*) . . .

Thus, there is a regular circulation of the vital fluid throughout our system, of which the Sun is the heart — the same as the circulation of the blood in the human body — during the manvantaric solar period, or life; the Sun contracting as rhythmically at every return of it, as the human heart does. Only, instead of performing the round in a second or so, it takes the solar blood ten of its years, and a whole year to pass through its *auricles* and *ventricles* before it washes the *lungs* and passes thence to the great veins and arteries of the system.

. . . The universe (our world in this case) breathes, just as man and every living creature, plant, and even mineral does upon the earth; and as our globe itself breathes every twenty-four hours. . . .

. . . Space is the real world, while our world is an artificial one. It is the One Unity throughout its infinitude: in its bottomless depths as on its illusive surface; a surface studded with countless phenomenal Universes, systems and mirage-like worlds. Nevertheless, to the Eastern Occultist, who is an objective Idealist at the bottom, in the *real* world, which is a Unity of Forces, there is "a connection of all matter in the *plenum*," as Leibnitz would say. This is symbolized in the Pythagorean Triangle.

— *The Secret Doctrine,* I, 541, 615

Intelligences are without beginning.
The Sphere hath an active Soul.
The heavens have neither rent nor seam.

— *The Desātīr,* "The Book of Shet Sasan the First," vv. 16, 17, 20
(Mulla Firuz Bin Kaus, trans.)

The heavy-moving stars are many, and each has an Intelligence, a Soul and a Body.

And in like manner every distinct division of the heavens and planets, hath its Intelligences and Souls.

— Ibid., "The Book of the Prophet, the Great Abad," vv. 23, 24

THE PHYSIOLOGY of the universe which we have been studying during the last few meetings should be understood in its relation to the psychology of the universe; and, at the same time, we should remember that beyond the psychological aspect of the kosmic life there is the pneumatology of the universe; these giving rise in their respective fields to the three essential vehicles through and in which, from which, and back to which, the universal life plays and flows and is — the three thus being the fountainheads of and therefore corresponding in man to his three general divisions of body, soul, and spirit. The physiology of the universe comprises the totality of all the imbodied or envehicled entities thereof; the psychology of the universe comprises the various hierarchies of spiritual beings which work in those hosts of bodies; and the pneumatology of the universe comprises all those divine beings standing behind, ruling and inspiring, the intermediate classes. Now the doctrines with regard to this third and last division are extremely difficult, as we all know, and hitherto we have had occasion merely to allude to them. Our studies, so far, have comprised only an attempt to understand something of the psychology and of the physiology of the spaces of kosmos.

Now one — and perhaps one of the greatest — of the functions or operations of universal nature is that which is expressed by our word evolution; and we use it in strictly the etymological sense, meaning the *unfolding* or the *unrolling*, or the *rolling outwards*, of what is, or has been, impacted in the original seed or root. We do not use the word evolution as that word is misused in modern biological science. In fact, biologists do not teach evolution; they teach what the French very correctly call *transformisme;* and the difference between the two senses is immense. As, at a later date, we shall go into this study more in detail,* we desire at present

---

*[Lectures given in 1927–9 and later issued as *Man in Evolution*.]

to call attention to this great difference of meaning merely in order to avoid a misunderstanding, that in using the words evolution or development as these are used in occultism, we use them in the sense used by modern biologists. Not at all. We employ the word evolution strictly in the etymological sense — the unfolding, the unrolling, the outgoing, of the forces lying latent, from its past karma, in the seed of the being or entity, whatever it may be, which enters upon a cycle of active existence.

This great principle was well illustrated in the case of kosmic evolution by what the ancient Stoics taught with regard to the evolving or development or evolution, the rolling out, of the four (or five) elements of the ancients, as those elements were understood in their day. They taught, as we pointed out at a former study, that the fifth element, the fifth essence or quintessence, called aether — which is our ākāśa — held in its bosom before their manifestation or evolving the seeds of the lower four; and that when the time came for these four to evolve, when the Deity, when Zeus, wished to send forth the worlds again into manifestation after a period of repose, the first that appeared was the element fire, rolling out from aether (or ākāśa), evolving, unwrapping itself, from it. Not fire as we understand it, but, as it were, the seed of fire, the spirit of fire, that primary and elemental kosmic force of which fire on our plane, this low plane, is a feeble manifestation. Then, when fire had run through its course of cyclic evolution, in the same way that it had proceeded forth from the bosom of aether or ākāśa, so did air from fire, unrolling itself from the bosom of fire which had contained in itself this element air; containing not merely its own *swabhāva,* or characteristic or quality of fieriness, as we say in Oriental thought, but containing in itself *also* the characteristic of its own parent aether, ākāśa. Then, next in sequence, from air rolled forth, was unwrapped, sprang forth in development, the element water. Not our water, which is absurd, but that which we might call the seed of water, the spirit of water, that which water or liquidity represents on our plane; and it held in its bosom somewhat of the quality or characteristic of air, its parent; and of fire, its grandparent; and also of aether or ākāśa. It contained also the forces, the potencies, and the powers, of these its predecessors, but feebler naturally in water than in their own respective realms; the qualities and potencies of each preceding one growing feebler as the evolution proceeds farther on, i.e., more largely into "matter." Then from water, from its bosom, evolved or rolled forth the seed of the element earth. When the turn of the cycle set in, when the evolution of these elements, when the building of globes and so forth, had come to an end, and Zeus wished to recall them all back to his bosom, then the reverse procedure began, and water took unto itself again its child, the element earth. Earth began to liquesce and to pass back into the element water. Then in its turn, in its due period, the element water began to aerify its particles and to pass into, or was gathered again into, the bosom of its parent, the element air. Then air in its turn began to ignify its nature and to pass into the bosom of its parent fire. Then, finally, fire aetherialized its nature and passed back into the bosom of the fifth essence or aether, its parent; and the cycle of kosmic evolution was ended for another period of repose.

Now we carry these five elements farther on at least to seven in number. But there is the principle of development inherent in the kosmos which we illustrate by using the word evolution as above outlined: the outgoing of the breath, the breathing forth, of Brahmā, as the archaic Indian thinkers said. The work done, then ensued the inbreathing, the ingathering, the involution, of Brahmā. Precisely the same illustration that we have just given from the Stoic philosophy you will find in the ancient Hindu literature, in the Upanishads, and more particularly in the Purānas.

Just so, after the same manner, with due changes made for circumstances and entities, are the globes of our planetary chain evolved. Globe A runs through its life cycle, and then evolves globe B, which in turn runs its life cycle, and then evolves globe C, which runs through its life cycle and evolves globe D, or our globe earth. Globe D runs through its life cycle and evolves globe E; and then are evolved globe F and then globe G, the last of the manifested seven, in the same manner. These globe-evolutions are the subject which we are now studying.

The questions that have been asked have been exceedingly helpful to the present speaker. They have shown him, for instance, that not enough has been said about the planes of kosmos and the principles of kosmos, and about the various ways and forces by which these twelve globes of our planetary chain are interrelated. Let us then illustrate these in the following diagram:

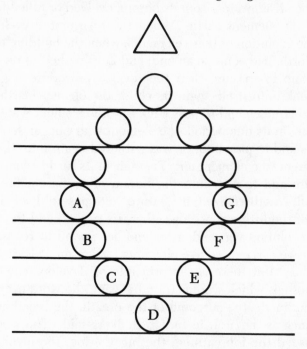

Here we have the seven kosmic planes represented by straight lines, and above them is shown a triangle, which will represent, if you please, the pneumatological or divine or superspiritual three planes about which it is needless now to speak, because even if anything were said about them it is very doubtful that it would be of assistance to us at the present time. The teachings with regard to them are too abstract. Below the triangle follow the three higher planes of the kosmic manifest seven, containing the five hid globes of our planetary chain; then below these follow the four lower planes of the kosmic manifest seven of the kosmos, containing our manifested seven globes, or what H. P. Blavatsky in *The Secret Doctrine* usually called the planetary chain of the earth. We have numbered them as in former studies, A, B, C, D, E, F, and G. In addition, each one of these seven kosmic manifest planes or worlds is itself a septenary, i.e., divided into seven subplanes or worlds. This fact will come in as a very important subject in our later studies.

You will notice that these twelve globes are on seven planes. You will next notice that in the diagram only seven manifest kosmic planes, and a triangle representing three divine planes, are given, which make ten. Now why do we not here show twelve kosmic planes or worlds? We have drawn the diagram in this way in order to call attention, by an apparent lack of something, to a fact which we wish to emphasize. You may remember the Latin poet, Martianus Capella, speaking of the sun, "whose sacred head is encircled with twice six rays." Now these twice six rays encircling the head of the solar god represent the twice six powers or the twice six globes in the spiritual sun. Our visible physical sun is but the body of the sun. There are seven manifest suns; actually there are ten and two polar "links." We see but one sun, the lowest; that sun, as a matter of fact, nonetheless being on *our* highest physical plane; but, as the storyteller says, "that is again another story"!

These twelve forces of the sun represent and are the twelve forces of the Logos, who is the manifest solar god; and, naturally, being twelve forces they must have their own homes to live in, their own spheres of appropriate action. They must have the appropriate matters or substances in which to work. As a matter of fact, *they are themselves their own homes!* They build their own houses with a part of themselves, even as a snail builds its own shell, remaining notwithstanding apart; in it, controlling it, each one to each, but yet not of it, as the spirit and the soul of a man remain apart from his body, in it yet above it, and in a true sense not of it.

These twelve forces represent and are, therefore, the twelve planes of the universal solar system; yet there are but ten planes in a hierarchy. What about the extra two, the eleventh and the twelfth? Now here is the solution of the riddle. All manifested being is a continuum. This means that universal being extends itself infinitely in all directions, most especially we say inwards and outwards, without break of continuity, yet graded into innumerable parts or steps or planes or worlds; and this continuum is, so to say, broken up into hierarchies manifesting in seven, ten, or twelve divisions or parts. The lowest seven parts are the *manifest* portion of any hierarchy, that portion which is builded below a certain plane of materiality, and these seven are the rūpa worlds or worlds of form; and of these seven, as a matter of fact, the three higher are *relatively* arūpa or "formless" — to *us,* to *our* cognition, please understand. The truly arūpa or so-called "formless" or divine worlds are the three highest above these manifest seven, thus making the ten worlds or planes or degrees.

Any hierarchy has of course its beginning and its end, its zenith and its nadir, its acme and its ground, its highest and its lowest, the first and the tenth counting downwards. But what is it that connects this first and this tenth with the other hierarchies, with the rest of the continuum? What is a hierarchy? It is an individualized entity. This entity is composed, in its turn, of hosts and multitudes of smaller or inferior entities, as man's body is an entity, and yet is composed of hosts of cells; and these cells again are entities, and in their turn are composed of molecules and of atoms; and the atoms in their turn are composite things; and yet they all live together, and function together, every one of them common to a hierarchy, within other hierarchies, and all interrelated and interlocking. But each one of these hierarchies nevertheless has its own acme or summit and its nether pole, its head and its foot, its beginning and its end.

That which connects a hierarchy, let us say at the acme or the beginning, with the rest of the continuum, is an intermediate or "critical" plane partaking of the nature both of the hierarchy beneath and of the hierarchy above it in the continuum, of which, of course, it is a part. With its foot, again, it is connected on an extra or twelfth plane, another intermediate or "critical" plane, with the highest plane of the hierarchy which is beneath it or follows it. Thus, then, we have a hierarchy consisting of ten, always ten, degrees or stages or planes or forces: seven manifest, and three hid or occult, or mystic — it matters not what word you use here; and these ten principles or planes, forming a hierarchy, are connected with the superior worlds and connected with the inferior worlds by two extra or intermediate planes, one below and one above, each to each.

Let us now take up our main study from the point where we

left it last week. A very interesting question was asked last week, as to whether our planetary chain formed the seven principles of the earth. And the answer was: "They do not, because each one of the seven globes is itself a distinct and separate planet and is itself a septenary." But the planetary chain forms a hierarchy of globes. Please remember that hierarchy does not mean any one particular thing. It means any possible collection of entities to the number of ten, which *form a unity*. You will recall how much emphasis we laid in a former study upon the differences between a *one*, a *monad*, a *unity*, and a *union*. It was stressed in anticipation of questions on studies like our present subject. If we have not these elementary ideas clear in our minds, there is bound to be confusion. A *union* is a more or less fast or loose aggregate or assemblage of diverse entities. A *unity*, as we shall use it, is a union in which the bonds are so tight that it functions not as an assemblage, but as a single being, as an individual. A hierarchy is a *unity*. A *monad* is the root of a hierarchy, a pure and permanent individual, like the characteristic life-center in a seed from which a tree springs. The tree functions as a *unity*, but if you take its individual leaves and branches, and roots, and consider it as a mere assemblage, it is only a *union*. Considered as an entity, as a hierarchy of less lives, smaller lives, it is a *unity;* and the spiritual center or seed from which it springs, its indwelling characteristic swabhāva, its peculiar life-seed, is the *monad*. And the *one* is that ultimate, purest, simplest, form of kosmic being which we call divine, and of which the old theologians sang: In which there is no shadow of turning, there is no manifestation or differences. It is pure being, as contrasted with differentiated substance. It is the *one*, in which are no opposites or no contrasts; pure being, pure bliss, pure consciousness — what the Upanishads call *sat-chit-ānanda;* beness-consciousness-bliss.

Now, then, the planetary chain being a unity or a hierarchy, functions as a single entity, and is a single entity; it is coadunated, because it is a unity; it is formed into one thing. Why? Because it is endowed with a soul and a spirit flowing forth from its generating monad. In other words, its consciousness is monadic.

Let us read from *The Secret Doctrine*, volume I, page 166, an extract as follows:

Hence it only stands to reason that the globes which overshadow our Earth must be on different and superior planes. In short, as Globes, they are in CO-ADUNITION *but not in* CONSUBSTANTIALITY WITH OUR EARTH *and thus pertain to quite another state of consciousness.*

Coadunition, or rather coadunation, the forming into a unity, does not mean that the entity so unated is a single (noncomposite) being in the ordinary popular sense; otherwise its component parts would not be conjoined in a unation. It means that the coadunated entity is a unity or a hierarchy in the same way that man's body is a unity and a hierarchy, if we consider that body as the vehicle through which works the indwelling monadic soul of the man, governing and controlling the hosts of smaller lives of which the body is made.

Now we take up the method or process by which our manifest seven globes of the planetary chain are evolved or "born," let us say. When the thrill of the incoming life-waves — consisting of ten classes, after their long pralayic rest, coming over from the moon-globe A that was and now is not — inaugurates the new earth-manvantara, those life-waves begin to differentiate on the plane of the globe A of the earth planetary chain to be, and to gather into themselves magnetically or gravitationally the hosts of life-atoms belonging to that plane and which are hanging in space, and which have been transmigrating during the long pralayic rest of the higher principles — transmigrating into other beings on that particular plane and out of them. And here is the real meaning of the ancient doctrine of transmigration: the life-atoms which a man throws off during life, and which his body at any moment consists of during his life, and which are left behind him after his death, and while he himself is resting in devachan, transmigrate according to their respective natures; pass into and inform the beasts, and the vegetable world, and the mineral, and the elemental — the three elemental worlds or kingdoms; and similarly those of his intermediate principles. But when that man returns to incarnation, passing through the various planes downward into physical incarnation, he makes for himself, at first, garments of light formed of his former life-atoms belonging to the higher planes, that is, he gathers into himself again the same life-atoms that he shed and cast off when he passed through those respective planes on his way "upwards"; and so, on each plane on his way downwards into incarnation. Similarly, when he reaches this earth, he gathers the life-atoms of this plane into himself again, not merely by the magnetic pull unconsciously to himself active during his antenatal life, but even more so after his birth. And so do these planets, the various globes of the various planetary chains. The life-waves gather again to themselves, for each globe in turn, as they pass down and through the four lower planes of the kosmos, the life-atoms that belonged respectively to the former moon-globes on the four lower planes, which life-atoms help to build the new "physical" globes or bodies of the new planetary chain to be, which the incoming life-waves or the seven principles of each of the globes of the moon that was, form and shape, and in which they are now to work in the new manvantara.

What does each one of these globes of our planetary chain, or any other chain, consist of? It consists of these life-atoms, *plus* the indwelling vital forces, the life-waves; and together they actually construct the globe, and *are* that globe. Man likewise builds his own body from within. There are secrets even in nutrition that our scientists have not yet solved. Man builds his own body out of himself, as often said before. He first secretes, and then excretes his various vehicles on the different planes of his being. He excretes his own body and bodies or vehicles from the secretions that come from within himself. And the globes of our chain are built in precisely the same way.

We have passed briefly under consideration, in other studies, the three elemental kingdoms as regards their work in forming globe A of our chain. Let us now return to that. The elemental kingdom no. 1 has finished its work, let us say, on what is now the first foundation of globe A. That globe, therefore, has begun to take form. It is one-seventh (or one-tenth) formed, formed to the extent of the range of the first elemental kingdom. That first elemental kingdom has now passed through its seven periods of work, of evolution, and then goes into obscuration — one of Mr. Sinnett's words. A far better word would have been *dormancy* or *sleep*, because this word obscuration actually rather obscures the sense. A man is not obscured when he sleeps. The body may be so, in a sense; but it is better actually to state in more appropriate words just what the real condition is. It is that of sleep, or latency — of dormancy, rather.

But what happens now? Instantly that elemental kingdom no. 1 goes into dormancy, elemental kingdom no. 2 begins its work on the foundation just laid for it by elemental kingdom no. 1. Meanwhile, the surplus of life of elemental kingdom no. 1 passes on to globe B, and lays there the first foundation of globe B as it did for globe A. Now what do we mean by the "surplus of life," and what, furthermore, is it that is left behind as the śishta or remainder, of the elemental kingdom no. 1 now dormant on globe A? (Nevertheless, the active life of the life-waves, a part of it, passes on and forms the beginning of globe B.) What is the surplus of life, then? Surplus of life, as here used, is that to which we alluded a few moments ago, when we spoke of the *unfolding* or *unrolling* of the elements which, before manifestation, are involved in each other. This *surplus of life* contained or involved in the elemental kingdom no. 1, on globe A, is *the 42 principles of all the other six globes* of the manifest seven, as regards the first elemental kingdom, enwrapped, enfolded, involved and dormant therein, so to say, and not yet ready to manifest, because of not being appropriate and fit for globe A, and therefore spoken of as sleeping, *resting* in the bosom of elemental kingdom no. 1, but more truthfully *overshadowing* it and infilling it with life, with the 42 "fires." As this surplus of life is unfolded, or evolved, sleeping spheres, sleeping forces or potencies — which are really the overshadowing 42 fires — pass down to the plane below as surplus of life, the passing "down" being due to the gravitational attraction or pull of the lower plane, as felt by their inferior *swabhāva* or *inherent characteristic.* Hence, as soon as they touch their own realms, so to say, the sleeping fires of the life-waves belonging by nature to those realms begin to awaken, the life-waves appropriate and belonging to that plane begin to work, and the elemental kingdom no. 1 *on globe B* begins its life cycle.

Let us go back to globe A. When the elemental kingdom no. 2 has finished its work on globe A, i.e., when it has run through its seven stock-races on globe A, then elemental kingdom no. 3 steps in as did no. 2, after no. 1. Immediately thereupon the gravitational pull on no. 2, after that elemental kingdom no. 2 on globe A has gone into dormancy, draws that surplus of life in elemental kingdom no. 2 down to globe B, where immediately no. 2 on globe B begins to awaken and to work, and to gather in the life-atoms *belonging to it on that plane.* Thus, on globe A we have elemental kingdoms 1 and 2 in dormancy, and no. 3 working out *its* life cycle on globe A. Elemental kingdom no. 1, when it has finished its sevenfold course of work on globe B, passes similarly on to globe C and begins to form it; while no. 2 coincidently is entering on its work on globe B; and no. 3 is on globe A, as said.

Thus, then, at the present stage we have elemental kingdom no. 1 beginning its work on globe C; elemental kingdom no. 1 in obscuration on globe B, where no. 2 is active; elemental kingdoms nos. 1 and 2 asleep, and elemental kingdom no. 3 active on globe A. After *its* — no. 3's — life cycle is completed on globe A, then comes the fourth or mineral kingdom on globe A, and there does precisely as did its predecessors, elemental kingdoms nos. 1, 2, and 3, i.e., it runs through its sevenfold stock-race or course on globe A. And instantly that this is finished, the mineral kingdom enters into dormancy or sleep or obscuration on globe A, and the vegetable kingdom begins to appear there. Meanwhile, when that happens, the mineral kingdom passes down to globe B, following the same rule or operation or function of nature as did the preceding kingdoms or life-waves. As the vegetable kingdom appears on globe A, elemental kingdom no. 3 passes on to globe C. No. 2 passes on to globe D, our earth; and no. 1 then passes on to globe E. Then, on globe A, appears the animal kingdom; and when it has run through its sevenfold course it passes down to globe B, and coincidently each of the five preceding kingdoms or life-waves makes a step forward to the next globe. Then, finally, comes the 7th, the human kingdom, on globe A. So that when the human on globe A appears, the first elemental kingdom is beginning its work on globe G — the last of the manifest seven. Thus, step by step, one kingdom or life-wave following the other *in turn*, the seven life-waves pass from globe A to globe G through all the intermediate globes; but when the 7th or human kingdom reaches globe G, the other kingdoms are also respectively com-

[handwritten note:] the no = globes E F G are invisible because 3 elemental kingdoms only have worked within

pleting their evolution there; the reason being the law of retardation operating to slow up the progress of the inferior kingdoms on the upward arc, because these inferior kingdoms ascend through the globes on the upward arc with more difficulty than the higher and more evolved kingdoms. The drag of matter holds them back.

This is the first chain-round. From the second chain-round on, the process is different, and we shall have to study that difference in detail next week, perhaps, or at a later meeting. Meanwhile, please get this clear. The march of the life-waves through the spheres represents one detail of the circulations of the kosmos — the passing of the life-entities from sphere to sphere. Furthermore, we have been speaking mostly of globe A; and therefore when we say mineral and vegetable and animal and human, we do not mean those things *as we know them on earth today,* on this globe D in this fourth round, in their already more or less evolved condition now. We are speaking of the *first* round of and through the *first* planet, or globe A; and those kingdoms as they then were would be to our present perceptions, even at their fullest development on globe A during the first round, the mere filmy and invisible and wholly imperfect presentments of what they are to be in the future — i.e., they would seem to us to be spiritual entities. And yet to their own globe, and to themselves, even in that first round and on that first globe A, they were as physical as our globe is now to us, and we are to each other.

At our last meeting, you will remember that we discussed the question: What is the basis of proof upon which our esoteric teachings rest? Whence came they, and how old are they? Let us take the first part of this question: "What is the basis of proof?" The answer to that is simple. The basis of proof is the operations and functions of universal nature, as we have repeatedly said. By nature we mean not physical nature alone, but all that is, inner and outer, higher and lower — everything; for that is truth, that is, the reality of being. Now that is the basis. How do we gain an understanding and a knowledge of these things and facts of universal nature? So far as the understanding is concerned, the argument in proof is presented on the same grounds on which any fact or truth of nature is presented and by an appeal to intelligence and common sense.

"Science" in our days is a word to swear by. Call a thing scientific and people will swallow it without much pretense of close analysis. It does not matter much to the average man whether the scientific allegation be true or not per se. He rarely examines it. It may be a "scientific fact" today; and then tomorrow it is replaced by some other "scientific fact." No men in the world, I venture to say, have more real reverence for true science, i.e., for classified and coordinated *knowledge*, than have ourselves; but for the theories and hypotheses of scientific researchers we have no more respect than those hypotheses are intrinsically worth. The day when science begins to dogmatize through its representatives, it becomes nothing more than a peculiar kind of church. I know of nothing that kills dogmatism more quickly and easily and naturally than these studies in our ancient wisdom; for the simple reason that no sooner do we understand one thing, and think that we have seized a final truth, than we learn from the expansion of our faculties and our knowledge, the very wholesome lesson that it is but a baby's introduction to a truth still more sublime. We learn that lesson very, very quickly; and if we have any tendency to dogmatize or to worship mental idols of any kind, that tendency is quickly killed in us by further study.

Here is our point: ask any scientist for proof of one of the established theorems of his science; let us put it even more forcibly, for proof of one of the more recondite facts of nature, and he will probably say to you: "When you come to me, after having pursued an adequate course of study, and your mind has been disciplined to understand what you are asking about, then I may be able better to aid you, for then you will be able to understand what I shall have to say." And the man would be absolutely right in giving such an answer, which is exactly in substance what our Teachers tell us. That answer comprises the basis of the argument in proof. When the questioner or aspirant is willing to discipline himself and to study, not merely to read, but to give adequate thought and study to the subject — mental study and mental and moral discipline, including physical care for the body, and above all else showing deep spiritual aspiration — when he has thus truly disciplined himself, because "discipline precedes the Mysteries"; when his nature is thus opened up and trained, all exactly in principle as the scientist tells the inquirer to do, then he shall *know,* for, as the Masters tell us: "Live the life, and ye shall know the doctrine, because knowledge will come to you naturally." And this living the life, let us say in passing, means not merely one thing, it does not mean merely morality of sex alone, however important that truly is; it means, if anything, far more than that. It means the full training of the interior man to be true, right, clean, aspiring; in other words, the good old-fashioned word righteousness, acting rightly because you are thinking rightly; because such training opens wide the doors within to the light. The man — and woman, too, of course — who has envy or jealousy or hatred or selfish ambition corroding his soul, or who nourishes revenge in his heart, or any other and all others of these denizens of the inner infernal regions, these hellions of the inner man, is utterly unfit to understand the doctrine; and for a very simple reason. His intellect is befuddled and beclouded. His psychic nature is thickened and rendered gross. His inner nature is cut off from its spiritual sun and its inspiration; and his very brain-mind becomes opaque to the millions of rays of the higher nature.

Now these are old reflections; we all know them; we have read them time and time again. But let us take home into our hearts this illustration: just as the scientist tells his inquirer, When you have studied and are prepared, then come to me, and we will begin investigation, for then you will be able to understand; so do our Teachers tell us, When you are disciplined and are ready, when you are prepared and trained, then come to us and we will investigate nature's secrets, and you will then have firsthand proof; because you yourself, your inner nature, will not merely have been so quickened that knowledge will come to you naturally and intuitionally, and you will know, but your soul, or rather spirit-soul, through the methods of training of the ancient wisdom, and of the ancient schools, will be sent into the very heart of being, of universal nature, and you will discover firsthand knowledge *for yourself* — a knowledge that will endure unchanged for aye!

This answer simply imbodies facts that we all know. Our teachings are based on, or rather are the codified expression, the formulated expression of, *the fundamental operations or functions of nature, of universal nature.* The argument in proof, or the demonstration, takes exactly the same form, and rests upon exactly the same grounds, as does the argument or proof of a fact in natural physical science. Fulfill the conditions, and you will have the knowledge, says the one; and so says the other.

Now as regards the *whence.* These teachings came to the first conscious human race on our globe in this round from semidivine beings who brought them over from a previous manvantara; and these semidivine beings were once men, as we now are. These beings or revealers are what we shall in our turn be when the sevenfold manvantara of our planetary chain shall have ended its course; and we shall then become the teachers and instructors on the future planetary chain, the child and offspring of this chain, of those vast hosts of less progressed entities who are now trailing along behind us on this chain.

This form of instruction was first communicated to the original thinking human race by direct passing; and then, as time went on, and the races of men sank more deeply into matter, there were established leaders of the people, priest-kings of the so-called divine dynasties, a fact which was the original source of what has now become a mere legend, the so-called divine right of kings, which was then an actual fact. There were then true priest-kings, leaders of men; spiritual souls, in other words, consciously working among men. Then, still later, when the races sank still more deeply into matter, these priest-kings, great and noble beings, geniuses of the first water, spiritual luminaries in every sense, were replaced by the priest-colleges, depositories of the primeval revelation; and then the Mysteries were inaugurated, to which chosen ones were taken from the masses of the people for initiation and for spiritual and intellectual training, in an era still more engrossed in matter.

This last happened at about the middle period of the fourth root-race, the race which preceded ours; and this system of the Mysteries has descended even to our own day.

But there is still one fact most difficult to explain, but which must be gone into at least shortly in order to complete our survey; and that is, that from the very beginning of our round on this

earth, from the very beginning of the first race, a race of empty
and mentally senseless "shells" — in the sense that the beasts are
"shells," not being enlightened by the inner intellectual light, the
inner rays, the mānasaputras — from the very beginning of human
race-life on this earth in this round certain entities, of far higher
grade than man will be even aeons upon aeons hence, had come
to earth and had watched over and guided the evolution of the
first and second and early third races. During the third stock-race
they created, by the power of will and yoga, by kriyāśakti, a
mystic body of high adepts and seers, a body which is the most
secret and hid; and this body has functioned and worked even
down to our own times, and it is what we today call the Lodge
of the Masters, its representative among men on earth today.
Those beings "created" by will and yoga, by kriyāśakti, were they
who carried on the mystic knowledge, the wisdom of the gods,
from age to age during the aeons that dropped, one after the
other, into the background of the past, passing that knowledge on
to their successors in turn, until it at present has reached our
own day.

Let us leave this, and take up the third point of query. How
old is the esoteric wisdom? We have already answered that question in the foregoing observations; but we might add this, that its
age is incomputable per se — it is, rather, *ageless*. Can you tell
me, please, how old are the functions and operations of universal
nature? Tell me that, and then I will tell you how old the ancient
wisdom is! It is ageless. This wisdom of universal nature, the
reality of being, is the same to an inhabitant of a planet circling
around Sirius or any other great or small star, as it is to us. It is
that wisdom which is in our day truly called theosophy, god-
wisdom, the wisdom of the gods — that which they themselves
study, we may say.

There was another question which came in a letter, and it
alludes to what is an apparent misunderstanding with regard to
the planet Mars. This questioner seems to have misunderstood,
or at least to be disturbed by, the fact that the planet Mars was
reckoned as one of the planets overseeing one of the globes on the
ascending chain of our system; in other words, the sixth globe
of the manifest seven of our chain, and also as overseeing one of

the globes of the hid five; and she asks: "Why is this, if Mars represents the principle of desire or kāma?" Let us point out first that we are not alluding to the physical planet Mars. We are alluding to the hierarchy Mars, when we speak of it as being the overseer or controller of two of our twelve globes.

Furthermore, as representing the principle of kāma or desire, please bear in mind that Mars is also a septenary; that it has its own seven, ten, or twelve globes, and that these globes are divine, and spiritual, and psychic, and one of them physical, as is our globe earth. Desire is dual. There is a divine desire as well as an evil desire. What is aspiration, for instance? Obviously, the globes correspond in the Martian chain to those which it affects in our chain, and it exercises on the globes of those two planes a corresponding influence, a noble one.

Whence comes that impulse in a man's nature which makes him eagerly desire to do good? Yes, remember the old Greek cosmogonic mythos, that the first divinity to stir in the bosom of Chaos, was Eros, divine desire. Everything has its opposite, desire included.

And this questioner further asks about Mars, Mercury, and the "four other planets," quoting H. P. Blavatsky that they "bear a relation to Earth, of which no master or high Occultist will ever speak, much less explain the nature." But I might say this, perhaps, that this special septenary represents a particular group whose function is to act in building another planetary chain.

There is another question that has been asked on the subject of man's entire inner constitution: whether this is also twelve-fold, as is the complete constitution of the planetary chain. We have said that man has seven manifest principles, which make of him a complete man. He also has three higher principles which, when they become manifest in him, make of him a divine being, a dhyān-chohan. In addition to all these, he has two more "links." I have avoided speaking of them as "principles," in order to avoid creating confusion. But he has two more links — one in his higher nature, and one beneath him — along one or the other of which it is his destiny to travel. Now you may call these two extra links principles if you like. I do not think that they should be so called because man is a self-conscious hierarchy. His entire nature is a denary, or composed of ten fundamental principles; and really this higher link is the root by which he is rooted into divinity. It is so high above him, that to say that it is one of man's principles sounds to me like a desecration of thought, or a blasphemy.

On the other hand, in the nadir of his being, beneath him, he has the other link, or the twelfth, if you like, counting downwards. This other link, this other body or field of matter or force, or both, or force-matter or energy-substance, along which it may be his awful destiny to travel, is his link with absolute matter, and is the opposite of his divine root.

The further question comes up: Can you call these two links principles or not? I can only say that if you call them principles, then man's twelve principles correspond in a general way each to each to the twelve globes of our chain. But otherwise we may say this, that the first (or the last) of these twelve globes symbolizes man's link with the divine; and our earth-globe, the lowest in the diagram on page 574, which is the copy in gross matter of the highest globe, is his link going downwards into absolute matter.

You remember what H. P. Blavatsky says in one of her beautiful works, *The Voice of the Silence,* where she speaks of the "men of Myalba." Now, Myalba is our earth, and it is also called a hell. It is so considered in the esoteric wisdom; and we have pointed out before and now once more say in concluding this answer, that of these hells some are described as being quite pleasant and agreeable to the beings who inhabit them; but to the beings who live on the superior globes above them they would be awful. The description of a globe as a hell must be properly understood, in order to get the meaning of this truly profound fact. "Hell" means the limitations and sorrows inevitable to spiritual entities passing through a globe of gross matter, such as our earth-globe is.

FORTY-SIX

THE CHELA LIFE. SEVEN AND TEN LIFE-WAVES: THE COURSE OF THE
MONADS AROUND THE SEVEN GLOBES; LAWS OF ACCELERATION
ON THE DOWNWARD AND OF RETARDATION ON THE UPWARD
ARC. FIFTH AND SIXTH ROUNDERS. THE SACRED WORD.

There are many sorts of chelas. There are lay chelas and probationary
ones; accepted chelas and those who are trying to fit themselves to be even
lay chelas. Any person can constitute himself a lay chela, feeling sure that
he may never in this life consciously hear from his guide. Then as to probationary chelas, there is an *invariable* rule that they go upon seven years' trial.
These "trials" do not refer to fixed and stated tests, but to all the events of
life and the bearing of the probationer in them. There is no *place* to which
applicants can be referred where their request could be made, because these
matters do not relate to places and to officials: this is an affair of the inner
nature. We *become* chelas; we obtain that position in reality because our
inner nature is to that extent opened that it can and will take knowledge: we
receive the guerdon at the hands of the Law.

— W. Q. JUDGE, *Letters That Have Helped Me,* pp. 54–5

"Verily! it is this noble eightfold path; that is to say: right views; right
aspirations; right speech; right conduct; right livelihood; right effort; right
mindfulness; and right contemplation.

"This, O Bhikkhus, is that middle path, avoiding these two extremes, discovered by the Tathâgata — that path which opens the eyes, and bestows
understanding, which leads to peace of mind, to the higher wisdom, to full
enlightenment, to Nirvâna!"

— *Dhamma-Chakka-Ppavattana-Sutta* (Max Müller, trans.),
(The Sacred Books of the East, vol. xi, 147–8)

Seek this wisdom by doing service, by strong search, by questions, and by
humility; the wise who see the truth will communicate it unto thee, and
knowing which thou shalt never again fall into error, . . .

— *Bhagavad-Gītā,* ch. 4 (W. Q. Judge Recension)

Let loyalty and truth be paramount with you. — CONFUCIUS

Be what you love. Strive after what you find beautiful and high, and let
the rest go. Harmony, sacrifice, devotion: take these for keynotes; express
them everywhere and in the highest possible way.   — W. Q. JUDGE

THERE IS something very beautiful and encouraging in the thought that the doctrines which we study have been studied with the same devotion in other ages, not only by learners such as we are, but by the greatest minds of all times; and, furthermore, that these being the doctrines of nature, of Mother Nature, they are essentially the same in all parts of the boundless spaces of the kosmos, so that kindred thinkers on the planets of other solar systems study the same essential thoughts that we do. As the mind of man grows in its comprehension of these wonderful doctrines, as his mind expands and his soul grows greater under the inspiriting rays of his inner spiritual sun, he comes to realize that the more he learns, the more does he know that there are endless knowledges ahead to learn; until, finally, the student reaches the point where his whole soul is infilled with a reverence and a love and a devotion for truth and his teachers that know no limits; and truly, that realization is the mainspring and the inspiration of what we call the chela life.

I have been hoping, before the present cycle of our studies is concluded, to touch upon this question of the inner life of the student, the chela life, because I know nothing that is more beautiful, nothing that is so encouraging, and at the same time nothing that calls for larger exercise of the truly spiritual will and of the higher understanding than do the requirements of soul needed in order to follow that chela life; because that life calls out everything that a man has in him, or a woman has in her — everything. You may remember that H. P. Blavatsky somewhere, in fact in several places, speaks of the chela life as being very, very beautiful, and at other times as being a "terrible" thing. And so it is, and for one simple reason which we shall mention, and then we shall turn to our evening's study.

The reason is this: beautiful we know it is. But why should it be "terrible"? Because no sooner does the student set his feet finally and firmly on that still small path, which we are told leads to the very heart of the universe, than everything that is in his karma and that would find expression through many future lives perhaps, comes down upon him all at the same time, more or less; and, as H. P. Blavatsky says, to succeed requires an inflexible will of iron and an undivided concentration of all his faculties upon the great work. He must face, and *conquer*, in one short lifetime perhaps, the karmic fruitages of bygone mistakes and failures falling upon his devoted soul; all at once, like horrible ghosts of the past. You can imagine what that means! He must face them, and conquer. Such is the working of nature and the karmic law; and *all* aspirants must go through the trial. Our Teachers as well as all others have had to face karmic circumstances, and conquer them; and these things have been a puzzle to the ignorant outside world, which inevitably has most unjustly blamed the aspirant. In H. P. Blavatsky's life, to take an instance, there are passages which, as anyone who knows of and who can understand them aright will realize, redound infinitely to her credit; but the ignorant and biased and cruel world does not see the originating karmic cause of past lives in those passages, and blames her as having originated them in this life as "weaknesses" in its blind view, because it does not know of what these greater souls have to face when their devoted feet are following the path to glory and success — "working out old karma," as the saying is.

I think that this is a very valuable truth which we should carefully reflect over; and to me it has always been a very practical and morally useful one, because it brings charity for others into our hearts, a greater kindliness, and a greater realization of the nobility, of the self-sacrifice, of those who tread this path — *not for themselves* but *for us*, a path which yet is pure joy; it is absolutely so; but, on the other hand, until the final victories have been won, and they must be won, it is often strewn with pitfalls and surrounded with circumstances which cause the treader of that path to be grossly and cruelly misjudged by the world, which sees but understands not.

We have been studying during the last few evenings the doctrine of the planetary chains, and we have arrived at the point where we are enabled to see how the various planets of our chain, as illustrating all the planetary chains, came into being as the off-throwings of the life-waves coming down from the rest to which they had gone when leaving the preceding planetary chain at its pralaya, or death.

Now what do we mean when we speak of life-waves, the seven — or the ten? We mean the collective hosts of the monads;

and in order to have a short and easy definition, which perhaps will best recall to our minds what a monad is, let us call it, if you please, a *spiritual ego*. It is, in fact, a consciousness-center, being in the spiritual realms of the universal life what the life-atoms are in the lower planes of form. Now these monads and life-atoms collectively are the seven (or ten) life-waves — these monads with the life-atoms in and through which they work; these life-atoms having remained — when the former planetary chain went into pralaya — in space as kosmic dust on the physical plane, and as corresponding life-atoms or life-specks of differentiated matter on the intermediate planes above the physical.

Out of the working of the monads as they come down into matter — or rather through and by the monadic rays permeating the lower planes of matter — are the globes builded: partly out of the substance of the monads themselves, thrown out from themselves; and partly from the ingathering of the life-atoms magnetically attracted to the incoming monadic life-waves, for these are the same life-atoms that formed the various vehicles of those identical monads in the preceding planetary chain, and therefore are now attracted to them again. These life-atoms had remained behind, when that former chain died, on each of the various planes: the physical, the astral, the psychic, the intellectual, the quasi-spiritual, the spiritual, and the divine; for all these planes or worlds have their various life-atoms (or building bricks) through and in which these spiritual egos or monads work.

We have already explained the building of the globe A, the first on the downward arc of our own planetary chain. Let us briefly recapitulate. The seven (or ten) hosts of monads, or the seven life-waves, consist of monads in seven degrees of advancement for each host, or in ten degrees, if we count ten. Let us say seven for purposes of easy illustration. Therefore, these seven main hosts with their seven subdivisions each, comprise the 49 "fires," or the 49 sublife-waves, which work and function through the globes of the planetary chain during the rounds after they have builded those globes. These seven main groups or hosts or hierarchies pertained each one to a respective one of the seven manifest globes of the planetary chain that was — of the moon in our case; and they build each one the respective new globe of the planetary chain that is or that will be — of the earth in our case. Yet all enter into the work of building each globe, for instance, globe A; and when globe A is builded, they all enter into the work of building globe B; and likewise so with globes C and D and E and F and G, which are all of the manifest seven.

In doing this work of building, first enter into the arena of activity, as said before, the three kingdoms of the elementals, one kingdom of which may perhaps be called a spiritual kingdom. The second kingdom of the elementals we may perhaps call a quasi-spiritual or ākāśic kingdom; and the third elemental kingdom is much more material, immediately preceding the mineral which is the fourth kingdom. The other life-waves or the hosts or hierarchies, outside of these four, are those of the vegetable, the beast or so-called animal, and the human; and then finally above these seven are three other kingdoms, thus forming ten; and these three highest are the kingdoms of the dhyān-chohans, the completed or fully evolved entities from the preceding lunar manvantara. About them there is a most fascinating detailed study, which we cannot go into tonight. It has reference to the reason why these particular dhyān-chohans failed to attain full dhyān-chohanship during the lunar manvantara, and therefore were obliged to take a hand in the building of the succeeding planetary chain, that of our earth, in which they actually function, however, as the inspiring spirits, the inspiring gods, so to say.

Now then: first enters elemental kingdom no. 1, and forms the basis or lays the foundation of globe A. When it has run through its sevenfold cycle, when its seventh subcycle begins, its first subclass is attracted to the plane below in order to form the foundation of globe B as it had done that of globe A. But it is the surplus of life which so descends. The actual elemental kingdom no. 1 belonging to globe A remains behind on globe A and goes into dormancy there; whereas the surplus of life which elemental kingdom no. 1 had in its bosom (latent as it were in globe A) is projected out or attracted to that spot of kosmos which is to develop into globe B, because the monads of this surplus of life belonged to globe B of the lunar chain, as the monads on globe A did to globe A of the lunar chain. Then follows on globe A, elemental kingdom no. 2; followed in turn by all the other kingdoms. As each new kingdom enters globe A, a step forward is taken by all the preceding kingdoms, each to its succeeding globe.

After elemental kingdom no. 2 ends its course, then on globe A follows elemental kingdom no. 3; and when its seventh subkingdom is running its course, its first subkingdom is projected to globe B, which also attracts the same. Meanwhile, the first subkingdom on globe B of no. 2 moves to globe C; and elemental kingdom no. 1 passes to globe D; and so it is that these kingdoms follow each other, step by step, globe after globe, up to globe G.

Then on globe A comes the mineral kingdom, or what may be called the mineral kingdom on such a spiritual globe as is globe A. We probably could not conceive of its condition on globe A, first round, in our *present* condition of existence here on globe D, fourth round, although we — our monads — passed through that condition on globe A. We ourselves as monads took a part in that building of the mineral on globe A, first round.

Each one of the kingdoms on the several globes below globe A, when the mineral kingdom enters globe A, now each in its turn moves a step forward to the next globe. Then appears the vegetable kingdom on globe A, and then the animal, and then the human. As each following one appears, each of the preceding kingdoms, each on its globe, moves one step forward to its next globe; so that it works out that when the first subkingdom of elemental kingdom no. 1 reaches the last manifest globe, or globe G, the first subkingdom of the human (or what is the "human" for globe A) reaches globe A and runs its course there. Then follow on globe A the three highest kingdoms, the dhyān-chohanic, but in a very peculiar way; and it would overload our minds, I think, at the present time, to go into the details of that study now. Let us get the main principles of the course of the monads around the seven globes clear first.

When these seven kingdoms — from elemental no. 1 to the human — have finished their evolution on globe A during this first round, globe A goes into what Mr. Sinnett called obscuration, that is, into dormancy; it goes to sleep. Everything on it is now dormant, is sleeping, awaiting the incoming of the life-waves when round no. 2 begins. Please remember that we are now studying round no. 1 only. Beginning with round no. 2, the process followed by the life-waves through the seven globes changes. Again when the life-waves have run their full sevenfold course, or their seven stock-races or root-races on globe B, then it in its turn goes into dormancy or obscuration, which is not *pralaya*, please. Technically not. It may be possible to call the state of dormancy by the name of pralaya in a general sense; but pralaya really means disintegration and disappearance, like that of death. But obscuration is sleep; it is, really, dormancy. And so is it with each one of these seven globes, one after the other. When the final or rather the last representatives of the last stock-race, i.e., of the last life-wave, leave it, each one in turn then goes to sleep or into dormancy.

But there is an interesting fact, due to what the Masters have called the law of acceleration operating on the downward arc, and the law of retardation operative on the upward arc. It so happens that the most evolved kingdoms, such as the human and the beast and the vegetable, pass through their various cycles more quickly than do the younger kingdoms or hosts of these seven life-waves or hierarchies, such as the mineral and the three elemental kingdoms. These latter are younger, and have not been over the ground before; whereas the more evolved kingdoms have to go over what is, in a certain sense, a more familiar path — unfamiliar only in this respect, that they are now running the round in a *new* planetary chain, on and in and through a *new* plane or world of the universal kosmos.

Remember that there are seven planes of kosmos, ten really; but we are now keeping our study limited to the seven manifest planes. With each new planetary chain, a new subdivision of one of those seven worlds or planes is entered upon, for this purpose: to gain experience in every world or plane that the universal solar system offers the evolving entities of the life-waves. So that when seven full chain-manvantaras have been run through — in other words, when seven planetary chains have been lived through — one complete plane of the kosmos has been traversed or experienced by the life-waves, and there then ensues what is called a solar pralaya. This is another deep subject which we reserve for future study.

Now, then, all the entities in our first round on our present planetary chain have reached globe G, the last of the manifest seven; the smaller and inferior and less evolved entities having had more trouble and difficulty in making the route, in running the round, on account of having had less experience in former great cycles. But as these less kingdoms, inferior kingdoms, come down the arc of descent, being more matter-full than the more evolved, i.e., the older and therefore more spiritualized, they run faster than do these latter; and this is the acceleration of the speed of development of the lower kingdoms on the downward arc. Conversely, on the upward arc, from our globe D or the earth, the rate of development is reversed; the higher kingdoms run faster, while there is for those lower kingdoms a law of retardation: acceleration for the higher kingdoms, such as the human, but a slowing down or retardation for the lower kingdoms.

Here is the reason why the process of evolution works out as I have tried to explain it: when all these seven hierarchies do finally reach globe G during this first round, they reach it all together, that is to say, they gather on that last globe G all together, globe G being the last globe of the manifest seven; and here they all finish the first round simultaneously before the interplanetary nirvana begins.

After this long interplanetary nirvana, when it is ended, then opens round 2 on globe A, and round 2 is the exemplar, or sets the example, of the evolutionary process for all the succeeding five rounds, seven rounds in all; and while, indeed, the same general procedure or plan of evolving on each globe, and from globe to globe, that was followed in the first round still holds, there is this immense difference: that all the "houses," the "tenements," used by the evolving entities in the second round were builded during the first round for them. They are ready and awaiting the incoming monads, as the śishtas, the remainders, of the first round. So that the entities, the host of monads, when they return to globe A and the other globes of the chain for the second round, have but to step into and thus awaken these sleeping bodies or houses, each host passing into its own class, instead of having to build anew and go through the lowest houses or bodies up to the highest, as was the case in the first round; for each kingdom now enters into its own appropriate bodies evolved during the first round and now waiting for the incoming monads. And so it is on each of the seven globes of the planetary chain. When round 3 begins, an identical procedure is followed; and likewise for all succeeding rounds.

Another immense difference, already alluded to, is this — that beginning with the second round, all the lines of evolution or activity now having been laid, and nothing having to be instituted *de novo,* from the ground up, as it were, the progress of the life-waves or hierarchies is relatively faster for those which are the most evolved: having this effect, that some smaller hosts of monads, and individuals too, outrun the others, run through their evolutionary course much more rapidly, and thus outdistance or precede the general body of the seven evolving hierarchies, so that, for instance, when they leave our own globe D, they pass on ahead of, or before, the bulk of the advancing army, to globe E, and then to globe F, and finally to G the last, and then have their interplanetary nirvana ahead of their more slowly evolving brothers; and return to globe A as advanced rounders. In our case, the case just cited, they would be fifth rounders, since our present round is the fourth. This is why we have fifth rounders now among us, although we as a human host are in our fourth round. As regards the sixth rounders — those whose spirituality is so high, and whose innate capacity acquired through long aeons of experience is so great that they outrun even the fifth rounders — they are very, very few in number. Our Teachers tell us that Gautama the Lord Buddha is the only *fully developed sixth rounder* in recorded history who has succeeded in attaining this exalted state, and he only — the noblest initiate in recorded history — he only succeeded by virtue of a mystery — a profoundly esoteric process.

. . .

There remain a few scattered thoughts for us to take up before we leave our study tonight. First: the seven so-called sacred planets are not all necessarily higher in degree or stage of evolution than is our earth-chain, although they do indeed actually build our earth-chain by their supervision and guiding influence as architects, and by and through the forces which they lend to the evolving hierarchies or life-waves belonging to our chain. Some of them, of our seven sacred planets, are actually lower than the earth is, spiritually. Others are higher. Others again are higher in degree but less evolved in time than we are; that is to say, they are spiritually higher, yet they are younger in years. As, for instance, a son is younger in years than is his father, but it is quite possible that the growing boy is, spiritually speaking, his father's superior; not necessarily so, but it could be so and often is. Gautama the Buddha is an example in point. He vastly outranked not merely his own family, but all human beings since his time, and also for ages preceding his time.

.   .   .

As has been said, the second round opened the new process of evolution for the remainder of the manvantara of our planetary chain; and at our next meeting we shall deal briefly with this; and then we shall turn to our own globe D and its evolutionary history; because it seems better to follow the lines of study laid down by H. P. Blavatsky in *The Secret Doctrine;* and, after having pointed out the general evolution of the planetary chain, to come to our own globe and specialize on it. Its history holds all that we can possibly manage to study and understand for months to come; and this study will, of course, involve the study of the seven great stock-races or root-races of our globe during this present fourth round.

.   .   .

I have before me three questions. The first is as follows:

What is the true esoteric explanation of the physiological and psychic effect or influence exerted by the vibratory movement set in motion by the sounding of the Word, upon the cerebral or nervous centers of the human body, and is there any special, definite musical note which ought to be sustained throughout the sounding?

This question we are not enabled to answer in full for two reasons: first, interesting as it is, it does not bear upon the subject of our present study; and the second reason is, that a full answer to this very interesting question would involve a virtually complete outline of practical theurgy, and that, of course, is impossible here and now. But we might say this: the main thing is not so much what musical note is sounded, as what is behind the sounding. If the sounding is to be merely a humming, or making a musical noise, or a vocal exercise, you might as well be still; but if there is behind the sounding the aspiration of the heart, and the uplifting of the mind, and the throwing of the will as a consciously exerted energy to everything that is spiritually noble, it matters very little, so far as we are concerned, on what note the voice is sounded. It is what is aroused by will and meditation in the inner man, or what the inner man is enabled to give out, that counts for good; but this does not mean that the proper sounding of this mystic word cannot be done so as to produce the most wonderful effects. It certainly can.

The next question is:

Is not our number 10 made of 6 and 4 instead of 7 and 3? The upper and lower globes are connecting or transition globes, as I understand. We have often been told that this earth is the real hell, so to speak, which is now more comprehensible. Some beings, I understand, may have to travel lower, which would mean backward, and this must be connected with the mystery of the moon, it would seem. I should also imagine that the lower globe at least, must have been formed or evolved or compounded differently from the others.

The answer to the last part of this question is, no. It has not been evolved differently. As regards "the upper and lower globes being connecting or transition globes," I presume the person who sent this question in meant the *uppermost* and *lowest;* in other words, no. 1 and our earth. They are so. The rest of the question has already been answered. The evolving entities are ever traveling, either lower or higher; and this is very truly connected in one direction very straitly with the "mystery of the moon"; but this is a subject which, for us at least, is and must remain absolutely tabu for the present.

I will in a few moments draw a diagram which will illustrate the question of the 6 and 4, or 7 and 3. Meanwhile, we will go on to the next question.

The moon must also have had twelve globes?

It did.

Are possibly our present globes the ones which held this position for the moon?

They are, yes, in a sense; not the actual *present* globes of our chain, but their "privations," as Aristotle would have said. That is to say, those spiritual-astral remnants or types or images which the lunar globes became when they went into pralaya, do reappear again when the new planetary chain comes into being, and around them are formed, as around a model, the 12 globes of the earth-chain. The answer, then, is both yes and no; the 12 globes of the moon that were, come out of "privation" as types or models for the 12 globes of the new chain to be — the earth-chain.

And those now above us the ones we shall next use, climbing as does the nautilus, who "left the past year's dwelling for the new"?

I do not fully, perhaps, understand this part of the question; because, obviously, we shall use next all the globes on the ascending arc, and of course we shall climb. Unless, indeed, the questioner means, perhaps, three of the five hid globes, the three on the ascending arc; in which case the answer is the same, yes.

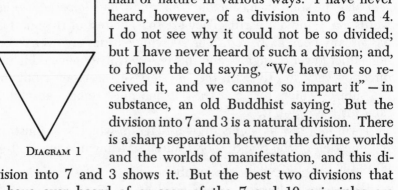

DIAGRAM 1

Now with regard to the 6 and 4, or 7 and 3. I might point out that it is quite possible theoretically to divide these ten principles of man or nature in various ways. I have never heard, however, of a division into 6 and 4. I do not see why it could not be so divided; but I have never heard of such a division; and, to follow the old saying, "We have not so received it, and we cannot so impart it" — in substance, an old Buddhist saying. But the division into 7 and 3 is a natural division. There is a sharp separation between the divine worlds and the worlds of manifestation, and this division into 7 and 3 shows it. But the best two divisions that I have ever heard of or seen of the 7 and 10 principles are this and one other, as seen in this first diagram. Here we have

an upper triangle (this diagram is a symbol, please understand,
a symbolic diagram), a triangle with its "horn" pointing upwards;
then an intermediate square below it; and then a triangle with
its horn pointing downwards. These three figures show the ten
innate or natural principles of man: the divine triad; the intermediate quaternary, showing the personal or individual entity
as a composite and complete "man"; and the lower triangle with
its horn, if you like, pointing downwards.

Now this is a very general diagram, but it does show how the
ten element-principles function: the divine, the purely material,

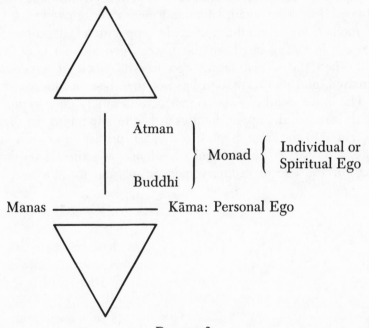

DIAGRAM 2

and the intermediate quaternary. But for practical purposes,
I think the best way is to divide the ten principles of man as
shown by diagram 2. First, of course, is the upper or divine
triangle, a figure which goes without saying. Then we divide the
intermediate quaternary into *two duads*. Please remember that
this composite drawing is a symbolic diagram used merely for
purposes of illustration. Here, then, we have, as before, the
divine triad above; then the duad of the monad, so to say, ātma-

buddhi. Then the second or personal or astral duad, which is manas and kāma. Then below is the inverted triangle representative of the mere vehicle, the body — that is to say, the sthūla-śarīra and the linga-śarīra and the prānas. The value of this division is, that if you study it, it will most admirably illustrate what happens to a man post mortem, or after death. This intermediate quaternary can be divided, as said, into these two duads, which separate naturally after death. They can be separated even in life, without a man's killing himself. When a man dies, the lower triangle disperses, simply goes to pieces. The psychological struggle after death, when the "second death" ensues, takes place between this lower duad, kāma and manas, or kāma-manas, and the monad, ātma-buddhi; and if the upper duad, ātma-buddhi, succeeds in taking out from this lower duad all that is of good in it, then the reincarnating ego has its stock of experience increased, and its incarnation has not then been a failure.

The lower duad likewise is mortal, and finally goes to pieces; but the monad, the upper duad, is at last indrawn into the divine triangle, into the three highest of the ten principles of man, and there it passes its postmortem experience, whether it be devachan for the ego of ordinary men or nirvana for the initiates.

FORTY-SEVEN

"1. To the earnest Disciple his Teacher takes the place of Father and Mother. For, whereas they give him his body and its faculties, its life and casual form, the Teacher shows him how to develop the inner faculties to the acquisition of the Eternal Wisdom.

"2. To the Disciple each Fellow-Disciple becomes a Brother and Sister, a portion of himself, for his interests and aspirations are theirs, his welfare interwoven with theirs, his progress helped or hindered by their intelligence, morality, and behavior through the intimacy brought about by their co-discipleship." — From the Book of Discipline in the Schools of Dzyan, quoted by H. P. Blavatsky

The WISE ONES tarry not in pleasure-grounds of senses.

The WISE ONES heed not the sweet-tongued voices of illusion.

Seek for him who is to give thee birth, in the Hall of Wisdom, the Hall which lies beyond, wherein all shadows are unknown, and where the light of truth shines with unfading glory.

That which is uncreate abides in thee, Disciple, as it abides in that Hall. If thou would'st reach it and blend the two, thou must divest thyself of thy dark garments of illusion. . . .

Thou canst not travel on the Path before thou hast become that Path itself. . . .

"UPADYA, the choice is made, I thirst for Wisdom. . . . Thy servant here is ready for thy guidance."

'Tis well, Srâvaka. Prepare thyself, for thou wilt have to travel on alone. The Teacher can but point the way. The Path is one for all, the means to reach the goal must vary with the Pilgrims.

— *The Voice of the Silence*, pp. 7, 12, 45

W E ARE GOING to interrupt the regular course of our studies tonight in order to take up a subject which undoubtedly is very dear to the hearts of all of us, and upon which we have touched more or less briefly at different times: that is to say, the subject of the relationship between teacher and pupil, between what the old Hindus called the guru and the chela. We are going to treat it from our standpoint, of course; not as that relationship has been all too often misunderstood in different countries and at different times in those periods which Plato called periods of spiritual barrenness. Our age is one of such periods or, perhaps better, is just emerging from one; and you all remember, doubtless, how in one of the most beautiful of the ancient Hindu writings, the *Bhagavad-Gītā*, the Logos Krishna states that at such periods he incarnates anew in order to save and establish the just and to overthrow the unjust and the wicked — for the reestablishment of righteousness on earth.

This relationship is an extremely sacred one, because it is a tie which binds closely heart to heart, mind to mind; and, according to the beautiful teachings of the ancient wisdom, the preceptor, the teacher, the guru, the master — call him or her by what name you will — acts as the midwife, bringing to birth, helping to bring into the active life of the disciple, the hid part of the disciple, the soul of the man. You remember that Socrates always refused to hear himself called a teacher in the ordinary sense. But he said: "I am a midwife to young men, because I bring their souls to birth. I help the inner being, the inner man, to express himself." And this is exactly the spiritual relation that the teacher holds to the disciples, to the pupils, to the chelas, the learners, the hearers — call them by what name you will.

The idea is, again, that the latent spiritual potencies in the mind and heart of the learner shall receive such assistance as the teacher can give, but it does not mean that the teacher shall do all the work that the disciple himself or herself must do. No child can be taught to walk merely by seeing its parents walk; and no parent can eat for its child, or drink for its child, or learn for its child. The child must do these things itself. You may remember that H. P. Blavatsky frequently points out that, according to the old teachings, the relationship of teacher and disciple is infinitely more sacred even than that of parent and child; because, while the parents give the body to the incoming soul, the teacher brings forth that soul itself and teaches it to see, and teaches it to know, and teaches it to become what it is in its inmost being — a divine thing.

Now we pointed out at our last meeting that the so-called chela life, or chela path, was a beautiful one, full of joy to its very end; however, as a warning, lest such an idea be taken in a light or frivolous manner, in a manner not sufficiently deeply understood, we endeavored also to point out that it called forth and needed everything noble and high in the learner or disciple himself or herself; for the powers or faculties of the higher self must be brought into activity in order to attain and to hold those summits of intellectual and spiritual grandeur where the Masters themselves live. For that, Masterhood, is the end of discipleship; not, however, that this ideal should be set before us merely as an end to attain to as something of benefit for one's own self, because that very thought is a selfish one and therefore a stumbling on the path. It is for the individual's benefit, of course; yet the true idea is that everything and every faculty that is in the man or the woman, in the soul of either, shall be brought out in the service of all humanity; for this is the royal road, the great royal thorough-fare of self-conquest. It actually is far easier to follow than is the path of self, the road of shadows. And, as we have often said before, the path of light, of self-conquest and growth, leads to the very heart of being, to the very heart of the universe; because, as the inner faculties develop, as they grow and expand under the inspiriting rays of the inner spiritual sun, they receive and com-prehend new knowledges, take wider and vaster insights into the secret chambers of Mother Nature. Each new insight, each intuition of great things, in its turn opens, as it were, new doors into chambers still more vast. The mind undertakes first to under-stand; and, finally, knows through immediate perception the realities of the universe, and this is Masterhood; and beyond those great Teachers, beyond the Masters themselves, are still greater ones who follow a path still more sublime!

But every footstep along that path is a footstep — now please listen carefully and do not judge before you hear the end — is a footstep of self-sacrifice, sacrifice joyfully made of the lower self's egoisms; the noblest, the most joyful, the most beautiful thing in the world, because it is the giving up at each such step of the shackles of the lower or inferior self with its multitudinous limitations, in order to pass into a greater light. Cooperation with others in the great work in that noble sense — and we mean by the use of that word no modern political shibboleth whatsoever — the mental and spiritual cooperation not merely between teacher and disciple, but between the disciples themselves and all the hosts of the spiritual beings of the universe, can come only when the lower selfish self is utterly forgotten; and it comes in exact proportion as this inferior self, our personal ego, is so forgotten, and the higher self takes over the reins of our destiny.

What is our greatest limitation? What is it that prevents us from seeing not merely truth itself, but also into futurity and into the past? What prevents us from knowing the secrets of being? It is the veils enshrouding the personal self, the concentration of our thoughts and ideas around the individual, around the personal, egoic center. We clasp these veils to our breast and thereby weave around us a web of māyā or illusion, because we wish for personal benefits, and will them, and want them, for the lower selfish self.

The real process of growth is the exact reverse of this. It is the casting down of these idols of the personality, the throwing away of these inner veils, so that the light may come in, that light and that peace, which latter, in the beautiful words of the Christian ritual, passeth all understanding of men.

What are some of the requisites of chelaship? First, perhaps, devotion, devotion to an ideal. Have first the ideal, then be devoted to it, follow it always. It will require your will fully in exercise, the spiritual will. Coincidently, perhaps, comes duty. Ask any man or woman who sincerely has tried to follow this path, whether duty be such an easy thing, and he will tell you truly that there is nothing like the right performance of duty, which brings into the soul such indescribable peace and rest. Think of what it means to have nothing behind you to undo, no mistakes of the personality which have to be remedied, rectified! And this can be done, and easily done. It can be accomplished by following that still old path, as the Upanishads put it, which leads into the haven of eternal joy, eternal peace, and to that enwrapping consciousness of universal presences and processes which to the nobler side of the intellect is supreme bliss.

Coincidently again with these two is the noble virtue of

loyalty. Can any man succeed in anything unless he be true? Fancy a man undertaking a noble work and being told to trust neither himself nor his fellows! How is it possible to succeed with one's own nature running in diverse directions, his very heart-strings pulled here and there, hither and yon, by the conflict of selfish desires and by the petty egoisms of his personality? It cannot be done.

These principles of chelaship rest on no vague or uncertain foundation, but on the vast experiences of the human race, which any man or woman can prove by looking within, looking into those founts of spiritual life, crystal clear and pellucid as the water of the mountain tarn; where he may see, as in the beautiful old mythos of Narcissus, his own reflection, the reflection of his own divine self. That can never be done when and as long as the mind is covered with the dust of its enshrouding veils. It is the dust of selfish actions, the cravings of these petty egoisms, the disturbed and untranquil surface of the mind blown upon by the windy gusts of passion, which unfit it utterly to reflect the higher self — the companion of stars. That which reflects the stars, itself must be in a sense starlike; and only that which is starlike in the soul can understand the lessons of the stars.

So far, then, as regards the teaching. But how about the teacher? What man would go upon a ship captained by another man in whom he had no confidence at all? What man would step into an automobile driven by another man whom he knew to be drunken? A trite simile, but a very true one, and directly applicable to the case in point. Where, then, shall we find these teachers, those in whom we can place such trust? We can, indeed, learn something from the books, the great scriptures of the old-time religions, written by great initiates. We can learn much even from their surface meanings; but there is a key which unlocks still deeper meanings in those scriptures, and that key can be imparted alone by one who knows, a teacher.

Now where shall we find such a teacher? A momentous question, one, probably, that is asked, would be asked, rather, by anyone who might hear us speaking as we do. The *insignia majestatis*, the "signs of spiritual majesty," cannot be mistaken. *Have them in your own heart, and you will know them when you see them*. And you can have them in your own heart; and how? Simply follow the noble old rules of conduct. Live as ye should, and ye shall know the truth, because ye shall see it; and, as our Teachers add, it will come to you naturally; and you will know the teacher when you see him or her, and you will also know better than to judge a teacher by superficial appearances, by the words of the day, the day's mere exercises and duties; having that light in your own heart, at least in some degree, you will perceive the kindred rays in the heart of the teacher, and know him.

Therein lies the meaning of the beautiful saying, ascribed to Jesus: "I am the way, the truth, and the life," and it is truly so, because no disciple, no man (or woman) desirous of leading a better and a nobler life, can put his foot on that path until he himself *becomes* it, at least in some degree.

You know that in olden times there were seven (and ten) degrees of initiation. Let us speak only of the seven. Of these seven degrees, three consisted of teachings alone, which formed the preparation, the discipline, mental and spiritual and psychic and physical; what the Greeks called the *katharsis* or "cleansing"; and when the disciple was considered sufficiently cleansed, purified, disciplined, quiet mentally, tranquil spiritually, then he was taken into the fourth degree. And this fourth degree likewise consisted partly of teachings, but also, as we have pointed out before, in part of direct personal introduction, by the old mystical processes, into the processes of the universe, by which truth was gained by firsthand personal experience. In other words, to speak in plain terms, his spirit-soul, his individual consciousness, was assisted to pass into other planes and realms of being, and to know and to understand by the process of *becoming* them. Because a man, a mind, an understanding, can grasp and see and thereby know only those things which *it itself is*.

Think over those words, they are full of meaning and truth. You can understand nothing that is not in you, nothing. No man, for instance, who is deprived of the mathematical faculty can understand even the mere elements of mathematics. Having this mathematical faculty within himself he understands something of the meaning of the rules of mathematics. No man can understand what right action is, what devotion and duty and loyalty are, unless he has at least something in his own soul of devotion and duty and loyalty; and the more he knows of these beautiful qualities the more he loves them, the more he wishes to follow them; and in following them, following them always farther on, he loves them the more and the more. These truths living in you lead you finally to a complete understanding of the hearts of your fellow men; giving you an ability to read their characters, an ability to understand the woes and troubles that they carry; and the power as well as the ability, and the desire as well as the power and the ability, to replace those sorrows and egoisms in the hearts of men with joy and peace and love and goodwill.

That is the noble work that is before us; and that is the work of the Masters themselves. You may remember that when Mr. Sinnett was in correspondence, through H. P. Blavatsky and two or three more of the chelas, with the Masters, he was told plainly that the last truths, even of the limited sphere of esoteric knowledge that it was permissible to give to him, could not be imparted to him because, as he himself confesses, he had no right comprehension of the meaning of universal brotherhood, and no love for that noble truth. Apparently, his utmost understanding of that sublime truth was a form of sentimental unity, or merely a political cooperation. He had, apparently, no sense of the meaning inherent in the words, the *spiritual brotherhood of all beings* and, particularly, of the fact that all human beings are linked together, not merely by the bonds of emotional thought or feeling, but by the very fabric of the universe itself, all men, as well as all beings, springing forth from the inner and spiritual sun of the universe, as its hosts of rays. We all come from one source, that spiritual sun, and are all builded of the same life-atoms on all the various planes. It is this interior unity of being and of consciousness, as well as the exterior union of us all, which enables us to grasp intellectually and spiritually the mysteries of the universe; because not merely ourselves and our own fellow human beings, but also all other things that are, are children of the same parent, great Mother Nature, in all her seven and ten planes or worlds of being.

After the fourth degree, there followed the fifth and the sixth and the seventh initiations, each in turn, and these consisted of teachings also; but more and more, as the disciple progressed, were there developed in him the faculties — and he was helped in this development more and more largely as he advanced farther — there were developed in him the faculties, still farther and more deeply to penetrate beyond the veils of māyā or illusion; until, having passed the seventh or last initiation of all of the "manifest" initiations, if we may call them that, he became one of those truly called *supermen* whom we call the Mahatmas, great soul-spirits, whose very nature is *magnanimity* — used here in the old Latin sense of "great souledness" — the word meaning exactly what *mahatmaship* does in the Sanskrit.

Loyalty to the teacher, devotion to the teacher, the complete fulfilling of all duties to the teacher, is the other side of this subject. Devotion, duty, and loyalty to truth and its behests, on the one side, unfailing, unchanging, never varying; and the same virtues living in our souls towards the teacher whom we have chosen, is the other side, because that teacher has given us inner light, yea, more, has given us inner life, inner life in a very real and practical sense, and not merely in a mystical one; because, by the processes of the ancient schools, such a teacher is enabled to carry the disciple, if uninterrupted in his studies, even over the gulf of what men call physical death; is enabled so to awaken the dormant powers of the spirit-soul in him that they function as it were automatically. The giver of inner light and the giver of inner life: such is the teacher. How rarely is this recognized or even known in the Occident today. This explains in part why the egoistic and so-called individualistic Occidental, self-satisfied in his blind folly, hurls against the devotion of teacher and pupil of the ancient Eastern schools, the devotion of the disciples to their teacher and of the latter to them, such unkindly and insulting epithets, calling such devotion mental servitude, calling it mental subservience, speaking of it in terms of mockery, proving, as said before, that the critic understands it not, because that noble virtue is not in his own soul in the sense we mean. How great and far-reaching is his spiritual loss!

There is something so beautiful in devotion and loyalty and duty, faithfully carried out, that all nations of men, in all times and in all countries, have placed those three qualities of the soul in the very forefront of manly and womanly virtues. I venture to say that if we follow these three noble virtues faithfully, undismayed by the many mistakes that we may make, and our courage never dampened by the falls that we may have, but always rising again to the battle — I venture to say that as time goes on, easier and easier, smoother and smoother, will become for us the path of wisdom and peace, and ever more joyful.

Fidelity is comprised in these things. *Semper fidelis,* runs the beautiful Latin motto, "always faithful"! What loveliness of thought there is in this! What man or woman can fail to despise the weakness in the weakling, the unfaithfulness in the unfaithful one! Indeed, such moral obliquity is a human characteristic; even the beasts have it not. Show me an unfaithful beast. It is only in us men that this petty vileness has its existence. And what can we learn from this little fact? Simply this, that we have, in addition to the innate love of the beast for its master, the divine gift of self-conscious intellection, which in too many of us is weakly allowed to remain uncultivated and undeveloped, so that we have but two or three feeble glimmerings or rays from the spiritual sun, so to say. And these two or three or more feeble glimmerings are just enough to put "sin," to use the old word, into our hearts. They are just enough to make us see and realize our self-importance, but not enough to make us see the truth and our inherent spiritual brotherhood; and here is where the human being fails and falls — the so-called "secret of Satan."

What, then, is the remedy? More light. What is the remedy for folly? Wisdom. What is the remedy for ignorance? More knowledge. With more light, with the flooding of the inner nature by the rays of the spiritual sun within, these feeble glimmerings and rays grow and expand, until finally the whole inner nature is deluged with this wonderful inner light that the mystics of all ages have talked of; and then unfaithfulness becomes impossible, utterly impossible. No man will sit down, childlike, and spend his time casting up sums in simple addition — two and two make four. He has passed that childish stage. He goes to higher things; and he looks upon the unfaithfulnesses and the failings of his less developed brothers with compassion, not with condemnation of the weakling himself. These weaklings are precisely like little children with their small sums in arithmetic. They are precisely like mentally undeveloped people. They have only a few poor glimmerings or rays in them of that glorious luminary within.

Now there is the actual psychologic fact. It is not a figure of speech or metaphor. That is what the criminal is in his inner nature: I mean the really criminal man or woman who chooses evildoing from love of it. That is what the poorly developed man has in him: just these poor feeble glimmerings of the inner sun, which are all that reach his undeveloped mind; just enough to make him see something, and to recognize, as he thinks, his own self-importance. But when the greater light, when the flooding, the deluging, of the inner nature with the larger illumination comes, then we see that all there is of us, in the sense of this petty self, is but a reflection of something nobler; and all our natures, our entire natures, are opened, when that realization comes, to an alliance with this inner and higher and nobler self, the spiritual sun of our inner being.

FORTY-EIGHT

THE HEART OF THE UNIVERSE. THE WAY TO PEACE, BLISS, UNDERSTAND-
ING, IS WITHIN. THE GREAT QUEST — KNOW THYSELF — THE WHOLE
SECRET OF INITIATION. OUR RESPONSIBILITY: ETHICAL VALUES
AND THE LAWS OF THE UNIVERSE; HARMONY.

Behold the truth before you: a clean life, an open mind, a pure heart,
an eager intellect, an unveiled spiritual perception, a brotherliness for one's
co-disciple, a readiness to give and receive advice and instruction, a loyal
sense of duty to the Teacher, a willing obedience to the behests of TRUTH,
once we have placed our confidence in, and believe that Teacher to be in
possession of it; a courageous endurance of personal injustice, a brave decla-
ration of principles, a valiant defence of those who are unjustly attacked,
and a constant eye to the ideal of human progression and perfection which
the secret science (*Gupta Vidya*) depicts — these are the golden stairs up
the steps of which the learner may climb to the Temple of Divine Wisdom.
— From the Book of Discipline in the Schools of Dzyan,
quoted by H. P. BLAVATSKY

The ancient narrow path that stretches far away
Has been touched by me, has been found by me.
By it the wise, the knowers of Brahma, go up
Hence to the heavenly world, released.
— *Brihad-Āranyaka Upanishad*, 4, 4, 8 (Hume, trans.)

The way to final freedom is within thy SELF.
That way begins and ends outside of Self.
— *The Voice of the Silence*, p. 39

The great secret is sympathy for the souls of men, the will to press forward to that which is true.
— KATHERINE TINGLEY

THIS evening's call for a resumption of our esoteric studies
was in one sense unexpected; and instead of following the
thread of our discourses where they were left off, I am
going to ask you to come, all of us together in thought and in
spirit, into an atmosphere of magical beauty, into an atmosphere

where the roots of our being live, and whence is drawn the sustenance, both spiritual and intellectual, from which the intermediate nature of man, and also man as he appears in the everyday affairs of life, finds its nourishment, its guidance, and its direction, and all the finer things which make man man.

In this spiritual and intellectual atmosphere, I refer first to some elementary propositions of the ancient wisdom, the first of which is that all men in their inmost spiritual essence are not merely in kinship, but in an utter and inseparable union. This does not mean that the hosts of monads who are the spiritual portions of men, one monad to one man, are but one monad; but, as you all must know, it means that the monads themselves also have a spiritual side, and that that spiritual side or nature of each one has its roots, finds its ultimate fountain of being, in the transcendent divine in which we live and move and have our being.

Therefore through each monad, if we so will it, run the streams of intellectual omniscience, which streams are transmitted to us even through the beclouding veils of the intermediate nature; for we derive both that spiritual life and that intellectual omniscience — in other words, bliss and pure consciousness and pure understanding — from the divine which is at the heart or core of every man and of every woman; yes, and also at the heart and the core of the beings beneath us, though they as yet have not evolved the sensitive vehicle which can translate those sublime and supernal mysteries into comprehensible thought-form through their lack of the necessary organ of thought, which in them has not yet expressed itself as a self-conscious faculty.

The human beings above us, I mean those who are the chelas of the Teachers, and the Teachers themselves, and the Teachers of the Teachers, are each one respectively a stage nearer than the preceding class to that divine, a degree or a step higher in the buddhic hierarchy, in the Hierarchy of Compassion.

Let us recollect that we are the outmost rank or ring of that buddhic Hierarchy of Compassion, and it depends upon each one of us, not only upon the life that we live, but upon the ideas that we hold inshrined in our minds and in our hearts, to how great a degree we may become faithful transmitters and manifesters of the divine streams from that supernal source. When we can transmit these in their native crystalline purity, when our minds become transmitters so limpid and clear, so high in their aspirations and so unadulterate in their natures that we can consciously receive and pass on these life-giving streams, the streams of understanding from the fountain of the universal life, then indeed we are saviors of men, saviors of our fellows; and this is the goal to which the Teachers call us.

For after all, is not this aim the one which the Teachers have told us is the lifework of themselves, and should be the lifework of us at the present time? It is. In some countries they speak of a Christ; in other countries they speak of a Buddha; elsewhere they speak of one who has found the Way, the Path, who has found Tao. And in each case the reference is to one who has so completely subordinated his individuality to the universe that he thereby becomes the faithful transmitter of the spiritual life.

All these various names and titles mean the same thing. What is this meaning? It is that the mind and the heart, the understanding and the consciousness, and therefore the example and the life, are all at one, all in unity working along the same pathway leading to the sublime goal at which we have hinted; and this life so led brings not only to the heart of each one of us a peace and a joy which pass all ordinary human understanding, but it likewise enables us to give that peace and that joy to others.

It is through and by the lessons that we learn in our daily life that come to us the opportunities of setting our feet upon this pathway. As all of us know, the noblest aim that we can have is to fit ourselves for this lifework. Now, how is it done? Is it by looking for mere mysteries and for weird tests and expected trials? What kind of a test or trial should such be, at a time when one is wrought up to a pitch of exaltation and high expectation so that in a certain sense he is temporarily abnormal and therefore has a transitory but nevertheless an abnormal strength to meet such tests or trials. Such would hardly be tests or trials at all and hence would be of very little profit and very little worth. The testing comes in the affairs of life that concern us daily, in the duties which we perform faithfully or perhaps unfaithfully, in never leaving our task for personal or selfish purposes; for here we are tested in every part of our being, and at every moment, and in the most unexpected and most unforeseen places, and at the most unexpected and most unforeseen times.

Our rejoicing passeth all ordinary comprehension when one, through long and faithful service and unswerving devotion which leads to inner development, which takes him far along the path, follows that still small path which leadeth to the heart of the universe; for we feel that what he then has attained we also may attain and should attain and must ultimately attain if we do as he did; it is a matter for joy to all when this happens.

I have just spoken of the pathway which leadeth to the heart of the universe. Now what is that heart? Is it "God"? What god can we conceive of which is not, after all, the noblest figuration of our own imagination? Such a god after all would be but a name, a breath, and nothing more, for it is a conception originating in our own minds. We do not mean by the phrase, "the heart of the universe," some divine being who after all is but an aggregate, a collection, a synthesized unity of the various individuals of the hierarchy of which it is the controlling head. We do not mean this, for what sense would it have since these hierarchical heads are more numerous than the sands on the shores of an infinite ocean, for they are infinite in number; and how should any one such be the heart of the universe? Nay, that is not our meaning. We mean by the heart of the universe that consciousness, that light, that understanding, that nature whose essence is bliss, which is the life of the universe — not a personal life but an impersonal life, from and through which the universe draws the forces which infill it, which forces are the gods, the spiritual beings, the playing of whose vitality we sense even through the shell of the physical world, and therefrom take the term so familiar to us, the forces working in matter.

This consciousness, this light, this understanding, this nature whose essence is bliss, are collectively what we mean by the heart of the universe, a heart which is nowhere in particular, because everywhere; called the "heart" only because it is the secret center in each one of us, the core of our being, and which is not only the source but also the passageway, or the canal, or the channel, through which those supernal forces of the divine do pass into us; and, reduced to the last analysis, we are they and they are we, because the recondite and secret fountains of our being are all these things.

You know the teaching of the old Eastern philosophy, the Vedanta of Hindustan, which in this respect is likewise the teaching of Northern Buddhism, and is also ours, to this effect: the universe is one vast organism, an organism which is composite of organisms still smaller, still more minute, not located in any particular place but spread throughout the spaces, indefinitely in all directions, and likewise inwardly and outwardly, in the inner worlds as well as in the outer worlds. And these are full of these still smaller, still more minute organisms, which in their aggregate form the vast organism of the cosmos.

I fancy that after all it is only a figure of speech to speak of the universe as one vast organism, for the reason that any organism, in strict logic, must be a limited entity, and the thought that we are endeavoring to express is dealing with *That* which is limitless in all senses. Hence the expression "vast organism" is a metaphor, a trope, a manner of speech in order to express an idea almost too subtil and high to put in ordinary language.

This vast organism of the cosmos then is an organism only by philosophic license, so to say. It is an organism in the sense in which the human race is an organism, formed, as the latter is, of individuals, composite of men, men who are minuter organisms of the corporate body we call humanity, of men whose bodies in their turn are composite of entities still more minute; and these entities still more minute are again composed of entities still smaller than they, and so forth indefinitely.

Let our minds pass in thought in the reverse direction towards macrocosmic spheres, and there also do we find the same law of unity in diversity, prevailing everywhere. We may reach in our imagination an ultimate point and say, this is the universe; but by a still stronger effort and looking beyond that point not only do we sense other universes still more remote, but our instinct, our intuition, alike tell us that through these more distant aggregates, as through our own universe, play the same deific forces that we know, the same divine energies, the same driving urge to progress, the same call to come up higher, having the same forces playing through them, their brother-universes or sister-universes, if you will. And there are indefinite numbers of such, incomputable hosts of them, hosts visible and invisible, hosts without and within. So that all that we can mean when using the phrase, "the universe is one vast organism," is to carry our thought ever onwards and to realize that it is boundless space, without limitations, without frontiers, without ending places.

Remember, furthermore, that any such organism exists only in periods of its own manvantara; for manvantara is a word which we may by analogy employ for both the great and the small. There may be a manvantara of a universe as well as a manvantara of an aggregate of universes; nor does any such universe, nor does any such aggregate of universes, necessarily have its period of manvantara or its period of pralaya contemporaneously with all other aggregate bodies.

Let us be cautious about this. When we speak of "universal manvantara" we mean the manvantara of our own cosmic aggregate; but another universe may be in pralaya while we are in manvantara; many other universes may be in pralaya, or in manvantara, while we may be conversely in manvantara or pralaya.

Let us be watchful over our thoughts, keeping close guard over our minds, for in this manner we shall never allow our minds to crystallize into a mere succession of phrases and thus make of the thought a dogma. We learn much by thus watching ourselves and by thus studying ourselves, and by reaching ever inwards into our own spiritual natures, guided by the teaching which the Masters have given to us; and the essence, or, so to say, the keynote of all these teachings is that the way to light and to life and to peace and to bliss and to understanding is within ourselves; and we obtain these wonderful things by reaching or striving ever farther inwards, inwards, inwards, endlessly. For the farther we reach into ourselves, so to say, the farther we follow that pathway leading inwards, the more we become conscious of still greater things, still wider visions, and the pathway thus followed becomes space itself.

Is this pathway a different path from that which leadeth outwards, outwards, outwards, still farther outwards to spaces and cosmoi which we can intuitively sense as existing beyond the boundaries of our own universe? No, it is the same path, exactly the same path; it is only our mind of matter, in which we of necessity must work in this our present period of evolution, that conceives of the mysteries of consciousness as occupying space, or as following lines of directional expansion. All these things exist in our consciousness, not along any material directions; it is consciousness which understandeth, and consciousness is neither forwards nor backwards, nor to the right nor to the left, nor up nor down, but *is*. It is all things at all times, and because it is everywhere, it is nowhere in particular.

Where then abides this consciousness which is in each one of us? It is within, it is found by reaching inwards; it is the great searching, the great quest; it is the seeking the light; it is likewise the finding it; it is seeking the life; it is the finding of it. This consciousness should be sought for by turning inwards therefore; yet when we say that the path is inwards, it is, after all, but a figure of speech; it is a manner of verbal expression, in order to convey an idea, and we must not let our minds crystallize around a mere figure of speech.

Do you remember when we spoke at a former meeting here on the nature of the ancient initiations, we then called attention to the very profound truth that there could be no initiations unless there were the awakened consciousness in the postulant or neophyte? What is initiation? The word itself really means a beginning, the first steps of a beginner, and there are many beginnings. There is the beginning for the man of the world; there is the beginning for the true chela; there is the beginning for the Mahatma; there is the beginning for his Teacher, and so on indefinitely. It is the opening of the course for development of a beginner, and he who guides his first steps will do so with much the same care and attention that a mother uses in guiding and watching the first steps of her little one.

It is an old Oriental saying, and a very beautiful one, too, that the initiator is both father and mother to his disciple, and more even than this: because whereas the father and the mother give the life of the physical body, and that body itself for the purpose of the incoming soul, and also give the love and the care and the attention necessary to save the child from dangers and perils in our physical world, the initiator in very truth gives you your soul, because he awakens it for you, acquaints you with yourself, opens the portals of your understanding, leads you forth to inspect and understand the universe surrounding us and the mysteries which it comprises. In brief, the teacher, the initiator, leads you inwards so that you may know yourself — in other words, as just hinted, watches over and attends to the growth and development of your expanding consciousness.

Γνῶθι σεαυτόν, said the Greeks: "Know thyself," an injunction carved over the temple of Apollo at Delphi; this mandate comprises in two words the whole secret of initiation and of the initiations, because it comprises the path which the expanding consciousness follows in its growth: *know thyself*.

Thyself — what is it? It is consciousness; it is also the heart of the universe. Thyself, that self which is the same in thee and in me, in you and in all others, which is not different in any one of us, as compared with any other one of us. It is the ultimate self, the spiritual oversoul; and therefore it is the one self, the heart of the universe. It is the consciousness in you which says simply "I am," and that same consciousness is in me and in all others: in the Teacher, in the chelas of the Teachers, in the Teachers of the Teachers, in the Silent Watcher of our supernal sphere — that overself is the same in all entities comprised in any hierarchy.

But while that overself is the same in you, and in me, and in all that is, not different anywhere from what it is anywhere else; yet this does not comprise all there is of us psychologically speaking. There is something else within us, not different from the oversoul but a ray of that oversoul, so to say, and this something else in each one of us is the individual ego: that part in each of us which says not merely "I am," but "I am I," and not you. Think over this psychological mystery as it is to those who are not well acquainted with the ancient wisdom; for truly one of the most wonderful mysteries of the ancient wisdom, of esotericism, lies in a correct understanding of this psychological mystery.

In order to make my meaning more clear, please remember that while it is a perfectly true statement that the inner nature of man is the seed of his individual consciousness, that consciousness is but a reflection, so to say, of the universal consciousness which abides in all other entities whatsoever and wheresoever they may be. It is quite true that we reach into this universal consciousness and partake of its universality by following the path leading inwards; but this is not a procedure of the consciousness; and the mind should not be allowed to crystallize around any idea of mere directional expansion.

A man, by considering the starry orbs which he sees over his head at night, may as easily follow the path inwards as another man may by sitting in a corner with his attention concentrated on his navel or the tip of his nose, in the manner of some exoteric yogis, so called. The truth is that it is an arousing of the consciousness to self-understanding, and to developing it towards the universal.

Therefore, once you begin that undertaking, and once you begin to follow that path, you will find that mere directional expansions are but words. The consciousness itself will give you the meaning of these things, and such meaning is always away from the directional limitations or particularities of the material world. It is a growth of consciousness actually, rather than a following of any path so called in any particular direction. As a man's consciousness expands he realizes that it is growing; but he will probably smile if he hears one, whose consciousness has not expanded equivalently, talking of any particular direction in space as being that which the pathway towards the light follows.

This relative I, this ego-self, this individual I in each one of us, is not the heart of the universe; but it is rooted in the heart of the universe, therefore rooted in the universal life, in the universal consciousness, for it is a ray of it. It is that part of us which, by the magic of evolution, by the wondrous magic which the gods work in their deific energies, forming and framing the cosmos as a wonderful web of being — it is that part of us, I say, which grows from unself-consciousness to self-understanding, to self-consciousness.

In the vast womb of eternities past it began its career as an unself-conscious god-spark; and its destiny is to flower out in due course as a self-conscious god, becoming so through the unwrapping or unfolding or evolving of the potentialities which are latent or inherent in its very nature as a spark of the universe. This is spiritual evolution, and can be considered as a building up of a god from the forces and faculties and powers inherent in its

own self, the pouring forth of the latent or sleeping energies
which intrinsically belong to it; yes, a self-conscious god, as it will
finally become, infilled with and by the heart of the universe,
which is the universal self. It is the building up of a god through
and by means of the ego-self, its periodic mirror or reflection.

As Katherine Tingley expresses it in her most beautiful invocation:

O my Divinity! thou dost blend with the earth and fashion for thyself
    temples of mighty power.
O my Divinity! thou livest in the heart-life of all things, and dost radiate
    a golden light that shineth forever and doth illumine even the darkest
    corners of the earth.
O my Divinity! blend thou with me that from the corruptible I may become
    Incorruptible; that from imperfection I may become Perfection; that
    from darkness I may go forth in Light.

The universal self is the heart of the universe, for these two
phrases are but two manners of expressing the same thing; it is
the source of our being; it is also the goal whither we are all
marching, we and the hierarchies above us as well as the hierarchies and the entities which compose them inferior to us. All
come from the same ineffable source, the heart of Being, the
universal self, pass at one period of their evolutionary journey
through the stage of humanity, gaining thereby self-consciousness
or the ego-self, the "I am I," and they find it, as they advance
along this evolutionary path, expanding gradually into universal
consciousness — an expansion which never has an end, because
the universal consciousness is endless, limitless, boundless.

Yea, in very truth, it is all a most wondrous mystery, using the
word "mystery" here in its Greek sense of something secret and
wonderful. We leave our deific source as unself-conscious god-
sparks, and our destiny is to become self-conscious gods, thereafter
taking a direct part in the vast cosmic labor.

But is this the limit which we reach, thereafter to go no farther
ahead? Do we then reach the frontiers of consciousness-space,
thereafter finding or discovering nothing still grander or greater
to know or to be? No indeed, the truth is the exact reverse of
this. The consciousness expands gradually, and the more it ex-

pands the more it learns, and that expanding is timeless, outside of time and space. It expands forever.

We have spoken of the hierarchies above us, that is to say, of the hosts of hierarchies who have passed through the human stage and who are marching along their own respective evolutionary pathways towards still greater destinies; but let us not forget that beneath us there are other hosts of hierarchies composed of lives innumerable, uncounted hosts of them, trailing after us, consciously or unconsciously looking up to us as we look up to those who have preceded us, even as we have trailed after, in former manvantaras, those who are now ahead of us, whom we look up to as gods or spiritual beings or, to use the term adopted from Buddhism, dhyān-chohans.

Of the hosts of these small and inferior entities who are trailing after us, one portion of them is comprised in the multitude of minute, even infinitesimal, lives which compose our bodies: that is to say, the physical body, the astral body, the mental body, the intellectual body, and the spiritual body, which aggregate hosts composing these respective bodies, being of different grades or in different stages in evolution, and each such host furthermore interlocking with each other and with all others, and with different hierarchies of the world around us — all the hierarchies composing these various bodies of man's septenary constitution together form the composite unity through which man's inmost self works, because in them, in another sense than that used by Paul of the Christians, we live and move and have our inferior being.

What is this inmost self? I have already said what it is this evening, and on many another occasion here. It is that part of us by which we conjoin with the heart of the universe — in very truth, it *is* the heart of the universe, limited only by the individualized expression of our spiritual nature; and this spiritual nature itself is the source of our ego.

Let us try briefly once more to sketch the construction or rather, perhaps, constitution of our inner nature, and I select us men as examples because we have developed up to the point where self-consciousness is beginning to manifest itself, and thereby we may illustrate more clearly and more easily how evolution proceeds.

First, then, is the universal self, the heart of being, which is the same in all of us. This universal self pours out its energies through the highest in man's constitution, which in each one of us is the monad, our inner spiritual god. The monad working through the various spheres builds up man's intermediate nature, which is the ego-self; and this ego-self, as its consciousness expands away from personality and limitations towards universality, spontaneously enters upon greater and ever greater spheres of life and activity, until this ego becomes in its turn a fully self-conscious expression of its inspiriting monad, which is but another way of saying that it rebecomes that monad itself, *plus* the experiences that the ego has acquired from absorbing the aroma of the various lives which it has had.

When the ego has thus rebecome monadic, in other words has become a monad itself — its own inspiriting monad meanwhile having itself advanced to spheres of life and activity still more sublime than it formerly had — the ego-monad then assumes a cosmic nature, and in its turn evolves an intermediate self or intermediate selves, which works or which work through our lower natures, helping thereby the lives beneath us and in us, in whom we live and move and have our inferior being, as I have already said. It is through these inferior lives composing our intermediate or lower natures that the ego-self finds its fields of self-expression; and when it finally becomes an egoic monad, it becomes to the hosts of lives on these intermediate and lower spheres their divine oversoul, the hierarch of their hierarchy.

Thus then, as a parting thought, let us realize the responsibility — spiritual, mental, psychical, emotional, astral, and physical — which is ours. And when I say "ours," I mean ours as self-conscious beings, egos. We are responsible for what these intermediate and lower lives undergo to a very large extent; we realize that as we impress them, so will they self-express themselves, until they have attained self-consciousness in their turn; we realize that we give them the initial impetus towards evolutionary unfolding, and that as we set their faces, so to say, so will they travel the path.

We realize, finally, that ethical values are in human life, and in the connections that I have just hinted at, what the laws of the universe are in the cosmos. Both signify harmony; both signify consistency in action; both signify an identic source; and both point to the fact that both we and they, these lower entities, are treading the path which they who have gone before us have trodden. This treading of the path is a growth of consciousness, it is an expansion of the conscious understanding; and hence it is that these entities ahead of us are where they are, because, having trodden that path, they have come to know.

The Buddhists have a most beautiful expression to illustrate this fact of the common nature of those who have gone before ourselves, and those who are coming after us. They speak of a Buddha as one who is a *Tathāgata,* a Sanskrit expression compounded of two words meaning either "thus come" or "thus gone," for the Sanskrit is susceptible of either translation; but the meaning is identical, signifying one who has followed the inward way, the inner pathway, the still small path coming down, so to say, from the universal self, passing through the human constitution onward until it disappears again in the heart of being from which we came.

All of you are that pathway. I mean that each one of you men and women is for yourself that pathway; there is no other for any one of you, because it is yourself traveling along the path of understanding consciousness, and reaching ultimately its evolutionary goal, when you become a god.

INDEX

INDEX

Absolute(s), 43, 184, 347
  defined, 182-3, 426
  evolved to present state, 185
  names for, in *Gītā*, 316-17
  no, in European sense, 165, 229, 231, 240-41
  sat, chit, ānanda state of, 188
Abstraction(s), 206
  entifying, 172-3, 476, 479, 481
  initiates' use of, 204
  nature an, 202
Acceleration, law of, 595-6
Acts, Unknowable God in, 31, 426
Ādām, as humanity, 100, 102, 106, 223
Ādām Qadmōn, 44, 87-8
Adept(s). *See also* Mahatma(s)
  defined, 259
  hierarchy of, 228, 231, 234
  lodge of, in third race, 586
Adhibhūta, 316-17
Adhidaivata, 316-17
Adhiyajña, 316-17
Adhyātman, 316-17
Ādi-bhūta, 347
Ādi-buddha, 283
  correlated with other terms, 404-5
  defined, 234-5, 274-5
  of fourth round, 236
Ādi-buddhi, 197, 304, 404-5
Ādi-tattwa, 347, 360, 404-5
Adonai, and Jewish polytheism, 71
Adwaita-Vedanta, 307, 440
Aeneid (Vergil), 179
Aeons (Aions), of Gnostics, 121, 478-9
Aeschylus, and Mysteries, 255
Aether. *See also* Ākāśa, Daivīprakriti
  as cosmic element, 141-2, 347, 408, 423-4, 428, 453, 572-3
  parallel terms of, 404, 406
Ages, relative, of planets, 207-8
Agnōstō theō, 426
Agrae, Mysteries at, 290-91
Ahher, 458-9
Ain Sōph. *See* Eyn Sōph
Air
  as cosmic element, 141-2, 347, 359, 408, 423-4, 428, 453, 572-3
  in Syrian hierarchy, 328, 341-2
  parallel terms of, 404, 407
Aitareya-Upanishad, 18
Ākāśa, 360, 593. *See also* Aether, Daivīprakriti
  aether or, 428, 572
  defined, 406
  swabhavat as, 196, 442-3
Ākāśa-tattwa, 404, 406
Albertus Magnus, 168
Alchemist, 142
Alexandria, 74, 260-61, 274

Al Farabi, 94
All, The
  man linked with, 14-15, 35-6, 58
  space, 214-15
America
  home of sixth race, 282
  new cycle with discovery of, 421-2
Americans, ancient, 418
  egg symbol among, 499
Amrita-yāna, 187, 189-90, 194
Analogy
  axiom on, 525, 537
  between atom and cosmos, 237-8
  between man and planetary chain, 552-3
  false, 360, 452, 472
  nature's fundamental law, 525, 545
  of thoughts and cosmic emanation, 383-4
  rationale for, 537-8
Ānanda, sat, chit, 188, 577
Ancients
  had universal philosophy, 203
  knew heliocentric system, 329
  taught anthropocentrically, 18, 435
Ancient Wisdom, 400
  advice in studying, 401-2
  antiquity of, 21
  Buddhism near to, 226
  no query unanswered in, 518
  same in other solar systems, 590
  seven keys to, 378-9
  source of, 21-2, 585-6
  used figures of speech, 17, 273-4, 438
  why held secret, 185-6, 529, 552-3
Androgyne, early man was, 106
Angel(s). *See also* Archangels
  atom is, 381, 389
  guardian, 416
  in Christian hierarchy, 86, 343
  in Dante, 176
  in Syrian hierarchy, 328, 341
  life-atoms will become, 552, 568
  we may be fallen, 154
Anglo-Saxon, 135
  epics, 4, 17
  etymology of "world," 478-9
  names for days of week, 250
Animal(s), 236. *See also* Beast(s)
  celestial bodies are, 80-81, 101, 207
  human souls were, souls, 185
  kingdom, first round, 564-5, 581, 593
Annihilation
  of life-atoms, 549-50
  of lost souls, 218-19, 221-2, 232, 269
  of man by sun, 365
Ansated cross, 471
Antarākāśa, 28
Ante-Purgatory of Dante, 176-8